Scotla███████████tion:
La█████████████

Scotland's Constitution: Law and Practice

Second Edition

C M G Himsworth
Professor of Administrative Law,
University of Edinburgh; Solicitor

and

C M O'Neill
Partner, Brodies LLP

Bloomsbury Professional

Bloomsbury Professional Limited, Maxwelton House, 41–43 Boltro Road, Haywards Heath, West Sussex, RH16 1BJ

© Bloomsbury Professional Limited 2009

A CIP Catalogue record for this book is available from the British Library.

ISBN: 978 1 84766 318 4

Typeset by Phoenix Photosetting, Chatham, Kent
Printed and bound in Great Britain by M&A Thomson Litho Ltd,
East Kilbride, Glasgow

Contents

Preface

In the preface to the first edition of this book we described the second elections to the Scottish Parliament as a milestone in Scotland's journey of constitutional development and one which was appropriately marked by the publication of a work focusing on the particular experience of Scotland within the United Kingdom and Europe. The passing in May 2009 of the tenth anniversary of the opening of the Scottish Parliament was another staging post in that journey, representing a new opportunity to reflect on the condition of 'Scotland's constitution' and the extent to which that constitution has developed since devolution.

This spirit of reflection is not, of course, unique to us. The desire to analyse and to assess the 'success' of the devolution project – and to advocate more or less radical reform – has found expression in academic work across a range of disciplines and in political and journalistic comment. In the realm of institutional politics, appraisals have been undertaken by the House of Commons Justice Committee and, through the Calman Commission, on behalf of the Scottish Parliament, while the Scottish National Party administration has sought to stimulate a 'National Conversation' which addresses explicitly the question whether Scotland's constitutional future lies in independence from the UK. Those appraisals have themselves provided us with much useful material.

As before, we have sought to provide a description and analysis of peculiarly Scottish institutions in a way which integrates them with a general background to constitutional law and the UK institutions which have a continuing relevance for the government of Scotland. We have sought to update and supplement the first edition by discussing not only aspects of the constitution which have changed or which have faced new challenges – for example in the operation of minority government at Holyrood – but others, such as the House of Lords and the civil service, where change is frequently heralded but seemingly impossible to implement. Our aim remains to provide an accessible and interesting introduction for all those with an interest in the constitutional law of Scotland.

As with the first edition, we are conscious that as soon as we have finalised what we hope to be an accurate account of contemporary conditions those conditions will change. Further development is inevitable and, for the constitutional lawyer, welcome. In general, we have done our best to incorporate material up to June 2009, with occasional later references. We have anticipated future change where that change is by now inevitable – for example by reference to the role of the new Supreme Court rather than to the House of Lords – but there are other predicted developments to which we cannot do justice: the anticipated reform of the MPs' pay and allowances scheme, the range of changes proposed in the Constitutional Reform and Governance Bill, a further Irish referendum on the Lisbon Treaty and even perhaps a further change of Prime Minister before the next UK general election. And it is too early to tell what the constitutional consequences of the global financial and economic crisis may be.

The final content of the book remains the shared responsibility of us both but has benefited immeasurably from the generous assistance of a number of colleagues at the University of Edinburgh Law School and Brodies. Of the former we are extremely grateful to Dr Niamh Nic Shuibhne for her European law expertise, to Dr James Harrison for the contribution of useful and illuminating material which would otherwise have been overlooked and, as ever, to Ms Myra Reid for her technical support. Of the latter special thanks are due to Mr Jim Colquhoun and Mr Alan Cumming for their research assistance and to Mrs Donna Watson for her patience in deciphering our obscure hieroglyphics.

Chris Himsworth
Christine O'Neill
20 August 2009

Table of Statutes

Table of European Legislation

Table of Statutory Instruments

Table of Cases

C

Bibliography

Adams, J, and Robinson, P, (eds) Devolution in Practice (2002)

Alson, P, The EU and Human Rights (1999)

Arthurs, HW, Without the Law (1985)

Bagehot, W, The English Constitution (1963) (Introduction by RHS Crossman)

Bamforth, N, and Leyland, P, (eds) Public Law in a Multi-Layered Constitution (2003)

Bankton, Lord, Institute of the Laws of Scotland (Stair Society, 1993–95)

Barker, A, (ed) Quangos in Britain: Government and the Networks of Public Policy-Making (1982)

Beard, CA, An Economic Interpretation of the Constitution of the United States (1913)

Bentham, J, Of Laws in General (HLA Hart (ed), 1970)

Bickel, AM, The Least Dangerous Branch (1962)

Birkinshaw, P, European Public Law (2003)

Birkinshaw, P, Freedom of Information (3rd edn, 2001)

Blair, S, Scots Administrative Law: Cases and Materials (1999)

Blaustein, AP, and Flanz, GH, (eds) Constitutions of the Countries of the World (1971–)

Boch, C, EC Law in the UK (2000)

Bogdanor, V, Devolution in the United Kingdom (2001)

Bogdanor, V, The New British Constitution (2009)

Boyle, A, et al (eds) Human Rights and Scots Law (2002)

Bradley, AW, and Ewing, KD, Constitutional and Administrative Law (14th edn, 2007)

Calvert, H, Constitutional Law in Northern Ireland (1968)

Calvert, H, (ed) Devolution (1975)

Campbell, T, et al (eds) Sceptical Essays on Human Rights (2001)

Clayton, R, and Tomlinson, H, The Law of Human Rights (2nd edn, 2009)

Cleland, A, and Sutherland, E, Children's Rights in Scotland (2nd edn, 2001)

Clyde, Lord, and Edwards, DJ, Judicial Review (2000)

Convery, J, Public Law (2nd edn, 2007)

Convery, J, The Governance of Scotland (2000)

Coppel, P, Information Rights (2nd edn, 2007)

Craig, P and de Burca, G, EU Law (4th edn, 2008)

Craig, PP, Administrative Law (6th edn, 2008)

Crick, B, The Reform of Parliament (1970)

Daintith, T, and Page, A, The Executive in the Constitution (1999)

Dalyell, T, Devolution: The End of Britain (1977)

De Lolme, JL, The Constitution of England (new edn, 1834)

De Smith, SA, Jowell, J, and Woolf, Lord, Judicial Review of Administrative Action (6th edn, 2007)

De Smith, SA, The New Commonwealth and its Constitutions (1964)

Dicey, AV, The Law of the Constitution (10th edn, by ECS Wade 1959)

Douglas-Scott, S, Constitutional Law of the European Union (2002)

Duchacek, ID, Power Maps: Comparative Politics of Constitutions (1973)

Ely, JH, Democracy and Distrust (1980)

Finnie, W, Himsworth, CMG, and Walker, N, (eds) Edinburgh Essays in Public Law (1991)

Forsyth, C, (ed) Judicial Review and the Constitution (2000)

Fraser, WIR, An Outline of Constitutional Law (2nd edn, 1948)

Gordon, GH, The Criminal Law of Scotland (3rd edn, 2001)

Grant, JP, (ed) Independence and Devolution: The Legal Implications for Scotland (1976)

Griffith, JAG, The Politics of the Judiciary (5th edn, 1997)

Hadfield, B, The Constitution of Northern Ireland (1989)

Hague, DC, Mackenzie, WJM, and Barker, A, (eds) Public Policy and Private Interests (1975)

Hailsham, Lord, The Dilemma of Democracy (1978)

Hall, W, and Weir, S, The Untouchables: Power and Accountability in the Quango State (1996)

Hanks, P, Constitutional Law in Australia (2nd edn, 1996)

Harden, I, and Lewis, N, The Noble Lie: The British Constitution and the Rule of Law (1986)

Harlow, C, and Rawlings, R, Law and Administration (3rd edn, 2009)

Hart, HLA, The Concept of Law (2nd edn, 1997)

Hartley, TC, The Foundations of European Community Law (6th edn, 2007)

Hazell, R, (ed) Constitutional Futures (1999)

Hazell, R, The English Question (2006)

Hazell, R, (ed) The State and the Nations (2000)

Hazell, R and Rawlings, R, (eds) Devolution, Law Making and the Constitution (2005)

Hewart, Lord, The New Despotism (1929)

Himsworth, CMG, and Munro, CR, Devolution and the Scotland Bill (1998)

Himsworth, CMG, and Munro, CR, The Scotland Act 1998 (2nd edn, 2000)

Himsworth, CMG, Local Government Law in Scotland (1995)

Hogg, PW, Constitutional Law of Canada (5th edn, 2007)

Hopkins, WJ, Devolution in Context: Regional, Federal and Devolved Government in the EU (2002)

Hume, D, Commentaries on the Law of Scotland Respecting Crimes (3rd edn, 1986)

Hunt, M, Using Human Rights Law in English Courts (1997)

Janis, MW, Kay, RS, Bradley, AW, European Human Rights Law: Text and Materials (3rd edn, 2008)

Jeffery, C and Mitchell, J, The Scottish Parliament 1999-2009 (2009)

Jennings, I, The Law and the Constitution (5th edn, 1959)

Jowell, J, and Oliver, D, (eds) The Changing Constitution (6th edn, 2007)

Keating, M, The Government of Scotland (2005)

Kellas, JG, Modern Scotland (2nd edn, 1980)

Kellas, JG, The Scottish Political System (4th edn, 1989)

Kelsen, H, Pure Theory of Law (2nd edn, 1970)

The Laws of Scotland, Stair Memorial Encyclopaedia, Reissues 'Administrative Law' (2000), 'Constitutional Law' (2002)

Lester of Herne Hill, Lord, and Oliver, D, (eds) Constitutional Law and Human Rights (1997)

Lester, A, Pannick, D and Herberg, J, (eds) Human Rights Law and Practice (3rd edn, 2009)

Loughlin, M, Legality and Locality (1996)

Loughlin, M, Sword and Scales (2000)

MacCormick, N, Institutions of Law (2007)

MacCormick, N, (ed) The Scottish Debate: Essays on Scottish Nationalism (1970)

Macdonald, IA, and Webber, F, Immigration Law and Practice in the United Kingdom (6th edn, 2005)

Macdonald, J, Crail, R and Jones, C, (eds) The Law of Freedom of Information (2nd edn, 2009)

McFadden J, and Lazarowicz, M, The Scottish Parliament (4th edn, 2009)

McHarg, A and Mullen, T, (eds) Public Law in Scotland (2006)

Mackay, W et al, Erskine May's Treatise on the Law, Privileges, Proceedings and Usage of Parliament (24th edn, 2004)

Mackinnon, J, The Constitutional History of Scotland (1924)

Mackintosh, JP, The British Cabinet (3rd edn, 1977)

Mackintosh, JP, The Devolution of Power (1968)

MacPhail, ID, Sheriff Court Practice (3rd edn, Welsh, T, 2006)

MacQueen, HL, (ed) Scots Law into the 21st Century) (1996)

Milne, D, The Scottish Office (1957)

Mitchell, JDB, Constitutional Law (2nd edn, 1968)

Munro, CR, Studies in Constitutional Law (2nd edn, 1999)

Norrie, KM, Children (Scotland) Act 1995 (Revised edn, 1998)

O'Neill, A, Judicial Review in Scotland (1999)

Oliver, D, Constitutional Reform in the UK (2003)

Ovey, C and White, RCA, Jacobs and White The European Convention on Human Rights (4th edn, 2006)

Paterson, AA, Bates, TStJN, and Poustie, MR, The Legal System of Scotland (4th edn, 1999)

Paterson, L, The Autonomy of Modern Scotland (1994)

Peers, S, and Ward, A, (eds) The EU Charter of Fundamental Rights: Politics, Law and Policy (2004)

Quekett, AS, The Constitution of Northern Ireland (1928, 1933, 1946)

Rasmussen, H, On Law and Policy in the European Court of Justice (1986)

Rawlings, R, Delineating Wales (2003)

Reed, R, and Murdoch, J, A Guide to Human Rights Law in Scotland (2nd edn, 2008)

Seneviratne, M, Ombudsmen: Public Services and Administrative Justice (2002)

Stair, Viscount, Institutions of the Law of Scotland (1981)

Sunkin, M, and Payne, S, (eds) The Nature of the Crown (1999)

Tierney, S, Constitutional Law and National Pluralism (2004)

Tomkins, A, Public Law (2003)

Trench, A, Devolution and Power in the United Kingdom (2007)

Trench, A, (ed) The State of the Nations 2001 (2001)

Trench, A, (ed) The State of the Nations 2008 (2008)

Tribe, LH, American Constitutional Law (3rd edn, 2000)

Turpin, C, and Tomkins, A, British Government and the Constitution (6th edn, 2007)

Wade, HWR, and Forsyth, CF, Administrative Law (10th edn, 2009)

Walker, DM, The Scottish Legal System (8th edn, 2001)

Weatherill, S, and Beaumont, PR, EC Law (3rd edn, 1999)

Weiler, PC, In the Last Resort: A Critical Study of the Supreme Court of Canada (1974)

Whatley, CA, Bought and Sold for English Gold? Explaining the Union of 1707 (2nd edn, 2001)

Wheare, KC, Federal Government (4th edn, 1963)

Wheare, KC, Government by Committee (1955)

Wheare, KC, Modern Constitutions (2nd edn, 1966)

White, RM and Willock, ID, The Scottish Legal System (4th edn, 2007)

Winetrobe, BK, Realising the Vision: a Parliament with a Purpose (2001)

Woolf et al, De Smith's Judicial Review of Administrative Action (6th edn, 2007)

Chapter 1

Constitutions and Constitutional Law

INTRODUCTION

1.1　　This is a book about constitutional law and, in particular, about constitutional law in Scotland. Before we can embark on the project in detail, however, there is a need for an initial familiarity with the domain of study. The terminology and the language of constitutional law must also be acquired, together with some knowledge of its general ideas and the cultures and traditions within which those ideas are discussed. One must know what is important to constitutional lawyers and why; what it is that interests and even excites them; and what difficulties they encounter. One must learn how constitutional lawyers analyse existing constitutional situations; what assistance they derive from constitutional events in the past; and what guidance they may acquire from systems of constitutional law in other parts of the world. One must understand too how constitutional lawyers speculate about possible future developments in Scotland or elsewhere, how the law they study differs from other branches of the law; and how the approach to their subject of study tends to be different from that of political scientists, sociologists and others.

This is not always straightforward or uncontroversial and although detailed discussion of the growing body of scholarship related to what might be described as inter-disciplinary approaches to law (including constitutional law) is beyond the scope of this book, that scholarship should not be overlooked.

How then to acquire the more traditional language and fundamental ideas of constitutional law rapidly? The method chosen in this introductory chapter is to enter the subject by way of discussion of a hypothetical written constitution for an independent Scotland. There is, of course, no such actual constitution because there is (at the time of writing) no independent Scotland but it is a useful exercise to make the imaginative leap required to consider what would be the principal component parts of such a written constitution. Because we know what other constitutions contain, we can engage in quite intelligent and informed speculation about what a Scottish version would look like. However, because this remains an exercise of the imagination, we can keep the model constitution quite simple. Then, with the hypothetical model in mind, we can develop two useful lines of discussion. On the one hand a process of comparison can do much to explain the function of constitutions in general, and to understand what influences the content of constitutional rules in different states. Secondly, we can compare and contrast the content of the hypothetical constitution with the reality of constitutional law in Scotland today.

A WRITTEN CONSTITUTION FOR SCOTLAND?

1.2 While emphasising once again that, in this section, it is a hypothetical constitution for Scotland which is to be discussed, it should also be borne in mind that some individuals and organisations have made it a very practical task to draft a constitution for adoption by Scotland if it were to become an independent state at some future point. Such constitution-making is to be distinguished from the processes which have led to the establishment of a Scottish Parliament within the United Kingdom and which are considered in some detail later in this book. The drafting of independence constitutions is a task which, in recent years, has fallen rather to a campaigning organisation known as the Scottish Secretariat following the meeting of a provisional National Assembly in 1962[1] and latterly to the Scottish National Party[2]. The inspiration underlying their drafts has obviously derived from a political impetus in the direction of an independent Scotland: the need for a new constitution would arise from Scotland's new status, once achieved. Here, some of the provisions in such earlier drafts have been taken into account but more dispassionately and without any underlying commitment to the desirability of any particular political future for Scotland. Ideas from these Scotland-based drafts are supplemented by others from draft models of a written constitution for the whole of the United Kingdom[3] and from the actual constitutions of other states. It would be reasonable to assume that our hypothetical constitution for an independent Scotland might consist of, at least, the following ten different parts or chapters.

1 *A Constitution for Scotland* (1964). It was reissued with a new introduction in 1993.
2 For the text of the SNP draft and a commentary by Professor Neil MacCormick, see his 'An Idea for a Scottish Constitution' in W Finnie, C M G Himsworth and N Walker (eds) *Edinburgh Essays in Public Law* (1991). More recently, in September 2002, the SNP published a revised version: *A Constitution for a Free Scotland*. For the current SNP Government's proposals on the route to be taken to independence see '*Choosing Scotland's Future: A National Conversation*' (2007) and p 62 below. See also V S MacKinnon 'The Constitution of an Independent Scotland' in J P Grant (ed) *Independence and Devolution: The Legal Implications for Scotland* (1976).
3 See, in particular, Institute for Public Policy Research *The Constitution of the United Kingdom* (1991) (hereafter '*IPPR Constitution*').

Part 1: A preamble

1.3 A written constitution is first and foremost a legal document. It has authority in the country to which it applies and is binding on the people, the governing institutions and the courts of that country. Very often, however, legal documents contain a preface, frequently referred to as a preamble, which may or may not have the same binding force as the rest of the document but which, in an introductory fashion, explains who the parties to the document are, why they are creating the document and the principal purposes underlying the document. In the case of a constitution, the preamble will often explain that it is 'the People' who declare the constitution to be made in their name. Frequently a constitutional preamble will refer briefly to the circumstances under which the constitution was adopted – the collapse of the previous constitutional regime (whether or not in revolutionary circumstances) or the gaining or regaining of independence after a period of subordination to another power. It would not be surprising for a new Scottish constitution to explain in its preamble that it is being made by 'the Scottish People' at a time when independence, lost at the time of the Treaty of Union with England in 1707, was being regained[1]. The preamble might then refer to a number of values to which 'the People' and their constitution aspire. These would be expressed at this stage in very general terms and might include, for instance, the importance of the permanent independence of Scotland; some statement about the future relationship of Scotland to the former United Kingdom, to Europe and to other nations; the importance within Scotland of the freedom and equality of its people and of fairness, justice, democratic government and, to use a phrase to be discussed later, the rule of law. In other states, the preamble is often the place in which to declare the nation's attachment to a particular god or strand of religious teaching. The Irish constitution of 1937 is declared to be made by the people, but in the name of 'the Most Holy Trinity'. The Saudi Arabian constitution of 1992 declares the kingdom to be 'a sovereign Arab Islamic state, with Islam as its religion'.

1 The SNP draft of 2002 bypasses a preamble but, in art 1, asserts the absolute right of the people of Scotland to self-determination and to sovereignty over the territory and natural resources of Scotland.

Part 2: General

1.4   Many constitutions contain provisions which define the territory of the state – a feature which might be particularly important in a new constitution for Scotland which would, for instance, have to be quite clear about the boundary between Scotland and England, both on land and, perhaps more problematically, at sea[1]. The constitution might then appoint a particular city as the capital of the country. It might describe the national flag and provide for the national anthem. Constitutions are often used to identify the country's official language or languages – for Scotland, in all probability, Gaelic, Scots and English.

Another provision of the greatest importance in any modern constitution is that which defines the status of the constitution itself. The constitution of an independent Scotland would probably declare itself to be supreme; that its terms should be treated as having a higher status than ordinary law; and that, in the case of any discrepancy between the constitution and any other law, it should be the rule in the constitution that would prevail and the ordinary law would have no effect[2].

1 This is not a purely hypothetical issue: the extent of Scotland's territorial waters was a matter of some controversy in the context of the current devolution arrangements. See p 122.
2 See p 18 below.

Part 3: Rights and freedoms

1.5   Nothing in this description of our hypothetical model constitution should suggest that, after the preamble and some general matters, the provisions should be set out in any particular order. There are, logically, many different possibilities. It may, however, be natural for constitutional drafters to place the matters they consider to be of greater political or social significance before matters of lesser significance. For many, this means that guarantees given to citizens and others that their fundamental rights and freedoms will be respected should appear at an early point in a written constitution. Such guarantees are often contained in what is popularly called a 'Bill of Rights' which typically consists[1] of a list of rights and freedoms[2] (eg the right to life; freedom from torture, slavery and forced labour; the right to liberty and security; the right to a fair and public hearing; the prohibition of retrospective criminal offences; respect for private and family life; freedom of thought and religion; the right to education; freedom of expression, of assembly and of association; and others). Each of these rights is briefly defined and is then followed, in most cases, by a reference to the limited circumstances (which have usually to be defined by another law) in which it is to be treated as justifiable to have a restriction placed on the original right. Thus, for example, a person has a right to his or her liberty – but not where it is taken away following conviction of a criminal offence by a court. There may also be other provisions offering rather softer guarantees of what are called 'social and economic rights' – eg rights to an adequate standard of living including adequate food, clothing and housing[3]; and sometimes a right of access to official information – thus providing 'freedom of information' – may be assured. In addition, there may well be further rules thought necessary to ensure the effective implementation and enforcement of the guaranteed rights. It should be remembered, however, that the constitution has already been stated to be the highest form of law in the country. The impact of that core characteristic of a written constitution is well illustrated by the support it provides for the upholding of basic rights and freedoms. They are 'fundamental' both in their intrinsic importance but also in the legal status guaranteed to them by the constitution. However, many constitutions do declare certain rights to be fundamental but then fail to provide mechanisms which are effective enough to sustain them. In such cases, the declarations amount to no more than that. They may be made in good faith or they may be made more cynically as window dressing but they can be expected to have little or no effect on the ground.

1 Quite apart from a list of rights specified in the constitution, it may be expected that an independent Scotland would be a party to the European Convention on Human Rights. This might have the effect of further expanding or strengthening the Bill of Rights. See also ch 12 below. For fuller discussion, see R Reed and J Murdoch *A Guide to Human Rights Law in Scotland* (2nd edn 2008); A Boyle et al (eds) *Human Rights and Scots Law* (2002); A Lester, D Pannick and J Herberg (eds) *Human Rights Law & Practice* (3rd edn 2009).
2 The list chosen is based on that in the *IPPR Constitution*.
3 The South African constitution provides that everyone has the right to have access to adequate housing (s 26) and to health care services, sufficient food and water, and social security (s 27).

Part 4: Nationality

1.6   Although many of the provisions (including human rights provisions) of a written constitution will apply to anyone present in the country, constitutions do, for some purposes, make separate provision for those who 'belong' there and those who do not, for instance in relation to the right to vote in elections[1]. Typically, such 'belonging' will be defined in terms of a concept of nationality or of citizenship[2]. It would, therefore, be for our hypothetical constitution to say who is to qualify for Scottish nationality or citizenship – usually done by reference to some prior nationality and then to place of birth, parentage or a rule of naturalisation by residence. Also included might be an acknowledgment of a Scottish citizen's wider citizenship of the European Union and of the rights of citizens of other European states in Scotland.

1 The right to vote is not necessarily confined to citizens. For current rules in Scotland, see pp 70-72.
2 Although, for some purposes, fairly permanent residence in the country may be sufficient, perhaps in combination with citizenship of some other specified state. See, in relation to electoral registration, p 72 below. On UK citizenship in general see ch 12.

Part 5: Head of state

1.7   Our hypothetical constitution might now be expected to include a series of parts or chapters which deal with the composition and functions of the principal organs of government. In relation to these we have to make certain assumptions about what these might be in our imagined version of an independent Scotland.

As far as the head of state is concerned, it can probably be assumed that, at least for a while, Scotland would remain a monarchy, with the king or queen inheriting the title by succession. Provision would be made for this[1]. The alternative would be for Scotland to follow Ireland and become a republic, with provision made for the election of a president for a specific period of years. Symbolically, much might hang on the choice that is made. A switch to a republic might carry with it the impression of a more far-reaching break with a monarchical past in the United Kingdom. In other respects, however, the distinction between the republican and monarchical models is less than might be expected because an almost certain characteristic of either model would be to restrict very sharply the real power of the president or monarch. He or she would have a ceremonial role; would preside on great occasions of state; and might have restricted and residual powers to act in circumstances not fully foreseen by the constitution. He or she would have what the English nineteenth-century writer Walter Bagehot called a 'dignified' rather than an 'efficient' role[2]. There are other possibilities and it is well known, for instance, that the presidents of the United States and of France do exercise real political and constitutional power. In all probability, however, our hypothetical head of state of an independent Scotland might have many important governmental powers allocated to him or her but these powers would, in almost all cases, be stated to be exercisable only on the instruction or recommendation of ministers who would be the people to whom most of the real powers are given.

1 The SNP's draft constitution provides that Queen Elizabeth (and her successors) would remain head of state, 'until such time as the people of Scotland decide otherwise'. The current SNP Government proposes that the Queen would remain the Head of State in Scotland (*Choosing Scotland's Future* (p 2 n 2 above) para 3.25).
2 *The English Constitution* (with introduction by R H S Crossman, 1963) p 61. See also p 152 below.

Part 6: The Executive

1.8   This and the next two parts of the constitution would probably make clear the three-partedness, the 'tripartism'[1], of most contemporary Western constitutions. For reasons to be developed later, constitutions tend to allocate different types of governmental power (usually dubbed executive, legislative or law-making, and judicial power) to different types of institution – the executive, the legislature (parliament) and the judiciary (courts). There must be a 'separation of powers'.

This terminology is not without difficulties and these are explored at a later stage[2]. For present purposes, however, there should be no difficulty in recognising executive powers as the powers vested in those who 'drive' the state – those who make plans, devise policies, make decisions, take action and compel others to act. Sometimes the terms 'government' and 'governmental' are used in ways which embrace the whole of executive, legislative and judicial power. More narrowly, the term 'government' can be confined to the executive branch alone and it is in this sense that, in all probability, our hypothetical constitution would identify the Prime Minister (or perhaps First Minister) and other ministers, as the 'Executive'[3]. There might also be provision for a Deputy Prime Minister and also for a 'cabinet' of senior ministers. There might be specific provision for these to include a Minister of Finance (or Chancellor of the Exchequer), a minister responsible for foreign or international matters, and a Minister for Justice. There would be separate provision for officials (who might or might not be ministers) known as 'Law Officers'[4]. There would have to be provision for the means of appointment of the Prime Minister and other ministers and also for the termination of their appointments. Almost certainly, these would be closely related, in the constitutional model we are describing, to the acceptability of the Prime Minister to the Parliament (or, if there are two houses or chambers in the Parliament, to the directly elected house) and then the acceptability of other ministers to the Prime Minister and perhaps also the Parliament. In other words, the Parliament would, directly or indirectly, choose the Prime Minister and dismiss the Prime Minister, along with other ministers, if they lost its confidence. The Prime Minister would have the power to appoint other ministers, probably with the agreement of the Parliament, and to dismiss them. The parliamentary connection would probably be continued in another constitutional rule which would require ministers including the Prime Minister to be accountable and responsible to the Parliament[5]. This parliamentary model of government, including a close relationship between the membership and operation of the executive and the legislature (sometimes called the 'Westminster model') is, again, not inevitable. Many constitutions draw a much stronger line between the executive and legislative branches of government. Elections to each are separately organised. Each branch exercises powers separately from the other. Neither branch is directly accountable to the other, although there may be points at which the two can interact in a system of 'checks and balances'. The US constitution provides a well developed version of this model. Its presidential rather than parliamentary form of government is defined by its directly elected president[6] and the allocation of executive authority, including the office of commander-in-chief of the armed forces, directly to the president.

Whichever general model of executive government is adopted, a constitution may make further provision for the public service, in part to give permanent civil servants some protection from political interference; there may be outline provision for the ways in which the government will be funded and its accounts independently audited; and there may be provision for the organisation and control of the armed forces. Separately, there may be a part of the constitution securing the position of local government, its guaranteed autonomy and status[7].

1 I D Duchacek *Power Maps: Comparative Politics of Constitutions* (1973).

2 See ch 3.

3 There are further terminology problems specific to the executive branch under the current devolution arrangements in Scotland. It was, during the first eight years of devolution, known as the Scottish Executive but was in 2007 styled the Scottish Government by the incoming SNP administration. That usage attracted negative comment from the UK government. For earlier discussion of the same issue, see *The Founding Principles of the Scottish Parliament* SP PR OR SP Paper 818 (2003), hereafter the '*CSG Inquiry*', paras 814–826.

4 Who, if the UK model were followed, would have formal responsibility for representing the government in legal proceedings and for providing government with authoritative legal advice.

5 What is meant by 'accountability' and 'responsibility' in this context is discussed in ch 9.

6 Actually, although the president is *separately* elected, the election is not wholly *direct*. Formally (and indeed in ways which have practical consequences), popular votes in states are for the membership of an electoral college which then elects the president. See US Constitution, art II and *Bush v Gore* 531 US 98 (2000).

7 The European Charter of Local Self-Government (1985), to which the UK and most of the other 47 members of the Council of Europe are parties, requires that a 'substantial share of public affairs' should be entrusted to local authorities (art 3(1)) and that the 'principle of local self-government shall be recognised in domestic legislation, and where practicable in the constitution' (art 2). See also ch 7.

Part 7: Legislature or parliament

1.9   As already mentioned, primary law-making powers are routinely allocated to a body which is different from the executive. This is the legislature or parliament. Under the parliamentary model of government, it is also usual to allocate to the same body powers of supervision and control of the executive, especially in relation to financial matters. Constitutions are typically designed to ensure that parliaments are representative of the people and, therefore, that their members are directly elected by the people. Essential to our hypothetical constitution, then, would be provisions determining the size of the parliament, how long each parliament would last between elections (and, therefore, the frequency of elections), who could vote in elections, and what the voting system and other arrangements would be. Quite separately, a decision must be made on whether a directly elected chamber would be supplemented by a second chamber constituted, probably, on a different basis. Some parliaments (including, of course, the present United Kingdom Parliament with both the House of Commons and the House of Lords) are made up in such a 'bicameral' way. However it is constituted, the functions of the second chamber and its relationship to the first chamber need to be defined.

Part 8: Judiciary

1.10   The third element in the tripartite structure is the judiciary. A constitution must make provision for judges (in particular, rules for their appointment, their tenure of office and termination of office) and for the structure of courts. On judges themselves, our hypothetical constitution may be expected to provide for appointments to the senior positions to be by head of state but on the recommendation of a minister (in some cases, the Prime Minister), perhaps after initial selection or screening by an independent body with special expertise. Importantly, the constitution would ensure that only in exceptional circumstances and by exceptional procedures could a senior judge be dismissed.

Part 9: Territorial division

1.11   One typical feature unlikely to be adopted into a Scottish constitution would be the division of the country into a number of states or provinces, each with its own constitutionally guaranteed autonomy, territory and governmental powers. This would be to go further than a system of local government and create a federal system for Scotland. Although a federation might be an appropriate model for a country the size of the United Kingdom, the small size of the territory and population would almost certainly preclude it for Scotland. Federal systems can, however, take a number of different forms[1] and, although classic models may be identified in, for instance, the United States or Canada, other models of federalism or quasi-federalism tending towards the form of devolution currently adopted in the United Kingdom are possible. There might, for instance, be a case for giving a constitutionally guaranteed autonomy to Orkney, Shetland or the Western Isles. More generally, the territorial division of the country and the installation of locally elected units of government can be used to give expression to the principle of 'subsidiarity'. This has been given formal recognition in the constitutional arrangements of the European Union but is of wider application. It asserts the value of conducting government at a level as close as possible to the people – whether that be for different purposes at the level of the European Union, state level, sub-state or regional level, or at the level of local government.

1 K C Wheare *Federal Government* (4th edn, 1963).

Part 10: Constitutional amendment

1.12   Two earlier features of the constitution make necessary this final part. One is the power of the Parliament to make laws. The other is the provision in part 2 which has made the law in the constitution supreme over other laws. From this it may be deduced that the Parliament cannot, in the ordinary way, make laws at variance with the rules in the constitution. The Parliament cannot simply amend the constitution by ordinary legislation.

It may, on the other hand, be anticipated that circumstances could arise in which it would be widely thought to be desirable that a particular provision of the constitution be amended. The need for amendments to a constitution can be linked to the point made earlier that a written constitution can be viewed as an expression of a community's values. Technological or social change may, for instance, demand revision of the constitution from time to time and we should expect that our hypothetical constitution would include a mechanism to achieve it[1]. This would almost certainly enable the Parliament to make the amendment but would also require it to adopt special procedures; or to proceed only if a special majority of Parliament agrees; or only if the amending law is also approved by a majority of the population of Scotland in a referendum. Sometimes different procedures are required for different provisions in a constitution, depending on how fundamental and how unalterable they are thought to be. Some provisions may be considered to be so fundamental that they are not amendable in any circumstances at all, although this can be taken to undesirable extremes.

1 In some measure, constitutions are, in effect, also amended when courts interpret and apply constitutional provisions in a different way. See ch 13.

VIRTUAL CONSTITUTION TO REAL CONSTITUTION

1.13   We should once again remind ourselves that the constitution whose terms we were quickly reviewing in this chapter was indeed a figment of our joint imagination. There is no separate or independent Scotland. Scotland does not have its own written constitution. What the provisions of the hypothetical constitution should, however, assist us in doing is two things. The first is to think a little further about what constitutions are and what constitutions and constitutional law do. The second is to draw comparisons between the imaginary and the real, the better to understand the real constitution of Scotland.

Constitutions and their function

1.14   With our hypothetical constitution in mind, we should have no difficulty at all in making sense of some quite cryptic definitions of constitutional law. Thus, from one source, we are told that United Kingdom constitutional law is that part of the law which 'governs the system of public administration of the United Kingdom, and relationships between the individual and the state'[1]. Another informs that 'constitution' refers to 'the whole system of government of a country, the collection of rules which establish and regulate or govern the government'[2]. And another that 'the word "constitution" [is] used to refer to the aggregate of those laws in a state which are styled collectively the public law'[3]. Professor Sir Neil MacCormick wrote of 'how powers and functions of government are divided among different agencies, and how checks and controls are then maintained between and within different branches of government'[4].

1 Lord Lester of Herne Hill and D Oliver (eds) *Constitutional Law and Human Rights* (1997) p 7.
2 A W Bradley and K D Ewing *Constitutional and Administrative Law* (14th edn, 2007) p 4, quoting from K C Wheare *Modern Constitutions* (2nd edn, 1966).
3 C R Munro *Studies in Constitutional Law* (2nd edn, 1999) p 1, quoting from Jeremy Bentham *Of Laws in General* (H L A Hart (ed), 1970).
4 N MacCormick *Institutions of Law* (2008) Ch 3 'Law and the Constitutional State' at p 45.

1.15   What these definitions have in common is, first of all, some idea of a state with a territory and people. Secondly, there is an assumption that such a state will have institutions whose purpose is to discharge the functions of the state – functions which impose important burdens on the state but which also require that substantial powers are exercised by the state's institutions. Thirdly, it is assumed that these state-related powers and responsibilities are different in character from the powers and responsibilities of individual people and non-state organisations such as businesses, partnerships and companies. Often the distinction is drawn between *public law* which governs relationships between such public bodies themselves and also between public bodies and private individuals and organisations and, on the other hand, *private law* which regulates relationships between individuals and private organisations.

Fourthly, it is the constitution that regulates, or at least provides a framework for, these state-based or public law relationships. Our hypothetical Scottish constitution is full of examples of this. The parts on the head of state, the executive, the legislature and the judiciary consist largely of rules which define the composition of the different institutions and define how the separate elements within each relate to each other and then how they relate to the other principal institutions and also, bearing in mind the part on rights and freedoms, how the institutions of government relate to the people. Thus the part on the legislature has to contain rules dealing with the powers and procedures of the parliament. As we have seen, rules have to define the composition of the parliament; they must state whether it is to be unicameral or bicameral and, if bicameral, determine the relationship between the two houses; they must provide for the separate functions of the presiding officer or chair of (each house of) the parliament. But rules in that part and in the part dealing with the executive must also define the relationship between the actual government in the shape of the prime minister and other ministers and the parliament itself. They must determine how far ministers may or must also be members of the parliament. They must provide the powers and mechanisms to enable the parliament to supervise the work of the executive and to ensure, if this is intended, that ministers are accountable or responsible to the parliament. Within the chapter on the executive, rules must define the relationships between prime minister, other ministers, the cabinet and the public service.

Meanwhile, the part on the legislature must also contain the rules which relate the people to the parliament through the election process and also by the opportunities provided for members of the public to question executive decisions and action by invoking the help of members of the parliament. Similarly, an important function of the part on the judiciary is not only to establish the courts themselves but also to provide a framework within which members of the public may then use the courts to question the legal validity of things done or decided by the executive and, probably, the parliament too. Significant for all these processes are the provisions which provide rights of access to information for members of the public and the part on rights and freedoms. A right to free expression or a right to liberty which is declared to be protected from restriction by the executive or by parliament or to be capable of restriction only in limited circumstances clearly does much to regulate the relationships between executive, parliament and people. In so far as the courts have a role in resolving any disputes that may arise when the limits of the guaranteed rights are challenged by either side, that relationship between the courts, the other branches of government and the people being regulated by the constitution has to be established.

It is unsurprising, in the light of what has been said so far, that many constitutional lawyers find it helpful to think of constitutions as 'maps'[1]. What constitutions are doing is charting, within the political system of a state, the formal distribution of power and authority in different sites and then showing the connections between the sites. Such a map is intended to be an accurate description of the present location of constitutional authority but it is also intended to endure. A constitutional earthquake might in a wholly unpredictable way destroy the map. This might be caused by a revolution within the state which overthrows the existing constitutional order. There may be circumstances in which, by agreement of all those with map-making authority, the map may be redrafted in the form of amendments to the constitution and the relocation of some constitutional authority to a different site. But the map should not be alterable in matters of substance simply at the hand of those who exercise power at only one point on it. Those who exercise power should not be free unilaterally to amend the map by extending their boundaries and staking out new territory on it.

1 See, in particular, I D Duchacek *Power Maps: Comparative Politics of Constitutions* (1973).

1.16   For some, the analogy of the map may be to adopt too flat an image of the functioning of a constitution. They may prefer a more sophisticated model in which the different relationships between constitutional sites are represented in a multi-dimensional way. The idea, however, that what constitutions do is to define limits of constitutional space; that they separate some elements (whether institutions or functions) from others; that they allocate areas of free movement or autonomy to people or to institutions and restrain the invasion of that autonomy by others is certainly at the heart of most people's conception of a constitution. The strategies, the techniques and the mechanisms of constitutional law are, above all, concerned with the definition and protection of areas of constitutional space within which autonomous but constrained authority may be exercised.

There is a fifth assumption that underpins almost every conception of constitutional theory. This is that there is an underlying purpose to constitutions and to constitution-making. Constitutional techniques and mechanisms do not exist for their own sake. Constitutional mapping is not *merely* an exercise in geometry or surveying. What provides the purpose and even the passion of constitutional law is a belief that important values can be injected into and sustained within a political system by constitutional means. This has two aspects. The first is the identification of the values themselves and frequently this is a cause of controversy. There is clearly no necessary reason to suppose that political and constitutional values will be identical across the great religious, cultural and ideological divides. If the same terminology is used, it may in fact relate to widely differing ideals. Even in the context of liberal democratic politics, the content of values such as equality, liberty, justice and democracy may be contested but it is, nevertheless, values such as these that constitutional lawyers usually have in mind at the point where they engage in constitutional redesign or in the evaluation of existing designs. These are matters to which we return (with more specific reference to Scottish, United Kingdom and European constitutional law) but it should at this stage be observed that it is probably three inter-linked groups of values that are most prominent: (1) those concerned mainly with the condition of the people in the state, including not only human rights, freedom, equality and procedural and social justice but also benefits such as shelter, education and a good environment; (2) those relating to the quality of government, for example that it be honest, fair, accountable, democratic and participatory but also efficient; and (3) those relating to the state itself, such as the wish that it be independent from or in closer union with other states or that it should operate in a highly decentralised way, with power formally and irrevocably divided between the institutions of the central and federal government and those of the states or provinces or, less rigidly, in a system of devolution; or, alternatively, in a much more highly centralised way. Choices (sometimes, of course, sharply constrained) have to be made as to both the ends and also the means to be adopted to achieve those ends but it is with considerations of these sorts in mind that constitutional lawyers will evaluate particular rules and the interrelationships between institutions and people.

The second consideration to be borne in mind in the pursuit of political and social values by constitutional means is the important question of the effectiveness of constitutions in achieving the purposes which they proclaim. What particularly prompts this question is the evident 'failure' of many constitutions worldwide. The list of twentieth-century failures was very long. Constitutions do not always achieve for their people the freedom or justice they seek. They fail to restrain dictatorial executive power or they fail to achieve the democratic conditions to which, on their face, they aspire. Failing constitutions are sometimes described as merely 'paper' constitutions. The reasons for failure are many and not always easy to understand. Often they may be the same reasons that lead to the failure of other sorts of law. Just as a law against drug abuse does not always end abuse, so a constitutional guarantee may often be ineffective and sometimes the reason for ineffectiveness is not hard to discern. It may be that blame can be attached to a particular provision that was inadequately thought about in advance. Sometimes ineffectiveness may be the result of inept 'borrowing' from other systems or from inept draftsmanship. It may simply have been too sloppily crafted. It may have been too general in its terms when greater specificity would have helped. In relation to constitution-making for former British colonies in the second half of the twentieth century, Professor S A de Smith wrote of the 'advantages of being explicit'[1]. On the other hand, there are strong arguments in favour of the use of general language (and, at the same time, fewer words) in constitutions, in contrast with other types of legal documentation. Constitutions intended to endure may be better written in general terms rather than in highly specific language which may date rapidly. Another factor to be taken into account at that point, however, is the role of the superior courts in their interpretation of the terms of the constitution. This will always have a bearing upon the practical application of the constitution and, therefore, upon its effectiveness in the light of the meaning attributed to its terms by courts. In principle, the more general the language of the constitution, the greater the scope of interpretative freedom, and therefore power, which rests with the courts[2].

1 S A de Smith *The New Commonwealth and its Constitutions* (1964) p 82.
2 See ch 13.

1.17 Rather differently, another reason for failure may be that a constitutional provision has from the start been included as a mere token and with a cynical or negligent lack of concern for its effective implementation. In such a case the 'failure' cannot be attributed to any weakness in the text of the constitution itself but to more fundamental flaws in the motivations of those who designed and established it. The 1936 Constitution of the former Soviet Union is often held up as a good example of constitutional deceit and manipulation. The rights it proclaimed for the citizens of the Soviet Union were always illusory, as was the declared right of states to secede from the union if they wished[1]. Such deliberate cynicism may be unparalleled but it has also to be acknowledged that, whether as a result of flamboyant overstatement of objectives sincerely wished or of baser motivations, many constitutions in the world have expressed an aspiration to create institutions or achieve goals which, on a more sober assessment, were never likely to be attainable. In such a situation the 'failure' of the constitution is incorporated from the outset. Although most striking examples of dislocation between the declared and more covert aims of constitutions are to be found in more distant systems[2] – in part because, in contrast with the United Kingdom, they put their purposes on the formal record – any critical inspection of the United Kingdom constitution will reveal similar failings[3]. Any such analysis is, in any event, complicated by the tensions in any pluralist liberal democracy between political and, therefore, constitutional goals. Although it may sometimes be hoped and asserted that the constitutional order maintains an impartial overview of social and political difference, this is never achievable. Constitutions may be expected to sustain some purposes and values at the expense of others.

1 See ch X (fundamental rights and duties of citizens) and art 17 (right freely to secede).
2 For a classic dissection of the US constitution, see C A Beard *An Economic Interpretation of the Constitution of the United States* (1913).
3 See I Harden and N Lewis *The Noble Lie: The British Constitution and the Rule of Law* (1986).

1.18 There are also more subtle and elusive ways in which constitutions may be said to fail. Constitutions are constitutions of states. They are primarily concerned, as we have said, with the regulation of the exercise of state power. Constitutions are, therefore, dependent upon the existence of states and state power and their role becomes problematic in times when the idea of the state is itself challenged, as may be said to be the case in the contemporary condition of 'globalisation'. If the power of states, whether benign or threatening, is declining in the face of larger economic and political forces, so too does the underlying rationale for constitutions. State power and its regulation decline in significance. The limits of personal liberty are determined less by state authorities than by supranational forces. To the extent that these trends occur, so the importance of national constitutional orders will decline. This is a development which is distinguishable from situations where states, most notably today the member states of the European Union, resolve to bind themselves by treaty to collective undertakings and the surrender of their separate sovereignties. There, state power is asserted but shared in ways which produce constitutional consequences of their own[1]. The impact of 'globalisation', on the other hand, is to force a reduction in the authority and significance of constitutions of any sort[2].

1 See ch 3.
2 See N Walker 'The Idea of Constitutional Pluralism' (2002) 65 MLR 317; C M G Himsworth 'In a State No Longer: the End of Constitutionalism?' [1996] PL 639; G Anderson 'Scottish Public Law in an Age of Constitutional Globalisation' in A McHarg and T Mullen (eds) *Public Law in Scotland* (2006).

Constitutional law in Scotland

1.19   The second introductory project within this section is once again to return to the hypothetical constitution for an independent Scotland and to rely on it to draw two rather obvious points of comparison and contrast between that imaginary model and the present reality of constitutional law in Scotland.

Scotland, the United Kingdom and the European Union

1.20   The first point is that, since constitutions are, for the most part, an aspect of statehood and Scotland is not an independent state but a part of the UK state, it is to the level of the United Kingdom that we have to look, for most purposes, for a 'national' constitution. That is not to say that it is wholly meaningless to talk about a Scottish constitution or Scottish constitutional law in conditions where national independence is lacking. Scottish constitutional law and public law in general have distinguishing features which have to be taken into account in any broader description of United Kingdom constitutional law. Since 1999 the most significant of these features has been devolved government under the Scotland Act 1998 (SA 1998) and, although this terminology is not widely used, that Act can quite reasonably be described as a constitution for Scotland[1]. In federations it is usual to have both a national constitution and then separate state or provincial constitutions at the local level. During the twentieth century, it was quite usual to acknowledge that Northern Ireland had a constitution of its own within the United Kingdom. The Government of Ireland Act 1920, which provided the basis of the Stormont Parliament and devolution in the Province from 1922 to 1972, was frequently referred to as a 'constitution'[2] and, although never fully implemented, it was the Northern Ireland Constitution Act 1973 which repealed much of the Government of Ireland Act 1920 and would have provided a new 'constitution'. SA 1998 may be seen in a similar way and the resulting constitutional context is further considered in Chapter 3 – as well as in the rest of the book, as more specific topics are considered.

1 Indeed, SA 1998, read in combination with the ECHR and European Community law, has been described judicially as a 'mini constitution' (see *Whaley v Lord Advocate* 2004 SC 78, para 37 (Lord Brodie)). It has also been said of SA 1998 that it 'may reasonably be expected therefore to contain everything that is needed by way of legislation for the proper working out of the system

that it lays down' (*Somerville v Scottish Ministers* 2008 SC (HL) 45 per Lord Hope of Craighead para 17).
2 See, eg, A S Quekett *The Constitution of Northern Ireland* (1928, 1933, 1946).

1.21   There is another important way in which our model constitution for an independent Scotland has to be contrasted with real constitutional conditions. Not only has Scotland to be seen for most important purposes as a part of the United Kingdom but the United Kingdom, along with the other 26 states of the European Union, has been constitutionally affected by membership of the Union. There is indeed a sense in which the treaties which establish the Union and create its institutions, including the European Court of Justice, serve as a constitution of the Union of which the United Kingdom and the member states are simply parts. Although the parallel is resented politically in many quarters, there are good reasons from a legal perspective for comparing the European Union with federations such as the United States, Canada or Germany. In those the federal constitution is the highest form of law and the constitutions of member states are subordinate to it. The parallel with the European Union, though not perfect, can readily be drawn and this and related matters are further addressed in Chapters 3 and 5.

The unwritten constitution of the United Kingdom

1.22   There is another immediate contrast to be drawn once we begin to look to the real United Kingdom constitution rather than the hypothetical Scottish version. Probably the best-known single characteristic of the United Kingdom constitution is that it is 'unwritten'. What this means is that there is, for the United Kingdom, no single document of high authority which, in the manner we have described, sets out the core rules of the British constitution. The United Kingdom is unique among modern states in having no written constitution[1] and the inconvenience of this situation is evident in compendia such as Oceana's *Constitutions of the Countries of the World*[2] where the editors struggle to find for the United Kingdom the documentation readily available for other states. Some would say that the lack of a written constitution is indeed merely an inconvenience. If we wish to identify for the United Kingdom the documents which, were we to assemble them in one place, would provide the equivalent of a written constitution, we can indeed draw together some (mainly statutory) material for the purpose. *Constitutions of the Countries of the World* does this and includes the (English) Magna Carta 1215, the (English) Bill of Rights 1689, the Parliament Acts 1911 and 1949, the Statute of Westminster 1931[3], the European Communities Act 1972 (ECA 1972), the Sex Discrimination Act 1975, the Race Relations Act 1976 and the British Nationality Act 1981, as well as SA 1998, the Government of Wales Act 2006 (GWA 2006), the Northern Ireland Act 1998, the Human Rights Act 1998 (HRA 1998) and the House of Lords Act 1999. There are, however, a number of problems with this. Partly because we lack a written constitution, we lack a definition of what counts as a constitutional statute or a constitutional document when drawn from another source. This is partly a question of what is important or significant enough to be included. The editors of *Constitutions* have made their choice but what were the criteria for including some documents and excluding others? One criterion might be the status or the degree of formal authority of one statute compared with others but, again, it is partly because of the lack of a written constitution that we also lack any formal hierarchical ordering of rules. In the case of *Thoburn v Sunderland City Council*[4], Laws LJ did find it useful to identify what he called 'constitutional statutes' and his list included Magna Carta, the Union with Scotland Act 1706, the Reform Acts 1832, the ECA 1972, HRA 1998 and as well as SA 1998 and the GWA 1998[5]. That list is, however, in no sense formally definitive and its content would be contested[6]. There is one formal statutory source which does provide an account of what may be defined as the essential elements of the UK constitution: for the purposes of defining and limiting the legislative powers of the Scottish Parliament, SA 1998 describes what is meant by the 'reserved aspects of the Constitution'. These include '(a) the Crown, including succession to the Crown and a regency, (b) the Union of the Kingdoms of Scotland and England, (c) the Parliament of the United Kingdom, (d) the continued existence of the High Court of Justiciary .... (e) the continued existence of the Court of Session'[7]. Clearly that list, assembled for a very limited purpose, does not, in itself, amount to a written constitution for the United Kingdom but it does suggest that, despite the difficulties of identification and selection, it may be argued that, once the choices have been made, the United Kingdom can muster a written constitution. The rules are not in a single document – in *Constitutions of the Countries of the World* the editors sometimes include for other countries more than a single text[8] – but they are written down. They may lack the coherence and convenience of a single text but the collected documents can perform the same function.

1 From time to time, of course, states may have only an 'interim' constitution prior to the adoption of a permanent constitution, as was the case in South Africa between 1994 and 1997. Elsewhere, states may lack a written constitution – sometimes for an extended period – when the former constitution has been suspended or revoked following a coup.
2 A P Blaustein and G H Flanz (eds).
3 Creating a new constitutional basis for the Commonwealth.
4 *Thoburn v Sunderland City Council* [2003] QB 151. See ch 5.
5 *Thoburn v Sunderland City Council* [2003] QB 151 at 186.
6 See ch 5.
7 SA 1998, Sch 5, Pt I, para 1.
8 This is, for instance, the case with Israel and New Zealand.

1.23   However, this would, be an unhelpful analysis for at least four reasons:

(1)   First, a collection of statutes, however put together, leaves gaps in the UK constitution. Many rules which, because of their constitutional significance, would have to be included in a full account do not derive from any statute or other formal documents at all. Their origin lies in the unwritten rules of the 'common law' rather than statute ranging from many of the rules which define police powers and the liberties of individuals through to the special 'prerogative' powers, formerly exercised by the monarch but now in the main by ministers, such as the power to declare war and manage foreign affairs, as well as the power to summon and dissolve Parliament. The common law as a source of constitutional rules is dealt with in Chapter 5 but, for present purposes, it is quite easy

to see that such rules are not readily defined as 'written' and yet they are important. It is true that rules of the common law may be articulated, developed or at least referred to in the written judgments of courts and such judgments are frequently cited as the written sources of the rules, but they would not lie easily alongside statutes as part of a written constitution.

(2)   The other principal omission from a documentary account of the UK constitution would be those rules or practices usually referred to as 'constitutional conventions'[1]. Many of these are central to the United Kingdom's institutional arrangements where formal legal rules are absent or provide only a partial picture. It may perhaps seem strange that key institutions such as the Cabinet and the Prime Minister are not formally established by law; the subordination of the Queen (despite possessing a range of formal legal powers) to the Prime Minister and other ministers is similarly unknown to the law; the relationship between ministers and Parliament is not legally regulated; and relationships between the two Houses of Parliament are only partially defined by legal rules. These are, however, institutions and relationships which are of sufficiently high constitutional importance to have been directly incorporated in the export version of the Westminster model when it travelled to former colonies in the second half of the twentieth century. To take one off the peg, the independence constitution of Lesotho in 1966 expressly provided that the Cabinet should be collectively responsible to the Houses of Parliament[2], a position which is regulated only by convention in the United Kingdom. When such provisions are indeed incorporated into a written constitution, their formal status as legal rules becomes clear[3]. It may be said that a similar but more partial process has occurred in the adaptation of Westminster-based procedures by SA 1998. This makes clear, for instance, that the Queen formally approves the appointment of members of the Scottish Executive, made by the First Minister[4]. That power to appoint is now statute-based. On the other hand, the Queen's obligation to approve the names tendered to her probably remains based on convention.

At the United Kingdom level itself, the position is less clear and accounts vary. It is possible to say that all that happens in the British constitution which is not directly regulated by law is 'mere politics'. One can, in other words, *describe* politically created institutions and their relationships but such descriptions can have no normative force. There are practices but no rules. At the other end of the spectrum are accounts which insist that rules do operate in these areas[5]. Such rules are not legal rules – no legal rule prescribes whom the Queen must appoint as Prime Minister[6] – but, as conventional rules or constitutional conventions, they operate to similar effect, save only that they are, by definition, unenforceable by courts. Courts may acknowledge the existence of political relationships within the constitutional order where these may have a bearing on what a related legal rule is or should be. For instance, the rules governing the ways in which judicial control is exercised over administrative action may take into account the political accountability of ministers to Parliament[7]. The politically based idea of collective responsibility within a Cabinet may influence the legally enforceable rule of confidentiality of Cabinet proceedings[8]. But courts will not adjudicate upon the substance of 'rules' which have only a political or conventional basis[9].

The answer to the question of whether conventional practice can be the source of rules (albeit non legal) probably lies at a point between the two more extreme positions. This acknowledges that, in the large area of political behaviour in the United Kingdom that currently lies beyond the reach of formal legal regulation, distinctions have to be drawn. In some areas, such as those which define the individual[10] and collective[11] responsibility of ministers, few 'rules' seem to operate beyond those determined by the flexible pressures of political power and survival. It is largely meaningless to characterise behaviour as constitutional or unconstitutional. In other areas, the most important of which determines the constraints on the Queen's behaviour vis-à-vis her ministers, it does make sense to describe her role as normatively constrained. There are rules which should be observed and the Queen would act unconstitutionally if she breached them. We shall find that a non-legal rule has already emerged to govern the circumstances in which the Westminster Parliament may use its power to make laws for Scotland in the areas for which the Scottish Parliament[12] has legislative competence. In accordance with what has been named the 'Sewel Convention', this should occur only with the consent of the Scottish Parliament. Although this could never be directly restrained by a court, an Act passed by Westminster without such consent might well be regarded as having been passed unconstitutionally.

(3)   The third objection to the idea that a group of statutory texts can be recognised in the United Kingdom as the equivalent elsewhere of a written constitution is that its lack of coherence, its lack of any statement of overall constitutional ideals and objectives and, above all, the fact that it has never been formally adopted into use mean that it has little chance of claiming the loyalty, and even the affection, of the people. It is not, it is true, a constitution imposed by a foreign power but it is a constitution which has been imposed by history and subjected to only incremental change.

(4)   The fourth objection is the most fundamental. One of the principal purposes of practically all modern written constitutions is to assert their own supremacy. This is not supremacy for its own sake but rather a supremacy which creates a hierarchy in which constitutional rules are at the top and all other rules, including, most importantly, the laws made by the Parliament, are subordinated to them. Parliamentary laws which are not in accordance with the constitution are invalid – a proposition which, in turn, almost inevitably, demands that the courts (or a single court) must have the power to determine the validity or not of the laws made by the legislature[13].

It is this which makes the difference. It is the lack of supremacy of the constitution and, therefore, the lack of a judicial power to review the validity of Acts of Parliament which most sharply distinguish the United Kingdom's constitutional arrangements from most written constitutions. Instead of an ultimate rule of the constitutional order (for Hans Kelsen[14], the *grundnorm*) which directs courts to obey the constitution and thus, if necessary, to defy Acts of Parliament, there is, in effect, a *grundnorm* which directs courts to obey all Acts of Parliament without the option of defiance. In the United Kingdom, it is Parliament which is supreme, rather than a written constitution[15]. This has profound consequences for the UK constitutional order and the position of Scotland within it. Constitutional amendment becomes a matter for Parliament itself in the ordinary process of legislation rather than some special procedure under the supervision of a controlling court[16]. It is for this reason that if, failing a court, a 'constitutional long-stop' is sought for the protection of the constitution from manipulation by the party politically dominated House of Commons, this is, for some, to be found in the United Kingdom Parliament's second chamber, the House of Lords. Although the formal capacity of that House to restrain the law-making powers of the House of Commons has been very largely confined to a power of delay rather than of veto, the House of Lords, equipped with a Select Committee on the Constitution to assist it in the process, is widely seen to perform a 'long-stop' role[17].

1   The term is not to be confused with the 'constitutional convention' which is a meeting of worthy people convening for the purpose of devising the terms of a new constitution, such as that held in Philadelphia in 1787 – and perhaps the European Convention which met during 2002–03 to discuss the constitution of the European Union.
2   Constitution of Lesotho (1966), s 73(2).
3   Although there *may* still be doubt about the justiciability and, therefore, the enforceability of such rules in the courts.
4   SA 1998, s 47(1), and see p 166.
5   I Jennings *The Law and the Constitution* (5th edn, 1959) ch III.
6   See, p 157 below.
7   See, eg the speech of Lord Mustill (although a dissent) in *R v Home Secretary, ex parte FBU* [1995] 2 AC 513 at 567.
8   *A–G v Jonathan Cape Ltd* [1976] QB 752.
9   Although, in Canada, the Supreme Court did rule on whether there had been a breach of convention in *Reference re Amendment of the Constitution of Canada* (1982) 125 DLR (3d) 1.
10 See p 254.
11 See pp 161 and 174.
12 See p 139.
13 For the confirmation of that power in the United States, see *Marbury v Madison* 5 US 1 Cranch 137 (1803).
14 *Pure Theory of Law* (2nd edn, tr M Knight, 1970).
15 See ch 5.
16 See discussion of this by the House of Lords Select Committee on the Constitution and its rejection of suggestions for the adoption of a special procedure for Bills of 'first class constitutional significance': *Changing the Constitution: The Process of Constitutional Change*, Fourth Report HL 69 (2001–02), paras 59–61.
17 See Report of the (Wakeham) Royal Commission *A House for the Future* (Cm 4543, 2000) ch 5; *Fifth Report of the House of Commons Public Administration Committee*, HC 49 (2001–02) paras 72–75; *First Report of the Joint Committee on House of Lords Reform*, HL 17, HC 171 (2002–03), p 10.

1.24   However, although it has generally been right to conclude that the British constitution is not one which has been policed by courts but has instead sought a political underpinning, things may now be in a state of flux. In ways to be discussed in Chapter 13, the courts have taken on a wider role, especially under HRA 1998 and the devolution Acts also of 1998, which may, for good or ill, expand into a broader capacity to undertake a form of constitutional review. It would be at that stage that, with an increasing part of the constitution committed to writing and a shift of final decision-making authority from the political to the judicial organs, the United Kingdom would become more closely aligned with other Western democracies. Until that stage is reached, however, constitutional developments will remain a matter, if not of political whim, of political debate and resolution.

Chapter 2

Constitutional Law and Constitutional Values

INTRODUCTION

2.1   As already mentioned in Chapter 1, it is often the case that written constitutions expressly incorporate a statement of principles or values which the constitution claims to uphold. Such statements may take different forms – sometimes quite short and simple, sometimes more elaborate. Often the statement will not be included in the text of the constitution itself but will instead take the form of a preamble to the constitution which claims to declare in advance the goals which the constitution makers are seeking to achieve by the substantive rules which follow. A list of principles or values inserted in this way can include principles which are not strictly legal in character but which are more broadly social or political; they may be intended to be not directly enforceable by courts, while still available to aid courts where difficulties in the interpretation of specific clauses in the constitution arise; and they may be cast in very general terms. An example of a constitutional preamble of this sort which is frequently cited is that of the Indian Constitution of 1950. It is committed to securing for all citizens:

> JUSTICE, social, economic and political; LIBERTY of thought, expression, belief, faith and worship; EQUALITY of status and opportunity; and to promote among them all FRATERNITY assuring the dignity of the individual and the unity and integrity of the Nation.

The Constitution of the United States provides:

> We, the People of the United States, in order to form a more perfect Union, establish Justice, insure domestic Tranquillity, provide for the common defence, promote the general Welfare, and secure the Blessings of Liberty to ourselves and our Posterity, do ordain and establish this Constitution for the United States of America.

The South African Constitution proclaims that it was adopted to:

> Heal the division of the past and establish a society based on democratic values, social justice and fundamental human rights; Lay the foundations for a democratic and open society in which government is based on the will of the people and every citizen is equally protected by law; Improve the quality of life of all citizens and free the potential of each person; and Build a united and democratic South Africa able to take its rightful place as a sovereign state in the family of nations.

These constitutional texts all provide interesting examples of preambles designed to give specific recognition to the values intended to be sustained by the provisions which follow. Such preambles are not, however, an inevitable element of a written constitution and, in many constitutions, they are omitted. Although the Indian Constitution did contain a substantial preamble, most of the other constitutions devised for newly independent states in the Commonwealth in the 1950s and 1960s did not[1]. This does not mean, however, that the constitution makers involved were any less concerned to ensure that their constitutional texts reflected similar constitutional values. It was simply that their preferred drafting technique led them not to include formal statements but instead to leave any underlying principles or values to be deduced from the rules of the constitution actually laid down; implied from the text, rather than expressly stated. Most obviously, a written constitution which includes a Bill of Rights makes a strongly implied commitment to the underlying value to individuals of the rights and freedoms it contains. The incorporation of rules for the popular election of a Parliament may be taken to imply a commitment to principles of representative democracy. The adoption of a model of federal government which divides powers between central and regional authorities implies a commitment to the values of a democratic system which deliberately seeks to avoid the concentration of political power in a single central government. A constitution which expressly or impliedly confers strong powers on a constitutional court or on the judicial system in general demonstrates a preference – sometimes stronger, sometimes weaker – for the resolution of certain types of dispute by a court rather than by politicians.

Thus, the fact that a written constitution does not include a declaration of values and principles expressly articulated in a preamble to the main text should not at all be taken to mean that the constitution, taken as a whole, makes no commitment to a set of principles which inform its operation. Certain problems, however, attach to this process, whichever method is adopted. The principles asserted, whether expressly or impliedly, may not be all they seem. They may have a very vague and general character and they may not be intended to be directly enforceable by courts. This may easily lead to big differences between the principles proclaimed by the constitution on the one hand and their actual realisation in practice on the other. Whether intentionally or not, statements of principle tend to tell only a part of the story. They attempt to conceal contradictions between values; they select heavily in favour of those principles likely to show the constitution in a good light; they tend to be aspirational and ideological; and, at worst, they are a complete sham. Discrepancies between the assertion and reality of constitutional values and goals may be much greater[2].

When we come to examine the constitutions of Scotland and the United Kingdom, we find that the lack of a written constitution clearly rules out the possibility of any single authoritative statement of constitutional principles and values. Similarly, the opportunity is denied to derive from a single constitutional text a group of implied principles which might be said to underpin the constitutional order. However, this should not prevent us from describing the values which are claimed to be inherent in British constitutional arrangements. The lack of a single document may complicate this process a little and there is the added complication of the long period of historical development which is such an important feature of the United Kingdom constitution. This is also true, of course, of other enduring constitutions but it is certainly the case that accounts of the principles which underpin the United Kingdom constitution have changed over time and they continue to change. Just as statements contained in written constitutions will tend to be a response to conditions of the time of their making and will reflect the concerns and aspirations of that time, so too do statements about the unwritten British constitution. They vary over time, if only in the degree of emphasis given to different aspects from one commentator to another. There is nothing politically neutral about constitutional principles. In a United Kingdom context, a nationalist will attach great importance to the recognition given by the constitution to the separate 'nations' of the United Kingdom. A unionist will take a different view. Republicans and monarchists will disagree. Different views will be taken of the value of human rights and their relative significance. Sometimes issues will divide the political left and right but, at other points, divisions will be along other lines. While such disagreements (whether about the principles themselves or the best means of pursuing them) are inevitable, they do nothing to diminish the need for any student of the constitution to have available a more or less coherent set of principles and standards against which the working of the constitution can be assessed and evaluated. They may not have any formal constitutional status but such principles and standards have an important bench-marking function as a tool of constitutional analysis. Thus, although the absence of a formal statement leaves us free to choose constitutional benchmarks of our own devising, there is merit in choosing standards associated with the liberal democratic tradition within which the United Kingdom constitution is claimed to operate and, if a written constitution were ever devised, would perhaps be asserted in its introductory preamble. For a start, despite the absence of a formal domestic constitutional statement, the United Kingdom has expressed itself bound by the standards imposed by many international documents. European Union law is of authoritative standing in the United Kingdom and it is the Treaty on European Union which, among other things, confirms in its preamble the Union's 'attachment to the principles of liberty, democracy and respect for human rights and fundamental freedoms and of the rule of law'[3]. The United Kingdom is a party to the European Convention on Human Rights (ECHR) which has been applied by the courts in both the period before and since its 'incorporation' by the Human Rights Act 1998 (HRA 1998)[4]. In addition to the rights themselves, the preamble to the Convention commits members of the Council of Europe to the 'profound belief in those fundamental freedoms which are the foundation of justice and peace in the world' and reminds of the 'common heritage of political traditions, ideals, freedom and the rule of law'. And all members of the Commonwealth, including the United Kingdom, have committed themselves to upholding certain fundamental principles in documents including the Harare Commonwealth Declaration 1991. In addition to wider undertakings, the Heads of Government pledged the Commonwealth and its member countries to 'democracy, democratic processes and institutions which reflect national circumstances, the rule of law and the independence of the judiciary, just and honest government'; and to 'fundamental human rights, including equal rights and opportunities for all citizens regardless of race, colour, creed or political belief'[5].

With commitments such as these as a backdrop, this chapter focuses discussion on three areas:

(1)   individual liberty and its protection (a short note only);
(2)   standards of good governance, integrating within these the idea of the separation of powers;
(3)   the distinctive idea of accountability of government to the law, often referred to as the rule of law. In this account, the idea of a 'right to law' is referred to.

1 S A de Smith, *The New Commonwealth and its Constitutions* (1964).
2 See the reference to the USSR at p 13 above.
3 See also the draft Constitution Treaty of June 2003, arts 1–2.
4 See ch 13.
5 See also the Commonwealth's Latimer House Principles on the three Branches of Government (2003).

INDIVIDUAL LIBERTY AND ITS PROTECTION

2.2   There is little doubt that most people would proclaim the attainment of the liberty of the individual as one of the most fundamental purposes of a constitution. State institutions, whether in the form of kings or modern bureaucracies, have a tendency to oppress and it should be the function of a constitution to protect individuals from that oppression. This is an imperative which has to be linked with the idea of good governance which is discussed below, at which point it will also be recognised that governments, while being restrained from oppression, must also be facilitated in the discharge of their lawful functions. The protection of individual liberty is also closely related to the idea of accountability to the law and the rule of law.

When indeed Professor Dicey propounded his analysis of the rule of law in 1885, he declared that it could at that time be said that the constitution was 'pervaded by the rule of law on the ground that the general principles of the constitution (as, for example, the right to personal liberty, or the right of public meeting) are with us the result of judicial decisions determining the rights of private persons in particular cases brought before the courts; whereas under many foreign constitutions the security (such as it is) given to the rights of individuals results, or appears to result, from the general principles of the constitution'[1]. For Dicey, personal liberty was very important. Whether or not he was right to say that it was better protected, as an aspect of the rule of law, by court decisions in their development of the common law than by express provision in a constitutional document is debatable. What is clear, however, is that, by the end of the twentieth century, there was a near consensus in the United Kingdom Parliament that this was insufficient, and the country's adherence from 1951 to the European Convention on Human Rights was relied on to provide the basis for the incorporation by HRA 1998 of a new system of rights protection. These developments are pursued further in Chapter 13.

1 A V Dicey *Law of the Constitution* (10th edn, 1959) p 195.

STANDARDS OF GOOD GOVERNANCE

Introduction

2.3   Constitutions are expected to deliver not only protection for the rights of individuals but, just as importantly, the conditions under which the institutions of government can secure social goods to the population at large. At some points the two objectives are entirely complementary. It is often through the delivery of public services that rights are also secured. At other points there is some tension between the two. The state acts in the general interest but only at the price of some interference with the rights of individuals. For many of its services, the state must have the power to obtain funding through the imposition of taxation. It must have the power to acquire land and to restrict the use of land and other property. The state also claims the power to license trades and professions and to regulate commercial and industrial activity in the interests of securing competitive conditions of operation, the health and safety of employees or the quality of the environment. In support of these powers, the state needs also to claim ancillary powers to enforce the governmental regimes that are established. At their most extreme, these involve imposing criminal penalties for non-compliance with the rules laid down. Thus, the administration and enforcement of governmental programmes often carry with them the danger of interference with the rights of individuals. The use of the state's powers and, even more, the abuse of those powers will always bring that possibility. And this is the case whatever the political tendencies of particular governments. The twentieth century saw fluctuations in the political programmes of governments including varying attitudes to how government in general should be conducted and the overall size of the government machine. But, whether one thinks of the period of nationalisation of industry after the 1939–45 war or of the Thatcherite determination to restrict the size and power of the state in the 1980s, similar questions are raised about how quality of governance is to be achieved. Nor is this merely a question of balancing public policy considerations against the rights of individuals, although that is clearly a matter of importance. Good governance also involves the attainment of standards of wider scope and it is these to which constitutions are also expected to aspire.

Traditionally, the emphasis in most accounts of constitutional values has been upon the dangers of abuse of governmental power and, therefore, upon the adoption of principles which might restrain those abuses. That approach remains important and some aspects of it are to be considered shortly. It is, however, important also to recognise that the point of restraining abuse of government is not ultimately to achieve no government at all but to achieve better government. This is not to suggest that there are objective criteria for the evaluation of particular governmental policies and programmes. These are matters on which, of course, reasonable people and, in particular, political parties, disagree. However, what can be agreed is that government should be enabled to be efficient and effective and a constitution which fails in this respect fails to meet the most important criterion of good governance. Beyond that, though, principles of good governance demand the injection of democracy; of decentralisation or subsidiarity[1]; of government which is free from corruption, unfair discrimination, illegality and maladministration; and of openness and transparency. Such a list is very general in nature and it is the stuff of constitutional debate to determine to what extent and in what ways these values should be represented in the institutions and procedures of a particular state. In the United Kingdom a particular focus has been placed in recent years upon the qualities which should be displayed by the public services. These have been expressed by the Committee on Standards in Public Life[2] as the 'Seven Principles of Public Life': selflessness, integrity, objectivity, accountability, openness, honesty and leadership. When the EC Commission published its White Paper on *European Governance* in 2001, its choice of 'principles of good governance' was openness, participation, accountability, effectiveness and coherence, all of which were stated to reinforce the further principles of proportionality and subsidiarity[3]. The UK Parliamentary Ombudsman has published The Principles of Good Administration[4].

1 See p 8 above.
2 Appointed on 25 October 1994 and currently chaired by Sir Christopher Kelly.
3 COM (2001) 428 ch II.
4 Revised, 2009.

The principle of accountability

2.4 Above all else, good governance necessarily implies a commitment to the principle of accountability – a quality common to both the lists above[1]. This takes several different forms. Perhaps the most important is accountability of government to the law which, as the rule of law, is considered in the next section. The *financial* accountability of government is also important and is reflected in the audit and other mechanisms established with a view to securing financial propriety[2]. Accountability to ombudsmen in respect of maladministration has been developed across much of British public administration[3]. Overriding all these, however, in any liberal democracy is the claim made by institutions of government to be *democratically accountable to the people*. Such accountability is typified by the responsibility of ministers to the Westminster and Scottish Parliaments[4] but it is represented too in the accountability of elected local councils[5]. Neither of these models – central or local – provides the basis for a direct or 'pure' democracy in which the people themselves are seen to govern. Frequent elections combined with mechanisms of accountability between elections provide only an indirect form of democracy. The intermittent, though perhaps increasing, use of referendums to test public opinion on specific issues of importance[6] does not alter this position significantly. Another important feature of this constitutional order which gives general recognition to democratic principles is that it incorporates substantial variations in their application. In some areas democratic accountability is much more immediate and direct than in others. A lack of direct accountability may be the result of systemic failure and, as an example, the difficulties of giving effect to the principle of ministerial responsibility are considered in Chapter 9. At other points, however, the reduced application of democratic accountability is the result of deliberate decisions that this should be the case. For varying reasons, those bodies, grouped collectively as 'intermediate government' or 'quangos', are deliberately intentionally placed at arm's length from direct democratic control[7]. To an extent, the emergence of 'executive agencies' within UK government departments and the Scottish Administration has the same effect[8]. At all those points where general principles of open government give way to exceptional restrictions on public access, the scope for direct democratic accountability is reduced[9].

1 See D Oliver *Constitutional Reform in the UK* (2003) ch 3.
2 See p 291.
3 See p 270.
4 See p 254.
5 See ch 7.
6 Recent instances have been the devolution referendums in Scotland and Wales in September 1997 (see p 58); and in Northern Ireland in 1998. A referendum might be held on the question of the UK's adoption of the euro currency. In 1975, a referendum was held on the UK's continued membership of the EC. In March 1979 referendums were held prior to the (non-) implementation of the Scotland Act 1978 and the Wales Act 1978. The SNP Government's National Conversation (see p 2 n 2 above) has proposed a referendum on whether the Scottish Government should negotiate with the UK Government to achieve independence.
7 See ch 7.
8 See ch 6.
9 See ch 9.

Separation of powers

2.5   Common to all relationships of accountability (democratic, legal and others) is the need to establish institutions whose membership, powers and procedures give them the degree of autonomy necessary to enable them to perform the function of holding to account which is allocated to them. To achieve the accountability of government to the law there must be a judiciary capable of acting sufficiently independently of the governmental bodies it is supposed to control. The principle of the independence of the judiciary, which is considered in Chapter 11 has a clear pre-eminence, despite its own complexities. That principle is, however, usually seen as one manifestation – and probably the most prominent manifestation – of a more general principle of the separation of powers. This is an idea of great antiquity in the history of thought about good governance – certainly one which predates modern conceptions of constitution-making and constitutionalism. Its age gives the doctrine of the separation of powers both its attraction as an honoured principle but also its crudeness as an analytical benchmark. Its limitations are particularly apparent in relation to constitutions based on the parliamentary form of government.

It is with the name of Montesquieu[1], the eighteenth-century French philosopher, that the doctrine of the separation of powers is principally associated. In his *De l'Esprit des Lois* (1748) he articulated a view of the British constitution as one which had achieved a separation of legislative, executive and judicial powers as the basis of securing the life and liberty of the subject. Even though a misleading description of the British constitution, then or now, the idea of the separateness of powers was enormously influential in constitution-making elsewhere, notably in the United States Constitution of 1787 whose opening articles are deliberately structured around the need for a separate legislature in the Congress[2], executive in the President[3], and judiciary in the Supreme Court and other federal courts[4]. Despite the superimposition on that division of institutions and functions of 'checks and balances' producing some interaction between the three sectors (eg the Senate's powers over presidential appointments to the Supreme Court and elsewhere) and the inevitable intermingling of party politics, the separation is real. The Supreme Court does have a large degree of independence and the separate elections to the presidency and the Congress ensure clear blue institutional water between the two. On the other hand, when export models of the United Kingdom constitution are committed to paper and also deal separately with the Parliament, government and judiciary, the separateness is, beyond its presentational convenience, much less secure. In systems of parliamentary government, there *are* good reasons for insisting on a principled independence of the judiciary but the merger of powers and personnel between the executive and legislature means that any true separation of those branches of government is elusive. Legislative power is substantially shared between the parliament (whether, for instance, at Westminster or Holyrood) and the executive. Governments dominate primary law-making and have broad powers of secondary law-making[5]. The accountability of government to parliament on the one hand denies a separation between the two but, to an extent, insists upon it[6].

However, this does not mean that, viewed more broadly, respect is not paid to the value of institutional autonomy. Indeed, a complex and sophisticated pattern of autonomies is readily detectable. Apart from the functional autonomy sought on a territorial basis by the local government system[7] and by devolution itself, most examples are to be found in those bodies whose raison d'être is the scrutiny of the executive or where, for other reasons, it is thought desirable that a body should be free from direct control of ministers. The separation of powers becomes a principle which is much more significant as a basis for division of authority *within* the executive branch of government than between the executive and the legislature. This has been one of the justifications for the creation of many quangos[8] which then depend for their autonomy upon their separately conferred powers and protection from overt political control over appointments to and dismissals from the senior positions. In turn, this is what has driven the work of the Committee on Standards in Public Life and the Commissioner for Public Appointments in Scotland when dealing with appointments to public bodies and, in the case of some high-profile bodies, statutory protections, similar to those afforded to judges, are built in. Thus the Scottish Public Services Ombudsman is appointed by the Crown but on the nomination not of the Scottish Ministers but of the Parliament. And he would be dismissible only following a resolution of the Parliament passed by a two-thirds majority of MSPs[9]. The Auditor General for Scotland is in a similar position[10]. In both cases, the official whose independence needs to be safeguarded is protected from dismissal on the whim of the government. Similarly, because the supervision of elections is plainly a sensitive area, the Electoral Commissioners are appointed by the Queen but only on an Address from the House of Commons and then only with the agreement of the Speaker and following consultation with leaders of the political parties[11]. A dismissal would require a House of Commons Address preceded by a report from the Speaker's Committee[12] specifying the justification for the dismissal on limited statutory grounds[13]. Another important area of institutional autonomy within the execu-

tive, and one of much greater antiquity, is that occupied by the law officers
– members of the government itself and yet independent from government for
the purpose of their major functions[14].

Separation of powers, broadly conceived, has also been important at the heart
of central government itself. Differentiating clearly between the role of elected
and politically driven ministers, on the one hand, and appointed, politically
neutral civil servants, on the other, and then regulating relationships between
the two groups, has long been a matter of constitutional concern[15]. There has
to be a 'separation' between ministers and civil servants in general and then
the creation of a relationship in which ministers can, subject to rules protecting their professional autonomy, direct civil servants in what they do. But, for
some purposes, particular civil servants are given an enhanced autonomy enabling instead the scrutiny of ministers by them. This is the position of accounting or accountable officers whose duty it is to monitor the financial propriety of
their own ministers[16]. Latterly, another element has been added – the civil servants who *do* have a political role or, as they have come to be known, 'special
advisers' – and this has heightened the need for careful thought about appropriate relationships within government. The problems were nicely explored in
a report, which explicitly incorporated the imagery of territorial relationships,
of the Committee on Standards in Public Life[17]. Entitled *Defining the Boundaries within the Executive: Ministers, Special Advisers and the Permanent Civil
Service*, the report discussed the boundaries and relationships, at one point the
'chemistry of relationships' (para 3.6), within the constitutional framework,
the changing landscape of government and the need for the boundaries to be
'secured', principally by means of a new Civil Service Act[18].

A feature of that Standards Committee report is its insistence on the need for
express regulation of a sector in which questions about boundaries had always
been there but had not, until recently[19], been the cause of great concern. Things
had, in the main, simply 'worked', despite some uncertainties and contradictions in the applicable rules. This reflects a wider approach in the United Kingdom to institutional analysis and reform of the 'If it ain't broke, don't fix it'
school. There had been a tendency to try to leave unreformed those aspects
of the constitution which, although on their face indefensible in principle,
were nevertheless thought to 'work'. Nowhere was this more apparent than in
the formerly combined roles of the Lord Chancellor – a senior minister who
appointed judges and was the head of the English judiciary and 'convener'
of the House of Lords – and, in particular, in the defence of those roles by a
former holder of the office[20]; Lord Irvine of Lairg:

> We are a nation of pragmatists, not theorists, and we go quite frankly for
> what works. I would say that for countries emerging for the first time and
> trying to gain the attributes of a mature democracy, a much stricter doc-
> trine of separation of powers would be appropriate than is appropriate for
> us who represent a very old and well-founded democracy in which those
> values are well understood and upheld ... We do not want to make changes
> for the sake of it or for academic reasons or to conform to some kind of
> universal paradigm of how we manage our affairs, but we should look to
> see what works[21].

But a more principled approach was shortly to prevail. The new UK Supreme Court, in which the Lord Chancellor (no longer a judge or necessarily legally qualified) does not sit, has been established[22]; and the Judicial Appointments Commissions/Boards have effectively become responsible for judicial appointments[23].

1   Charles de Secondat, Baron de Montesquieu.
2   US Constitution, art 1.
3   US Constitution, art 2.
4   US Constitution, art 3.
5   See ch 8.
6   See ch 9.
7   See ch 7.
8   See ch 7.
9   Scottish Public Services Ombudsman Act 2002, sch 1, para 4(1)(d).
10 Scotland Act 1998 (SA 1998), s 69(1), (2). The Comptroller and Auditor General is similarly protected. See Exchequer and Audit Departments Act 1866, s 3.
11 Political Parties, Elections and Referendums Act 2000 (PPERA 2000), ss 1 and 3.
12 The Speaker, two ministers, the chairman of the Home Affairs Committee and five other MPs.
13 PPERA 2000, s 2 and Sch 1.
14 See N Walker 'The Antinomies of the Law Officers' in M Sunkin and S Payne (eds) The Nature of the Crown (1999).
15 See p 182.
16 See p 291.
17 Ninth Report, (Cm 5775 (2003)).
18 For further discussion, see p 183.
19 See Eighth Report of the House of Commons Public Administration Select Committee: Three Unfortunate Events (HC 303) (2001–02).
20 Currently the role is combined with that of Secretary of State for Justice.
21 Evidence to the House of Commons Select Committee on the Lord Chancellor's Department, 2 April 2003 paras 28, 46. See also the evidence of Mr E Jurgens to the same Committee on 27 March 2003.
22 See p 296.
23 See p 302.

THE RULE OF LAW

Introduction[1]

2.6   Like the doctrine of the separation of powers, the rule of law is a long-standing concept in the history of constitutional theory. But, again, it is an idea whose meaning and utility have changed greatly over time. Aristotle's notion of government by laws being superior to government by men may carry little meaning today. On the other hand, Voltaire's preference for a land 'where men were ruled by law and not by caprice'[2] is wholly comprehensible. Professor Dicey gave a central position to his version of the rule of law but it is one which now has a much-reduced relevance. For him, the idea of the supremacy or the rule of law included at least three 'distinct though kindred conceptions'. It meant, first, that 'no man is punishable or can be lawfully made to suffer in body or goods except for a distinct breach of law established in the ordinary legal manner before the ordinary Courts'; second that 'not only ... with us no man is above the law, but (what is a different thing) that here every man, whatever, be his rank or condition is subject to the ordinary law of the realm and amenable to the jurisdiction of the ordinary tribunals'; and, third, that 'the general principles of the constitution (as for example the right to personal liberty, or the right of public meeting) are with us the result of judicial decisions determining the rights of private persons in particular cases brought before the Courts'[3].

Over a century later, some aspects of this account still have attractions as a grounding for good governance. It is underpinned by assumptions that government should be conducted in accordance with the law; that the law should be administered by independent courts; and that the law should be administered in accordance with basic principles of equality. On the other hand, Dicey's insistence on a privileged but piecemeal role for the common law has lost its meaning today. His reliance on the 'ordinary' courts as the sole guardians of liberty needs much qualification, although the assurance of access to the sheriff court and Court of Session (and their equivalents in other parts of the United Kingdom) in civil actions against public bodies and on appeal or review from proceedings in tribunals remains important. Perhaps the least resonant aspect of Dicey's doctrine for the modern reader is his idea that governments and their officials should be made subject to the *same* law and, therefore, the *same* legal restrictions as the 'ordinary' citizen. Understandable as this may be as a first line of defence raised by a nineteenth-century commentator with a minimalist view of governmental power and who was concerned about the growth of government with collectivist and interventionist tendencies, it appears too crude a response today. An expanded, complex and legitimate role for government demands a more subtle approach. It has also come to be recognised that the rule of law, while retaining its utility as a portmanteau concept, is easily capable of abuse as a mere political slogan and is certainly capable of attracting a variety of different meanings. What follows is a brief account which might capture mainstream views.

1 See J Jowell 'The Rule of Law and its Underlying Values' in J Jowell and D Oliver (eds) *The Changing Constitution* (6th edn, 2007).
2 Quoted by Dicey *Law of the Constitution* (10th edn, 1959) pp 189–190.
3 Dicey pp 188–205.

The principle of legality

2.7   In the first place, the rule of law represents and endorses a simple principle of legality[1]. Public bodies and their officials must act in accordance with the law as it is for the time being. For this purpose, it is irrelevant whether the relevant rules of law are 'good' or 'bad' rules, whether they are outdated and in need of reform, or whether they were made in accordance with procedures which, while legally unchallengeable, were unsatisfactory. All that is required is that the rules be valid in the system in which they are located. If they are, the rule of law, in this first aspect, insists that there is value in their being observed by and enforced against public bodies. Public bodies are as much bound by the law as anyone else and, unless specifically conferred, they have no power to suspend the application of the law in relation to themselves. They cannot make new law to benefit themselves or, indeed, for any purpose, without legal authority to do so.

This idea of legality has a number of important consequences which serve to ensure the very high priority accorded to the rule of law. It secures the general liability of public bodies to actions arising out of a breach of contractual obligations or delict[2]. It is also the principle of legality and, in this sense, the rule of law which is sustained when the limits of the executive powers of the police or army or other public officials are tested in the courts. This was reflected in a statement by a former Minister for Justice to the Scottish Parliament when he said:

> This country does not operate by way of executive diktat. It is proper that [challenges on grounds of human rights] are a matter for the courts, despite the fact that the Executive may occasionally find itself on the wrong side of their decisions. That is part and parcel of belonging to a country in which the rule of law applies[3].

In particular, it is the principle of legality which is invoked in the process of judicial review where the courts' role is to assess the lawfulness of the act or decision of a public body by reference to the source of legal authority, usually statutory, on which the body purports to rely[4]. This may involve a difficult interpretative exercise but the point is to uphold the terms of the law as laid down.

Although these procedures are available not only to individuals but to other public bodies as well, it is the rule of law, in this initial sense, which has been regarded as the historic guardian of civil liberties. Until the more 'interventionist' approach to individual rights was adopted by HRA 1998 (and SA 1998), such rights were protected only to the extent that they were not reduced by the powers conferred on public bodies. In Dicey's day these limits were defined principally by common-law rules – a position well illustrated by the famous English case of *Entick v Carrington*[5] in which the court held unlawful a search of private premises which, though done under a warrant issued by a Secretary of State, had no legal justification in statute or in common law. A claim that 'state necessity' could legitimate the search was rejected. More recently, however, it is the limits of statutorily conferred powers which are more significant. To take an uncontroversial example, once the limits of the Mental Health (Scotland) Act 1984 had been clarified[6] it would have been unlawful, as the law then stood, for the Scottish Ministers to continue to detain a person who had murdered in the past, who might still be dangerous but whose condition was untreatable. It was, however, the Executive's belief that the public interest demanded that such persons should be detained and the Mental Health (Public Safety and Appeals) (Scotland) Act 1999 was promptly passed by the Parliament in order to change the law.

A further minimum requirement of the rule of law as the principle of legality is its implementation by the courts. The law must be interpreted; it must be applied to the circumstances of particular cases; and it must, if necessary, be enforced. This requires courts which have the necessary skills but, more importantly, the ability to take an impartial and independent view of the facts and law before them. An independent judiciary, especially one which is not subordinated to the control of the executive, is an important ingredient of the rule of law. Without that, the principle of legality would unravel.

1 This is to be distinguished from the 'principle of legality' recently developed (though claimed to be of historic origins) in cases including *R v Home Secretary, ex parte Simms* [2000] 2 AC 115; *R (Daly) v Home Secretary* [2001] 2 AC 532; *R (Morgan Grenfell Ltd) v Special Commissioner* [2003] 1 AC 563. See also *R (Mohammed) v Foreign* Secretary [2009] EWHC 152. In these the rather narrower principle means that Parliament may derogate from fundamental principles of human rights only in express terms or by necessary implication.
2 Legally defined exceptions occur where, for instance, the Local Government (Contracts) Act 1997 overrode the general law on the validity of local authority contracts. The Crown Proceedings Act 1947 removed many earlier immunities attaching to the Crown, but leaves some in place. See also, however, *Davidson v Scottish Ministers* 2006 SC (HL) 41.
3 SP OR 11 November 1999, col 508, Jim Wallace MSP.
4 See ch 13.
5 (1765) 19 St Tr 1030.
6 *Ruddle v Secretary of State for Scotland* 1999 GWD 29-1395.

Beyond legality: the rule of law and justice

2.8 While it is difficult to overstate the value of the rule of law and the legitimacy which adherence to the law confers, it is plain that legality is not sufficient in itself to ensure a just society. It is, for this reason, that there is a reluctance to describe a state as complying with the rule of law if its laws are themselves unjust. Observing and enforcing the law then brings injustice rather than justice. Easy examples occur in manifestly dictatorial regimes where laws are made to suit the purposes of the dictator. The apartheid regime in South Africa prior to 1991 pretended an observance of the rule of law. There was a sophisticated legal system and a judiciary which could make claims to independence but many of the rules which were applied by the courts were not only undemocratic in origin but were deliberately discriminatory between the racial groups in the country. Huge injustices were done in the name of the law. Nearer to home, however, while the degree of systemic persecution may be less, similar complaints may be heard about recent terrorism legislation because of the breadth of the police powers conferred or indeed, earlier, about the Abolition of Domestic Rates etc (Scotland) Act 1987 which brought to Scotland the short-lived poll tax. The capacity, within the UK system of executive domination of a supreme Parliament, to produce laws which attract sharp and often widely shared criticism is apparent. It was in the face of the threat to the rule of law from 'elective dictatorship' that Lord Steyn once said that 'in exceptional cases...the rule of law may trump parliamentary supremacy'[1]. Nor is the Westminster Parliament alone in this. If Westminster can be criticised on 'rule of law' grounds for the authorisation of broader powers to intercept communications[2], so too can Holyrood[3].

Examples such as these have led to expanded views of the rule of law in perhaps three main directions. Most dominant has been a tendency to pack into the concept of the rule of law the whole gamut of human rights protection. Thus, rules of law which are profoundly and unjustifiably unequal in their terms or their impact are, like the apartheid rules, said to be contrary to the rule of law. But, similarly, rules which are in breach of other fundamental human rights, such as those articulated in the ECHR, are non-compliant. Beyond that, however, it may be argued that even more fundamental than those civil and political rights are the social and economic rights which guarantee education, employment, housing and an absence of poverty. The state which fails its citizens in these areas too may be regarded as failing to comply with the rule of law. Nor may the unequal protection of the rule of law be tolerated. 'That…is not the way the rule of law works. The lesson of history is that depriving people of its protection because of their beliefs or behaviour, however obnoxious, leads to the disintegration of society……The rights and fundamental freedoms that the [ECHR] guarantees are not just for some people. They are for everyone. No one, however dangerous, however disgusting, however despicable, is excluded. Those who have no respect for the rule of law – even those who would seek to destroy it – are in the same position as everyone else.'[4]

Secondly, the concept of rule of law can impose obligations on state institutions not only to respect the rights of citizens but also to obey wider obligations of 'institutional morality'[5] which would encompass qualities characterised in this chapter as 'good governance'. Principles of democracy, transparency and accountability can be restyled as aspects of the rule of law.

And, thirdly, the terminology of the rule of law is available to all those who, without any pretension at all to conceptual precision, will use the language of non-compliance with the rule of law to castigate a government or official for any extreme failure to act fairly or justly. This is especially the case where the threat of anarchy and lawlessness looms as, for instance, was the case when Keith Raffan MSP concluded a speech describing patterns of intimidation and electoral fraud in Zimbabwe by saying that '[i]nstead of the rule of law, there has been the rule of the mob'[6].

It is clearly impossible to define a single correct use of the concept of the rule of law. It can be used to refer to a number of specific qualities in a system of law or as an umbrella term to capture all that is good in a legal or political system. However, there is a strong case for saying that the rule of law may be best understood as a right to law – a right to the legal accountability of government. This is, in the main, to return to a narrow principle of legality but it is also to insist on the effective application and enforcement of laws by courts. There must be nowhere within the state to which the jurisdiction of the courts does not extend[7] – nor, for that matter, places beyond the limits of the state. There should, in principle, be no persons and no institutions who are immune from the law or the courts – even those at the highest level in the constitution[8]. Exceptionally, immunities or indemnities from the normal application of the law may be justified, as may, occasionally, the retrospective imposition of new legal vulnerabilities[9] but the standard expectation of the right to law is that the formal equality of subjection to, and treatment by, the law will prevail. This includes an understanding that review by courts is not excluded[10]; that governmental powers are not conferred in terms so broad that they are unreviewable by courts; and, as important as anything, that the law is enforceable. The former Scottish Executive said: 'Enforcement plays an important and integral role within the Scottish civil justice system. Without means to enforce them the orders of our civil courts would be but 'as bees without stings' and the rule of law could not be upheld.'[11] Not only should the law be enforceable but it should in fact be enforced, and enforced even-handedly. The legal system should be resourced adequately and access to the system must be assured, with the assistance of the legal profession as necessary. That, in turn, presupposes a measure of guaranteed independence for the profession itself. The Law Society of Scotland has said in evidence to the Justice 1 Committee of the Scottish Parliament: 'An independent Scottish solicitor profession is an important aspect of democracy and the Society believes that the independence of the legal profession is a central feature of the rule of law.'[12]

It may be contended that all these issues fall within the familiar territory of fundamental rights protection. The rights guaranteed by ECHR, art 6 to a fair trial go a very long way to ensure a right to law. The right to law, however, should extend to beneficiaries beyond the 'victims'[13] recognised by the ECHR, including, in particular, public bodies themselves. Public bodies rely as much as anyone upon the power of the courts to enforce the law. They need to be able, in the public interest, to ensure that suspected criminals are prosecuted, that action is enforceable against those who breach licensing or other regulatory rules, and that taxes are gathered. It would be contrary to the rule of law if this enforcement power were abused but it would also be wrong if the power were not available. Equally, public bodies may need the law's protection from the unlawful acts of other public authorities. A power conferred by the Local Government in Scotland Act 2003 enables the Scottish Ministers to take steps to enforce a duty imposed on Scottish local authorities to secure 'best value' in the performance of their functions[14]. From a local authority point of view, it is important that they know that such enforcement action can be taken only within the limits of the rules laid down.

There are many other features of a 'right to law' which could be developed but one which is important relates to the timing of the operation of the law. It is often said that 'justice delayed is justice denied' and it is certainly true that the issue of delay in relation to legal proceedings can raise a range of (rule of law related) issues. Several were mentioned in the speech of Lord Hope in the English case of *R (Burkett) v Hammersmith and Fulham London Borough Council*[15]. Firstly, he reminded that, until reforms in the 1980s, the Scottish procedure for judicial review of governmental action[16] 'was of little use in practice, as it took so long ... to obtain a decision of the court'[17]. Secondly, and conversely he dealt with the principle of 'promptitude' which demands that judicial review proceedings, in either Scotland or England, although the rules differ in detail between the two, should be brought without undue delay – mainly to protect the interests of the public authority concerned. Thirdly, however, those rules of 'promptitude' should themselves be sufficiently precise and certain to avoid the loss of a deserving action against a public authority because of confusion over the procedural rules to be applied[18]. It is in the texture of the rules which acknowledge procedural concerns such as these that respect for the rule of law can be said to be found.

Thus, it is the availability of law and the access to remedies in courts of law which are the essential ingredients of the rule of law. The courts must have an independence and impartiality discussed later in Chapter 11. They must have a range of powers – in turn opening up a range of legal avenues to those who access them – and these are addressed principally in Chapter 13. The courts offer, above all, the conditions of the legal accountability of government to complement the political accountability already discussed, and to be developed further in Chapter 9. It is the balance (or, at some points, the opposition) between the two – the one placing emphasis on political and democratic mechanisms and the other on judicial mechanisms – that best characterises the condition of the constitutional order. However, it is ultimately in the political realm that the balance, adjusted from time to time, is secured[19].

1   Attlee Foundation lecture, 11 April 2006.
2   Regulation of Investigatory Powers Act 2000. See eg Surveillance: Citizens and the State, 2nd report of the HL Committee on the Constitution (2008-09) HL Paper 18.
3   Regulation of Investigatory Powers (Scotland) Act 2000.
4   Lord Hope of Craighead, *RB v Home Secretary* [2009] UKHL para 210.
5   See eg, J Jowell 'The Rule of Law and its Underlying Values' in J Jowell and D Oliver (eds) *The Changing Constitution* (6th edn, 2007).
6   SP OR 13 March 2002, col 10206.
7   But, for an interesting exploration of this, see H W Arthurs *Without the Law* (1985).
8   For Crown immunity, see M Sunkin and S Payne (eds) *The Nature of the Crown* (1999). See also A Tomkins,'The Crown in Scots Law' in A McHarg and T Mullen (eds) *Public Law in Scotland* (2006).
9   But the War Damage Act 1965 operated retrospectively to undo the effect of *Burmah Oil Co (Burma Trading) Ltd v Lord Advocate* 1964 SC (HL) 117, as did the Education (Scotland) Act 1973 in relation to *Malloch v Aberdeen Corpn* 1974 SLT 253. The War Crimes Act 1991 has retrospective effect. See also the Erskine Bridge Tolls Act 2001 and the Damages (Asbestos-related Conditions) (Scotland) Act 2009.
10 Although review is sometimes excluded: see p 383.
11 *Enforcement of Civil Obligations in Scotland* (2002). 'Bees without stings' is attributed to Stair Institutions II, 4, 47.
12 *Report on Regulation of the Legal Profession Inquiry* SP Paper 700(2) 2002, Annex D.
13 See ch 13, n 383.
14 See Local Government in Scotland Act 2003, ss 1, 23–27.
15 *R (Burkett) v Hammersmith and Fulham LBC* [2002] 3 All ER 97.
16 See p 369.
17 [2002] 3 All ER 97 at 115.
18 [2002] 3 All ER 97 at 115–117.
19 Cf M Loughlin *Sword and Scales* (2000).

Chapter 3

The Scottish Constitutional Context

INTRODUCTION

3.1   In Chapter 1 it became clear that the general function of all modern constitutions is the same. A constitution maps institutions and their interrelationships, and defines the position of individual citizens and others. Equally, in Chapter 2, the purposes and values promoted or permitted by constitutional orders, whether directly or indirectly, were seen to share a common core in the Western liberal tradition. But, within those very broad parameters, there is, of course, scope for very wide variations between one set of national constitutional arrangements and another. The constitution of the United Kingdom and then, within that, the constitutional position of Scotland have characteristics which, at a general level, are shared with other national constitutions but which also have peculiarities in their structure and content which are determined by the context in which they are situated.

The context within which a constitution is located is defined by reference to the complex interaction of the political, social and economic forces which shape the state to which the constitution relates. Sometimes these are fairly easily understood by reference to some recent event producing radical change and a new start. The current constitution of the Republic of South Africa was the product of deliberation over the period between 1990 and 1996 and the terms of the 1997 constitution clearly reflect the radically changed political circumstances in which it was born. Its preamble opens with a recognition of 'the injustices of the past'. But even that constitution was not written on a wholly clean slate and its terms also reflect some political and legal continuities in South Africa – for instance, the role of provinces in government, although in expanded numbers. The same is true of other states where circumstances have brought abrupt change but also a constitution which nevertheless owes something to the state's constitutional past, for example the constitution of the Federal Republic of Germany of 1949; the constitution of the Fifth French Republic of 1958; the post-Franco constitution of Spain of 1978 or the constitution of Montenegro after its separation from Serbia in 2006. In other states, such as the United Kingdom, where constitutional change has been more evolutionary, the continuities tend to overshadow the effect of the specific occasions where change has occurred. Our task is an understanding of the modern constitution but there is no avoiding the incorporation into a contemporary account of some of the features of its historical development where these continue to affect its current shape. For some, this points to the need for a substantial historical story and this was indeed the fashion in constitutional analysis at one time. But constitutional histories tend to distort. They give an illusion of constitutional continuity, of constitutional cause and effect, which ignores the much more significant impact of other changes over time. On the other hand, there are indeed some historical events which, though reshaped by the passage of time, still loom large in any modern account. It would be difficult to understand the modern constitutional situation of Scotland without absorbing the impact of the creation of the United Kingdom of Great Britain in 1707; the accession of the United Kingdom to the European Union[1] in 1973; and the launch of devolution and the Scottish Parliament under the Scotland Act 1998 (SA 1998). These three historical events and, in each case, their aftermath have had the greatest effect on defining the context in which we now study the constitutional law of Scotland. In subsequent sections of this chapter, each receives introductory treatment[2].

This is, of course, to be selective, and other choices might be made and added to the list. There is, for instance, no doubt that the United Kingdom's imperial past greatly affected its constitutional development and some might include modern Commonwealth relationships as one of the continuing defining characteristics of the modern United Kingdom constitution[3]. Some would attach particular significance to relationships between church and state as they have developed over time. Nor is there any doubt about the importance of the historical circumstances which brought the arrival of cabinet government in the eighteenth century or of a measure of democracy in the shape of the Reform Act 1832 and the extension of suffrage to women in 1918 and 1928. Another choice might be the United Kingdom's accession to the European Convention on Human Rights in 1951 or the passing of the Human Rights Act 1998[4] (HRA 1998). Certainly all these were events or circumstances of significance in their time and all have a continuing resonance. However, they lack the 'constitutive' impact for Scotland of the formation of the United Kingdom, accession to the European Union and devolution.

1 Accession at that time was to the different 'Communities', subsequently known together as the European Union (see below).
2 For fuller treatment, see J Mackinnon *The Constitutional History of Scotland* (1924); J D B Mitchell *Constitutional Law* (2nd edn, 1968); J G Kellas *Modern Scotland* (2nd edn, 1980); J G Kellas *The Scottish Political System* (4th edn, 1989); L Paterson *The Autonomy of Modern Scotland* (1994); C R Munro *Studies in Constitutional Law* (2nd edn, 1999); *SME Reissue* Constitutional Law (2002).
3 A survivor has been the (declining) role of the Judicial Committee of the Privy Council as a court of appeal from certain Commonwealth countries, as to which see ch 13.
4 See ch 13.

The formation of the United Kingdom of Great Britain

3.2   The Westminster Parliament elected in May 2005 is the 54th Parliament of the United Kingdom. The numbering of Parliaments dates from 1801 when, by the Union with Ireland Act 1800, the United Kingdom of Great Britain and Ireland was formed. Prior to that, however, and more significantly from a Scottish point of view, it was in 1707 that the Articles of Union brought Scotland, together with England and Wales[1], into the initial United Kingdom of Great Britain. The Articles laid down the terms on which the two countries – which had shared the same monarch (in 1707, Queen Anne) since the Union of the Crowns in 1603 – would come together. The Articles provided for a single flag combining the crosses of St Andrew and St George; for the succession to the throne to be to the House of Hanover as already determined for England by the Act of Settlement 1700; and for the United Kingdom to 'be represented by one and the same Parliament, to be styled, the Parliament of Great Britain'. There would be single systems of coinage and of weights and measures. Many of the other Articles dealt with the harmonisation of taxes and of the regulation of trade.

Clearly of momentous impact in its own time, the Treaty and the circumstances of its making might now be thought, some three hundred years later, to be of very limited continuing significance. The Treaty did not create Great Britain as a federal state under which governmental responsibilities would be formally divided between London and Edinburgh, but it created instead the conditions under which London-based institutions could govern across an expanded territory. That would, however, be to underrate the Treaty's continuing relevance which might be summarised as follows:

(1)   In the first place, the very fact that in 1707 the new state of Great Britain was created by voluntary merger (but with consent perhaps corruptly obtained[2]) keeps alive arguments that, should it be the wish of the people of Scotland, a demerger could legitimately be negotiated, thus producing an independent Scotland once again. Such arguments are enhanced by claims that the original merger was based upon a distinct lack of democratic approval, and by the ease with which the territorial division between Scotland and England could be restored. It has been the declared policy of the Scottish National Party that its victory in a Holyrood general election would trigger a popular referendum across Scotland on the issue of independence although that has proved difficult to implement[3]. The mechanisms that might be adopted for the undoing of the Union have been the subject of discussion[4], as has the future relationship with the European Union of an independent Scotland and the continuing United Kingdom[5].

(2)   An important consequence of the terms of the Union Treaty has been the survival of the separate legal system of Scotland. The Treaty, while establishing a single legislature at Westminster and thus enabling Parliament to amend the law of Scotland or to introduce new laws, did not itself make general amendments to the previously existing laws, except to the extent that they were contrary to or inconsistent with the Treaty itself. It did not, for instance, simply unify the legal systems by extending English law wholesale to Scotland. Indeed, the opposite was true. The continued existence and jurisdiction of the Court of Session and of the High Court of Justiciary were preserved (Art XIX) and the Treaty provided that, while Parliament might make laws 'concerning public right, policy and civil government' the same throughout the United Kingdom, no alteration could be made to 'laws which concern private right, except for the evident utility of the subjects within Scotland' (Art XVIII). In addition, the Treaty declared that 'no causes in Scotland [might] be cognoscible by the Courts of Chancery, Queen's Bench, Common Pleas[6] or any other court in Westminster Hall' (Art XIX) although the impact of that provision was in effect undermined by the emergence, very soon

after the Union, of the practice of taking civil appeals from the Court of Session to the House of Lords.

The principal effect of these Treaty provisions has nevertheless been to ensure the preservation of the 'mixed' (civilian and common law) system of private law in Scotland with clear continuing consequences, for instance, for property law. The divergence of public law rules may have been less noticeable but common law rules affecting, for instance, civil liberties and judicial review[7] have remained different from those in England. More prominently, the court systems themselves have remained quite distinct and rules relating to judicial tenure in Scotland trace back to the pre-Union Claim of Right (1689) rather than to the (English) Bill of Rights (1688) or the Act of Settlement 1700. Senior judges hold office *ad vitam aut culpam* (for life or until serious fault) although this is a position which has been substantially qualified by statute in recent years[8].

(3)   Extending beyond the legal system itself, the Treaty and the conditions under which the United Kingdom was created also influenced the general shape of governmental institutions in Scotland. The Treaty sought to preserve the position of the old royal burghs in the local government of Scotland (Art XXI) and, although much change was brought to them and surrounding institutions, they survived until 1975[9]. While their position was not directly protected by the Treaty, sheriffs exercised local administrative functions in addition to their dominant judicial role which, to a limited extent, they retain today[10]. More significantly, the eighteenth century brought the distinctive role of the Lord Advocate in Scottish government. Later, the conditions of 'board' government in the nineteenth century gave way to the Scottish Office, created in 1884. There also emerged the general practice of making separate legislation at Westminster in respect of the public administration of Scotland, which endured until the arrival of devolution in 1999.

(4)   Another, periodically revitalised, issue raised by the Treaty is its status as a written constitution, albeit only partial in its scope, for the United Kingdom. The case has been made[11] that, because the Articles of Union created a new state and one of its principal institutions – a *new* UK Parliament rather than merely an expanded English Parliament – the Treaty and the Acts of Union passed by the old Scottish and English Parliaments which implemented it should be regarded as *constitutive* of the new United Kingdom and not be treated as merely *legislative* in character. The point of seeking to establish a status of this sort for the Treaty is to establish also the basis for an argument that some, at least, of the terms of the Treaty are not, or should not be, amendable today simply by an Act of the Westminster Parliament. Put in this way, the argument for 'constitutional' status for the Treaty is an argument for its being treated as entrenched against incompatible legislation enacted by Westminster and, therefore, a challenge to that Parliament's claim to supremacy or sovereignty. Despite the apparent initial force of the arguments in support of the Treaty's special status, there are also formidable counter-arguments. These are addressed in Chapter 5.

These considerations taken together have placed Scotland in a constitutional relationship within the United Kingdom which must be unique in the world.

It is a relationship which, since 1999, has been substantially restructured by the devolution arrangements introduced by the SA 1998 which are discussed in chapters 4–6 below and indeed in most of the rest of this book. Important as these new arrangements are, however, they are heavily conditioned by the broader constitutional circumstances dating back to 1707. It is these which, though not creating a federation, permitted the United Kingdom to be called 'unitary' in only a highly qualified sense. Many have preferred the terminology of the 'union' state, to acknowledge the special quality of Scotland's autonomy. It is for similar reasons that, although Scotland has for many purposes, before and since devolution, been described as a 'region' of the United Kingdom, the title of 'nation', albeit a substate nation, has often been preferred. This is, of course, to draw terminological distinctions which have a stronger political than purely legal resonance, but they have an important constitutional foundation.

1   Wales had been subject to the English Crown from 1283.
2   C A Whatley *Bought and Sold for English Gold? Explaining the Union of 1707* (2nd edn, 2001).
3   See p 62 below.
4   A J Allan *'Talking Independence'* (2002) and The National Conversation, Chapter 3 – see below 62. See also D Sinclair *Issues Around Scottish Independence* (1999) Constitution Unit.
5   See R Lane 'Scotland in Europe' in W Finnie et al (eds) *Edinburgh Essays in Public Law* (1991); M Happold 'Independence: in or out of Europe? An independent Scotland and the European Union' (2000) 49 ICLQ 15.
6   The courts later to be reconstituted as the English High Court.
7   See ch 13.
8   See ch 11.
9   The Local Government (Scotland) Act 1973, subsequently overtaken by the Local Government etc (Scotland) Act 1994, removed the powers from the royal (and later statute-created) burghs.
10 See ch 11.
11 See especially N MacCormick 'Does the United Kingdom have a Constitution? Reflections on *MacCormick v Lord Advocate*' (1978) 29 NILQ 1.

THE EUROPEAN UNION

Introduction

3.3   On 1 January 1973, the United Kingdom, together with Ireland and Denmark, became members of three international organisations known as the European Coal and Steel Community, the European Economic Community (or Common Market) and the European Atomic Energy Community (Euratom). Already members since the foundation of the three Communities in 1951 and 1958 were Belgium, France, (West) Germany, Italy, Luxembourg and the Netherlands. In the period since 1973, membership has grown to a total of 27 with the addition of Greece in 1981, Portugal and Spain in 1986, Austria, Finland and Sweden in 1995, Cyprus, Estonia, Hungary, Latvia, Lithuania, Malta, Poland, Slovakia and Slovenia in 2004, and Bulgaria and Romania in 2007. Over the same period, under changing treaty relationships negotiated between the parties, the principal Community, the European Economic Community, was restyled as the European Community to recognise an expansion of its competences beyond the merely economic and the European Union was created[1]. Both changes were made under the terms of the (Maastricht) Treaty on

European Union 1992. The European Union, a term often (though strictly not correctly) now used interchangeably with the European Community, embraces not only the Community itself but also two other sets of inter-governmental arrangements, known as 'pillars', concerning a common foreign and security policy and police and judicial co-operation in criminal matters[2].

It is anticipated that membership of the Union may expand in the coming years. Negotiations for the admission of Croatia, Macedonia (FYROM), Montenegro and Turkey are underway. Iceland is a recent entrant upon the process.

At the time of their inception, the original Communities, as children of the post-Second World War European Movement, had the declared aims of laying the foundations of 'an ever closer union among the peoples of Europe'; ensuring 'the economic and social progress of their countries by common action to eliminate the barriers which divided Europe'; and 'pooling their resources to preserve and strengthen peace and liberty'[3]. Those broad aims have been retained but the aims of the Union have been greatly expanded to include the achievement of 'balanced and sustainable development'; the assertion of the identity of the Union on the international scene (including the implementation of a common foreign and security policy); the introduction of a citizenship of the Union; and the maintenance and development of the Union as an area of freedom, security and justice[4].

Currently debate about the future of the Union is focused on the fate of the Lisbon Treaty of 2007(see below).

1 In July 2002 the Treaty establishing the European Coal and Steel Community expired.
2 The intermingling of the institutional and policy arrangements for the Community and Union short of complete integration is reflected in the Treaty provisions. Rather than moving to a single text, the EC Treaty and the Treaty on European Union (TEU) have operated in parallel, producing abbreviated references in this chapter to articles of both the EC and the TEU. If the Lisbon Treaty (see below) is implemented the EC Treaty will be renamed the Treaty on the Functioning of the European Union. The pillars would be merged.
3 Preamble to the EEC Treaty 1957.
4 TEU, art 2.

The UK and the European Union – a unique relationship

3.4   The European Union is one of the many international organisations of which the United Kingdom is a member under the terms of treaties into which it has entered. The United Kingdom is a member of the Council of Europe; it is a member of the Commonwealth and of the United Nations; and a member of countless other organisations conferring benefits but also imposing membership obligations in terms of their constituent treaties. The power to enter into such treaty relationships is clearly a significant aspect of the general governmental authority of the state. In a state such as the United Kingdom, which is generally to be regarded as 'dualist' rather than 'monist' (in that the terms of international treaties require specific legislation to implement their terms domestically rather than affecting the legal rights and obligations of those within the state automatically), many treaties do bring with them the need for an Act of Parliament to ensure that they work effectively and that the state's new obligations are met. For this reason, the treaty-making power has some constitutional significance. It is of importance to identify who has the power to bind the state in treaty obligations – in the case of the United Kingdom, a prerogative power of the Crown – and also to take account of the procedures necessary for their domestic implementation. Much more rarely, however, does the actual content of particular treaties or the organisations they create have substantial constitutional consequences[1].

There are, however, very good reasons for treating accession to the European Union as in a category of its own. The first of these derives from the unique strength and sophistication of its institutions. At the core of the Union, there are four principal bodies: the Council (of the European Union), the Commission, the European Parliament and the European Court of Justice. There are others in addition: while the Council brings together ministerial representatives from each of the member states, so the separate 'European Council' comprises all the heads of government who meet at summit conferences at least twice a year with the responsibility to 'provide the Union with the necessary impetus for its development and ... [to] define the general political guidelines thereof'[2]. The Commission exercises important executive responsibilities in the Union but its functions are supplemented by a number of agencies responsible for specific policy areas, including, for example, the Copenhagen-based European Environment Agency. Separately, there are the European Central Bank, the Court of Auditors with audit responsibilities across the Union's institutions, and the European Ombudsman whose principal function is the investigation of complaints of maladministration. Another body, currently of greater potential than actual importance, is the Committee of the Regions which has consultative functions and is representative of the regions and local authorities of the Union. Scottish membership (four full and four alternate members) had earlier been drawn entirely from elected councillors but, since January 2002, representatives have been drawn from the Scottish Executive, the Scottish Parliament and local authorities[3].

1 But see the European Convention on Human Rights (ECHR), discussed in ch 12.
2 TEU, art 4.
3 On this and other aspects of Scottish representation, see *Fifth Report of the Scottish Parliament's European Committee: An Inquiry into Scotland's Representation in the European Union*, SP EU OR SP Paper 676, 2002.

The institutions of the European Union

3.5   Returning to the principal institutions, they present a curiously idiosyncratic picture. Although, for some purposes, it is helpful, if also provocative, to compare the Union with a federal state and, therefore, tempting to compare its institutions with analogous federal bodies, such comparisons quickly break down. Mapping by reference to constitutional functions is difficult because, to an even greater extent than with domestic constitutions, the separation of legislative and executive powers is elusive – although judicial functions are, as one might expect, allocated to the Court of Justice and the Court of First Instance. The Union's institutions, although much changed over half a century, still retain the shape and division of functions originally appropriate for a small, limited-purpose, inter-governmental organisation. No doubt they will evolve further in the light of the current initiative for the reform of the Union but, in the meantime, the institutions have a curious mix of functions and interrelationships both with each other, and then with the governments and peoples of the member states. In turn, this results in obscure lines of democratic accountability. The richness of this strange constitutional situation cannot be pursued here[1] but, in summary form, the principal institutions have the following membership and functions:

1 For full accounts see, eg, JHH Weiler *The Constitution of Europe* (1999); S Douglas-Scott *Constitutional Law of the European Union* (2002); T C Hartley *The Foundations of European Community Law* (6th edn, 2007); S Weatherill and P R Beaumont *EC Law* (3rd edn, 1999). See also C Boch *EC Law in the UK* (2000); P Birkinshaw *European Public Law* (2003); P Craig and G de Burca *EU Law* (4th edn, 2008); P Craig 'Britain in the European Union' in J Jowell and D Oliver *The Changing Constitution* (6th edn, 2007).

The Council of the European Union[1]

3.6   Formerly known as the Council of Ministers (and not to be confused with the European Council mentioned above[2]), the Council is composed of a minister from each of the member states and is attended by the minister relevant to the subject matter of a particular meeting. EC Treaty, art 202 defines the functions of the Council as ensuring the co-ordination of the general economic policies of the member states, with the power to take decisions and confer powers of implementation on the Commission. The Council is the political power house of the Union; it directs policy and is, with participation from the Commission and the Parliament, the Union's principal law-maker. With membership drawn directly from the governments of the member states, the Council, overshadowed from time to time by the summits of the European Council, is the principal focus for political initiative and for political dispute. Such disputes take place in conditions of pressure, compromise and trade-off within a framework which assures individual states of a veto on certain important matters but otherwise permits majority voting, almost exclusively qualified majority voting (QMV). This model of voting lifts the curb on activity which a unanimity rule would impose but, subject to detailed adjustments incorporated over the years, gives added weight to national votes by reference to the population of each member state. Current rules, deriving from the Treaty of Nice[3], produce a situation in which voting strengths in the Council will range from France, Germany, Italy and the United Kingdom with 29 votes each to Malta with 3 out of a total of 345, with 255 votes by a majority (sometimes a two thirds majority) of members constituting the qualified majority[4].

Very important to the practical working of the Council are the contributions of the Commission (below) and also of a body known as the Committee of Permanent Representatives (COREPER). This is an organisation which consists of senior members of the permanent missions maintained in Brussels by the member states and whose principal responsibility is preparing the Council's agenda. In practice, much of the burden on the Council is lifted by the prior discussion undertaken and agreements reached in COREPER. The Council is further assisted by its Secretariat-General, headed by the Secretary-General. One of the biggest curiosities of the organisation and working of the Council is its constantly changing presidency. A principal target for reform, the presidency – and, with it, the responsibility for setting the political agenda and for the management of meetings – rotates among member states at intervals of only six months. The Swedish presidency of July to December 2009 gives way to the Spanish presidency of January to June 2010 and thereafter to Belgium and Hungary. The next UK presidency is predicted in 2017.

1 Terminology is in flux here. It appears that 'Council of Ministers' has given way to 'Council'. See now the text of the Treaty of Lisbon.
2 Nor, of course, with the *entirely* separate Council of Europe which has, among other things, responsibility for the administration of the European Court of Human Rights.
3 The Treaty was signed on 26 February 2001 and came into force on 1 February 2003.
4 The Lisbon Treaty would adjust the majority required and would introduce the opportunity for any four states to block a proposal.

The Commission

3.7   Even with its Secretariat-General, the Council, as the principal policy- and decision-making body of the Union, could not undertake all the associated tasks of prior policy development and subsequent implementation. It would need additional administrative resources which, in state-based constitutions, would be represented by a permanent civil service. This function, at the Union level, is undertaken by the Commission, one of whose responsibilities is indeed to exercise powers conferred on it by the Council for the implementation of rules laid down by the Council[1].

But the Commission has an independence and significance which go far beyond the supporting role of a civil service. It is a distinctive Union institution, in that both its functions and composition are central to the working of the Union as a whole. The Commission is expected to ensure the proper functioning and development of the Common Market by ensuring the application of Treaty provisions and measures taken by the institutions; to formulate recommendations or deliver opinions on matters dealt with by the Treaty; and both to have its own power of decision and to participate in the shaping of measures taken by the Council and by the European Parliament in the manner provided for in the Treaty[2]. These formal powers provide the authority for the Commission to play a primary role in policy initiative and to be the primary source of Union legislation[3], in that only the Commission may initiate legislative proposals even if, for the most part, their eventual approval becomes a matter for the Council and the Parliament. As the 'guardian of the treaties', it is also the body competent to take enforcement action against member states in the Court of Justice[4]. The autonomy of the Commission derives not only from its separately conferred functions but also from its membership. The Commission is currently a college of twentyseven Commissioners drawn from the member states, (currently Baroness Ashton from the United Kingdom)[5]. Commissioners are appointed by means of a process involving nomination by member states, adoption of a proposed list of Commissioners (including a President) by the Council by QMV, and approval, following scrutiny, by the Parliament. The Parliament retains a power to dismiss the Commission by motion of censure[6]. Commissioners, assigned to different policy portfolios, have an obligation, despite the prior involvement of most in national politics[7], to act independently of political pressures.

There is, of course, much more to the operation of the Commission than the collective work of the Commissioners themselves. The Commission is supported by sectoral Directorates-General and also by an elaborate system of committees, composed of member state representatives, in a process known as comitology. Although this has the capacity to contribute positively to the decision-making process, it also produces some confusion in lines of accountability within the Commission and a lack of transparency.

1 EC Treaty, art 211.
2 EC Treaty, art 211.
3 Although much legislation is in practice generated by the Commission following a request by the Council under EC Treaty, art 208 or the Parliament under EC Treaty, art 192.
4 EC Treaty, art 226.
5 The Lisbon Treaty would reduce Commission membership to only 2/3 of the number of member states, selected on a rotating basis.
6 EC Treaty, art 201. Dismissal was threatened but not carried out in relation to the ill-fated Santer Commission in 1998–99. See S Douglas-Scott *Constitutional Law of the European Union* (2002); A Tomkins 'Responsibility and Resignation in the European Commission' (1999) 62 MLR 744.

The Parliament

3.8   It is the Parliament which injects an element of elected representative democracy into the working of the Union. The Parliament's role has been greatly strengthened since its early days as an Assembly whose members were not directly elected and, although its legislative functions as formally defined may still fall short of those attributed to national parliaments, it now has, in practice, powers both of legislation and administrative and financial scrutiny which are comparable, given the obvious institutional differences, with those of their national counterparts.

The Parliament is now directly elected by proportional representation on a five-year cycle in elections held on a national basis across the Union. Currently 72 MEPs (out of a total of 736) are elected from the United Kingdom[1] with the country divided for this purpose into 12 electoral regions. Scotland is defined as a single region for the election of six members. The European Parliamentary Elections Act 1999[2] which took effect for the elections held in that year provided for voting on the 'closed' regional list system with votes cast for political parties rather than for named individuals[3].

As we have seen, the principal law-making body of the Union is the Council. The Parliament's role is never formally to initiate legislation but it becomes involved in law-making under three different procedural arrangements. In the first place, the Parliament may at least have the right to be consulted on a proposed piece of legislation. Then there is the 'co-operation' procedure[4] which enables the Parliament first to submit an opinion on a piece of draft legislation which may be rejected only after a further 'reading' in the Parliament, and then only by a unanimous Council. Finally, the 'co-decision' procedure, now widely used, removed the opportunity for an overriding veto by the Council. If the Council does not adopt a Commission draft initially approved by the Parliament, it may submit a second draft to the Parliament whose decision to approve or reject outright is then final. If the Parliament proposes amendments, these are considered by a joint conciliation committee of the Parliament and Council which is empowered to negotiate on an agreed text. If it fails, the legislation is dropped.

In addition to its powers of intervention in the legislative process, the Parliament has formal powers in relation to the approval of the Union's budget and the scrutiny of expenditure[5]. It also imposes a measure of accountability on the Commission, both in respect of appointments (and, by censure, of dismissal) and by mandatory systems of reporting, and also, to a lesser extent, on the Council. The Parliament has the power to inject a further measure of democratic pressure into institutions – renowned for their general lack of democratic responsiveness – by the public conduct of its debates, its power to establish committees of inquiry to investigate 'alleged contraventions or maladministration in the implementation of Community law'[6], and by its system of public petitions under which individuals[7] may submit grievances in the hope of redress.

1 EC Treaty, art 190.
2 Amending the European Parliamentary Elections Act 1978 and since consolidated in the European Parliamentary Elections Act 2002.
3 With the exception of Northern Ireland which uses the STV voting system.
4 EC Treaty, art 252.
5 EC Treaty, art 272.
6 EC Treaty, art 193.
7 'Any citizen of the Union, and any natural or legal person residing or having its registered office in a member state' (EC Treaty, art 194).

The Court of Justice[1]

3.9   There are two courts of the Union which sit in Luxembourg – the Court of Justice proper and the Court of First Instance (CFI)[2] which has a more limited jurisdiction (some of it concerned with actions brought by staff against Community institutions) and from which an appeal lies to the Court of Justice. Both courts are composed of judges appointed by the governments of the member states. Formally appointments are collective decisions[3] but, in reality, they are on the nomination of each member state, albeit that a judge need not be a national of the nominating state. Appointments are for renewable periods of six years. Currently the UK judge at the ECJ is Konrad Schiemann, and at the CFI, Judge Nicholas Forwood, an English QC. The ECJ is assisted by a team of eight Advocates General (also drawn from the member states) whose role is to assist the court by producing an often substantial written opinion on the arguments prior to the Court's own judgment.

The functions of the Court include adjudication upon challenges by member states and others to the validity of decisions by Community institutions, enforcement actions against member states, and references under EC Treaty, art 234 on points of Community law from national courts. Much of the work of the ECJ, as with that of national courts, may be described as largely technical

in character as the Court has been required to provide its authoritative interpretation of the texts of the treaties and of Community legislation. It is also,
however, a court which at some periods of its history has been viewed as a
body with a strong integrationist agenda and has been subjected to a degree of
criticism for that[4]. Inevitably, it has also been dubbed the 'constitutional court'
of the Community or Union because of its role in the resolution of disputes
between institutions and states, with the effect of strongly raising its profile
among the Union's institutions.

1 The Court of Justice of the European Communities, to be renamed the Court of Justice of the
    European Union by the Lisbon Treaty.
2 It would be renamed 'the General Court' under the Lisbon Treaty. There is also an EU Civil
    Service Tribunal.
3 EC Treaty, art 223.
4 See especially H Rasmussen *On Law and Policy in the European Court of Justice* (1986).

The European Union and the UK constitution

3.10   Even this summary account should be sufficient to reveal that the
European Union is an organisation distinguished by the sophistication of its
institutions. Other international organisations, notably the United Nations and
the Council of Europe, have quite highly developed structures and, like the
European Union, accommodate policy-making bodies, broadly representative
assemblies, institutions for the implementation of policies and programmes
and courts or tribunals for the adjudication of disputes. But, measured in terms
of the financial and other resources devoted to it and the domestic impact of
its policies, the European Union stands far ahead of any other international
organisation. It is not for these reasons, however, that the European Union is
accorded its very high constitutional significance. There are at least three further factors.

The treaties and the supremacy of EU law

3.11   Much the most important is the status accorded to European Union/
Community treaties and legislation made under the treaties. It is a necessary
aspect of the European project that European law should apply uniformly
throughout the Union with predictable evenness, except in those situations
where the institutions themselves have approved a lack of uniformity. There
should, in principle, be a 'level playing field'. This demands that two main
conditions be satisfied. In the first place, European law contained in the treaties, and the regulations, directives and decisions made under the treaties, has
to flow into all the (member) states of the Union. Rules contained in the treaties
and regulations are to be 'directly applicable' – without the need for separate
legislation made by the parliaments of individual states – by all courts within
the states. That is a position which has been strengthened by the ECJ which
has held that some of those rules contained in EC directives which, on their
face, require domestic legislation for their implementation are nevertheless of
'direct effect' and must be enforced by domestic courts once the commence-

ment date has passed, even though the implementing legislation has not yet been made. This, in itself, means that the impact of the EU treaty regimes far exceeds that of any other international treaty.

It is, however, a position substantially reinforced by the other necessary consequence of the need for the uniformity of application of rules across the Union. The ECJ has also insisted on the 'supremacy' of European law. Not only must the rules flow into the domestic legal systems and become enforceable by the courts of those systems but they must also be given priority over any conflicting domestic law. Even if that domestic law is contained in a statute of the national parliament or (in the states other than the United Kingdom) in the written constitution, it is the European rule which must prevail and be enforced[1]. This is the position which has been adopted by the ECJ itself and which must be followed and applied by domestic courts. The mechanism which has particularly assisted the ECJ in the promulgation of this doctrine of supremacy – and also of direct effect – has been the EC Treaty, art 234 (formerly art 177) reference procedure. This enables, and in the case of final courts in member states requires, a domestic court to request a ruling by the ECJ on any question relating to the interpretation of the Treaty or the validity or interpretation of acts of Community institutions which is necessary to enable judgment to be given. The Court's decision must then be applied and implemented. The power to respond to references under EC Treaty, art 234 has given the ECJ the opportunity to dispense its views, with mandatory effect, across the Union. From a constitutional point of view, it is the impact of this new source of supreme lawmaking, backed by a court to enforce that supremacy, which has been the most significant consequence of EU membership.

The framework within which the status of European Union law has been achieved within the United Kingdom is to be found in the European Communities Act 1972 (ECA 1972) and then, within Scotland, in SA 1998. ECA 1972 provides that '[a]ll such rights, powers, liabilities, obligations and restrictions from time to time created or arising by or under the Treaties[2] ... as in accordance with the Treaties are without further enactment to be given legal effect or used in the United Kingdom shall be recognised and available in law, and be enforced, allowed and followed accordingly'[3]. It also enables the implementation of Community obligations by delegated as well as by primary legislation[4] Courts are required to take judicial notice of the Treaties and of 'any decision of, or expression of opinion by' the ECJ[5].

Of all ECA 1972's provisions, the most problematic has been s 2(4) which requires that 'any enactment passed or to be passed, other than one contained in this Part of this Act, shall be construed and have effect subject to the foregoing provision of this section'. From what has been said about the logic of the hierarchical demands of the European Union, there should be nothing surprising about a domestic United Kingdom provision which, when read with ECA 1972, ss 2(1) and 3, does appear to require a United Kingdom court to give precedence to European law where there is a conflict with a United Kingdom statute, even if that statute is of later date and thus, chronologically at least, in a position to displace the European provision. However, such a provision produces a conflict with a principle of the British constitution which, prior to ECA

1972, was assumed to be fundamental and inviolable – the legislative supremacy of the Westminster Parliament. On the face of it, that Parliament cannot be restricted in its law-making powers by previous laws from any source, including the terms of its own earlier Acts. The way in which that conflict has been resolved is explored in Chapter 5.

The impact of SA 1998 is less momentous and less problematic. It reinforces the supremacy of European law by imposing upon the Scottish Parliament – a parliament which is, in any event, one of restricted competence – a prohibition on the making of any law which is incompatible with Community law[6]. The same restriction is applied to the Scottish Executive[7].

1 For discussion of the ECJ case law in this area and the response of UK courts, see ch 5.
2 Updated by successive amendments to ECA 1972, s 1, to include the Nice Treaty.
3 ECA 1972, s 2(1).
4 ECA 1972, s 2(2) and Sch 2.
5 ECA 1972, s 3(2). ECA 1972, s 2(3) authorises expenditure on Community obligations to be charged on the Consolidated Fund. See p 280.
6 SA 1998, s 29(2)(d).
7 SA 1998, ss 54 and 57(2).

Ministerial accountability

3.12   Another consequence of the expansion of European Union activity, especially legislative activity, since the United Kingdom's accession in 1973 has been the growth of the involvement of government ministers in the making of legislation by the Council of Ministers and the promulgation of that legislation, as necessary, in domestic instruments. In turn, this creates a need for parliamentary scrutiny of that process[1].

These are functions which have taken on a new significance since the arrival of devolution in 1999. Ministerial representation at the Council of Ministers is a matter for the national level of government of the member state of the Union. It is a United Kingdom view of the policy under discussion – whether, for instance, energy, agriculture or fisheries – which has to be represented. Prior to devolution this did not at all stand in the way of some of the UK's ministerial team being drawn from the Scottish Office, the UK department of government with Scottish responsibilities, where this was appropriate and especially where peculiarly Scottish interests (eg fisheries) were at stake. Since July 1999, it has continued to be possible for Scottish ministers – drawn from the Scottish Government rather than from a department of the United Kingdom government – to form part of the United Kingdom's team at Brussels[2]. It remains a single United Kingdom position which has to be represented, however, and this is a matter of some political sensitivity. There is a concern that Scottish interests, where different from United Kingdom interests taken as a whole, may be inadequately represented[3]. Implementation and enforcement of European law have become the responsibility of the Scottish Government within the devolved areas of government[4]. Responsibility for the parliamentary scrutiny of legislative proposals by the European Commission and Council of Ministers has, again within the devolved areas, become shared between Westminster and Holyrood[5]. The scrutiny of implementing legislation made by the Scottish Executive as Scottish statutory instruments is also a Holyrood responsibility[6].

One general consequence of these arrangements and of the introduction of devolution at a time when much of the control of important areas of national policy has been transferred from the United Kingdom to the European Union is that the scheme of devolution in SA 1998 does not tell the full story. That scheme is set out in Chapter 5 and it is a scheme under which, for example, agriculture and fisheries are matters devolved to the Scottish Parliament and Executive. It will be apparent, however, that with both of these policy areas substantially 'devolved' to the EU and with United Kingdom control substantially exerted by United Kingdom ministers in the Council of Ministers, the effective extent of domestic devolution to Scotland is much diminished.

1 Scrutiny arrangements are in the hands of the House of Commons Select Committee on European Scrutiny and the House of Lords European Union Select Committee. The Commons Committee can refer EU documents for debate in a European Standing Committee while the Lords Committee has seven sub-committees.
2 This was anticipated in *Scotland's Parliament* (Cm 3658) ch 5.
3 See p 44.
4 See p 126.
5 For the UK Parliament, see n 1 above. In the Scottish Parliament, scrutiny is undertaken by the European and External Relations Committee.
6 See p 249. Such implementation has been the subject of legal challenge: see *Infant and Dietetic Foods Association Ltd, Petitioners* 2008 SLT 723.

The EU Charter of Rights

3.13   Another quite different development has been the EU's 'solemn proclamation' of a Charter of Rights at the European Council in Nice in 2000[1]. Until the emergence of the procedure which led to the Charter, it had not been an express element in the project of the Community or Union to guarantee the rights of citizens. Many of the terms of the Treaties, though designed to establish the Common Market, did have a rights aspect to them – for instance, in the way they assured freedom of movement of persons[2] or equality of treatment[3] but there was no comprehensive rights agenda. This had been left to the quite separate institutions of the Council of Europe in Strasbourg, especially that Council's promotion of the ECHR and the European Social Charter. Thought had earlier been given to the possibility of the Community's own accession to the ECHR, but without positive outcome[4].

Instead, at European Council meetings in 1999 the proposal was made to establish a Convention[5] which would meet to develop a text of the Union's own making. The result was the Charter of Rights proclaimed at Nice. Both its content and its status are important. The Charter consists of six chapters containing a total of fifty substantive articles, with a seventh chapter of general provisions. The substantive articles are spread across Dignity (including the right to life and the prohibition of slavery and forced labour); Freedoms (ranging through the right to liberty and security of the person, protection of personal data, freedom of thought, freedom of the arts and sciences, and freedom to conduct a business); Equality (including reference to the rights of the child, the elderly and persons with disabilities); Solidarity (workplace rights, social security, health care, environmental protection, and consumer protection); Citizens' Rights (the right to stand and vote in European Parliament and municipal elections, the right to good administration, the right to petition the Parliament); and Justice (fair trial and presumption of innocence). All the guaranteed rights derive from those assured by other international obligations common to the member states, especially the EC Treaty and the TEU, the ECHR and the European Social Charter[6]. The Charter is stated to be

> addressed to the institutions and bodies of the Union with due regard for the principle of subsidiarity and to the Member States only when they are implementing Union law. They shall therefore respect the rights, observe the principles and promote the application thereof in accordance with their respective powers[7].

Since its proclamation at Nice, the Charter has been of only declaratory effect, a result of caution on the part of those nervous about making it legally binding. That, however, is a situation which seems likely to change. The Nice summit was famous not only for its adoption of the Charter but also for its commitment to adoption of a new constitutional basis for the Union, which subsequently produced the Lisbon Treaty. The Treaty would raise the Charter to legally-binding status although it also permits 'opt-outs' from the Charter by the United Kingdom and Poland.

1 For a full account, see S Douglas-Scott *Constitutional Law of the European Union* pp 470–478.
2 EC, art 39.
3 EC, arts 12, 13, 141.
4 The Constitution Treaty (and now the Lisbon Treaty) revived that option by requiring the Union to seek accession. It was the view of the ECJ (Opinion (ECJ) 2/94 [1996] ECR I–1759) that a Treaty amendment was required.
5 In the sense of a body meeting to establish a constitution. See p 19, n 1.
6 For an account of the background of each article, see the 'Explanations' published with the Charter.
7 Charter of Fundamental Rights, art 51(1).

A constitution for Europe

3.14   It is not difficult to understand why many people are inclined to describe the Treaties which establish the institutions of the European Union as a constitution. The Treaties allocate law-making functions to the Council and the Parliament; executive authority to the Commission; and judicial powers to the Court of Justice in ways which are analogous to those used in the constitutions of nation-states. The description of the Treaties as a constitution has become increasingly common and there have, for a long time, been those who are perfectly comfortable with the notion of the European Court of Justice as a constitutional court. Its powers to adjudicate on the compatibility of national laws with Community laws are entirely comparable with those of a constitutional court within a federation. Judges in the Court of Justice are making decisions similar to those made by constitutional judges elsewhere.

While the similarities of function between the Treaties and national constitutions may be admitted, however, there are objections to the comparison being pressed too far. For some, the idea of a constitution without an identifiable state or 'demos' is intrinsically unsound[1]. For others, it is the assumption that a constitution would formalise the creation of a state as the goal of the European project that is anathema. For 'Eurosceptics' the emergence of a federal state, a superstate, is to be resisted and talk of a constitution is, for them, a step in the wrong direction.

Be that as it may, the European Union did commit itself to a process intended to lead to the emergence of a more formal constitution. Responding to general pressures for institutional reform, a sense that public confidence in European institutions needs to be rebuilt[2] and the need to reform institutions in advance of the anticipated expansion of the Union, a White Paper on European Governance[3] was launched in July 2001 to pave the way for the European Council meeting held in Laeken, Belgium in December 2001. The White Paper contained the Commission's proposals for greater involvement and openness in the workings of the Union, better procedures for policy-making and policy delivery, better external relations for the Union and what it called 'refocused institutions' in the Union itself. It enunciated principles of good governance, and anticipated a wider process of constitutional reform to be initiated at Laeken. In due course, the Laeken Council did indeed establish a Convention on the Future of Europe under the chairmanship of former French President Valéry Giscard d'Estaing.

The Convention had 105 members, including representatives of all the governments of the member states and candidate states, representatives of national parliaments, and MEPs. It conducted its consultations and discussions until 12 June 2003 when it published its draft of a new Constitution Treaty[4] for presentation to the European Council and for eventual consideration by an Inter-Governmental Conference. For some, a bold new step in the development of the Union, for others a 'tidying-up' exercise, the draft contained much of interest. It proclaimed a commitment to a new restatement of values and objectives; a new legal personality for the Union; recognition of the Charter of Fundamental Rights; and a commitment to seek accession to the ECHR. It restated the principles of the primacy of Union law (and of the Constitution), the categories of exclusive and shared competence, and the principles of subsidiarity and proportionality. In a protocol on those principles, there was a commitment to consultation with national parliaments on EU legislative proposals, subject to the possibility of application to the ECJ for breach. The European Council would acquire a new President (for a maximum period in office of five years), thus ending the circulating presidency.

In due course, the Constitution Treaty was signed (in 2004) but the ratification process suffered a fatal set-back when the French and Dutch populations rejected the text in referendums in May and June 2005. Subsequently, further negotiations produced the successor Lisbon (or Reform) Treaty which drew heavily on the Constitution Treaty but deliberately omitted the language of the 'Constitution' as well as the more ambitious aims of the earlier text. The Treaty aims to increase efficiency (eg by more qualified majority voting in the Council) and the involvement of the Parliament in extended codecision procedures. There would be a new President of the EU and a High Representative for Foreign and Security Policy. It was signed in December 2007 but, like the Constitution Treaty before it, suffered a set-back – this time with the negative

Irish referendum of June 2008. At the time of writing, a further Irish referendum is expected.

For Scotland[5], the interest in this exercise in constitutional reform is two-fold. In the first place, there is the interest shared by the United Kingdom as a whole and by other member states in any new relationship between the states and the Union. Any tendency towards more formal federal-style arrangements will be watched closely by supporters and opponents alike. Secondly, Scotland will join other regions in Europe in observing any reinforcement at the European level of the recognition of the principle of subsidiarity[6] at the substate level. For regions, the application of subsidiarity should be seamless and operate at all levels. In particular the threat that greater European integration may dilute the effect of domestic federalism or devolution should be reversed. Already Scotland has participated in meetings of the presidential conferences of regions with legislative power[7]. In December 2002, the Committee on Constitutional Affairs of the European Parliament chaired by Giorgio Napolitano produced an important report on the role of regional and local authorities in European Integration[8] which was adopted by the Parliament on 14 February 2003. The Parliament committed itself to the principle of bringing the European Union closer to its citizens through regional and local bodies; the desirability of strengthening participatory representation through the incorporation of the European Charter of Local Self-Government into the body of Union law and a mediating role for regions; and access for regional and local authorities to the ECJ. These were not, however, proposals which were taken up by the Constitutional Convention, with one exception. The Constitution Treaty included within the Protocol on subsidiarity not only an obligation to consult national Parliaments on legislative proposals but also a provision that those Parliaments should themselves 'consult, where appropriate, regional Parliaments with legislative powers'. The same requirement has been retained in the Lisbon Treaty[9].

1 For general discussion, see, eg, P Craig '*Constitutional Law, Constitutions, Constitutionalism and the European Union*' (2001) ELJ 125.
2 Especially in the light of the initial Irish 'no' vote on the Nice Treaty in June 2001.
3 *Enhancing Democracy: A White Paper on Governance in the EU* (COM (2001) 428).
4 CONV 797/1/03.
5 For the views of the Scottish Parliament's European Committee at an earlier stage, see SP EU OR SP Paper 705, 2002.
6 A principle operating mainly in the relationship between the states and the Union to ensure that, in the absence of an exclusive Union competence, the Union will act 'only if and in so far as the objectives of the intended action cannot be sufficiently achieved by the member states, either at central level or at regional and local level, but can rather, by reason of the scale or effects of the proposed action, be better achieved at Union level'.
7 Most recently, at Brussels in December 2008.
8 A5-0427/2002.
9 Protocol on the application of the principles of subsidiarity and proportionality, Art. 6.

DEVOLUTION AND THE SCOTLAND ACT 1998

Introduction

3.15   Today the constitution of Scotland and of the United Kingdom as a whole would be incomprehensible without full account being taken of the pattern of arrangements for devolved government established not only in Scotland itself but also Wales, Northern Ireland and, indeed, in Greater London. An important issue in contemporary constitutional debate is where devolution goes from here. Will the regions of England join in? Will the devolved institutions grow in strength, in comparison with the central institutions in Westminster and Whitehall? Will there be a tendency to greater uniformity in the provision of devolution across the United Kingdom – perhaps in combination with a strengthening of devolution in the direction of a 'truly' federal model? Might an English Parliament be created? Will there, on the other hand, be a pattern of continuing divergence and asymmetry? What will be the contribution of nationalist pressures, especially in Northern Ireland and in Scotland itself? Although none of these questions is wholly new, they have taken on a new vigour.

Prior to the developments of 1997–99, the British constitutional tradition was one which emphasised the unitary character of the state. The United Kingdom was a country with a single 'supreme' legislature at Westminster. The executive branch of government was, again, a single entity headed formally by the monarch but effectively driven by the Prime Minister and other ministers. Certainly a sharp contrast could be drawn between the unitary United Kingdom and federalist constitutions elsewhere. Dicey sang the praises of the unitary state and especially its sovereign Parliament. He elaborated their advantages over the divisions, weakness and litigiousness of federal government in the United States and elsewhere[1]. But Dicey's was an interpretation clouded by his staunch unionism. For him, the retention of Ireland within the United Kingdom was the political goal and essential to that project was a single supreme Parliament.

Whether or not distorted in this way, however, the legacy of the Diceyan unitary state and supreme Parliament has came to dominate constitutional thought[2]. At the same time, the United Kingdom, while formally unitary in its structure, has always been a state with strong decentralising tendencies. Local government has traditionally been a great strength and, although the structure of the systems of local administration varied across the different parts of the United Kingdom and they varied over time, local bodies have borne many of the responsibilities of government which elsewhere have passed to the central state. Local government has acted as a counterweight to central government, in particular in the period since the democratisation of local councils in the late nineteenth century. In Scotland, the royal burghs first established in the twelfth century, the parishes and sheriffs were joined by, and ceded power to, the elected country councils created in 1890 and then to the other local authorities established in successive reforms in the twentieth century. Although local authorities would, at most, be described as junior partners in their relationship with central government, they have undoubtedly had an important decentralising influence.

Another significant challenge to the unitary model of the UK constitution was represented by the operation for half of the twentieth century of the Stormont system of devolved government in Northern Ireland from 1922 to 1972. This was not federalism in a classical form but the Parliament of Northern Ireland, although formally subordinate to Westminster and ultimately abolished by an

Act of the Westminster Parliament[3], enjoyed very wide legislative powers. It was a substantial inroad into the unitary system. Stormont was created out of the special circumstances of Ireland within the United Kingdom, and pressures for independence or for home rule for the whole of Ireland. The Government of Ireland Act 1920 which was designed to devolve powers separately to the North and to the South of Ireland but its implementation was pre-empted by civil war and the creation of the Republic of Ireland in 1922. The struggle for home rule during the period from the 1880s to 1920 was not, however, a process wholly confined to Ireland itself and, for much of that period, there were parallel pressures in Scotland. There was a succession of home rule Bills and there was a joining of forces in 1913 for a Government of the United Kingdom Bill which would have brought 'home rule all round'[4].

Although these developments were ultimately abortive in that they did not bring a Parliament to Scotland at that time and significant moves in that direction were not to be revived until the 1970s, they were taking place against a background in which Scotland was, in other ways, acquiring distinctive institutions of government of its own. Indeed, from the time of the Union itself, the arrangements for the government of Scotland had their own character. The Union, even if it established a formally unitary state, never created a uniformity of provision and was the basis of much of the ensuing diversity.

Much of the government of Scotland fell to the Lord Advocate in the eighteenth century and then to appointed boards (eg the Board of Supervision (for poor relief) and the Prison Commissioners) in the nineteenth century. Later landmarks were the establishment of the Scottish Office under a Secretary for Scotland in 1885[5], the aggregation of functions in that Office which came to be headed by a Secretary of State in 1926, the physical relocation of much of the Scottish Office to St Andrew's House in Edinburgh in 1939[6], and the subsequent transfer to the Scottish Office of further powers (including, for instance, responsibility for major roads) in the 1950s[7].

1 Dicey, ch 3.
2 Including, for a long time, in Scotland. See W I R Fraser *An Outline of Constitutional Law* (2nd edn, 1948).
3 Northern Ireland Constitution Act 1973, s 31.
4 For an illuminating account of all the devolutionary proposals up to the 1970s see A G Donaldson 'Administrative and Legislative Devolution' in J P Grant (ed) *Independence and Devolution: The Legal Implications for Scotland* (1976). See also J P Mackintosh *The Devolution of Power* (1968).
5 H J Hanham 'The Creation of the Scottish Office, 1881–7' 1965 JR 205; D Milne *The Scottish Office* (1957).
6 Committee on Scottish Administration (Gilmour Committee) (Cmd 5563, 1937). A London base was retained at Dover House, now the London home, within the Ministry of Justice, of the Scotland Office.
7 Royal Commission on Scottish Affairs (Balfour Commission) (Cmd 9212, 1954). See also report of the Royal Commission on the Constitution (Cmnd 5460, 1973) ch 4 and written evidence to the Commission by A W Bradley.

The home rule movement

3.16 As a background to this process of deconcentration of executive authority, political pressure for more radical change in the government of Scotland was building – especially at the hand of the Scottish National Party.

Founded in 1928 as the National Party of Scotland[1] the SNP grew in influence in the period after the 1939–45 war, with its Scottish Covenant of 1945 and subsequent victories in the polls. It was, in particular, the SNP's victory in the parliamentary by-election in Hamilton in 1967 that triggered the creation of the Royal Commission on the Constitution in 1969. The remit of the Kilbrandon Commission[2] was to examine the present functions of the central legislature and government in relation to the several countries, nations and regions of the United Kingdom; to consider, having regard to developments in local government organisations[3] and in the administrative and other relationships between the various parts of the United Kingdom, and to the interests of the prosperity and good government of Our people under the Crown, whether any changes are desirable in those functions or otherwise in present constitutional and economic relationships ...'.

The Commission reported in 1973[4]. The enduring impact of the Commission's report has been, first, in its articulation of the late twentieth-century case for constitutional change in Scotland. There was, above all, a case for an elected assembly or parliament in Scotland with law-making powers. The separate Scottish legal system and the tendency for Westminster to make much separate legislation for Scotland required a new legislature which should also have the important task of holding the Scottish Office to account. Secondly, however, the Commission legitimised, in modern times, a constitutional design for the United Kingdom which would recognise different needs for Scotland, Northern Ireland, Wales and the English regions and provide different responses for each[5]. It was unnecessary to contemplate a fully federal model of government – a solution firmly rejected by the Commission – and the preferred model of devolved government would clearly have to be asymmetric.

1 See D Young 'A Sketch History of Scottish Nationalism' in N MacCormick (ed) *The Scottish Debate: Essays on Scottish Nationalism* (1970).
2 Lord Kilbrandon succeeded to the chair of the Commission in 1972, on the death of Lord Crowther.
3 For Scotland, the (Wheatley) Royal Commission on Local Government in Scotland and, eventually, the Local Government (Scotland) Act 1973. See ch 7.
4 Cmnd 5460, 1973.
5 It was also, however, a Commission divided within itself. A strong dissent was recorded by two members.

The Scotland and Wales Acts of 1978

3.17   Growing political pressure on the returning Labour government in the 1970s led to its producing proposals for devolved government in Scotland and Wales[1]. A Scotland and Wales Bill[2] failed to make progress, however, and separate Bills were introduced and enacted, in due course, as the Scotland Act 1978 (SA 1978) and the Wales Act 1978. The latter contained a model of executive devolution (ie lacking primary law-making powers) to an elected assembly. On the other hand, SA 1978 would have produced an elected assembly with law-making powers and an executive (headed by a First Secretary) drawn from it. The assembly and executive were to be given a range of devolved powers spelled out in a Schedule to SA 1978. However, the two Acts of 1978 were never implemented. Lacking adequate political control over the House of Commons, the government had been forced to concede the need for the arrangements to be approved by a referendum held in the two countries affected and approved by not merely a majority of those voting but by at least 40 per cent of those entitled to vote[3]. Both referendums held on 1 March 1979 were lost[4] and, following the demise of the government itself in the general election of May 1979, the Acts were repealed[5].

The incoming Conservative government was hostile to devolution. It, and its successors, suppressed legislative proposals for devolution until their own demise in 1997. Politically, the Conservatives were in retreat in Scotland during this period, eventually returning no Scottish MPs at all in the 1997 general election. Constitutionally, they were prepared to 'take stock'[6] and made limited proposals for altering the handling of Scottish business at Westminster, including new rules for the Scottish Grand Committee of the House of Commons[7].

1 At that time England was quiescent and Northern Ireland in the midst of a series of constitutional experiments following the collapse of the Stormont Parliament in 1972 and its replacement by direct rule from London.
2 Following *Our Changing Democracy: Devolution to Scotland and Wales* (Cmnd 6348, 1975).
3 SA 1978, s 85.
4 In the case of SA 1978, a small majority of those voting were in favour of its implementation, but not enough to clear the 40% hurdle.
5 Scotland Act 1978 (Repeal) Order 1979, SI 1979/928; Wales Act 1978 (Repeal) Order 1979, SI 1979/933.
6 *Scotland in the Union: a Partnership for Good* (Cm 2225, 1993).
7 C M G Himsworth 'The Scottish Grand Committee as an Instrument of Government' (1996) 1 Edin LR 79.

The Scottish Constitutional Convention and subsequent developments in Scotland and the United Kingdom

3.18   Outside government, however, the flame of devolution was kept alive. In particular, a broad coalition, which had its origins in a body formed after the 1979 referendum and known as the Campaign for a Scottish Assembly, came together in 1989 as the Scottish Constitutional Convention, following the publication in 1988 of *A Claim of Right for Scotland*[1]. The Convention had a largely political membership drawn from Labour and Liberal MPs, MEPs and councillors and with representatives from other parties, though not the SNP. There was also a sprinkling of representatives from the Scottish Trades Union Congress, the churches, ethnic minority communities and some others. In 1990 the Convention published a report, *Towards Scotland's Parliament*, containing initial proposals for a new Parliament. It went on to refine these in a final report, *Scotland's Parliament: Scotland's Right*, in 1995.

Although not presented in the form of a draft Bill and lacking some of the detail eventually needed, the Convention's report was highly influential as a blueprint for adoption by the Labour government elected in 1997 with a manifesto commitment to legislate for a Scottish Parliament. The government's plans were in the Queen's Speech delivered in the Westminster Parliament on 14 May 1997. Legislation was proposed for a devolved Scottish Parliament and also for a Welsh Assembly, and a directly elected authority for London. There was also a commitment to the need for referendum approval but, astutely, referendums were to be held not after the Acts were passed but before the Bills were even introduced into Parliament, in the light of legislative proposals to be published as White Papers. Public support in referendums would erode political opposition in Parliament. In the event, the referendum held in Scotland on 11 September 1997[2] saw the general question 'that there should be a Scottish Parliament' approved by 74.3 per cent of those voting and a second question 'that the Scottish Parliament should have tax-varying powers' approved by 63.5 per cent[3].

The Scottish White Paper *Scotland's Parliament*[4] to which approval had been given contained detailed proposals for the new arrangements for devolved government. It dealt with the composition and electoral arrangements for the new Parliament, an outline of how it would be expected to operate, the Parliament's relationship to a new Scottish Executive, financial arrangements and the relations between the devolved Scottish institutions and the European Union and other Scottish bodies such as local authorities. In December 1997, the government published its Scotland Bill[5], whose first clause read, in a way which retains a power to excite: 'There shall be a Scottish Parliament'. Thereafter, the Bill contained the provisions which, after some changes made during its parliamentary passage[6], form the basis of many of the later chapters of this book. SA 1998 reached the statute book on 19 November 1998 and was brought into effect in stages up to 1 April 2000[7]. In parallel with the passing of the Act itself, some important discussions were taking place within a body known as the Consultative Steering Group (CSG) on the Scottish Parliament[8]. This was set up by Donald Dewar MP, as Secretary of State for Scotland, in November 1997 with the task of reporting by the end of 1998 on its consideration of the operational needs and working methods of the Parliament and to produce proposals which would inform the preparation of the Parliament's initial standing orders. The CSG was chaired by Henry McLeish MP, at that time Minister of State at the Scottish Office, and contained representatives of all the main political parties as well as some former members of the Constitutional Convention. In December 1998, the CSG produced a substantial report, *Shaping Scotland's Parliament: Report of the Consultative Steering Group on the Scottish Parliament*, which was indeed highly influential in the making of the new Parliament's Standing Orders[9]. Perhaps of equal significance was the Group's generation of the four key principles which guided its own work and, as a manifestation of the 'new politics' intended to operate in devolved Scotland, have had a lasting importance. In summary, the principles were that (1) the Parliament should embody and reflect the sharing of power between the people of Scotland, the legislators and the Scottish Executive; (2) the Scottish Executive should be accountable to the Scottish Parliament and the Parliament and Executive should be accountable to the people of Scotland; (3) the Parliament should be accessible, open, responsive, and develop procedures which make possible a participative approach to the development, consideration and scrutiny of policy and legislation; and (4) the Parliament in its operation and its appointments should recognise the need to promote equal opportunities for all. It was against the background of these principles that the Procedures Committee of the Parliament conducted its 'CSG inquiry' during 2002–03, leading to the publication of its report in March 2003[10]. The CSG principles have had an enduring appeal, featuring most recently in the work of the Calman Commission, see page 63.

In addition to the creation of devolved government in Scotland have been developments in Wales, Northern Ireland, London and the English regions. The emergence of a wider pattern of asymmetric devolution across the United Kingdom as a whole has provided the context within which Scotland's own arrangements have developed. The Government of Wales Act 1998 (GWA 1998)[11] provided a weaker form of devolution than that operating in Scotland. It created the National Assembly for Wales but gave it no primary legislative powers equivalent to those conferred on the Scottish Parliament. Instead, Wales became a country of 'executive devolution' by which it was meant that there were transferred to the Assembly[12] executive powers in defined areas[13] including education, social services, health services and agriculture, formerly exercised by the Secretary of State for Wales. These include powers to make delegated legislation[14]. All primary law-making authority for Wales remained at Westminster. Later, however, the Government of Wales Act 2006 (GWA 2006) was passed[15] to enhance (in two stages) the legislative powers of the Assembly; to reform its electoral arrangements; and to introduce a formal separation between the legislative and executive branches. As a result, the Assembly already has wider powers to make subordinate legislation and the power to make Assembly measures within areas defined by Order in Council[16]. There are elections on a four-yearly cycle on the Additional Member System[17] and the Welsh Assembly Government (the Welsh Ministers) is established as a separate entity[18]. GWA 2006 also makes provision for a referendum on the transfer to the Assembly of broader powers of law-making by way of Assembly Acts[19]. In the meantime, an independent All Wales Convention is enquiring into the strength of opinion in favour of such broader powers.

The different arrangements in Wales produce somewhat different relationships between the National Assembly and the United Kingdom government. The retention of primary legislative power at Westminster means that the continuing role of the Secretary of State for Wales (who, unlike his Scottish counterpart, is authorised to participate in Assembly debates[20]) and also of Welsh MPs is different. There is no immediate pressure to reduce Welsh representation in the House of Commons, but there is specific provision for the consultation of the Assembly by the United Kingdom government on its legislative programme for Wales (GWA 1998, s 31). On the other hand, some of the other over-arching structures of devolution apply in the same way in Wales as in Scotland. Devolved government in Wales is financed by a grant under the same 'Barnett formula' arrangements[21] and 'devolution issues' raising questions about the lawfulness of the exercise of Assembly functions may be taken by reference or appeal to the UK Supreme Court[22].

Although Northern Ireland must be included within any contemporary survey of devolution within the United Kingdom and the institutions created under the Northern Ireland Act 1998 (NIA 1998) provide the basis for close comparison with those in Scotland, there are also difficulties which place such a study beyond the scope of this book[23]. The Assembly and Executive established under NIA 1998 and the powers potentially conferred produce a strong form of legislative devolution similar to that in Scotland. It is, however, a system strongly coloured by the previous history of devolution in the province (producing, for instance, a pattern of excepted, reserved and transferred powers reminiscent of that contained in the Government of Ireland Act 1920) and, more importantly, by the province's political history and present condition. NIA 1998 gives effect to the Belfast (or Good Friday) Agreement of April 1998[24] whose terms were subsequently approved by referendums held in both Northern Ireland and the Republic of Ireland. The Assembly is elected by the single transferable vote system[25] and the Executive is formed according to a sophisticated power-sharing formula[26]. However, progress towards the full implementation and operation of the Northern Ireland scheme of devolution has been badly stalled because of substantial disagreements between the principal political parties on such fundamental issues as the decommissioning of arms. The Assembly was formally suspended for four periods during 2000 to 2003 following which the Northern Ireland Act 2006 created a non-legislative Assembly which was followed by a "Transitional Assembly" established under the Northern Ireland (St Andrews Agreement) Act 2006.

It may be that, in due course, Scottish devolutionary arrangements will be more affected by the development of regional government in England rather than by the current settlements in Wales and Northern Ireland. The Greater London Authority Act 1999[27] created the London Assembly and the separately elected Mayor of London in 2000. In May 2002, the United Kingdom government published its proposals for regional government in the rest of England[28]. These would enable the creation of directly elected assemblies in any or all of the eight regions outside London currently established for the purpose of decentralising governmental agencies. Nothing in the proposals, however, compels the creation of an assembly in a particular region. That would be the consequence of a regional referendum on the issue held under the terms of the Regional Assemblies (Preparations) Act 2003. The Act enables the Secretary of State to hold a referendum in a region where he has first 'considered the level of interest' in a referendum and he has also received recommendations on consequences for local government in the region[29]. If, as a result of these proposals and the testing of local opinion, regional government in England were to take off in a strong way, there would almost certainly be consequences for Scotland. In the longer term, assuming the continued existence of the United Kingdom, new possibilities for the redistribution of authority within the state might emerge, including perhaps renewed consideration of a federal solution and, less radically, other ways of representing the nations and regions in the United Kingdom Parliament[30]. It is also almost inevitable that regional government in England would compel the reconsideration of the financing of devolution across the United Kingdom[31] and might lead to wider reforms of intergovernmental relationships[32]. However, developments in this direction are currently wholly stalled in the light of the crushing defeat for the government's proposals for an assembly in north-east England in 2004.

1   In due course the *Claim of Right* was formally 'received' by the Presiding Officer of the Scottish Parliament on 29 June 1999.
2   Referendums (Scotland and Wales) Act 1997; cf C R Munro 'Power to the People' [1997] PL 579.
3   For the tax-varying power as passed, see p 285.
4   Cm 3658, 1997.
5   See C M G Himsworth and C R Munro *Devolution and the Scotland Bill* (1998).
6   See C M G Himsworth and C R Munro *The Scotland Act 1998* (2nd edn, 2000) xiii–xvii.

7 Scotland Act 1998 (Commencement) Order 1998, SI 1998/3178.
8 See also P Grice 'The Creation of a Devolved Parliament' (2001) 7(3) *Journal of Legislative Studies* 1.
9 Initially contained in the Scotland Act 1998 (Transitory and Transitional Provisions) (Standing Orders and Parliamentary Publications) Order 1999, SI 1999/1095.
10 *The Founding Principles of the Scottish Parliament*, SP PR OR SP Paper 818 (2003).
11 Pursuant to proposals in *A Voice for Wales* (Cm 3718, 1997) and a referendum held on 18 September 1997.
12 GWA 1998, s 22 and then, principally by the National Assembly for Wales (Transfer of Functions) Order 1999, SI 1999/672.
13 GWA 1998, Sch 2.
14 Mainly as statutory instruments and published, unlike Scottish SIs, in the UK series.
15 This implements proposals made in the (Richard) Report of the Commission on the Powers and Electoral Arrangements of the National Assembly for Wales (2004) and the White Paper 'Better Governance for Wales' (Cm 6582, 2005).
16 GWA 2006, ss 93–102 and Sch. 5.
17 GWA 2006, Pt. 1.
18 GWA 2006, ss 45–55.
19 GWA 2006, Pt. 4.
20 GWA 2006, s 32.
21 GWA 2006, s 117 and see ch 10.
22 GWA 2006, s 149, Sch. 9, and see ch 12.
23 On the situation prior to 1998, see H Calvert *Constitutional Law in Northern Ireland* (1968); B Hadfield *The Constitution of Northern Ireland* (1989). On more recent events, see B Hadfield 'The Implementation of the Belfast Agreement, in part or in whole' (2002) EPL 22.
24 Cm 3383, 1998.
25 Northern Ireland (Elections) Act 1998, s 2.
26 NIA 1998, ss 16–20.
27 After a referendum held in May 1998 under the Greater London Authority (Referendum) Act 1998.
28 *Your Region, Your Choice: Revitalising the English Regions* (Cm 5511, 2002).
29 Regional Assemblies (Preparations) Act 2003, s 1(4), (5).
30 For proposals in relation to the House of Lords, see p 83.
31 See ch 10.
32 See p 188.

The Future of the Scottish Constitution

3.19   If recent years have been a period of rapid constitutional change in Scotland, the period since the formation of the minority SNP Government in 2007 has raised the most acute questions about Scotland's constitutional future. These are poignantly characterised by two, largely conflicting, constitutional projects, both still underway at the time of writing. On the one hand there has been the Scottish Government's own 'National Conversation' launched in August 2007[1]. This offers the prospect of an extension of Scottish devolution, in particular by strengthening the powers of the Parliament. More significantly, the project proposes a route to an independent Scotland by means of the opening of negotiations on independence with the UK government following approval in a national referendum. A draft Bill designed to establish the machinery for such a referendum has been published[2]. There have been discussions and meetings as a part of the Conversation, although in March 2009, the Parliament itself approved a motion urging that the Scottish Government should abandon its referendum plans[3]. In the meantime, from the Parliament itself, but with the support of the UK government, has come the establishment in April 2008 of the Commission on Scottish Devolution chaired by Sir Kenneth Calman. This was given a remit to consider ways of changing present constitutional arrangements to enable the Scottish Parliament to serve the people of Scotland better. In December 2008, the Commission published an interim report[4] in which it set out its provisional thoughts, to that point, on the emerging practice of devolution and on the powers and funding of the Parliament and in June 2009 it published its final report[5], recommending a number of changes to the Parliament's powers and its financial autonomy. Much uncertainty surrounds the implementation of these recommendations and how they may interact with the National Conversation. An extraneous feature, unforeseen at the launch of the two projects but one which will undoubtedly affect future developments, has been the banking and general financial crisis of 2008–09.

1 *Choosing Scotland's Future: A National Conversation.*
2 Ibid Annex B.
3 SPOR 5 March 2009, col 15578.
4 *The Future of Scottish Devolution within the Union: A First Report*, 2008.
5 Serving Scotland Better: Scotland and the United Kingdom in the 21st Century.

Chapter 4

The UK and Scottish Parliaments: the Institutional Framework

INTRODUCTION

4.1   In any study of a parliament in a working constitution the main focus is inevitably on what that parliament does. Thus, in a system of parliamentary government, the role of parliament in the process of government formation and then in the process of holding governments to account are a central concern. So too are the parliament's legislative powers and the procedures by which laws are made, especially in so far as law-making is guided, or indeed dominated, by the executive. The ways in which the limits of the powers of the parliament may be tested in courts are also of great importance. These parliamentary powers and procedures and the involvement in them of the executive and the judiciary provide the defining characteristics of the constitution itself. For Scotland, since July 1999, those characteristics have included the phenomenon of two working parliaments and to the constitutional relationships already mentioned there has to be added the relationship which has been created and which continues to develop between them.

As a preliminary to the study of the workings of the Parliaments, however, it is necessary to put in place the rules governing their structure and composition. The ways in which their membership is defined and the rules by which they are brought into existence or may be terminated do much to establish whether they have the autonomy and legitimacy necessary to carry out effectively the functions constitutionally allotted to them. Particularly important in the assessment of the work of the Parliaments is the question of how far they discharge their most distinctive function which is that of injecting the quality of democracy into the constitutional system as a whole. That, above all, is the task of parliaments and one to which other constitutional organs contribute much more weakly. The democratic benchmark is that against which the Parliaments are primarily to be tested.

It is for that reason that the main focus in pp 67–82 of this chapter is on the two elected chambers – at Westminster the House of Commons and then the Scottish Parliament itself. At pp 82–87, however, there is a brief coverage of the House of Lords and account is taken of the stage presently reached in the reform of that House. It has, for the past decade, been the subject of considerable attention. The existence of the House of Lords has important consequences for the working of the Westminster Parliament: inevitably a bicameral parliament operates, and is intended to operate, differently from a unicameral parliament. In the Scottish Parliament the lack of a second chamber has consequences for its operation and, when compared with Westminster, it needs to look elsewhere for the performance of functions carried out there by the House of Lords. Some, however, have argued for a bicameral Scottish Parliament and brief discussion of that possibility concludes this section. At pp 87–90 is an introduction to parliamentary committees, although the main committee functions are dealt with in Chapters 8 and 9. For most purposes the Parliaments operate as collective bodies – whether as whole chambers or as committees of those chambers – but the status and function of individual members are also important. Pages 91–96 concern such matters as pay and allowances – an area which at the time of writing has become one of the most controversial in British politics – and with the standards required of individual members and the privileges they claim, both individually and collectively. Pages 97–98 deal with the management and administration of the Parliaments. Finally, pp 98–99 address, with particular reference to the Scottish Parliament, the question of public accessibility and openness.

It will be observed that this chapter involves – sometimes quite explicitly, sometimes implicitly – comparisons between the Westminster and the Scottish Parliaments. This is useful despite the obvious differences between the two. The Westminster Parliament is ancient while the Scottish Parliament is modern. The Westminster Parliament is bicameral and is much larger than its Scottish counterpart. The Westminster Parliament formally incorporates the Queen into its membership, whereas the Scottish Parliament does not. Many of those who campaigned for a Scottish Parliament had in mind that it should in no way become a mere replica of Westminster[1]. It was argued that it should be more responsive to the people, it should be less bound by ceremonial pomp and tradition, it should contain members who were less antagonistic to each other and less bound by party rivalry and discipline, and the Scottish Parliament should be more family friendly, especially in its working hours.

The most recent formal setting within which attempts have been made to assess how the Scottish Parliament has 'measured up' to this agenda declared devolution a 'remarkable success' having heard praise for the 'transparency and openness' of the Scottish Parliament and its 'greater democratic scrutiny of public life in Scotland and of legislative proposals'[2]. This assessment will not be universally accepted and there are many who would compare the Scottish Parliament unfavourably with Westminster[3]. Furthermore, for as long as the present devolutionary settlement subsists, there will be some ways in which formal comparisons between the Parliaments cannot truly be drawn. At the first meeting of the Scottish Parliament in May 1999, Winnie Ewing MSP said, when called upon to chair the initial proceedings, as the Parliament's most senior member, that she had always wanted either to say or to hear someone else say: 'the Scottish Parliament, which adjourned on 25 March 1707, is hereby reconvened'[4]. But, despite these brave words, the Scottish Parliament cannot readily be seen as the successor to the Parliament which went out of existence in 1707. It is not the Parliament of an independent Scotland. In all formal constitutional respects it is the statutorily created child of the Westminster Parliament – a point emphasised by Lord President Rodger in *Whaley v Watson*[5] when he referred to 'the fundamental character of the Parliament as a body which – however important its role – has been created by statute and derives its powers from statute. As such, it is a body which, like any other statutory body, must work within the scope of its powers'[6]. Although this may be unsurprising within the general context of devolution, it may also be regarded as irksome by those who aspire to a greater autonomy for the Parliament. Thus far, however, this formal subordination of the Scottish Parliament does not appear to have created significant public concern[7].

1 See the Scottish Constitutional Convention's Report, *Scotland's Parliament: Scotland's Right* (1995) p 24; *Report of the Consultative Steering Group on the Scottish Parliament* (1998) (*CSG Report*); section 2.
2 Commission on Scottish Devolution ('the Calman Commission'), *The Future of Scottish Devolution within the Union: a First Report* (2008) ('First Report'), para 4.6.
3 For further discussion see also Jeffrey C and Mitchell J, The Scottish Parliament 1999–2009: The First Decade (2009).
4 SP OR, 12 May 1999, col 5.
5 *Whaley v Watson* 2000 SC 340.
6 *Whaley v Watson* 2000 SC 340 at 348.
7 Statistics reproduced by the Calman Commission suggested that in the ten years to 2007 public support for a devolved Parliament had increased, while there had been a corresponding decrease in support for independence and the pre-1999 position. See the Calman Commission, *First Report*, paras 2.1–2.4.

THE ELECTED CHAMBERS

Structure and composition

4.2   The structure of the House of Commons and the Scottish Parliament is, in each case, determined by the rules which govern the number of members (MPs and MSPs), the election of members and the period for which the chambers are elected. These rules are, however, interrelated and the rules which apply to the Scottish Parliament are, to an extent, shared with those that apply at Westminster or are dependent upon them.

Elected members

4.3   Here the Scottish Parliament is taken first. The size of the Parliament is determined by reference to the number of constituencies (electoral areas) in Scotland – from each of which one MSP is elected – and the eight regions[1] – from each of which seven MSPs are elected[2]. The constituencies were identical to the Westminster parliamentary constituencies which existed when SA 1998 was passed, save that the Orkney Islands and Shetland Islands, which share a Westminster constituency, were separated to give each a constituency (and, therefore, a separate MSP) at Holyrood. There were 72 Westminster constituencies, producing 73 for Holyrood and, with the 56 regional members, 129 MSPs in total. The mechanisms by which the constituency and regional MSPs are elected are considered below but it may be noted that the original provisions of SA 1998 tying of the number of Holyrood constituencies to the number of Westminster constituencies (subject to the adjustment for Orkney and Shetland) would have had consequences going beyond mere administrative convenience in the management of elections – although that is, in itself, an important consideration. The reasons for the number of Westminster constituencies in Scotland having fallen in recent years (and, therefore, the number of

Scottish MPs) are discussed below but the impact on the size of the Scottish Parliament could not be justified on the same grounds. The case was made that the rules governing the size of the two Parliaments should be decoupled in the interests of maintaining the present size of the Scottish Parliament and, therefore, the same number of MSPs to serve on the Parliament's committees and to carry out its other functions[3] and the Scottish Parliament (Constituencies) Act 2004 gave effect to that change. The reduction in the number of Scottish Westminster constituencies to 59 as a result of the Fifth Periodical Review of the Boundary Commission for Scotland has therefore had no impact on the number of MSPs[4].

The size of the House of Commons is a matter determined by reference to the number of single-member constituencies currently defined for electoral purposes. There are at present 646 parliamentary constituencies across the United Kingdom as a whole (including the 59 in Scotland referred to above) but this is a figure which is subject to variation[5].

1 The same as those formerly used as constituencies for elections to the European Parliament.
2 Scotland Act 1998 (SA 1998), s 1(2), (3) and Sch 1.
3 SP OR 27 March 2002, col 10653; Scottish Grand Committee 12 June 2000.
4 See Fifth Periodical Report of the Boundary Commission for Scotland, Cm 6427, 30 November 2004.
5 See p 77 below.

Parliaments and parliamentary sessions

4.4   The length of each session of the Scottish Parliament[1] is four years. It is a fixed-term Parliament, with each general election falling four years after the last, on the first Thursday in May[2], the Parliament being dissolved twenty-one days before the election[3]. That is a rule which the Scottish Parliament cannot itself amend but it is subject to two exceptions, one of which is narrow and technical in nature but the other of wider constitutional importance. The Queen may, following a proposal by the Presiding Officer, by proclamation adjust the dates of the dissolution and the general election by no more than a month[4]. It is important that the power to propose such a change is to be exercised by the Presiding Officer and not by someone on behalf of the Scottish Government (or, indeed, by the opposition where a minority government might be put out of office): it should be exercised not for party political reasons but simply because the originally prescribed date was, for some reason, inappropriate. The other circumstance is where political paralysis has occurred and the Presiding Officer is required to shorten a session of the Parliament by proposing that the Queen dissolves the Parliament and calls a general election. One of the principal distinctions between the United Kingdom and the Scottish Parliaments is that, whereas the length of the Westminster Parliament is open-ended, subject to a maximum of five years, and can be dissolved, within that period, at any time by decision, in effect, of the Prime Minister, the Scottish Parliament must normally see out its fixed four-year session. The principal merit claimed for such a fixed-term arrangement is that it reduces the power of the government to manipulate the date of general elections to party advantage by choosing a time favourable to itself and maintaining party discipline meantime – both standard features of the Westminster Parliament. Having a fixed-term Parliament forces its members to seek the resolution of political conflict (including conflict over the making and unmaking of governments) within its own membership and without recourse to an early general election and a probable change of membership. The disadvantage of a Parliament of absolutely fixed terms is the risk that parliamentary and governmental activity could be brought to a complete halt if party political conditions prevented the formation (whether by coalition or otherwise) of a majority of members in support of a government and its policies. Political paralysis could indeed occur. This difficulty is met, in the case of the Scottish Parliament, by provisions which require the Presiding Officer to intervene where either (a) the Parliament with the support of two-thirds of MSPs resolves that it should be dissolved or (b) the Parliament fails to nominate a person for appointment as First Minister within the prescribed period and thus fails to allow an Executive to be formed[5]. In either of these circumstances an extraordinary general election is to be held. Such an extraordinary election does not disturb the normal four-year cycle of ordinary elections which remains in place, save that, if an extraordinary election takes place within six months of the date scheduled for the next ordinary election, that election does not take place[6].

As already mentioned, a fundamental difference between the two Parliaments is that, while the Scottish Parliament is (under normal circumstances) of fixed term, the Westminster Parliament is of variable length, subject only to a maximum duration of five years. That is a limit statutorily prescribed by the Parliament Act 1911 and is subject to adjustment only by another Act of Parliament. The 1911 Act repealed an earlier seven-year limit[7] and was itself temporarily overridden to enable the extension of the length of the Parliaments during the two World Wars of the twentieth century[8].

The time limit set by the Parliament Act 1911 is a restriction imposed by statute on rules which otherwise derive from the royal prerogative, as modified by convention. It is, in law, for the Queen to summon or dissolve a Parliament by proclamation. The same applies to the proroguing of Parliament between annual sessions. These are, however, decisions which, by convention, are made only on the advice of the Prime Minister[9]. It is this rule, for better or for worse, which gives the Prime Minister and the government of the day very substantial political control over the working of Parliament. The power to control the length of sessions within a Parliament is largely managerial but is important in the conduct of legislative business[10]. However, the Prime Minister's power to determine the overall length of a Parliament and the date of the next general election is of the greatest importance in planning the government's business, diminishing the power of the opposition, and maintaining discipline and control within the party of government[11].

1   In relation to 'sessions', terminology differs between the two Parliaments. At Westminster, a new Parliament is elected, following the dissolution of the last and the holding of a general election. Counting from 1801, the current Westminster Parliament is the 54th. The length of each parliamentary term is then divided into annual sessions, usually beginning and ending in November. In relation to the Scottish Parliament, the language of SA 1998 does not include reference to separate 'Parliaments'. Instead, the whole period between an election and the following dissolution is a 'session' of the Parliament. See the Standing Orders (SOs), r 2.1.
2   SA 1998, s 2(2).

3   SA 1998, s 2(3) and the Scottish Parliament (Elections etc) Order 2002, SI 2002/2779, art 85.
    Saturdays, Sundays and certain other holidays are disregarded in the calculation of the period.
4   SA 1998, s 2(5).
5   SA 1998, s 3(1), (2). See p 167 below for the appointment of the First Minister.
6   SA 1998, s 3(3), (4).
7   Septennial Act 1715. Earlier there was a three-year limit: Meeting of Parliament Act 1694.
8   The length of a Parliament cannot be extended by an Act of Parliament passed by the House of
    Commons alone under the Parliament Acts 1911 and 1949. See p 223 below.
9   See p 68.
10 See p 224.
11 The present government's Green Paper, The Governance of Britain (Cm 7170, 2007), indicated
    an intention to institute a new 'constitutional convention' in terms of which the government
    would seek the approval of the House of Commons before seeking a dissolution. No steps have
    been taken to implement that proposal.

ELECTIONS

Introduction

4.5   There is nothing more symbolically significant in a democracy than
the ballot box[1]. The exercise of each individual's right to choose, in the secrecy
of the voting booth, who should be his or her representative in an elected
assembly is the guarantee which underwrites the democratic system. There is,
however, nothing simple about the means of securing the working of fair and
free elections in a sophisticated democracy dominated by political parties. This
account focuses on elections to the Westminster and Scottish Parliaments but
much of the United Kingdom electoral law relevant to national parliamentary
elections is also used as the basis for the systems of election to local authorities and to the European Parliament. It covers entitlement to vote; entitlement
to be a candidate and member; voting systems; candidates, political parties
and constituencies; the tenure of members and the filling of casual vacancies;
and a note on the conduct of elections themselves. There are some concluding
remarks on Parliaments and political parties.

1   Although even that symbol can be the subject of controversy: the use of 'cardboard' ballot boxes
    during the Scottish Parliament and Scottish local government elections of 2007 was one of
    many aspects of these elections which were the subject of criticism. The security of ballot boxes
    during those elections was much debated: see Electoral Commission, Independent Review of
    the Scottish Parliamentary and local Government Elections 3 May 2007. N Ghaleigh, 'The
    Scottish Parliament elections 2007: what kind of hackery is this?' (2008) 12 Edin LR 2008 137.

Entitlement to vote

4.6   An individual's entitlement to vote in an election depends on that
person's name being on the electoral register for the area in which he or she
intends to vote[1]. Registers are compiled by electoral registration officers
throughout the United Kingdom and have to be available for an election called
at any time, since the dates of elections to the Westminster Parliament are not
fixed and by-elections, at any level, are unpredictable. Since 2001, registers
have been maintained as permanent records, with adjustments made on a 'rolling' basis reflecting day-to-day changes caused by people moving in or out of
the area or coming of age[2]. For an individual, being on the register is absolutely

essential to the right to vote in that area, although, in the case of absence from the address at the time of an election, it may be possible to vote by proxy or by post. Prior to 2001, electoral registers were compiled not on a rolling basis but annually and by reference to residence at an address on a particular date (10 October). Annual registers became out of date towards the end of their lives and, as a result, probably reduced voter participation. Although of less significance for the new rolling registers, an annual canvass of residents must still be carried out by registration officers, with 15 October as the operative date.

Admission to the electoral register depends on being resident in the constituency. RPA 1983, s 5 (as substituted by the Representation of the People Act 2000 (RPA 2000)), in which this test is laid down, does not, however, offer precise guidance on the meaning to be given to 'residence'. It does, on the other hand, seem clear that the physical quality of the fabric of the accommodation in which a person claims to reside may range widely. Certainly conventional bricks and mortar are not required and, in *Hipperson v Newbury District Electoral Registration Officer*[3], it was held that the tents and vehicles in which protestors at a peace camp slept would suffice. Certain other issues have been considered. RPA 1983 itself makes it clear that residence at an address will not be affected by temporary absence[4]. A person remains correctly registered at the home address rather than residence being interrupted temporarily by a holiday, business or educational absence. On the other hand, it has been recognised that, where a person acquires 'a considerable degree of permanence'[5] at some other address, residence there may also satisfy the test. In *Fox v Stirk*[6] it was held that university students could qualify at their university address. In *Hipperson* the protestors qualified at their peace camp, and in *Dumble v Borders Electoral Registration Officer*[7] weekend use of a cottage for political purposes sufficed. In *Scott v Phillips*[8], though, the summer use of a holiday cottage did not confer residence[9]. The idea of 'residence' has, at all events, acquired a special meaning in this electoral context. Physical presence[10] in a place is not the determining factor. The degree of permanence in a place (and more controversially its 'quality') is more significant.

The courts have created another dimension to the concept of residence, almost certainly not foreseen when it was first formulated and which is presumed to have survived the amendments of RPA 2000. This too derives from *Fox v Stirk* and is that a person may, in law, be resident in two places (and perhaps more) at once. Students may acquire a 'considerable degree of permanence' at both their university and 'home' addresses and this may apply to other voters as well. Dual registration does not confer the right to vote twice in a general election[11] but it does provide the option of voting in one place rather than another to groups whose numbers may be politically more significant in the more marginal of the two constituencies.

Special rules on residence apply to certain categories of potential voters. The right to vote is extended to British citizens now living overseas by permitting them to remain, for up to 15 years, on the register for the address at which they formerly resided[12]. Provision is also made for patients resident in mental hospitals except those who are detained offenders[13] and for prisoners held on remand[14]. Special provision is also made for certain homeless persons to make a 'declaration of local connection' to establish residence for electoral purposes[15].

Residence apart, admission to the electoral register depends upon the satisfaction of certain other criteria. Being on the register does not, however, guarantee a right to vote in all elections. Thus:

(1)   While persons aged 16 or over may be placed on the register, only those over 18 on the date of an election may vote[16].

(2)   Persons who are Commonwealth citizens (ie British citizens and citizens of other Commonwealth countries) and citizens of the European Union may be registered[17]. However, only Commonwealth citizens and citizens of the Republic of Ireland may vote in elections to the House of Commons. Citizens of other states in the European Union may vote only in elections to the Scottish Parliament, in local government elections, and in elections to the European Parliament[18].

(3)   Members of the House of Lords may be registered and may vote in all elections, except elections to the House of Commons. Prior to the House of Lords Act 1999, this exclusion extended to all hereditary peers. Now, only those hereditaries who have retained their membership of the House of Lords are barred from voting in elections to the House of Commons.

(4)   Despite registration, no person convicted and serving a sentence in prison may vote[19]. This blanket ban has been held by the European Court of Human Rights to be disproportionate to the UK's legitimate aim of encouraging 'responsible citizenship' and a breach of ECHR Article 3 of Protocol 1 (pre elections)[20]. The UK Government is still considering its response to this ruling[21].

(5)   Persons convicted of corrupt or illegal practices at an election have restricted voting rights[22].

(6)   People who are subject to a legal incapacity (eg serious mental impairment) may not vote[23].

Entitlement to be a candidate and member

Until recently, there were no rules directly defining who might stand in an election to the House of Commons. However, there were rules which disqualified certain categories of person from membership and rules which might be used to exclude people who were subject to a disqualification, either at the point of election or subsequently. These rules remain and the same approach has been adopted for the Scottish Parliament, although with the use of a modified list of disqualifications. A consequence, however, of the introduction of the new voting system for the Scottish Parliament has been the need to introduce new rules directly governing candidature, and these are mentioned below[24].

The list of persons disqualified from membership of the House of Commons includes:

(a)   aliens but not those who are citizens of the Republic of Ireland or of Commonwealth countries[25];

(b)   persons under 18[26];

(c)   certain detained mentally ill persons;

(d)   members of the House of Lords[27];

(e)   undischarged bankrupts and persons against whom sequestration of their estate has been awarded[28];

(f)   those convicted of treason or of other offences and serving a term of imprisonment of more than a year[29];

(g)   persons guilty of corrupt or illegal practices at elections[30].

It will be observed that these disqualifications are founded on a miscellany of historically based reasons[31], some of which are of dubious continuing constitutional significance. Of more general importance, and invoking broader principles of constitutional propriety and the separation of powers, are rules which (a) disqualify certain persons holding positions in the public service and (b) restrict the number of holders of ministerial office who may be MPs. The ancestor of both rules was a section of the Act of Settlement 1700 which would have[32] barred all holders of an 'office of profit' under the Crown from membership of the Commons. As far as the holders of non-political office are concerned, the spirit of that restriction is maintained in the House of Commons Disqualification Act 1975 (HCDA 1975) which prevents all members of the civil service, the armed forces and any police force from being MPs. Equally, holders of judicial office including sheriffs principal and sheriffs are barred, as are a large number of holders of public offices specified in HCDA 1975[33]. These disqualifications sustain important elements of the principle of the separation of powers by drawing a line between the judiciary and large sectors of the executive on the one hand and the legislature on the other. In addition, there has been retained, as a device to enable an MP to resign his or her seat (for which no other direct provision is made[34]) certain disqualifying offices of profit under the Crown, notably the Stewardship of the Chiltern Hundreds, appointment to which has the indirect effect of a resignation.

However, the disqualifications do not extend to ministers of the Crown, which permits the constitutionally most important exception to any pure idea of the separation of powers. Ministers may, and according to convention must, be drawn from one or other House of Parliament, and with most of them from the House of Commons[35]. Notionally in the interests of restraining governmental dominance of the House of Commons, however, a limit is placed on the number of paid ministerial offices to be held at any one time in that House. HCDA 1975 and the Ministerial and Other Salaries Act 1975 together have the effect of restricting the number of ministerial offices in the Commons to 95 and also determine maximum numbers at prescribed salary levels in the Commons and Lords together.

Similar rules on disqualification and on ministerial offices apply in the Scottish Parliament. The general disqualifications are the same, save that there is no bar to membership of members of the House of Lords. Lord Steel of Aikwood, the Parliament's first Presiding Officer, and Lord Watson of Invergowrie have both been MSPs[36]. Nor is there any formal bar on a person's combining membership of the Scottish Parliament with that of the House of Commons. Neither body has a disqualifying rule to this effect and that enabled several MPs elected in 1997 to the Westminster Parliament to be elected to Holyrood in 1999, including Donald Dewar and Jim Wallace. Although rules subsequently adopted by several parties forbade such 'dual mandates' the current First Minister, Alex Salmond, retains the Westminster seat which he occupied before being (re) elected to the Scottish Parliamant in 2007.

Rules equivalent to those at Westminster bar certain office-holders from membership of the Scottish Parliament[37].

The inclusion of all ministers (with the exception of the two Law Officers[38]) as MSPs is a statutory, rather than a merely conventional, requirement at Holyrood[39] but there is no overall limitation on the number of ministers in the Parliament.

1 Representation of the People Act 1983 (RPA 1983), s 1.
2 Cut-off rules operate to crystallise the state of the register at the final date for nominations before elections. Individuals may appeal against their exclusion from the register to an Electoral Registration Court.
3 [1985] QB 1060.
4 RPA 1983, s 5(3)–(5).
5 *Fox v Stirk* [1970] 2 QB 463.
6 *Fox v Stirk* [1970] 2 QB 463.
7 *Dumble v Borders Electoral Registration Officer* 1980 SLT (Sh Ct) 60.
8 *Scott v Phillips* 1974 SLT 32.
9 See also *Ferris v Wallace* 1936 SC 561.
10 Or 'actual residence', as the RPA 1983 unhelpfully has it.
11 RPA 1983, s 1(2).
12 Representation of the People Act 1985, s 1.
13 RPA 1983, s 3A and s 7.
14 RPA 1983, s 7A.
15 RPA 1983, ss 7B, 7C.
16 RPA 1983, s 1(1).
17 RPA 1983, S 4.
18 RPA 1983, ss1 and 2 and see SI 1994/342; SI 1995/1948.
19 RPA 1983, s 3.
20 *Hirst v United Kingdom* (2006) 42 EHRR 41. See also *Smith v Scott* 2007 SC 345 in which the Court of Session sitting as the Registration Appeal Court made a declaration of incompatibility under HRA 1998 in relation to Section 3 of RPA 1983.
21 See the 31st Report of the Joint Committee on Human Rights, (2007–08) HL 173, HC 1078.
22 RPA 1983, s 160.
23 RPA 1983, s 1.
24 The Political Parties, Elections and Referendums Act 2000 (PPERA) as amended by the Electoral Administration Act 2006) also contains rules on the description of the party affiliation of candidates on ballot papers. See p 81.
25 Act of Settlement 1700, s 3; British Nationality Act 1981, Sch 7. For fuller discussion of this and the other categories of disqualification, see Erskine May *Parliamentary Practice* (23rd ed, 2004) ch 3.
26 Electoral Administration Act 2006 s 17(1). Section 17(8) 'disapplies' section 6 of the (English) Union with Scotland Act 1706 which imposed a minimum age requirement of 21.
27 The terms of this disqualification were adjusted on the passing of the House of Lords Act 1999. Peers who are not members of the House of Lords are not disqualified. See p 84 below.
28 Insolvency Act 1986, s 427.
29 Forfeiture Act 1870; Representation of the People Act 1981 (RPA 1981).
30 RPA 1983, ss 159, 160.
31 Another was the disqualification of ordained clergy and Church of Scotland ministers, until lifted by the House of Commons (Removal of Clergy Disqualification) Act 2001.
32 But for its repeal by the Succession to the Crown Act 1707.
33 See the lists in the schedules to HCDA 1975 which are frequently amended.
34 Indeed, resignation from the English Parliament was prohibited by resolution of 2 March 1623.
35 See p 160.
36 In evidence to the House of Lords Committee on the Constitution, Lord Steel expressed his

support for Presiding Officers of the Scottish Parliament (and also of the Welsh Assembly) being made peers: HL Paper 28 (2002–03).
37 SA 1998, s 15 and the Scottish Parliament (Disqualification) Order 2007, SI 2007/285.
38 SA 1998, ss 27, 48.
39 SA 1998, ss 45, 47.

Voting systems: candidates, political parties and constituencies

4.7   Defining the electorate does not define the way in which they elect their representatives. That depends on how elections are organised; who may stand for election as a candidate; whether the electorate is divided into constituencies and, if so, whether one or more than one member are to be elected from each; how many votes each person has and how the votes are counted; and, perhaps most important of all, the ways in which voting for individual candidates is combined with a process of voting for political parties. As a result of a number of developments in recent years there are now four different types of voting system operating in the United Kingdom[1]. Elections to the Westminster Parliament are conducted on a constituency-based 'first past the post' (FPTP) system. Elections to the Scottish Parliament and the Welsh Assembly (and also the London Assembly) are held on the additional member system (AMS) which combines constituency-based FPTP with a system of electing additional regional members drawn from a party list[2]. Elections to the European Parliament are conducted on a regionally based 'closed list' system, except in Northern Ireland where the *Single Transferable Vote* (STV) system is used. This latter system has also been used for the election of the Northern Ireland Assembly and, since 2007, is also the system used for local government elections in Scotland. It is discussed in more detail below.

This diversity of practice has developed largely as a result of a long-standing dissatisfaction with the way in which FPTP has operated at Westminster. That system satisfies some of the widely accepted criteria for a good voting system but fails in other respects. The Labour government elected in 1997 had a manifesto commitment to a review which was conducted by the (Jenkins) Independent Commission on the Voting System, reporting in 1998[3]. It will be useful to consider the findings of that review and also the systems enacted for elections to the devolved Parliaments and the European Parliament but, as a starting point, the principal features of FPTP for the Westminster Parliament should be put in place.

One of its claimed advantages is its simplicity: each constituency returns one MP; at each election (whether a general election or a by-election to replace an MP who has died or retired) voters have one vote which they cast for one candidate identified by name and, almost always, political party; the candidate with the largest number of votes wins and is returned as MP for the constituency. Counting in the constituencies is simple and the overall consequences of a general election are easily seen in the new membership of the House of Commons. All MPs have a formal equality of status and all voters know, or have the means of knowing, who their single elected representative is. These simplicities do, however, produce what is, for many, a profound unfairness represented by the inevitable tendency of a FPTP system to leave the many constituency voters (often a majority) who did not vote for the winning candidate feeling that they are without representation in Parliament and also to produce an overall pattern of representation skewed in favour of the party which happens to have come first most often, and against parties which may have attracted large number of votes but for candidates placed second or lower in their constituency contests. On the whole, smaller parties are disproportionately badly represented. In the 2005 general election the Labour Party won 356 seats (55 per cent) on 35 per cent of the total vote while the Liberal Democrats won 62 seats (9 per cent) on 22 per cent of the vote.

The overall lack of proportionality and the apparently unfair results it produces are not, for some, decisive. For them, the system's simplicity and straightforwardness of representative effect are important and these are coupled with its tendency to produce a single overall winning party in the House of Commons which eases the process of government formation from that party and often, because of its distorted majority, 'strong' government thereafter. However, it is the arguments against the disproportionality of the FPTP system which have produced reforming proposals which have borne fruit in recent years.

There have been proposed two principal models of voting to provide a solution. The first is the Single Transferable Vote (STV) system. This achieves its higher degree of proportional representation by (a) the creation of a small number of larger multi-member constituencies, with each returning, say, three or five or seven MPs and thus capable of ensuring that members of more than one significant party represent the constituency in Parliament; and (b) the opportunity for each voter to cast votes for the three, five or seven candidates, in order of preference, coupled with a counting system which gives weight first to first-preference votes and then to lower-preference votes. The capacity of this system for a higher degree of proportionality of outcome is obvious. Its disadvantages, when compared with FPTP, are its reduced capacity to deliver 'strong' government, with a greater possibility of the need for coalition rather than single-party governments; the loss of local representation because of the increased size of constituencies; the loss of personal directness of representation and accountability because of the multi-member team sent to Parliament; and the relative complexity of the voting and counting systems[4]. The other principal route to proportionality is by way of a 'list' system. In its purest form, this involves the abolition of separate constituencies, and in a single nationwide poll, the opportunity for all voters to cast votes for persons and/or parties on lists of candidates submitted (in the main) by political parties. The system operates to ensure, as precisely as possible, a matching of percentage support expressed by votes in the country against the percentage of representation in Parliament. In this, its purest all-country version, local representation is entirely lost but may be reinstated to a degree by the organisation of elections on a regional basis; and it may admit to Parliament MPs representing tiny (and perhaps extreme) political parties, a feature which can be curbed by imposing a preliminary requirement to achieve a minimum (eg 5 per cent) of the total poll. The list system tends to lead to coalition governments. The system[5] deployed on a regional basis – with Scotland returning six[6] MEPs – is used for elections in the United Kingdom to the European Parliament. It is a modified list system which is used to provide the 'regional' members of the Scottish Parliament.

At the third general election in May 2007 (which produced a far less 'diverse' Parliament than had the 2003 election) this enabled the Scottish Conservative Party to supplement its four constituency MSPs with thirteen regional members and, critically for the overall result, added 26 regional seats to the SNP's 21 constituencies. The system also produced two regional members for the Greens and one independent[7]. On the other hand, the Labour Party added only nine regional members to its thirty-seven constituency MSPs and the Liberal Democrats added five to their eleven.

The Jenkins Commission conducted a review of electoral systems as they might be applied to the House of Commons and, in their recommendations[4], expressed a preference for neither STV nor a list system as the primary means of reform. Instead, the Commission proposed a two-vote mixed system with the majority of MPs elected on an individual constituency basis, not by FPTP but by use of the Alternative Vote (which is not a means of achieving proportional representation but does offer voters the opportunity to express second and further preferences). Remaining MPs would be elected from open lists (ie lists giving the opportunity for the selection of individuals rather than simply of parties) based on small regions. There has, however, been no movement towards the adoption by government of the Jenkins proposals or, indeed, of any others albeit that in May 2009 Secretary of State Alan Johnson MP expressed his support for the 'AV plus' system and called for a referendum on electoral reform[8].

1 For a discussion of each and of the various reviews of the different systems which have taken place since 1997 see The Government of Britain, Review of Voting Systems: The experience of new voting systems in the United Kingdom since 1997, Cm 7304, 24 January 2008.
2 AMS systems are also be described, elsewhere in the world, as MMP (mixed-member proportional representation) systems.
3 Cm 4090.
4 As to which, and its consequences for the 2007 Scottish local government elections, see p 198.
5 'Closed list' rather an 'open list' which gives voters the choice of allocation of votes only by party rather than a named individual: European Parliamentary Elections Act 2002, s 2.
6 Reduced from eight by the European Parliament (Number of MEPs and Distribution between Electoral Regions) (United Kingdom and Gibraltar) Order 2008, SI 2008/1954.
7 *Report of the Independent Commission on the Voting System* (Cm 4090, 1998).
8 The Times, 25 May 2009.

Constituencies and their boundaries

4.8   Any electoral system short of one adopting a list-system vote across the entire territory of the nation relies upon the division of that territory into separate (and roughly equal-sized) constituencies and, because of the vagaries of population shifts, that division needs to be kept under review. The need for the division and review to be done scientifically and in the light of objective criteria in the interests of rationality and fairness suggests that the tasks should be allocated to bodies with a degree of independence from governments. That need for independence is enhanced by the peculiar susceptibility of constituency boundaries to party political manipulation. Especially in the constituencies required for the elections to the Westminster and Scottish Parliaments – small and, under FPTP, with single winners – quite slender boundary adjustments moving small populations of potentially friendly or hostile voters in or out of constituencies may produce quite different results. It is for this reason that the duty to review boundaries and to make recommendations for change has been placed in the hands of appointed boundary commissions for England, Northern Ireland, Scotland and Wales[1]. Although chaired *ex officio* by the Speaker of the House of Commons, the Boundary Commission for Scotland is, in practice, chaired by a Court of Session judge (currently Lord Woolman) with two other members appointed by the Secretary of State. The principal task of the Commission is to undertake periodic boundary reviews for both the Westminster and Scottish Parliaments. Its first periodic review of Scottish Parliament boundaries is underway – with the Commission having published revised recommendations for constituencies and provisional proposals for regions on 21 May 2009. The overriding principle, so far as Westminster is concerned, is to produce constituencies across Great Britain of equivalent size and thus with an electorate of about 70,000, but subject to special geographical considerations such as size, shape and accessibility as well as boundaries of local government areas[2]. A local inquiry may be held into the published provisional recommendations of the Commission which then submits its report in final form. It is then for the Secretary of State to lay the report before Parliament together with a draft Order in Council implementing the report, with or without modifications. As noted above[3], the 2006 Commission review of the Westminster constituencies was of much greater than usual significance because SA 1998, s 86 removed the long-standing statutory requirement that Scotland should be disproportionately well represented at Westminster with a minimum of 71 MPs. As a result of that review the number of Scottish MPs was reduced to 59.

THE WEST LOTHIAN QUESTION. There is one issue affecting the composition, and also the powers, of the two Parliaments which defies precise categorisation. It is captured by the question posed originally by Tam Dalyell MP (formerly for the West Lothian constituency and latterly for Linlithgow) at the time of the debate leading to the Scotland Act 1978[4] but which has a continuing relevance. As he put it, it was a question about why he, as a Westminster MP for a Scottish constituency, could legitimately be expected to participate in, or vote on, business in relation to Blackburn in the English county of Lancashire but not in relation to Blackburn in West Lothian because that business would, for Scotland, be devolved (and has now been devolved by SA 1998) to the Scottish Parliament. Dalyell viewed this as a fatal flaw in any system of devolution constructed on an asymmetrical basis. Forcing the Westminster Parliament to be both a United Kingdom Parliament dealing with 'reserved' matters across the whole country and also an English (and Welsh) Parliament in relation to the matters devolved to Scotland (and Northern Ireland) created inevitable and unacceptable tensions – in particular the possible use by a United Kingdom government to secure legislation for England by a Commons majority dependent upon Scottish MPs. This was a position exacerbated by the 'overrepresentation' of Scotland in the House of Commons, a matter now addressed by the boundary changes discussed above. Notwithstanding those changes, the West Lothian Question refuses to go away and has in recent years – particularly following the SNP's victory in the 2007 Scottish Parliament elections – become a frequently kicked political football. Current Conservative Party policy, for example, is to 'address the West Lothian question and give English MPs a decisive say on laws that affect only England', a policy which might be given effect by legislation in similar terms to Lord Baker of Dorking's Parliament (Participation of Members of the House of Commons) Bill – a private member's bill introduced in 2006 which would have given the Speaker discretion to exclude categories of MPs (including all Scottish MPs) from speaking and voting on a Bill. In its May 2009 report 'Devolution: A Decade On', the House of Commons Justice Committee recognised the force of the West Lothian Question but described the 'English question' as being about far more than the voting by Scottish, Welsh and Northern Irish MPs on matters of importance only to England. Rather, it 'encompasses the wider issue of how England should be governed post-devolution'[5]. The Committee noted the range of possible solutions to the 'English question' depending on how that question is characterised:

> 'First, there are those solutions which seek to address the constitutional imbalance seemingly brought about by devolution, for example, through the creation of an English Parliament. Second, there are those solutions which seek to amend the role, practice and status of Westminster as a means of addressing the West Lothian Question, for example, schemes of English votes for English laws. However, others consider that the West Lothian Question could be best addressed by a change in the party political balance at Westminster, for example, through reform of the electoral system or a reduction in the number of MPs from Scotland and Wales. These approaches could be described as all-England solutions. The final category of solutions are those which attempt to tackle the centralised nature and relative size of England through decentralisation or devolution within England'[6].

Having identified this range of possible solutions, however, the Committee was unable to endorse any one of them. It expressed concern about the question of 'balance' which would arise in the event of the creation of a new English Parliament, given the 'sheer size of the English population'. The suggestion had been made to the Committee that in the context of what would have become a more explicitly quasi-federal structure it would be extremely unusual to see one federal unit representing 80% to 85% of the total population of the state. Limiting the right to vote on 'English-only matters including health and education, to MPs with English seats' would require more careful drafting of new legislation to isolate English provisions from those extending to other parts of the UK and would also demand reform of the current system of allocating public spending in terms of which funding allocations for Scotland, Wales and Northern Ireland are calculated by reference to the amount determined for England. Changes in the electoral system or a reduction in the numbers of 'devolved' MPs with seats at Westminster were felt not to address the issue of principle at the heart of this debate – i.e. what voting rights ought to be enjoyed by those MPs – while it was felt by the Committee that regional devolution within England would be unlikely to answer the demands of those who 'want an English solution to the West Lothian question'. The Committee concluded that there remained 'major political as well as constitutional questions which are for Parliament as a whole to consider. It is our belief that as devolved government in Scotland, Wales and Northern Ireland develops in profile and substance, Parliament will come under pressure to consider these questions'[7]. Meanwhile, north of the border the Calman Commission (see p 63) concluded that it was 'not for us to discuss where or how power might be decentralised or devolved in England…nor…how England's laws should be made'[8]. The 'West Lothian Question affects all of the UK, and is a matter for the UK Parliament, not a matter for the Commission'[9].

1 Parliamentary Constituencies Act 1986 (PCA 1986), s 2. The Boundary Commission for Scotland is responsible for review of Scottish Parliament boundaries by virtue of S1 and Schedule 1 SAA 1998, as amended by the Scottish Parliament (Constituencies) Act 2004. Statutory provision has been made for the transfer of the powers to the Electoral Commission (PPERA 2000, s 16) but this seems unlikely to affect the Scottish Commission for the foreseeable future.
2 PCA 1986, Sch 2.
3 See p 95.
4 T Dalyell *Devolution: The End of Britain* (1977) pp 245–251.
5 Devolution: A Decade On, Fifth Report of Session 2008–09, HC 529-I, para 158.
6 Ibid, para 163.
7 Ibid, para 230.
8 The Calman Commission, Serving Scotland Better: Scotland and the United Kingdom in the 21st Century (*'Serving Scotland Better'*) (2009), para 2.13. For further discussion see R Hazell (ed), The English Question (2006) and The Constitution Unit, Towards a New Settlement?, Report to the Commission, July 2008.
9 *Serving Scotland Better*, p 155, n 4.92.

The tenure of MPs and MSPs and the filling of vacancies

4.9   MPs and MSPs are elected for the period of the Parliament. In the Scottish Parliament, an MSP's term of office is stated to begin on the day on which the member is declared to be returned[1]. Before a member can take part in any proceedings of the Parliament he or she must take the oath of allegiance[2]. Thereafter, membership lasts until dissolution unless a member acquires a characteristic incompatible with membership[3] or dies or resigns. The device for enabling resignation from the House of Commons has been mentioned[4]. In the Scottish Parliament, resignation is by written notice to the Presiding Officer[5]. In both Parliaments, there is provision for the filling of casual vacancies. In the House of Commons, a by-election is held on the authority of a warrant issued by the Speaker, following a motion on behalf of the party which formerly held the seat[6]. In the Scottish Parliament, a 'constituency vacancy' is filled by a by-election held within three months on a date fixed by the Presiding Officer[7]. There cannot be the same option of a by-election in the case of a 'regional vacancy'. In the interests of maintaining proportionality of representation, the seat is to be filled by the person next in line at the last election on the relevant political party's regional list, who is willing and able to serve[8]. If the seat was held by an individual who is not a party representative, it is to remain vacant until the next general election[9].

1 SA 1998, s 13.
2 SA 1998, s 84.
3 See pp 72–73.
4 The Stewardship of the Chiltern Hundreds see p 73.
5 SA 1998, s 14.
6 Erskine May *Parliamentary Practice* (23rd edn, 2004), p 40.

7 SA 1998, s 9.
8 For example, in the current Parliament Shirley-Anne Somerville MSP replaced Stefan Tym-
   kewycz as an SNP list member for Lothians on 31 August 2007 following the latter's resignation. Anne McLaughlin became an MSP on 9 February 2009 following the death of Bashir
   Ahmad on 6 February 2009.
9 SA 1998, s 10.

The conduct of elections

4.10 Detailed rules for the conduct of elections are prescribed in regulations. For elections to the Scottish Parliament, rules about the registration of
voters, registration appeals (to the sheriff and thence to a registration appeal
court of three judges), the manner of voting (including absent and proxy
voting), election campaigns (including election agents and the control of campaign expenses), the regulation of broadcasting during campaigns and the legal
challenge of election results are contained in the Scottish Parliament (Elections
etc) Order 2007[1].

1 SI 2007/937 as amended by SI 2008/307. For UK parliamentary elections, the source of many
   of the equivalent rules is the Representation of the People (Scotland) Regulations 2001, SI
   2001/497, as amended.

Parliaments and political parties

4.11 The written constitutions of the world do not have much to say
about political parties[1]. They may take care to ensure that freedom of political
thought and freedom of political association (including the right to form and
belong to political parties) are guaranteed to citizens but, in the text of a constitution itself, few clues are given as to the dominant role of political parties
in the actual working of constitutional rules. Political parties and even whole
systems of party organisation may come and go while constitutions, remaining
above the political fray, have an enduring character and display a neutrality
and impartiality in their silence. Politics should be left to be conducted in the
shadow of the constitution.

Historically, United Kingdom constitutional rules gave hardly any direct recognition to the participation by political parties in the system. Electoral candidates were permitted to identify their party affiliation on the ballot paper
and, on the other hand, since 1974, certain political organisations have been
proscribed under the Prevention of Terrorism (Temporary Provisions) Act
1974 (now the Terrorism Act 2000, Pt II). For two main reasons, this situation
has changed to produce the rules for the registration of political parties under
PPERA 2000[2]. The introduction of proportional representation involving the
use of lists of party candidates for the devolved assemblies and Parliaments
and for the European Parliament required official recognition for the parties.
Secondly, registration was required by the wish to extend constraints on individual candidates in respect of election funding to constraints on parties as a
whole; the wish to monitor donations to political parties; and the wish to facilitate (so far) limited public funding assistance for political parties. Since 1975,
some funding assistance ('Short' money) has been made available to opposi-

tion parties at Westminster and this facility was extended to Holyrood at its inception, but additional forms of assistance required more formal structures. Under PPERA 2000, s 12 policy development grants are available to registered parties represented in Parliament. The Act also introduced mechanisms for the monitoring and control of donations to parties.

The changes introduced by PPERA 2000 serve only limited purposes, however, and go only a little way to regulate by law the party system which dominates the working of the Westminster and, in a different way, the Scottish Parliament. It is the ways in which parties determine who forms governments, how those governments are maintained in power and enabled to carry out their business, and the peculiar relationship of control and accountability between governments and Parliaments which loom largest but party domination of the electoral process is an essential initial element.

1 But the former Constitution (1977) of the USSR gave a leading role to the Communist Party.
2 Originally under the Registration of Political Parties Act 1998.

THE HOUSE OF LORDS AND THE CASE FOR BICAMERALISM IN THE SCOTTISH PARLIAMENT

Introduction

4.12   The most obvious structural difference between the Westminster and Scottish Parliaments is that, in addition to its elected chamber, the Westminster Parliament includes the unelected House of Lords. It is bicameral rather than unicameral and this has clear consequences for law-making procedures at Westminster, and for government formation and accountability. The debate over the case for abolition of the House of Lords or for the reform of its composition and powers was an important element in constitutional discourse throughout the last century and, although several reforms were indeed made (including most recently the restrictions on membership by virtue of a hereditary peerage enacted by the House of Lords Act 1999), there is considered to be unfinished reforming business carried forward into the twenty-first century.

It may be helpful to begin with an account of the composition of the House of Lords before the recent reforms were launched following the election of the Labour government in 1997. Much the largest single contingent was that of the hereditary peers and peeresses of whom there were about 759 (with nine of original creation and the remainder of the second or later generation). They would all have expected to retain membership for their lifetimes, with transmission to their successors[1]. Secondly, there were some 500 life peers created by virtue of the Life Peerages Act 1958. One question raised in the process of reform is whether all should be retained as members of the House of Lords for their lifetimes, with at least short- to medium-term consequences for the prospects of securing a reduction in total membership. Then in much smaller numbers, there were the Lords of Appeal in Ordinary (the senior judges who, until the advent of the Supreme Court (see p 296) sat in the Appellate Committee of the House of Lords and the Judicial Committee of Privy Council and, prior to 1958, the only 'life peers')[2] and retired Lords of Appeal, some 27 altogether.

And finally, there were the 'Lords Spiritual': 26 archbishops and bishops of the Church of England.

The actual functions of the House of Lords are dealt with elsewhere in this book. The House of Lords participates in the making of Acts of Parliament but principally in a 'revising' capacity and subject ultimately to the discipline of the Parliament Acts 1911–49, according to which the will of the House of Commons prevails[3]. In the approval of secondary legislation, the Lords normally defer to the Commons but with occasional rebellions[4]. The Lords may hold individual ministers to account but they cannot bring down governments as a whole[5]. The Lords exercise their functions in a way which does not seriously challenge the primacy of the Commons, despite their being the 'Upper' House.

1 Prior to the Peerage Act 1963, the disclaimer of a title was not possible (*Re Parliamentary Election for Bristol South East* [1961] 3 WLR 577) but that Act enabled disclaimer for the lifetime of the incumbent, enabling, eg, Tony Benn and Sir Alec Douglas Home to become MPs.
2 Created under the Appellate Jurisdiction Acts 1876 and 1887 and the Administration of Justice Act 1968, s 1.
3 See p 223.
4 See *A House for the Future* (Cm 4534) ch 7.
5 *The House of Lords – Completing the Reform* (Cm 5291) para 23.

The House of Lords: reform or abolition

4.13 If one were to start with a clean slate, the case for a bicameral (or even multicameral) legislature would be made in terms of a mixture of arguments concerning both the composition and functions of an additional chamber[1]. A second chamber designed to have weak, perhaps only advisory, functions attracts few serious questions about its membership. A second chamber designed to discharge important functions, including, for instance, the power to amend or veto legislative proposals, needs strong arguments for its very existence and provokes debate about its membership. Probably the most obvious justification for second chambers in general has been the wish to see state or provincial interests represented and given power in federal constitutions[2].

Whatever the general arguments, however, debate in the United Kingdom has never been permitted to start from a clean slate but has been conducted instead on the basis of more piecemeal reforms of the peculiarities of the historical heritage. The twin considerations of functions and membership have been important but they have been clouded by history, a commitment to the need for change to command broad support in Parliament, and political expediency. The starting point for the incoming Labour government in 1997 was a manifesto commitment to reform which was followed, in December 1998, by a White Paper outlining the way forward[3]. The first stage would be the removal of the right of all but a small number of hereditary peers to sit and vote in the House of Lords. This would produce a 'transitional' House which would be accompanied by a new independent Appointments Commission to recommend non-political appointments to the transitional House. As far as longer-term reform was concerned this would be, as originally proposed in the manifesto, a matter for a Joint Committee of both Houses of Parliament but that Committee's work would be prefaced by a Royal Commission to consider possible alternatives for reform.

Thus, the next step taken was the passing of the House of Lords Act 1999 which provides that no one shall be a member of the House of Lords by virtue of a hereditary peerage, save for up to 92 hereditary peers for their lifetimes or 'until an Act of Parliament provides to the contrary'[4]. The government concession to allow some hereditary peers to remain was negotiated to prevent a stalling of the Bill by opposition in the House of Lords itself[5]. A non-statutory Appointments Commission was established with powers to recommend non-political life peers and to vet all nominations.

By January 2000, the Royal Commission on Reform of the House of Lords, under the chairmanship of Lord Wakeham, had reported[6], with recommendations for a largely nominated membership and offering three different models for the election, on a regional basis, of the remainder. There would be a new Appointments Commission established by statute. At this point, however, the pace of reform slackened as it became apparent that a division of opinion was opening as to the way forward. In particular, the Royal Commission's preference for a mainly nominated membership of the reformed House was found to be unacceptable to many outside (and some inside) the government. It was not until after the May 2001 general election that the government itself provided a considered response to Wakeham. In *The House of Lords – Completing the Reform*[7], the government broadly accepted Wakeham but invited views on a number of outstanding issues. A very substantial contribution to the developing debate came from a report, in February 2002, of an inquiry held by the House of Commons Public Administration Committee[8] to which the government responded in April[9]. This was followed by the revival of the proposal, originally made in 1998 but thought to have been abandoned through the lack of sufficient parliamentary consensus, for a Joint Committee of both Houses on reform. That Committee (under the chairmanship of Jack Cunningham MP) met for the first time on 9 July 2002 and in December 2002 the Committee reported[10] that it was its view that there was broad agreement on the role, functions and powers of a reformed second chamber. The self-restraining conventions governing relations with the House of Commons should be continued as a vital part of any settlement. No new or additional powers should be conferred on the House of Lords but consideration would later need to be given to its treatment of secondary legislation. The composition of the House was the principal outstanding issue. There should be about 600 members, although with a larger number for a transitional period. Tenure for all members of 12 years was proposed and there would need to be further consideration of the position of bishops, the Law Lords, and the judicial function of the House of Lords. What was required before further progress could be made was a debate, and later a vote, in each House on the same list of seven options for the composition of a new House of Lords ranging from fully appointed to fully elected via different percentages of each. The debates were scheduled for 21 January 2003 and the votes on the options took place on 4 February. In the House of Lords there was a majority for a fully appointed House but for no other option. In the House of Commons, however, there was no majority for any of the seven options and there was a danger of paralysis once again.

In May 2003 the Joint Committee returned to the fray with the publication of a further report[11] summarising the extent of progress already made, the degree of consensus already achieved, even on some aspects of the future composition of the House, and the work still to be done. The report, from a divided Committee, concluded with an appeal to the government for an early response which could lead to an acceptance by both Houses that the work of the Committee should continue. That appeal went largely unheeded and such proposals as have been put forward by the government since 2003 for reform of membership of the Lords have failed to get off the ground[12].

The then Lord Chancellor Lord Falconer announced in September 2003 the government's intention to remove all remaining hereditary peers from the upper chamber but that proposal was not taken forward before the 2005 general election. Following the election, a cross-party group on Lords reform was established and its work led ultimately to the publication in February 2007 of a further White Paper – The House of Lords: Reform[13]. The White Paper described its role as being to 'set the stage for the free votes on the composition of a future House of Lords, promised in the Government's 2005 manifesto'[14]. It recommended a 'hybrid House' comprising a mix of elected and appointed members but offering a range of options on the precise balance of the two. A form of proportional representation would be introduced in relation to elected members, while appointees would be chosen by a statutory appointments commission reporting directly to Parliament. It was also proposed that at least 20% of the total membership of the Lords should be non party-political. Remaining life and hereditary peers would disappear but in a gradual way. There followed a government sponsored debate in the Commons on 7 March 2007[15] at the conclusion of which a large majority of MPs voted in favour of a wholly elected second chamber – only to be followed a week later by the Lords themselves voting against all options involving elections and favouring, instead, an all-appointed chamber[16].

Perhaps inevitably, this impasse was followed by the appointment of a further cross-party working group and the publication in July 2008 by the Ministry of Justice of another White Paper – An Elected Second Chamber: further reform of the House of Lords[17] – which advanced the case for a 100% or 80% elected chamber, with members serving a single term of between 12 and 15 years and being elected in 'thirds' with elections taking place on three electoral cycles. Hereditary peers would be removed, as would Church of England Bishops. It then appeared that reform was off the agenda until after the next general election. However on 10 June 2009 Prime Minister Brown announced that "The government will come forward with published proposals for the final stages of House of Lords reform before the summer break – including the next steps we can take to resolve the position of the remaining hereditary peers and other outstanding issues"[18].

It remains, as it was nearly six years ago when the first edition of this book was published, unclear when and how the process of reform of the Lords will be progressed and concluded.

1   M Russell *Reforming the House of Lords: Lessons from Overseas* (2000); special issue of *Journal of Legislative Studies* (2001) vol 7 (Spring).

2   The US Senate performs that role on behalf of the states.
3   *Modernising Parliament: Reforming the House of Lords* Cm 4183, 1998.
4   House of Lords Act 1999, ss 1–2. The allocation of these peers was according to prior party strength in the Lords and the standing orders of the House contain the procedures for replacing deceased members. Since the end of the first session of the last Parliament (ie November 2002) this has been by election. The first election (of Lord Ullswater) was held in March 2003.
5   A challenge to the Bill in the House of Lords Committee for Privileges on grounds including an asserted obligation to protect Scottish hereditary peers under the Articles of Union failed. See *Lord Gray's Motion* 2000 SC 46 (HL) and pp 112–113.
6   *A House for the Future* (Cm 4534, 2000).
7   Cm 5291, November 2001.
8   *The Second Chamber: Continuing the Reform* (HC Paper 494 (2001–02)).
9   HC Paper 794 (2001–02).
10 HL Paper 17, HC Paper 171 (2002–03).
11 HL Paper 97, HC Paper 668 (2002–03).
12 A notable exception was the Constitutional Reform Act 2005 which focused on the judicial role of the Lord Chancellor and Lords of Appeal in Ordinary and created the new Supreme Court.
13 Cm 7027.
14 Para 1.1.
15 HC Debs, 7 March 2007, Col 1524 *et seq.*
16 HL Debs, 14 March 2007, Col 741 *et seq.*
17 Cm 7438.
18 HC Debs, 10 June 2009, Col 798.

Bicameralism and the Scottish Parliament

4.14   Despite the occasional calls for abolition, the principal debate at Westminster has focused on the reform of the House of Lords. In relation to the Scottish Parliament, on the other hand, where a second chamber has been lacking from the start, there had been until recently virtually no serious discussion about creating one. It was not on the agenda of the Scottish Constitutional Convention nor did it appear in the process of the creation of the Parliament[1]. This is, arguably, for the good reasons that Scotland is a relatively small country; the range and volume of the Parliament's business were never likely to warrant its division across two chambers; there is no compelling reason for regional representation in Scotland beyond that provided in the first chamber; and there was no wish unnecessarily to incur the complexity and expense a second chamber would bring. Only two arguments in favour of the addition of a second chamber have been made. The first is that existing procedures, especially in the committees of the Scottish Parliament, are failing to provide a sufficiently strong 'revising' role on Bills. It is an argument which begs many questions about the meaning of both 'failure' and the legitimacy of a strong revising role for a chamber which might be largely unelected. The answers should almost certainly be sought instead by revision of the Parliament's existing procedures. The second argument derives, in effect, from a plea for the direct involvement in Scottish politics of the unelected great and good. The House of Lords provides a location (to include also ministers) for those who have retired (or been expelled) from elected politics or have never aspired to election, and a second chamber at Holyrood could perform a similar function. The democratic insistence on drawing only on elected politicians as ministers does, for better or for worse, restrict the field. Lord Steel, having been interpreted initially as proposing a second chamber, has instead suggested that there is a need for an 'external review panel', appointed by the Parliament to undertake a legislative scrutiny role[2]. The Calman Commission (see p 63) has recently considered both these arguments and representations made to the Commission in favour of introducing a second chamber for the Scottish Parliament. It concluded, however, that those submissions did not provide 'the weight of evidence that would be required as a basis for serious contemplation of such a fundamental change'.

1 There was a second chamber in the (Stormont) Parliament of Northern Ireland. See A G Donaldson 'The Senate of Northern Ireland' [1958] PL 135.
2 Lecture on 'The State of the Nation', 29 January 2003. For consideration of the wider case for a second chamber proper, see H MacQueen 'The case for a second chamber' in *What Future for Scotland?* (2003) Policy Institute.
3 *Serving Scotland Better*, para 6.13.

PARLIAMENTARY COMMITTEES

4.15   In a remarkable analysis of constitutional practice of 50 years ago, Sir Kenneth Wheare wrote that committees were such a familiar feature of both social and governmental organisations as to be part of 'the British way of life'[1]. Since then the popularity of committees in different aspects of governmental activity has been maintained, although their dominant role in local authorities may now be being questioned[2]. Certainly, however, the importance of committees in the Westminster Parliament has grown since Wheare's time and they have now assumed a significant role at Holyrood.

The case for committees is largely based upon the simple proposition that some, at least, of a Parliament's principal functions are not well discharged in a chamber of the whole membership of the House or Parliament, whether that be 646 MPs or 129 MSPs. The plenary session may serve well as the forum in which the great issues of the day can be debated by all members; where ministers can make significant statements and be questioned on them; where ministers can also be publicly questioned and harangued on matters chosen by members; and where the massed ranks of the political parties represented in a Parliament can be seen to confront each other. A plenary session lends itself to ceremony when this is called for and tends to demand a high degree of formality of procedure. If the principal functions of a Parliament are to contribute to the enactment of legislation and to scrutinise the work of the Executive, much of this can appropriately be done in plenary session. There are good reasons to expose Bills (and their proponents) to general debate and also to ensure that, if they are to pass, they do so at a meeting at which all members are entitled to be present and to vote. Equally, it is valuable to have ministers being called to account, from time to time, before meetings of the whole Parliament.

There are, on the other hand, reasons why, on some occasions, the handling of business in plenary sessions is inappropriate and the reference of such business to smaller groups is to be preferred. Detailed scrutiny of Bills is more efficiently done by a smaller group, whether the debate is then conducted by the members of the committee themselves in response to amendments proposed by them or, in investigative mode, by the interrogation of experts or other witnesses. Similarly, the detailed and systematic scrutiny of Executive action is better conducted by committees with powers to call for relevant papers, to take evidence from ministers and other witnesses, and to sit in places other than the Parliament building itself. Not only does the use of committees make these functions more efficient in themselves, by the use of smaller and more focused groups, but it also takes pressure off the House or Parliament as a whole. Committees can function, with different memberships, at the same time as other committees and even at the same time as plenary sessions.

1 K C Wheare *Government by Committee* (1955) p 1.
2 See pp 199–200.

Westminster committees

4.16   At Westminster, the tradition of the House of Commons has been to draw a sharp line between the functions of *legislation* and *scrutiny of the Executive*. A 'public bill committee' is established for a Bill as it progresses through the House. Normally the powers of a public bill committee do not extend to taking evidence from external witnesses[1]. On the other hand, select committees are established for the full term of a Parliament and, with a remit covering a single government department, take on the functions of executive scrutiny and proceed in the main by investigations involving the taking of written and oral evidence[2]. The functions of the two sets of committees do not formally overlap, although proposals for the greater integration of select committees into the legislative process have been made[3]. There would be as many advantages in using the expertise of the policy-focused select committees in the scrutiny of Bills as in the scrutiny of the administrative activity of the department they monitor.

1 But see p 220.
2 For details, see p 268.
3 See *First Report of the Modernisation Committee: The Legislative Process* HC Paper 190 (1997–98) and more recently the *First Special Report of the House of Commons Modernisation Committee: Committee Stage of Public Bills: Consultation on Alternative Options* HC Paper 810 (2005–06).

Holyrood committees

4.17   From the outset, it was assumed that an integrated committee system would be adopted by the Scottish Parliament. Scotland's Parliament envisaged that the 'committees might for example initiate legislation, scrutinise and amend the Scottish Executive's proposals as well as having wide ranging investigative functions'[1]. The functions of the House of Commons' standing and select committees would be combined and allocated to a single set of 'subject committees' and provision for these was made in the Parliament's standing orders[2]. Such committees are established by resolution of the Parliament, on a motion of the Parliamentary Bureau. The precise nomenclature and remit of subject committees varies from Parliament to Parliament. Currently the Parliament has the following seven subject committees: Economy, energy and tourism (to include enterprise and a range of other matters falling within the remit of the Cabinet Secretary for Finance and Sustainable Growth); Education, Lifelong Learning and Culture, Health and Sport; Justice; Local Government and Communities (including planning, housing and regeneration); Rural Affairs and Environment; and Transport, Infrastructure and Climate Change.

In addition, standing orders require the appointment of seven mandatory committees[3]. There must be a Standards, Procedures and Public Appointments Committee (dealing with compliance with the MSPs' Code of Conduct, practice and procedures of the Parliament and matters relating to public appointments in Scotland), a Finance Committee, Public Audit Committee (audit of public expenditure), a European and External Relations Committee (European Union and international matters), an Equal Opportunities Committee, a Public Petitions Committee and a Subordinate Legislation Committee (considering subordinate legislation and powers to make such legislation). In addition to the mandatory and subject committees, the Parliament may appoint other committees of a more ad hoc nature. The Review of SPCB Supported Bodies Committee was established in January 2009 to review the structure and functions of a number of bodies supported by the SPCB including the Scottish Public Services Ombudsman, the Scottish Information Commissioner and the Scottish Parliamentary Standards Commissioner. The Committee reported on 21 May 2009[4]. It is also possible for the whole Parliament to sit as a committee for the consideration of Bills.

Appointments to membership of committees are made by the Parliament on a motion by the Parliamentary Bureau[5]. In proposing appointments the Bureau must have regard to the qualifications and experience of MSPs when they have expressed an interest in membership[6]. In the first two sessions, control by the Bureau and the Parliament led to a situation in which MSPs from one or other of the coalition Executive parties had a majority on all committees although the non-Executive parties were compensated by the allocation of a number of committee convenerships and deputy convenerships. The current minority SNP administration cannot, of course, achieve the same dominance of committee membership and convenerships and deputy convenerships are divided fairly evenly amongst the main parties[7]. Political control by Executive parties does not, in itself, undermine the capacity of committees to act in a relatively impartial and cross-party way where the subject matter demands this (eg in relation to audit, standards or petitions) but the political composition of committees is clearly an issue, whatever efforts are made to mitigate or suppress its effects, when, for instance, subject committees are considering Bills or scrutinising Executive action[8].

The functions of the Parliament's committees are largely determined by reference to their specific remits as listed above. In addition, all committees have general functions including the consideration of the policy and administration of the Scottish Administration, the need for law reform in their area, and the power to initiate Bills[9]. It has already been mentioned that, in the closing stages of the first session of the Parliament, the Procedures Committee carried out its 'CSG Inquiry' and it is not surprising, in the light of the emphasis placed by the CSG on the potential contribution to be made by committees to the work of the Parliament, that large sections of its report[10] focused on how the committees had worked in practice. Notwithstanding discussion of a number of areas where improvement was thought possible, the inquiry report expressed satisfaction that, as committees had been expected to be a major component in the Parliament's mission to achieve the goals of accountability and power-sharing, they had indeed established themselves as a 'key part of the Parliamentary landscape'[11].

More recently, the Parliament's Committee system has been looked at by the Calman Commission as part of its review of the operation of devolution. Like the earlier CSG inquiry, the Commission heard 'very considerable evidence … that the Scottish Parliament's committees generally work well'[12] but also found concerns raised about the effectiveness of committees in holding the government to account and, indeed, about the system of 'dual-purpose' committees which have been fundamental to the Parliament since its creation. In relation to this latter concern, the Commission observed that in order to fulfil this scrutiny role it was important for committee members to build up expertise in the subject area which, in turn, "requires a relatively low rate of turnover of members"[13]. They wished to 'encourage' political parties to do what they could to minimise the 'churn' of committee members. Echoing concerns expressed elsewhere, the Commission also referred to the problem of 'legislative overload'[14] and while recognising that it was a difficult issue to address suggested more use of sub-committees and that the standing orders should no longer require sub-committees to have the approval of the whole Parliament[15].

Over and above the committees formally established under the Parliament's standing orders, there has also emerged a pattern of 'cross-party groups'. These provide an opportunity for MSPs of all parties and members of the public to discuss matters of shared interest. Although not created by the Parliament under its standing orders, such groups are subject to the supervision of the Parliament's Standards, Procedures and Public Appointments Committee and are regulated under the terms of the MSPs' Code of Conduct[16].

1   Cm 3658, para 9.10 and see also the *CSG Report*, section 2 'Sharing the Power: the Role of Parliamentary Committees' paras 9–16.
2   SOs, r 6.1.4.
3   SOs, r 6.1.5. Reduced from eight in September 2007 by the merging of the functions of the Procedures Committee with those of the Standards Committee.
4   See p 206.
5   SOs, r 6.3.
6   SOs, r 6.3.4.
7   The Green Party's Patrick Harvie MSP is Convener of the Transport, Infrastructure and Climate Change Committee, the promise of which convenership to the Greens was widely reported in May 2009 as a condition of the party's support for the SNP in forming an administration, and for Mr Salmond as the Parliament's nominee as First Minister.
8   *CSG Inquiry* para 584.
9   SOs, r 6.2.2.
10 *CSG Inquiry* para 830.
11 *CSG Inquiry* paras 596–658.
12 *Serving Scotland Better*, para 6.22.
13 Ibid, para 6.35.
14 Ibid, para 6.37.
15 Ibid, para 6.39.
16 See 11th Report of the Standards, Procedures and Public Appointments Committee of 2008, SP Paper 185.

MPS AND MSPS[1]

General

4.18   It would be surprising if, in the examination of the work of a modern parliament, the institution were thought to be organised entirely on the basis of groups or blocks of members. Committees clearly perform an important role and political parties, although accorded a formally less significant position, give a structure and dynamic to the working of parliaments. Apart from key individuals such as the Presiding Officer of the Scottish Parliament and the Speaker of the Commons and perhaps the conveners of parliamentary committees, the role of individual members is diminished. For many parliamentary purposes, the member exists only as part of a party block; party discipline curbs the freedom to speak or vote as the member might wish; and opportunities for independence of action, or even of thought, may be few. This is particularly true of those MPs and MSPs who hold office in the UK or Scottish governments but the expectation of loyalty on the part of back benchers is almost as great. It is much less true, of course, in the case of independent MSPs in the Scottish Parliament.

Even in the case of members of large party groups, however, the constitutional identity of individual MPs and MSPs is maintained, as well as some opportunities for individuality of function. At Westminster respect has been paid to the enduring theory that the role of an MP is that of a *representative* of his or her constituents rather than their *delegate*. An MP cannot be mandated to speak and vote simply as their constituents, or indeed any other organised group, might wish[2]. And, while party policy will usually dominate, opportunities for a 'free vote' on a matter of conscience do occur in both the House of Commons and the Scottish Parliament[3]. Equally, the chance to promote a (private) member's Bill is evidence of the possibility of some freedom of manoeuvre but, even there, unless the chosen subject matter of the Bill is genuinely non-political, party pressures are not likely to be far away. Similarly, the opportunity to launch an adjournment debate in the Commons or a members' business debate in the Scottish Parliament and to ask parliamentary questions provide some scope for autonomous action. On the whole, the opportunity for such autonomy increases the further MPs or MSPs are from issues of high political concern and the nearer they are to personal or constituency matters. And, of course, it is in their constituencies, the correspondence and other work on behalf of constituents, and in the surgeries they hold that many MPs have traditionally found most fulfilment. This is not a wholly disinterested endeavour, however, and may, in marginal constituencies, be motivated as much by a concern for an MP's own re-election as for the welfare of his or her constituents. The same pressures are felt by MSPs and, although there might have been some expectation on the part of constituency members that this would be a role for them rather than their regional counterparts, both classes of MSP seem committed to 'constituency' work. Indeed this is a feature of the work of MSPs as a whole. There is less evidence than might have been expected of a two-tier membership, with the constituency MSP claiming to be the 'real' member. The Parliament's own *Code of Conduct* for Members insists that all MSPs have equal formal and legal status and provides guidance on relationships between them[4].

1   This section does not really deal with members of the House of Lords. Although there are many parallels, party discipline is less rigorous in that House and the position of individual members varies much more, according to their category of membership.
2   On which, see p 95 below.
3   For instance, in the Scottish Parliament, on the matter of hunting: SP OR 19 September 2001, cols 2586, 2589. Perhaps more a matter of politics than of conscience, a free vote was also allowed by the Labour/Liberal Democrat coalition in September 2008 on whether to endorse the Standards Committee's decision to impose a one day suspension from the Parliament on the Scottish Labour leader Wendy Alexander in connection with a failure properly to declare campaign donations in the register of members' interests: SP OR 4 September 2008, col 10437 et seq.

MPs' and MSPs' pay and allowances

4.19   It is inevitable that some sensitivity will attach to the process of determining the remuneration of parliamentarians, especially where, as is the case, this is a matter left for MPs and MSPs themselves to decide. Although steps were taken to defuse this sensitivity in relation to absolute salary levels, the systems for payment of additional allowances and expenses have recently been the subject of intense scrutiny and criticism. At Westminster the independent Senior Salaries Review Body recommends levels of MPs' pay in line with increases in Civil Service salaries. SA 1998 gives the Parliament[1] the power to determine the salaries of MSPs (s 81) and, in March 2002, the Parliament accepted a recommendation[2] that salaries would be tied at 87.5% per cent of Westminster salaries[3], ie £54,093 from 1 November 2007.

Allowances are payable to MPs and MSPs in respect of office, travel and other expenses with detailed rules having been developed by each Parliament describing what can and cannot be claimed. As described in chapter 12, although it has been the practice of the Scottish Parliament for some years now to publish very detailed information about expenses and allowances claims by individual MSPs, the Westminster Parliament had not been similarly proactive in and, indeed, resisted attempts by journalists and others to obtain access to such information using freedom of information legislation. Preparations were being made for the orderly release by House of Commons authorities of detailed allowances information when in early 2009 the Telegraph newspaper obtained full details of MPs' claims – it is believed in exchange for a substantial payment – and published, over a number of weeks, extracts from those claims. The published material, which focused particularly on the 'Additional Costs Allowance' which entitles MPs to certain costs associated with the need to live for part of the week in London, was the cause of embarrassment to members from across all political parties. The office of the Speaker of the House of Commons is largely responsible for the administration of the expenses allowances and expenses scheme and the failure of the then Speaker, Mr Michael Martin, to maintain the confidence of the House in his ability to carry through proposals for reform led ultimately – and highly unusually – to his resignation[4]. On 23 June 2009, the Leader of the House of Commons, Ms Harriet Harman, announced proposals to introduce, as part of a new Parliamentary

Standards Bill, criminal offences relating to making false claims or submitting false or misleading information as part of a claim for allowances and expenses. Meanwhile, the Committee for Standards in Public Life[5] is, following a request from Prime Minister Brown in March 2009, also in the process of reviewing MPs' expenses.

1 SA 1998, s 81, after initial arrangements made by SI 1999/1097.
2 SP OR 21 March 2002, col 10577.
3 SP OR Paper 554.
4 HC Debs, 19 May 2009, col 1323.
5 See below.

Standards and privileges

4.20   A feature of the historical development of the House of Commons has been the recognition that an efficient system of election is a necessary but not sufficient condition for the creation of a House able to discharge the functions assigned to it. Over the three centuries to the late twentieth century the principal object was to secure to parliamentarians the conditions of independence and freedom from interference necessary for the work of Parliament to be done. This originally derived from a continuing fear on the part of parliamentarians that the Crown would encroach upon their freedoms in an oppressive way and this is the fear still reflected in the ceremonial declaration of the privileges of the House of Commons which is made at the beginning of each Parliament. These privileges, represented in a special freedom of expression and freedom from arrest, have lost some their constitutional piquancy. Some are seen now as reflecting past battles fought and won on behalf of the House of Commons, although this by no means removes all continuing significance.

In the closing years of the twentieth century, however, there was an abrupt shift of emphasis. It became clear that the principal barriers to parliamentary business came not from threats to freedoms and privileges from outside but from misbehaviour and abuse of these privileges, or at least perceptions of misbehaviour and abuse within the House of Commons itself. There had always been a recognition that privileges could be abused by MPs and it was part of the task of the Privileges Committee to investigate such internal abuses. Now, however, there were calls for something much stronger and more positive to counteract the dangers of 'sleaze' and corruption to which some MPs had become vulnerable. The 'cash for questions' affair in which the Committee criticised the conduct of two MPs willing to accept up to £1,000 from a journalist pretending to be a businessman, in return for their asking a parliamentary question, led to the setting up of the Committee on Standards in Public Life under Lord Nolan. That committee produced a first report[1] which led to a strengthening of House of Commons procedures. The post of Parliamentary Commissioner for Standards was established and the former Committee on Privileges became the Standards and Privileges Committee, with a new remit.

The Standards and Privileges Committee is concerned with the conduct of MPs and not with peers, the latter being regulated by the House of Lords Committee for Privileges. That Committee was faced, just over a decade after the original 'cash for questions' debacle, with novel and difficult questions about the sanctions which were available to it where a serious complaint is made against a peer. In January 2009 the Sunday Times published allegations that several peers had accepted payments from business interests in return for which they had taken steps to secure amendments to legislation going through Parliament for the benefit of those businesses. The Leader of the House asked the Committee to investigate the allegations and to consider what powers the House of Lords had to suspend a peer in the event of misconduct. The Committee sought legal advice from the Attorney General, Baroness Scotland of Asthal in February 2009. The Attorney General noted first that the letters patent by which a peer is appointed provides that a peer 'may have, hold and possess a seat, place and voice in the Parliaments' and, second, that individuals may be disqualified from membership of the House of Lords by virtue of certain statutory provisions. There was considerable doubt as to whether the Lords had the inherent power to create sanctions – such as suspension – of its own, particularly in light of it having been resolved in 1704 that 'neither House of Parliament hath any power, by any vote or declaration, to create to themselves any new privilege that is not warranted by the known laws and customs of Parliament'. The Attorney General considered previous debates and discussion about powers of expulsion and concluded that there was no inherent power of expulsion available to the Lords. On the question of suspension, the position was 'less clear' but she considered 'on balance, that the House does not have such a power... the key factor against this argument is that a suspension would interfere with the rights of a peer conferred by the Crown to attend, sit and vote in Parliament (albeit to a lesser degree than permanent exclusion). This is a fundamental constitutional right and any interference with that right cannot be characterised as the mere regulation of the House's own procedures. Accordingly...if a power to suspend a member for misconduct is sought, the safer course is to create a legislative framework to confer such a power on the House'. Perhaps realising that this conclusion was likely to present more difficulties than it would resolve, the Committee sought a second opinion – from the former Lord Chancellor, Lord Mackay of Clashfern. In his opinion, of April 2009, Lord Mackay took a different approach. On the issue of the rights conferred on peers when they are appointed, he concluded that those rights were more limited than the Attorney General had described and did not include a 'right' to sit in the House of Lords as such (but rather a right to receive a 'writ of summons' at the commencement of each session). On the issue of the power of the House of Lords to suspend its own members, Lord Mackay agreed with the Attorney General that the House had no power to create new privileges for itself but concluded that, based on his analysis of the history of proceedings in the Lords, 'the House's existing power to adopt the procedures necessary to preserve "order and decency" includes a power to suspend, for a defined period within the lifetime of a Parliament, a Member who has been found guilty of clear and flagrant misconduct'. Unsurprisingly, Lord Mackay's view prevailed[2] and on the same day as the Committee reached that view it also published its report on the peers involved and recommended the suspension of two of them[3]. Lord Truscott and Lord Taylor of Blackburn were suspended on 20 May 2009[4].

Similar arrangements for standards and privileges exist in relation to the Scottish Parliament. SA 1998 makes no provision for the 'privileges' of the

Parliament or its Members, save to protect in some measure proceedings of the Parliament and parliamentary papers from actions in defamation and in relation to contempt of court[5]. While the Consultative Steering Group did not address its attention to the privileges of MSPs[6], it did recommend that parliamentary standing orders should provide for a Standards Committee[7]. This recommendation was adopted in the making of the transitional standing orders and a Standards Committee was set up. That has now been replaced by the Standards, Procedures and Public Appointments Committee[8].

The Committee's remit, so far as standards are concerned, is to consider and report on (a) whether an MSP's conduct is in accordance with the Parliament's standing orders, (b) the Code of Conduct for Members (the adoption, amendment and application of which is expressly placed within the Committee's remit), (c) matters relating to members' interests, and (d) any other matters relating to the conduct of members in carrying out their parliamentary duties[9]. The initial rules on the declaration of members' interests were laid down in an order made by the Secretary of State to meet the requirements of SA 1998, s 39 which was replaced by the Interests of Members of the Scottish Parliament Act 2006 (which began life as a Committee Bill promoted by the then Standards Committee). The Act puts on a statutory footing the Register of Interests of Members of the Scottish Parliament which is maintained by the Clerk of the Parliament. MSPs are required to register 'registrable interests' (a range of different financial interests including gifts, sponsorships and remuneration), they are also obliged to make an oral declaration prior to participating in proceedings of the Parliament, and there is a prohibition on paid advocacy. The Act provides for a range of sanctions, including measures to be taken by the Parliament itself to suspend or exclude MSPs who have breached the rules and, in some circumstances, criminal prosecution.

The Committee is not the only enforcer of standards of conduct for MSPs. The Scottish Parliamentary Standards Commissioner Act 2002 (SPSCA 2002) created the eponymous Commissioner. The Commissioner is appointed for a period not exceeding five years – the current Commissioner Stuart Allan having been appointed for a period of 2 years in April 2009 – (extendable for one further such period) by the Parliamentary corporation with the agreement of the Parliament[10] and may be removed from office by the corporation only if the Parliament so resolves with not less than a two-thirds majority[11]. A person is ineligible for appointment as Commissioner if he or she is an MSP or a member of the Parliament's staff (or has been within the previous two years)[12]. There is provision for an acting Commissioner[13]. The functions of the Commissioner are investigating and reporting on complaints about the conduct of MSPs, his principal task being to decide whether the conduct complained about has been committed by the member and, if so, whether it has breached a 'relevant provision' of the Parliament's standing orders, the Code of Conduct or the members' interests rules.

Both the Committee and the Commissioner have been involved in dealing with a number of complaints against MSPs, perhaps none more controversial than those made against the then Scottish Labour leader Ms Wendy Alexander at the end of 2007[14]. The complaint, made by an SNP researcher, was that

Ms Alexander had failed to register several 'gifts' – donations to help fund her campaign for leadership – in the Register of Interests. The complaint was first considered by the Commissioner who, amongst other things, reported the matter to the procurator fiscal in line with rules which require such reporting where the Commissioner reaches the view that the conduct complained of might constitute a criminal offence[15]. The fiscal having indicated that no prosecution would be brought, the Commissioner concluded his investigation and found that Ms Alexander's conduct constituted a breach of section 5 of the Interests of Members of the Scottish Parliament Act 2006. The Standards, Procedures and Public Appointments Committee considered the Commissioner's report and decided, but only by a majority, that it agreed with the Commissioner's findings. It was divided as to what if any sanction ought to be imposed on Ms Alexander but determined by division that she should be suspended from Parliament on the first Wednesday of the 2008–2009 parliamentary session. This determination, in July 2008, was regarded by many as being driven solely by political motives which, if it was, were satisfied by the resignation of Ms Alexander as Scottish Labour leader. However, the saga did not end there. On 4 September 2008 the Parliament debated the Committee's determination and voted to 'quash' the Committee's recommendation that Ms Alexander be suspended. In an acrimonious debate it was suggested by a number of MSPs that members of the Standards Committee had been influenced by party whips in reaching their verdict on Ms Alexander's conduct and on the sanction which should be applied[16]. This was undoubtedly a low point in the Committee's history and a reflection, perhaps of the fact that, as with all other activities of the Parliament, politics can never be removed entirely from the mix.

1   Cm 2850, 1995.
2   See Committee for Privileges, First Report, HL 87, 14 May 2009, and the memoranda from the Attorney General and Lord Mackay of Clashfern which are appended to the Report.
3   Committee for Privileges, Second Report, HL 88, 14 May 2009.
4   See HL Debs, 20 May 2009, col 1418.
5   SA 1998, ss 41–42, Sch 8, para 33. See C Munro 'Privilege at Holyrood' [2000] PL 347.
6   Save again in relation to contempt and the need for a workable *sub judice* rule; see paras 38–42.
7   Paras 75, 76.
8   SOs, r 6.4
9   SOs, r 6.4.
10 SPSCA 2002, s 1(2).
11 SPSCA 2002, s 1(7).
12 SPSCA 2002, s 1(3).
13 SPSCA 2002, s 2.
14 For a full account see the Sixth Report of the Standards, Procedures and Public Appointments Committee of 2007-2008, SP Paper 142.
15 Scottish Parliamentary Standards Commissioner Act 2002 (Procedures, Reporting and Other Matters) Directions 2002, issued by the then Standards Committee of the Parliament. In this case the 'potential' offence was the participation by Ms Alexander in proceedings of the Parliament while having failed to register registrable interests.
16 SP OR 4 Sept 2008, col 10439 *et seq.*

THE MANAGEMENT AND ADMINISTRATION OF THE PARLIAMENTS

4.21   So far considered in this chapter have been the different elements of the parliamentary structure – chambers, committees and individual members – and the distribution of functions, to be dealt with in later chapters, between them. There is also a need in both Parliaments for some overall co-ordination, support and management to enable parliamentary purposes to be achieved. On the one hand, there is a need for the dispassionate and non-political assistance of officials whose job it is to hold the ring between the different interests represented and to ensure that they are provided with all the advice and administrative support necessary to discharge the individual and collective functions. On the other hand, it has also to be ensured that the work of a parliament is managed politically, broadly in accordance with the wishes of the political majority. At Westminster and, in particular, in the House of Commons, these are functions carried out by the Speaker, together with a substantial staff responsible to the Clerk of the House and, on the political front, largely through informal processes of mediation and control between the parties known as the 'usual channels'.

In the Scottish Parliament, there are slightly more formal arrangements which derive, in the first instance, from SA 1998 itself, including its specification of some of the content of the Parliament's standing orders[1]. On the 'non-political' side, the administration is headed by the Presiding Officer and two deputies elected by the Parliament at the first meeting of each session[2]. The elections are by secret ballot and there is a requirement that all three officers be not drawn from the same political party[3]. They must act impartially[4]. The Parliament's standing orders confer the general functions of the Presiding Officer which are to chair meetings of the Parliament, the Parliamentary Bureau and the Conveners' Group as well as to determine and rule on questions arising under the standing orders. The Presiding Officer also represents the Parliament 'in discussions and exchanges with any parliamentary, governmental, administrative or other body, whether within or outwith the United Kingdom'. In parliamentary debates, the Presiding Officer must exercise a casting vote in the event of a tie. Such occasions caused occasional controversy where the vote resulted in defeat for the government[5]. The Presiding Officer is a member (along with four other MSPs elected by the Parliament) of and chairs the Scottish Parliamentary Corporate body (or Parliamentary corporation) which is established as a distinct legal entity with the functions of providing the Parliament with property, staff and services and representing the Parliament in legal proceedings by or against it[6]. It is also for the Corporate Body to appoint the Clerk of the Parliament[7] who acts as chief executive of the Parliament's administrative service.

On the 'political' side, the principal body is the Parliamentary Bureau which has no statutory basis but, following recommendations of the Consultative Steering Group for a business committee, is established under standing orders[8] to make proposals to the Parliament for its business programme and for the remit and membership of committees. The Bureau's own membership comprises, in addition to the Presiding Officer, one member per political party[9]. The Parliamentary Bureau, formed in May 2007, has four members, representing the SNP, Labour, Conservative and Liberal Democrat Parties. Political control, however, derives from the voting system which gives each member a vote for each of the party's MSPs, thus normally ensuring a majority for the governing party or parties. The Presiding Officer has a casting vote, a privilege of no practical consequence[10]. It is the Bureau's ability to control the Parliament's programme, subject, of course, to any political majority in the Parliament itself, which ensures the government's broad control over the content and pace of the Parliament's agenda. The principal criticism of the CSG Inquiry was of the Bureau's lack of transparency[11].

1 Principally, SA 1998, s 22 and Sch 3. Periodically, there are representations from within the Parliament that it should be freed from the restrictions imposed by this Act.
2 SA 1998, s 19.
3 SOs, r 3.3.7.
4 Lord Steel, the Parliament's first Presiding Officer, announced on 28 July 1999 that he had resigned from the Countryside Alliance.
5 Most recently when the Presiding Officer's vote defeated the SNP government's budget for 2009–10 (see SPOR 28 January 2009).
6 SA 1998, ss 21, 40 and Sch 2.
7 SA 1998, s 20.
8 Ch 5.
9 Of five or more MSPs or group of smaller parties.
10 As pointed out by the Presiding Officer in evidence to the Procedures Committee's CSG Inquiry, para 754.
11 *CSG Inquiry*, paras 743–783.

THE OPENNESS AND ACCESSIBILITY OF THE PARLIAMENTS

4.22   If maintaining high standards of conduct is an important precondition of a functioning Parliament, another general requirement is public access to the Parliament's deliberations and its papers. It has been largely uncontroversial that the work of the representatives of the people should be open to inspection by the people. Law-making should be done in public and scrutiny of an executive which may itself have tendencies to secrecy should, as a matter of principle, bring information into the public domain. In addition, the exposure of parliamentary business to scrutiny by the public and the press serves as an important check on standards of behaviour. There should at least be the right of public access and this has been ensured, formally at least, at Westminster by long-standing rules which ensure public rights of access to the two chambers and to committee meetings and which require the publication of (*Hansard*) reports of proceedings[1]. Increasingly, there has been pressure to extend this to a positive obligation to provide publicity and an important theme in the emergence of the Scottish Parliament was that of public involvement in the Parliament's work. One of the four guiding principles of the CSG was that of ensuring access and participation.

SA 1998 itself requires that proceedings of the Parliament (which includes committee proceedings) be held in public, except in circumstances provided for in standing orders[2]; and for the reporting of proceedings[3]. These requirements have been elaborated in standing orders giving unqualified rights of public access (subject to public order considerations) to the Parliament[4], but subject to permitted restrictions in the case of committees. There is a requirement for the Corporate Body to produce the Scottish Parliament Official Report[5]. The Parliament and the Corporate Body are, as public authorities, subject to the information regime provided by the Freedom of Information (Scotland) Act 2002[6]. In addition, provision may be made for the broadcasting of proceedings[7].

However, when the CSG urged that the Parliament should be accessible, open and responsive and that it should develop procedures which make possible a participative approach[8], it meant more than minimal guarantees of access to information and, in due course, the *CSG Inquiry*[9] was able to report on a large number of initiatives which have included the extensive use of an attractive website, the education service of the Parliament, and open days. Institutionally, the same spirit has been evident in the use by committees of their power, where resources permit, to meet outside Edinburgh and to involve members of the public in their inquiries. The petitions procedure[10] has also been important and so too has the encouragement given to the cross-party groups, many of which have sought to engage with the Scottish public.

1 But, for expressions of concern about participation in the UK parliamentary process, see reports of the House of Commons Public Administration Committee: HC Paper 373 (2000–01); HC Paper 334 (2001–02). For discussion of the resistance of the Westminster Parliament to the coverage of its activity by the Freedom of Information Act 2000, see p 355 n 11.
2 SA 1998, Sch 3, para 3.
3 SA 1998, Sch 3, para 4.
4 SOs, r 15.2.
5 SOs, r 16.2.
6 See p 353.
7 SOs, r 16.4.
8 *CSG Report* (1998), section 2.
9 *CSG Inquiry*, paras 61–206.
10 See p 275.

Chapter 5

Law-making Competences for Scotland

INTRODUCTION

5.1   A primary function of any constitution is the identification of those bodies which are competent to change the law. This hardly requires explanation. It is the existing state of the law which defines the legal rights and obligations of individuals in all aspects of their lives. The law defines relationships within and between bodies such as limited companies, partnerships and unincorporated associations and it determines the functions of governmental bodies too. They, like individuals and companies, may act only within the limits of the law and the introduction of major new policies and programmes by public authorities, at whatever level, must normally be preceded by the making of new laws to confer new powers. New powers for ministers, or for local and other public authorities also frequently attract the need for new administrative bodies to be established; new procedures for implementing the policies concerned; new systems of enforcement, including the creation of new criminal offences for defaulters; and, perhaps above all, the authority to spend money. All of these require legal change and this makes the allocation of law-making power of prime importance. Above *all else*, the distribution of legislative power determines the constitutional character of the state. In a federal system it is the division of powers amongst the central legislature and the legislatures of the states or provinces that most clearly defines its structure. For Scotland, within the devolved structure of the United Kingdom and within the European Union, it is to the distribution of legislative power that one looks first as a guide to the working of the constitution as a whole.

The formal division of powers does not, of course, tell the whole story. As mentioned in Chapter 1, apparently autonomous states are subject to *external* influences which restrain their powers, including their law-making powers at all levels. These same influences also constrain the day-to-day operation of internal legal rules. Similarly, the activities of political parties across the constitutional order and the rules which govern access to and the distribution of public funding are just two of the many *internal* constraints on the exercise of legislative power. Above all, it is the conditions which determine *who* has effective control over the exercise of law-making power that determine what new laws are produced. Formal legislative power may be vested in the Westminster or the Scottish Parliament but the operation of parliamentary government at Westminster has long served to transfer substantial control over the legislative programme from Parliament to ministers. The Scottish Government has also achieved a substantial degree of control over Holyrood, albeit tempered by the constraints of coalition or minority government.

These are matters to which we return in Chapter 8 which deals with law-making procedures. In this chapter, the focus is on formal law-making competences and these are dealt with at pp 104–149. By way of introduction, however, pp 102–104 provides a brief examination of the sources of law in Scotland before we consider how the existing body of law may be changed.

SOURCES OF LAW IN SCOTLAND

5.2   In this context, the 'law of Scotland' is to be understood as the law applied by the courts of the Scottish legal system[1]. It is the 'positive' law, as opposed to 'natural' or 'moral' law. Sources of law are 'the answer to the question: where do I find authoritative statements of the principles and rules which the courts must apply to determine my rights and duties, my remedies and liabilities, in various circumstances?'[2] They are, then, the documents[3], judgments[4] and principles[5] which courts treat as authoritative for the purposes of deciding cases brought before them. It is on the basis of legal propositions derived from such sources that cases are argued by counsel and that statements of the current state of the law are made by legal advisers and commentators. In situations in which the current law is uncertain, it is still to these formal sources of the law that lawyers must look in order to make their best predictions – sometimes, in truth, no more than a well-informed guess – as to what the law is or how it is likely to develop in the future. In other contexts, the terminology 'source of law' may be used in a less formal sense to denote, for instance, a historical event or document explaining the emergence of the present law; a religious or philosophical idea from which, arguably, the 'positive' law applied by the courts has been derived; or, in a comparative way, a related rule in another system of law which has had an influence on the way the law has developed in Scotland. Such 'non-formal' sources are not treated as strictly authoritative in Scottish courts but they are frequently called in aid to assist the reasoning process where formal domestic sources are lacking or are uncertain. This is particularly true in times of substantial legal change where new rules are introduced but the courts have little or no home-grown guidance on how to interpret them.

The experience of other jurisdictions where similar rules may have operated for a long time can be very helpful, although care must be taken to keep in mind not only the similarities but also the differences between the two systems. An example has been the use made of Canadian human rights cases in the Scottish courts since the coming into force of domestic protection for human rights by the Scotland Act 1998 (SA 1998) and the Human Rights Act 1998 (HRA 1998)[6]. Such cases may be helpful because they deal with similar facts and similar rules of law but they are not formally authoritative and they must be applied with great care by courts in Scotland[7]. Such examples nicely illustrate the difficulties often encountered in distinguishing between the formal and non-formal sources of law. The distinction is drawn and is important, especially in the lower courts of a hierarchical system. In the higher courts, however, where they are called upon to decide issues of great uncertainty and they have more freedom to select sources of guidance, the non-formal sources (in particular, rules from other systems) may have a greater influence.

It is appropriate to list the formal sources of authority for Scottish courts as a preface to considering the legislative bodies competent to make new law and to amend the existing law. No more than a snapshot of the sources of law can be provided, avoiding the many complexities which courts confront as they interpret rules from different sources and, in assessing the status of those rules, decide which to apply when conflicts arise. Essential to any account of sources of law is the notion of *hierarchy*: the degree of authority to be attributed to a rule of law derived from one source and the susceptibility of that rule to being overtaken or replaced by a rule deriving from another source. This question of hierarchy is explored below. A simple listing of sources produces, first, a distinction between the *'common law'*[8] developed at the hand of the courts, and, on the other hand, *statute law* – the product of a formally authorised legislature. The common law in Scotland is supplemented by the works of the *institutional writers*[9] (though with little direct impact upon contemporary public law) and, it seems, by customary *international law*[10]. Statute law comprises *Acts of the Westminster Parliament*[11], as supplemented, since 1999, by *Acts of the Scottish Parliament* and legislation made by others under the authority of such Acts. In a special category, since 1973, has been *European Community law*.

1   Including some courts, eg the Supreme Court, located outside Scotland.
2   D M Walker *The Scottish Legal System* (8th edn, 2001) p 408.
3   For example, a written constitution or an Act of Parliament.
4   Of courts, tribunals and other bodies with the power to give authoritative decisions on legal questions.
5   Which may be derived from, for example, the work of institutional writers or from historical sources.
6   See, for example, *Starrs v Ruxton* 2000 SC (JC) 208 (discussed in more detail in ch 11); *Clancy v Caird* 2000 SC 441, *Brown v Stott* 2000 SLT 379 (Appeal Court of the High Court of Justiciary) and 2001 SC (PC) 43 (Privy Council) and *MG, Petitioner*, an unreported decision of Lord Brodie of 13 August 2008. Reference has been made also to South African and New Zealand jurisprudence, eg *Vervuren v HM Advocate* 2002 SLT 555.
7   'It is necessary, generally, to exercise considerable discretion in the application of decisions relating to different legal systems ... There is always an initial and possibly fundamental difficulty that one is unfamiliar with the legal systems involved and with the structure of the courts and the inter-relationships between the courts and other branches of government in the several countries in relation to which apparently similar issues have been considered:' *Clancy v Caird* 2000 SC 441 per Lord Penrose at 479.
8   This term is problematic. Here, it is used to mean court-made, non-statutory law in general and is a term shared by the Scottish and English legal systems. In other contexts, it is used as a term specifically to identify English common law and the common law world beyond in most of the United States and the Commonwealth and to be opposed to the 'civil law' in most jurisdictions of continental Europe. On this analysis, Scotland's system is often described as 'mixed'. See W D H Sellar 'Scots law: mixed from the very beginning? A tale of two receptions' (2000) 4 Edin LR 3; R Evan-Jones 'Receptions of law, mixed legal systems and the myth of the genius of Scots private law' (1998) 114 LQR 228; and C M G Himsworth 'Devolution and the mixed legal system of Scotland' 2002 JR 115.
9   See, for example, Stair's *Institutions of the Law of Scotland*; Bankton's *Institute of the Laws of Scotland*; and Hume's *Commentaries on the Law of Scotland Respecting Crimes*. For discussion see 22 *Stair Memorial Encyclopedia*; DM Walker *The Scottish Legal System* (8th edn, 2001); AA Paterson, TStJN Bates and MR Poustie *The Legal System of Scotland* (4th edn, 1999); R M White and I D Willock *The Scottish Legal System* (4th edn, 2007).
10 *Lord Advocate's Reference No 1 of 2000* 2001 JC 143 following the decision of Sheriff Gimblett at Greenock to acquit three anti-nuclear protestors of charges of malicious damage to a vessel used as part of the UK's Trident missile programme: 'A rule of customary international law is a rule of Scots law' (per Lord Prosser at 512). It was held by the Appeal Court of the High Court of Justiciary that customary international law provided no justification for criminal damage to property even where that property was to be used for purposes which were 'illegal' under international law. See also S C Neff 'International law and nuclear weapons in Scottish courts'

11 And some still-surviving Acts of the Scottish Parliament passed before 1707.

THE WESTMINSTER PARLIAMENT

5.3   Despite the priority which courts have to give, in appropriate circum-stances, to European Community law, it makes sense to most Scottish constitu-tional lawyers to consider first the powers of the Westminster Parliament. The powers of the Scottish Parliament, the delegated legislative powers of ministers and other bodies, and the law making competences of the European Commu-nity are best understood by reference to those of Westminster. Treatment of those other sources of law-making power is therefore deferred until later sec-tions of the chapter. On the other hand, the United Kingdom's accession to the European Communities on 1 January 1973 brought profound consequences for the competence of the Westminster Parliament itself and these should be dealt with here. The only way to understand the consequences of EC accession is first to explain how things were prior to January 1973 and then the effect of accession.

Pre-1 January 1973

5.4   In the classic accounts of the UK constitution of the nineteenth and twentieth centuries, treatment of the powers of Parliament achieved a central position[1], and for good reason. In the absence of a written constitution, it was Parliament's apparently unconstrained law-making capacity which served as the ultimate source, the *fons et origo*, of the UK constitutional order. The con-dition which created this situation was the political victory of the English Par-liament of the seventeenth century, a victory whose fruits were inherited by the combined UK Parliament from 1707. It was a victory over royal power, including royal law-making power, and it was a victory over any competing law-making or law-declaring power of the courts. The courts could still apply the common law but they were committed to a recognition that all other forms of law would yield to the superior statutory law of Parliament. Under a written constitution it is routinely the case that it falls to the courts – as they interpret the provisions of the constitution – to define the extent of the powers of the legislature[2]. Indeed, no working constitution, written or not, is entirely free from the interpretative hand of the courts as they shape the limits of legislative power.

In the United Kingdom, without any authoritative constitutional document conferring and defining law making powers, the responsibility for that defini-tion fell even more squarely upon the courts and it was the courts which came to give recognition to Acts of Parliament as the highest form of law. There is something circumlocutory here: Parliament achieved pre-eminence in the con-stitutional order but relied on the courts to exercise a 'self-denying ordinance' to preserve that status[3]. The courts have in the past trenchantly defended this position:

'It is often said that it would be unconstitutional for the United Kingdom Parliament to do certain things, meaning that the moral, political and other reasons against doing them are so strong that most people would regard it as highly improper if Parliament did these things. But that does not mean that it is beyond the power of Parliament to do such things. If Parliament chose to do any of them the courts could not hold the Act of Parliament invalid ... Their Lordships in declaring the law are not concerned with [the political relationship between the UK and Southern Rhodesia]. They are only concerned with the legal powers of Parliament.'[4]

When, at p 119, we turn to consider the powers of the Scottish Parliament, we shall find that we start with certain provisions of SA 1998 which define those powers. It is plain that, when a new Parliament is established, it is necessary to lay down what its law-making powers shall be. SA 1998 serves as a constitution: it 'constitutes' the Scottish Parliament and defines its powers. In this respect, it performs a very similar function to that of a written constitution of a state, one of whose primary functions is to establish the legislature and then to set out its powers. The French Constitution defines the powers of the Assemblée Nationale[5]. The US Constitution establishes the Congress and then defines its powers[6]. One of the principal consequences of the lack of a written constitution for the United Kingdom is that there is no formal written definition of the powers of the Westminster Parliament[7].

How, then, do we know what its powers are? One simple answer is that we should take account of (a) the record of what Parliament has done and (b) the reaction of the courts to that record. Our concern is with the *legal* powers of Parliament and the primary test (the same test adopted under a written constitution) of the lawfulness of the exercise of law-making powers is how the courts react. Of course, we may, in any given case, question whether the courts have reacted correctly. There will be room for debate about how they would or should respond to some particular hypothetical Act of Parliament in the future. There is also room for discussion of whether the courts are now revising their view of some aspects of parliamentary power and, if so, in what direction. These considerations affect our assessment of the judicial record but they do not dislodge the courts as the ultimate authority on questions of interpretation of what the law is.

There are, however, two problems with a focus on courts and what they decide. In contrast with a general constitutional statement of the sort found in a written constitution, court decisions tend to be sporadic and issued only in reaction to particular cases raised. Courts are not usually called upon to provide systematic statements of the law and, if they do so, they may be accused of going beyond the sphere of their legitimate authority. Secondly, therefore, when courts do engage in general statements of the law, these are almost inevitably obiter (ie not decisive of the question at hand) and not strictly authoritative. We need to keep in mind what Parliament does as well as what courts do.

1 See, for example, A V Dicey *The Law of the Constitution* (10th edn, 1959); I Jennings *The Law and the Constitution* (5th edn, 1959).
2 See ch 1.
3 It was not a logical or even legal necessity which compelled the courts to adopt this position of subordination: the most oft-cited example of an alternative approach is *Marbury v Madison* 5

US (1 Cranch) 137 (1803) in which the US Supreme Court asserted its right to declare unconstitutional an Act of Congress.
4 *Madzimbamuto v Lardner-Burke* [1969] 1 AC 645 per Lord Reid at 723.
5 Title IV.
6 Art 1.
7 Equally, there is no formal constitution of Parliament itself.

Legislative supremacy of the UK Parliament[1]

5.5   With these considerations in mind, how do we describe the rules governing the legislative competence of the Westminster Parliament? The powers
of the Scottish Parliament are defined by reference to a list of restrictions on
its legislative competence. Even though no constitutional document defines
such a list for the Westminster Parliament, could one be constructed from our
knowledge of constitutional history and current practice? If so, it would be
a much shorter list. The principal restrictions on the Scottish Parliament are
defined by reference to subject matter: it may legislate on education but not
energy; tourism but not trade. Subject, however, to possible exceptions mentioned below, there are no such restrictions on the Westminster Parliament.
The Scottish Parliament's power to legislate has geographical limits: it may
not legislate for a country or territory other than Scotland[2]. By contrast, the
Westminster Parliament may legislate not only for the United Kingdom (either
for the whole of the country or for some specified part[3]) but also for the Channel Islands and the Isle of Man[4]; it may legislate for the oil industry in the
North Sea[5]; and, historically, it made laws for those parts of the world which
formed the British Empire and, subsequently, the Commonwealth. For most
former colonies, the final Act of the UK Parliament was that which conferred
independence[6]. In the case of the former dominions, it has been assumed that,
since the Statute of Westminster 1931, Westminster would not legislate for
them except with the consent of the country concerned. This principle enabled
the passing of the Canada Act 1982[7]. The same assumption that local consent
would be required for legislation had been extended to the former colony of
Southern Rhodesia (now Zimbabwe) but, in the circumstances of the Unilateral
Declaration of Independence coup led by Ian Smith in 1965, the authority of
the Westminster Parliament was asserted to make laws for Southern Rhodesia
without the consent of its (illegal) government[8]. Such laws were accepted as
having undoubted effect by the British courts[9] although they were not observed
by the Southern Rhodesian courts[10]. The same principle applies where the UK
Parliament passes laws creating criminal offences based on activities on the
high seas or on the territory of other states[11]. Such laws bind UK courts but
may be given little or no recognition in other parts of the world. It was Sir Ivor
Jennings who wrote that the UK Parliament could, if it wished, ban smoking on
the streets of Paris[12]. Subject to constraints possibly now imposed by European
Community law, that proposition remains true but now, as then, it is subject to
the very real limitation that such a no-smoking law would have no noticeable
impact on the French courts.

It is not difficult to see that examples such as these lead quickly to the proposition that the legislative competence of the Westminster Parliament is unlimited.
It was the Swiss jurist J-L de Lolme who wrote that Parliament could do any-

thing except make a woman a man or a man a woman[13]. He was distinguishing Parliament from the Roman jurisconsults who could call a daughter a son. Presumably, however, Parliament *could*, as a matter of law, do the same.

Any Act of Parliament – but not some lesser measure, even if approved by one or both Houses of Parliament[14] – will attract the loyal obedience of courts in the United Kingdom. The courts have considered it inappropriate to scrutinise the legislative procedure leading to the passing of an Act. Even if there have been allegations of fraud in that process, an Act of Parliament will be applied by the courts[15]. If an Act has reached the statute book, if it is on the parliamentary roll[16], it will be given effect by the courts.

Another clear proposition in the law of the United Kingdom is that Acts of the Westminster Parliament have the capacity to override rules of international law. 'Conventional' (treaty-based) rules of international law are not, in any event, accorded any formal status by UK courts[17], although their existence may be acknowledged as an interpretative aid. Acts of Parliament are frequently used to give domestic effect to the terms of treaties but, equally, Acts of Parliament may be passed in defiance of the United Kingdom's treaty obligations[18]. In the rather special case of the European Convention on Human Rights (ECHR) prior to its incorporation by HRA 1998, the English courts were inclined to take the terms of the Convention as an interpretative aid where a statute was thought to be ambiguous but, despite a presumption that Parliament would not intend to override the fundamental rights the Convention sought to guarantee[19], would acknowledge the superiority of a conflicting Act of Parliament where its terms were clear. The Scottish courts were initially reluctant to attribute any role to the Convention even as an interpretative aid[20] but later adopted a position in line with that taken in England[21]. The new status conferred on Convention rights by HRA 1998 is considered in Chapter 12[22].

A further consequence of according an apparently unlimited competence to the Westminster Parliament is that, in principle, the Parliament of today can always amend or repeal an Act passed by Parliament at any time in the past. Once again, questions of interpretation will arise. *Express* words of amendment or repeal will always prevail. Modification deriving from an *implied* intention to amend or repeal will depend upon a court's interpretation of the later Act. However, the general rule is clear: subject to consideration of the special case of the European Communities Act 1972 (ECA 1972)[23], Parliament cannot, in law, be constrained from amending or repealing earlier Acts[24]. There are some Acts whose amendment would, in practice, be highly improbable, except perhaps with the consent of those affected[25], but there would be no doubting, in the eyes of the UK courts, the formal competence of Parliament to make such amendments. Sometimes this principle is expressed in its inverted form – the rule that Parliament cannot 'bind its successors'. A provision in an Act of Parliament which purports to restrict the legislative freedom of a future Parliament is viewed as ineffective[26]. That, at least, is believed to be true of attempts to limit the *substantive* content of future legislation.

Questions have, however, been raised about the competence of an Act of Parliament to impose *procedural* conditions on the manner in which a future Parliament may repeal or amend its terms. Could an Act of Parliament impose conditions on a future Parliament requiring an amendment of that or other legislation to be made only following a positive referendum? Or by a procedure involving the two Houses sitting together? Or requiring special majority voting in both Houses?[27] While the arguments which have been made in favour of such limitations may be persuasive, they have not been founded on any clear and unambiguous support from the courts.

The most recent such attempt to challenge Westminster legislation on the grounds that procedural requirements had not been complied with also failed but provided the opportunity for the House of Lords to comment more generally on the concept of sovereignty of Parliament, particularly where that concept may appear to conflict with 'fundamental' principles of the common law. Before turning to the case itself, it may be useful to summarise the traditional approach of the courts to this issue.

The recognition given by the courts to the apparently unlimited competence of the UK Parliament has led to the primacy of statute law over law from almost any other source. Thus, a provision in an Act of Parliament will always be accorded a higher status than a common law rule and it has been accepted that Parliament may amend or override the common law and courts will always give effect to such changes provided that they are made explicitly. The impact of a statutory provision on a common law rule will, however, always be a matter of interpretation for a court. The words of the Act, the presumed intention of Parliament and the impact – for example on personal freedom – of modifying the common law will all be relevant. In principle, the courts will acknowledge that, by express words, Parliament can make any change. They will be less inclined to accept that an important common law rule has been displaced if Parliament's intention to do so has not been made explicit and can be derived only by implication[28].

These principles were the subject of some discussion in *R (Jackson) v Attorney General*[29] which concerned a challenge to validity of the Hunting Act 2004 on the grounds that having been passed pursuant to the Parliament Act 1949 which was itself invalid the 2004 Act was also invalid. The arguments about the validity of the 1949 Act are discussed in more detail in Chapter 8[30] but in the course of rejecting the challenge a number of their Lordships made observations which cast doubt on the "absolutist" view of parliamentary sovereignty described above. While Lord Bingham of Cornhill described 'the supremacy of the Crown in Parliament' as the 'bedrock of the British constitution' without departing from the traditional view, Lords Steyn and Hope of Craighead took different approaches. Expressing the view that 'we do not in the United Kingdom have an uncontrolled constitution', Lord Steyn referred to the impacts of Britain's membership of the EU – discussed below – and the Human Rights Act 1998 and also noted that the supremacy of Parliament is 'a construct of the common law. The judges created this principle. If that is so, it is not unthinkable that circumstances could arise where the courts may have to qualify a principle established on a different hypothesis of constitutionalism. In exceptional circumstances involving an attempt to abolish judicial review or the ordinary role of the courts, the Appellate Committee of the House of Lords or a new Supreme Court may have to consider whether this is a constitutional fundamental which even a sovereign Parliament acting at the behest of a complaisant House of Commons cannot abolish'[31]. Lord Hope's perspective was similar, observing in particular that the principle of absolute legislative sovereignty was an English one and that, in fact, 'the rule of law enforced by the courts is the ultimate controlling factor on which our constitution is based'[32].

Such developments apart, the idea of legislative supremacy as it was understood prior to EC accession in January 1973 remains very much intact. Legislative supremacy has never meant that Acts of Parliament are the only source of law: to the extent that they have not been displaced by statute, common law rules and, indeed, rules deriving from Scotland's institutional writers remain good law. Some common law rules, including those which define the royal prerogative, have significant constitutional effect. Similarly, rules made by authorities to whom power has been delegated by Parliament (including, indeed, powers to amend Acts of Parliament themselves[33]) are, of course, good law. Acts of the Scottish Parliament are, to take the most prominent example, becoming more and more important as sources of law in Scotland.

1   See A Bradley 'The Sovereignty of Parliament – Form or Substance' in J Jowell and D Oliver *The Changing Constitution* (6th edn, 2007) and J Jowell 'Parliamentary Sovereignty under the New Constitutional Hypothesis' [2006] PL 562.
2   SA 1998, s 29(2)(a).
3   See, for example, the Civil Evidence (Scotland) Act 1988 and the Disabled Persons (Northern Ireland) Act 1989.
4   See, for example, the United Nations Act 1946, s 1 and the Al-Qa'ida and Taliban (United Nations Measures) (Channel Islands) Order 2002, SI 2002/258.
5   Continental Shelf Act 1964, and orders thereunder.
6   Eg Ghana Independence Act 1957; Jamaica Independence Act 1962.
7   The Preamble to the Canada Act 1982 stated that 'Canada has requested and consented' to the Act. A challenge to its enactment was brought by two representatives of Canadian 'aboriginal' [sic] communities who argued that certain provisions of the Act would prejudice their rights and that they had not given their consent. The Court of Appeal held that in order to comply with the requirement of consent in the Statute of Westminster, s 4 it was necessary only that there was an express declaration of consent in the legislation concerned and, if there was, the Court would not go behind that declaration: *Manuel v A-G* [1983] Ch 77. The Court did not rule on the question of whether the Canada Act 1982 would have been invalid had a declaration of consent been omitted altogether.
8   Southern Rhodesia Act 1965. The Southern Rhodesia (Constitution) Order 1965, SI 1965/1952 rendered null and void – at least so far as the UK was concerned – all laws passed by the new regime.
9   *Madzimbamuto v Lardner-Burke* [1969] 1 AC 645.
10 In *Madzimbamuto v Lardner-Burke* [1969] 1 AC 645, the High Court of Southern Rhodesia took the view that the Smith regime was unlawful but that as it was then the only effective government of Rhodesia, it was necessary to give effect to regulations made by it.
11 See *Mortensen v Peters* (1906) 8 F(J) 93 concerning the Herring Fishery (Scotland) Act 1889 and for more recent examples see the Proceeds of Crime Act 2002 (confiscation of property abroad), the Anti-terrorism, Crime and Security Act 2001 (extra-territorial effect of biological and nuclear weapons offences) and *R (Al-Fawwaz) v Governor of Brixton Prison* [2002] 1 AC 556 on the interpretation of the Extradition Act 1989.
12 I Jennings *The Law and the Constitution* (5th edn, 1959) pp 170–171.
13 *The Constitution of England* (new edn, 1834) p 117.
14 See *Bowles v Bank of England* [1913] 1 Ch 57. For statutory instruments approved by one or both Houses, see p 388.
15 *British Railways Board v Pickin* [1974] AC 765. Lord Denning, part of the Court of Appeal Bench whose decision was reversed by the Lords, had suggested that the question of whether (private) legislation had been obtained improperly was 'a triable issue' and that the court may, if it were to conclude that an Act had been so obtained, be under a duty to report the matter

to Parliament's attention. He did not suggest that the Act could be struck down by the court ([1973] QB 219 at 230–231).

16 *Martin v O'Sullivan* [1984] STC 258.
17 See, for example, *Malone v Metropolitan Police Commissioner* [1979] Ch 344. However, it does appear to be accepted that customary rules of international law are part of the law of Scotland: cf p 103, n 10 above.
18 *Cheny v Conn* [1968] 1 All ER 779.
19 *R v Secretary of State for the Home Department, ex p Brind* [1991] AC 696
20 See especially Lord Ross in *Kaur v Lord Advocate* 1980 SC 319.
21 *T, Petitioner* 1997 SLT 724 and *Advocate General for Scotland v MacDonald* [2001] 1 All ER 620.
22 See p 390. For the relationship between Acts of the Scottish Parliament and (a) Convention rights and (b) international law in general, see pp 126 and 139 respectively.
23 See p 115.
24 Or indeed authorising ministers to do so: see, for example, HRA 1998, s 10. However, a power to modify or repeal primary legislation which is conferred by secondary legislation will not be implied: there should be an express provision and this will be construed strictly and narrowly (*Hyde Park Residence Ltd v Secretary of State for the Environment, Transport and the Regions* [1999] 3 PLR 1).
25 For example, the Canada Act 1982, discussed above.
26 See *Vauxhall Estates Ltd v Liverpool Corpn* [1932] 1 KB 733; *Ellen Street Estates Ltd v Minister of Health* [1934] 1 KB 590; *Thoburn v Sunderland City Council* [2003] QB 151.
27 Requirements for special majority voting in the Scottish Parliament are included in SA 1998 (see p 69) but, as we shall see, the Scottish Parliament does not enjoy the same Westminster-style 'supremacy'.
28 See, for example, *Beattie v Royal Bank of Scotland plc* 2003 SLT 564.
29 *R (on the application of Jackson) v Attorney General* [2006] 1 AC 262.
30 p 223.
31 p 302–303.
32 p 304.
33 For such powers, see p 145.

The Treaty of Union and the Westminster Parliament

5.6   Notwithstanding the comments of Lords Steyn and Hope in *Jackson*, what the concept of legislative supremacy *has* done in practice is to establish the UK Parliament as the *highest* source of law. It establishes that the highest rule known to a British court, the ultimate rule of recognition[1] or *grundnorm*[2] is that the law contained in the most recent Act of Parliament on a particular subject is to be obeyed. We turn shortly to examine whether, and to what extent, that position has been changed by ECA 1972. Before doing so, we should examine the one serious challenge to the doctrine of legislative supremacy which was launched much earlier. This is the challenge of the Articles (or Treaty) of Union concluded between Scotland and England in 1706 and enacted into law by the separate Parliaments of the two countries in 1707[3]. The arguments in favour of according higher law status to the Treaty are three:

THE 'CONSTITUTIVE' CHARACTER OF THE TREATY   There are good reasons in constitutional logic to attribute a special status to the Treaty provisions. Although the Treaty was made in an age before written constitutions, as we would now understand them, were devised, there is no doubt that it had constitutive characteristics[4]. Article I provided for the two Kingdoms of Scotland and England to become united into one Kingdom of Great Britain. Article II provided for succession to the monarchy; and Article III for the United Kingdom to 'be represented by one and the same Parliament, to be styled the Parliament of Great Britain'. Article III is particularly important because it clearly points to the creation of a *new* Parliament and, therefore, one which should expect to operate subject to the terms laid down in the document by which it was created. At all events, the Treaty was certainly not itself a legislative product of the Parliament of Great Britain and has a strong claim, perhaps the strongest claim, to be a document which, unlike mere Acts of Parliament, could bind succeeding Parliaments.

THE LANGUAGE OF THE TREATY A separate argument in favour of the Treaty's status lies in the claims made by its own provisions. There is frequent use of the phrases 'for ever' and 'in all time coming'[5] subject to the qualification, in some articles, that alterations to the provisions laid down may be made by the Parliament of Great Britain. The Treaty concluded (in Art XXV) with a declaration that prior law and statutes which were contrary to or inconsistent with the Treaty would 'cease and become void'.

Two provisions have a special significance. One is Article XIX which provides for the Court of Session to 'remain in all time coming within Scotland as it is now constituted by the laws of that kingdom; and with the same authority and privileges as before the Union, subject, nevertheless, to such regulations, for the better administration of justice, as shall be made by the Parliament of Great Britain'. Its predecessor (Art XVIII) provides for laws in Scotland to remain in force 'but alterable by the Parliament of Great Britain; with this difference betwixt the laws concerning public right, policy, and civil government, and those which concern private right, that the laws which concern public right, policy and civil government may be made the same throughout the whole United Kingdom, but that no alteration can be made in laws which concern private right, except for evident utility of the subjects within Scotland'.

JUDICIAL RECOGNITION OF THE TREATY The third argument in favour of according the Treaty special status is the degree of recognition given to it by the courts[6]. The attitude adopted by courts is potentially, of course, of the highest importance. They have the authority to translate constitutional speculation into real rules. Unfortunately, however, there have been mixed signals given in the small number of cases (which have been prompted in the main by a wish for increased prominence for a political cause) that have come before the courts. Despite the passing of 50 years since it was decided, *MacCormick v Lord Advocate*[7] retains its iconic status for it was in that case, in which the title of the Queen as 'Elizabeth II' was challenged in the Court of Session, that Lord President Cooper gave significant support to the higher status of the Treaty. Referring to the principle of the unlimited sovereignty of Parliament as 'a distinctively English principle which has no counterpart in Scottish constitutional law'[8] he noted that the Treaty and the associated legislation, by which the Parliament of Great Britain was brought into being as the successor of the separate Parliaments of Scotland and England, contain some clauses which expressly reserve to the Parliament of Great Britain powers of subsequent modification, and other clauses which either contain no such power or emphatically exclude subsequent alteration by declarations that the provision shall be fundamental and unalterable in all time coming. He concluded that he had 'not found in the

Union legislation any provision that the Parliament of Great Britain should be 'absolutely sovereign' in the sense that that Parliament should be free to alter the Treaty 'at will'. The significance of these dicta is, however, severely undermined by two further aspects of the case. In the first place, they are obiter and therefore lack any formal precedential authority because the case itself, dismissing the challenge, was decided on other grounds. Secondly, and more importantly from the point of view of the wider impact of Lord Cooper's opinion, what he gave with the right hand he took away with the left. Instead of moving forward from asserting the right and indeed the duty of the Court of Session to uphold and enforce the Treaty's pre-eminence against a future statute of the Westminster Parliament, he reverted to a position in which he declared: 'This at least is plain, that there is neither precedent nor authority of any kind for the view that the domestic Courts of either Scotland or England have jurisdiction to determine whether a governmental act of the type here in controversy is or is not conform to the provisions of a Treaty'[9].

By doubting the justiciability of the issue, Lord Cooper undermined the strength of his initial position on the status of the Treaty itself. Those doubts remain, along with rather more specific reservations about the justiciability of such terms in the Treaty as the 'evident utility of the subjects within Scotland'. Whether a court could be expected to determine the 'utility' of a measure (and, if so, according to what criteria) was doubted in the later case of *Gibson v Lord Advocate*[10] in which the pursuer claimed that an EC fishing regulation was contrary to the Treaty of Union. The court's rejection of the claim was on the ground that this was a question of public rather than private right and, therefore, that the 'evident utility' test was not engaged. In later cases arising out of challenges to the imposition of the poll tax in Scotland, attempts to invoke the Treaty failed but on grounds, inter alia, that it could not be used to question the validity of the statute under which the appeals were brought. There appeared to be a background assumption of the higher status of the Treaty, if only its terms could be successfully invoked[11].

That background assumption has not been completely dispelled by the most recent 'judicial' consideration of the status of the Treaty. Following the introduction of the House of Lords Bill[12] at Westminster in 1999 – intended to remove the rights of hereditary peers to sit and vote in the Lords – the House of Lords, on the motion of Lord Gray, referred to its Committee for Privileges the question: 'Whether the House of Lords Bill ... would ... breach the provisions of the Treaty of Union between England and Scotland'. It was argued on behalf of Lord Gray that the Bill would, if enacted, contravene Article XXII which provided, inter alia, that 16 of the peers of Scotland would be entitled to sit and vote in the House of Lords. The opinions of Lords Slynn, Nicholls and Hope of Craighead[13] deal with a wide range of matters including the existence of a 'Treaty'[14] of Union and whether, and by whom, the provisions of such a Treaty could be enforced given that neither of the contracting parties 'has existed as such since 1707'[15]. While their lordships were in agreement that the Treaty of Union, Article XXII had, in fact, been altered by subsequent Acts of the UK Parliament[16] and that Article XXII did not have the status of 'fundamental law' they were equivocal on the question of whether certain other articles might enjoy such status.

Lord Hope reviewed the earlier cases and noted that, rather than expressing any clear and unambiguous view on the capacity of the Treaty to bind the Parliament which it had created, each court faced with such a question 'has always been able to find another route for the disposal of the argument'[17]. His own view was that 'the argument that the legislative powers of the new Parliament of Great Britain were subject to the restrictions expressed in the Union Agreement by which it was constituted cannot be dismissed as entirely fanciful'. However, rather like the courts to which he had referred, Lord Hope did not think it necessary for the Committee to decide whether there might be circumstances in which 'the basic rule of legislative supremacy by qualified by judicial decision'[18]. That was a matter for the courts to decide.

As it stands, then, the debate as to the 'fundamental' nature of the Treaty of Union remains – at least at the level of constitutional theory – unresolved. While unwilling to concede that it imposes no limits whatsoever on the powers of the Westminster Parliament, it seems likely that the courts (and Parliament) will continue to deal with questions as to the Treaty's status in a pragmatic fashion by finding – in Lord Hope's words – an alternative route for their disposal[19].

1   H L A Hart *The Concept of Law* (2nd edn, Bulloch and Raz eds, 1997).
2   H Kelsen *Pure Theory of Law* (2nd edn, tr M Knight, 1970).
3   See the material referred to at p 38 and see also *SME Reissue* Constitutional Law paras 60–66.
4   N MacCormick 'Does the United Kingdom have a Constitution? Reflections on *MacCormick v Lord Advocate*' (1978) 29 NILQ 1.
5   See, for example, Arts I, II, VI, VII, and XIX.
6   In addition to the Scottish cases cited below, the relevance of the Treaty has been acknowledged in English cases. See, for example *R v Commissioner of Police, ex p Bennett* [1995] QB 313.
7   *MacCormick v Lord Advocate* 1953 SC 396.
8   *MacCormick v Lord Advocate* 1953 SC 396 at 411.
9   *MacCormick v Lord Advocate* 1953 SC 396 at 413.
10 *Gibson v Lord Advocate* 1975 SC 136.
11 *Pringle, Petitioner* 1991 SLT 330; *Murray v Rogers* 1992 SLT 221; *Stewart v Henry* 1989 SLT (Sh Ct) 34; *Fraser v MacCorquodale* 1992 SLT 229. See NC Walker and CMG Himsworth [1991] JR 45.
12 Now the House of Lords Act 1999.
13 *Lord Gray's Motion* 2000 SC (HL) 46. The Committee had a membership of seven but only the three 'Law Lords' gave written reasons for the unanimous decision of the committee to answer the question in the negative.
14 In the sense of a treaty binding on the two contracting states as a matter of international law rather than simply separate Acts of the independent Parliaments.
15 *Lord Gray's Motion* 2000 SC(HL) 46 per Lord Slynn at 49.
16 And eventually repealed by the Statute Law Revision (Scotland) Act 1964 and the Statute Law (Repeals) Act 1993.
17 *Lord Gray's Motion* 2000 SC (HL) 46 per Lord Hope of Craighead at 59.
18 *Lord Gray's Motion* 2000 SC (HL) 46 per Lord Hope of Craighead at 59.
19 In June 2003 Lord Hope was reported as having made comments to the effect that any new Supreme Court (as to which see ch 13) would require independent funding, management and accommodation to avoid breaching the Treaty of Union, Art XIX which prohibits the hearing of Scottish cases in 'the Courts of Chancery, Queen's-Bench, Common-Pleas or any other Court in Westminster-hall' *The Times*, 19 June 2003. See also Lord Hope's comments in *R (Jackson) v Attorney General* [2006] 1 AC 262 at pp 303–304.

Post-January 1973

5.7   In Chapter 3 it was explained that the United Kingdom's accession to the European Union has had a substantial impact on Scottish and UK constitutional law. The biggest single practical consequence is that, in line with the wider requirements of the Union, the European treaties as well as all the laws promulgated under the treaties as regulations and directives have to be given effect within the United Kingdom. They become part of UK law and must be implemented and enforced by UK courts. This, in itself, creates no major difficulties in principle and the incorporation of EC law was one of the main purposes of ECA 1972. ECA 1972, s 2(1) provided that all the then existing rights and obligations, and all *future* rights and obligations, 'created or arising by or under the Treaties ... are without further enactment to be given legal effect'. This was sufficient at the time to enable the United Kingdom to comply with the treaty requirement to 'take all appropriate measures to ensure fulfilment of the obligations arising out of this Treaty or resulting from action taken by the institutions of the Community'[1]. In addition, ECA 1972, s 3 required that UK courts should determine any question of the meaning or effect of any provision of EC law in accordance with the principles established by, and decisions of, the European Court of Justice.

But, of course, Community law changes and the treaties require that such changes must also be incorporated by member states. In the United Kingdom an Act of Parliament (or an Act of the Scottish Parliament) can be used to do this. Alternatively, ECA 1972, s 2(2) provides for a special form of delegated legislation by which ministers (UK or Scottish) may give effect to the terms of an EC regulation or directive[2]. These procedures, taken as a whole, are straightforward enough to use although good questions can be asked about how sufficient democratic control can be maintained over the process, especially given the sheer quantity of European legislation which has to be incorporated each year.

1 EC Treaty, art 5.
2 For delegated legislation generally, see p 143.

Supremacy of EC law – the EU perspective

5.8   There is, however, a further requirement which the EU treaty regime imposes. Not only must EC rules be incorporated but they must take precedence over all other laws within the member state. The economic and political reasoning behind this is clear: to achieve a common market and to realise the other objectives of the Union, there is a necessity to achieve a high degree of uniformity of legal provision. This was an imperative which the European Court of Justice (ECJ) adopted with enthusiasm. In cases decided before the UK accession, but whose principles have been reinforced repeatedly ever since, the ECJ asserted a principle of supremacy designed to ensure that the Court itself, and also all courts applying EC law in member states, will, in the case of any conflict between EC and domestic rules, uphold and enforce the EC rule:

'As opposed to other international treaties, the Treaty instituting the EEC has created its own order which was integrated with the national order of the member-states the moment the Treaty came into force; as such, it is binding upon them ... The transfer, by member-states, from their national order, in favour of the Community order of the rights and obligations arising from the Treaty, carries with it a clear limitation of their sovereign right upon which a subsequent unilateral law, incompatible with the aims of the Community, cannot prevail'[1].

1 *Costa v ENEL* [1964] CMLR 425 (at 455–456).

Supremacy of EC law – the UK perspective

5.9   In the United Kingdom, this supremacy rule is one which the courts must apply, in accordance with ECA 1972, s 3 and, in many situations, this need not cause any difficulty. The status of ECA 1972 itself ensures that the rules which it incorporated at accession override any previous rule in UK law, even if contained in an Act of Parliament. This, however, does not answer the question of what a court must do if it confronts a situation, as is more likely almost 40 years after accession, in which an Act of Parliament is passed whose provisions clash with Community law. If the Act is an Act of the Scottish Parliament there is, as we shall find, no problem for the court: SA 1998 provides that Community law must prevail[1]. However, in the light of our earlier discussion of the legislative supremacy of Parliament, there would appear to be a greater problem if the Act is an Act of the Westminster Parliament. We have concluded that the highest rule of law known to a UK court, the rule which defines the very basis of the UK constitution, is that the most recent Act of Parliament stating the law on any given subject must prevail over any other law from whatever source. This principle is, on the face of it, plainly at odds with the Community rule which requires Community law to prevail. The traditional pre-1973 theory of the authority of the UK Parliament left no room for compromise. The probable need for *future* compromise had, however, been anticipated by Parliament itself in ECA 1972, s 2(4) which provided that 'any enactment passed or to be passed, other than one contained in this part of this Act, shall be construed and have effect subject to the foregoing provisions of this section'.

It did not take long for the meaning of ECA 1972, s 2(4) to become the focus of judicial scrutiny as, inevitably, tensions between UK and EC law became the subject of litigation. Unsurprisingly, in light of the traditional approach to the legislative supremacy of Parliament, the courts were somewhat reluctant to adopt the ECJ's approach of subordinating national legislation to the rule of EC law. No doubt aware of the very difficult political and constitutional issues at stake, courts faced with an apparent conflict between domestic and European law preferred, at least initially, to recast the issue before them as one essentially of statutory interpretation: UK legislation would be given whatever (sometimes strained) construction necessary to give effect to EC law[2].

This approach to resolving differences between UK and EC law did not directly address the more fundamental issue at the heart of these disputes: which source of law would be accorded supremacy by the UK courts in the case of a clear conflict? An answer to *that* question was eventually given in 1990 following the challenge by a number of British companies – including Factortame Ltd – to the provisions of the Merchant Shipping Act 1988 (MSA 1988). It was argued that MSA 1988, by according certain benefits to companies which were owned and operated predominantly by British nationals, breached EC law prohibiting discrimination on grounds of nationality. The remedies sought by the applicants were a declaration that the provisions of MSA 1988, if applied, would contravene EC law and an order (including an interim order) prohibiting the Secretary of State from enforcing the UK legislation. The complex procedural history of the *Factortame* case cannot be fully described here but after an interim injunction was granted by the High Court and then revoked in the Court of Appeal, the case reached the House of Lords. The Lords initially held that as a matter of UK law they had no power to suspend the operation of an Act of the UK Parliament but referred to the European Court of Justice the question whether – in the case of a clear breach of EC law by domestic legislative provisions – the domestic courts were obliged or empowered to grant the remedy sought. The ECJ was unequivocal: 'a national court which, in a case before it concerning Community law, considers that the sole obstacle which precludes it from granting interim relief is a rule of national law it must set aside that rule'.[3]

When the case returned from the ECJ to the House of Lords their Lordships granted the interim relief sought, thereby preventing the Secretary of State from invoking the provisions of MSA 1988. In explaining their decision to do so, their Lordships made clear their view that their decision in this case was a necessary consequence of Britain's accession to the European Community, and one which should have been anticipated by the Westminster Parliament:

> 'If the supremacy within the European Community of Community law over the national law of member states was not always inherent in the EEC Treaty it was certainly well established in the jurisprudence of the Court of Justice long before the United Kingdom joined the Community. Thus, whatever limitation of its sovereignty Parliament accepted when it enacted the European Communities Act 1972 was entirely voluntary. Under the terms of the 1972 Act it has always been clear that it was the duty of a United Kingdom court, when delivering final judgement, to override any rule of national law found to be in conflict with any directly enforceable rule of Community law.'[4]

However clear the duty of the court may have been thought to be, Lord Jauncey was rather more explicit about the significance of the decision. The court was, here, 'faced with the wholly novel situation of determining whether in the circumstances of this appeal interim relief against the application of primary legislation should be granted to the applicants'[5]. That it decided that such interim relief ought to be granted was, it has been suggested, a declaration that the ultimate rule of recognition – or *grundnorm* – of the UK legal system(s) had altered and to that extent at least the description of the *Factortame* decision as 'revolutionary' is an apt one. On the other hand, it is certainly arguable that the Lords in *Factortame* behaved in a manner entirely in keeping with their predecessors who, 300 years earlier, had recognised Parliament's position of constitutional pre-eminence and sought to ensure that the law reflected, and sustained, the political settlement reached within and beyond the state. Moreover, the revolution was only partial: while there was a clear modification of the traditional rule that the provisions of a later statute will impliedly repeal those of an earlier one, at least as far as ECA 1972, s 2(4) was concerned, there was no question of this marking the end of the supremacy of the UK Parliament. The effect of ECA 1972 was of that Parliament's doing and the ability of the same Parliament to undo ECA 1972 in its entirety was not questioned.

Since *Factortame*, the courts have been more willing to assert their right to review the compatibility of UK legislation with EC law[6] and to provide remedies where it is alleged that there is a breach of the latter by the former, even to the extent of finding those affected by the incompatibility of UK legislation with EC law entitled to damages directly caused by the breach[7].

1 SA 1998, s 29(2)(d). See p 139 below.
2 See, for example, *MacCarthys v Smith* [1981] 1 QB 180; *Marshall v Southampton and South West Hampshire Area Health Authority* [1986] 2 All ER 584.
3 *Factortame Ltd v Secretary of State for Transport* (No 2) [1991] 1 AC 603 at 644.
4 *Factortame Ltd v Secretary of State for Transport* (No 2) [1991] 1 AC 603 per Lord Bridge of Harwich at 658–659.
5 *Factortame Ltd v Secretary of State for Transport* (No 2) [1991] 1 AC 603 at 676.
6 *R v Secretary of State for Employment, ex parte Equal Opportunities Commission* [1995] 1 AC 1.
7 *R v Secretary of State for Transport, ex p Factortame Ltd* (No 5) [2000] 1 AC 524.

The European Communities Act 1972 as a 'constitutional statute'

5.10   An interesting addition to the cases in which the status of EC law has been raised is *Thoburn v Sunderland City Council*[1]. There were, in fact, four different cases (all involving 'Metric Martyrs') of some complexity but each turned on the validity of regulations made in 1994 under ECA 1972, s 2(2) to outlaw the use of imperial (rather than metric) units of measurements of weight by amendment of the Weights and Measures Act 1985 (WMA 1985) and of other regulations, some of which were made under that Act itself. The principal argument raised by the Martyrs was that WMA 1985, s 1 which permitted the parallel use of imperial units of measurement, had, as a later statute, impliedly repealed ECA 1972, s 2(2) to the extent that it empowered the making of subordinate legislation that would be inconsistent with it. That argument was rejected by Laws LJ in the English Administrative Court. He took the view that (a) no such question of implied repeal could arise because there was no actual *inconsistency* between anything in WMA 1985, s 1 and ECA 1972, s 2(2) and that (b) there was no general limitation on the power of Parliament to confer a 'Henry VIII' power[2] to amend primary legislation which would be effective not only in respect of existing (in this case pre-1972) legislation but also later Acts. More importantly, however, he set out the proposition that ECA 1972 was a 'constitutional statute' which, in contrast with 'ordinary' statutes and by force of the common law, could *never* be impliedly repealed. It was a statute of the sort which either '(a) conditions the legal relationship between citizen and state in some general, overarching manner, or (b) enlarges or diminishes the scope of what we would now regard as fundamental constitutional rights'. To amend such a statute would require 'express words in the later statute, or ... words so specific that the inference of an actual determination to effect the result contended for was irresistible'[4]. In the light of that test, WMA 1985, s 1 (which was, in any event, a consolidation of an earlier pre-1972 Act) could never have impliedly repealed – and thereby restricted the effect of – ECA 1972, s 2(2).

Such a conclusion is not, in itself, surprising. The idea that an implied repeal might have occurred was highly improbable. Also within the mainstream of opinion on the status of the rules in ECA 1972 and of EC law within the United Kingdom was the view of Laws LJ that these were matters to be judged entirely by principles inherent in UK law itself. He was invited to adopt the view that it was now EC law itself that determined the legal relationship between the EU and the United Kingdom but such a proposition was, he said, false. The *grundnorm* had not, in other words, shifted: 'The conditions of Parliament's legislative supremacy in the United Kingdom necessarily remain in the United Kingdom's hands. But the traditional doctrine has in my judgement been modified. It has been done by the common law, wholly consistently with constitutional principle'[5]. However, as Laws LJ moves into the language of 'constitutional statutes'[6] in relation to ECA 1972, two rather different concerns arise. In this first place, it is not really clear what additional understanding it contributes. In particular, it appears to add little to the debate about how far ECA 1972 may 'bind successors'. At another part of the judgment, the traditional doctrine is invoked[7] but equally the force of *Factortame and R v Secretary of State for Employment, ex parte Equal Opportunities Commission* is sustained. The courts will uphold EC law against subsequent conflicting UK law and that, says Laws LJ, is to sustain the primacy of substantive EC provisions. But the limitation of sovereignty 'has no application where the question is, what is the legal *foundation* within which those substantive provisions enjoy their primacy, and by [sic] which the relation between the law and institutions of the EU law and the British state ultimate rests. The foundation is English law'[8]. This approach does not, however, answer the question about how a court would or should respond if ever there were to be a statute passed which was stated to be in conflict with EC law *and* 's 2(4) of the 1972 Act notwithstanding'.

The other problem with the constitutional statute and its status is that it is a category extended by Laws LJ to include such examples – it was not a definitive list – as Magna Carta, the (English) Bill of Rights 1689, the Union with Scotland Act 1706, the Reform Acts 1832, HRA 1998, SA 1998 and the Government of Wales Act 1998. The difficulty with such a listing is that, although the concept of the 'constitutional statute' may be useful for some purposes[9], in seeking to equate these other statutes with ECA 1972 important distinctions may be blurred. There has been no general avoidance of implied repeal of these measures in the past[10]. There would be difficulties in the identification of which provisions in them are protected.

1 *Thoburn v Sunderland City Council* [2003] QB 151.
2 See p 145 and G Marshall 'Metric measures and martyrdom by Henry VIII clause' (2002) 118 LQR 493.

3   *Thoburn v Sunderland City Council* [2003] QB 151 at 185.
4   *Thoburn v Sunderland City Council* [2003] QB 151 at 185.
5   *Thoburn v Sunderland City Council* [2003] QB 151 at 185.
6   See D Campbell and J Young 'The metric martyrs and the entrenchment jurisprudence of Lord Justice Laws' [2002] PL 399.
7   With reference to *Vauxhall Estates Ltd v Liverpool Corpn* [1932] 1 KB 733 and *Ellen Street Estates Ltd v Minister of Health* [1934] 1 KB 590.
8   *Thoburn v Sunderland City Council* [2003] QB 151 at 188.
9   This terminology is also used in the *First Report of the Joint Committee on House of Lords Reform* (HC Paper 171, HL Paper 17 (2002–03)) para 15 and in the report of the (Wakeham) Royal Commission on reform of the House of Lords (Cm 4534, 2000).
10 See the discussion of the Acts of Union at p 110 above.

THE SCOTTISH PARLIAMENT

General

5.11   The creation of the Scottish Parliament by SA 1998 does not, of course, eliminate the Westminster Parliament as a law-making body for Scotland. From the discussion in the last section of the powers of the UK Parliament, it should be clear that, whatever powers Westminster confers on the Scottish Parliament, it retains its powers to legislate for Scotland – even in terms which contradict the (letter or) spirit of SA 1998. That it remains formally competent to amend or even to repeal SA 1998 is a position which derives, regardless of any provision in SA 1998 itself, from the general theory of the supremacy of the Westminster Parliament. Despite this, it is also explicitly stated in the section which confers general law-making authority on the Scottish Parliament that it 'does not affect the power of the Parliament of the United Kingdom to make laws for Scotland'[1]. The legal and political repercussions of the retention of these powers by Westminster – the constitutional consequences of a settlement which is devolutionary rather than federal in character – are considered below[2].

In the meantime, however, we should examine the law-making powers of the Scottish Parliament. In broad terms, it was the Blair government's intention to establish a Parliament which would extend democratic control over the widespread responsibilities then exercised on an administrative basis by the Scottish Office and other Scottish departments[3]. This in turn reflected the proposals earlier made by the Scottish Constitutional Convention[4] and was intended to confer rather broader powers than those which would have been devolved under the abortive Scotland Act 1978 (SA 1978). As we move on to consider the limits on the Parliament's legislative competence, however, we should bear in mind that these determine only what the Parliament may do in its *law-making* mode. They do not, dictate any general limits on what may be discussed by the Parliament, a fact which has sometimes been a matter of some sensitivity – for instance in the debate held on 16 January 2003 on the 'international situation' (Iraq)[5]. The Parliament has also held debates on the succession to the throne[6], the Scottish regiments[7] and repeatedly on the detention of illegal immigrants, particularly children, at Dungavel House Immigration Removal Centre in Lanarkshire[8]: matters on which it concedes it cannot legislate.

As to legislative competence itself, what was required was a statutory scheme which would enable the new Parliament to legislate for Scotland but which would then draw a line between the devolved matters on which the Scottish Parliament would be competent to legislate and, on the other hand, the reserved matters in respect of which Westminster would have sole legislative authority. The line would be drawn between devolved matters such as health, education, housing, economic development, the environment, agriculture and the police and, on the other hand, reserved matters relating to foreign policy, fiscal and social security policy and the constitution of the United Kingdom. It was the government's belief that reserving powers in those and other areas listed in their proposals would safeguard the integrity of the United Kingdom and produce the benefits for the United Kingdom – as a whole – of a consistent and integrated approach to those policy areas[9].

The translation of these political ambitions into the language of SA 1998 itself starts simply but then becomes more complex. SA 1998, s 28(1) provides that the Scottish Parliament may make laws to be known as Acts of the Scottish Parliament (ASPs). Procedures in the Parliament leading to the passing of a Bill and its receiving the royal assent are considered in Chapter 8 but it should be noted here that, with a view to giving an ASP the same sort of protection from procedural challenge that the courts extend to Westminster Acts[10], SA 1998, s 28(5) provides that the validity of an ASP is not affected by any invalidity in the proceedings leading to its enactment[11].

That protection extends to certain procedural defects but it does not, of course, render immune to challenge an ASP whose provisions exceed the substantive limits of the Parliament's powers. On the contrary, the general law-making power in SA 1998, s 28(1) is stated to be subject to SA 1998, s 29 which provides that an ASP 'is not law so far as any provision of the Act is outside the legislative competence of the Parliament'[12]. Such a provision is unlawful and SA 1998 creates special procedures by which the validity of a provision suspected of being unlawful may be challenged in the courts[13].

1   SA 1998, s 28(7).
2   See 140.
3   *Scotland's Parliament* para 2.1. For the background to devolution, see ch 3.
4   See *Towards Scotland's Parliament: a report to the Scottish people by the Scottish Constitutional Convention* (1990); and *Scotland's Parliament: Scotland's right* (1995).
5   SP OR 16 January 2003, cols 17013–17087 and, in relation to the Scottish Parliament's lack of legislative competence in this area, see the exchange between Tom McCabe MSP and Margo MacDonald MSP at col 17021.
6   SP OR 16 December 1999, cols 1633–1680: 'The Parliament is the voice of Scotland. If the voice of Scotland wishes to make its position plain, it should not consider itself silenced merely by virtue of the fact that our vote cannot change the law' (Roseanna Cunningham MSP, col 1680).
7   SP OR 31 May 2001, cols 1243–1258.
8   SP OR 11 September 2003, col 1582; SP OR 22 September 2005], col 19358 SP OR 5 September 2007, col 1413.
9   *Scotland's Parliament* para 3.4.
10 See p 107.
11 See p 226.
12 SA 1998, s 29(1).
13 See p 398. There are also procedures for challenging provisions in Bills prior to enactment. See p 233.

The legislative competence of the Scottish Parliament – an outline

5.12 SA 1998, s 29 goes on to define the 'legislative competence' of the Parliament by listing a number of ways in which a provision in an ASP is outside that competence. In neither SA 1998, s 28 nor s 29 is there any positive qualification of the general power to 'make laws'. There is not, for instance, any statement that the Parliament's use of its legislative powers should be for the 'peace, order and good government' of Scotland – a formula which was often used in the definition of the powers of parliaments of newly independent states in the Commonwealth and also of the Stormont Parliament in Northern Ireland[1]. Rather, the definition of competence is entirely cast in negative terms by reference to matters which are outside competence. Foremost among the limitations on competence are those which were anticipated in the government's original proposals – an ASP must apply only to Scotland and must not relate to 'reserved matters'. The legislative competence of the Parliament is, however, also restricted in certain other ways and these are considered below.

Before moving on to these express *restrictions* on competence, however, it may be useful to mention certain implied positive aspects of that competence. First, it has been assumed that the power to make laws includes the power to delegate substantial law-making powers to others[2]. Second, the law-making power includes the power to amend or repeal provisions in Acts of the Westminster Parliament, whether made before or after 1 July 1999. Third, the power to make laws includes, of course, the power to amend and repeal the Scottish Parliament's own Acts[3]. It should be assumed that, like the Westminster Parliament, the Scottish Parliament cannot 'bind its successors' although it may enact the procedures which, subject to future modification, it expects the Parliament to adopt for legislating on certain matters in the future. For example, the Public Finance and Accountability (Scotland) Act 2000, s 4 authorises expenditure of sums allowed by the Budget Acts which have been passed annually since then[4] but this Act could not prevent the Parliament from adopting a different legislative device for the allocation of funds at a later date. Fifth, the Parliament's competence could, presumably, not be restricted by the terms of any agreement entered into between the Parliament and a third party. Such agreements are not likely to arise often, if at all, but it appears that the prospects for the Parliament's entering into a 'covenant' with Scottish local authorities during the first session may have foundered, in part, because of doubts about whether it would be appropriate for the Parliament to fetter, in any way, the freedom to use its law-making powers[5]. Finally, it appears that the Scottish Parliament has the power to legislate with retrospective effect[6] including (it appears with respect to events which may have taken place before 1 July 1999[7].

1 Government of Ireland Act 1920, s 4.
2 See p 143.
3 See, for instance, the repeal of the Abolition of Poindings and Warrant Sales Act 2001 by the Debt Arrangement and Attachment (Scotland) Act 2002.
4 See pp 288–291.
5 See 'Legacy Paper' of the Parliament's Local Government Committee, 25 March 2003. There

was no such obstacle to the entering into a 'Concordat' between Scottish Government and COSLA in 2007: see p 204.

7 Erskine Bridge Tolls Act 2001.

8 See the Damages (Asbestos-related Conditions) (Scotland) Act 2009 which provides that sections 1 and 2 of that Act are 'to be treated for all purposes as having always had effect'. The Act is at the time of writing the subject of judicial review proceedings which seek its reduction (see *AXA Petitioners* [2009] CSOH 57 for Lord Glennie's opinion on the interim orders application determined on 27 April 2009).

Limitations on legislative competence – territory

5.13   Returning to SA 1998, s 29, the restriction of the Parliament's powers to apply to Scotland only may seem straightforward enough. It would, on the face of it, be surprising if the Scottish Parliament could legislate on matters outside Scotland and SA 1998 provides that a provision of an ASP is indeed outside the Parliament's legislative competence if 'it would form part of the law of a country or territory other than Scotland, or confer or remove functions exercisable otherwise than in or as regards Scotland'[1]. Although the reasons for this restriction may seem obvious, the result is that legislative proposals which require co-ordination with others for England or other parts of the United Kingdom may attract the need for legislation at Westminster rather than at Holyrood[2]. In addition, the need to define 'Scotland' for the purposes of conferring legislative competence in respect of the regulation of sea fishing was the cause of some difficulty and controversy[3]. It has also been interesting to see the use made, in some examples of delegated legislation to which the same territorial restriction applies[4], of the formula: 'Insofar as it extends beyond Scotland, this Order does so only as a matter of Scots law'[5]. There must be room for some doubt about how legislation admitted to extend beyond Scotland is permitted to do so 'as a matter of Scots law'[6].

1 SA 1998, s 29(2)(a).

2 See p 140.

3 'Scotland' is defined to include 'so much of the internal waters and territorial sea of the United Kingdom as are adjacent to Scotland' (SA 1998, s 126(1)). An Order in Council may, however determine the boundaries of internal waters and territorial sea for this purpose (SA 1998, s 126(2)) and the lines drawn by the Scottish Adjacent Waters Boundaries Order 1999, SI 1999/1126 did cause political controversy. See SP OR 3 June 1999. An Order in Council may also be made to specify functions as being 'exercisable in or as regards Scotland' (SA 1998, s 30(3) and the Scotland Act 1998 (Functions Exercisable in or as Regards Scotland) Order 1999, SI 1999/1748). See also the Marine and Coastal Access Bill which was introduced in the Westminster Parliament in December 2008.

4 See p 147.

5 See, for example the Pet Travel Scheme (Scotland) Order 2003, SSI 2003/229 and the Plant Health (Scotland) Order 2005, SSI 2005/613.

6 For discussion, see SP Paper 504 (2002) para 12.

Limitations on legislative competence – reserved matters

5.14   The discussion in *Scotland's Parliament* of the need for SA 1998 to define the boundary between reserved matters and devolved matters has already been mentioned. The same document also gave an indication of how this was to be done. Put simply, the choice was between two possible mechanisms. Either SA 1998 should contain a list of all the matters to be devolved to the Parliament, stating also that anything not so specified was to be reserved; or it should specify the matters to be reserved, leaving all else devolved. Whichever mechanism was chosen, there would also be the question of the form the lists should take and the degree of detail they should contain. The argument in favour of some precision is that ambiguity and doubt should be avoided for the benefit of parliamentarians and citizens alike: uncertainty may give rise to unreasonable amounts of litigation in the courts. On the other hand, attempts at precision can themselves be the cause of great complexity and may in time produce more uncertainty and litigation.

The model for allocating powers in the SA 1978 was one which (a) listed devolved matters rather than reserved matters; and (b) did so in great detail and by reference to long lists of specific statutory provisions[1]. In 1997, when making their own proposals, the government was critical of the 1978 model. It thought that, because of its high level of specificity, the scheme would have required frequent updating and might have given rise to regular legal arguments about whether particular matters were or were not devolved. The objective of ensuring maximum clarity and stability was best served, in its view, by listing the matters to be reserved to the UK Parliament rather than specifying the devolved matters, an approach which had been adopted in the Northern Ireland Constitution Act 1973[2].

In SA 1998 itself, the scheme for defining the Parliament's law-making powers on this basis starts from s 29(2)(b) which states that a provision in an ASP is outside the Parliament's legislative competence if 'it relates to reserved matters'. The reserved matters themselves are set out in SA 1998, Sch 5[3] which is, as a result, at the core of the devolution settlement: by listing the reserved matters, its terms define the principal boundaries of the Parliament's powers. The government's explanation of the reasoning leading to the choice of the list of reservations was set out briefly in *Scotland's Parliament*: 'There are many matters which can be more effectively and beneficially handled on a United Kingdom basis. By preserving the integrity of the UK, the Union secures for its people participation in an economic unit which benefits business and provides access to wider markets and investment and increases prosperity for all. Scotland also benefits from strong and effective defence and foreign policies and a sense of belonging to a United Kingdom'[4].

This statement led fairly quickly to the identification of some subjects which should unproblematically be reserved. *Scotland's Parliament* listed such things as the constitution of the United Kingdom; UK foreign policy, defence and national security; and the stability of the United Kingdom's fiscal, economic and monetary system[5]. On the other hand, a test of what can be 'more effectively and beneficially handled on a United Kingdom basis' also leaves some matters unresolved. There are questions about what should logically fall on each side of the line. Should the National Health Service be reserved or not? Should legislation on social security policy be made at Westminster or Holyrood? And what about the police service? Or, in a different sector, broadcasting?

Another series of questions follows quickly behind. It might, for instance, be appropriate to reserve *some aspects* of a particular topic but to devolve

123

others. In SA 1978, school education was devolved but university education was not. How were these to be treated in 1998? Could the universities still be handled more effectively and beneficially on a UK basis or should they join school education in being devolved? Transport, especially in respect of safety and regulation, may tend to attract the need for UK legislation but should not some aspects be devolved to Holyrood? Within the health sector, which might in general be devolved, should different considerations apply to abortion, human fertilisation, genetics, xenotransplantation and vivisection? It was the government's view that all of these special aspects should be reserved 'in view of the need for a common approach'[6]. It will not be surprising, however, that the content of SA 1998, Sch 5, in which all these borderline questions were exposed, was the focus of some of the most sustained debate as the Scotland Bill went through Parliament. The borderline between reserved and devolved was fraught with issues on which reasonable people would disagree and on which the differences between political parties would be substantial.

Another outcome of the process of demarcation between reserved and devolved matters is technical complexity. A simple listing of reserved matters in SA 1998, Sch 5 may have been the aim but the Schedule has become a substantial document of reservations and exceptions to reservations (such exceptions being, of course, areas which are devolved to the Scottish Parliament[7]). Its terms are, in some respects, further complicated by SA 1998, Sch 4 which is considered below. SA 1998, Sch 5 itself is divided into three Parts. Part I contains what are called 'General Reservations' and Part II lists 'Specific Reservations', although it is not always obvious why each item falls into the category it does. The offence of treason is, for instance, listed as a 'general' reservation while the currency is listed as 'specific' in Part II. Schedule 5, Part III is headed 'General Provisions' but contains five paragraphs which supplement the provision already made in Parts I and II. Three of those paragraphs deal with 'Scottish public authorities' and 'reserved bodies'[8] and para 4 makes specific supplementary provision in relation to financial assistance to industry. Part III, para 5 provides an important interpretative aid relevant to Parts I and II: much of the detail in the lists of reserved matters in those Parts is provided by reference to the subject matter of a named Act of Parliament and para 5 confirms that such references are to be read as references to the subject matter of those enactments as at 1 July 1999[9].

1   SA 1978, s 18 and Sch 2, s 63 and Schs 10–12.
2   *Scotland's Parliament* para 4.3. See also the Constitution Unit's *Scotland's Parliament: Fundamentals for a New Scotland Act* (1996) chs 3 and 4.
3   Given effect by SA 1998, s 30(1).
4   Para 3.2.
5   Para 3.3.
6   Para 3.3.
7   So, for example, while the broad subject area of intellectual property is reserved to Westminster, the exception to that reservation (and in relation to which Holyrood is competent to legislate) is the subject matter of the Plant Varieties Act 1997 Pts I and II (plant varieties and the Plant Varieties and Seeds Tribunal): SA 1998, Sch 5, Pt II, S C4.
8   On which see p 207.
9   ie the 'principal appointed day' – see SA 1998, s 130 and SI 1998/3178. If the subject matter of an Act had ceased to have effect at any time between the passing of SA 1998 (ie 19 November 1998) and 1 July 1999, it should be read as a reference to the subject matter of the enact-

ment immediately before that time. For an informed view of the potential difficulties with this scheme see the written evidence of Iain Jamieson to the Calman Commission (available at www.commissiononscottishdevolution.org.uk).

Scotland Act 1998, Schedule 5, Part I – general reservations

5.15   Returning to the substantive provisions of SA 1998, Sch 5, Part I lists the general reservations under six headings: the constitution; political parties; foreign affairs; public service; defence; and treason.

THE CONSTITUTION   A number of aspects of the constitution are declared to be reserved matters, beginning with the Crown, including succession to the Crown and a regency (although the Parliament has debated the question of the exclusion of Catholics from succession to the Crown by the Act of Settlement 1700, while acknowledging that any statutory change would be for Westminster)[1]. The general reservation of the Crown is qualified by other provisions in SA 1998, Sch 5 which produces a rather complex situation overall. Most importantly, though, SA 1998, Sch 5 recognises the position established elsewhere in the Act that the Scottish Executive has had functions transferred to it which are within devolved competence and which are prerogative or other executive functions exercisable on behalf of the Queen[2]. Such functions are not, therefore, reserved by the reservation of the Crown[3]. On the other hand 'honours and dignities' are reserved, as are the functions of the Lord Lyon King of Arms so far as relating to the granting of arms but not his judicial functions which, like most aspects of the judicial system, are devolved[4]. The management of the Crown Estate is stated to be reserved[5] and the reservation of the Crown also reserves the functions of the Security Service (MI5), the Secret Intelligence Service (MI6) and the Government Communications Headquarters[6].

Another line which has to be drawn by SA 1998, Sch 5 lies between the reserved and devolved aspects of 'Crown' property. The general reservation of the Crown does not reserve 'property belonging to Her Majesty in right of the Crown' or belonging to any person acting on behalf of the Crown[7], although the compulsory acquisition of property held or used by a UK minister or government department[8] is reserved. On the other hand, the ultimate superiority of the Crown is not reserved[9], with the consequence that the Bill to abolish the feudal system was squarely within the Scottish Parliament's competence[10] and property held by the Queen in her private capacity is not reserved[11]. The hereditary revenues of the Crown *are* reserved[12], as are the royal arms and standard[13]. Finally, the Schedule reconfirms the non-reservation of the Scottish Seal[14].

Also reserved under the head of 'the Constitution' are the Union of the Kingdoms of Scotland and England[15]; and the Parliament of the United Kingdom. SA 1998 and the continued existence of the High Court of Justiciary and the Court of Session as, respectively, a criminal court and civil court of first instance and of appeal. This last reservation does, however, leave the Scottish Parliament free to legislate to amend the powers and procedures of the two courts and, of course, the Parliament would have wider powers in relation to the lower courts (although Sch 5, Pt II includes the reservation of judicial remuneration including that of sheriffs principal and sheriffs[16]). It is not clear whether it would be competent for the Parliament to legislate to curtail or abolish appeals to the House of Lords: senior judicial opinion is at odds with the views of the Parliament's Presiding Officer on the question [17].

POLITICAL PARTIES The second 'general reservation' made by SA 1998, Sch 5 is the registration and funding of political parties, although this is stated not to reserve the making of payments to parties for the purposes of assisting MSPs to perform their parliamentary duties[18].

FOREIGN AFFAIRS Thirdly, SA 1988, Sch 5 reserves 'foreign affairs', defined as international relations, including relations with the European Communities and international organisations, the regulation of international trade and international development assistance[19]. The conduct of foreign affairs is a function readily associated with the United Kingdom as a whole rather than its constituent parts and joins the 'defence of the realm' (see below) as an obvious matter for reservation. International relations are to be conducted at the national level and this includes relations with the European Communities. Despite argument that it would be appropriate for the Scottish Parliament and Executive to have an autonomous representation in Europe, the formal line was held. On the other hand, the text of the reservation makes an exception of 'assisting Ministers of the Crown' in their conduct of international relations[20] which opens the door to Scottish participation in international and European negotiations including representation in the Council of Ministers[21]. Another exception recognises the dual character of international relations. While the negotiation and conclusion of treaty obligations is reserved, it is important that observing and implementing those obligations is not: within their own areas of competence, the Scottish Parliament and Executive are not prevented from observing and implementing obligations deriving from international treaties, the European Convention on Human Rights (ECHR) and Community law[22]. In the case of the ECHR and Community law, this is reinforced elsewhere in SA 1998 by specific prohibitions against the Parliament and the Scottish Ministers legislating or acting incompatibly with Convention rights or Community law[23] and by the transfer to the Scottish Ministers of powers to implement Community law within their own areas of competence[24]. SA 1998 does not formally place the failure to observe other types of international obligations beyond the competence of the Scottish Parliament or Executive, although the Secretary of State's powers of intervention under SA 1998, ss 35 and 58 may be used on those grounds[25].

PUBLIC SERVICE Further reserved by SA 1998, Sch 5 is the civil service of the state[26]. Separate provision is, however, made for appointments to the staff of the Scottish Administration and for other aspects of civil service management[27].

DEFENCE The general reservation of the 'defence of the realm' and related matters is not surprising[28]. All the armed forces (including reserve forces) are reserved matters, as are visiting forces, international headquarters and defence organisations, and trading with the enemy and enemy property. On the other hand, the exercise of civil defence functions (by persons other than members of the armed forces) is not reserved; nor is the conferral of enforcement powers in relation to sea fishing[29].

TREASON   The final 'general reservation' is of the offence of treason[30].

1   SP OR 16 December 1999, cols 1633–1680.
2   SA 1998, s 53(2). See p 154.
3   SA 1998, Sch 5, Pt I, para 2(1). Similarly, a public authority which has no reserved functions does not become a reserved body simply by virtue of the reservation of the Crown: SA 1998, Sch 5, Pt III, para 2.
4   SA 1998, Sch 5, Pt I, para 2(2).
5   SA 1998, Sch 5, Pt I, para 2(3).
6   SA 1998, Sch 5, Pt I, para 2(4).
7   SA 1998, Sch 5, Pt I, para 3(1). SA 1998 contains separate provisions for the transfer, by subordinate legislation, of property belonging to any Minister of the Crown or government department to the Scottish Ministers (SA 1998, ss 60, 90 and 109), the Lord Advocate (SA 1998, s 62) and the Scottish Parliament (SA 1998, Sch 2, para 2). See SIs 1999/1104, 1999/1105 and 1999/1106. SA 1998, s 116 also provides a mechanism by which ambiguities as to the transfer of property may be resolved by a certificate issued by the Secretary of State which is 'conclusive evidence' that a transfer has or has not taken place.
8   SA 1998, Sch 5, Pt I, para 2(3)(c).
9   SA 1998, Sch 5, Pt I, para 3(2).
10 See the Abolition of Feudal Tenure etc (Scotland) Act 2000, especially ss 58–61 and discussion at Stage 1 (SP OR 9 November 1999, cols 339–370) and Stage 3 (SP OR 3 May 2000 cols 213 357) of the Bill's progress.
11 SA 1998, Sch 5, Pt I, para 4(1).
12 SA 1998, Sch 5, Pt I, para 3(3)(a). Though not revenues from bona vacantia, ultimus haeres and treasure trove.
13 SA 1998, Sch 5, Pt I, para 3(3)(b).
14 SA 1998, Sch 5, Pt I, para 5. See also SA 1998, ss 28, 38.
15 SA 1998, Sch 5, Pt 1, para 1(b) and (c). The (English) Union with Scotland Act 1706 and the (Scottish) Union with England Act 1707 are declared to have effect subject to SA 1998, s 37, and see p 110 above. SA 1998, Sch 4, para 1(2)(a) also makes specific provision protecting the Union with Scotland Act 1706 and the Union with England Act 1707, Arts 4 and 6 from modification by the Scottish Parliament, so far as they relate to freedom of trade.
16 SA 1998, Sch 5, Pt II, Section L1.
17 Compare Lord Hope of Craighead 'Taking the case to London – is it all over?' 1998 JR 135. with the treatment of Adam Ingram MSP's Civil Appeals (Scotland) Bill discussed at p 228.
18 SA 1998, Sch 5, Pt I, para 6. And see p 81.
19 SA 1998, Sch 5, Pt I, para 7(1).
20 SA 1998, Sch 5, Pt I, para 7(2)(b).
21 See p 50.
22 SA 1998, Sch 5, Pt I, para 7(2)(a).
23 SA 1998, ss 29(2)(d), 57(2), (3).
24 SA 1998, ss 53, 57(1).
25 See pp 178, 235. In debates on the Scotland Bill, the government argued that it would be inappropriate to make compatibility with international law a test of legislative or Executive competence as this would present courts with issues inappropriate for resolution by them. See p 235.
26 SA 1998, Sch 5, Pt I, para 8. Para 8(2) excepts from reservation the subject matter of the Sheriff Courts and Legal Officers (Scotland) Act 1927, Pt I and the Administration of Justice (Scotland) Act 1933, Pt III which are, respectively, concerned with the appointment of sheriff clerks and procurators fiscal, and officers of the High Court and the Court of Session. The current SNP administration's consultation Scotland's Future records its desire to see Scotland given greater powers in relation to the civil service but the Calman Commission has so far rejected the idea that there should be any change (see Commission on Scottish Devolution, The Future of Scottish Devolution Within the Union: A First Report (2008), para 5.27 and the discussion of those proposals at p 63).
27 See SA 1998, s 51 and p 187.
28 SA 1998, Sch 5, Pt I, para 9.
29 SA 1998, Sch 5, Pt I, para 9(2). For other aspects of sea fishing, see p 122.
30 SA 1998, Sch 5, Pt I, para 10. The reservation includes constructive treason, treason felony and misprision of treason.

Scotland Act 1998, Schedule 5, Part II – specific reservations

5.16   Part II of Sch 5 to the Scotland Act 1998 contains a list of 'specific reservations'. They are arranged under a series of Heads from A to L as follows:

A   Financial and Economic Matters;
B   Home Affairs;
C   Trade and Industry;
D   Energy;
E   Transport;
F   Social Security;
G   Regulation of the Professions;
H   Employment;
J   Health and Medicines;
K   Media and Culture;
L   Miscellaneous.

Under each Head, the style of the Schedule is to include a number of Sections each of which contains a description of reserved matters either by reference to one or more subject areas (eg coinage, legal tender and bank notes) or by reference to the subject matter of a specific piece or pieces of UK legislation (either primary or secondary) or, in one case, an EC Directive[1]. Such specific statutory references make the Schedule vulnerable to change over time to reflect subsequent amendments[2] although the terms of the Schedule itself make clear that the subject matter of any enactment referred to is to be read as a reference to the subject matter as at 1 July 1999[3]. In the text of many of the reservations, the reservation itself is followed by one or more exceptions. Thus, in Section A1 there is a reservation of 'fiscal, economic and monetary policy, ... taxes and excise duties' but there is an exception for 'local taxes to fund local authority expenditure (for example, council tax and non-domestic rates)'. The Scottish Parliament could not legislate to raise general taxes but it could use the special tax-varying power under SA 1998, Pt IV[4] and it could legislate to amend or replace the council tax as a source of local authority revenue.

Other reservations imposed by SA 1998, Sch 5, Head A prevent the Parliament from legislating on the currency, financial services (but bank holidays *are* within the Parliament's competence), financial markets and money laundering. Head B (Home Affairs) reserves the misuse of drugs, data protection and elections for membership of the Scottish Parliament, the House of Commons and the European Parliament, although local government elections, with the exception of the franchise, are not reserved. Also under Head B are reservations of firearms, entertainment (including video recordings and film classification), immigration and nationality, national security, gaming, emergency powers and extradition. Under Head C (Trade and Industry) are reserved business associations (but not charities), most aspects of insolvency, competition (but not the regulation of the legal profession), intellectual property, sea fishing outside the Scottish zone (except Scottish fishing boats)[5], consumer protection, most aspects of product standards and safety (excluding food), weights and measures, telecommunications, the Post Office and postal services, and the research councils.

A list of reservations under Head D (Energy) covers electricity, and most aspects of oil and gas, coal and nuclear energy. The reservation of Transport (Head E) includes most aspects of road traffic regulation, rail[6], marine and air transport. Practically all aspects of social security are reserved under Head F, while Head G reserves the regulation of architects, health professions and auditors. Head H reserves most of employment law and health and safety law[7]. While the provision of health services is not generally reserved, Head J (Health and Medicines) reserves abortion, xenotransplantation, embryology, surrogacy and human genetics as well as medicines. Head K reserves broadcasting, including, controversially, the BBC itself[8] which is combined with lesser matters such as the public lending right under the general heading of Media and Culture. The list of reservations closes with Head L (Miscellaneous). This reserves the constitutionally significant matter of judicial remuneration[9] but that is joined by 'equal opportunities, the control of weapons of mass destruction, the Ordnance Survey and 'time'. By that is meant time scales and time zones[10] and the calendar, units of time and the date of Easter. On the other hand, the computation of periods of time and bank holidays and Quarter Days are not reserved. The regulation of activities in outer space is reserved.

1   See Section B2 (Data Protection), referring to Council Directive (EC) 46/95.
2   See, for example, the insertion of a new para (a) of Section B3 of Part II of Sch 5 by the European Parliamentary Elections Act 2002.
3   See SA 1998, Sch 5, Pt III, para 5. But see also Section B2 which provides, in relation to the reservation of the Data Protection Act 1998, that if any provision of the Act was not in force on 1 July 1999, it was to be treated as if it were. While parts of SA 1998 came into force at the date of royal assent (16 July 1998), the majority of the remaining provisions were brought into force on 1 March 2000 (SI 2000/183).
4   See p 285.
5   See above.
6   The reservation concerning rail has been the subject of amendment to increase the scope of rail powers devolved in Scotland. Nevertheless, the Provision of Rail Passenger Services (Scotland) Bill which was introduced by Tommy Sheridan MSP in September 2006 was stated by the Presiding Officer to be outside legislative competence by virtue of the reservation of rail services. See p 229 n 5.
7   This reservation, somewhat controversially, led the Scottish Executive to conclude in July 2006 the introduction of a new criminal offence of corporate homicide was a reserved matter: see the Corporate Manslaughter and Corporate Homicide Act 2007.
8   See also p 208.
9   See p 309.
10 Including the subject matter of the Summer Time Act 1972.

Devolved and reserved matters: a flexible boundary

5.17   The list of reserved matters contained in SA 1998, Sch 5 is not fixed for all time. The Schedule could be (and occasionally has been) amended by primary legislation passed at Westminster. That, however, might be a cumbersome process and SA 1998 itself anticipated the need for a simpler method by secondary legislation, but with protection against its use simply to serve the interests of the UK government. Thus, SA 1998, s 30(2) enables Sch 5 (and also Sch 4) to be modified by Order in Council for purposes considered 'necessary or expedient' by Her Majesty but any such Order must first be approved in draft by resolution – not only of both Houses at Westminster but also the Scottish

Parliament itself. The procedure has been used on a number of occasions to make amendments to the Schedule[1]. One Modifications Order[2] included the insertion of a new reservation of 'Access to information' but with an exception which paved the way for the Scottish Parliament to pass the Freedom of Information (Scotland) Act 2002. A subsequent adjustment of the transport reservation[3] enabled the grant of new railway services planning powers to local authorities by the Transport (Scotland) Act 2001 and another[4] permitted the introduction in the first session of the Stirling–Alloa–Kincardine Railway and Linked Improvements Bill. An adjustment to the insolvency reservation[5] enabled the Parliament to provide for the insolvency of social landlords[6]. General guidance has been issued to Whitehall departments on the use which may appropriately be made of SA 1998, s 30(2)[7]. It is suggested, for instance, that orders under the subsection should not routinely be used simply to resolve doubts about the precise boundaries of a reservation. That should generally be left to the courts but an exception might be where it is known that the Scottish Executive has proposals to initiate legislation in an area and 'the Executive and UK government see the risks and consequences of a successful legal challenge as being significant in the wider context'[8]. Finally, it is to be noted that consequential amendments to Schedule 5 have been made by 'ordinary' subordinate legislation made by the UK government[9].

The Calman Commission has recommended a number of discrete changes to the reserved/devolved boundary which recommendations may in due course be taken forward using the mechanisms described above. So, for example, the Commission has recommended devolution of the regulation of airguns and the power to determine the level of the national speed limit in Scotland but the 're-reservation' of rule-making powers relating to insolvency[10].

1 The Scotland Act 1998 (Modifications of Schedules 4 and 5) Order 1999, SI 1999/1749; the Scotland Act 1998 (Modifications of Schedule 5) Order 2000, SI 2000/3252; the Scotland Act 1998 (Modification of Schedule 5) Order 2001, SI 2001/1456; the Scotland Act 1998 (Modifications of Schedule 5) Order 2002, SI 2002/1629; the Scotland Act 1998 (Modifications of Schedule 5) Order 2004, SI 2004/3329; the Scotland Act 1998 (Modifications of Schedule 5) Order 2005, SI 2005/865; the Scotland Act 1998 (Modifications of Schedule 5) (No 2) Order 2005, SI 2005/866; the Scotland Act 1998 (Modifications of Schedule 5) Order 2006, SI 2006/609.
2 SI 1999/1749.
3 SI 2000/3252.
4 SI 2002/1629.
5 SI 2001/1456.
6 Housing (Scotland) Act 2001, s 64 and sch 8.
7 Devolution Guidance Note 14 (which at the time of writing was available on the Ministry of Justice website at http://www.justice.gov.uk/guidance/devolutionguidancenotes).
8 Devolution Guidance Note 14, para 6 (ii).
9 See the Legislative Reform (Health and Safety Executive) Order 2008, SI 2008/960.
10 See Commission on Scottish Devolution, *Serving Scotland Better: Scotland and the United Kingdom in the 21st Century* (2009).

Reserved matters: problems of interpretation

5.18   Although the line drawn by SA 1998, Sch 5 between devolved and reserved powers broadly achieved the political objectives of the UK government of 1998, the means by which this was done is not without difficulties.

Some of these derive simply from the problems inherent in any attempt to define powers in the only way we have available – the use of language. Some are particularly associated with the adoption of the method of definition of powers by reference to the reserved matters rather than by a listing of the devolved powers themselves. We might identify four particular difficulties:

(1)   At the most abstract level (and the level least likely to raise practical difficulties), one problem of definition by reservation is that, because there is no defined outer boundary of the limits of legislative power, reservations in SA 1998, Sch 5 have been chosen by reference to conventional categories of Westminster legislation, extended as an afterthought to such matters as time scales and the calendar. But what, for instance, of other matters of natural or scientific definition? Could the Scottish Parliament redefine for Scotland the periodic table of the elements; could it provide a new scale for the measurement of temperature or wind speed in Scotland; could it redefine categories of cattle or horses or cats or dogs? Less fancifully, could the Scottish Parliament intervene to legislate not only on the use of Gaelic or the resources to be allocated to it[1] but also on its orthography? And if on Gaelic, Lallans? And if on Lallans, the use of English in Scotland? Could the Scottish Parliament abolish the apostrophe?

(2)   Of more obvious practical application is the question of whether the line between the devolved and the reserved has been correctly defined. The White Paper explained the case for reserving powers in these terms:

>   'There are many matters which can be more effectively and beneficially handled on a United Kingdom basis. By preserving the integrity of the UK, the Union secures for its people participation in an economic unit which benefits business and provides access to wider markets and investment and increases prosperity for all. Scotland also benefits from strong and effective defence and foreign policies and a sense of belonging to a United Kingdom'[2].

It is not difficult to see that many of these criteria for the reservation of particular areas to the Westminster Parliament are reflected in the terms of SA 1998, Sch 5. Most of the 'general' reservations can be seen to have a 'UK' aspect to them and, if the need for 'participation in an economic unit' taking the form of the United Kingdom is accepted, many of the 'trade and industry' and 'employment' reservations may be fairly unproblematic. The same goes for some other categories such as 'social security' and the 'financial and economic' matters. More problematic are reservations such as broadcasting and abortion. It is less clear that these are dictated by the criteria laid down. They were controversial at the time the Scotland Bill was debated in Parliament[3] and have remained so[4].

(3)   Even if the boundaries between what is devolved and what is reserved were not themselves controversial, problems would remain for Parliaments and governments because, in many policy areas, there are inevitable overlaps between those parts which are reserved and those which are devolved. From the point of view of the Scottish Parliament, this makes it impossible for a wholly comprehensive and integrated policy

position to be adopted, even in those areas which are, on the face of it, devolved. The education system, including universities, is devolved but the research councils and, therefore, research council funding of universities are not. Housing is generally devolved but housing benefit, upon which so much of contemporary housing policy depends, is, as an aspect of social security, reserved. Environmental protection is generally devolved but most aspects of energy policy (including nuclear energy) and transport policy are not.

Some of the problems of overlap are addressed by means made available under SA 1998 itself or left for resolution by extra-statutory negotiation between the two tiers of government. SA 1998 makes provision for the 'executive' devolution of powers which, for legislative purposes, are reserved. It also makes special provision for public bodies whose powers straddle the divide. The power retained by the Westminster Parliament to legislate in areas which have been devolved to Holyrood allows legislation to be enacted across the reserved–devolved boundary, although normally only with the consent of the Scottish Parliament[5]. One of the aims of the concordat regime between the Scottish and the UK governments is to enable the co-ordination of policy[6].

One overarching overlap is represented by the reservation to Westminster of a near monopoly in matters of taxation. With the exception of the tax-varying power provided by SA 1998 itself[7] and the power of the Scottish Parliament to make laws on 'local taxes to fund local authority expenditure'[8], all the powers of the Parliament have to be read subject to the financial controls lying ultimately with Westminster and Whitehall[9]. Even if the extent of those powers is, despite the reservations in SA 1998, Sch 5, formally very broad, they are, in practice, exercisable only subject to external financial constraints.

(4)   Finally, it has to be remembered that any exercise of legislative power by the Scottish Parliament is potentially challengeable in the courts. Such challenges have to date focused on human rights issues but it is probable that at some point, despite the procedural precautions imposed by SA 1998[10], there will be challenges based on the interpretation of the reserved matters defined in Sch 5[11]. The circumstances in which such challenges may arise and the way in which courts will handle them are considered later[12] but it should be noted that SA 1998 itself provides some interpretative assistance in s 29(3) which states:

> 'For the purposes of this section, the question whether a provision of an Act of the Scottish Parliament relates to a reserved matter is to be determined, subject to subsection (4), by reference to the *purpose* of the provision, having regard (among other things) to its effect in all the circumstances'.

The importance of this subsection is that 'purpose' is prescribed as the defining test of whether a provision 'relates to' a reserved matter or not. It addresses the difficult question of overlap presented by any provision in an ASP which may 'affect' – to use a neutral term – both matters which are plainly not reserved but also, to an extent, some which are. SA

1998, s 29(3) states that a provision will not 'relate to' a reserved matter unless that is its purpose. This should operate to save not only provisions which have a merely trivial impact on a reserved matter: even if the impact of a provision on a reserved matter is quite substantial it will be saved provided that its 'purpose' can be held to be within the devolved area. Of course, the purpose of a provision is itself to be determined with regard, 'among other things' to its 'effect in all the circumstances'. These supplementary tests are by no means wholly clear. Despite the centrality of 'purpose', how does one, for instance, determine the 'effect' of a provision in advance of its implementation[13]. What are 'all the circumstances' by reference to which one must judge the effect of a provision? What are the 'other things' to which one must also have regard?

There seems little doubt that there will, over time, be difficulties of interpretation in these areas. Some examples of legislation in certain overlapping areas were, however, provided by ministers at the time of debate on the Scotland Bill and these might provide an indication of how both the legislature and the courts may behave[14]. As one example, Lord Sewel suggested that in a Bill which dealt in general with pollution control (a devolved area) but which also contained provisions dealing with water pollution from coal mines or dust from open cast mining, those provisions would be saved by their anti-pollution purpose despite their touching upon the reserved matter of coal mining. Similarly, a Bill dealing with local government reorganisation should be saved by its devolved purpose, despite its ancillary impact on the administration of local functions relating to reserved matters such as weights and measures and the provisions of housing benefit. A recurring hypothetical example with a high political profile is that of a Bill to authorise the holding of a referendum on independence for Scotland. Because its 'purpose' could be interpreted as the testing of opinion rather than the amendment of the constitution, such a Bill would almost certainly be within the Parliament's powers.

Despite the reservations expressed above on the lack of precision of the 'purpose' test, it may be that the broad-brush solutions proposed by Lord Sewel will work well enough in most situations. Much will depend on the general approach taken by the courts to the interpretation of ASPs and especially to the question of whether they fall within the Parliament's competence. This is treated briefly in Chapter 13. At this point, however, it may be noted that, since 'purpose' is prescribed as the prime determinant of competence at the reserved/ devolved divide, courts may well be swayed, in cases where the 'purpose' is not unambiguously revealed on the face of the Act, by evidence of 'purpose' revealed in debates in the Parliament at the time of the passing of the Bill[15]. Since the case of *Pepper v Hart* in 1993[16] the courts, departing from previous practice, have been prepared, in circumstances of ambiguity, to take into account the content of ministerial statements in the Westminster Parliament indicative of an Act's meaning, including its purpose[17]. There appears to be no confirmation so far that the courts have been prepared to extend the principles of *Pepper v Hart* to statements in the Scottish Parliament but it seems probable that there would be no barrier to their doing so[18]. A generally more liberal approach would be expected and there have been indications in the Parliament itself that *Pepper v Hart* statements might usefully be incorporated into the record of the Parliament's proceedings to assist future interpretation[19]. Although not finally determinative of the issue in future legal proceedings, it might well assist a court to take a view that a provision is competent if ministers (and perhaps other MSPs) declared it to have a devolved purpose[20]. Even if a judgment is taken, whether in the Parliament or in the Supreme Court[21], that a provision in a Bill does not, in the light of the purpose test, relate to reserved matters it should be borne in mind that executive intervention by the Secretary of State cannot be ruled out if he (reasonably) believes it would 'have an adverse effect on the operation of the law as it applies to reserved matters'[22].

In addition to the provision made by SA 1998, s 29(3), there is one particular category of overlapping provision which receives special treatment. SA 1998, s 29(4)[23] provides that a provision in an ASP which would *otherwise not relate* to reserved matters (ie on application, as necessary, of the test in SA 1998, s 29(3)) but makes modifications of *Scots private law* or *Scots criminal law*, as it applies to reserved matters, is normally to be treated as relating to reserved matters. As a general statement, this is, of course, unsurprising. Modifications of law applying to reserved matters would be expected to 'relate to' reserved matters and thus be beyond the Parliament's competence. However, SA 1998, s 29(4), which has to be read with provisions in Sch 4 discussed below, is important for the exception to the general rule which it also contains. Thus, where the purpose of the provision is 'to make the law in question apply consistently to reserved matters and otherwise' that provision is *not* to be treated as relating to reserved matters.

The point here is to take account of the need to ensure that the Scottish Parliament is competent to take on the stewardship of the legal system of Scotland including the broad fields of private and criminal law. The division between devolved and reserved matters places some private and criminal law clearly within the Parliament's competence but some would plainly relate to reserved matters, for example the law of banking, insurance, consumer protection and employment or criminal offences relating to the misuse of drugs. A law whose purpose was to reform legal provision in those areas would plainly be beyond the competence of the Scottish Parliament. By virtue, however, of SA 1998, s 29(4), an ASP which, while modifying the law in those areas because it extended across the devolved/reserved divide, had, as its purpose, the making of 'consistent provision' across the divide, would be saved. An ASP touching upon the general principles of contract (including those contracts which are reserved) or the general principles of delictual or criminal liability could be competent on the grounds of making 'consistent provision'.

SA 1998, Sch 4 apart, two other provisions have to be noted in connection with s 29(4). The first is contained in SA 1998, s 126(4) and (5) which define the terms 'Scots private law' and 'Scots criminal law'. The former is defined to include the general principles of private law, the law of persons, the law of obligations, the law of property and the law of actions (including judicial review). 'Criminal law' includes criminal offences, jurisdiction, evidence, procedure and penalties and the treatment of offenders. Secondly, it should be remembered that SA 1998, s 35 might be invoked by the Secretary of State[24].

1   See, for instance, the Gaelic Language (Scotland) Act 2005.

2   Cm 3658, para 3.2.
3   See D Stockley 'The Increasingly Strange Case of Abortion: Scots Criminal Law and Devolution' HC Debs 31 March 1998, col 1093; HL Debs 3 November 1998, col 203. HC Debs 31 March 1998, (1998) 2 Edin LR 330–337 and the Scotland Bill debate on this issue.
4   For discussion of abortion issues and the reservation of abortion to Westminster see, for example, the Public Petitions Committee, SP PE OR, 6 November 2001, col 1396. First Minister Alex Salmond was reported in September 2007 to support the creation of a commission to consider whether abortion should cease to be a devolved matter.
5   As to Sewel motions, see p 141.
6   See p 191.
7   As to which, see ch 10, p 285.
8   SA 1998, Sch 5, Pt II, S A1.
9   See ch 10.
10 See ch 8.
11 Although 'reserved matter' questions have not arisen in litigation, they have arisen as issues for discussion within the Parliament. The Preliminary Stage Report of the Committee on the (private) Robin Rigg Offshore Wind Farm (Navigation and Fishing) (Scotland) Bill discussed certain competence issues (SP Paper 721, paras 9–12) concerning the reservation of 'navigational rights and freedoms' by SA 1998, Sch 5, Pt II, s E3.
12 See ch 13. See especially the treatment (p 400) of SA 1998, s 101.
13 In a slightly different but related context, s 126(3) of SA 1998 (concerning whether Executive functions relate to reserved matters) uses the formula 'likely effects in all the circumstances'. Are 'likely effects' different from an 'effect'?
14 This is, of course, to be read subject to judicial views for the time being on the extent to which the courts should have regard to parliamentary debates under the rules in *Pepper v Hart* [1993] AC 593. For indications of a restrictive approach, see, for example, *Robinson v Secretary of State for Northern Ireland* [2002] NI 390. The other problem with ministerial statements on the Scotland Bill is that they were much affected by reference to the 'pith and substance' doctrine applied (from Privy Council cases on Canada) by Lord Aitken in the Northern Ireland case of *Gallagher v Lynn* [1937] AC 863 at 870 and the 'respection' doctrine developed by H Calvert in *Constitutional Law in Northern Ireland* (1968) ch 11 and applied in *R v Londonderry Justices* [1972] NILR 91. See also B Hadfield *The Constitution of Northern Ireland* (1989). Despite ministerial encouragement to look to 'pith and substance' and 'respection', it is uncertain how they relate directly to the 'purpose' test now incorporated into SA 1998.
15 A drafting technique which has been adopted in some ASPs has been to define terms by reference to the specific language of SA 1998, for example the Local Government in Scotland Act 2003, s 59 which defines 'equal opportunities' by reference to SA 1998, Sch 5, Pt II, S L2.
16 *Pepper v Hart* [1993] AC 593.
17 For example, in *Chief Adjudication Officer v Foster* [1993] AC 754, statements made by government ministers in both Houses were held to be relevant to the interpretation of the Social Security Act 1986, s 22(4) which empowered the Secretary of State to make regulations prescribing the circumstances in which a person would be treated as 'severely disabled' for the purposes of the Act. See also *Short's Trustee v Keeper of the Registers of Scotland* 1994 SLT 65 and *R v Deegan* [1998] 2 Cr App R 121 in which the English Court of Appeal declined to take account of ministerial statements because they, themselves, were not sufficiently unambiguous.
18 Interestingly, however, in *Thomson v Thomson* 2002 SLT (Sh Ct) 97, Sheriff Principal Nicholson was prepared to consider the explanatory notes prepared in connection with the Scottish Parliament's Protection from Abuse (Scotland) Act 2001: 'While those notes have not been endorsed by the Parliament, they have, I believe, some persuasive authority in terms of indicating the intention of the legislation in question' (at 98). The Inner House of the Court of Session has expressed doubt about the propriety of having regard to explanatory notes in relation to the interpretation of a statutory instrument: 'We should make clear at the outset that we have considerable reservations about having regard to such a note in relation to the interpretation of statutory provisions, since it is specifically stated in the note itself that it is not part of the regulations' (*Scottish Water v Clydecare Ltd* 2003 SLT 333 per Lord Osborne at 341).
19 See, for example. SP OR 29 March 2000 col 1092 and SP OR 11 January 2001 col 141, although in neither of these points nor in references to *Pepper v Hart* in committee proceedings have questions of competence been at issue.
20 Thus reinforcing the statements of competence formally made by a minister and the Presiding Officer at the time of a Bill's introduction. See p 228. Note, too, that explanations of a

Bill's competence are now attached to proposals from the Scottish Law Commission. See, for example, the Joint Report of the Law Commission and the Scottish Law Commission, *Third Parties–Rights Against Insurers* 2001 (Scot Law Com 184) para 1.30.
21 See p 233.
22 SA 1998, s 35(1)(b) and see p 235. See also SA 1998, s 58(4)(b), discussed at p 189.
23 See also SA 1998, Sch 4, discussed below.
24 See p 234 below.

Limitations on legislative competence: Scotland Act 1998, Sch 4

5.19   SA 1998, s 29(2)(c) provides that a provision in an Act of the Scottish Parliament is outside the Parliament's competence if it is in breach of the restrictions in SA 1998, Sch 4. As originally drafted, SA 1998, Sch 4 had a very simple purpose: it was designed to protect the Act itself from amendment by the Scottish Parliament. It would make a nonsense of a constitutional arrangement designed to structure the Parliament in a particular way, and to limit its powers, if the Parliament itself could amend SA 1998 at will. The terms of the Act needed to be 'entrenched'[1] against amendment, or at least, many of the Act's provisions require such protection – especially those which define the Parliament's powers. Arguably, other sections of SA 1998 need not be protected for all time. They provide some initial rules for devolved government which can quite reasonably be amended or repealed by the Scottish Parliament without jeopardising the integrity of the devolution scheme as a whole. Such qualified protection of SA 1998 is provided by Sch 4, para 4(1) which states that an 'Act of the Scottish Parliament cannot modify, or confer power by subordinate legislation to modify, this Act'. The paragraph goes on, however, to set out a list of exceptions to that prohibition[2]. Thus, for instance, the Scottish Parliament could, if it wished, modify[3] the rules governing legal proceedings against the Parliament itself, defamation and contempt of court in relation to proceedings of the Parliament and corrupt practices in the Parliament which are contained in SA 1998, ss 40, 41, 42 and 43 respectively. Similarly, the Scottish Parliament is able to amend many of the financial provisions in SA 1998, Pt III. On the other hand, it is not permitted to amend core rules such as that which secures judicial salaries and thus assists in the protection of judicial independence[4]. Another specific protection given by SA 1998, Sch 4 is of the provisions under which by s 56 executive powers are reserved on a shared basis even though they would otherwise be wholly devolved to the Scottish Ministers[5]. Once again, the point here is to protect from amendment provisions which are fundamental to the devolution scheme itself.

The restrictions on the modification of SA 1998 have themselves been amended recently to enable the Scottish Parliament to legislate in response to the decision of the House of Lords in *Somerville v Scottish Ministers*[6] which confirmed that the one year time limit under the Human Rights Act 1998 for bringing claims for breaches of Convention rights did not apply to claims brought for breach of Convention rights against the Scottish Ministers under SA 1998. The UK government made the Scotland Act 1998 (Modification of Schedule 4) Order 2009[7], extending the legislative competence of the Scottish Parliament in a very specific manner and this was followed by the passing by the Scottish Parliament of the Convention Rights Proceedings (Amendment) (Scotland) Act 2009, the terms of which mirrored that extension of legislative competence[8].

In addition to protecting most of SA 1998 itself from amendment by the Scottish Parliament, Sch 4 serves two other main purposes as a result of changes made during the passing of the Scotland Bill. First, it prevents the Parliament from amending certain other specified pieces of legislation. It entrenches provisions in the Acts of Union concerning freedom of trade, certain provisions of ECA 1972 and HRA 1998 as well as some other Acts of the UK Parliament[9]. Thus, although human rights are not a reserved matter under SA 1998, Sch 5, the particular mode of incorporation of the ECHR by HRA 1998 is protected by SA 1998, Sch 4[10].

The other main purpose of SA 1998, Sch 4 is to augment the provision made elsewhere in relation to reserved matters. As we have seen, SA 1998, Sch 5 identifies the reserved matters which are beyond the legislative competence of the Scottish Parliament and SA 1998, s 29(3) provides that the question of whether a provision of an Act of the Scottish Parliament 'relates to a reserved matter' is to be determined by reference to the purpose of that provision. This enables legislation to be passed by the Parliament which might well have an impact upon a reserved matter but, because its 'purpose' is to make law in a devolved area, the legislation will be competent. Now, however, SA 1998, Sch 4, para 2 adds a further restriction by protecting from modification 'the law on reserved matters' regardless of the 'purpose' of the Act of the Scottish Parliament. The 'law on reserved matters' – defined to include Acts of the UK Parliament, subordinate legislation or non-statutory rules of law (ie the common law) whose subject matter is reserved – is entrenched in much the same way as most of SA 1998 itself and the other enumerated Acts such as HRA 1998. Thus, to take an example mentioned earlier, an Act of the Scottish Parliament could legitimately affect coal mining, provided that its purpose is to prevent pollution. That Act could not, however, modify UK legislation whose subject matter is the coal industry.

That general rule is subject to two qualifications. One allows a small exception in the case of modifications which are 'incidental to, or consequential on' provision made (by the same Act or another enactment) which does not relate to reserved matters. To be permissible, such modifications must not 'have a greater effect on reserved matters than is necessary to give effect to the purpose of the provision'[11]. Thus to stay with the mining example, an Act of the Scottish Parliament cannot in principle amend the Coal Industry Act 1994, even if the general purpose of the legislation is to prevent pollution. If, however, the amendment can be treated as merely 'incidental' and 'necessary' to achieve the pollution prevention purpose, such an amendment *is* permitted.

The other qualification raises once again the special status accorded by SA 1998 to Scots private law and Scots criminal law to take account of their inherent propensity to straddle the divide between reserved and devolved subject matter. Here in SA 1998, in Sch 4, the effect is to limit the restriction on the Scottish Parliament's powers to modify 'the law on reserved matters' where that law is such a rule of Scots private or criminal law[12]. If this is the case, the rule against modifying reserved matters applies only to the extent that the rule in question is *'special to a reserved matter'* or the subject matter of the rule is one of a defined list. That list[13] includes 'interest on sums due in respect of taxes or excise duties and refunds of such taxes or duties' and 'the obligations, in relation to occupational or personal pension schemes, of the trustees or managers'.

As to rules which are *'special to a reserved matter'* SA 1998, provides no further guidance. In parliamentary debate on the Bill, however, the Minister explained that it is 'important to ensure that the Scottish Parliament can legislate on the general rules of Scots private law and criminal law across the board and without fragmenting the general principles which distinguish Scots law as a separate system of law. The new test in SA 1998, Sch 4 applies generally. In the case of Scots private and criminal law, however, it applies only to certain specified aspects of private law and to the rules of Scots private and criminal law which are special to reserved matters – those which result in a distinct and separate treatment of a reserved matter[14].

Three examples of rules 'special to a reserved matter' were suggested: the Copyright, Design and Patents Act 1988, s 90 which provides for assignation of copyright; the rule that gaming contracts cannot be enforced because they are *sponsiones ludicrae*; and the Proceeds of Crime (Scotland) Act 1995 which provides for confiscation of proceeds of drug trafficking.

On the other hand, an example of rules lacking such a 'special' character were those defining how a person may sign a document under Scots law – rules which may apply to both reserved and devolved areas. The dividing line between the 'special' and the 'non-special' may not, however, always be easy to discern.

In addition to providing a form of protection for these three categories of 'entrenched' provisions – SA 1998 itself, the particular named enactments, and the law on reserved matters – Sch 4 makes two other types of provision. The first is to enact some general exceptions to the restrictions the Schedule has imposed on the powers of the Scottish Parliament. In particular, none of those restrictions prevents the Parliament from merely restating (eg by codification) the law in ways which would otherwise be prohibited by the Schedule[15]. The other set of provisions concern the transfer of *Executive* powers. They permit powers to pass to the Scottish Ministers even though legislative power is prevented by SA 1998, Sch 4 from passing to the Scottish Parliament[16].

1   Not the language actually used in SA 1998 itself, but, in equivalent circumstances, the Northern Ireland Act 1998 does refer to 'Entrenched enactments' (see Northern Ireland Act 1998, s 7).
2   Sch 4, para 4(2)–(5), as modified by the Scotland Act 1998 (Modifications of Schedules 4 and 5) Order 1999, SI 1999/1749 and the Scotland Act 1998 (Modifications of Schedule 4) Order 2000, SI 2000/1831.
3   Including modification by amendment or repeal: SA 1998, s 126(1).
4   SA 1998, Sch 4, paras 4(3) and 5(a). See ch 11.
5   SA 1998, Sch 4, para 6. See p 178.
6   2008 SC (HL) 45 and see p 410.
7   SI 2009/1380.
8   For discussion of the Bill's designation as an emergency bill see p 232.

9 Private Legislation Procedure (Scotland) Act 1936; Local Government, Planning and Land Act 1980; and Social Security Administration Act 1992.
10 See C Himsworth 'The Hamebringing: Devolving Rights Seriously' in A Boyle et al (eds) *Human Rights and Scots Law* (2002). The reservation did not prevent the Parliament from enacting the Scottish Commission for Human Rights Act 2006 : see p 340 but did apparently allow the UK Parliament to legislate in connection with the definition of public authority in the Human Rights Act 1998 without the need for a legislative consent motion : see Health and Social Care Act 2008, s 145.
11 SA 1998, Sch 4, para 3(1) and as to the assessment of what is 'necessary' to give effect to the purpose of a provision see SA 1998, Sch 4, para 3(2).
12 Whether contained in a statute or the common law.
13 This list was expanded by the Scotland Act 1998 (Modifications of Schedule 4) Order 2000, SI 2000/1831 to take account in particular, of the Welfare Reform and Pensions Act 1999. All relate to aspects of fiscal, pension and social security regimes reserved by SA 1998, Sch 5.
14 HL Debs 21 July 1998, col 821.
15 SA 1998, Sch 4, para 7. In addition, other provisions of SA 1998, Sch 4, Pt II permit the Parliament to change the titles of judges and certain public officials and to change procedures for the making of subordinate legislation.
16 SA 1998, Sch 4, para 12.

Limitations on legislative competence: Convention rights and Community law

5.20   In addition to the restraints imposed by SA 1998, Sch 5 on legislation relating to reserved matters (as elaborated by s 29(3)) and Sch 4 in relation to private and criminal law, there remain three further limitations on legislative competence imposed by s 29 itself. Two are prescribed by SA 1998, s 29(2) (d) which states that a provision in an ASP is beyond the competence of the Parliament if it is incompatible with any of the Convention rights[1] or with [European] Community law[2].

The justification for these constraints, against the wider background of the incorporation of the ECHR by HRA 1998[3] and of the implementation of Community law in the United Kingdom by ECA 1972 is quite straightforward. Both regimes demand a subordination of UK law-making to the 'higher' rules they introduce and, although difficulties have been encountered on the road to accepting the subordination of UK Acts to Community law[4] and UK Acts are given a form of protected status under HRA 1998[5], there is no doubt about the obligation to read the terms of ASPs subject to rules of the two European regimes. In the case of HRA 1998, ASPs are specifically defined as 'subordinate legislation', which parallels the effect of SA 1998, s 29(2)(d): there is room for an argument that ASPs, as the product of a parliament rather than merely the decisions of public officials, should have been treated more like Westminster Acts[6] but the enacted rules reject that.

1 Defined by s 126(1) as having 'the same meaning as in the Human Rights Act 1998'. It was intended that there would be symmetry between SA 1998 (and indeed the Northern Ireland Act 1998 and the Government of Wales Act 1998) and the HRA 1998. The latter defines 'Convention rights' as those described in articles of the ECHR set out in HRA 1998, Sch 1.
2 Defined by SA 1998, s 126(9) as '(a) all those rights, powers, liabilities, obligations and restrictions from time to time created or arising by or under the Community Treaties, and (b) all those remedies and procedures from time to time provided for by or under the Community Treaties'.
3 In fact, however, HRA 1998 was not fully implemented until 2 October 2000, over a year after the Scottish Parliament acquired its powers on 1 July 1999. Provision was made in SA 1998

itself for relevant provisions (including s 29(2)(d)) to have effect during that period, despite the non-implementation of HRA 1998 upon which they relied SA 1998, (s 129(2)). For discussion of activity during 1999–2000 and the relationship between the two Acts, see I Jamieson 'Relationship between the Scotland Act and the Human Rights Act' 2001 SLT (News) 43 and C Himsworth 'Rights versus Devolution' in T Campbell et al (eds) *Sceptical Essays on Human Rights* (2001). See also p 390 below.

4 See p 115.

5 HRA 1998, s 4 enables a 'declaration of incompatibility' to be made in respect of 'primary legislation' (the definition of which excludes ASPs) but does not empower the courts to 'strike down' an Act of the UK Parliament which is incompatible with Convention rights. See p 391.

6 See C Himsworth 'Rights versus Devolution' in T Campbell et al (eds) *Sceptical Essays on Human Rights* (2001). For litigation which has challenged ASPs on grounds of incompatibility with Convention rights see p 396.

Limitations on legislative competence: the position of the Lord Advocate

5.21   The final restriction on the legislative competence of the Parliament relates specifically to the position of the Lord Advocate. It should be noted that, although the Lord Advocate is a member of the Scottish Executive and she is competent to exercise powers allocated collectively to the Scottish Ministers[1], she also has quite separate functions to be exercised independently[2]. These are the decisions made in the Lord Advocate's capacity as head of the systems of criminal prosecution and investigation of deaths in Scotland in which her independence[3] and freedom from political interference are at a premium. By SA 1998, s 29(2)(e), the Lord Advocate's independence is also placed – with a prominence which would not have been achieved by its inclusion simply as a reserved matter in Sch 5 – beyond the legislative reach of the Parliament. However, while the general justification for the protection of the Lord Advocate's powers may be clear, it might stand in the way of the adoption of a policy to confer a power to prosecute statutory offences on certain regulatory authorities – an area in which there is currently a marked difference between Scotland and England[4].

1 See p 180.

2 SA 1998, s 48(5).

3 See ch 2.

4 In environmental matters, for instance, the Environment Agency can prosecute while the Scottish Environment Protection Agency must refer potential prosecutions to the procurator fiscal.

WESTMINSTER LEGISLATION ON DEVOLVED MATTERS

5.22   It has already been pointed out that SA 1998 expressly preserves the power of the Westminster Parliament to make laws for Scotland[1] which includes the possibility of laws which are within the legislative competence of the Scottish Parliament. As former First Minister Dewar stated, 'in a devolved system, it could not be otherwise'[2]. This rightly implies that Westminster could, in theory, use its powers either to reform the structure of devolved government or, leaving that in place, to make legislation which could override the wishes of Holyrood. It was, however, explained, as the Scotland Bill proceeded through Parliament, that the UK government did not expect that the powers would be used other than with the Scottish Parliament's consent[3]. It was assumed that a convention would be established to that effect. In accordance with such a convention it might, for instance, be convenient to use Westminster legislation to incorporate the terms of an international treaty which covered both reserved and devolved matters[4].

Since the setting up of the Scottish Parliament, this approach has been reaffirmed in both Parliaments and the 'Sewel convention' has become an established part of the architecture of devolution. In particular, First Minister Dewar restated the understanding that the UK government would not introduce proposals to legislate, without consent, on devolved matters and would oppose any private member's Bill which sought to do so[5]. Any UK government proposal would have to be placed before the Scottish Parliament and Westminster business adjusted accordingly. An initial example of such legislation which was immediately taken forward on that basis was the Food Standards Act 1999[6], the justification being that a single regime of regulation across the UK would be appropriate. Consent is given by the Scottish Parliament by passing a 'legislative consent motion'[7]. A legislative consent motion is debated following the lodging by the Scottish government of a legislative consent memorandum which summarises the provisions and policy objectives of the UK Bill in question, specifies those provisions which are within the competence of the Parliament or the Scottish Ministers and explains why it is thought appropriate for the Bill to make such a provision. A legislative consent memorandum is also required in relation to the UK Bills which include such provisions even where the Scottish Government does not intend to lodge a legislative consent motion.

It remains open to the Scottish Parliament to amend or repeal measures enacted by Westminster pursuant to a legislative consent motion so far as they fall within the Parliament's competence. There can, in other words, be no question of inferring that an encroachment by Westminster into the devolved area produces a permanent enlargement of the reserved matters and an implied amendment of SA 1998, Sch 5. The terms of SA 1998, s 28(7) plainly accommodate the possibility of such Westminster legislation within the devolution settlement's own terms[8].

There has been over the last decade greater use of the Sewel convention than might have been anticipated and a considerable amount of debate about that use within the Scottish and UK Parliaments[9] and elsewhere. So, for example, early research showed that in the period to 30 April 2002 30 Sewel motions were debated in the Scottish Parliament to approve the extension of provisions in Westminster Bills to Scotland in areas of devolved subject matter[10]. Perhaps ironically, though Sewel motions provided a ready target for the (SNP) opposition in the Scottish Parliament[11] on the basis that they demonstrate a dependence on Westminster and a surrender of autonomy inappropriate to the devolution scheme, since the minority SNP administration took office in May 2007 a greater number of Bills affecting Scotland have been passed at Westminster than at Holyrood[12]. The use of legislative consent motions raises interesting questions relevant to the overall relationship of 'partnership' between Edinburgh and London. They are part of the regime of co-operation under the Memorandum of Understanding and concordats established between the UK and devolved governments[13] and may be understood as part of that wider pattern of inter-governmental relationships. There remains, however, a legitimate interest in (1) the extent and purposes of the use of legislative consent motions; (2) an explanation of why they have occurred so often; and (3) an understanding of the problems raised by their use. As to (1), the extent of use has been mentioned. While the types of legislation for which such motion may be used would include legislation to alter the legislative competence of the Scottish Parliament[14] or the competence of the Scottish Executive[15], the main purpose has been that originally conceived – to legislate for devolved purposes. In turn, this last category subdivides, in the analysis of Alan Page and Andrea Batey[16], into five suggested justifications: to include Scotland in UK-wide reforms; to implement international obligations; to enable Scottish participation in UK arrangements; to give UK bodies the same powers (or constraints on powers); and to give Scottish bodies the same powers as those enjoyed elsewhere in the United Kingdom.

On (2), explanations for frequency of use, Page and Batey see these principally in terms of a higher-than-predicted quest for uniformity of provision, whether because of high electoral expectation of similar rules, the need for regulatory equivalence, or because of the similarity of political commitment of governments in Edinburgh and London. Even these rationales for uniformity do not, however, justify legislation at Westminster rather than Holyrood the explanation for which may derive from a preference for immediate action on a Westminster initiative rather than a probable delay while a Holyrood Bill is drafted and enacted; a wish to avoid disruption of the Executive's own legislative programme; and perhaps to avoid challenge in the courts (whether by an individual or even the UK government) to a Scottish Bill close to the limits of legislative competence.

Even if the use of legislative consent motions to enable legislation at Westminster is justifiable or, at least, explicable in these ways, it does not mean that the practice is free from difficulties. At a purely practical level, the frequent use of Westminster legislation is aggravating the problems of a divided statute book. Reserved matters quite apart, even law on devolved matters is uneasily split between UK Acts and ASPs. More important is the surrender of scrutiny of 'Sewel' Bills to the Westminster Parliament[17] where they may receive little attention from a specifically Scottish perspective. And there are also problems with the Sewel motion procedure itself. At the time a motion is passed in the Scottish Parliament, it may be unclear what exactly is being approved and difficulties have arisen, unsurprisingly, over the extent to which a Sewel motion can be taken to accommodate significant changes at Westminster to the Bill as first conceived.

1 SA 1998, s 28(7) and p 119.
2 SP OR 9 June 1999, col 358.
3 HL Debs 21 July 1998, col 791 (Lord Sewel).
4 *Scotland's Parliament* para 4.4.
5 SP OR, 9 June 1999, col 358. See also House of Commons Procedure Committee Fourth Report, *The Procedural Consequences of Devolution* HC Paper 185 (1998–99).
6 For the Sewel motion see SP OR 23 June 1999, col 675.
7 This terminology was introduced in 2005 following an inquiry conducted by the Parliament's Procedures Committee, see SP Paper 428 (2005) and SOs Chapter 9B.

8   For a contrary view see N Burrows 'This is Scotland's Parliament; let Scotland's Parliament legislate' 2002 JR 213, based on the assumption that, '[i]t is outwith the competence of the Scottish Parliament to amend UK legislation' (p 236). For examples of such amendments, including amendment of post-devolution UK legislation, see the Mental Health (Care and Treatment) (Scotland) Act 2003, sch5. Interestingly, SA 1978, s 17(2) had provided expressly that 'A Scottish Assembly Act may amend or repeal a provision made by or under an Act of Parliament'.

9   See the Procedures Committee report referred to at note 7 above; the report of the House of Lords Select Committee on the Constitution *Devolution: Inter-Institutional Relations in the UK* HL Paper 28 (2002–03); the report of the House of Commons Scottish Affairs Committee on The Sewel Convention: the Westminster perspective HC (2005-06) 983; A Page and A Batey 'Scotland's Other Parliament: Westminster Legislation about Devolved Matters in Scotland Since Devolution' [2002] PL 501, (upon which this section draws heavily); B K Winetrobe 'Counter-Devolution? The Sewel Convention on Devolved Legislation at Westminster' 2001 SLPQ 6(4) 286; J Munro, Thoughts on the Sewel Convention, 2003 SLT News 194; *CSG Inquiry* and SP OR 11 June 2002, col 1620.

10 Page and Batey, p 503.

11 See for example K MacAskill and M Curran, 'Is Holyrood passing the buck' 2005 JLSS 50(3) 20.

12 Seven bills enacted by the Scottish Parliament compared with ten legislative consent motions to enable Westminster to legislate.

13 See p 191. Note also the use of SA 1998, s 57(1) to implement Community obligations. See p 178.

14 Not so far done, except by the alternative route of an Order in Council under SA 1998, s 30(2).

15 See the Learning and Skills Act 2000, s 104 and the Electronic Communications Act 2000, ss 8–9.

16 See n 9 above.

17 Including, for instance, scrutiny of delegated powers which would normally be undertaken by the Subordinate Legislation Committee at Holyrood.

SUBORDINATE LEGISLATION MADE BY MINISTERS AND OTHERS

General considerations

5.23   It has been a well-known feature of law-making at the UK level that far more legislation is made each year by ministers than by Parliament. In purely quantitative terms, ministers[1] (mainly as 'the Secretary of State') make many more rules, regulations, schemes, orders and other forms of subordinate legislation – a great range of terminology is used – than is made by Parliament as Acts of Parliament. Some powers are formally exercisable by 'Her Majesty by Order in Council' but effective power lies, of course, with ministers[2]. In 2008, the number of statutory instruments, which include almost all subordinate legislation made by UK ministers, was about 3,000; the number of Public Acts of the Westminster Parliament, was 33. Ministers make virtually all subordinate legislation under powers delegated to them (hence 'delegated legislation') by Parliament, although, in a very small number of cases, the authority derives from the royal prerogative[3]. It is, of course, fundamental to the idea of the rule of law that there should be such a primary source of authority for any rule-making power of ministers and it would be considered intolerable if ministers were to purport to make rules or regulations, other than in the exercise of powers conferred upon them. This was an abuse ended when completely discretionary law-making powers were wrested from the Crown and its ministers in the seventeenth century[4]. Today, the courts take a strict view of ministers who purport to exercise powers they do not have[5]. On the other hand, the courts cannot question the authority of Parliament to delegate law making powers to ministers if it chooses to do so. Under the terms of a written constitution, a legislature may be constrained in the powers it delegates[6] but the 'supreme' Westminster Parliament is not.

The question has still to be asked why the Westminster Parliament, even with the authority to do so, chooses to give legislative powers to ministers to produce delegated legislation on the scale already indicated. Why should Parliament wish to appear to breach the principle of the separation of powers by conferring legislative powers on the executive to such an extent? In part, the answer is technical in that what is formally promulgated as delegated *legislation* is frequently no more than a series of executive decisions. Each year until 1999, ministers[7] made a Local Government Finance (Scotland) Order[8] which allocated an amount of grant to each local authority in Scotland. This was really executive decision-making but it took the form of delegated *legislation*.

In most other cases, however, subordinate legislation is more clearly *legislative* in character. Ministers are entrusted with powers to make rules and this requires some justification. The official explanation has remained broadly the same since the early part of the twentieth century and dates back to the Report of the Committee on Ministers' Powers in 1932[9]. In the period following the 1914–18 war, there developed a panic about what was perceived to be the rapid and uncontrolled expansion of executive power. Lord Hewart, the Lord Chief Justice of England, published his polemic *The New Despotism* in 1929 and the (Donoughmore) Committee on Ministers' Powers was set up in response. While making a number of proposals for the reform of governmental procedures, the Committee did acknowledge that executive power was not simply going to go away. The process of delegated law-making could be better structured and ministers could be made more accountable to Parliament but the case for extensive powers of delegated legislation had to be recognised. Central to that case was the argument that Parliament had no alternative but to delegate. The sheer quantity of the legislation required would be unmanageable if it had to be treated as primary legislation and taken as Bills through all their parliamentary stages. There would simply not be sufficient time. As we shall find[10], some delegated legislation does attract the need for limited parliamentary supervision but this is much less than would be required if it all made its way through Parliament as Bills. Other justifications which were offered by the Ministers' Powers Committee for bypassing full parliamentary scrutiny included the technicality of the subject matter of much delegated legislation, which made it less appropriate for discussion by parliamentarians and the need for flexibility. It is impossible for any government, when introducing primary legislation, to tie up every detailed aspect of its operation for all time. Occasions will arise when further changes to the law will be required to alter rules in response to events; to alter the terms of earlier legislation which may affect the operation of the new rules in unexpected ways; and to alter the pace of introduction of the new rules. One way in which this is done is by making the operation of most primary legislation dependent upon the making of commencement orders by ministers to bring them into effect, often in a number of separate stages according to a timetable which can be adopted and amended, as required, after the primary legislation itself has been passed. A special need for flexibility justifies the conferring of particularly wide powers on ministers in times of emergency. Parliamentary procedures do permit the accelerated passage of Bills and this is sufficient to meet the needs of some forms of emergency situation[11] but more aggravated civil emergencies may demand a response which is even more rapid. This is an area which has seen significant legislative activity recently. The Emergency Powers Act 1920[12] which empowered the Queen to make a *proclamation of emergency* when, or when it is anticipated that, 'events of such a nature as to be calculated, by interfering with the supply and distribution of food, water, fuel, or light, or with the means of locomotion, to deprive the community, or any substantial portion of the community, of the essentials of life'[13] has been replaced with the Civil Contingencies Act 2004 which imposes duties and confers powers to deal with events or situations which threaten serious damage to 'human welfare in a place in the United Kingdom', 'the environment of a place in the United Kingdom' or 'war or terrorism which threatens serious damage to the security of the United Kingdom[14].

Despite the substantially changed circumstances of British government in the 70 years or so since the 1932 Report, broadly the same justifications for the use of delegated legislation tend to be offered today. One consequence of this has been that, when the Scottish Parliament was proposed and thought given to how its business would be done[15], the assumption was made that the delegation of law-making powers to the Scottish Ministers would be a necessary part of the package[16]. Certainly, no doubts were ever expressed that the general legislative competence of the Parliament included the power to delegate to ministers, although there was discussion of the use to which the powers might be put[17].

This continued acceptance of the case for subordinate legislation at both the UK and Scottish levels does not mean, however, that some of the explanations for the need for ministerial law-making power should not be looked at quite sceptically. Ministers will always tend to be attracted by this relatively uncontrolled power and the Westminster Parliament and the Scottish Parliament have shown themselves to be alert to some of the dangers. The sheer quantity of delegated legislation is a principal concern while powers given to ministers to amend primary legislation cause a particular constitutional frisson. Such powers have been dubbed 'Henry VIII clauses' at Westminster because of the potential threat they present, but they vary greatly in significance. At one end of the scale they are a necessary and merely technical adjunct to major new primary legislation. Powers to make delegated legislation are required to enable ministers to amend existing statutes to allow full effect to be given to the new provisions. At the other end of the scale are the very substantial powers which were conferred by, for instance, the Deregulation and Contracting Out Act 1994 and the Convention Rights (Compliance) (Scotland) Act 2001[18].

Another area of sensitivity is the delegation of powers which might release direct parliamentary control of financial matters. There has been a reluctance to delegate powers to vary rates of taxation and, at Holyrood, the power of the

Scottish Ministers to authorise appropriations under the Public Finance and Accountability (Scotland) Act 2000 by Budget Acts raised rather similar concerns[19]. It was eventually accepted that, once initial appropriations had been made in the annual Budget (Scotland) Act, variations could be made by order by the Scottish Ministers. Other concerns can arise in relation to the use of subordinate legislation with retrospective effect or in such a way as to exclude review by the courts.

Another principal concern at Westminster and Holyrood has been the tendency for primary legislation to delegate to ministers not only matters of detail but also matters of core legislative provision. The Scottish Parliament's Education (Graduate Endowments and Student Support) (Scotland) Act 2001 made provision, in one section, for the endowment scheme itself and left all else to regulations to be made by the Scottish Ministers. SA 1998 itself provides several examples of potentially wide-ranging law making powers delegated to ministers which might, on their face, by vulnerable to abuse. The power in SA 1998, s 30(2) to amend, by Order in Council, the terms of Schs 4 and 5[20] avoids the need for primary legislation but gives substantial power to UK ministers. The powers contained in SA 1998, ss 63 and 108 to transfer executive functions from UK ministers to the Scottish Ministers and vice versa[21] are also significant; and the power in SA 1998, s 107 'to remedy ultra vires acts' of the Scottish Parliament or the Scottish Executive is another[22]. These and many others are listed in SA 1998, Sch 7 but what is also important about the Schedule is that it prescribes the model of parliamentary scrutiny (mainly at Westminster but, in some cases, also at Holyrood) for each class of instrument. It is this parliamentary accountability, discussed in Chapter 8, and also the legal accountability (Chapter 13) of delegated law-making which lift much of the constitutional concern which would otherwise attach to the allocation of broad powers to ministers.

1   For executive powers in general, see ch 6.
2   The number of *devolved* powers exercisable by Order in Council is not large but, for instance, the Census (Scotland) Order 2000, SSI 2000/68 is an example. New powers to legislate by Order in Council conferred by ASPs have, again, not been numerous but the power in the Scottish Public Services Ombudsman Act 2002, s 3 to amend the Ombudsman's jurisdiction is an example.
3   As explained on p 183, one continuing prerogative legislative power is that used to regulate the civil service, currently the Civil Service Order in Council 1995. It was an instruction made under the Civil Service Order in Council that was unsuccessfully challenged in *CCSU v Minister for the Civil Service* [1985] AC 374.
4   See Claim of Right 1689.
5   See ch 13 below.
6   In the United States, see inter alia *Schechter Poultry Corp v United States* 295 US 495 (1935).
7   From 2000, the Scottish Ministers: see below.
8   See Local Government Finance (Scotland) Order 1999, SI 1999/364.
9   *Report of the Committee on Ministers' Powers* (Cmd 4060).
10 See ch 8.
11 See, for example, the Mental Health (Public Safety and Appeals) (Scotland) Act 1999 and p 231.
12 As amended by the Emergency Powers Act 1964.
13 EPA 1920, s 1.
14 Civil Contingencies Act 2004, s1.
15 As earlier explained it can be argued that all ASPs are themselves subordinate legislation of a

sort. HRA 1998, for its purposes, does so classify them and ASPs are judicially challengeable, although on grounds different from rules made by ministers (see ch 14). For present purposes, ASPs are better regarded as primary legislation.

16 See the *Report of the Consultative Steering Group on the Scottish Parliament* (1998), paras 27–33.
17 See C Himsworth 'Subordinate Legislation in the Scottish Parliament' (2002) 6 Edin LR 356.
18 And see Part 2 of the Public Services Reform (Scotland) Bill introduced in the Scottish Parliament on 28 May 2009.
19 See SP SL or SP Paper 69 (2000).
20 See p 129.
21 See p 178.
22 See p 189.

Delegated law-making powers in Scotland

5.24   The implementation of SA 1998 creates a situation in which there are now four different categories of ministerial subordinate legislation in relation to Scotland:

(a)   *Subordinate legislation made by Ministers of the Crown* (including legislation made as Orders in Council) in relation to reserved matters. Existing powers of UK ministers continue in relation, for instance, to social security.

(b)   *Subordinate legislation by the Scottish Ministers under powers conferred by Acts of the Scottish Parliament.* Many such ASPs have been passed. There is no doubt about the formal competence of the Parliament to delegate law-making powers to the Scottish Ministers and to others, provided, of course, that the powers would, in other respects, be within the Parliament's legislative competence. It is not competent for the Parliament to purport to enable others to legislate on matters on which the Parliament itself could not legislate[1]. It might further be speculated that an ASP which was itself skeletal but which conferred extremely wide powers on ministers might be challengeable – in a way that a Westminster Act would not – on the ground that the Parliament was failing to perform the duty to 'make laws' laid down by SA 1998, s 28(1).

(c)   *Subordinate legislation under powers transferred from UK ministers to the Scottish Ministers under SA 1998.* Many of the powers exercisable by the Scottish Ministers are not powers conferred directly by the Scottish Parliament but are the powers transferred, within 'devolved competence', from UK ministers under SA 1998, ss 53–54[2] and also those transferred, as additional Executive powers, under SA 1998, s 63. This pattern extends to powers of delegated law-making (including legislation by Order in Council), most of which has so far been made under the transferred powers. These include the power, under ECA 1972, s 2(2)[3] to implement Community law in Scotland[4]. The very first Scottish Statutory Instrument – the Environmental Impact Assessment (Scotland) Regulations 1999, SSI 1999/1 – was such a measure.

There is no general power retained by UK ministers to exercise law-making functions in the areas transferred to the Scottish Ministers (and, therefore, no scope for a general equivalent of the Sewel convention[5] to govern when that retained power might be exercised) but it should be recalled that certain specified powers[6], including some powers of delegated law-making, are *shared* powers which may be exercised by ministers at both levels. A special instance of shared power is that conferred on UK ministers, as well as the Scottish Ministers, by SA 1998, s 57(1) to implement Community obligations. Instances of the agreed use of this power by UK ministers – for instance because the impact of an instrument would be minor and technical, or because there is no particularly Scottish interest in it – are routinely reported to the European and External Relations Committee of the Scottish Parliament.

(d)   A final category of ministerial subordinate legislation includes *powers conferred directly on the Scottish Ministers by post-devolution Acts of the Westminster Parliament.* Examples include the powers conferred by the Energy Act 2008, s34[7], enabling the Scottish Ministers to transfer functions relating to the licensing of carbon capture and storage schemes to another body (e.g. SEPA). Although the most important powers to make delegated legislation (both in constitutional and purely quantitative terms) are those exercisable by ministers, other public bodies enjoy *byelaw-making powers* to enable them to carry out their functions. Scottish local authorities have general powers (subject to confirmation by the Scottish Ministers) to make byelaws under the Local Government (Scotland) Act 1973, s 201 for the 'good rule and government' of their areas and for the 'prevention and suppression of nuisances' and they have certain, more specific, powers under the Civic Government (Scotland) Act 1982[8]. The national park authorities have powers to make byelaws and management rules[9] and bodies such as rail operators[10] also have byelaw-making powers.

1   That is a consequence expressly prohibited by, for example, SA 1998, ss 29, 54.
2   Most such powers are contained in 'pre-commencement enactments', a category which may be extended to include powers in post-devolution UK Acts which expressly declare themselves to be such 'pre-commencement enactments'. See, for example, Pollution Prevention and Control Act 1999, s 5(3).
3   See SA 1998, Sch 8, para 15 which amends ECA 1972 for this purpose. Although the generally implied assumption in SA 1998 that any Orders in Council in devolved areas would be made on the advice of Scottish (rather than UK) ministers, para 15 does make specific reference to Orders 'made on the recommendation of the First Minister'.
4   See p 49.
5   See p 141.
6   SA 1998, s 56(1), (2).
7   Such powers are to be distinguished from those transferred under 'pre-commencement enactments'. See n 2 above.
8   SA 1998, ss 112–118 (management rules), s 121 (byelaws to control seashore).
9   National Parks (Scotland) Act 2000, sch 2, paras 8–10.
10 Railways Act 2005, s 46 and Sch 9.

THE EUROPEAN UNION

5.25   The impact of the European Union upon law-making in the United Kingdom has already been noted in earlier sections of this chapter. EC law has successfully asserted superiority over Acts of the UK Parliament[1] and, as a result, the most fundamental rule of the constitution has been changed. It is also clear that all legislation made by the Scottish Parliament and by the Scottish Ministers is subordinate to Community law but that Acts of either Parliament or delegated legislation by UK ministers or the Scottish Ministers under ECA 1972 are used to implement Community rules. The superior status of Community law should not, however, lead us to conclude that the Community can issue legislation on any subject whatever. The Community's law-making competence is bounded by the terms of the EC Treaty[2] and the tasks of the European Court of Justice include ruling not only on the compatibility of national law with Community law but also on the compatibility of Community legislation with the Treaty.

The treaties allocate powers to the Community in both fairly specific and more general terms[3]. A limited number of competences are exclusive to the Community. Others are competences shared between the Community and the Member States. Among the exclusive competences are powers in relation to the common commercial policy (towards third countries), the customs union, and some aspects (marine biological resources) of the common fisheries policy. Shared competences include those in relation to the internal market, agriculture and fisheries, transport, energy, social policy, the environment and consumer protection[4]. These are supplemented by a clause which enables the Council to take 'appropriate measures' to attain the objectives of the Community for which no specific power has been provided by the treaties[5]. Additionally, the Union's powers extend to the competences in relation to the common foreign and security policy[6].

1 See pp 114–117.
2 See p 41.
3 For discussion, see S Douglas-Scott *Constitutional Law of the European Union* (2002) ch 4.
4 A restated list of these competences appears in the Treaty on the Functioning of the European Union (TFEU), by which name the EC Treaty will be known provided the Lisbon Treaty (2007 OJ C306/1) is eventually ratified by all Member States: TFEU Art 4.
5 EC Treaty, Art 308 (TFEU Art 352) and for discussion see 29th Report of 2006–07 of the House of Commons European Scrutiny Committee, HC 41.
6 See p 42 above and TFEU Art 2.

Chapter 6

The UK and Scottish Governments

INTRODUCTION[1]

6.1   The Scottish campaign for devolution was primarily a campaign for a Scottish Parliament. Although the language was that of 'self-*government*', the principal focus was on establishing an elected assembly or Parliament. Politically, that was what would make a difference. A Parliament is a powerful symbol and, if given sufficient law-making competence, could bring real change. But Parliaments, contrary to some generally held beliefs, do not govern. Parliaments do not, on the whole, have policies or programmes – although they may have some power to influence or control those who do. Parliaments do not themselves even implement policies and programmes. They do not, in the main, make decisions directly affecting the lives of individuals – although they may make the laws which provide the framework within which such decisions are made. Parliaments do not spend money – although, once again, they may give the authority to spend to those who do.

Those who make and implement policies; who make decisions; and who spend money are the holders of the executive powers of the state. The importance of these functions and, therefore, of the executive branch is self-evident and it is perhaps surprising that, in the run-up to constitutional reform in Scotland, the emphasis was so strongly upon the new Parliament rather than upon the new institutions of executive government that would also have to be created. In part, this is to be explained by the commitment simply to replicate for Scotland the model of parliamentary government already operating at the United Kingdom level rather than to create an executive on a presidential model with a much sharper differentiation of institutions and a stronger commitment to the separation of powers. Had a presidential model been sought, much more attention would have been paid to procedures for the election of a Scottish president, the powers of that president and the president's relationship to the Parliament. The adoption instead of a parliamentary model of government meant that the institutions required could be taken, with necessary modifications, from the Westminster peg. This is, on the other hand, no reason for belittling the significance of the executive branch of government on the parliamentary or Westminster model. Despite the absence of the formal prominence which would be given to a president, it is often the case that a government on the parliamentary model has greater overall power. In the relationship between government and Parliament, the balance tends to tip in favour of the government. Constitutional formalities apart, the principal driving force lies in the executive branch. An account of parliamentary government is one in which the executive is viewed as central, with Parliament as a, sometimes supporting and sometimes restraining, secondary force.[2]

151

The subject matter of this chapter is, in brief, the executive at the United Kingdom level and then, more substantially, the executive in Scotland. The principal focus is, therefore, upon the teams of ministers and supporting civil servants headed by the UK Prime Minister and the Scottish First Minister. However, this focus has, to be qualified in two ways. In the first place, it has to be recognised that at neither the UK nor the Scottish level is all executive authority concentrated at the centre. Much executive power is dispersed to other bodies. Local authorities have extensive executive authority within their localities. Their responsibilities for matters such as school provision and social work are directly conferred on them by statute. The provision of police services is an important executive function and is one in which local authorities have a role but where ministers have a strong supervisory function and most decision-making is in the hands of local chief constables[3]. In addition, a large number of executive functions are distributed at an 'intermediate level' (ie between central and local government) to public bodies – frequently dubbed 'quangos'. Some of these, such as health authorities, have local responsibilities. Others have a national remit. Traditionally, the primary distinction between local authorities and quangos is that members of local councils are elected while members of the governing boards of quangos are appointed. That distinction remains in most cases, although it has been blurred a little recently by the passing of the Heath Boards (Membership and Elections) (Scotland) Act 2009 which provides for the election of some members of health boards. Both local authorities and quangos are dealt with in Chapter 7.

The other qualification to an account of executive authority which places the primary focus upon ministers and their civil servants is that the constitution continues to accord functions to the Sovereign (or to the 'Crown'). This may seem to be a strange way to introduce a person and institution whose formal role is often described as the head of state and the fount of executive authority. It was, however, the nineteenth-century commentator Walter Bagehot who, in 1867, provided us with a useful distinction in our analysis of the constitution which is nowhere better illustrated than in relation to the Queen. That was the distinction between the 'efficient' and, on the other hand, the merely 'dignified' aspects of the constitution[4]. The efficient aspects are those which are based on the actual working of the constitution. They reflect actual power and authority. The dignified aspects, on the other hand, are those which have a purely formal character in the modern constitution. Typically, they derive from historically founded constitutional relationships which were once real and efficient but have long since ceased to be so. The functions of the Queen may be described today as almost entirely dignified rather than efficient but no account can completely ignore the limited efficient aspects. Nor can one ignore the contested nature of the account at some points. There is some debate about what the working rules of the constitution actually are. There is also debate about what they *should* be. Some would argue strongly for a greater reduction of the real power and authority of the Queen and, in some cases, ultimately in the direction of a republic. Others would argue for a retention and even expansion of monarchical power, as a check on the power of politicians.

At all events, it is necessary in this account of executive government in the United Kingdom and in Scotland to start with some remarks on the role of the monarch. Thus comments on the Queen and the UK government (pp 153–155) precede observations on the UK government itself (pp 155–165) and on the Queen and the Scottish Government (pp 166–167) precede the Scottish Executive itself. Pages 176–182 deal with sources of executive power and pp 182–188 with government departments including, in particular, the Scottish Administration. Pages 188–193 address relations between Whitehall (the London home of much of the UK government) and St Andrew's House (the building in Edinburgh where the Scottish Government has its principal building[5]).

1 Terminological difficulties arise immediately and should be acknowledged. SA1998 recognises and defines both the 'Scottish Executive' (see p 167) and 'Scottish Administration' (p 187) but not 'Scottish Government'. During the first two terms of the Scottish Parliament, the governing coalition was known in Scotland and elsewhere, colloquially, as 'the Executive'. When the SNP took office in 2007 it styled itself – to the consternation of some – as the Scottish Government. Stationery, websites and official documents have been re-branded accordingly. We use both Scottish Executive and Scottish Government in this book, using one or other as we consider appropriate in the particular context. Needless to say, any particular usage is not to be read as indicating any particular political predisposition.
2 The centrality of the executive is well recognised and explored in T Daintith and A Page, *The Executive in the Constitution* (1999).
3 Police (Scotland) Act 1967, as amended by the Criminal Justice (Scotland) Act 2003. See also Chapter 12.
4 W Bagehot, *The English Constitution* (1963) p 61.
5 The term 'St Andrew's House' is, for this reason, generally adopted in this book, although 'Victoria Quay' (Leith) does have a competing claim to provide the name for the Government's (or Administration's) home.

THE QUEEN AND THE UK GOVERNMENT

6.2   It has been mentioned that discussion of the role of the monarch is complicated by the effect of history largely to 'hollow out' that role in such a way as to remove from it virtually all effective constitutional authority. In broad terms, rules relating to the monarch may be divided into three categories[1]:

In the first place, certain 'efficient' rules define who shall be king or queen. The Act of Settlement 1700 and the Acts of Union 1707 confirmed the line of succession to the House of Hanover and thence, eventually, to the House of Windsor and Queen Elizabeth II. The right to succeed is barred to Roman Catholics and to those married to Roman Catholics – a rule which has been the cause of some debate over the last decade[2]. Funding of the monarchy is split between sums charged directly to the Consolidated Fund[3] and sums voted annually by Parliament[4]. Similarly efficient rules include the Queen as part of the United Kingdom (but not the Scottish) Parliament and, in both Parliaments, require her assent to legislation: an Act of either Parliament is not valid without that assent. In law, ministers are appointed by the Queen. Efficient rules also define the composition of the Privy Council and prescribe the requirement that certain measures be formally made or agreed by the Council[5].

Secondly, however, a long list of powers formally vested in the monarch are best described as merely dignified because the substantive power to decide is, for all efficient purposes, transferred elsewhere. Thus, while the Queen's assent to Bills passed by the Houses of Parliament *is* required before they become law as Acts of Parliament, the Queen must not withhold that assent[6].

The Queen makes virtually no contribution to the appointment or dismissal of ministers, beyond a formal involvement. The Queen must approve measures placed before the Privy Council. And the same applies to virtually all other powers vested by statute in the Queen. The Queen plays no 'efficient' part in the appointment of judges[7], the Parliamentary Ombudsman or the Scottish Public Services Ombudsman[8]. The Queen cannot, at her own hand, dismiss ministers even though they 'hold office at Her Majesty's pleasure'.

Similarly, the Queen does not, in an 'efficient' way, exercise any of the great range of powers vested in her not by statute but by virtue of what is called the royal prerogative[9]. Formally the Queen makes war and peace, conducts relations with foreign countries, and regulates the civil service. Such powers are mostly ancient in origin and are the survivors, often heavily modified and circumscribed by statute[10], of a much longer list of genuinely monarchical powers. Even the survivors, however, are only in a dignified sense powers of the Queen. Like the statutory powers, prerogative powers have, by convention, become a part of the efficient powers of ministers. Ministers are the ones who make the choices and the decisions for which they subsequently take responsibility. A web-based document issued by the Scottish Executive has referred to some public appointments being made 'by the Queen on behalf of Ministers', which captures nicely both the formal primacy but also the practical subordination of the Queen's position.

One constitutional consequence of the elision of the functions of ministers and monarch (whether involving total transfer of functions – statutory or prerogative – to ministers or the Queen acting wholly on ministerial advice), and also of the vagaries of language and conceptual imprecision over time, has been the emergence of the concept of the 'Crown'[11]. Sometimes a term used to refer simply to the person of the sovereign, sometimes to the sovereign as an institution of government and sometimes to the entire collectivity of sovereign and ministers (of the Crown), the concept of the 'Crown' has been useful in defining a distinct governmental entity for legal purposes – although an entity which is divisible between the tiers of government, hence the acknowledgment by the Scotland Act 1998 (SA 1998) of both 'the Crown in right of Her Majesty's Government in the United Kingdom' and also 'the Crown in right of the Scottish Administration'[12]. Confusion has arisen over the extent to which immunities from legal proceedings possessed by the sovereign personally[13] extend also to ministers[14] and what remedies may be available against the Crown in legal proceedings[15].

Thirdly, in a few very limited respects, however, the general transfer of effective power to ministers has to be qualified. The Queen does, we believe, retain a personal power of decision-making in relation to members of the royal household and certain honours such as appointments to the Orders of the Garter and the Thistle and the Order of Merit. Of greater constitutional significance, it is arguable that the Queen retains a residual power of choice of a new Prime Minister which might become exercisable in the conditions of a hung Parliament[16]. On the same basis, it is thought by some that the Queen retains a power to refuse a Prime Minister's request to dissolve Parliament or even a power to dissolve Parliament herself[17]. In addition, it was declared by Bagehot that the Queen had the right to 'be consulted, the right to encourage and the right to warn' her government[18]. Although that position has not since been seriously contradicted, it probably amounts to something of an overstatement of the Queen's power in the twenty-first century.

1 Many other models of analysis are, however, possible. See eg R Brazier 'Constitutional Reform and the Crown' in M Sunkin and S Payne (eds) *The Nature of the Crown* (1999) (Sunkin and Payne).

2 See eg SP OR, 16 December 1999, col 1633 and the raising of the issue by Alex Salmond MP at Prime Minister's Questions in 2006 (HC Debs, 28 June 2006, Col 259) Prime Minster Brown was reported to be in discussions with the Queen in March 2009 in relation to possible reform.

3 See ch 10.

4 Civil List Acts 1952, 1972 and 1975.

5 For the Order in Council as delegated legislation, see pp 143 and 247.

6 See p 222.

7 Ch 11.

8 Ch 9.

9 In March 2004, the Public Administration Select Committee of the House of Commons published its report 'Taming the Prerogative: Strengthening Ministerial Accountability to Parliament (HC 422, 16 March 2004) in which it examined the range of prerogative powers exercised by ministers and recommended legislation first to list, and thereafter to put in place safeguards to apply to the use of, those powers. The Governance of Britain Green Paper (Cm 7170, 2007) proposed a number of reforms relating to the use of prerogative powers by ministers, including in some cases placing those powers on a statutory footing and in others giving Parliament a more formal role (for example in relation to decisions to deploy the armed forces). The 2009 draft Constitutional Renewal Bill (Cm 7342, 2009) included provisions relating only to the ratification of treaties and not to the other prerogative powers discussed by the Select Committee and in the Green Paper. See too the Constitutional Reform and Governance Bill 2009.

10 *A-G v De Keyser's Royal Hotel Ltd* [1920] AC 508.

11 For constructive criticism of the treatment of this subject in the first edition of this book, and for more detailed discussion than space here permits, see A Tomkins, The Crown in Scots Law in A McHarg and T Mullen (eds), *Public Law in Scotland* (2006). See also Sunkin and Payne.

12 See A Twomey, 'Responsible Government and the Divisibility of the Crown' [2008] PL 742 and its discussion of *R (Quark Fishing Limited) v Secretary of State for Foreign and Commonwealth Affairs* (No 2) [2006] 1 AC 529.

13 Even these deserve critical scrutiny. See D Pannick [2003] PL 201.

14 *M v Home Office* [1994] 1 AC 377.

15 See *Davidson v Scottish Ministers* 2002 SC 205, *Beggs v Scottish Ministers* 2007 SLT 235.

16 See p 159.

17 See p 159.

18 *The English Constitution* p 111.

THE UK GOVERNMENT

6.3   Turning now from the almost entirely 'dignified' to the 'efficient', the essence of parliamentary government on the Westminster model is to be found in an executive consisting of a team of ministers, headed by the Prime Minister and drawn from the party (or occasionally parties) which has secured political domination of the House of Commons. The most senior ministers are appointed as Secretaries of State[1] and junior ministers are styled Ministers of State and Parliamentary Under-Secretaries. Governmental powers are mainly vested (principally by statute but also by virtue of the royal prerogative) in the Secretaries of State and are exercisable by them and the junior ministers allocated to their departments. Certain powers and responsibilities are also vested directly in the Prime Minister[2]. The separateness of the exercise of these powers is, however, heavily modified in practice by a collectiveness of governmental activity imposed upon senior ministers by their membership of the Cabinet; by a wider notion of political and perhaps constitutional collective responsibility which touches all ministers; and then by the control exercised by the Prime Minister over the entire government. Governmental activity at ministerial level is assisted and implemented by the civil service distributed between departments and executive agencies[3].

What follows is a short summary of the current practice of government formation at the United Kingdom level. In many respects, this is an account of a system which has, in its most important aspects, remained reasonably stable for over a century. It should, however, be borne in mind that many of the current rules and practices are heavily dependent upon wider constitutional and political conditions. In particular, they depend upon the rules which govern the composition of Parliament – including the composition of the House of Lords and the system of elections to the Commons – and the relationship, expressed in terms of both control and accountability, between government and Parliament. Changes in these areas would undoubtedly produce consequential change for the composition, powers and operation of the executive itself.

1 And occasionally there may be a 'First Secretary of State', the title being honorific and denoting the political weight carried by its holder. Lord Mandelson (see below) was created First Secretary of State on 5 June 2009.
2 See eg the Prime Minister's power under SA 1998, s 95 to recommend the appointment of Scotland's two most senior judges.
3 See below.

The Prime Minister

6.4   The position of Prime Minister is central to the functioning of British government. Constitutionally and politically, the Prime Minister is head of government. Prime Ministers have powers of appointment, patronage and leadership in government which place them head and shoulders above their political colleagues. However, this is a position which is achieved more by the operation of politics and constitutional practice than as a result of specific legal rules. Indeed, the office and powers of the Prime Minister receive only very sketchy recognition from the law. Legal provision is made for pay, pension[1] and house in the country[2] and certain of the Prime Minister's powers of appointment are specified in statute but these are marginal considerations. The prominence of the Prime Minister derives much more from his or her political profile as leader of the majority party; the power to hire and fire fellow ministers; and his or her presence in Parliament, the country, in the European Union and abroad.

1 Ministerial and Other Salaries Act 1975 (as amended by the Ministerial and Other Salaries Act 1997).
2 Chequers Estate Act 1917.

Appointment of the Prime Minister

6.5   A new Prime Minister is needed whenever the post falls vacant. The circumstances in which a vacancy may occur vary widely but they may be broadly grouped under two heads: (a) circumstances where the majority political party (or coalition) retains its support in and control of the House of Commons but the Prime Minister dies or resigns on grounds of illness or other personal or political reasons (Churchill (1955), Eden (1957), Macmillan (1963) Wilson (1976) and Blair (2007)) or because of loss of support of or dismissal by the ruling party (Thatcher (1990)). The party continues in control but the leader has to be replaced.

On the other hand, (b) following the dissolution of Parliament and loss of the ensuing general election. These events may occur in a range of situations but all will be triggered by the Prime Minister's decision to request of the Queen a dissolution of Parliament[1]. All Parliaments are, in practice, terminated by prime ministerial request and none runs to its full term of five years. However, such requests for a dissolution and election again fall into two groups.

One is where the Prime Minister's hand is forced by severely adverse conditions in the House of Commons, for example where the government loses a vote of no confidence or, on some other issue treated as a matter of confidence, the Prime Minister must seek a dissolution and general election, as Mr Callaghan did in 1979. There would be the alternative possibility of the Prime Minister's tendering the resignation of his or her government instead of seeking a dissolution of Parliament, but that is an option not pursued since the 1939–45 war[2].

Secondly, the Prime Minister, although not forced to do so, may seek a dissolution for tactical reasons usually associated with his or her assessment of the prospects of success in an early election and, therefore, a continuation in office thereafter. Such a dissolution may occur relatively early in a Parliament (Wilson 1966 and 1974) or, more often, as the end of the five-year term draws nearer and the Prime Minister, sometimes by this time under a degree of pressure, makes a choice of when best to seek a renewal of the government's mandate (Douglas Home (1964), Wilson (1970), Heath (1974), Thatcher (1983) and (1987), Major (1992) and (1997) and Blair (2001) and (2005)). In all these situations of a dissolution and election, it is the outcome of the election which decides whether a prime ministerial resignation and replacement are necessary. Until the result is known, the Prime Minister and the government as a whole remain in office and, if their party wins the election, they continue to do so. There is at no stage a vacancy in the office of Prime Minister and the incumbent continues (Wilson (1966), Thatcher and Blair (both twice)). If, however, the incumbent Prime Minister loses the election, his or her position becomes politically and constitutionally untenable and resignation must follow (Douglas Home (1964), Wilson (1970), Heath (1974), Callaghan (1979) and Major (1997)). A rule, derived from recent practice and which is expressed in terms of 'winning' and 'losing' elections, works clearly where election outcomes are, themselves, clear but might, of course, present difficulties where the outcome is a more finely balanced House of Commons. In the last half-century, the only problematic outcome, in this respect, was when, in 1974, Mr Heath lost his own overall Conservative majority but Labour too had failed to win overall. It was not considered constitutionally improper, in those circumstances, for Heath briefly to explore the prospect of securing an arrangement for support by the Liberals before, on failing to secure that support, offering his resignation. Indeed, such suspension of decision-making might reasonably be carried forward, if necessary, to a testing of the Prime Minister's continuing support at an early meeting of the new Parliament. It is likely that such problematic election outcomes and, therefore, uncertainties as to the obligations of Prime Ministers to resign would increase if British politics ceased to be a mainly two-party affair and a third significant party or group of parties emerged – whether or not consequential upon the adoption of a system of proportional representation.

Such uncertainties aside, however, this account of the circumstances which produce a vacancy in the office of Prime Minister and the need for a successor are seen to be underpinned by two main principles. The first is that, purely personal conditions such as health apart, a Prime Minister's tenure is dependent upon political support in the House of Commons and the second that, although as a matter of law the Queen has the power to appoint and dismiss her ministers including the Prime Minister, that power is wholly subordinated to the party political imperative and must be exercised in deference to it. Short of the sort of crisis unknown in the working of the modern constitution, there is no room for an independent discretionary power to dismiss her Prime Minister.

The same principles are carried forward into the appointment process itself. The formal appointment of a Prime Minister occurs when he or she receives the Queen's warrant but the rules which propel the appointee into the Queen's presence are political. Thus, in the circumstances grouped under (a) above – ie conditions in which the ruling party remains in control but its leader has to be replaced, it is entirely for the internal electoral procedures of the party to produce the name of the successor[3]. Interim arrangements can be made. In circumstances (b), where a general election has produced the need to replace a defeated Prime Minister, the leader of the party now commanding an overall majority in the Commons must be invited by the Queen to be Prime Minister and to form a government. Questions similar to those raised above about the consequences of an election which produces uncertainty have provided much scope for debate among commentators despite, or perhaps because of, the absence of any such live instances. If the largest post-election party lacks an overall majority but appears able to secure the support of a smaller party, it seems clear (Wilson (1974)) that the leader of that largest party should be appointed as Prime Minister. Even in the absence of such a coalition or pact, it seems clear that the same person should be invited to form a government. If, after a shorter or longer period, that government is defeated on a significant issue in the House of Commons, the Prime Minister would be entitled to seek a further dissolution and election[4].

1 A request that cannot be refused by the Queen – see p 159 below.
2 Such resignations might become more frequent if the conditions for more coalition governments were created.
3 In the case of Prime Minister Brown, his succession to Mr Blair was the result of an unopposed candidature for leadership of the Labour Party in 2007.
4 J Rasmussen 'Constitutional Aspects of Government Formation in a Hung Parliament' (1987) 40 Parl Aff 139. See also S Kalitowski, 'Hung-up over Nothing? The Impact of a Hung Parliament in British Politics' (2008) 61 Parl Aff 396.

Prime Minister's functions

6.6   Once appointed, the Prime Minister has the following principal functions:

(a)   To form a government by the appointment of ministers, a process discussed below and one which the Prime Minister may have to repeat following decisions to dismiss or relocate ministers in subsequent 'reshuffles'.

(b)   To make many other public appointments responsibility for which, whether authorised by statute or in the exercise of the prerogative, is allocated to the Prime Minister.

(c)   To lead and co-ordinate the functions of government as a whole, including the chairmanship of the Cabinet and many of its committees[1].

(d)   To be the principal representative of the government in the House of Commons, the country, the European Union and abroad.

(e)   To lead his or her political party in Parliament and in the country and, in particular, to play a leading role in elections.

(f)   To determine the length of the Parliament (within the five-year maximum) in the exercise of the power to request from the Queen a dissolution.

1 See p 162.

The Cabinet and other ministers

6.7   Although all ministers are, like the Prime Minister, formally appointed by the Queen, and are formally dismissible by her, the choice of who should join and, in due course, be removed from the government is one for the Prime Minister. However, it is very much a constrained choice. The Prime Minister will be seeking the best team available: people who are politically able, who have the qualities necessary to present and defend policies in Parliament and in the country, people who will not be vulnerable to personal attack (perhaps on grounds of earlier misdeeds) or otherwise be damaging to the government as a whole. Politics dominates the choice and, with occasional exceptions to the rule, it is almost inevitable that ministers will be members or supporters of the governing party. Within that party[1], appointees are likely to be political allies and friends but with room for some former opponents, perhaps to forestall any opposition on the government's back benches. There may be a need for balance between left and right, 'pro-European' and 'Euro-sceptic', old and young, male and female, black and white, and between the nations and regions of the United Kingdom. There is also, however, an overriding constitutional constraint which insists that all ministers must be drawn from one or other House of Parliament[2]. This is what is meant by parliamentary government. Inevitably, most ministers will be MPs rather than peers because the House of Commons, despite proposals for the reform of the Lords (as to which see chapter 4), remains the constitutionally and politically dominant House and expectations of appointment are high among MPs who are members of the majority party. It would be unthinkable for the Chancellor of the Exchequer to be anywhere but the Commons, and although in recent years a number of other Secretaries of State have been drawn from the Lords that may still be regarded as an exception to the general rule.

As a consequence of the Constitutional Reform Act 2005 it is no longer essential that the Lord Chancellor be a member of the House of Lords[3] but it remains necessary for the conduct of the government's business in the House of Lords to have ministers located in that chamber. The Lords is, in any event, a source of party allies, often with previous government experience in the Commons. Another reason for drawing some ministers from the Lords is that there is a statutory numerical cap on numbers of ministers in receipt of a salary who may be members of the House of Commons. The House of Commons Disqualification Act 1975, s 2 currently restricts that number to 95[4] whereas recent governments have tended to consist of about 115 ministers. Ministers are allocated to their departmental portfolios by the Prime Minister and the distribution of posts can provide him or her with the opportunity to reorganise the departmental conduct of business[5].

Ministers hold office on an 'open-ended' basis and their period of office may be brought to an end by death; their removal by the Prime Minister, whether to move to another post or to leave the government altogether; or their resignation, which might be on grounds of health or other personal reasons, or in response to adverse political pressure, or a mixture of these. In some cases, resignation may be to forestall dismissal by the Prime Minister or may be the consequence of a strong Prime Ministerial suggestion. During their period of office, ministers discharge the functions deriving from either statute or the royal prerogative which are either directly conferred on them (although few modern statutes do identify a specific minister, with a preference instead for the generic formula 'Secretary of State'), or are, less formally, allocated to ministers, including junior ministers, by the Prime Minister. Thus, typically, executive powers (including powers to make subordinate legislation) relating to social security (eg the jobseeker's allowance or income support) are conferred by legislation on the 'Secretary of State'; they are, therefore, exercisable, by the Secretary of State for Work and Pensions but with many responsibilities delegated in practice to the relevant junior minister – for example, the Minister of State for Employment and Welfare Reform.

For their services, ministers are rewarded by salaries on a statutory scale[6]. There is, however, a category of ministerial assistants to whom no salary is paid. These are the parliamentary private secretaries who hold office under conditions prescribed by the *Ministerial Code*. As a form of trainee ministers, they are MPs who, in terms of the demands of political discipline, occupy a position half-way between that of minister and back-bencher. Their equivalent at Holyrood is the parliamentary liaison officer[7].

1 On his appointment as Prime Minister in 2007 Mr Brown referred to a desire to create a government of "all the talents" which would not be restricted to those who supported the government. Five ministers were appointed who were not members of the Labour Party: Admiral Sir Alan West (former First Sea Lord who became Parliamentary Under Secretary of State for security and counter terrorism); Professor Sir Ara Darzi (a practising surgeon who became Parliamentary Under-Secretary of State for Health); Shriti (now Baroness) Vadera (an investment banker appointed as Parliamentary Under Secretary of State in the Department for International Devel-

opment); Sir Digby Jones (former director general of the CBI appointed as Minister of State for trade and investment); and Sir Mark Malloch Brown (former UN deputy general secretary appointed Minister of State at the Foreign Office). Of the five appointees, four remain in the government. In addition, in June 2009, Prime Minister Brown announced his attention to include in the Cabinet – with a seat in the Lords – Sir Alan Sugar, a businessman and 'star' of the BBC television programme 'The Apprentice'.

2 But ministers remain in office after the dissolution of Parliament and a short-term absence from Parliament pending election to the Commons may be tolerated. A standing *exception* to the general rule prior to devolution was the Scottish Solicitor-General who was frequently a member of neither House. The usual means by which 'outsiders' are brought into the government is by conferring a life peerage on them: hence Peter Mandelson was created Baron Mandelson of Foy and Hartlepool in October 2008 to enable him to leave his post as EU Trade Commissioner to become Secretary of State for Business, Enterprise and Regulatory Reform.

3 The current incumbent is Jack Straw MP who is also Secretary of State for Justice.

4 This provision has its origins in the Act of Settlement 1700 which, if implemented, would have excluded all ministers.

5 For departments in general, see p 182 below.

6 Ministerial and Other Salaries Act 1975 (as amended by the Ministerial and Other Salaries Act 1997 which ties ministerial salaries to civil service salaries).

7 See p 172.

Law Officers of the Crown

6.8   In a special category as ministers are the three UK Law Officers: the Attorney-General, the Solicitor-General[1] and the Advocate General for Scotland. Although owing a political loyalty to the government, the Law Officers are obliged to adopt a more dispassionate stance in their roles of providing legal advice to government, representing the government in court and, in the case of the Attorney-General and the Solicitor-General, in their overarching responsibility in England and Wales for the independent Crown Prosecution Service, headed by the Director of Public Prosecutions[2]. The Advocate General for Scotland is a position created at the time of devolution in 1999 when the original Scottish Law Officers, the Lord Advocate and the Solicitor-General for Scotland, were transferred to the Scottish Executive[3]. The Advocate General advises the UK government on matters of Scots law and has special functions under SA 1998 in relation to 'devolution issues[4].

1 J LL C J Edwards *The Law Officers of the Crown* (1964); N Walker 'The Antinomies of the Law Officers' in Sunkin and Payne.

2 For discussion of recent difficulties to the giving of advice and in relation to prosecutions see The Governance of Britain: A Consultation on the Role of the Attorney General, Cm 7192 (2007). Non-legislative changes to the role of the Attorney General were announced in March 2008. Further changes were outlined in the government's draft Constitutional Renewal Bill.

3 See p 180.

4 See p 232. L Clarke 'The Role of the Advocate General for Scotland' in A Boyle et al (eds) *Human Rights and Scots Law*; 2002 SLT (News) 139.

Ministerial conduct

6.9   How ministers conducted themselves in office was once a matter simply for administrative regulation by the Prime Minister. An internal document, *Questions of Procedure for Ministers*, gave guidance on a number of managerial matters, including some which touched on ministerial behaviour.

The 1990s brought publication of the document as the *Ministerial Code* but also, with the creation in 1994 of the Committee on Standards in Public Life, a much higher profile for questions of conduct. The content of the *Code* has, from 1999, been substantially reproduced in the *Scottish Ministerial Code*, discussed below[1]. In so far as either Code requires enforcement, this remains a matter for the Prime Minister or First Minister, a perceived weakness in the system of enforcement which has led to criticism.

In response to these criticisms and in partial implementation of recommendations made by the (Wicks) Committee on Standards in Public Life Prime Minister Brown announced changes in July 2007[2] including the appointment of a new independent adviser who, at the Prime Minister's request, can investigate alleged breaches of the Code[3].

1 See p 174.
2 The Governance of Britain, Col 7170.
3 The first Independent Adviser on Ministers' interests is Sir Philip Mawer. His first annual report was published in March 2009. See also Chapter 4.

Cabinet government

6.10   An idea central to the concept of parliamentary government is its collective character. In contrast with, for example, the United States government in which executive power is constitutionally concentrated in the President and all other executive members have a deliberately subordinate role, the emphasis in the historical emergence of the parliamentary Westminster model has been on the executive's functioning as a collectivity. This is the yardstick against which modern governments are measured and, though they may be found to be wanting, it endures. The principal emblem of the collective nature of parliamentary government is the Cabinet. The Cabinet retains some of the functions of Bagehot's 'hyphen' – joining executive and Parliament – but has become even more strongly the 'board of control'[1], the executive committee of the government. Like other boards of directors and executive committees, its work may be sidelined to an extent by a strong chairman or chief executive in the form of the Prime Minister but its position at the centre remains important. All senior ministers (including the Secretary of State for Scotland and the other 'territorial' Secretaries of State) are members of the Cabinet which meets weekly at the centre of a network of Cabinet committees in which much of its work is done. Once protected by secrecy, the remits and membership of Cabinet committees (including, for instance, those responsible for the government's legislative programme) are now well publicised. The Cabinet is serviced by the Cabinet Office, headed by the Cabinet Secretary who is also the Head of the Home Civil Service.

A frequently asked question is whether the collective style of government is, in practice, maintained, and much depends here on political contingency, varying according to general political conditions and the temperament of the Prime Minister. The model of Cabinet government enables but does not guarantee collective decision-making. It also enables or, at least, does not prevent prime ministerial government. Three closely related factors will contribute to an assessment:

(a) the collective responsibility of ministers;
(b) the dominance or not of the Prime Minister;
(c) the relationship of ministers to Parliament and especially the relationship of accountability. This last aspect is something treated separately in Chapter 9 but the others may be addressed here.

1 *The English Constitution* pp 67–68.

Collective responsibility[1]

6.11   There are strong pressures within a system of parliamentary government for ministers, whether in the Cabinet or not, to act collectively. Sometimes these pressures are elevated by commentators to the status of a constitutional convention or doctrine of 'collective responsibility' but they derive almost entirely from political expediency. Ministers may enjoy separately conferred statutory powers. They may operate in separate departmental units for most policy-making and policy-implementing purposes. Ministers may have the distinctive status of MP or peer, or prestige within their party. Personally, they may have large egos and career ambitions which involve the displacement, if the opportunity presents, of their senior ministerial colleagues. And yet, it will almost always be advantageous to almost all members of a government to be collectively loyal to the team they have joined for the time being. This implies a degree of pooling of information and discussion prior to the making of important decisions[2]; the opportunity for that information and discussion – especially where it involves dissent on controversial matters – to be kept secret; and, perhaps above all, a commitment on the part of all ministers publicly to defend decisions when made and to present a united front to Parliament and to the public, whatever the degree of earlier anguish and dissent. Sometimes it will suit a government's purposes to depart from this model of internal secrecy and external unity. It may be useful for some ideas under discussion to be 'leaked' by one means or another to test public reaction prior to a final decision or to soften up public opinion for bad news (perhaps not as bad as the version which was leaked) to be announced later. Sometimes the impression of a lively debate between ministers rather than that of sullen acquiescence may be advantageous instead of destructive. To have a minister who briefly appears 'greener' than most[3] or appears more sympathetic to the plight of underfunded university students[4] is not necessarily harmful. Publicly declared differences – agreements to disagree – may occasionally be the best that can be achieved without total collapse of the government[5].

For the most part, however, it is the need for solidarity which dominates and it is team discipline which keeps in place the package of obligations associated with 'collective responsibility'. Ministers must remain 'on message'. Ministers who step out of line, especially by publicly revealing dissent on important issues without authority to do so, may expect to be reprimanded or to lose their jobs. However, it will be open to the Prime Minister to be more tolerant of misdemeanours if personal or political considerations demand. In all important respects, these 'rules' of political solidarity apply as much to the principal opposition party as to the party in government. The shadow team of ministers is almost as much concerned to present a united front as the government[6]. Sanctions are applied to dissidents in the same way and this reinforces the political rather than any constitutional underpinning of the concept of collective responsibility. Political expediency keeps both teams together. It is true that some aspects of governmental collective responsibility are given structure by the *Ministerial Code*[7]. It is also true that the parliamentary device of the motion of 'no confidence in Her Majesty's Government' reinforces the collective nature of the sanction invoked. Either the government falls or it survives as a whole. And the idea of collective responsibility was given some recognition as the basis of the English High Court's decision to uphold the confidentiality of Cabinet business in the 'Crossman diaries' case in 1976[8].

These phenomena do not, however, deny the political character of collective responsibility itself – a feature clearly illustrated by events at the time of the Iraq war of 2003. Because of his disagreement with the government's decision to commit forces, Robin Cook MP resigned from his ministerial position as Lord President of the Council (Leader of the House of Commons). On the other hand, the International Development Secretary, Clare Short MP, first described her own government's policy in the lead-up to the conflict as 'reckless' but neither resigned, nor was dismissed by the Prime Minister. Nor did Ms Short resign as the war began or, at a later stage, when she was again critical of the government's aid policy on Iraq. Eventually, however, she did resign and, amid great acrimony, used her resignation speech on 12 May 2003 to condemn the state of Cabinet government as she saw it. In Bagehot's terms, the Cabinet had become, like the Privy Council, merely a 'dignified' part of the constitution. In her words there was 'no collective responsibility because there is no collective, just dictats from the Prime Minister'[9]. Whatever the rights and wrongs of this judgment, there is no doubt that events surrounding the Iraq crisis posed many questions about the condition of Cabinet government.

More recently Prime Minister Brown suffered a number of resignations from his Cabinet in the days leading up to the European and English local government elections on 4 June 2009. The political dimension to these resignations was particularly evident : no specific policy issue divided the Cabinet, rather those who resigned made known their concerns that Mr Brown's continued leadership would lead inevitably to defeat at the next general election.

1 For a discussion of the history and content of the concept see O Gay 'The collective responsibility of Ministers' HC Research Paper 04/82 2004.
2 In June 2003, the consultation document accompanying the draft Civil Contingencies Bill (Cm 5843) explained that powers formally exercisable by a single Secretary of State 'would be exercised by Ministers in accordance with the normal principles of Cabinet collective responsibility' (p 29).
3 Eg the Environment Secretary, Michael Meacher MP at the time of the Johannesburg summit in August 2002.
4 Clare Short MP, November 2002.
5 The best example of this being the presentation by the Labour government in 1975 of separate options on whether or not to withdraw from the EC.
6 For example, Kenneth Clarke MP, as shadow business secretary, caused embarrassment to the Conservative opposition in March 2009 by appearing to depart from party commitments on reform of inheritance tax, leaving the party leadership to 'restate' their official position.
7 It should also be noted that 'collective responsibility' has received statutory recognition in the Freedom of Information Act 2000, s 36 and the Freedom of Information (Scotland) Act 2002, s 30.

8 *A-G v Jonathan Cape Ltd* [1976] QB 752.
9 HC Debs, 13 May 2003, col 38.

Prime Ministerial government

6.12   As already indicated, an important question about the modern functioning of Cabinet government in the United Kingdom relates specifically to
the role of the Prime Minister. No one would seriously suggest today that he
or she is merely *primus* or *prima inter pares*, the 'first among equals'. The
political dominance of the Prime Minister within the governing party; the
Prime Minister's leading role on the government's behalf in Parliament and
the media; the role as statesman abroad; ultimate responsibility for the use
of nuclear weapons; and certainly the Prime Minister's power to hire and
fire ministers and to exert pressure on colleagues and MPs by the power to
decide the date of the next general election, are all factors which give the
Prime Minister an inevitable pre-eminence. And yet, the idea of the Cabinet as a team lingers[1]. There is a widespread belief – one that goes back
many years[2] – that the Prime Ministerial position is open to abuse and that
it is, in fact, abused by some incumbents. Prime Ministers may use technical tricks to dominate colleagues – by determining the agenda, length and
content of the minutes of Cabinet meetings and Cabinet committees. They
may hector and bully. They may snub and sideline and use their substantial
powers to 'spin' information. They may demean colleagues by assuming lead
responsibility for *their* functions – whether health, or education or foreign
affairs. They may dominate party campaigns, especially at general elections.
Such features tend to be accompanied by others which suggest that Prime
Ministers – especially those with large and virtually unassailable majorities
in the Commons – not only dominate Parliament but may also be tempted
to ignore it. Together, these produce the apprehension that Cabinet government has been replaced not merely by prime ministerial government but by
presidential government. Most frequently, such suggestions are merely political rhetoric intended both to charge Prime Ministers with abuse of power
and shedding their accountability to party, Parliament and people and, on the
other hand, to deride other senior ministers for their feeble subordination. On
the other hand, the charge of presidentialism has sometimes to be taken seriously as a critique of the operation of the modern constitution. The manner
in which executive power is exercised *is* important and it is especially important to be aware of the consequences of any change for the accountability of
government to Parliament and the people. We may provisionally conclude
that, while modern technology and communications and a heightened sensitivity of Prime Ministers to changing expectations of the media and the
general public have undoubtedly affected prime ministerial behaviour, most
of the institutional rules forcing a dependence upon party support and electoral success ensure a continuing distinction between prime ministerial and
presidential government.

1 Harold Wilson's description, in the 1960s, of his ministers as a football team with himself as a
   centre half has become more than a little quaint.
2 J P Mackintosh *The British Cabinet* (3rd edn, 1977). See also C Foster, 'Cabinet government in
   the twentieth century', 2004 67 MLR 753.

THE QUEEN AND THE SCOTTISH EXECUTIVE

6.13   SA 1998, s 45(1) provides that '(t)he First Minister shall be appointed by Her Majesty and ... shall hold office at Her Majesty's pleasure'. The section goes on to make provision for the First Minister's resignation – to be tendered to Her Majesty[1] – and subsequent sections require the approval by the Queen of the appointment of the other ministerial members of the Scottish Executive[2]. It is to the Queen that recommendations are to be made for the appointment (and removal) of the Lord Advocate and Solicitor-General for Scotland[3]. On the face of it, therefore, SA 1998 confers very substantial constitutional powers on the Sovereign. As already explained, it is, however, one of the best known features of the United Kingdom constitution that the involvement of the Sovereign at this and many other points is more apparent rather than real. It is formal rather than substantive. Hers is the role of the figurehead or, more dismissively, the rubber stamp. In some instances, this is made clear by the statutory context in which the powers are conferred. There is no doubt, for instance, that the rules on the formation of the Scottish Executive are intended to confer the substantive powers to choose on the Parliament (subject to political forces within it) and (once appointed) on the First Minister and to leave the Sovereign with only the formal role of accepting the recommendations made to her. It would be unconstitutional for her to do otherwise. The same position is reached in the non-statutory procedure for the appointment of the United Kingdom government, as already described[4]. The principle that the Sovereign's role should be merely formal applies, with only very limited exceptions, across the full range of the functions conferred upon her, whether by statute or by virtue of the prerogative.

Certain 'dignified' functions are assured by SA 1998 itself. Not only are the First Minister, other members of the Scottish Executive and junior ministers formally appointed by the Queen but their functions are formally exercised on behalf of the Queen[5]. In relation to the Parliament, the Queen is formally empowered in defined circumstances to order a dissolution and require a poll and subsequent meeting[6]; and a Bill, when passed by the Parliament, becomes an Act when it has received Royal Assent[7]. While not deriving from SA 1998, the Queen attended the opening ceremony of the first Parliament on 1 July 1999, and attended a Kirking Service in St Giles' Cathedral on the previous day. The Queen addressed the Parliament when it met in Aberdeen in May 2002, her jubilee year[8], and she addressed the Parliament again after the beginning of the second session in June 2003[9], its third session in June 2007[10] and on the tenth anniversary of its opening on 1 July 2009. The practice of using a 'Queen's Speech' has not been adopted and the First Minister himself has presented the Executive's legislative programme to the Parliament[11]. It has become the practice of the Privy Council to involve Scottish Privy Counsellors, in particular the First Minister, in business including the making of Orders in Council required by the Scottish Executive and it is an indication of the formality of these proceedings that Orders in Council promoted by either the UK or the Scottish government may be conducted in the presence of ministers from both administrations.

Arrangements are made for the Queen to receive papers from the Scottish Cabinet[12] and there has emerged a practice of meetings between the Queen and the

First Minister, although these have not achieved the frequency or regularity of the Prime Minister's audiences[13]. It is, therefore, acknowledged that the Queen has the right to be informed about Scottish government. Whether, in line with Bagehot's formula, she has a right to advise or warn has yet to emerge.

1 SA 1998, s 45(2).
2 SA 1998, s 47(1).
3 SA 1998, s 48(1).
4 See p 158.
5 SA 1998, ss 52–53.
6 SA 1998, ss 2–3.
7 SA 1998, s 28(2)–(4)
8 SP OR 28 May 2002, col 12125.
9 SP OR 3 June 2003, col 317.
10 SP OR 30 June 2007, Col 3.
11 See p 227.
12 Guide to *Collective Decision Making*, para 4.25. For the *Guide* more generally, see below.
13 First Minister Jack McConnell said that he had 'audiences with Her Majesty the Queen from time to time' (SP OR S2W-1283, 28 July 2003) and it is known that First Minister Salmond also has such audiences.

THE SCOTTISH EXECUTIVE

6.14   SA 1998 creates a Scottish Executive, the members of which are (a) the First Minister; (b) ministers appointed by the First Minister: and (c) the two Scottish Law Officers, the Lord Advocate and the Solicitor-General for Scotland[1]. SA 1998 further states that the 'members of the Scottish Executive are referred to collectively as the Scottish Ministers'[2] and the 'Scottish Ministers' is the term used elsewhere in SA 1998 to describe the body in which statutory powers are vested[3]. A person who 'holds a Ministerial office' (i.e. a UK government minister) may not be a member of the Scottish Executive[4].

1 SA 1998, s 44(1).
2 SA 1998, s 44(2).
3 SA 1998, s 52(1).
4 SA 1998, s 44(3).

Appointment and tenure of the First Minister

6.15   SA 1998 has established a parliamentary form of government similar to that at the United Kingdom level, in that the First Minister and the Ministers he or she then appoints are drawn from the membership of the Scottish Parliament itself. They owe their appointment and subsequent retention of office to the political support they have in the Parliament. In a purely formal sense, however, the appointment of the First Minister is made by the Queen by royal warrant. He or she is to be 'appointed by Her Majesty from among the members of the Parliament and shall hold office at Her Majesty's pleasure'[1]. However, SA 1998 makes it clear that the Queen does not have a free choice in her selection of the First Minister. She receives a recommendation from the Presiding Officer of the Parliament and that recommendation must, in turn, be of the person nominated by the Parliament itself[2]. On appointment, the First

Minister must take the official oath, tendered by the Lord President at a sitting of the Court of Session[3].

There was more use of these procedures in the early years of the Parliament than might have been expected. The initial appointment of Donald Dewar as First Minister in May 1999 was followed, on his death, by the appointment of Henry McLeish in October 2000 and then, on his resignation, by the appointment of Jack McConnell in November 2001. In each case, the nomination was contested, producing a vote and victory for the Labour/Liberal Democrat partnership candidate. At the beginning of the second session, Jack McConnell was renominated as First Minister against opposition from candidates from the SNP, the Conservatives, the Greens and the Scottish Socialists as well as Dennis Canavan MSP and Margo MacDonald MSP[4]. The third session of Parliament produced, for the first time, a First Minister leading a minority government. Alex Salmond faced opposition from the Conservatives, Labour and Liberal Democrats but secured the nomination when the two Green MSPs elected in May 2007 voted with the SNP block (SP OR 16 May 2007, col 20). Once an appointment has been made, the First Minister holds office until one of four events occurs:

(1)   The First Minister may at any time voluntarily tender his or her resignation[5]. This is what brought Mr McLeish's tenure to an end on 8 November 2001. SA 1998 does not indicate in so many words whether the Queen is obliged to accept the First Minister's tendered resignation. However, it may be assumed that she must do so in all imaginable circumstances[6]. The sort of circumstances in which a First Minister might resign are also not expressly anticipated in SA 1998 but clearly they might include personal circumstances such as illness. They would also include circumstances in which the First Minister feels[7] that his or her own conduct or personal responsibility for the failures of the Executive requires resignation or where, in any event, the pressure to resign from colleagues (including fellow members of the Executive) or from the Parliament becomes irresistible. One thing not made completely clear in SA 1998 is whether, in the case of a 'voluntary' tendering of resignation, that resignation must take immediate effect.

(2)   If the degree of dissatisfaction felt by the Parliament towards the First Minister and the Scottish Executive reaches the level at which the Parliament formally 'resolves that the Scottish Executive no longer enjoys the confidence of the Parliament', then the First Minister has no option. The First Minister must tender his or her resignation to the Queen[8] and, in such an event, all ministers in the Scottish Executive must also resign[9]. So too must the junior Scottish Ministers[10]. It is assumed that, in the case of such an involuntary tendering of resignation, it would have to take immediate effect.

(3)   SA 1998 also provides that the nomination procedure is triggered if the office of First Minister becomes vacant, otherwise than in consequence of a resignation. This is what happened in the sad circumstances of Donald Dewar's death on 11 October 2000.

(4)   Finally, SA 1998 formally assures adherence to the parliamentary model of government by providing that, if a First Minister should cease to be an

MSP (other than by dissolution of the Parliament), the Parliament must nominate a successor. In the more routinely predictable circumstances of the dissolution of the Parliament, dissolution does not, of itself, bring to an end a First Minister's tenure of office. The First Minister (and the rest of the Scottish Executive) may remain in office through the period of the dissolution and subsequent general election. The First Minister's fate hangs on the result of the election and then of the process of nomination which the Parliament must undertake thereafter. If the First Minister is renominated (as Mr McConnell was in May 2003), he or she is to be reappointed. If not, and some other person is nominated for appointment, the existing First Minister ceases to hold office once his or her successor is actually appointed[11].

In some of these circumstances where a vacancy produces the need for the nomination of a new First Minister, there will also be the need for a temporary replacement, as was the case on Donald Dewar's death and the resignation of Henry McLeish. In such circumstances, First Ministerial functions are to be exercised by a person designated by the Parliament's Presiding Officer. Such an Acting First Minister must be an MSP or, if the Parliament has been dissolved, someone who was an MSP prior to the dissolution[12]. In both instances mentioned, Jim Wallace, who served as Deputy First Minister throughout the first session of the Parliament but, as leader of the junior partner, was not a candidate for the First Ministership itself, was so designated. An Acting First Minister may also be designated if the First Minister, while still in office, is 'for any reason unable to act'. It may be, however, that there will in practice be very little use of this option. There is, no elaboration of what is meant by the First Minister's being 'unable to act'. Presumably, a short-term illness, acknowledged by the First Minister to be disabling, might be a relevant condition – although Donald Dewar's heart surgery and recuperation in the summer of 2000 did not prompt the need for a formal replacement. Jim Wallace stood in on an informal basis.

These general rules are supported by the procedural requirement that, if one of four specified events occurs, the Parliament must make its nomination within a period of 28 days beginning with the date of the event[13]. The four events are: (1) the holding of a poll at a general election; (2) the First Minister's tendering of his or her resignation; (3) a vacancy in the office of First Minister, other than by resignation; and (4) the First Minister's ceasing to be an MSP (other than by dissolution of the Parliament itself). There is, however, provision for the period of 28 days to begin to run again if another 'event' occurs. The running of time would be brought to a halt if the Parliament used its exceptional power under SA 1998, s 3 to pass a resolution for its own dissolution[14] but with the procedure triggered once again by the poll at the ensuing general election. In the unlikely event that, for whatever reason, the Parliament fails to make a nomination for appointment as First Minister within the statutory period, the Presiding Officer must initiate a dissolution and general election[15].

1   SA 1998, s 45(1).
2   SA 1998, s 46(1),(4).
3   SA 1998, s 84(4); Promissory Oaths Act 1868, s 5A.
4   SP OR 15 May 2003, col 18.
5   SA 1998, s 45(2).

6   An assumption reinforced by SA 1998, s 46(2)(b).
7   As in the case of Mr McLeish.
8   SA 1998, s 45(2).
9   SA 1998, s 47(3)(c).
10 SA 1998, s 49(4)(c).
11 SA 1998, s 45(3). As happened to Mr McConnell on 16 May 2007, some two weeks after the general election in which the SNP secured the largest number of seats in the Parliament.
12 SA 1998, s 45(4), (5).
13 Although 28 days may be enough for most appointments where a party leader is already available, it puts great pressure on the ruling party, in the case of a death or resignation, to elect a successor.
14 See p 69.
15 SA 1998, s 3(1)(b). The categorical terms of the section appear to impose an absolute duty on the Presiding Officer, although in the different rules of the Northern Ireland Act 1998 under which the Assembly must elect a First Minister and deputy First Minister within six weeks and in the different political conditions in the Province, a majority in *Robinson v Secretary of State for Northern Ireland* [2002] NI 390 held that the Secretary of State did not act unlawfully in not dissolving the Assembly, despite breaching the deadline by a few days.

Government formation by the First Minister

6.16   Once appointed, the most important initial task of the First Minister is to form a government by appointing the other members of the Scottish Executive (including the Law Officers[1]) and the junior Scottish Ministers. It may, of course, be the case that, as with Mr McConnell in May 2003, a First Minister is reappointed following success in a general election and, with many ministers continuing in office during the election period, will have few adjustments to make to the original team. The same could happen, following the retiral of the predecessor First Minister on, for instance, health grounds.

Whether starting with a clean slate or with a partially formed group of ministers, it is for the First Minister to appoint the further ministers required, such appointments being made with the formal approval of the Queen[2]. Ministers must all be drawn from the membership of the Parliament[3] – it is, again, a government on the parliamentary model which is being formed – and, in addition, the Parliament maintains further controls over the appointments process, some more formal than others. Most prominent is a formal requirement that the Parliament should agree to each appointment of a minister. This is a form of parliamentary involvement which does not apply at Westminster. There it is for the Prime Minister to make his or her own selection of ministerial colleagues, without the need for each individual minister to be approved by Parliament. The requirement in SA 1998 that such approval should be obtained derives from the recommendations of the Constitutional Convention[4]. It should be borne in mind, however, that the formal rule requiring parliamentary approval of appointments is to be understood within the broader operation of the party system in the Parliament. The First Minister often will have emerged from a particular alignment of political parties, acting as a coalition. The same coalition of forces may, at the same time, impose conditions on the party balance to be achieved in the subsequent appointment of the Executive and indeed upon the choice of individual ministers[5]. In the course of the current minority SNP administration the other main parties did not support Mr Salmond's ministerial choices but did not use their voting power to frustrate him[6]. The Parliament cannot itself determine the allocation of portfolios to ministers[7], although views may be expressed to the First Minister[8]. On appointment, a minister must take the official oath.

In formal terms, a minister holds office, like the First Minister, at Her Majesty's pleasure[9] but SA 1998 also provides that a minister may be removed from office by the First Minister[10] and such removals from office are not required to have the consent of the Parliament. The First Minister has a freer hand at the point of dismissal than on appointment. On the other hand, if the ministry as a whole loses political support and the Parliament resolves that the Scottish Executive no longer enjoys its confidence, then all ministers must resign[11]. At any other time, a minister may resign[12] and, whatever the circumstances of a resignation, the minister ceases to hold office immediately[13]. A minister also ceases to hold office if he or she ceases to be an MSP 'otherwise than by virtue of a dissolution'[14]. Like the First Minister, ministers do not immediately go out of office once a dissolution has occurred prior to a general election. They remain in office to perform the functions of the Scottish Executive until a successor First Minister and ministry are appointed – with the exception of any minister who has lost his or her own seat in the Parliament. Such a minister may be expected to resign, as did Iain Gray after failing to be re-elected on 1 May 2003[15]. Ministers are paid at rates approved by the Parliament under the authority of SA 1998, s 81. Different rates have been set for ministers and junior ministers but the prescribed rates are stated to be maxima and lower salaries may be paid[16].

1   The Law Officers are dealt with separately below.
2   SA 1998, s 47(1).
3   SA 1998, s 47(1).
4   *Scotland's Parliament: Scotland's Right* (1995) p 25.
5   For the formation of the first Executive in 1999, subsequent developments and the formation of the second Executive in 2003, see p 172 below.
6   See SP OR 17 May 2007, col 37. The two Green MSPs in the Parliament supported the First Minister while all other parties (and the sole independent MSP) abstained.
7   Or indeed how they may style themselves. Following the 2007 election, the SNP administration adopted the title 'Cabinet Secretary' for Ministers.
8   See eg the discussion by the Transport and Environment Committee of the desirability of a *separate* minister for the environment, 4 April 2001.
9   SA 1998, s 47(3)(a).
10 SA 1998, s 47(3)(b).
11 SA 1998, s 47(3)(c).
12 SA 1998, s 47(3)(c).
13 SA 1998, s 47(3)(d).
14 SA 1998, s 47(3)(e).
15 A resignation might be thought unnecessary. Had he not now ceased to be an MSP 'otherwise than by virtue of a dissolution'? Perhaps not, because his ceasing to be an MSP occurred at the date of the dissolution? But, in that case, perhaps his departure from office could not have been enforced, save by the First Minister?
16 SP OR 21 March 2002, cols 10577, 10596; resolution adopting SP Paper 554. Subsequent salary increases have been in line with the scheme adopted in 2002.

Junior Scottish Ministers

6.17   SA 1998 enables the First Minister to appoint what it dubs 'junior Scottish Ministers' – although they are, in current practice, described as ministers (in contrast to ministers who are, as noted above, currently known as Cabinet Secretaries). Such appointments are to be made with the approval of Her Majesty and, like their senior colleagues, the candidates must be MSPs[1] and must be agreed by the Parliament. Once appointed, junior Scottish Ministers have the same formal tenure of office as their seniors[2]. They may be removed by the First Minister. SA 1998 states that junior Scottish Ministers are 'to assist the Scottish Ministers in the exercise of their functions'. They often act formally on behalf of the Scottish Ministers (eg by signing statutory instruments) and answer oral questions in the Parliament. Ministers are further assisted in their duties by 'Parliamentary Liaison Officers' (PLOs). These were previously known as 'ministerial parliamentary aides' and have a role equivalent to that of parliamentary private secretaries at Westminster[3]. Like them, they are unpaid and are required to assist Cabinet ministers in the discharge of their parliamentary duties. Appointments require the approval of the First Minister.

1 SA 1998, s 49(1).
2 SA 1998, s 49(4).
3 *Scottish Ministerial Code* paras 4.6–4.11.

Scottish Cabinet government

6.18   The provisions of SA 1998 just described provide the formal framework within which the Scottish Executive must be constituted. However, they do not tell the whole story. SA 1998 is silent on the matter of party political representation in the Executive which is something left to be determined in the light of political conditions in the Parliament. It is, moreover, only a skeleton of legal rules which needs to be fleshed out with the combination of non-legal rules, guidance and practice which are adopted by First Ministers and the Executive as a whole, as they take office. After ten years of devolved government in Scotland, it is possible to draw upon the experience of the formation of the first three Scottish Executives in 1999, 2003 and 2007. These are illustrative of the ways in which SA 1998's provisions can be applied in the formation and operation of government within quite different political conditions.

The result of the general election held on 6 May 1999 produced the conditions for the first 'Partnership Government' in which a coalition drawn from the Scottish Labour Party and the Scottish Liberal Democrats took office. Unable to command the support of an overall majority in the Parliament from the membership of his own party, Donald Dewar sought agreement with Jim Wallace, leader of the Scottish Liberal Democrats, under which ministerial offices would be shared, following commitment to a programme of policies as a basis for joint working. Such an agreement was by no means an inevitable outcome, an all-Labour Executive with only minority support in the Parliament being another possibility, as occurred in the early days of the Welsh Assembly.

The *Programme for Government* agreed between the leaders of the two parties included a list of 'principles' and 'initiatives' across a range of policy areas such as education, health, enterprise and justice. There was a declared commitment to building communities, enhancing rural life and integrating principles of environmentally and socially sustainable development into all government policies. Scotland's culture would be promoted. One controversial policy matter was admitted to divide the parties – that of student tuition fees. There was a commitment to set up a Committee of Inquiry[1] and to consider the evidence and conclusions of the Committee. The Liberal Democratic members of the Executive would not be 'bound in advance'. Elsewhere, however, the parties declared a commitment to introducing a 'new style of politics based on partnership and consensus building'. There were commitments to local government, equal opportunities, strong and independent parliamentary committees and the development of the 'Civic Forum'. The Parliament's tax-varying power would not be used. There were commitments to collective responsibility and to the nomination of Jim Wallace as Deputy First Minister. The allocation of ministerial portfolios between the two partners would be agreed by the party leaders and appointments would be made by the First Minister, following consultation with his Deputy.

It was on the basis of this partnership agreement that the appointments of ministers and junior ministers were made in May 1999. In addition to being Deputy First Minister, Jim Wallace became Minister for Justice. Another Liberal Democrat was appointed as Minister for Rural Affairs and two others became deputy ministers. All other positions – another seven ministers, eight junior ministers and the two Law Officer posts – were held by Labour Party nominees. In the course of the first session of the Parliament, the principal reshuffle of ministers occurred following the appointment of Jack McConnell as First Minister.

In May 2003, the political balance in the Parliament produced a situation in which the Labour Party and the Liberal Democrats were again attracted to the negotiation of a coalition agreement. The Labour Party had only 50 seats (compared with 56 prior to the dissolution) but the Liberal Democrats had increased their representation to 17. Negotiations were rather more protracted than in 1999 but were completed, in the shape of *A Partnership for a Better Scotland*, between the election on 1 May and the nomination of Jack McConnell as First Minister on 14 May with the support of both parties. The new *Partnership* document was longer and more sophisticated than its predecessor but it served similar purposes. It listed a substantial number of policy commitments, including the commitment not to use the Parliament's tax-varying power and, more controversially, the undertaking to introduce proportional representation (by single transferable vote) in local government. The principles of collective responsibility were reaffirmed and there was a commitment to update and publish the *Scottish Ministerial Code* and the *Guide to Collective Decision Making*. On ministerial portfolios, the Liberal Democrats would have a share at least equal to their share of partnership MSPs. The roles of the (Labour) First Minister and the (Liberal Democrat) Deputy First Minister were spelled out, with other appointments by the First Minister, subject to consultation with and, in the case of a Liberal Democrat minister, nomination by the Deputy First Minister. Nominations of the Law Officers had to be *agreed*. A substantial section of the document reinforced the mechanisms designed to strengthen support for the Executive by the partnership MSPs. In the first session of the Parliament it had been a recurring concern in the Labour Party that Liberal Democrat MSPs had lacked discipline in maintaining support for the coalition.

It was on the strength of *A Partnership for a Better Scotland* that the First Minister brought forward his proposals for the new ministerial team. With most former members of the Executive and deputy ministers continuing in office, there was a need on 21 May 2003 for the Parliament to approve the appointment of only three new ministers and two junior ministers. The May 2007 general election produced, for the first time, a Scottish Executive formed from a 'minority' party in the Parliament. As in the 1999 and 2003 elections, no single party secured an overall majority but, in a change from the first two sessions of Parliament, the distribution of seats was such that the 'traditional allies' of Labour and the Liberal Democrats combined could not achieve such a majority and the SNP was, by a single seat, the largest single party. Following several days of discussions the SNP secured limited support from the Scottish Green Party but fell short of a formal coalition with them or any other parties. The First Minister therefore appointed a ministerial team from amongst the SNP's 47 MSPs. Making a virtue out of necessity, Mr Salmond reduced the number of Cabinet Ministers – to be known from then on as Cabinet Secretaries – from nine to five and appointed a further ten junior ministers (to be known simply as ministers). At the time of writing, the Cabinet comprises the First Minister, Alex Salmond, Deputy First Minister and Cabinet Secretary for Health and Wellbeing, Nicola Sturgeon, and Cabinet Secretaries for Finance and Sustainable Growth, Education and Lifelong Learning, and Rural Affairs and the Environment. Although a new Solicitor General was appointed, perhaps unusually, the Lord Advocate was not replaced by Mr Salmond.

In the course of the early months of the first government, two new procedural guides were developed and in August 1999 the *Scottish Ministerial Code* and *The Scottish Executive: A Guide to Collective Decision Making* were published. These have been updated and re-issued a number of times, the Code most recently in June 2008 and the Guidance in November 2008[2]. The Code in large measure replicates for the Scottish Government the *Ministerial Code* developed by the UK government and contains a mixture of administrative guidance and guidance on propriety. At its core is a statement of principles of ministerial conduct: the principle of collective responsibility must be upheld; Ministers have 'a duty to the Parliament to account, and be held to account, for the policies, decisions and actions taken within their field of responsibility'; they must give accurate and truthful information to the Parliament – 'Ministers who knowingly mislead the Parliament will be expected to offer their resignation to the First Minister'; openness is encouraged; and Ministers must ensure that conflicts of interest are avoided. These principles are then spelled out further in sections dealing with the conduct of Executive business; ministers and the Parliament (including the priority to be given to making public announcements first to the Parliament); ministers and their responsibilities, including the use of special advisers (up to 12 in all[3]) and the making of appointments; and procedures governing the party interests of ministers, ministerial visits, the presentation of policy and ministers' private interests. Guidance is given on the need to dispose of any financial interest giving rise to an 'actual or perceived conflict' of interest or to take alternative steps to prevent it. Although it need not do so, the *Code* reminds Ministers that they must also comply with the Interests of the Members of the Scottish Parliament Act (2006). A criticism that had been made of the *Ministerial Codes* is that enforcement procedures, over which the Prime Minister and First Minister ultimately preside, are weak. The UK government response to these criticisms is described above (p 162). North of the border, the *Scottish Ministerial Code* now provides for the First Minister to request that investigations into alleged breaches be carried out by a panel of advisers comprised of former Presiding Officers of the Parliament. This innovation was used for the first time in January 2009, when Tavish Scott MSP, leader of the Liberal Democrats, asked the First Minister to request that the panel consider whether Mr Salmond had breached the *Code* by misleading Parliament about the future of the Scottish Interfaith Council. The panel considered he had not[4].

The need to observe collective responsibility[5] is elaborated first in the *Code* and then in the *Guide*. These largely repeat principles contained in the equivalent UK documentation[6]. The *Guide* states that

> 'the Scottish Executive operates on the basis of collective responsibility and every effort must normally be made to ensure that every Minister with an interest in an issue is kept fully informed and has a chance to have his or her say – in an appropriate forum or manner – before a decision is taken. Collective responsibility also means that, once a decision has been announced, all Ministers are required to abide by it and to defend it as necessary. The doctrine of collective responsibility bites after a decision has been reached; it does not mean that there must be unanimity (or even consensus) beforehand. Ministers can express their views frankly in internal discussion of an issue, but their membership of the Executive requires them to maintain a united front once decisions have been reached; to ensure that the privacy of opinions expressed in internal discussions is maintained; and to ensure that the internal processes through which a decision has been made are not disclosed'[7].

It was on the basis of these rules that the Partnership Executive operated during the first session of the Parliament – symbolically most prominently, perhaps, in its survival of two votes of no confidence, first on the handling of management of the Scottish Qualifications Authority in December 2000[8] and then on road transport policy in February 2001[9]. A collective solidarity was generally maintained on Executive policies although it was noticeable that, perhaps because of the special circumstances of the case, there was no uniformity of response on the (reserved) issue of the Iraq war[10]. When Tavish Scott resigned as a Deputy Minister in March 2001 because he disagreed with the fisheries policy then being pursued, he said: 'Let me be clear: when one is a minister, one supports the Government. If one cannot support the Government, one resigns'[11]. The current Cabinet has continued to observe the convention.

The vulnerability of government and individual ministers to a successful vote of no confidence might, initially, be thought to be greatly increased where – as has been the case since May 2007 – that government represents a minority within the Parliament. Paradoxically, though, the minority government may be more secure than its predecessors given that all concerned understand that a successful vote of no confidence would require the formation of a new administration, which failing an extraordinary general election[12].

1   In due course, the Cubie Committee Inquiry into Student Finance. See *Student Finance: Fairness for the Future* (1999).
2   The latter now titled 'The Scottish Government: Guide to Collective Decision Making.
3   See p 184 below.
4   See Ministerial Code Inquiry: Complaint by Tavish Scott MSP regarding exchanges at First Minister's Questions, Report by Independent Advisers to the First Minister, The Rt Hon George Reid and the Rt Hon Lord Steel of Aikwood, 1 March 2009. A further reference to the panel was made by the First Minister in June 2009 following complaints that he had misled Parliament in relation to prisoner escapes: see SP OR 3 June 2009, col 18070. The Standards, Procedures and Public Appointments Committee of the Parliament (see chapter 4) has also called for a protocol to be developed between the Parliament and the Scottish Government as to the accuracy of members' contributions in the Chamber: see 5th Report 2009, SP Paper 254.
5   See B K Winetrobe 'Collective responsibility in devolved Scotland' [2003] PL 24.
6   Ministerial Code section 2 'Ministers and the Government'.
7   Paras 2.1–2.2. For consideration of the situation which arose in the special circumstances of Northern Ireland in which certain ministers had specifically declared themselves not to be bound by collective responsibility, see *Morrow's Application* [2001] NI 261.
8   SP OR 13 December 2000, col 841. On the SQA, see also p 258.
9   SP OR 15 February 2001, col 1279.
10 See SP OR 16 January 2003, col 17013.
11 SP OR 15 March 2001, col 601.
12 For further discussion see p 68.

SOURCES OF EXECUTIVE AUTHORITY

General

6.19   Ministerial functions must have a basis in legal authority[1]. It is a characteristic of modern government that the majority of functions exercised by United Kingdom ministers derive their legal authority from statute. Indeed the principal purpose of much legislation is to confer new powers on ministers or to modify existing powers. This includes the grant of extensive powers to make subordinate legislation[2]. As already mentioned, however, ministers may also derive powers from the common law which include those special powers originating in the royal prerogative but also powers enjoyed by ordinary persons, such as powers to enter into contracts, to employ staff and to convey property. In this respect, ministers exercising powers of the Crown are, again like ordinary persons, permitted in principle to do all those things which are not prohibited by law[3]. Ministers, unlike statutory bodies, are not restricted to the exercise of powers positively conferred by statute.

Although the powers of the Scottish Executive are similarly based, they are moulded by SA 1998 to suit the devolution settlement. SA 1998 provides for functions to be conferred on the Scottish Ministers, except for those conferred specifically upon the First Minister[4] or the Lord Advocate[5], and that statutory powers of the Scottish Ministers are exercisable by any member of the Scottish Executive[6]. This method of conferring powers collectively upon the Scottish Ministers[7], rather than upon individual ministers, has consequences which are discussed below[8].

The actual powers exercisable by the Scottish Ministers fall into four main categories[9]. In the first place, they may be given powers by the Scottish Parliament itself. Over time, this may be expected to be the largest group of powers and many of the Acts of the Parliament have conferred powers on ministers. Nevertheless it remains fair to say that most of the functions now exercisable by the Scottish Ministers fall into the second category and are those devolved to them at the launch of devolved government on 1 July 1999. Just as law-making powers were transferred, within limits defined by SA 1998, to the Parliament[10], executive powers were transferred to the Scottish Ministers. Thus functions which had previously been exercised by Ministers of the Crown (ie Ministers in the UK government and especially the Secretary of State for Scotland) were transferred to be exercisable *instead*[11] by the Scottish Ministers 'so far as they are exercisable within devolved competence'[12]. The functions may be either statutory[13] or from a prerogative (or other common law) source[14] but, just as the powers of UK ministers are nearly all statute-based, so too are the powers transferred to the Scottish Ministers. Common law powers such as the Crown's power to contract, are, however, available and so would be any of the remaining prerogative powers exercisable within devolved competence[15]. 'Devolved competence' is defined by reference to the legislative competence of the Parliament. Those things which are beyond the Parliament's legislative competence are beyond the executive competence of the Scottish Ministers. Thus, it is stated to be 'outside devolved competence' to make subordinate legislation if it would be outside the Parliament's competence, if the power were included in an Act of the Scottish Parliament (ASP); and, in the case of other types of function, if a provision of an ASP conferring the function would be outside the competence of the Parliament[16]. There are certain additional categories of functions which were devolved to the Scottish Executive from 1 July 1999 but which are hidden from sight because of their conventional rather than legal basis. These occur in those areas where the Queen must receive ministerial advice on the making of appointments and where no statute prescribes who should offer the advice, and on the use of the royal prerogative. In such areas, advice would formerly have been given by the Prime Minister or another UK minister but now this falls to the First Minister, not by virtue of any formal order but by virtue of administrative arrangement announced by the Prime Minister in June 1999[17]. Thus, in respect of functions within devolved competence such as the royal prerogative of mercy or the appointment of regius professors in Scottish universities, the Queen is advised not by the Secretary of State but by the First Minister. Advice on many other appointments is similarly transferred[18], as well as certain other functions, including the issue of congratulations on 100th and succeeding birthdays[19]. It was, at the same time, indicated that, in respect of some appointments, advice would continue to be given by the Prime Minister or another UK Minister but the First Minister would be consulted[20]. Guidance was also given on the submission of ministerial advice in relation to Scottish business of the Privy Council. Much of that relates to the making of subordinate legislation by Order in Council[21] but certain other functions, relating, for example, to universities and special bank holidays, are also transferred.

Returning to the transfer of competence under SA 1998, it was the UK government's intention to base the boundaries of executive competence on the legislative powers of the Scottish Parliament but then to extend them further. The Scottish Ministers should be able to discharge some statutory functions which, as reserved matters, remained within the legislative competence of the Westminster Parliament[22]. Thus, the third category of powers are those transferred to the Scottish Ministers under SA 1998, s 63[23]. That section enables the transfer (by Order in Council approved by both Parliaments) of further functions 'so far as they are exercisable by a Minister of the Crown in or as regards Scotland'[24] and the power was used to make a substantial transfer with effect from 1 July 1999[25]. Subsequent transfers have been made[26]. Large numbers of powers in relation, for instance, to the interception of communications, extradition, road traffic regulation, abortion (approval of clinics) and many others have been transferred to the Scottish Ministers. The final, and fourth, category of powers are those which have been directly conferred on the Scottish Ministers in post-devolution primary legislation at Westminster[27].

The functions of the Scottish Ministers are declared to be 'exercisable on behalf of Her Majesty'[28] and to be exercisable by any member of the Scottish Executive[29]. Powers may be exercised by junior ministers and, in principle, by civil servants on behalf of the Executive[30]. But UK ministers are not permitted to discharge the functions of the Scottish Ministers. For them to purport to do so would be an abuse of power[31]. However, there are three qualifications which have to be made to this general position. First, SA 1998, s 58 does provide the UK government with specific powers to intervene to prevent or, indeed, to require action on the part of the Scottish Executive. It has some parallels, as a constitutional longstop, with SA 1998, s 35 which enables the UK government to intervene in the law-making process[32]. One ground of intervention is to secure compliance with international obligations (other than EU or ECHR obligations) and if the Secretary of State has reasonable grounds to believe that it is required he or she may order that action proposed by the Scottish Executive be not taken; or direct that action should be taken; or he may revoke subordinate legislation. Such an order must be reasoned and would be subject to annulment by either House of the Westminster Parliament. The other circumstance in which a revocation order could be made is where a provision in subordinate legislation makes 'modifications of the law as it applies to reserved matters and which the Secretary of State has reasonable grounds to believe have an adverse effect on the operation of the law as it applies to reserved matters'. No such orders have been made so far.

The second qualification to the general rule against intervention by Whitehall ministers is that certain functions are deliberately stated to be shared between the two levels of government. SA 1998, s 56 lists a number of powers including powers to give financial assistance to industry and to others which, while devolved to the Scottish Ministers, may continue to be used by UK ministers[33]. Of greater significance is the specific power conferred by SA 1998, s 57(1) which declares that, despite the general transfer to the Scottish Ministers of functions within devolved competence, 'in relation to observing and implementing obligations under Community law', the functions continue to be exercisable by UK ministers. Although measures to implement Community directives are, in practice, almost entirely made by the Scottish Ministers, a few are made, with the agreement of the Scottish Executive, by UK ministers where, for instance, uniformity of provision is sought or no Scottish interest is affected[34]. An additional rationale for the availability of the power in SA

1998, s 57(1) is that it is ultimately for the UK government itself to ensure the full implementation of Community measures and any penalty imposed by the Community for non-compliance would fall, in the first instance, on the United Kingdom as the member state[35].

The third general qualification arises where, under SA 1998, s 93, 'agency arrangements' are made between the two governments for specified functions to be exercised by one on behalf of the other. Such arrangements have been made for administrative transfers in both directions[36]. In contrast with SA 1998, s 63, they do not have the effect of transferring the function itself. It is expressly stated that an agency arrangement 'does not affect a person's responsibility for the exercise of his functions'[37].

1 For the need for authority for expenditure, see p 280.
2 See p 143.
3 This is sometimes known as the 'Ram doctrine', after Grenville Ram, First Parliamentary Counsel, whose memorandum of 2 November 1945 was published in January 2003 – see HL Debs, 22 January 2003, col (WA) 98. See also A Lester and M Weait [2003] PL 415.
4 See eg the powers to recommend the appointment of ministers and judges (pp 170 and 280).
5 See p 180 below.
6 SA 1998, s 52(1)–(3).
7 In some instances, Acts of the Scottish Parliament have, in fact, conferred powers simply on 'Ministers', a term then defined to mean the Scottish Ministers. See eg the Land Reform (Scotland) Act 2003, s 98.
8 At p 258.
9 There are also certain 'shared' and other powers. See below.
10 See p 119.
11 It is the entire competence which is transferred. With the exception of the few instances of expressly shared competence (see below), the UK minister retains no continuing competence in the devolved area.
12 SA 1998, s 53(1).
13 Ie conferred by a 'pre-commencement enactment', a term defined in SA 1998, s 53(3) to include mainly Acts passed before it. Some subsequent Westminster Acts and Orders have, however, defined themselves as a 'pre-commencement enactment' in order to ensure the distribution of powers to the Scottish Ministers. See, for example, The Environmental Protection (Controls on Ozone-Depleting Substances) Regulations 2002, SI 2002/528 made under the Environmental Protection Act 1990.
14 '[T]hose of Her Majesty's prerogative and other executive functions' or functions conferred by a prerogative instrument: SA 1998, s 53(2) (a), (b). The formula 'prerogative or other executive power' was the means used for the statutory transfer of common law powers in the Government of Ireland Act 1920, s 8(2).
15 Eg the power to arm and supply police forces in order to keep the peace. See *R v Home Secretary, ex parte Northumbria Police Authority* [1989] QB 26. These categories of prerogative and other common law powers are usefully discussed in *Government Accounting*. See also the 'Ram' doctrine at n 3 above.
16 SA 1998, s 54. For analysis of the concept of devolved competence see in particular *Somerville v Scottish Ministers* 2008 SC (HL) 45, discussed in more detail in chapter 13.
17 HC Debs 30 June 1999, cols 215–216 (WA). The announcement was repeated in the House of Lords at HL Debs 1 July 1999 cols WA 50–51.
18 Eg H M Inspectors of Fire Services and of Constabulary.
19 Also 60th and succeeding wedding anniversaries!
20 Eg Lords Lieutenant and members of the Royal Commission on Environmental Pollution and the Forestry Commission.
21 See 247.
22 *Scotland's Parliament* para 2.7.
23 SA 1998, s 108 provides for a 'reverse' redistribution, ie the allocation, subject to the agreement of both Parliaments, from the Scottish Ministers to a UK minister.
24 Powers may also be transferred to the Scottish Ministers to be exercised concurrently with a

Minister of the Crown or may be left with a Minister of the Crown but subject to the agreement of, or consultation with, the Scottish Ministers.

25 Scotland Act 1998 (Transfer of Functions to the Scottish Ministers etc) Order 1999, SI 1999/1750.
26 Including SIs 1999/3321, 2000/1563, 2000/3253, 2001/954, 2001/3504, 2002/1630, 2003/415, 2006/1040, 2007/2915, 2008/1776.
27 Eg Energy Act 2008, ss 18, 26.
28 SA 1998, s 52(2).
29 SA 1998, s 52(3). The subsection refers to 'statutory functions', ie 'conferred by virtue of any enactment' (subs (7)). Even if not conferred by virtue of an enactment, the transferred prerogative and other executive powers are also exercisable on behalf of Her Majesty.
30 See p 187 n 8 and p 188 n 5 below.
31 And challengeable as a 'devolution issue' under SA 1998, Sch 6.
32 See p 234.
33 See also the Scotland Act 1998 (Concurrent Functions) Order 1999, SI 1999/1592(as amended).
34 Reports on the extent of use of SA 1998, s 57(1) are made to the European and External Relations Committee of the Scottish Parliament.
35 But the penalty might be recovered from the Executive. See *Scotland's Parliament* para 5.8.
36 Eg SIs 1999/1512 and 2000/745 both of which included the specification of certain environmental functions for discharge by UK departments. SI 2003/407 specified housing mobility functions.
37 SA 1998, s 92(2).

The Scottish Law Officers

6.20   The two Scottish Law Officers, the Lord Advocate and the Solicitor-General for Scotland, are members of the Scottish Executive[1]. They are appointed (and are removable) by the Queen on the recommendation of the First Minister, with the agreement of the Parliament[2]. A Law Officer may resign at any time and must do so, like other members of the Executive, if the Scottish Executive loses the confidence of the Parliament. Law Officers must, by virtue of the demands of their offices, be legally qualified. Historically, both offices were occupied by advocates but the current Lord Advocate (Ms Elish Angiolini) is the first solicitor to have held successively both posts[3].

The two Law Officer positions are of long standing[5], but their functions underwent a significant transformation on the implementation of devolution[6]. Until the implementation of SA 1998, they were the Scottish Law Officers of the UK government. Since then, they have been the Law Officers of the Scottish Administration and a new Scottish Law Officer of the UK government, the Advocate General for Scotland, was appointed[7].

The Lord Advocate and the Solicitor-General[8] have two broad areas of responsibility:

1 SA 1998, s 44 (1). The Solicitor-General is not, however, a member of the Cabinet. The Lord Advocate ceased to be a voting member of the Cabinet from November 2001 and has not attended any meetings of the Cabinet since the current SNP government entered office. The Guide to Collective Decision Making provides that the Lord Advocate does not 'normally' attend Cabinet Meetings (para 4.2), leaving open the possibility of exceptions to that general practice.
2 SA 1998, s 48(2).
3 But created a QC on appointment as the Solicitor General in 2001.
4 See *SME Reissue* Constitutional Law, paras 425–436.
5 For the purposes of their 'retained functions' (see below), the transfer of powers was on 20 May 1999 rather than 1 July 1999. See SI 1998/3178.

6 SA 1998, s 87.
7 The Solicitor-General may perform 'functions authorised or required, by any enactment or otherwise, to be discharged by the Lord Advocate': Law Officers Act 1944, s 2(1).

Legal advice

6.21   As members of the Scottish Executive, they act as the Government's most senior legal advisers and provision is made in the *Scottish Ministerial Code* and the *Guide to Collective Decision Making* to ensure that the law officers are 'consulted in good time before the Government is committed to critical decisions involving legal considerations'. Normally their opinion is to be obtained on a reference from the Scottish Government Legal Directorate[1]. There is no requirement that the Law Officers be MSPs but, to the extent permitted by standing orders, they may participate in its proceedings (but not vote)[2] and, exceptionally, to make statements to Parliament about specific prosecutions which may have given rise to public debate[3]. In this way, a Law Officer may represent the Government in answering questions or in support of a Bill, although it should be borne in mind that, in relation to the presentation of broader aspects of policy, the Cabinet Secretary for Justice has a general responsibility. The Lord Advocate has a role in judicial appointments[4] and SA 1998 gives him or her specific responsibilities in relation to the reference of Bills to the Supreme Court[5] and devolution issues[6]. The Lord Advocate is also the representative of the Crown in legal proceedings brought by or against the Scottish Administration[7]. As members of the Scottish Executive, the Law Officers are formally entitled to exercise any of the functions vested in the Scottish Ministers[8]. At the time of the implementation of SA 1998, many functions formerly allocated directly to the Lord Advocate became exercisable instead by the Scottish Ministers[9]. These functions largely involve appointments or rule-making (sometimes simply in a consultative role) for tribunals with responsibilities in Scotland and (it may be assumed that) the Law Officers have retained a lead responsibility in these areas.

1 *Code* paras 2.26–2.30; *Guide* Annex B. It is stated that the expectation is that the written opinions of the Law Officers, unlike other ministerial papers, will generally be made available to succeeding administrations. But the fact and content of their opinions must not be disclosed publicly without the authority of the Law Officers.
2 SA 1998, s 27. See also SOs, r 4.5.
3 The current Lord Advocate, for example, made a statement defending the Crown's decision to bring prosecutions in the 'World's End' case which collapsed when the trial judge Lord Clarke determined that there was 'no case to answer'. This statement provoked an unusual public exchange between the Lord Advocate and the Lord Justice General. See SP OR 13 September 2007 col 1763 and Lord Hamilton's letter to the Lord Advocate of 26 September 2007. See also p 311.
4 See p 302.
5 SA 1998, ss 32, 33. See p 233.
6 SA 1998, s 98 and Sch 6. See p 396.
7 Crown Suits (Scotland) Act 1857, as amended by SA 1998, Sch 8.
8 SA 1998, s 52(3).
9 This was achieved in a two-stage process. Powers were first transferred by the Transfer of Functions (Lord Advocate and Secretary of State) Order 1999, SI 1999/678, and then secondly by the general transfer of functions by SA 1998, s 53 or s 63 and the Scotland Act 1998 (Transfer of Functions to the Scottish Ministers etc) Order 1999, SI 1999/1750.

Retained functions

6.22   The second group of Law Officers' functions are different in that they are reserved entirely to them and not shared by other members of the Executive. SA 1998 refers to these as the 'retained functions' of the Lord Advocate[1]. They are the functions left to the Lord Advocate after the transfer of others to the Scottish Ministers, and are exercisable exclusively by the Law Officers[2]. They are the functions of the Lord Advocate as head of the systems of criminal prosecution and investigation of deaths in Scotland[3] and SA 1998 goes to some lengths to preserve the Law Officers' independence in these areas. The powers must be exercised separately to avoid political interference and the importance of this principle is recognised by the protection of the Lord Advocate's position against amendment by Act of the Scottish Parliament[4]. This independence is important at both the Scottish and UK levels because the Lord Advocate prosecutes in relation to criminal offences within the legislative competence of both Parliaments. In addition, the Scottish Parliament's powers of scrutiny of the Lord Advocate and the Solicitor-General in relation to particular legal cases is restricted[5]. In operational terms, the process of criminal prosecution is the responsibility of the Crown Office. The investigation of deaths is a responsibility assigned to sheriffs in fatal accident inquiries[6].

1   SA 1998, s 52(6).
2   Specific provision is also made for property and liabilities to be transferred to the Lord Advocate in respect of these functions. See SA 1998, ss 61, 62.
3   The formula used in SA 1998, s 29(2)(e).
4   SA 1998, s 29(2)(e). See p 140 above.
5   SA 1998, s 27(3).
6   In terms of the Fatal Accidents and Sudden Deaths Inquiry (Scotland) Act 1976. A Scottish Government sponsored review of the operation of the Act is underway : see Review of Fatal Accident Legislation Inquiry: a consultation paper (November 2008) and Review of Fatal Accident Inquiry Legislation: report on consultation (June 2009).

UK GOVERNMENT DEPARTMENTS AND THE SCOTTISH ADMINISTRATION

6.23   Ministers are appointed and given their powers in the ways already explained. It is, however, self-evident that these Ministers, whether at the UK or the Scottish level of government, cannot act alone in carrying out the great range of responsibilities allocated to them. The answer lies in the core institutions of executive government which combine ministers, in whom powers are formally vested, with a civil service whose numbers and organisation are intended to enable the functions to be discharged. It is a combination of the political ministers with the non-political civil servants: the public and high-profile with the, relatively, anonymous. It combines those whose tenure of office depends on the will of the relevant Parliament and Prime or First Minister with those whose tenure, as part of the 'permanent' civil service, is more secure.

Two main purposes are intended to be achieved by these arrangements. The first, as already implied, is operational efficiency. By providing ministers with the resources of expert guidance and advice and then the means to put into effect the ministers' policy programmes and to provide the machinery that all governments need, the civil service is an essential element of the primary function of government, which is to govern[1]. Second, this combination of ministers with civil servants is fundamental to the principal mechanisms relied on to provide accountability in government. Inevitably, most things done by governments are done by civil servants. As a practical matter, it would be impossible for things to be otherwise. On the other hand, it is also a system which, for almost all important purposes, insists that ministers remain legally and politically responsible for acts and decisions (and omissions to act or decide) across the board. The ways in which these lines of responsibility or accountability operate, and with what measure of success, are considered in Chapter 9.

The degree of autonomy sustained by the modern civil service in making its particular contribution to government is as difficult to analyse and explain as it is important. The absence of a written constitution, here as in other sectors, brings a situation in which there are no formal constitutional guarantees of the relative independence and impartiality which have been achieved. Concerns about this state of affairs, particularly in light of what has been described as New Public Management (one aspect of which is the creation of next steps agencies (see p 186 below)), have led to calls for a Civil Service Act establishing a legal framework for the public service[2]. The case for a Civil Service Act was accepted by the current Labour government in 2002[3] but such progress as there has been towards the introduction of a Bill has been slow, resulting in regular prodding and criticism by the House of Commons Select Committee on Public Administration. The Committee consulted on its detailed proposals for an Act in 2003, describing legislation as 'long overdue' and producing its own Draft Bill and recommending that the government publish its own (promised) draft legislation without further delay[4]. In November 2004 a draft Bill was published by the government[5] for consultation but legislation was not introduced before the 2005 general election. After that election the Select Committee, in a report on the politicisation of the civil service, concluded that the government 'has prevaricated long enough about a Civil Service Act; it should now introduce one.'[6]. The Governance of Britain Green Paper[7], published in 2007, included a commitment to bring forward legislation in the following session of Parliament and was followed by publication in 2008 of a draft Constitutional Renewal Bill as part of the White Paper 'The Governance of Britain – Constitutional Renewal'[8]. The 2008 draft Bill includes provision for defining the civil service (a negative definition which excludes the intelligence and security services and the Northern Ireland Civil Service); establishment of a Civil Service Commission; management of the civil service by the Minister for the Civil Service[9] (i.e. the Prime Minister); and requiring the publication of a 'civil service code'. This code would replace the existing *Civil Service Code*[10] which lays down principles for the accountability and ethical behaviour of civil servants. The provisions of the draft Bill which concern appointment of Civil Servants would replace the *Civil Service Management Code* made under the prerogative-based Civil Service Order in Council 1995[11]. The Bill would require most appointments to be made 'on merit on the basis of fair and open competition'; for 'recruitment principles' to be published by the new Commission and for the Commission to monitor and review recruitment practices.

The draft Bill also contains specific provisions concerning 'special advisers' (defined rather cryptically as civil servants 'appointed by a minister directly' to 'assist that minister' but recognisable as those officials increasingly imported into the civil service expressly to provide political advice and whose role has been the subject of considerable debate[12]. Although special advisers would be exempted from the requirement that appointments are made on merit after open competition, it is made explicit that their appointment must end when the appointing minister demits office and requires the laying before Parliament of an annual report about special advisers.

In an acknowledgement of the particular issues which arise as a consequence of devolution (see below), the draft Bill also includes provision for the publication of separate civil service codes for Scotland and Wales and for separate arrangements for Scottish and Welsh special advisers.

On 20 July 2009, the Constitutional Reform and Governance Bill (containing provision for those matters) was introduced.

1   In September 2007, the total number of civil servants in the UK Home Civil Service stood at 532,000, 9.6% of which were based in Scotland.
2   For a useful discussion of the background and issues see G Drewry, The Executive: Towards Accountable Government and Effective Governance, in J Jowell and D Oliver, The Changing Constitution (4th ed, 2007). As Drewry notes, calls to put the civil service on a statutory footing can be traced as far back as the Northcote-Trevelyan Report of 1854 (Parl Papers vol xxviii).
3   HC Debs, 22 May 2002, cols 279–280. See also HL Debs, 1 May 2002, col 691 et seq.
4   A Draft Civil Service Bill: Completing the Reform (HC 128 (2004))
5   Cm 6373.
6   Third Report of Session 2006-07, HC 122 (2007).
7   Cm 7170.
8   Cm 7342.
9   Excluding the diplomatic service which is to be the responsibility of the Secretary of State.
10 First introduced on 1 January 1996 but revised on 13 May 1999 to take account of devolution to Scotland and Wales.
11 See also the Civil Service (Management Functions) Act 1992 (which would be amended by the draft Bill); and the protection afforded to civil servants by the Employment Rights Act 1996, s 191.
12 See Drewry, op cit.; 'Special Advisers: Boon or Bane' Fourth Report of the HC Public Administration Committee (HC Paper 293 (2000–01)); (HC Paper 463 (2001–02)) (government's response); and HC 122 (2007) op. cit.

UK government departments

6.24   At the level of United Kingdom government, the structure which has come to encapsulate the combination of ministers and civil servants has been the government department. Ministers, as already discussed, do operate collectively as a team, whether at the centre of government as the Cabinet or, more broadly, as the ministry as a whole. Civil servants are part of a unified Civil Service[1] subject to centralised regulation[2]. For the purpose of the conduct of government business, however, a minister (or a small group of ministers) combines with civil servants to carry out functions within a specific sector. Together, as a department, they carry out the functions assigned to the Cabinet (or sometimes more junior) minister at their head. Thus the Secretary of State for the Home Department, with a team of junior ministers (Ministers of State or Parliamentary Secretaries), heads the Home Office with responsibilities including immigration in respect of the whole United Kingdom, and prisons in respect of England and Wales. The Foreign Secretary heads the Foreign and Commonwealth Office; the Secretary of State for Transport heads the Department for Transport; the Chancellor of the Exchequer heads the Treasury; and so on.

Importantly, from the point of view of the government of Scotland, there continues to be a Secretary of State for Scotland although the arrangements for the administration of that Minister's responsibilities have been the subject of regular change over the past ten years. Until 1999, the Scottish Secretary headed the Scottish Office and was responsible for the administration of a very substantial part of Scottish public affairs[3] and, in the period immediately prior to devolution, for all the legislative and administrative reforms required. From 1999[4], the office of Secretary of State was retained but with the name of the department changed to the Scotland Office and, since most of the former responsibilities had been devolved to the Scottish Ministers, with a much smaller range of functions. Elections and the electoral system in Scotland (in respect of both Holyrood and Westminster) are reserved matters and, therefore, part of the Secretary of State's remit[5]. Other reserved responsibilities for Scotland, however, remained with other UK departments, such as the Department for Work and Pensions and, in relation to immigration, the Home Office. In June 2003, these arrangements were shaken up. In the ministerial reshuffle of 12 June, Mrs Liddell resigned and was replaced as Secretary of State by Alistair Darling. Mr Darling, however, did not become a full-time Secretary of State for Scotland but combined the post with his existing post of Secretary of State for Transport. From the same time, Peter Hain combined the posts of Leader of the House of Commons and Secretary of State for Wales. Alongside the ministerial changes, the Scotland Office[6] and also the Wales Office ceased to exist as separate departments of government but were subsumed within the new Department for Constitutional Affairs, created mainly out of the former Lord Chancellor's Department and headed by the Secretary of State for Constitutional Affairs. In further changes in May 2007, the Department for Constitutional Affairs was itself abolished and its functions transferred to the Ministry of Justice. The Scotland Office is described as a 'distinct entity within the Ministry of Justice' and the Secretary of State for Scotland has been revived as a stand alone Cabinet post, currently occupied by Jim Murphy MP. The Secretary of State represents Scottish interests in the House of Commons while the Scotland Office's official spokesperson in the House of Lords is Lord Davidson of Glen Clova QC (the Advocate General for Scotland).

Some of the other UK departments have long histories, with functions changing only to reflect changes in the emphasis of government policies and programmes. Others are of more recent creation, to reflect changing views of whether large departments are to be preferred over small departments and, if large, then representing which preferred combinations of functions. In May 2009 there were two departments with responsibility for education: the Department for Children, Schools and Families and the Department for

Innovation, Universities and Skills. As a consequence of a Cabinet reshuffle and re-allocation of ministerial responsibilities in June 2009, a new Department of Business, Innovation and Skills was created into which many of the previous responsibilities of the Department for Innovation, Universities and Skills were subsumed. Until 2002 there was a single large Department of the Environment, Transport and the Regions but now there is a separate Department for Transport and a Department of Energy and Climate Change – encompassing the responsibilities of the former Department for Environment, Food and Rural Affairs and energy policy while regional matters are handled within nine Government Offices for the Regions and the Regional Co-ordination Unit. Whatever the particular structure of government departments has been, however, the principal characteristics of departments have, subject to what is said below about Executive agencies, remained the same. They are established as separate entities and with separate functions assigned to each. There are formal lines of demarcation between departments which bring the strengths of concentration on certain defined areas of government activity but also the weaknesses of heightened departmental rivalries in their competition for funding and other resources such as access to parliamentary time for their legislative programmes. Such departmental demarcation tends to undermine the co-ordination of government programmes and to prevent what is today called 'joined-up government'. This division of governmental activity is not greatly affected by the modern practice of designating most ministerial heads of department as Secretaries of State. If a function is allocated by statute to 'the Secretary of State', any person so designated may, in law, exercise the function[7]. This has certain procedural benefits but has little impact on departmental practice. Decisions are made by the minister responsible for the relevant department, or rather, in the case of most decisions, by civil servants in that department. The law recognises that functions vested in ministers may be competently exercised by their civil servants[8].

Probably the most significant adjustment to the department-based architecture of the Civil Service in management terms has been the creation, within the domain of most departments, of 'executive agencies'. Pursuant to recommendations originally made in a report by Sir Robin Ibbs, *Improving Management in Government: The Next Steps* (1988), the delivery of services has been separated from policy formulation and placed in the hands of agencies, each of which is headed by a chief executive and is subject to performance targets defined annually under the terms of framework documents issued by the department. It is a means of seeking to achieve a degree of efficiency in service provision short of privatisation and in a way which also stops short of the further degree of 'hiving off' which is achieved by the creation of a separately constituted non-departmental public body or quango[9]. One consequence of keeping the agencies within the overall direction and control of existing departments is that, in contrast with quangos, they remain formally within the area of accountability of ministers, although the heightened profile of agency chief executives has given rise to some adjustments of practice and perhaps also a contribution to the wider case for seeking a distinction between ministerial accountability and responsibility[10].

1　The Home Civil Service. Organised separately are the Northern Ireland Civil Service and the Diplomatic Service.
2　Although much diversity is achieved under the Civil Service (Management Functions) Act 1992.
3　See p 56.
4　For an assessment, see 'Devolution: Inter-Institutional Relations in the United Kingdom' *Second Report of the House of Lords Select Committee on the Constitution* (HL Paper 28 (2002–03)) paras 54–78.
5　See, for instance, the debate about the future size of the Scottish Parliament at p 67.
6　Linked to the Scotland Office is the Office of the Advocate General for Scotland.
7　See Interpretation Act 1978 and *Agee v Lord Advocate* 1977 SLT (Notes) 54.
8　*Carltona v Commissioners of Works* [1943] 2 All ER 560.
9　See ch 7.
10　See pp 254–259.

Scottish Administration departments

6.25　Devolved executive government in Scotland has been established on a rather different legal basis and, for reasons of the scale and scope of functions exercised, it will never be possible to make precise comparisons between St Andrew's House and Whitehall. Historically, the Scottish Office, as a territorially rather than functionally defined department of the UK government, was always different from most of its Whitehall cousins[1]. The creation of the new Scottish Administration[2] has at the least emphasised the distinct identity of the Scottish Government. Powers are conferred collectively on the Scottish Ministers and we have already noted the ways in which these powers have been distributed between ministers appointed to the Executive in May 2007. In the first two sessions of the Scottish Parliament the responsibilities of the senior ministers (as members of the Scottish Cabinet) were reflected in the work of the six departments mirroring in general terms the Westminster model of matching Ministers with departments. The current SNP administration has adopted a slightly different model. Beginning by defining the remit of each Cabinet Secretary, there has been created a large number of 'Directorates' for which each Cabinet Secretary is responsible. Overall management of the Directorates is allocated to six 'Directors-General' who, together with the Permanent Secretary Sir John Elvidge and two non-executive directors, comprise the Scottish Government's Strategic Board. So, for example, the Cabinet Secretary for Justice, Kenny McAskill MSP, is supported by the Director-General for Justice and Communities, Robert Gordon, and has responsibility for Directorates for Criminal Justice, Police and Community Safety, Constitution, Law and Courts and Courts, Judicial Appointments and Finance – Mr McAskill is also responsible for a number of agencies – including the Accountant in Bankruptcy and the Scottish Prison Service – and Inspectorates – including HM Inspectorate of Prisons for Scotland and the Scottish Fire and Rescue Advisory Unit.

These Directorates are different from those established at Whitehall. They are created not by any statutory or prerogative order but simply by administrative decision (of the Scottish Ministers). Civil servants within the Scottish Administration are members of the Home Civil Service[3] and the civil service is a reserved matter[4]. The general rules, including those in the *Civil Service Management Code* and the *Civil Service Code*, therefore extend to the staff of the

Scottish Administration[5] but with the appointment function and, as with UK departments, many management functions delegated to the Scottish Ministers[6]. As noted above, the government's Constitutional Reform and Governance Bill 2009 gives some recognition to the realities of devolution by providing for separate civil service codes for Scotland and for Wales. Some consequences of the current accommodation of the Administration's civil servants within the Home Civil Service, rather than the adoption of the Northern Ireland model of a separate service, are considered below in discussion of relations between St Andrew's House and Whitehall[7]. The Scottish National Party had called for a separate Scottish civil service before it took office, although since forming the current administration in 2007 the issue appears to have lost a degree of urgency for the SNP – perhaps because in practice Scottish civil servants have proved themselves more independent than the government anticipated.

1 D Milne *The Scottish Office* (1957).
2 A term used to include ministers, 'office-holders' and their civil servants: SA 1998, s 126(6)–(8).
3 SA 1998, s 51(2). Although see below for discussion of recent proposals for reform of that status.
4 SA 1998, Sch 5, Pt I, para 8.
5 See also the extension of the *Carltona* principle (p 187 n 8 above) by *Scottish House Builders Association Ltd v Scottish Ministers* 2002 SLT 1321; *Westerhall Farms v Scottish Ministers* (25 April 2001, unreported) and the limitations of the principle explored in *Beggs v Scottish Ministers* 2007 SLT 235. See also *Somerville v Scottish Ministers* 2008 SC(PC) 45.
6 SA 1998, ss 51(1) and (5), extending powers under the Civil Service (Management Functions) Act 1992, s 1.
7 See p 190. See also the *CSG Inquiry* consideration of civil servants' relations with the Parliament, at paras 513–548.

RELATIONS BETWEEN ST ANDREW'S HOUSE AND WHITEHALL

6.26   In this concluding section of the chapter we draw together some of the material already considered and try to assess how the Scottish and United Kingdom governments relate to each other under the devolution settlement established by SA 1998[1]. At the core of their relationship is the framework for the allocation of legislative powers to the Scottish Parliament to which the Scottish Executive has access and, on the other hand, the powers retained as 'reserved matters' to the Westminster Parliament[2]. Similarly, there is the statutory scheme for the division of Executive powers. The powers transferred to the Scottish Ministers by SA 1998 itself, by transfer of functions orders or by agency agreements have already been considered and so too have the powers shared between the two governments and the powers which require consultation between governments before they can be exercised[3]. The creation of the two, constitutionally distinct, governments or administrations[4] and the formal division of powers between them provide the principal foundations of the intergovernmental relationship.

But the initial allocation of powers is only a starting point. SA 1998 contains many other provisions which define the way in which the two tiers of authority share in the government of Scotland. Most tend to confer powers of scrutiny and control upon UK ministers, although, as we have seen, adjustments of the powers of the Scottish Parliament or the Scottish Ministers do require the formal agreement of *both* Parliaments[5]. UK departments scrutinise Bills in the Scottish Parliament with, in the background, the possibility that the Law Officers might initiate a challenge by way of reference to the Supreme Court[6]. The Secretary of State also has the power under SA 1998, s 35 to intervene to block the progress of a Bill[7], and, as earlier noted[8], similar powers under SA 1998, s 58 to prevent or require action by the Scottish Government.

The Secretary of State's powers under SA 1998, ss 35 and 58 are potentially very intrusive. They may have been considered a necessary element in a system of devolution which may require central government rather exceptionally to assert its authority in support of some wider UK interest. However, the powers take on a restraining and even disciplinary aspect when seen from the point of view of the Scottish Government. There is another provision in SA 1998 which enables UK ministers to make subordinate legislation to make provision considered necessary or expedient in consequence of (a) an Act of the Scottish Parliament which is not, or may be, within its legislative competence or (b) any purported exercise by a member of the Scottish Executive of functions 'which is not, or may not be, an exercise or a proper exercise of those functions'[9]. Because of its potentially very broad application, this power too could be very intrusive although to date it has been used only once to make a minor technical adjustment[10]. Nor are the powers which could be available to the UK government confined to those set out in SA 1998. SA 1998, s 28(7) reminds of the continuing power of the UK Parliament to make laws for Scotland. On the initiative of UK ministers, the Westminster Parliament can, for instance, amend SA 1998 itself[11].

Most of these powers may be seen as available for use only in exceptional circumstances. If used at all, other than with the consent of the Scottish Government and Parliament, it would probably be in circumstances of crisis or feared breakdown of government. Much more routinely, however, the UK government continues to exert a measure of control over Scottish government. It can exert its powers in reserved areas (such as taxation or social security) in ways which affect devolved government and, very importantly, it retains the power to regulate the financing of the work of the Scottish Government and Parliament. Finance is a principal determinant of the reality of power[12].

But, even when all the statutory rules are taken into account, the legal framework still tells only a part of the story of inter-governmental relationships. That framework is a necessary, but far from sufficient, condition of good governance. Devolution also demands practical good relations between governments. As it was put in *Scotland's Parliament*, the 'Scottish Executive will need to keep in close touch with Departments of the UK Government'[13]. There would be a need to 'develop mutual understandings covering the appropriate exchange of information, advance notification and joint working'[14].

The extent to which these mutual understandings and joint working have in fact developed has been considered, formally, several times over the last ten years. Early on, the House of Lords Select Committee on the Constitution considered the impact of devolution on inter-institutional relations in the UK while, more recently, the House of Commons Justice Committee and the Calman Commission have considered the first ten years of devolution from a whole UK and a Scottish perspective respectively[15].

Of undoubted importance is the maintenance of good working relations between officials of the two administrations. We have already noted suggestions for a separate Scottish civil service (p 188) but there has also been support from other quarters for the continuation of a single Home Civil Service to which all belong. The House of Lords Select Committee on the Constitution considered the consequences of a single civil service for inter-institutional relations and the arguments for separation and concluded that retention of the single service strengthened the guarantee of civil service impartiality; provided a 'brand' recognised within and beyond the service; provided opportunities for interchange and linkage between staff; and enabled close working and a ready flow of information[16]. More recently, the House of Commons Justice Committee recognised that reform of the civil service to give greater recognition to the demands of devolution may be inevitable but concluded that there was an 'overwhelming case for a more systematic programme of secondments between Whitehall, Cardiff and Edinburgh' which would help raise awareness of devolution, promote best practice and allow for shared learning across all three administrations[17]. The Calman Commission found that the 'evidence on the civil service has overwhelmingly been to retain a unified service' with '[c]ommon working practices, staff secondments and ease of communication' being cited in support of the status quo[18].

Of greater importance is relationships between ministers, the political representatives of the two governments. Here, party political considerations loom large, particularly where, as now, the two governments are of different political persuasions. There have been reports of 'clashes' between First Minister Salmond and Prime Minister Brown and in April 2008 John Swinney, Cabinet Secretary for Finance, reportedly described the UK Treasury as attempting to 'bully' the Scottish Government in relation to the block grant . But party politics will not be the only consideration. Differing views on the desired future government of Scotland – whether ultimate independence, federation, stronger devolution, stronger unionism – may also be relevant. More broadly, the future condition of the Scottish and UK economies, developments in the European Union, and relations (bilateral and multilateral) between all the devolved administrations of the United Kingdom will all have their impact.

Another feature of the relationship between the Scottish and UK governments is that is has developed partly on an incremental basis in response to events – an example of the constitution being simply what happens – but partly also on the basis of more structured agreement between the parties. The White Paper proposals for devolution recognised that, at points where the interests of the two governments would most obviously overlap – for instance at the margin between reserved and non-reserved matters, and where European Union and international relations were at issue – there would be a need for special arrangements to be made[19]. As the Scotland Bill proceeded through Parliament, the UK government indicated that these arrangements would take the form of a Joint Ministerial Committee[20] and a series of agreements as to working relationships in the form of 'concordats'[21].

The initial arrangements were published on 1 October 1999[22]. There was an overarching Memorandum of Understanding agreed by the UK government, the Scottish Ministers and the Cabinet of the National Assembly for Wales which contained the general arrangements. There was then a series of supplementary agreements to establish the Joint Ministerial Committee; a concordat on co-ordination of European Union policy issues (including separate sections on Scotland and Wales and with a common annex); a concordat on financial assistance to industry; a concordat on international relations (again with separate sections on Scotland and Wales and a common annex); and a concordat on statistics. The document also anticipated that UK government departments would be entering into bilateral concordats with their counterparts in Scotland and Wales[23].

The Memorandum of Understanding describes itself as 'a statement of political intent, and should not be interpreted as a binding agreement. It does not create legal obligations between the parties. It is intended to be binding in honour only'[24]. The Memorandum then sets out the main principles on which it and the dependent concordats are based – the need for good communication and consultation (especially on policy proposals); the importance of co-operation; the need for the exchange of information, statistics and research; and also, to a degree, the need for confidentiality in the handling of official information. Meetings of Joint Ministerial Committees, under the terms of the Memorandum, have been held to discuss common issues in the fields of education, local government, transport and crime, and sub-committees have been established on matters such as health and European policy. The Scottish Executive has concluded a large number of bilateral concordats with individual UK departments. These too emphasise their non-legal character and the need for good communications and then pick out specific policy areas in which co-operation is expected. To supplement the Memorandum and the concordats there have been published a series of Devolution Guidance Notes. These start with a general Note on 'Common Working Arrangements' and then deal with rather more specific matters such as the handling of parliamentary business and the attendance of UK ministers at committees of the devolved legislatures.

Several attempts have been made to assess the contribution made by the concordat regime to relations between the different administrations. In 2002 the House of Lords Committee noted that 'although the value of having the concordats is unquestioned, their usefulness in practice is more questionable'[25]; and that it had been suggested that the UK government's view was that 'the chief value of the concordats is the process of making them, rather than actually using them to facilitate intergovernmental relations'[26]. It was the Committee's own view that concordats should, in the future, be renegotiated on a fixed-term basis and that the Prime Minister's annual statement about intergovernmental relations should be accompanied by a full list of agreements concluded during the previous 12 months or in force at the date of the annual plenary meeting of the Joint Ministerial Committee[27].

The House of Lords Committee's recommendations were not, in fact, taken forward and the Calman Commission noted that there had been no plenary meetings of the Joint Ministerial Committee between 2003 and 25 June 2008[28].

The Commission cited several reasons for the irregularity of JMC meetings including the fact that for the first eight years of devolution in Scotland the same party was in government at Westminster and at Holyrood, leading to a situation where 'informal and party-level contacts, and pre-existing relationships, shouldered the burden that would otherwise have relied on more formal arrangements'[29]. This hints at the explanation for the timing of the meeting which took place in June 2008: it followed a formal request to the Prime Minister (and to the Secretary of State for Scotland) by First Minister Salmond[30]. The meeting, held in London and attended by representatives of the UK government, Welsh and Northern Irish assemblies and Scottish Government, is widely regarded as having been a success: both the Calman Commission and the House of Commons Justice Committee noted its contribution to the reaching of an agreement on a UK wide approach to marine planning, an area which spans the devolved/reserved boundary in complex ways[31].

It should be noted that the relative inactivity of the plenary JMC does not tell the whole story. There are also Joint Ministerial Committees dealing with specific policy areas including finance, domestic affairs and European issues, the latter in particular having met fairly regularly over the past ten years[32].

Both the Calman Commission and the House of Commons Justice Committee made recommendations to revitalise and enhance the role of the JMC although it remains to be seen how those will be taken forward.

1   In the discussion which follows, the focus is almost exclusively upon inter-governmental relationships. Including, as necessary, reference to executive access to the Parliaments for legislation and other authority for use of powers, it is these which define the working conditions of the devolution settlement. The theory and practice of relationships between *Parliaments* are much more problematic. For earlier discussion of relations between Holyrood and Westminster, see 'Devolution: Inter-Institutional Relations in the United Kingdom' *Report of the House of Lords Select Committee on the Constitution* (HL Paper 28 (2002–03) hereafter 'Inter-Institutional Relations') and Appendix 5 (B Winetrobe) and the UK government response to the report, Cm 5780 (2003). More recently, this area has also been considered by the House of Commons Justice Committee in *Devolution: A Decade On* (House of Commons Justice Committee, Fifth Report of Session 2008-09, HC 529, ch 6 – hereafter, *Devolution: A Decade On*) and by the Calman Commission in *Serving Scotland Better* (Final Report of the Calman Commission, 15 June 2009, Part 3 – hereafter, *Serving Scotland Better*).
2   See ch 5.
3   See p 178.
4   For the purposes of giving formal recognition to their separate rights and liabilities and enabling proceedings between them, the 'Crown in right of Her Majesty's Government in the United Kingdom' and the 'Crown in right of the Scottish Administration' are identified by SA 1998, s 99.
5   See p 129.
6   See p 232.
7   SA 1998, s 35. See p 234 below.
8   See p 178.
9   SA 1998, s 107.
10 The Scotland Act 1998 (Regulation of Care (Scotland) Act 2001) Order 2001, SI 2001/2478 which repealed Regulation of Care (Scotland) Act 2001, sch 3, para 24, which sought to amend the Finance Act 2000.
11 Apart from the orders to amend SA 1998, Schs 4, 5 (see ch 5), SA 1998 has been amended in small ways to update it in the light of other developments, eg the amendment of SA 1998, ss 5 and 12 by the Political Parties, Elections and Referendums Act 2000 and the repeal of s77(8) (relating to the mechanism for accounting for additional Scottish income tax where the Parliament has resolved to raise the basic rate) by the Commissioners for Revenue and Customs Act

2005. It has also been amended, perhaps more fundamentally, by the Scottish Parliament itself by the Convention Rights Proceedings (Amendment) (Scotland) Act 2009 – see p 412.

12 See ch 10 below.

13 Cm 3658, para 4.13.

14 Cm 3658, para 4.13. SA 1998, s 96 gives the Treasury the statutory power to require information from the Scottish Ministers.

15 See *Inter-Institutional Relations; Devolution: A Decade On*; and *Serving Scotland Better*.

16 *Inter-Institutional Relations*, ch 5.

17 *Devolution: A Decade On*, paras 77 to 87.

18 *Serving Scotland Better*, paras 4.91 to 4.94.

19 *Scotland's Parliament* (Cm 3658) paras 4.12–4.21 and ch 5.

20 HL Debs 28 July 1998 col 1487.

21 See eg HC Debs, 31 March 1998, col 1158.

22 SE/99/36; Cm 4444. Subsequent versions have been published as Cm 4806 (2000) and Cm 5240 (2001), mainly to take account of the varying situation of Northern Ireland within the arrangements. The Calman Commission recorded its understanding that a revised version was under discussion (as at June 2009): *Serving Scotland Better*, p121, n 4.7.

23 For general discussion see R Rawlings 'Concordats of the Constitution' (2000) 16 LQR 257; J Poirier 'The Functions of Intergovernmental Agreements: Post-Devolution Concordats in a Comparative Perspective' [2001] PL 134; A Scott 'The Role of Concordats in the New Britain: Taking Subsidiarity Seriously?' (2001) 5 Edin LR 21.

24 Para 2. The Memorandum of Understanding was approved by the Scottish Parliament on 7 October 1999.

25 *Inter-Institutional Relations*, para 38.

26 Para 40.

27 Paras 43 and 45. For the government's response, see Cm 5780.

28 *Serving Scotland Better*, para 4.28.

29 *Serving Scotland Better*, para 4.120. The Commission also noted that some departmental concordats were 'clearly out of date and may not properly reflect the political or administrative changes since they were agreed' and that the regular reviews of concordats which were envisaged had not taken place.

30 *Devolution: A Decade On*, para 111.

31 See *Serving Scotland Better*, para 4.29 and *Devolution: A Decade On*, para 112.

32 See *Serving Scotland Better*, paras 4.31–32. In addition, there have been several meetings of the 'British-Irish Council', which was created following the Good Friday Agreement and involves representatives of the UK and Irish governments and the devolved Scottish, Welsh and Northern Irish administrations.

Chapter 7

Local Authorities and other Public Bodies

INTRODUCTION

7.1 Central government – government, that is, by ministers and civil servants – has never been the whole of executive government in Scotland or the United Kingdom at large. In particular, local authorities have been responsible for much of the planning and delivery of public services and their importance continues. The legal status of local authorities has changed since David I first established burghs in Scotland by charter in the early twelfth century. They once had a legal and constitutional autonomy[1] which has become more precarious today. The structure of local government was changed at many points during the nineteenth and twentieth centuries and the responsibilities of local authorities have, similarly, been modified to reflect the changing needs of increasing urban populations and changing perceptions of the appropriate balance to be achieved between the functions of central and local government. The structure and responsibilities of the 32 councils established by the Local Government etc (Scotland) Act 1994 (LG(S)A 1994) with effect from 1 April 1996 are sketched at pp 196–202. The passing of the Scotland Act 1998 (SA 1998) and the implementation of devolved government from 1 July 1999 did not, in themselves, bring major change to local government. It was, however, anticipated that the new powers of the Scottish Parliament and the Scottish Executive would have important consequences for local authorities and, in particular, their relationship with the new forms of central government[2]. Those consequences, and their treatment by a Commission on Local Government and the Scottish Parliament under Neil McIntosh, are considered at pp 202–204.

Occupying a sort of middle ground between central and local government, there is what has been called 'intermediate government' (pp 204–206). This consists of a somewhat chaotic grouping of bodies which (a) are mainly created by statute but some by virtue of the prerogative or, more informally, by decision of central government; (b) are not a part of central government in that, unlike 'executive agencies', they are not contained within central departments but are 'non-departmental public bodies'[3]; (c) do, for the most part, have executive (ie decision-making) functions but some have an adjudicatory, advisory or consultative role; and (d) are headed not by ministers who are members of an elected government nor by elected local councillors but by persons, typically constituting a 'board', appointed by ministers. Such bodies have been established for a variety of different reasons and with different justifications for their independence from direct political accountability – often, but not always, based on reasons of commercial efficiency. In many individual instances this type of government has been unproblematic but the lack of direct accountability, the risks of abuse of patronage that appointment by ministers can bring, and the secrecy that sometimes accompanies their operation have all meant that government by 'quango' has acquired many negative attributes. Intermediate government has attracted close scrutiny by the Committee on Standards in Public Life[4] and also by the House of Commons Select Committee on Public Administration[5]. Pages 206–211 of the chapter consider the consequences of devolution for intermediate government. As with local authorities, many quangos with responsibilities in Scotland were initially unaffected by the implementation of SA 1998, save that some are now within the competence of the Scottish Parliament and Executive. Others remain United Kingdom responsibilities. Some, however, have functions that straddle the line between reserved and non-reserved matters and there has been the need to create a new category of 'cross-border public authority' to which special rules apply. Pages 211–215 are headed 'Reforming intermediate government' and deal, inter alia, with the Commissioner for Public Appointments in Scotland. Finally, at pp 215–216, the Ethical Standards in Public Life etc (Scotland) Act 2000, which applies to both local government and other public bodies, is considered.

1 Articles of Union, Art XXI (royal burghs).
2 *Scotland's Parliament* (Cm 3658) ch 6.
3 In the UK government's annual publication Public Bodies, the term 'public body' is defined to include nationalised industries, public corporations, NHS bodies and non-departmental public bodies.
4 *Fourth Report* (1997).
5 *'Mapping the Quango State'*, *Fifth Report* (HC Paper 367 (2000–01)); *'Government by Appointment: Opening up the Patronage State' Fourth Report* (HC Paper 165 (2002–03)).

SCOTTISH LOCAL GOVERNMENT SINCE 1996

Introduction

7.2   Although the present structure of local government in Scotland dates back only to April 1996, it is a system whose principal formal characteristics remained broadly the same throughout the twentieth century[1]. The period to 1975 saw the long rise of the county councils, from their statutory creation in 1890, alongside the burgh authorities which were mostly of much earlier date[2]. Local authorities were elected; they were multipurpose bodies rather than existing simply for the discharge of a single function; they were financed from both grants from central government and from rates collected locally; and decision-making was mainly by committees of the authority. Following the 1939–45 war, the range and importance of the services provided by local authorities increased. New responsibilities for town and country planning and social work combined with expanding responsibilities for education, housing, roads, water and sewerage to give local authorities a very substantial role. At the same time, however, their structure and organisation were failing to keep pace. In the view of the Wheatley Royal Commission which reported in 1969, something was seriously wrong[3]. There were too many authorities (some 643) and of too many (5) different types. This led to inefficiencies which could be remedied only by reform implemented, in due course, in May 1975 under the terms of the Local Government (Scotland) Act 1973. With the declared aim of achieving both greater democracy and greater effectiveness, the number of authorities was greatly reduced. Across mainland Scotland a two-tier structure was created. There were nine regional councils, taking responsibility for functions including education, social work, roads, structure planning and water supply; then 56 district councils, with responsibility for housing, environmental health and local planning. This, it was believed, would be a system coming closest to providing authorities of a size appropriate to the efficient delivery of the different services while, at the same time, linking the authorities to identifiable communities across the country. In the three islands areas of Orkney, Shetland and the Western Isles, however, single-tier authorities were created, with responsibility for all local functions save that they were amalgamated with the Highland Region for the provision of police and fire services. It was interesting that, whereas prior to the 1975 reorganisation the all-purpose authorities had been in the four major cities, after that reorganisation all-purpose authorities shifted to the islands. In the next reorganisation, however, single-tier authorities were introduced uniformly across Scotland.

The reorganisation of 1996 took place in very different circumstances from that of 1975. In the earlier period, there was an acknowledgment that the organisation of local government needed a substantial overhaul but there was no serious challenge to the idea of local government itself. Local self-government was essential to the delivery of local services and the structures had to be reformed to sustain the ideal. There were tensions between central government and local authorities, in relation to the funding of local government in particular, but it was still credible to refer to the relationship between the two as a 'partnership'. By the early 1990s, however, these conditions had changed substantially. From 1979, in particular, the Thatcher governments were less tolerant of the political independence of local authorities; they sought to restrict the authorities' freedom to spend money; and they removed many local authority powers. In the privatising ideology of the times, local authorities came to be viewed not as the essential providers of local services but as enablers of service provision. This led, for instance, to the removal of local authority responsibility for further education in 1992[4] and, at the point of reorganisation in 1996, of responsibility for water and sewerage services and the Children's Reporter service[5]. Just as importantly, however, central government imposed on local councils an expanding regime of 'compulsory competitive tendering' (CCT)[6] under which councils were required to compete with private-sector providers in the supply of services.

This approach to local government as a whole produced a different approach to how to achieve its most desirable structure. The big regional authorities, especially Strathclyde Regional Council and Lothian Regional Council in the central belt, had become symbolic of old-style big government and, particularly since they tended to be controlled by central government's political opponents, could readily be dispensed with. Two-tier local government, it was argued, was, in any event, confusing and unnecessary and produced uncertain lines of accountability. There was no involvement of a Royal Commission or other equivalent of the earlier Wheatley Commission but instead a direct move to

197

consultation papers[7] and the Bill which became LG(S)A 1994. Leaving the three islands councils intact, LG(S)A 1994 replaced the 9 mainland regions and 53 districts with 29 councils – roughly replicating the number of pre-1975 county councils but without the added complications of burgh or district councils. Subject to initial transitional arrangements, elections were originally to be held on a three-yearly cycle with effect from May 1999. Since then, however, these arrangements have been changed in two ways. First it was decided to synchronise local elections with those for the Scottish Parliament, and the Scottish Local Government (Elections) Act 2002 introduced a new four-yearly cycle with effect from May 2003. Later the local elections were disengaged from the parliamentary cycle by the Scottish Local Government (Elections) Act 2009 which provides for elections in 2012, 2017 and then every fourth year after that. Since the implementation of the Local Governance (Scotland) Act 2004 in 2007, elections have been held using the single transferable vote system of proportional representation[8] with council areas divided into multi member wards for the purpose. The electorate is the same as for elections to the Scottish Parliament and the European Parliament and thus includes members of the House of Lords and citizens of EU countries, provided that they are resident and on the electoral roll[9]. Since 1975, and surviving the reorganisation of 1996, there have also operated in Scotland bodies known as community councils[10]. These have no executive powers but consist of local people, mainly elected, whose task is consultative, especially on planning matters.

1   For a fuller account, see C M G Himsworth *Local Government Law in Scotland* (1995): C Himsworth, 'Local Government in Scotland' in A McHarg and T Mullen (eds), *Public Law in Scotland* (2006). See also *SME Reissue* Local Government; and *SME Reissue* Constitutional Law, paras 438–467.
2   Local Government (Scotland) Act 1889; Local Government (Scotland) Acts 1929 and 1947.
3   Cmnd 4150, paras 1, 2.
4   Further and Higher Education (Scotland) Act 1992.
5   LG(S)A 1994, Pts II, III.
6   Local Government, Planning and Land Act 1980; Local Government Act 1988; Local Government Act 1992. See now the obligation to secure 'best value' p 199 below.
7   *The Structure of Local Government in Scotland: The case for change, principles of the new system* (1991) and *Shaping the New Councils* (1992).
8   The Executive appointed the (Kerley) Renewing Local Democracy Working Group which reported in June 2000 – with a majority of the Group recommending the adoption of the single transferable vote (STV) system of election from multi-member constituencies. Subsequently, the Executive consulted further and, after it renewed its commitment in principle in September 2002, proposals for the introduction of STV were included in the draft Local Governance (Scotland) Bill published in February 2003. A commitment to proportional representation was included in the Liberal Democrat manifesto prior to the general election of May 2003 and, although the Labour Party manifesto expressed a preference for no change, the agreed coalition document, *A Partnership for a Better Scotland,* of May 2003, contained a promise to introduce, by the time of the 2007 elections, the STV system with multi-member wards of either three or four members, depending on local circumstances.
9   Local Government Elections (Changes to the Franchise and Qualifications of Members) Regulations 1995, SI 1995/1948.
10 Local Government (Scotland) Act 1973, Pt IV.

Powers

7.3   Local authority powers derive from statute[1], as passed mainly by the Westminster Parliament but increasingly by the Scottish Parliament. In the

British tradition of local government, powers tend to be conferred in quite specific terms and this means that the legal authority for most local authority functions is contained in statutes which deal with a particular functional area. Thus, local authorities derive their powers in relation to schools from the Education (Scotland) Act 1980 and subsequent legislation[2]; their powers to construct and maintain roads from the Roads (Scotland) Act 1984; their social work functions from the Social Work (Scotland) Act 1968; their planning powers from the Town and Country Planning (Scotland) Act 1997, and so on. Other powers are contained in statutes such as the Civic Government (Scotland) Act 1982 which provides for certain licensing and public order functions[3] and some are conferred by the Local Government Acts themselves.

The tradition of conferring powers by specific statutory provision has meant that, until very recently, local authorities have not had general or residual powers to do things of their choice for the good of their local communities. They have not had a 'general competence'. Their only flexibility has derived from two rather restricted sources. The Local Government (Scotland) Act 1973 (LG(S)A 1973), s 69 confers a power on authorities 'to do any thing ... which is calculated to facilitate, or is conducive or incidental to, the discharge of any of their functions'[4]. Then, LG(S)A 1973, s 83 conferred what was, at first sight, a much wider power. It permitted any authority to incur expenditure which in its opinion is in the interests of its area (or any part of it) or all or some of its inhabitants. The apparent breadth of that power was qualified in a number of ways but it was, in any event, replaced by the Local Government in Scotland Act 2003 (LG(S)A 2003), s 20. That responded to the calls for a power of general competence, a new power to do anything which a local authority considers is likely to promote or improve the well-being of its area and/or persons within that area). Local authorities were also given the duty to adopt a leadership role (community planning) within their areas in the shape of an obligation to maintain and facilitate a process by which public services are planned for and provided (LG(S)A 2003, s 15). Authorities have been subjected to a new duty to secure 'best value', ie the 'continuous improvement in the performance' of their functions (LG(S)A 2003, s 1).

1 An exception may be the very limited powers by virtue of the 'common good' enjoyed by some councils under LG(S)A 1994, s 15(4).
2 See, for example, the Standards in Scotland's Schools etc Act 2000.
3 See also the Licensing (Scotland) Act 2005.
4 But see *McColl v Strathclyde Regional Council* 1983 SC 225.

Internal structure and organisation

7.4 The powers of a local authority are almost exclusively vested in the elected council itself[1]. Traditional British practice has not been to adopt a model of local government involving an elected council or assembly and then, separately, an elected provost or mayor in whom some or all of the powers of the authority are vested. Local government has not had a 'presidential' character of this sort. Equally, there has not been a practice of conferring powers on a 'Cabinet' of senior politicians forming an administration separate from, but accountable to, the council at large. Nor has there been a tradition of conferring powers upon a 'manager' or chief executive as the head of the paid service of the council. Rather, the principal model for local government administration has been one giving pre-eminence to government by committee. Until recently most local authority decision-making was by committees organised on functional lines (ie with an education committee, a planning committee etc) and controlled politically by the party having a majority on the council itself. Since the 1975 reorganisation, most councils have also had a co-ordinating committee of senior councillors – typically a policy and resources committee; and many took some advantage of a power to delegate decision-making to officers[2].

Developments since devolution have brought change to the management of local authorities. It was a concern of the McIntosh Commission[3], followed up in the report of the (MacNish) Leadership Advisory Panel[4], that government by committee had become inefficient and unaccountable. The option of directly elected mayors or provosts which has been permitted (subject to local referendum) in England[5] has not found favour in Scotland, but many councils have modified their structures to produce a form of 'Cabinet' decision-making. Powers are formally exercised by an executive committee of senior councillors, with other committees assuming a more advisory or scrutinising role.

1 Exceptionally, powers are vested directly in an officer, for example assessors for the purposes of valuation for rating and the council tax.
2 LG(S)A 1973, s 56.
3 See p 202 below.
4 *Scottish Local Government's Self-Review of its Political Management Structures: Report of the Leadership Advisory Panel* (April 2001).
5 Local Government Act 2000, Pt II.

Local government finance

7.5   The continuing commitment to entrusting large volumes of local service provision to elected local authorities makes the work of those authorities expensive (in 2006–07, £18.9 bn across Scotland as a whole[1]) and the question of funding them important. Authorities must have sufficient funds to meet their needs but they should also be funded in a way which preserves a degree of autonomy in their decision-making and which encourages local accountability.

Local councils are funded today in three principal ways[2]. A small amount of revenue derives from charges made for services provided. Secondly, councils impose a local council tax on domestic properties, based largely on the value of the property concerned. Thirdly, councils receive from central government (since 1999, the Scottish Executive) annual grants allocated according to formulae designed to reflect their needs, by reference principally to their population (adjusted to take account of its special features) and to their own tax-raising capacity. Although certain grants attach to specific services (for example, the police), most grant funding is general and, notionally at least, may be spent in accordance with a council's own priorities. The general grant funding is provided in terms of an annual Local Government Finance (Scotland) Order[3] under the authority of the Local Government Finance Act 1992 and consists of two elements. The *revenue support grant* is funded from the Scottish Executive's general revenues while the second element, the proceeds of *non-domestic rate* income, redistributes to local authorities the sums initially collected by them from commercial ratepayers at a level fixed by the Scottish Ministers. The funding of local government – not only in terms of overall levels but also the lack of robust and buoyant sources under the control of local authorities and, therefore, their heavy dependence upon central grants – has been a matter of controversy for many years. Central government has been reluctant to make radical reform, for instance in the direction of a local income tax which was an option considered positively by the Layfield Committee on local government finance as long ago as 1976[4]. There was also the grave error made in the poll tax experiment of the Thatcher government from 1989 to 1991[5] which left much bitterness.

Expenditure by local authorities and their accounts in general are audited by the Accounts Commission for Scotland[6]. Auditors are required to monitor for good accounting practice but also for illegal expenditure and good value for money[7].

1 The figure published in the official Government statistics for that year.
2 Discussion here is of the funding of recurrent or revenue expenditure. Councils may also fund capital expenditure by borrowing. See LG(S)A 1973, s 69 and Local Government in Scotland Act 2003, ss 35–39.
3 For 2009–10, see SSI 2009/50. Curiously named 'The Local Government Finance Act 1992 (Scotland) Order 2009' because of the need to replace a previously made invalid order.
4 Cmnd 6453.
5 Himsworth *Local Government Law in Scotland* (1995) pp 113–115.
6 LG(S)A 1973, s 97 (as amended).
7 LG(S)A 1973, s 99.

Central–local relations

7.6   The most important constitutional issue in local government is the relationship which exists between local authorities, both individually and collectively (principally in the form of the Convention of Scottish Local Authorities (COSLA)), and central government. The reason for this is that the point of local government – the justification for the delivery of local services by way of independently elected local authorities rather than field administration by local offices of central government – lies in its freedom to act autonomously on behalf of local people. Local authorities could never be wholly independent, of course. Equally, however, they should not be mere pawns in the hands of central government. An appropriate balance must be struck and frequently the preferred language to describe the relationship has been one of 'partnership'[1]. Essential prerequisites of that partnership are that local authorities do have substantial powers vested in them; that, as we have seen, they have the financial and other resources to discharge their functions; and that they are not subjected to unnecessary supervision and control by central government.

Although there was much room for disagreement, it was generally conceded that in the final quarter of the twentieth century the status of local government in Scotland, in common with conditions elsewhere in Great Britain[2], was in decline. In particular, the Conservative governments from 1979 had removed functions from local government[3]; they had reorganised local government in ways likely to weaken it[4]; and had mismanaged local finance, especially during the poll tax experiment. On the local government side of the relationship, there had built up substantial anger and resentment – not ideal conditions under which to launch the devolution project in 1997.

1 See (Wheatley) Royal Commission Report (Cmnd 4150, 1969).
2 In Northern Ireland, the loss of many local services from local authorities to unelected boards in the 1970s had produced an ever starker picture.
3 For example, water services and the Children's Reporter service in 1996.
4 Again, in Scotland, in 1996. In England and Wales, the Greater London Council and the metropolitan counties were abolished in 1986.

LOCAL GOVERNMENT AND DEVOLUTION[1]

7.7   SA 1998 did not in itself bring immediate change to local government. It did not reorganise the structure; nor did it adjust the functions or financing of local government. However, it did bring with it the prospect of future change and, in particular, of a changed relationship with central government which, for these purposes, has now become the Scottish Government.

Local government is not, in the terms of SA 1998, a reserved matter. Nor are practically all the functions discharged by local authorities[2]. This means that it is within the legislative competence of the Scottish Parliament to reorganise local government or take away or add to the functions of local authorities[3]. Although the Parliament cannot in general legislate on matters of taxation, it can legislate for 'local taxes to fund local authority expenditure'[4]. The Scottish Parliament can also amend the system of local elections, although not the franchise[5]. Similarly, the Scottish Government has taken over the former functions of the Secretary of State for Scotland in relation to local authorities, including the determination of levels of financial assistance through grant.

Anticipating these transfers of power, the White Paper *Scotland's Parliament*[6] foresaw that they might produce the undesirable consequence that the Scottish Parliament would take the opportunity to accumulate a range of new functions at the centre which should instead continue to be more appropriately and efficiently delivered by other bodies, especially local authorities. The principle that decisions should be made as close as possible to the citizen (ie the principle of subsidiarity) held good *within* Scotland as it did *between* Scotland and the United Kingdom government. The UK government had just signed the Council of Europe Charter of Local Self-Government and the Scottish people would be served best by the Scottish Parliament and Executive working closely with strong democratically elected local government. That relationship with local authorities was particularly crucial to the good governance of Scotland and the effective provision of services to its people[7].

To assist the emergence of this relationship, the UK government established a Commission on Local Government and the Scottish Parliament under the chairmanship of Neil McIntosh. It had a remit to consider (a) how to build the most effective relations between local government and the Scottish Parliament and Scottish Executive and (b) how councils could best make themselves responsible and democratically accountable to the communities they served. The Commission carried out a substantial consultation exercise and reported in June 1999 to recommend that central and local government should commit themselves to joint agreements setting out working relationships. Rather like the concordats now agreed between the Scottish and UK ministers[8], there should be a 'covenant' between the Scottish Parliament and the 32 local councils, supported by a standing joint conference to consider matters of mutual concern. There should be a separate formal agreement between local government and the Scottish Ministers. In addition, the Commission recommended a new statutory power of general competence for local authorities; a review of local government finance; the reform of election arrangements and the electoral system; the review by councils of the way in which they conduct their business, including the formalisation of political leaderships as council executives; and the strengthening of community councils.

Some of these recommendations were carried forward. A Partnership Framework between the Scottish Executive and the Convention of Scottish Local Authorities was agreed in May 2001. This was a document based on 'parity of esteem and the principles of subsidiarity underlying the European Charter of Local Self-Government' and which committed the Executive to consultation, the exchange of information and meetings on matters of local government concern. In the Scottish Parliament, the first substantive policy debate was on local government[9] and the Parliament's Local Government Committee devoted some time in the 1999–2003 session to the discussion of a covenant between the Parliament and local government. A draft was prepared which provided, as with the Partnership Framework, for consultation in a relationship which was to be 'effective and meaningful'. A Standing Joint Conference would be established to undertake periodic reviews of the relationship and of the working of the covenant. However, the covenant was not concluded in the first session because of a number of unresolved difficulties. While the committee thought it possible that its successor in the second session might wish to pursue the matter further, it also thought that events had demonstrated that the Parliament was not, in practice, likely to 'absorb' local government powers. Perhaps more fundamentally, following legal advice, it referred to the retention of the Parliament's powers to legislate on local government matters 'irrespective of the views of local government representatives, or others. Any covenant could not alter this fundamental legislative position'. The committee was questioning the case for a covenant purporting to bind the Parliament. On the other hand, the Local Government Committee, in the face of Executive reluctance to set up a general inquiry into local government finance at that time, conducted its own inquiry – making recommendations that the balance between central and local funding of local government should be put on a 50:50 basis rather than 80:20; that properties should be revalued regularly for council tax purposes; that the non-domestic rate should be returned to local control; and that a further inquiry should be held into the feasibility of introducing a local income tax[10]. The coalition document of May 2003 committed the Executive to establishing an independent review of local government finance[11]. In due course, the report of the (Birt) Committee[12] was published but its findings (including the recommendation of a new local property tax) were rejected by the Executive.

When the SNP Government entered into its concordat with COSLA in November 2007 the principal focus was on the important issue of local government finance. In return for a 'freeze' on council tax levels during to years to 2010–11, the Government, in recognition of 'the unique position held by local government in the governance of Scotland', would seek to ensure a general increase in funding with less 'ring-fencing' of specific grants. At the same time, however, a Single Outcome Agreement[13] committing to specified policy objectives would be negotiated with each authority. A related SNP initiative[14] to abolish the council tax altogether and to replace it with a local income tax – at a single rate fixed nationally across the country and thus leaving authorities with no discretionary tax rate of their own – was subsequently abandoned because of lack of parliamentary support from other parties[15].

There has been a Scottish Government commitment not to engage in an early reorganisation of local government[16].

1 For a recent analysis see J Gallagher et al *Rethinking Central Local Relations in Scotland: Back to the Future?* (David Hume Institute, 2007).
2 An exception is weights and measures: SA 1998, Sch 5, Pt II, S C9.
3 See SA 1998, Sch 5, Pt III.
4 SA 1998, Sch 5, Pt II, S A1.
5 SA 1998, Sch 5, Pt II, S B3.
6 Cm 3658.
7 Cm 3658, ch 6.
8 See p 190.
9 SP OR, 2 July 1999, col 878.
10 SP Paper 551, Session 1 (2002).
11 *A Partnership for a Better Scotland* p 46.
12 *A Fairer Way*, November 2006.
13 See *Single Outcome Agreements: Guidance, format and indicators* issued by COSLA, the Scottish Government and others in February 2008.
14 *A Fairer Local Tax for Scotland*, March 2008.
15 For their discussion of the proposal, see the proceedings of the Local Government and Communities Committee of 28 May and 25 June 2008.
16 Most recently in the concordat of 2007.

INTERMEDIATE GOVERNMENT

7.8   In Chapter 1 we were introduced to the idea of constitutions as maps on which are located a state's institutions and their interrelationships. In the territory of intermediate government, map-making has been only partial and, therefore, unreliable. As we have seen, starting descriptions are negatively cast. Intermediate government occupies that space not occupied by central government or elected local authorities. Prior to devolution, 'central departments' were all located at the UK level. Post-devolution, 'central government' must include the 'devolved administrations' since it would be inappropriate to relegate elected assemblies or bodies accountable to elected assemblies and Parliaments into intermediate government. The definition of what, therefore, constitutes central departments is tolerably clear, although 'department' is not a term of art and central departments collectively are far from monolithic. Non-ministerial departments and offices[1] and executive agencies are part of a varied pattern. But then, even with central government identified, the negative style of definition breaks down in that it does little to help identify the field of intermediate government nor, more importantly, to categorise its occupants[2]. A simple listing of bodies would be possible but not very enlightening. Analysis could be chronological – certainly, some bodies have a much longer history than others – but, again, to little analytical effect. Classification by function is more useful – bodies may be categorised as having adjudicative, regulatory, supervisory, licensing, advisory, service provision or other characteristics – but this can obscure more important distinctions. Similarly, classification by reference to the supposed rationale for the creation and continued existence of public bodies separated from central and local government may be only fairly helpful. It is true that most justifications for intermediate government may be offered by reference to the need for efficiency (for example, the reason for giving the (decreasing numbers of) nationalised industries a commercial independence from government); or the need for a higher degree of independence from political control and political accountability in the provision of certain services (such as the BBC, the NHS or Scottish Water or the Scottish Court Service in its support of the judiciary); or the need for a quasi-judicial independence for licensing or regulatory bodies (such as the Scottish Environment Protection Agency) and for those who have to scrutinise the functions of government itself (such as the National Audit Office and Audit Scotland). But objective classification on this basis would be elusive. The present pattern of public bodies owes much to the contingencies of history – whether the rise and fall of nationalisation and privatisation; the politics of health care provision; varying climates of friendliness or hostility to local government; or variations in views on the optimum size of the 'state' – and to political expediency.

Probably the most useful guides to the field are those which facilitate contemporary constitutional analysis. This tends to focus on the efficacy of governmental processes (such as economic regulation), accountability (whether of public bodies themselves or of those whom they hold to account), transparency, and the vulnerability of intermediate government to abuse, especially political patronage by ministers in the appointments process. Concerns about quango[3] government and successive promises, in response, from politicians to launch 'bonfires of quangos' are mainly located in these areas. Thus certain potential admissions to the field of intermediate government are fairly quickly excluded. The armed forces, though interestingly different from standard government departments, remain within central government. Police forces, though with a structure of their own, are best seen as a limb of local government, and courts of law are excluded, because they lack 'governmental' characteristics. On the other hand, tribunals, whose functions and composition may be very similar, would probably be included. Ombudsmen would probably be excluded, like courts, on functional grounds – although, from the point of view of the risk of abuse of political patronage, their position may not be immediately distinguishable from some others. Universities vary in their formal status and, although probably not immediately recognisable as quangos, they are 'public bodies' in receipt of substantial public funding. Certainly their function as education providers does not exclude them. Further education colleges are more easily grouped as quangos[4] and so are 'opted-out' schools[5] the Scottish Funding Council (further and higher education) and the research councils[6]. Regulators such as those dealing with the privatised industries (for example, the Office of Rail Regulation, OFGEM (gas and electricity)), the Drinking Water Quality Regulator, SEPA and the Electoral Commission are within the sector. Service providers including the remaining nationalised industries (such as CalMac Ferries Ltd), Scottish Water and, above all, the health boards[7], health service trusts and other bodies within the National Health Service are certainly within intermediate government. Purely advisory bodies such as the enduring Royal Commission on Environmental Pollution[8], the (Scottish) Judicial Appointments Board or the Scottish Law Commission, whose situation, because lacking executive powers and serious public funding, are less exposed, would also be included.

One constitutionally distinct group which may be identified are the six 'SPCB' Supported Bodies' all of whom are appointed by the Queen on the nomination of the Scottish Parliament rather than of ministers and are supported by the Scottish Parliament Corporate Body. They are the Scottish Public Services Ombudsman, the Scottish Information Commissioner, the Commissioner for Public Appointments, the Scottish Commission for Human Rights and the Scottish Parliamentary Standards Commissioner. During 2008-09 they were the subject of a review by an ad hoc committee of the Parliament. The committee reported in May 2009[9], recommending the merger into a single 'standards' body of the Standards Commissioner and Public Appointments Commissioner. A committee bill was to follow.

1   For example, those identified by SA 1998 as 'offices in the Scottish Administration which are not ministerial offices'.
2   For one attempt at definition and classification, see Sixth Report of the Public Administration Committee (HC Paper 209-I (1989–99)) paras 8–25.
3   The term originated misleadingly as an acronym for 'quasi non-government organisation'. For discussion, see A Barker 'Governmental bodies and the neutral of mutual accountability' in A Barker (ed) *Quangos in Britain: Government and the Networks of Public Policy-Making* (1982). See also D C Hague, W J M Mackenzie and A Barker (eds) *Public Policy and Private Interests* (1975); W Hall and S Weir *The Untouchables: Power and Accountability in the Quango State* (1996); and D Oliver *Constitutional Reform in the UK* (2003) ch 17.
4   See *Governance and Accountability in the Further Education Section* (Scottish Executive, May 2002).
5   Although abolished in Scotland since the Standards in Scotland's Schools etc Act 2000, ss 17–23.
6   For example, the Economic and Social Research Council (ESRC).
7   See Health Boards (Membership and Elections) (Scotland) Act 2009.
8   Appointed by royal warrant in 1970, that Commission has open-ended terms of reference. Other Royal Commissions, such as the (Kilbrandon) Royal Commission on the Constitution (1973) or the (Sutherland) Royal Commission on Long Term Care of the Elderly (1998), have had a time-limited remit.
9   SP 266.

PUBLIC BODIES AND DEVOLUTION (INCLUDING CROSS-BORDER PUBLIC AUTHORITIES)

7.9   The implementation of SA 1998 has brought important changes to the constitutional position of intermediate government and many of the consequences of those changes are still being worked out. The allocation of legislative powers to the Scottish Parliament means that, for the future and within the limits of those powers, the Parliament can decide whether or not to establish new public bodies; their powers; their membership; and their methods of working. Questions of whether to allocate such new business to local authorities, to the Scottish Ministers or to a quango are for the Parliament to decide. Since 1999, the Parliament has created a number of bodies including Audit Scotland[1], the national park authorities[2], the Scottish Commission for the Regulation of Care[3], a Bus Users' Complaints Tribunal[4] , a Risk Management Authority[5]; the Scottish Commission for Human Rights and the Scottish Legal Complaints Commission[6]. On the other hand, Scottish Homes was abolished[7] and its functions subsumed into a new executive agency, Communities Scotland. The former three separate water authorities have been merged into Scottish Water[8]; predecessor bodies were merged into the Scottish Further and Higher Education Funding Council[9] and the constitutions of the Scottish Qualifications Authority[10] and the Scottish Court Service were adjusted[11]. Similarly, new bodies, which can appropriately be established by means other than primary legislation by the Parliament, may also be created. The use of the prerogative, for instance, to establish a new royal commission to inquire into some problem or the appointment of a commission or committee on a more informal basis is within the competence of the Scottish Ministers[12]. By the same token, it remains competent for the Westminster Parliament and UK ministers to establish new public bodies with responsibilities in relation to reserved matters affecting Scotland and, at the same time, decide whether or not to involve the Scottish Ministers, for example by specifying that they will be consulted on certain appointments[13]. It should also be borne in mind that the Westminster Parliament retains the power to legislate on any matter, reserved or not[14], and it could use this power to create a new authority with responsibilities which include devolved matters. It is unlikely that this power would be used other than with the consent of the Scottish Ministers and the Scottish Parliament[15] and an early example was the setting up of the Food Standards Agency in 2000. It would have been within the powers of the Scottish Parliament to establish such a body separately for Scotland but, by agreement, this was done for the United Kingdom as a whole[16]. This was, however, rather a special 'transitional' case, in that preparations for the Agency were already under way prior to devolution.

A rather more complex position presents itself in relation to those public bodies which were *already in existence* prior to 1 July 1999. The main questions raised are (i) how far the Scottish Parliament may affect such bodies by amending or repealing the legislation under which they operate; (ii) what involvement the Scottish Ministers have in relation to appointments or other aspects of the operation of these bodies, including their financing; and (iii) what influence the Scottish Parliament and its committees have on their operation. For these purposes, existing public bodies may be divided into three broad categories:

1 Public Finance Accountability (Scotland) Act 2000.
2 National Parks (Scotland) Act 2000.
3 Regulation of Care (Scotland) Act 2001.
4 Transport (Scotland) Act 2001.
5 Criminal Justice (Scotland) Act 2003.
6 Legal Profession and Legal Aid (Scotland) Act 2007 s 1.

7   Housing (Scotland) Act 2001. See also the dissolution of the Water Industry Commissioner by the Water Services etc (Scotland) Act 2005 and SSI 2007/399.
8   Water Industry (Scotland) Act 2002.
9   Further and Higher Education (S) Act 2005.
10 Scottish Qualifications Authority Act 2002.
11 Judiciary and Courts (Scotland) Act 2008.
12 See, for example the Report of the (Cubie) Independent Committee of Inquiry into Student Finance, *Student Finance: Fairness for the Future* (1999); and the Reports of the Jandoo and Campbell Inquiries into the Chhokar Affair (SP Papers 424 and 425 (2001)); the Report of the (Crerar) Independent Review of Regulation, Audit, Inspection and Complaints Handling of Public Services in Scotland 2007; and the Report of the (Sutherland) Review of Free Personal Care 2008.
13 See, in relation to appointment to the Strategic Rail Authority, the Transport Act 2000, s 202(3), (5).
14 SA 1998, s 28(7), and see p 140 above.
15 See ch 5, p 140.
16 Food Standards Act 1999.

(a) Public bodies with responsibilities entirely connected with reserved matters

7.10   A large number of public bodies, whose responsibilities fall outwith the legislative competence of the Scottish Parliament, are within this category[1]. They include such bodies as the BBC, the Independent Television Commission, the Health and Safety Executive, the Office of the Rail Regulator and the Equal Opportunities Commission. Such bodies are beyond the legislative competence of the Scottish Parliament. At first sight, they would also be wholly beyond the competence of the Scottish Ministers but some adjustments have been made in the process of expanding executive competence under SA 1998, s 63[2]. In, for instance, the field of broadcasting, the powers under the Broadcasting Acts 1990 to make payments to the Gaelic Media Service[3] for the financing of programmes in Gaelic has been transferred to the Scottish Ministers[4] and, in making certain appointments to the Independent Television Commission, to the Radio Authority and to the Broadcasting Standards Commission, the Secretary of State must consult the Scottish Ministers[5]. There is also an undertaking to consult on the appointment of the Scottish Governor of the BBC[6].

Despite the reservation of the functions of these bodies, the Scottish Parliament's powers to monitor their activities has been a live question since the proceedings on the Scotland Bill at Westminster, especially in relation to such institutions as the BBC[7]. The full extent to which the Parliament will become engaged in these issues is still emerging, although some early interest was, for instance, expressed in the appointment of a Scottish Governor of the BBC in July 1999[8]. SA 1998 does not confer any power on the Parliament to demand documents or the presence of witnesses in relation to a reserved body[9] but witnesses may be invited to attend on a voluntary basis[10].

1   A small number of these are specifically identified as 'reserved bodies' in SA 1998, Sch 5, Pt III but the category extends much more broadly than that.
2   See p 178.
3   S183. See also the Communications Act 2003 s 208.
4   Scotland Act 1998 (Transfer of Functions to the Scottish Ministers etc) Order 1999, SI 1999/1750.

5 Scotland Act 1998 (Transfer of Functions to the Scottish Ministers etc) Order 1999, SI 1999/1750.
6 For advice on royal appointments, see p 247. A Scottish Executive news release of 23 July 1999 confirmed that the First Minister had been consulted on the appointment of a new Scottish Governor.
7 See HC Debs, 13 January 1998, col 185.
8 See motion (SPOR) SIM-81 by Mike Russell MSP, asking that the Parliament be consulted on the matter by the Scottish Ministers. One section receiving attention from the Calman review is broadcasting.
9 SA 1998, s 23(6).
10 The Education, Culture and Sport Committee took evidence from the Scottish Governor of the BBC and others on 1 March 2000; the Equal Opportunities Committee took evidence from the Commission for Racial Equality on 16 April 2002; and the Local Government and Transport Committee heard from the Rail Regulator on 25 May 2004.

(b) Public bodies with responsibilities within the competence of the Scottish Parliament

7.11   Again, a very large number of bodies fall into this category. It includes, for instance, the health service bodies, the water authorities (which became Scottish Water) and many others mentioned above. A list was attached as Annex A to the White Paper *Scotland's Parliament*[1]. For these bodies the Scottish Parliament has full legislative competence and their powers could be amended or the bodies themselves could be abolished by the Parliament and their powers ended or transferred elsewhere. In those cases where the bodies exist by virtue of administrative decision only, the same powers to amend or abolish are now held by the Scottish Ministers – to whom have also been transferred the powers to appoint, to give directions and to provide funding that were previously within the responsibility of UK ministers[2]. As far as the scrutiny function of the Parliament is concerned, the power to call for the necessary witnesses and documents is provided[3]. One of the highest-profile investigations of the first session of the Parliament was that conducted by the Enterprise and Lifelong Learning Committee and the Education, Culture and Sport Committees into mismanagement at the Scottish Qualifications Authority[4].

1 Cm 3658.
2 For the general transfer of executive responsibilities, see p 176 above.
3 SA 1998, s 23.
4 See p 269.

(c) Public bodies with mixed responsibilities

7.12   This is the most complex group because the mixture of functions within the remit of a single existing body causes inevitable problems for the working of the devolved scheme of government, although some of the problems are only transitional and will be gradually removed over time. Bodies may have mixed functions in two different ways. They may be based entirely in Scotland and yet have responsibilities which are both reserved and devolved. It appears that there may not be very many of these but they include the Scottish Consumer Council, the Rail Users' Consultative Committee for Scotland and the Scottish Association of Citizens Advice Bureaux[1]. The other form of mixture of functions occurs where bodies have responsibilities in both Scotland and other parts of the United Kingdom and these responsibilities include devolved matters, whether or not also in combination with some reserved matters. This is a much longer list and includes such bodies as the British Tourist Authority, the Criminal Injuries Compensation Authority[2], the Forestry Commissioners and many others[3].

In the case of all these bodies, it would, in principle, be open to the Scottish Parliament to make new provision for them within its legislative competence[4]. As with Scottish local authorities, the Parliament could carry out substantial adjustments to their structure and it could abolish functions or transfer them elsewhere. However, in order to make that process work more smoothly and also to regularise the running of most of these mixed authorities (for which administrative responsibility has, in some way, to be shared between Scottish and UK ministers), SA 1998 created the new category of 'cross-border public authority' (CBPA)[5]. With effect from 1 July 1999, CBPAs[6] were specified in an Order in Council[7]. Others have since been designated as CBPAs on their creation[8]. Then, in relation to those specified CBPAs, the standard rules transferring executive responsibilities, within devolved competence, to the Scottish Ministers are disapplied, leaving responsibilities with UK ministers who are required to consult the Scottish Ministers in matters of appointments and the exercise of functions affecting devolved matters on Scotland[9]. Reports relating to CBPAs must be laid before the Scottish Parliament as well as the UK Parliament and the rights of the Scottish Parliament to call for witnesses and documents in relation to CBPAs are established[10]. In order to fine-tune these arrangements and, in particular, to define which ministerial responsibilities are allocated to which ministers (whether on a separate or shared basis or involving consultation), further provision has been made to adapt the functions of some CBPAs and ministers[11]. The specification of a body as CBPA does not prevent the Scottish Parliament from legislating to remove a function from a CBPA (in so far as exercisable in Scotland), perhaps in order to establish a separate body in Scotland. SA 1998 does, however, make provision for the property consequences of such a change[12] if it is made.

CBPAs are institutions which, because of the regime of shared responsibility imposed upon them, are not within the immediate control of the Scottish Parliament and Executive. On the other hand, the position of Scottish quangos with devolved or mixed functions (but not designated as CBPAs) has already been under review.

1   These all appear in the Schedule to SI 1999/1319. See below. Because they are not included in the category of intermediate government, local authorities are not further treated here, although they too have mixed responsibilities.
2   The earlier Compensation Board was abolished from 1 April 2000.
3   Also listed in SI 1999/1319.
4   The Tourist Boards (Scotland) Act 2006 changed the name of the Scottish Tourist Board to Visit Scotland but retained its connection with the British Tourist Authority under the Development of Tourism Act 1969.
5   SA 1998, ss 88–90. See *Scotland's Parliament* (Cm 3658, paras 2.8–2.11).
6   Which may include not only the quangos we have been discussing but also other government departments, offices and office-holders.
7   SA 1998, s 88(5), (6). See Scotland Act 1998 (Cross-Border Public Authorities) (Specification) Order 1999, SI 1999/1319.

8   For example, the Food Standards Agency by the Foods Standards Act 1999 and the Climate Change Committee by the Climate Change Act 2008. On the other hand, the pre-devolution (Wicks) Committee on Standards in Public Life and the post-devolution Electoral Commission have not been designated.
9   SA 1998, s 88 (1), (2). See eg SI 2007/447.
10 SA 1998, s 88(3) and s 23.
11 SA 1998, s 89 and see the Scotland Act 1998 (Cross-Border Public Authorities) (Adaptation of Functions etc) Order 1999, SI 1999/1747. Particularly extensive provision has been made in relation to the Forestry Commissioners (SI 2000/746).
12 SA 1998, s 90.

REFORMING INTERMEDIATE GOVERNMENT

7.13   Under this heading it is appropriate to return to some of the constitutional concerns which have been associated with intermediate government and to take account of some of the measures taken to address them. The main emphasis here is upon initiatives taken by the Scottish Executive and Parliament since 1999 but the underlying issues have been familiar for much longer and they continue to be addressed with some vigour at the UK level[1]. One such initiative has focused upon the question of maintaining ethical standards in public bodies and that is considered, along with parallel developments in local government, at pp 215–216 below.

Otherwise, the main political and constitutional concerns are with other possible forms of abuse of the quango system. What they have in common is the fear that quangos may be created and funded, and appointments made, not to serve the public interest represented by the ostensible purposes of the bodies themselves but to serve much narrower political purposes. The concerns which have arisen may be divided under three broad heads. There may, firstly, be questions about whether certain quangos are needed at all. Could they not be abolished and their functions given either to a merged quango or to central or local government? Secondly, and perhaps most prominently, there is the vexed question of appointments. There is a long-standing fear that appointments by ministers to quangos may be used as an improper form of political patronage. Thirdly, there are questions about the accountability of bodies whose very justification is based in part upon a wish to avoid direct political accountability but which must nevertheless be kept within some reasonable boundaries of supervision and control.

1   See, for instance, Fourth Report of the House of Commons Select Committee on Public Administration 'Government by Appointment: Opening up the Patronage State' (HC Paper 165 (2002–03)).

The need for quangos

7.14   To take these concerns in order, the extent of Scottish government by quango was the subject of some attention by the Executive during the first parliamentary session. In January 2001, a review of public bodies was launched. It was concluded in June with the publication of *Public Bodies: Proposals for Change*. This report surveyed a field of some 180 public bodies; it sought to generate principles according to which their continued existence (and the creation of other bodies) should be judged; and made proposals for a number of abolitions and mergers, and, in some cases, for further review. The principles adopted by the Executive started from the need for ministers to be directly accountable to the Parliament for the overall policy and strategic framework within which all devolved functions were carried out. Functions such as giving specialist advice and making quasi-judicial decisions apart, only where it was clear that ministers should be distanced from the execution of a function should it be allocated to some body outwith the Executive, and then only when subject to clear strategic direction. Bodies had to be properly run, efficient and effective. Overall the review produced proposals for the abolition or merger of 52 bodies and the more detailed review of a further 61. Seventy bodies were to be retained. The Public Appointments and Public Bodies etc (Scotland) Act 2003, s 4 dissolved five quangos, including the Ancient Monuments Board for Scotland and the Scottish Conveyancing and Executry Services Board. The current SNP Government has a commitment to reducing the number of public bodies in Scotland through a programme of 'Simplifying Public Services' launched in January 2008. A Public Services Reform Bill has been introduced, one of whose targets is quangos. The specific project to establish a new body Creative Scotland (and to dissolve the Scottish Arts Council) suffered a set-back when the Bill failed at Stage 1 in June 2008 but that project is revived in the new Bill.

Appointments to quangos

7.15   On appointments, the starting point was an extension to devolved public bodies in Scotland of the regime created for UK public bodies under the Commissioner for Public Appointments. That office was created by (prerogative) Order in Council following a recommendation by the Committee on Standards in Public Life[1]. When the UK Government published *Scotland's Parliament*, it included the commitment that the Scottish Executive would be required to put arrangements in place to ensure that appointments to Scottish public bodies were subject to independent scrutiny and conform to the Commissioner's *Code of Practice*[2]. The *Code* lays down certain general principles including the statement that the ultimate responsibility for appointments rests with ministers; selection must be made on merit; appointment panels must include an independent assessor; and principles of equal opportunity, probity, transparency and proportionality must be observed. Thereafter the *Code* contains detailed rules about the stages of the appointments process, auditing performance, the handling of complaints and the collection of statistics and information. There was no statutorily imposed obligation to adhere to these standards, but the 1999 coalition document, *Partnership for Scotland* contained a commitment to 'encourage the Parliament to review and monitor public appointments' and, in the meantime, the pre-devolution arrangements for public appointments were retained and extended to include appointments made by the Scottish Executive. The Commissioner for Public Appointments continued, therefore, to have a UK-wide role and the Scottish Ministers followed her guidance when making appointments[3]. In February 2000, the Minister for Finance launched a review of the system by issuing a consultation paper[4].

That paper contained a statement of key objectives of the public appointments system. It should enjoy public confidence through being fair, open and transparent; the system should be proportionate (ie appropriate to the nature of posts and the extent of their responsibilities); it should secure quality outcomes; it should encourage a wider range of people to apply; and should be accessible and informative. The paper then went on to elaborate on the ways in which these objectives might be achieved by means of reforms to the existing system. Among specific options considered was the creation by prerogative Order in Council of a new Scottish Commissioner for Public Appointments[5]. Although the role and powers of such an office would be broadly similar to those of the UK Commissioner, there would be scope for differences and it might be appropriate to place the obligation of the Scottish Ministers to observe the Commissioner's code of practice on a statutory basis[6]. The consultation paper referred to 'a possible, although not insurmountable, disadvantage' of establishing a Scottish Commissioner in the potential for inconsistencies in the appointments process across the United Kingdom. There might, in particular, be difficulties with the cross-border public authorities where the monitoring of appointments would at least require liaison. An answer might be for the existing UK Commissioner to be appointed also as the first Scottish Commissioner for an initial period of two years[7]. Another group of suggestions in the paper were for a strong role for the Parliament in the review and monitoring of public appointments[8]. In due course, the Executive brought forward proposals not for a prerogative-based Commissioner but for a statutory solution in the form of the legislation enacted just before the end of the first session of the Parliament in March 2003 as the Public Appointments and Public Bodies etc (Scotland) Act 2003 (PAPB(S)A 2003). It establishes (PAPB(S)A 2003, s 1) the office of Commissioner for Public Appointments in Scotland, to be appointed by the Queen on the nomination of the Parliament and subject to formal guarantees of independence including immunity from dismissal except by resolution of the Parliament passed with a two-thirds majority[9]. The principal duty of the Commissioner is to prepare and publish a code of practice for appointments to be made by the Scottish Ministers to any of a scheduled list of offices and bodies[10]. It is then for the Commissioner to examine the appointments methods and practices employed by the Executive and to investigate complaints. Ultimately the Commissioner is required to report failings under the code to the Parliament, with a related power to direct ministers to refrain from making an appointment subject to investigation 'until the Parliament has considered the case'[11].

1 *First Report* (Cm 2850, 1995).
2 Cm 3658, para 6.8.
3 *Appointments to Public Bodies in Scotland: Modernising the System* (Scottish Executive, February 2000) para 1.8.
4 *Appointments to Public Bodies in Scotland* para 1.8. See also SP OR 30 March 2000, col 1240.
5 *Appointments to Public Bodies in Scotland* ch 6.
6 *Appointments to Public Bodies in Scotland* para 6.5.
7 *Appointments to Public Bodies in Scotland* para 6.6.
8 *Appointments to Public Bodies in Scotland* ch 7.
9 PAPB(S)A 2003, sch 1.
10 PAPB(S)A 2003, s 2 and sch 2. The Code came into force in April 2006.
11 PAPB(S)A 2003, s 2(8).

Accountability and control of quangos[1]

7.16   As to questions of the supervision, control and general accountability of public bodies, many of the mechanisms[2] applicable to the Scottish Administration have been extended to them. Scottish quangos have been made subject to the audit arrangements introduced under the Public Finance and Accountability (Scotland) Act 2000. Health service bodies were removed from the supervision of the Accounts Commission and join other public bodies subject to scrutiny by the Auditor General for Scotland. Accountable officers must be designated within each body[3]. Intermediate government is also subject to the ombudsman regime. Practically all devolved Scottish bodies are within the jurisdiction of the Scottish Public Services Ombudsman[4]. Most reserved bodies and cross-border public authorities with executive powers remain within the jurisdiction of the UK Parliamentary Ombudsman. Reserved bodies are included within the scope of the (Westminster) Freedom of Information Act 2000 and devolved bodies fall under the Freedom of Information (Scotland) Act 2002[5]. As with local authorities, another significant change in the legal environment of quangos (both reserved and devolved) was brought about with the implementation of the Human Rights Act 1998 (HRA 1998)[6]. For the purposes of that Act, they are 'public authorities' and they must, therefore, act in a manner compatible with the (ECHR) Convention rights[7]. Bodies with regulatory powers, in particular, found it necessary to adjust the ways in which they implement and enforce the statutory regimes they supervise. It may be expected that there will be some impact on quangos if and when the recommendations of the Crerar Review of regulation, audit, inspection and complaints handling of public services in Scotland (2007)are implemented.

Overarching this catalogue of ways in which the accountability of intermediate government is to be established and maintained is the role of the two Parliaments. We have taken note of their formal legislative powers and the division of responsibility between them. The structure and operation of devolved bodies and, if they are dissolved, the devolved elements of CBPAs are for the Scottish Parliament. Reserved bodies remain the responsibility of Westminster. But what should be the role of the Parliaments in the routine monitoring of public bodies? There are, of course, strong arguments in favour of a very limited role. The point of intermediate government in the first place is to put it at arm's length from ministers and, therefore, to exempt it from the normal rigours of ministerial responsibility to Parliament. Equally, as a practical matter, it would be simply impossible, even if desirable, for the Parliaments to take a close supervisory interest in quangos. It is true that, at Westminster, select committees of the House of Commons include departmentally related quangos within their remit and some investigations have necessarily centred on these. The same possibilities are open to the Scottish Parliament, as evidenced by the SQA inquiries, but it would be impossible to maintain a regime of systematic scrutiny. This was a point powerfully made in the report of the House of Commons Public Administration Committee in November 1999[8]. On the other hand, conditions in the Scottish Parliament may turn out to be rather different. There may be both a willingness to take on a broader remit and, subject to other pressures, the scope to do so in practice[9].

1   See R Parry, ' Quangos, Agencies and the Scottish Parliament' in C Jeffery and J Mitchell (eds) *The Scottish Parliament 1999–2009* (2009).
2   See chs 9 and 10.
3   Public Finance and Accountability (Scotland) Act 2000, s 15(3), (4). For fuller discussion of audit arrangements, see p 291.
4   See p 273.
5   See p 353.
6   See p 333.
7   HRA 1998, s 6.
8   'Quangos', *Sixth Report* (HC Paper 209 (1998–99)) para 41.
9   For discussion, see Procedures Committee *CSG Inquiry*, paras 549–557. In the Scottish Executive's consultation paper *Appointments to Public Bodies in Scotland* in February 2000, ch 7 was devoted to the Parliament's potential role. Committees do consider the work of quangos from time to time. See eg the Education etc Committee (the Scottish Broadcasting Commission) on 7 November 2007 and the Transport etc Committee (Scottish Water) on 20 November 2007.

ETHICAL STANDARDS IN LOCAL GOVERNMENT AND PUBLIC BODIES

7.17   Another early initiative of the Scottish Executive was to introduce the Bill enacted as the Ethical Standards in Public Life etc (Scotland) Act 2000 (ESPL(S)A 2000). With origins first confined to local government, the Executive's proposals were expanded to embrace other public bodies and took forward the non-statutory codes of practice which the UK government had developed in response to proposals from the (Nolan) Committee on Standards in Public Life[1].

The Executive took the view that, although a statutory method of regulation of public bodies had been rejected by Nolan, such a system would now be appropriate. The principle that the highest standards of conduct should apply across the public service was paramount and there was no reason to believe that people genuinely committed to public service values would be deterred by a statutory system. Indeed a clear and strong framework of control, backed up by transparent and readily understood sanctions, would offer assurance to members of public bodies themselves[2].

Thus ESPL(S)A 2000 extends not only to all Scottish local authorities but also to a scheduled list of executive public bodies (including NHS bodies), but not advisory bodies or bodies such as local enterprise companies, university courts and nationalised industries. These were all thought to be sufficiently regulated in other ways[3]. The Scottish Ministers were required to issue a code of conduct for councillors[4] and, separately, a model code of conduct for members of devolved public bodies[5]. Both had to be approved by the Parliament by resolution and, in the case of the model code, each public body was required to submit for approval by the Scottish Ministers its own version of the code to be applied to it[6]. Both codes of conduct were issued in 2002 and urged general principles of selflessness, integrity, openness, honesty and others; there are 'general conduct' rules on, for instance, compliance with regulations on allowances, accepting gifts and hospitality; rules on the registration and declaration of interests; and on lobbying of councillors and members. The councillors' code concludes with an additional section on how to deal with planning applications. The machinery provided for the enforcement of the codes of conduct is the Standards Commission for Scotland[7], supported by a chief investigating officer[8] who is given extensive powers to investigate and report on alleged contraventions of the codes. Such reports may lead to a hearing before the Commission which has the power to impose sanctions ranging from censure, through suspension, to disqualification[9]. An appeal is available to the sheriff principal and thence to the Court of Session[10]. In practice, most complaints and investigations have related to the activities of local councillors.

1   First Report on Standards in Public Life (Cm 2850, 1995); *Guidance on Codes of Practice for Board Members of Public Bodies* (Cabinet Office, 1997).
2   *Standards in Public Life* (November 1999).
3   *Standards in Public Life* (November 1999).
4   ESPL(S)A 2000, s 1.
5   ESPL(S)A 2000, s 2.
6   ESPL(S)A 2000, s 3.
7   ESPL(S)A 2000, s 8.
8   ESPL(S)A 2000, s 9.
9   ESPL(S)A 2000, s 19.
10 ESPL(S)A 2000, s 22.

Chapter 8

Law-making Procedures

INTRODUCTION[1]

8.1   An essential part of the devolution project was to deliver a Scottish Parliament which not only had substantial law-making powers but which would also be in a position to use these powers to good effect. Its location in Scotland and its ability to focus entirely on Scottish issues in a way that Westminster plainly could not would provide the separate legal system of Scotland with a legislature dedicated to its needs. But more was required. It was hoped that the opportunity would also be taken to improve on Westminster's performance as a law-making machine. Law-making should become a more open and accessible process; and it should involve more consultation on the terms of proposed legislation, both in the Parliament itself and in the stages prior to its introduction into the Parliament. There should be less governmental domination of legislation and more opportunity for back-bench participation; and many of the time constraints and technicalities of procedure at Westminster should be avoided. Much of this depended on devising appropriate procedures and recommendations on the legislative process were an important element of *Shaping Scotland's Parliament*, the report of the Consultative Steering Group, in 1998. The Parliament's original standing orders[2] reflected many of those recommendations. Over the past ten years, as the Parliament has become well established as a law making body, those original standing orders have been subject to review and revision[3]. The procedures of the Scottish Parliament have become, like those of Westminster, the focus of inquiry and debate inside and outside the Parliament[4].The largest section of this chapter (pp 218–236) is devoted to a comparative discussion of the procedure on government or Executive Bills in the Westminster and Scottish Parliaments[5]; pp 236–240 deal with Members' Bills and, in the Scottish Parliament, Committee Bills[6]; and pp 240–245 with Private Bills. Pages 245–252 cover procedures for the making of subordinate legislation. In the concluding pages, some brief comparisons are drawn between Holyrood and Westminster.

1 For an outline of EU law-making procedures, see pp 44–47.
2 Initially the Scotland Act 1998 (Transitory and Transitional Provisions) (Standing Orders and Parliamentary Publications) Order 1999, SI 1999/1095, replaced by the Parliament's own standing orders in December 1999.
3 The current version of standing orders (the 3rd Edition, 3rd Revision) came into force on 24 April 2009.
4 For internal inquiries see example the Procedures Committee's 6th Report of 2004, a New Procedure for Members' Bills, SP Paper 193 and for external debate see the work of the Calman Commission (p 231).
5 Some procedural aspects of 'Sewel' or 'legislative consent' motions are dealt with in ch 5.
6 For Westminster see p 240, n 2.

GOVERNMENT AND EXECUTIVE BILLS[1]

General

8.2   This section describes the essential elements of legislative procedure at Westminster and then, by way of comparison, looks at the procedures adopted in the Scottish Parliament. However, this is not without difficulties. In neither Parliament do the formal procedural rules tell the whole story. Much depends on their practical application in conditions dominated by party politics. Comparisons are further complicated because Westminster and Holyrood procedures are subject to revision in light of the particular needs of each and without necessary reference to the other.

Common to the process of legislation in both Parliaments are procedures intended to subject legislative proposals to successive stages of debate. Some stages are designed to encourage debate on the principles of the proposals, their general desirability or undesirability. Other stages are designed to encourage detailed scrutiny. If the proposals are approved at all relevant stages, they then require the formal approval of the Queen (royal assent) to become an Act[2]. In both Parliaments the legislative proposals, once introduced into the Parliament, are known as Bills[3]. Prior to their introduction they may have taken the form of a 'draft Bill'. In other respects, the legislative procedures in the two Parliaments necessarily diverge. Most significantly, there are the complications at Westminster produced by the need to involve and, if necessary, to resolve differences between, both Houses of Parliament, rather than a single chamber as at Holyrood. In the Scottish Parliament there are the special forms of procedure laid down by the SA 1998 to enable challenge, if appropriate, to the validity of a Bill when passed by the Parliament but prior to its submission for royal assent[4].

1 Notwithstanding the use by the current Scottish administration of the term 'Scottish Government', the Parliament's standing orders continue to refer to "Executive Bills".
2 For Acts of the Scottish Parliament (ASPs), see Scotland Act 1998 (SA 1998), ss 28(2)–(4), 32.
3 For ASPs, SA 1998, s 28(2).
4 SA 1998, ss 32–35 and see p 233 below.

The passing of a public Bill at Westminster

8.3   Bill procedure at Westminster takes a variety of different forms. It is useful to consider first the course of one which may be regarded as of 'standard' form. This would be a 'public' Bill – one of general application (even if confined to specific subject matter and perhaps to only certain parts of the United Kingdom), rather than a 'private' Bill restricted in its application to particular persons or bodies or places[1]. It would be a public Bill introduced by a minister as a member of the government, rather than by a 'private member'[2]. It would be a Bill introducing new law (while also amending or repealing existing law) rather than consolidating existing law scattered over a number of statutes. It would be a Bill introduced first into the House of Commons, although others start their procedural life in the Lords.

One of the curiosities of legislative procedure at Westminster is the terminology used to describe the stages through which a Bill must pass in both Houses. The stages of a Bill are marked by a series of 'readings', usually taken in plenary session on the floor of the House, supplemented by a committee stage, usually taken away from the floor of the House but sometimes not, and a report stage at which the outcome of that committee stage is 'reported' to the House. 'Readings' are not, however, occasions on which a Bill is actually read. Instead they mark the points at which the House authorises further procedural progress – usually after a vote (division) which, in turn, usually follows a debate.

1 See p 236.
2 See p 240.

First reading

8.4   The first reading stage of a Bill is, however, an exception. In Westminster practice, this is the stage at which a Bill is introduced. A motion that the Bill be read for a first time is formally moved by a minister in the case of a government Bill. There is no debate. The procedure takes only a few seconds but it provides authority for the Bill to be published and it may also be the occasion for intimating the date of the next stage, the second reading. Although the first reading of a Bill is the occasion on which the House receives formal notice of the Bill and, shortly afterwards, its contents, the Bill's introduction will not usually be a surprise. The government's intention to introduce the Bill in that annual session of Parliament will usually have been announced in the legislative programme set out in the Queen's Speech at the beginning of the session. In turn, that announcement will usually be consequential upon statements of the government's commitment to the policy programme from which the Bill derives, often contained in the governing party's manifesto prior to the previous general election and for which it will, therefore, claim to have a democratic mandate to enact into legislation. Not all of a government's Bills, however, will have their origin in an election manifesto. Often a government will adopt new policies as the life of the Parliament proceeds and these too will require new legislation to bring them to fruition. At other points, a government will simply be responding to events, sometimes with an element of emergency. The Criminal Evidence (Witness Anonymity) Act 2008 was a response to the judgement in *R v Davis*[1] in which the House of Lords held that the use of anonymous witness evidence could be a breach of article 6 ECHR[2]. Other government Bills include measures to implement law reform proposals from the Law Commissions[3] (the independent bodies established to make proposals for law reform[4]) and the enactment of annual financial legislation[5].

Whatever the origins of a Bill, the traditional position at Westminster is that its content, especially its detail, will not be well known to parliamentarians or the public prior to its formal introduction at first reading. The Bill will usually, of course, have been subject to much discussion in the government department from which it originates. There will have been consultation between policy-makers, ministers, legal advisers, draftsmen and, where necessary, other departments which may be affected. Decisions on the co-ordination and time-tabling of the government's legislative programme will have been made by the relevant Cabinet committees. There is, however, no formal obligation on governments to expose their legislative proposals to wider scrutiny by the public or by affected interests until a Bill's formal introduction, although *some* consultation may be undertaken informally and there is a developing practice of publishing draft Bills well in advance of their formal introduction – see below.

1 [2008] 1 AC 1128; [2008] HRLR 35.
2 See p 334.
3 Since the creation of the Scottish Parliament, the implementation of Scottish Law Commission proposals at Westminster will be very infrequent, the only examples since 1999 being the Statute Law (Repeals) Act 2004 and the Parliamentary Costs Act 2006 both of which resulted from joint reports of the Law Commission and the Scottish Law Commission. Proposals for reform of certain aspects of partnership law and insurance law have not been taken forward. The Chairman of the SLC, Lord Drummond Young, has expressed concern that the number of Commission reports which have not been implemented have risen significantly since devolution: see SLC Annual Report 2008, SG/2009/13.
4 Law Commissions Act 1965.
5 See ch 10.

Second reading

8.5   The giving of approval in principle occurs at the 'second reading' of a Bill. On the motion that it 'be read a second time', a minister from the relevant department introduces the Bill; outlines its clauses; and commends its merits to the House. In a debate which will usually last some four or five hours, the views of leading spokespersons of the opposition parties as well as some backbench MPs will be heard before a division in which MPs usually vote strictly along party lines. The government, therefore, wins and it would indeed be a set-back probably sufficient to prompt resignation or consequential recourse to a vote of confidence in the government if it did not.

The standing orders of the House of Commons do permit the possibility of holding the equivalent of a second reading debate in a committee rather than on the floor of the House. This is an opportunity infrequently taken but the rule is indicative of the desirability, where appropriate, of lifting the pressure on plenary sessions in the House, a feature of much debate on procedural reform. A special instance of the use of a 'second reading committee' was the use made in relation to exclusively Scottish legislation, before SA 1998, of the Scottish Grand Committee, despite the problems with its political composition (ie its Labour majority) in the period 1979–97[2].

2 C M G Himsworth 'The Scottish Grand Committee as an Instrument of Government' (1996) 1 Edin LR 79.

Committee stage

8.6   The next stage in the progress of a Bill through the Commons is when it is sent to a committee for detailed scrutiny. Typically, this stage is taken in a public bill (formerly 'standing') committee, consisting usually of about 20 MPs reflecting the party balance in the House. It is a committee formed specifically for the consideration of a particular Bill but, although it will include the relevant junior minister, opposition spokespersons and perhaps a few other

MPs with a known interest in the Bill's subject matter, the membership of a public bill committee is predominantly non-specialist in character. The business of a standing committee is the detailed consideration of the clauses of a Bill. Often misleadingly called 'line-by-line' scrutiny of a Bill, debate is given a structure by a focus on amendments proposed (usually by opposition members of the committee) to individual clauses and then on the approval of each clause taken as a whole. The political composition of public bill committees means that amendments are rarely made without the approval of the government majority. In a small number of cases, the committee stage of a Bill may be taken on the floor of the House. This occurs where Bills are brief and uncontroversial and a separate committee stage is unnecessary. At the other end of the scale, it also occurs on Bills of high constitutional importance, such as the Scotland Bill, where the Bill justifies the attention and time of the whole House. Previous restrictions on the power of standing committees to hear evidence from outside Parliament led to provision being made, though rarely used in practice, for the committal of Bills to a 'special' standing committee which has the power both to debate amendments in the ordinary way but also, in advance of that, to hear evidence for and against the Bill's provisions[1]. Following changes to the Parliament's standing orders in 2006 public bill committees have the power to take such written and oral evidence ('to send for persons, papers and records').

At the end of the committee stage, the Bill proceeds to report stage back on the floor of the House. This stage provides another opportunity for debate on proposed amendments, often including amendments proposed by the government in the light of developments since the Bill was introduced or in the light of undertakings given in committee to amend the Bill in response to criticisms at that stage. The report stage usually leads straight on to the third reading which is a last opportunity for the House to debate and vote on the general acceptability of the Bill before it proceeds to the House of Lords.

Procedures on a Bill in the Lords follow the same overall pattern as in the Commons. The principal formal difference is that there is no general use of public bill committees in the Lords, although it has become more common in recent years to refer a Bill to a public Bill committee which sits away from the chamber of the House itself but which all peers remain eligible to attend. Following a Bill's approval by the House of Lords, the Bill must still receive royal assent before it becomes an Act. If, however, the Bill has been amended in the Lords, royal assent must be postponed until both Houses have approved it in precisely the same terms. For this purpose, the Bill must first return to the Commons where either any Lords amendments are accepted, in which case royal assent can follow, or if they are rejected, the Bill must go back to the Lords, with the possibility of further ping-pongs between the two Houses before a final text is agreed by both. When parliamentary proceedings on a Bill are complete, royal assent is given under the terms of the Royal Assent Act 1967. As noted earlier[2], this is, in modern times (ie since 1708), a purely formal matter.

---

1 A special standing committee was used for the Adoption and Children Bill in 2001–02; and see p 224 below.
2 See p 154.

House of Commons and House of Lords

8.7   The procedures sometimes required to obtain the agreement of both Houses to a single text of a Bill prior to royal assent are only one illustration of the complexity caused by having a bicameral legislature in which the mix of political composition and constitutional status of one House is very different from that of the other and in which legislative activity must usually to be conducted within the confines of annual parliamentary sessions.

However, one effect of bicameralism with straightforward consequences is that a Bill may start life in either House. Governments use this facility to distribute business between the two Houses at the beginning of the session, though usually taking care not to introduce Bills first in the Lords which, constitutionally or politically, it would be more appropriate to start in the Commons. Bills of 'first class constitutional importance', finance Bills and politically controversial Bills would not start life in the Lords. The different composition and traditions of the two Houses then affect procedures on Bills. In the House of Commons, the government will usually be able to secure a majority in all divisions on a Bill by applying the discipline of the party whip to its own MPs. This applies to divisions on substantive motions but it also applies to divisions on procedural matters. In particular, the government often uses its Commons majority to impose a timetable on a Bill according to which progress must be made at committee or report stage, failing which the 'guillotine' falls and large blocks of the Bill are formally approved with either very little debate or none at all. The restriction of debate by use of a timetable motion has consequences for the quality of scrutiny of a Bill and it routinely attracts accusations from the opposition that democracy is being suppressed, however much opposition MPs may themselves have been guilty of obstruction by earlier time-wasting! Such business management by use of the government party majority does ensure that government Bills make progress through the Commons. In the House of Lords, however, governments cannot always rely upon the same degree of co-operation – a situation which has not changed greatly since the reforms of the House of Lords Act 1999.

It is indeed in the legislative process that the problematic relationship between the two Houses of Parliament[1] is most apparent. In purely formal terms, the Houses have an equality of status and it might even be conceded that the House of Lords, as the 'upper' House, is superior. It is there that the Queen's Speech is delivered at the beginning of each session and MPs are merely summoned to attend. On the other hand, the Commons has an undoubted political pre-eminence. In some respects, this disjunction need not be a cause of difficulty. Peers recognise, for instance, that Bills which they introduce in their own House may make very little progress in the Commons. However, tension can arise around the handling of the government's own Bills. Sometimes the existence of the second chamber serves the government's purposes very well. The introduction of some Bills in the House of Lords before going to the Commons eases the government's programme, and the facility of the House of Lords as a revising chamber is of as much benefit to the government as others: they have the opportunity to revise their own Bills by proposing amendments in the Lords.

On the other hand, the formal requirement that Bills do need the approval of both Houses, including that of the Lords where the government's enemies may outnumber its friends – and even its friends are not subject to the same discipline as MPs – does provide the House of Lords with the opportunity to threaten to withhold its consent and to disrupt the government's programme. Although, by the end of the nineteenth century, it was generally accepted by the Lords that they should not play their joker to thwart the intentions of a government seeking to implement its democratic mandate – the Salisbury convention – it was the actual resort to the threat in the early twentieth century that prompted a formal amendment of the rules[2]. The Parliament Act 1911 (PA 1911) provided that a public Bill could reach the statute book without the need for the approval of the House of Lords if certain conditions were met. A 'money Bill' (a Bill certified as such by the Speaker of the Commons) may be passed, after only a month's delay in the Lords, by the Commons alone – a rule which reflects the special position of the Commons on financial matters. Then, in relation to all other Bills (except a Bill to extend the maximum length of a Parliament beyond five years), PA 1911 (as since amended by the Parliament Act 1949 (PA 1949)[3]) enables a Bill which has been passed by the Commons in two successive sessions to proceed to royal assent without the consent of the Lords, provided also that a period of 12 months has passed between the initial second reading and the second third reading stages in the Commons. In recent years, the Parliament Acts have been invoked to pass the War Crimes Act 1991, the European Parliamentary Elections Act 1999 and the Sexual Offences (Amendment) Act 2000. The most recent use of the Acts – to pass the Hunting Act 2004 – provoked litigation which resulted in the examination by the House of Lords of the validity of the 1949 Act itself. In *Jackson v Attorney General*[4] opponents of the 2004 Act – which banned hunting with dogs – argued that it was 'not of legal effect' because it had been made using the 1949 Act which, it was said, was itself invalid. This was because the 1949 Act had been made using the procedures contained in the 1911 Act whereas – so it was contended – the 1911 Act could be amended only with the consent of the Lords. Sitting as a panel of nine, the Lords rejected this novel attempt to strike down an Act of the Westminster Parliament holding that section 2(1) of the 1911 Act, which allowed the amended procedure to be used in relation to 'any public Bill' (other than a money Bill), was wide enough in application to comprehend an Act which amended the 1911 Act itself. On the broader question of the legitimacy of the 1911 and 1949 Acts, Lord Bingham of Cornhill observed that:

> 'It has been a source of concern to some constitutionalists...that the effect of the 1911, and more particularly the 1949, Act has been to erode the checks and balances inherent in the British constitution when Crown, Lords and Commons were independent and substantial bases of power, leaving the Commons dominated by the executive, as the ultimately unconstrained power in the state. There is nothing novel in this perception. What, perhaps, is novel is the willingness of successive governments of different political colours to invoke the 1949 Act not for the major constitutional purposes for which the 1911 Act was invoked (the Government of Ireland Act 1914, the Welsh Church Act 1914, the 1949 Act) but to achieve objects of more minor or no constitutional import

223

(the War Crimes Act 1991, the European Parliamentary Elections Act 1999, the Sexual Offences (Amendment) Act 2000 and now the 2004 Act). There are issues here which merit serious and objective thought and study. But it would be quite inappropriate for the House in its judicial capacity to express or appear to express any opinion upon them, and I do not do so'[5].

Perhaps one reason perhaps for what Lord Bingham notes as the relatively scare use of the Parliament Acts is that they clearly do not remove all problems for a government faced with a rebellious House of Lords. It may be very inconvenient to have to contemplate the year's delay and in a system which, at present, usually requires Bills to be passed within a single annual session, the government's opponents in the House of Lords may be in a position to force the government to the brink[6] and extract concessions in return for their approval of a Bill.

1 At the heart of the reform proposals discussed in ch 4.
2 And also the wider process of House of Lords reform. See ch 4.
3 By PA 1949 (itself enacted under the terms PA 1911), the original period of two years' delay was reduced to the present one year.
4 [2006] 1 AC 262. The case is also discussed at p 108 in the context of the legislative supremacy of the Westminster Parliament.
5 Ibid pp 286–287.
6 SA 1998 itself was subject to brinkmanship of this sort, on the matter of the Presiding Officer's power to pronounce on the legislative competence of a Bill.

Modernising legislative procedures at Westminster

8.8   When the Modernisation Committee of the House of Commons issued its report on the legislative process in 1997, it acknowledged that much work on the subject had been done by others in the past[1]. The Committee noted a number of perceived defects in the process which had become familiar. There was too little consultation on the content of Bills prior to their formal introduction; communication between the government, MPs and interested persons outside Parliament was patchy and spasmodic; ministers had become so dependent on Bills being approved largely unchanged that there was an inevitable disposition to resist alteration; committee stages of Bills were failing to be an occasion for constructive and systematic scrutiny but rather for politically partisan debate and struggles to extend or curtail discussion, leading to the use of the guillotine and a failure to consider large parts of a Bill; special standing committees were rarely used because of the perception, perhaps misconceived, that the extra time they required put additional pressure on the legislative timetable; report stages were frequently unconstructive, with the opposition using proposed amendments as pegs on which to hang debates on politically controversial issues and the government sometimes tabling hundreds of amendments, both technical and substantive, often to correct initial drafting faults; there was a marked imbalance in legislative activity at different times in the session, producing unacceptable pressures early in the year for the Commons and then, at the end of the year, for the Lords; and the absolute cut-off on the progress of public Bills imposed by prorogation at the end of the session frequently produced chaos amid the attempts to complete the government's legislative programme, and consequent scope for confusion and error.

The Committee's criticisms could easily be expanded into an even longer list of failings in the Westminster legislative process, especially in the House of Commons. Viewed dispassionately, many existing procedures are inefficient and irrational. Time is wasted and the task of detailed scrutiny often goes undone. Government appears sometimes to treat as important only the stages of the legislative process after the introduction of a Bill into Parliament. There has been governmental resistance to the intrusion of extra-parliamentary views by extending the government's own consultative processes into pre-legislative hearings or by the expanded use of the opportunities offered by special standing committees. There has been a government intolerance of criticism, backed by the assumption made by both government and opposition that weakness in the face of criticism quickly becomes a matter of confidence. Progress on long and complicated Bills has been marred by technical defects requiring correction by substantial numbers of amendments, sometimes not introduced until the Lords stages and, therefore, with the capacity to cause confusion in the closing stages in the Commons.

The weight of tradition makes any thought of reform difficult. Entrenched attitudes and practices are difficult to displace, especially when they continue to reflect the systemic balance of power and authority[2]. Reforming proposals need to take account of how far they seek to disturb that balance or how far, on the other hand, they seek to be accommodated within it. 'Modernisation' is a process which tends to hide this ambivalence. It is a process which avoids explicit statements about the degree of change assumed to be possible and, therefore, attracts suspicions of a 'hidden agenda' which might either be more ambitious than stated or might be an intention merely to tinker. 'Modernisation' at the hand of a committee of the House of Commons is especially problematic because any proposals it makes have to be interpreted not just as a contribution to the rules of the procedural game but also as playing the game itself.

In ways which anticipated procedures to be adopted later by the Scottish Parliament, the Modernisation Committee's original proposals ranged widely and many have since been implemented, at least in part[3]. The Committee proposed more pre-legislative scrutiny of draft Bills and, by November 1999, was able to record six instances of drafts referred to select committees (including the draft Bill on Freedom of Information sent to the Public Administration Committee), ad hoc committees or joint committees of both Houses. The Committee urged the greater use of special standing committees and later noted the reference of the Immigration and Asylum Bill in 1998–99 to such a committee; and also the greater use of committee stages split between a Committee of the Whole House and standing committees (used for the Greater London Authority Bill and the Sexual Offences (Amendment) Bill, as well as for Finance Bills). All Bills should be accompanied by full explanatory notes written in plain English[5], a recommendation adopted from the start of the 1998–99 session[6]. There should be more use of agreed motions to programme Bills[7], rather than having guillotines imposed; and the possibility of the 'carry over' of certain Bills from one session to another should be explored[8].

The Committee revisited these issues in 2006, producing reports on the legislative process generally and, in a special report, on the committee stage of public Bills[9]. In the former, the Committee focused on recommendations which would make it easier for the general public, representative bodies and other stakeholders to become more involved in the drafting and passing of legislation. It noted that pre-legislative scrutiny of Bills had proved 'one of the most successful Parliamentary innovations of the last ten years' and recommended that this should become more widespread. In addition, amongst other recommendations, the Committee was of the view that as 'a matter of routine, Government bills should be referred to committees which have the power to take evidence as well as to debate and amend a bill, and these committees should be named public bill committees'. We have noted above that this proposal has now been given effect.

1 See *The Legislative Process* (HC Paper 190 (1997–98)) para 2. Perhaps the earliest (unimplemented) reform proposal referred to was one on the 'carry-over' of public Bills made in 1928–29 (para 68).
2 See B Crick *The Reform of Parliament* (1970).
3 The Modernisation Committee's First Special Report of 1998–99 (HC Paper 865), issued in November 1999, recorded progress on the implementation of proposals for the reform of legislative and other procedures to that date.
4 HC Debs, 20 May 2003, col 842.
5 *Second Report* (HC Paper 389 (1997–98)).
6 Following enactment, the explanatory notes are revised and published on the HMSO website.
7 The first Bill subject to an (unofficial) programme motion was the Scotland Bill. Temporary standing orders have since made provision for such motions.
8 *Third Report* (HC Paper 543 (1997–99)).
9 HC 1097, HC 810 (2006).

A public Bill in the Scottish Parliament

8.9   The absence of the need to accommodate the wishes of a second chamber is what most distinguishes legislative procedure in the Scottish Parliament. However, it was recognised in advance that the lack of a revising chamber would place higher obligations of scrutiny upon the Parliament itself[1]. It was also assumed that Bills would be more widely consulted on in draft form prior to their introduction to the Parliament and more information about the purposes of a Bill and explanation of its content would be supplied[2].

SA 1998 itself made only outline provision for the stages of Bills, leaving the details to be supplied by the Parliament's standing orders[3]. During the early months of the Parliament, however, procedure was governed by temporary standing orders made by the Secretary of State in advance of the Parliament's first meeting[4]. These were replaced by the Parliament's own standing orders (SOs) in December 1999[5] (most recently updated in April 2009: see p 217 n 3 above). Although the rules contained in the standing orders are, of course, expected to be followed by the Parliament, a breach of the procedural rules will not usually be fatal. Indeed, SA 1998, s 28(5) specifically provides that '[t]he validity of an Act of the Scottish Parliament is not affected by any invalidity in the proceedings of the Parliament leading to its enactment'[6]. However, it is not clear that SA 1998, s 28(5) could save from invalidity a Bill which the Parliament failed to pass in accordance with the procedures laid down by SA 1998 itself – for example, the requirements of stages of Bills in SA 1998, s 36.

As at Westminster, the rules in the Scottish Parliament assume that most legislation will be introduced by the government as Executive Bills but separate provision is also made for Members' Bills (the equivalent of Private Members' Bills at Westminster)[7]; for Committee Bills introduced on the initiative of a committee of the Parliament[8]; Budget Bills (the equivalent of Consolidated Fund (or Appropriation) Bills at Westminster[9]); and Private Bills[10]. There are also special rules for Consolidation Bills, Codification Bills, Statute Law Repeals Bills and Statute Law Revision Bills[11]. It may now be regarded as a historical curiosity that the very first Bill introduced in the Scottish Parliament was the Bill which became the Mental Health (Public Safety and Appeals) (Scotland) Act 1999: this was an Emergency Bill and was dealt with under special rules.

Such emergencies apart, Executive Bills are usually drawn from the Executive's previously announced legislative programme. There is no provision for a 'Queen's Speech' to be used as a vehicle for announcing the programme. Nor, in the Scottish Parliament, is the programme tied to the annual timetable which, at present, imposes such a tight discipline on proceedings at Westminster. At Holyrood, a 'session' of the Parliament is the full period of the Parliament up to its dissolution[12]. Nevertheless, there is now a fairly well established practice of First Ministers making annual announcements as to the government's legislative intentions for the forthcoming year. The last such statement was made by Alex Salmond MSP in September 2008. Noting that it was "the programme of a minority government" and that for its progress the Government remained "as always, dependent on the support of other parties across this Chamber"[13]. Mr Salmond announced fifteen Bills, one of which (a Bill concerned with flood risk management) had been carried over from the previous year's programme. Other proposed Bills included a Council Tax Abolition Bill, a Scottish Climate Change Bill, Marine Bill and a Health Bill to control the availability and promotion of tobacco. By June of 2009 most of the fifteen Bills had been introduced but an inability to "put together a stable majority" had forced the Government to 'postpone' its proposals for abolition of the Council Tax until after the 2011 general election[14].

1   *CSG Report* section 3.5 para 3. Concerns about the extent to which the Parliament has discharged those obligations were reflected most recently in submissions to the Calman Commission (see p 87) suggesting the establishment of an unelected 'senate' to provide 'detached and expert scrutiny of legislation'. The prospect of an elected or unelected second chamber was rejected by the Commission in its first report. (The future of Scottish Devolution within the Union: A First Report, December 2008, para 8.14).
2   *CSG Report* section 3.5 paras 4–7.
3   SA 1998, ss 22, 36.
4   Scotland Act 1998 (Transitory and Transitional Provisions) (Standing Orders and Parliamentary Publications) Order 1999, SI 1999/1095.
5   The standing orders are supplemented by the more informal *Guidance on Public Bills* (and also *Guidance on Private Bills*) prepared by the Parliament's officials.
6   See the Presiding Officer's announcement in the Parliament's Business Bulletin 106/2000 of 21 June 2000 acknowledging an earlier breach of the rules on 'manuscript amendments' at Stage 3.
7   See p 237.

8 See p 239.
9 See p 289.
10 See p 242.
11 SA 1998, s 36(3) and SOs, rr 9.18–9, 20. Reference to Codification Bills had been removed from the Standing Orders in 2001 but was re-instated following a recommendation by the Procedures Committee. See 8th Report, 2006 SP paper 676.
12 SOs, r 2.1.
13 SP OR 3 September 2008, col 10301.
14 Cabinet Secretary John Swinney's statement to Parliament, SPOR 11 February 2009, col 14896).

Introduction of a Bill

8.10 A Bill formally starts life on introduction to the Parliament[1]. A Bill's structure and style must be in line with rules laid down by the Presiding Officer[2] and it must be accompanied by a number of other documents:

PRESIDING OFFICER'S STATEMENT OF COMPETENCE. A written statement signed by the Presiding Officer, as required by SA 1998, s 31(2), declaring whether or not, in his view, the Bill's provisions would be within the legislative competence of the Parliament. If any provision is declared not to be competent, reasons must be given[3]. Such statements, while rare, have been made. On 21 September 2006 the Presiding Officer made a statement that a large number of the provisions on the Civil Appeals (Scotland) Bill – a Members' Bill introduced by Adam Ingram MSP which was intended to abolish the final right of appeal to the House of Lords in Scottish civil cases – were outside the legislative competence of the Scottish Parliament. The Presiding Officer was of the view that the majority of provisions related to reserved matters, i.e. 'the Constitution', by virtue of SA1998, Sch 5, paragraph 1(c). One further provision was in his view incompatible with Article 6 ECHR[4].

As a direct consequence of the Presiding Officer's statement the lead committee considering the Bill – the Justice 2 Committee – recommended that the Bill's general principles not be agreed to and the Bill fell on 20 December 2006 when that recommendation was accepted by the whole Parliament[5].

FINANCIAL MEMORANDUM. A financial memorandum, containing estimated costs of the Bill's proposals[6].

In the case of an Executive Bill, there must also be:

EXECUTIVE STATEMENT OF COMPETENCE. A statement by the member of the Scottish Executive in charge of the Bill that the provisions of the Bill would, in his or her view, be within the Parliament's legislative competence, as required by SA 1998, s 31(1).

EXPLANATORY NOTES which 'summarise objectively' the effects of the Bill.

POLICY MEMORANDUM policy memorandum which sets out the Bill's policy objectives, any alternative strategies considered, consultations undertaken and an assessment of the Bill's effects on equal opportunities, human rights, island communities, local government, sustainable development and any other matters the Scottish Ministers consider relevant. It is by means of this policy memorandum and the scrutiny it may later receive that it has been hoped that a more open legislative process will be achieved.

Once introduced, the Bill and its accompanying documents are to be printed and published. The Bill then embarks on the procedure consisting of three stages (not confused with Westminster's language of 'readings') as required by SA 1998, s 36(1) and elaborated in the Standing Orders. The three stages are: Stage 1 for the consideration of a Bill's general principles (equivalent to a second reading at Westminster); Stage 2 for the consideration of details (a committee stage); and Stage 3 for final consideration and a decision on whether the Bill is to be passed (a third reading at Westminster). There follows the royal assent, with the possibility, however, of a reference to the Judicial Committee of the Privy Council or intervention by the Secretary of State, discussed further below.

The Bill's stages proceed according to a timetable laid down in the business programme of the Parliament, although the Standing Orders provide for standard minimum periods of 11 sitting days between Stages 1 and 2 and 9 sitting days between Stage 2 and Stage 3. The business programme is itself a matter for the Parliament to decide, on a motion from the Parliamentary Bureau[7].

1 SOs, r 9.2.
2 See *Guidance on Public Bills*, Annex A.
3 The terms of SA 1998, s 31(2) were a matter of controversy during the passage of the Scotland Bill. For debate at the final stage, see HL Debs, 17 November 1998, cols 1171–1175.
4 For the treatment of Mr Ingram's request, under the Freedom of Information (Scotland) Act 2002, for details of the legal advice given to the Presiding Officer in relation to his statement see Decision 209/2007 of the Scottish Information Commissioner (www.itspublicknowledge.info).
5 SPOR 30 December 2006, col 30752 et seq. This was not the first occasion on which the Presiding Officer had made such a statement. He had done so earlier the same year in relation to the Provision of Rail Passenger Services (Scotland) Bill. For a discussion of both see CMG Himsworth, Presiding Officer Statements on the Competence of Bills, (2007) 11 Edin LR 397.
6 In the case of a Bill which would charge expenditure on the Scottish Consolidated Fund, there must also be a report by the Auditor General for Scotland.
7 SOs, r 5.4.

Stage 1

8.11   The principal decision to be made by the Parliament at Stage 1 is whether it agrees to the general principles of the Bill and whether it should, therefore, proceed. The debate and decision on this take place on the floor of the Parliament but they may do so only after the Bill's provisions have been considered by an appropriate committee (the 'lead committee') of the Parliament (and, if necessary, the Subordinate Legislation Committee[1] and any 'secondary' committee or committees[2]). The lead committee must provide a report on the Bill and (in the case of Executive Bills) on the policy memorandum for the assistance of the Parliament. For that purpose it may proceed by discussion but also by the taking of evidence.

The Stage 1 reports of lead committees have proved influential particularly in highlighting to the promoter parts of a Bill which the Committee would expect to see improved by amendment at Stage 2. Lead committees have on occasion been unwilling or unable to endorse the general principles of a Bill. In the case of the Scottish Commissioner for Human Rights Bill the Committee was divided on which of three options ought to be pursued in order to fulfil the policy objective of the Bill. Because 'none of these options enjoys the support of a majority of Members of the Committee' the Committee was not 'in a position to recommend to the Parliament whether the general principles of the Bill should be agreed to or not'[3]. The Bill was nevertheless passed – as the Scottish Commission for Human Rights Act 2006[4]. Even where a committee recommends agreement to the general principles of a Bill, it may not secure the support of the whole Parliament. The Creative Scotland Bill was the first Executive Bill to fall at stage 1, the Parliament having agreed its general principles but not the financial resolution ancillary to the Bill (see SP OR 18 June 2008, col 9842).

1 See p 246.
2 SOs, r 9.6
3 Justice 1 Committee, 1st report, 2006, SP Paper 508.
4 See also the Stage 1 report on what became the Graduate Endowment Abolition (Scotland) Act 2008, SP Paper 37, 13 December 2007.

Stage 2

8.12   If the Parliament agrees to the general principles of the Bill at Stage 1 and the Bill has, if necessary, been the subject of a financial resolution to approve any expenditure it may impose on the Scottish Consolidated Fund[1], the Bill proceeds to Stage 2 which is usually to be taken in the same 'lead committee' as at Stage 1 but may, on a motion of the Parliamentary Bureau, be taken, in whole or in part, by some other committee or by a Committee of the Whole Parliament, chaired by the Presiding Officer[2]. If Stage 2 is taken in a committee, other MSPs may attend, and propose and debate amendments but may not vote. Procedure is by debate on a section-by-section basis, triggered by the proposal of amendments as at Westminster, except that amendments, though they may be grouped to assist debate, are not subject to selection by the convener.

1 For the role of the Finance Committee in relation to such resolutions, see p 290.
2 Bills in the first session of the Parliament which attracted Committees of the Whole Parliament were the Mental Health (Public Safety and Appeals) (Scotland) Bill; Census (Amendment) (Scotland) Bill; Scottish Local Authority (Tendering) Bill; Erskine Bridge Tolls Bill; Police and Fire Services (Finance) (Scotland) Bill; Criminal Procedure (Amendment) (Scotland) Bill; and Fur Farming (Prohibition) (Scotland) Bill. In session 2, the Senior Judiciary (Vacancies and Incapacity) (Scotland) Bill and in session 3 the Budget (Scotland) Bill were dealt with by such a Committee.

Stage 3

8.13   Following Stage 2, the Bill, if amended, is reprinted[1] and proceeds to Stage 3 which takes place in the full Parliament and a decision must be made, following debate, on whether the Bill is passed. At this stage, however, amendments may still be proposed or, on the motion of the member in charge of the Bill, it is possible for a Bill to be sent back for further Stage 2 consideration in committee. If, on the other hand, amendments are made at Stage 3 it is open to that member to propose an adjournment of the proceedings to another day before a final decision on the passing of the Bill is made. These are procedural devices intended to prevent insufficiently scrutinised provisions from reaching the statute book but they have not been regarded by all as having fulfilled that purpose effectively. The Calman Commission noted that the practice of timetabling the whole of Stage 3 to take place on a single day had the consequence that 'the debate on passing the Bill usually begins immediately after the disposal of the last amendment. With some more controversial Bills, this has sometimes resulted in a final decision being taken to pass a Bill only very shortly after some quite significant changes to its details have been agreed'[2]. In response to concerns that this leaves little room for reflection on the final shape of the Bill the Commission recommended that Stage 3 be limited to consideration of final amendments by the whole Chamber and a further Stage 4 introduced for the final debate on whether to pass the Bill in its final form[3].

1 Together with any revised or supplementary Explanatory Notes and revised or supplementary Financial Memorandum: SOs r 8A, 8B and 8C.
2 The Calman Commission, Serving Scotland Better: Scotland and the United Kingdom in the 21st Century (2009) para 6.58.
3 Recommendation 6.2.

Special forms of public Bill in the Scottish Parliament

8.14   While the standard procedure described may serve well across the generality of public Bills promoted by governments, whatever their particular subject matter, certain Bills demand a different procedure[1]. In the standing orders of the Scottish Parliament, special provision[2] is made for the following categories of Bill:

1 Recognised, in relation to the Scottish Parliament, in SA 1998, s 36(2), (3).
2 See also the provision made for Budget Bills: ch 10.

Emergency Bills[1]

8.15   Where urgency is required, the Executive may propose that a Bill be treated as an emergency Bill. If that motion is agreed by the Parliament, all stages of the Bill are to be taken in a single day[2]. Such an abbreviation of normal procedures carries risks, of course, but sometimes a particularly rapid response to a problem is necessary. The Parliament's very first Bill, which became the Mental Health (Public Safety and Appeals) (Scotland) Act 1999, was an emergency response to a significant court decision[3]. Emergency Bill procedure was invoked in respect of the Senior Judiciary (Vacancies and Incapacity) (Scotland) Act 2006 (allowing for the functions of the Lord President and the Lord Justice Clerk to be carried out by others should either be incapacitated by reason of ill health or their office be vacant). The procedure also used in February 2009 to enable the (eventual) speedy passage of the Budget (Scotland) Act 2009 one week after the minority administration's Bill had been rejected on the casting vote of the Presiding Officer[4]. Failure to secure the passage of the Bill would have led to the provisions of the Public Finance and Accountability (Scotland) Act 2000 for emergency funding being invoked[5] Most recently, and perhaps most controversially, the Emergency Bill procedure was used in June 2009 when the Convention Rights Proceedings (Amendment) (Scotland) Bill was dealt with by the Parliament in a single day. The Cabinet Secretary for Justice, Kenny McAskill, explained that the Bill was intended as a response to the decision of the House of Lords in *Somerville v Scottish Ministers*[6] and would impose a one year limit on the bringing of claims for breach of Convention rights against the Scottish Ministers[7]. Mr McAskill observed that the decision had created uncertainty and had led to tens of millions of pounds being set aside to meet possible compensation claims arising as a result of the decision. He stated that it was 'generally agreed that the situation needs to be resolved as quickly as possible'[8] but gave no explanation for the fact that the 'emergency' to which the Bill was responding was a judgment handed down some 20 months earlier – indeed, he observed (in explaining why there had been no public consultation on the proposed new legislation) that the government had 'stated publicly our desire for a change in the law as long ago as November 2007, so the change should not come as a surprise to anyone' (col 18521).

1 SOs, r 9.21.
2 Extendable, as in the case of the Mental Health (Public Safety and Appeals) (Scotland) Act 1999, on a motion by the Parliamentary Bureau: SOs, r 19.21.2.
3 *Ruddle v Secretary of State for Scotland* 1999 GWD 29-1395.
4 See SPOR 4 February 2009 col 14644.
5 See p 289. See also the Erskine Bridge Tolls Act 2001 (correcting an administrative error which had removed the power to levy tolls on the bridge).
6 2008 SC (HL) 45.
7 For further discussion of the case see p 410.
8 SP OR 18 June 2009, col 18517.

Consolidation Bills[1]

8.16 Although the whole point of most Bills is to change the law, sometimes in very significant ways, the purpose of a consolidation Bill is to restate existing law. This may involve the merging and reordering of existing statutes or the codification of the common law. In either case, some degree of amendment of existing law is permitted, on the recommendation of the Scottish Law Commission[2]. Because the consideration of a consolidation Bill is a largely technical exercise, the Parliament's standing orders require that such Bills are to be dealt with by a special consolidation committee, instead of a lead committee[3]. Amendments to consolidation Bills are confined to those necessary to achieve an accurate restatement of the law (or to implement the Law Commission recommendations). Only one consolidation Bill has reached the statute book: the Salmon and Freshwater Fisheries (Consolidation) (Scotland) Act 2003[4].

1 SOs, r 9.18. See also the provision made in SOs, rr 9.19–9.20 for Statute Law Repeals Bills and Statute Law Revision Bills. For the competence of Acts restating the law, see SA 1998, Sch 4, para 7 and p 139 above.
2 Or joint recommendation from the Scottish Law Commission and the (England and Wales) Law Commission.
3 In the Westminster Parliament, a joint committee of both Houses is used.
4 Proceedings on the Salmon and Freshwater Fisheries (Consolidation) (Scotland) Act 2003 were not without difficulty. The Committee appointed to consider the Bill, after having heard evidence on both the procedure to be adopted and on particular sections from the Scottish Law

Commission and the Scottish Executive (including the Lord Advocate), proposed a number of amendments. Following comparison with procedures at Westminster, the Committee expressed uncertainty about the scope of consolidation procedures at Holyrood and recommended further consideration by the Procedures Committee in the light of its experience on this Bill. See SP Paper 764.

Royal assent and pre-assent challenge to Bills

8.17 To become an Act, a Bill which has been passed by the Parliament needs to receive the royal assent. SA 1998 makes provision for this and states that '[a] Bill receives Royal Assent at the beginning of the day on which Letters Patent under the Scottish Seal signed with Her Majesty's own hand signifying Her Assent are recorded in the Register of the Great Seal'[1]. Beyond that formal stipulation, the Act is silent on the Queen's role but it has to be assumed that the Queen has no discretion as to whether to grant or withhold assent. If there is a discretion, it should be exercised on the advice of the First Minister.

SA 1998 does, however, specify that it is for the Parliament's Presiding Officer to submit Bills for royal assent[2], and this is important. The Presiding Officer's duty to submit a Bill arises once it has been passed but, in the ordinary way, he must delay the submission for a period of four weeks because it is within that period that an intervention may be made by either a Law Officer to secure a reference to the Supreme Court (formerly the Judicial Committee of the Privy Council) or by the Secretary of State to prohibit the submission of the Bill for assent[3]. Neither of these procedures has any counterpart at Westminster as both derive from the Scottish Parliament's status as a Parliament of restricted competence. The power to refer to the Supreme Court the question of whether a Bill (or any provision of a Bill) is within the legislative competence of the Parliament at this pre-assent stage complements the other procedures available under SA 1998 to ensure compliance[4]. Pre-assent challenge does not provide the last word on legislative competence since an ASP may be reviewed by the courts at a later stage. There has been a number of this latter type of challenge to ASPs[5] but, so far, no pre-assent references.

1 SA 1998, s 2(3), (4) and the Scottish Parliament (Letters Patent and Proclamations) Order 1999, SI 1999/737.
2 SA 1998, s 32(1).
3 SA 1998, ss 32(2), (3); 33–35.
4 See the obligations imposed on members of the Scottish Executive and on the Presiding Officer at a Bill's introduction at p 228 above.
5 See p 403.

References to the Supreme Court

8.18 A reference may be made by either the Advocate General or the Attorney-General on behalf of the United Kingdom government or by the Lord Advocate on behalf of the Scottish Government. The possibility of a reference by one of the UK Law Officers might arise in circumstances where their government doubts the competence of the Bill. This is, unlikely in relation to an Executive Bill where broad political partnership between the two governments exists and prior consultation on the terms of Scottish Bills is routine.

Even where, as has recently been the case, no such political partnership exists, such a reference would be an exceptional step. The reference of a Member's Bill passed by the Parliament without Government support might, on the other hand, be more likely. The reference of a Bill by the Lord Advocate, unless also in relation to a Member's Bill, is unlikely in practice although a 'friendly' reference of a Bill to clarify a point of interpretation, perhaps in consequence of an Executive undertaking to do so as the Bill was debated, would not be unthinkable. Whatever the motivation of the reference, it proceeds under rules laid down under SA 1998[1]. If the Supreme Court decides that a Bill (or one of its provisions) would not be within the competence of the Parliament[2], the Bill cannot proceed to royal assent in its initial form. There is, however, provision[3] for a 'reconsideration' stage in the Parliament[4]. If the Bill is passed by the Parliament, and subject to the possibility of a further Law Officer reference to the Supreme Court, it may be submitted for royal assent. If the Supreme Court decides that the Bill is not outwith the legislative competence of the Parliament, the Bill may proceed to royal assent[5]. Whatever the Supreme Court's decision, this reference procedure may be the cause of some delay in securing the final enactment of an ASP and, as already noted, royal assent must usually be delayed, in any event, for the four-week period within which a reference is competent. The only circumstance in which the four-week period may be shortened is if all the Law Officers (and also the Secretary of State[6]) have given the Presiding Officer notice of their intention not to exercise their powers under SA 1998[7].

1 SA 1998, s 103(3)(c). See (for the rules in force at the time of writing) The Judicial Committee (Devolution Issues) Rules Order 1999, SI 1999/665 (as amended by SI 2003/1880 and SI 2005/1138).
2 For discussion of how courts including the Supreme Court approach questions of legislative competence, see p 403 below.
3 SA 1998, s 36(4)–(6) and SOs r 9.9.
4 A Bill may also be reconsidered if, having been referred by the Supreme Court to the ECJ, the Parliament itself resolves to reconsider rather than await the outcome. See SA 1998, s 34(2).
5 Where Bills are passed by the Parliament immediately prior to a dissolution, royal assent can, of course, be expected only after the dissolution. But could any 'reconsideration' stage, if one were required, take place in the next session of the Parliament?
6 See below.
7 As was the case, for example, with the first ASP. The Mental Health (Public Safety and Appeals) (Scotland) Act 1999 was passed by the Parliament on 8 September and received the royal assent on 13 September 1999. Similarly, the Senior Judiciary (Vacancies and Incapacity) (Scotland) Act 2006 was passed by the Parliament on 15 June and received the royal assent on 27 June 2006.

Intervention by the Secretary of State

8.19   The Secretary of State's power under SA 1998, s 35 (unused since the creation of the Parliament) is very different from that of the Law Officers under SA 1998, s 33. Described there as a 'Power to intervene in certain cases', it is a power to make an order prohibiting the Presiding Officer from submitting a Bill for royal assent. The 'certain cases' are not cases of suspected legislative incompetence and it is for this reason that a power of control by United Kingdom ministers over the Scottish Parliament – compared by some with the powers of a colonial Governor General[1] – is a matter of some sensitivity. On the other hand, the three circumstances in which the Secretary of State – any Secretary of State, not just the Secretary of State for Scotland – may intervene are quite narrowly defined and it may, in any event, be assumed that the power is a long-stop, to be used extremely sparingly if at all[2]. Prior consultation between the two governments will in most cases have removed provisions which might attract intervention. The first situation for intervention under the section is where the Secretary of State has reasonable grounds to believe that provisions in a Bill would be incompatible with any of the United Kingdom's 'international obligations'. These are defined[3] to include obligations *other than* those arising under the EC treaties or the ECHR (incompatibility with which would, in any event, take the Scottish Parliament beyond its competence). Incompatibility with any *other* international obligations may be restrained by the power under SA 1998, s 35: in the drafting of the Act, it had been thought more appropriate to leave judgments in this area to ministers rather than to courts. Secondly, the Secretary of State may intervene on grounds of incompatibility with 'the interests of defence or national security'; and the third power to intervene is closely interwoven with the rules in SA 1998, s 29 and Schs 4 and 5 which define the competence of the Scottish Parliament by reference to reserved matters[4].

Although the Parliament is, in general, restrained from enacting legislation which relates to reserved matters, those provisions do enable incursions into reserved matters where, for instance, the 'purpose' of the legislation is to deal with devolved matters. However, if a Bill does make modifications of the law as it applies to reserved matters and the Secretary of State has reasonable grounds to believe that it 'would have an adverse effect on the operation of the law as it applies to reserved matters', he may order that the Bill be not submitted for royal assent. The timetable for a Secretary of State intervention is similar to that for Supreme court references – it must be made within four weeks of the passing of the Bill or, if the Bill is referred to the Supreme Court, within four weeks of a determination of that reference. The order prohibiting submissions for royal assent must not only identify the offending provisions but also state the Secretary of State's reasons for making the order. Such orders are subject to annulment in either House of the Westminster Parliament[5] and would also be subject to challenge by judicial review[6].

1 An image carried over from the event stronger powers which would have been available under SA 1978, s 19.
2 See p 189.
3 SA 1998, s 126(10).
4 See p 120.
5 SA 1998, Sch 7. For annulment procedures, see p 250.
6 See ch 13.

Procedures Committee reviews of the legislative process

8.20   In the first decade of the Scottish Parliament's life the procedures and processes which it has adopted in making new laws have been the subject of scrutiny by the Parliament's own procedures committee. A number of inquiries have been conducted and reports produced – leading in many cases to revision of the Parliament's standing orders. So for example, at a relatively early stage, the legislative process received attention in 2002–03 from the Procedures Committee in its CSG Inquiry[1]. The Committee did not report comprehensively at that time but recommended that a further review of all aspects of both primary and subordinate legislation procedures should be undertaken by the Committee in the next session[2]. It did, however, respond to some concerns which had been expressed and most of these focused on Executive Bills although it did also refer to an expectation that the balance between Executive and non-Executive Bills should shift in favour of Members' and Committee Bills[3]. Such Bills should be further supported with time and resources.

The principal concerns about Executive Bills were directed towards the severe timetabling pressures which had been imposed, especially but not exclusively in committees. There was a perception of there being too little time allocated for outside consultation before and during the legislative process and too little time for the proper consideration of amendments to Bills. Research had indicated average times spent on Executive Bills as 33 days for Stage 1; and 8 days for Stage 2 (with an average gap between those Stages of 14 days); and the gap between Stages 2 and 3 about 12 days[4]. But principles for time allocation were unclear and the Committee made a series of recommendations that the periods allocated during and between stages should be increased. Special care should be taken to ensure proper opportunities for debate at Stage 3, the last opportunity to amend a Bill[5]. If necessary, more time should be allocated and timetables extended to afford proper speaking opportunities for members[6]. These themes were taken up by Committee again in session 2 when it conducted a major inquiry into Timescales and Stages of Bills. In its subsequent report[7] a number of recommendations for changes to the standing orders were made to allow greater time for scrutiny of Bills, many of which recommendations have been implemented[8] and the increase in the minimum number of sitting days between stages 1 and 2 from seven to eleven (SO r 9.5.3A)). Since then the Procedures Committee has conducted inquiries into a number of other areas including private legislation[9], consolidation bill procedure[10] and circumstances in which it might be appropriate for an MSP who has introduced a bill to be a member of a committee considering that bill[11].

1   *The Founding Principles of the Scottish Parliament* SPPR OR SP Paper 818 (2003). See p 86.
2   SP Paper 818, Recommendation 37.
3   SP Paper 818, paras 305 and 695–714.
4   SP Paper 818, para 343.
5   SP Paper 818, para 357.
6   SP Paper 818, paras 358–362.
7   7th report, 2004: Timescales and Stages of Bills, SP Paper 228.
8   See for example the recommendation that a minimum period of one week should elapse between publication of the Stage 1 report and the stage 1 debate (SO r 9.6.3A).
9   SP Paper 334 (2005).
10 SP Paper 676 (2006).
11 SP Paper 652 (2006).

MEMBERS' BILLS

8.21   Although it is an almost inevitable feature of the 'Westminster model' of parliamentary government that the legislative programme of the Parliament is dominated by government Bills, the opportunity must be given to individual members to introduce Bills of their own. That opportunity reflects an assertion of autonomy on the part of the Parliament and of its individual members. The Parliament is not merely at the beck and call of the executive branch but may also initiate legislative proposals of its own. Such freedom represents an important principle and has great symbolic significance. In practice, however, the principle is much eroded, at Westminster at least, by executive pressure.

Private Members' Bills at Westminster

8.22　In the House of Commons, thirteen Fridays are allocated in each session to private members' business. That time is given initially to second reading debates on Bills whose promoters have won a high place in a ballot of MPs held at the beginning of the session[1]. Successful MPs use the opportunity to introduce a Bill on a topic of their choice, often one prepared in advance by a pressure group waiting for its chance for legislative reform. Such Bills are usually short, single-issue measures which, while not attracting governmental hostility, might never acquire sufficient priority for adoption into the government's own programme. However, governments do frequently support private members' Bills by the offer of drafting assistance, sometimes to the extent of a complete remodelling of the Bill. Conversely, government opposition to a Bill, or indeed resistance from any individual MP, will usually be fatal to a private member's Bill. Without the discipline of an assured majority or timetable motions, private members' Bills are vulnerable to being simply 'talked-out' at second reading, in which case, although they may be reintroduced, they lose their place in the queue. As with practically all other public business[2], private members' Bills lapse at the end of the session.

Those private members' Bills which survive the second reading stage are committed to a public bill committee (selected to ensure a majority in favour of the Bill) from which they return for remaining stages during Friday business before moving on to the Lords.

1 An alternative procedure for airing a proposal for a Bill is under the 'ten minute rule'.
2 Although promoted by private members, these Bills are 'public' Bills. For private Bills, see p 240.

Members' Bills in the Scottish Parliament

8.23　The Consultative Steering Group (CSG) was clear in its report on the need for MSPs to be enabled to make proposals for legislation which, if they had the support of a minimum number of members – the CSG suggested 10 per cent of the total – could then be brought forward as Bills. The Group recommended that no member should be able to introduce more than two Bills in any four-year parliamentary session[1]. These recommendations have been carried forward into the standing orders of the Parliament which contain provision for what are known at Holyrood as 'members' Bills', as opposed to the *private* members' Bills at Westminster[2]. Following the launch of the Parliament in July 1999, there was some enthusiasm for the initiation of Bills by MSPs.

In the course of the first session some 45 proposals for Bills were lodged, but most did not proceed to formal introduction. There was a decline, towards the end of the session, in the numbers of supported proposals taken forward to the stage of introduction into the Parliament as a Bill. Only one proposal for a Bill introduced after the end of 2001 was enacted. In all, eight Members' Bills reached the statute book. The first Act was the Sea Fisheries (Shellfish) Amendment (Scotland) Act 2000. Although it was very brief and it made only a small technical amendment to earlier legislation, it was hailed as a triumph for the Parliament. It managed very quickly to make a small but locally much-appreciated change in the law without fuss and without the opportunity for the procedural blockages which had earlier thwarted attempts at Westminster to achieve similar legislative change. No single MSP could simply shout 'Object' in the Scottish Parliament[3]. The second Member's Bill to reach the statute book was that introduced by Tommy Sheridan MSP and which became the Abolition of Poindings and Warrant Sales Act 2001. That too was hailed as a parliamentary triumph over the preferred position of the Scottish Executive on debt enforcement. The Executive had, however, managed to ensure the inclusion of a section delaying implementation of the Act for nearly two years, before which it was repealed by the Executive's own Debt Arrangement and Attachment (Scotland) Act 2002. Other Members' Bills which were successfully introduced and carried through to the statute book became the Protection of Wild Mammals (Scotland) Act 2002[4], the Leasehold Casualties (Scotland) Act 2001, the Mortgage Rights (Scotland) Act 2001, the Dog Fouling (Scotland) Act 2003, the University of St Andrews (Postgraduate Medical Degrees) Act 2002 and the Council of the Law Society of Scotland Act 2003. The apparent enthusiasm with which MSPs embraced members' bills did, however, give rise to cause for concern in some quarters. In 2004 the Procedures Committee conducted an inquiry into the use of the mechanism, driven in large part by evidence that the ease with which members could introduce bills was putting pressure on the Non-Executive Bills Unit and supported by the Parliamentary Bureau. The Committee's subsequent report[5] led to changes to the standing orders which appear to have played at least a part in reducing the number of members' bills being introduced. In session 2 only three members' bills made it to the statute book[6] and there have been two thus far in session 3 (the Disabled Persons' Parking Places (Scotland) Act 2009 and the Scottish Register of Tartans Act 2008).

An MSP who is not a member of the Scottish Executive[7] and wishes to introduce a Member's Bill must first lodge with the Clerk a 'draft proposal' consisting of the proposed short title of the Bill and a brief explanation of its purposes together with either a consultation document which will form the basis for a public consultation on the policy objectives of the draft proposal or a written statement of reasons why, in the Member's opinion, a consultation is unnecessary. The draft proposed must be published in the Business Bulletin with details of the consultation period or, alternatively, information about the statement of reasons for not having consulted. The draft proposal is then referred to an appropriate committee of the Parliament which can require the lodging of a consultation document within two months, which failing the Bill falls. Thereafter the member must lodge a 'final proposal' together with such consultation responses as have been received. The final proposal is published in the Business Bulletin for a month, during which time any other member may notify the Clerk of his or her support. If, by the end of the prescribed month, at least 18[8] other members (which number includes members of at least half of the political parties represented in the Parliament Bureau) have notified support for the final proposal, the Bill may be introduced. If, on the other hand, insufficient support is forthcoming, the proposal falls and no proposal in the same or similar terms may be made by any member within the succeeding six months. As recommended by the CSG, a member is restricted to a maximum of two Bills per session[9]. When a member's Bill is introduced, it follows the same procedural track as a standard (Executive) Bill[10]. An important facility available to MSPs as they prepare their Bills is the Parliament's Non-Executive Bills Unit (NEBU) which offers procedural advice and arranges for the drafting of Bills by experts recruited for the purpose. The NEBU offers similar facilities for committee Bills (see below).

1 *CSG Report*, para 3.5.21.
2 SOs, r 9.14.
3 See SP OR 28 September 2000 cols 829-834.
4 See pp 404–406.
5 SP Paper 193 (2004).
6 The Breastfeeding etc (Scotland) Act 2005, the St Andrew's Day Bank Holiday (Scotland) Act 2007 and the Christmas Day and New Year's Day Trading (Scotland) Act 2007.
7 Apparently a junior or deputy minister is not formally excluded.
8 Increased from eleven as a result of the Procedures Committee's recommendations.
9 Including for this purpose, a Bill deriving from a draft proposed by an MSP but then adopted as a Committee Bill – see below.
10 But there is no requirement under SA 1998, s 31(1) for a statement by the member that the Bill is within the legislative competence of Parliament.

COMMITTEE BILLS IN THE SCOTTISH PARLIAMENT

8.24   A special feature of procedure in the Scottish Parliament is the power given to committees of the Parliament to initiate legislation. The standing orders provide for what are known as 'committee Bills'[1]. At Westminster, it is often the case that select committees of the House of Commons make recommendations for the introduction of legislation and it is open to the government, if it accepts the recommendation, to introduce a Bill. Similarly, individual MPs, whether members of the committee or not, could take the initiative[2]. At Holyrood, however, it was envisaged from the outset, that, as part of the overall strategy to give committees a strong role in the work of the Parliament, the committees themselves would have the power to introduce Bills[3]. The CSG developed the idea with recommendations that committees of the Parliament should be able to conduct inquiries into the need for legislation in any area within their terms of reference and take proposals to the Parliament[4]. The CSG's views were incorporated into the standing orders.

A committee may make a proposal for a Bill. This might arise out of the committee's own business but standing orders also permit any MSP to submit, via the Parliamentary Bureau, a draft proposal for consideration by a relevant committee. Prior to making a proposal for a Bill (which may contain a draft of the Bill itself) the committee may hold an inquiry into the need for a Bill. The proposal must be accompanied by an explanation of that need. If the Parliament accepts the proposal, the Scottish Government has the opportunity to indicate that an Executive Bill will be introduced to give effect to that proposal. If, on the other hand, no such indication is given within five sitting days, then the convener of the originating committee may introduce the Bill. Thereafter, a committee Bill follows normal procedures, save that, at Stage 1, it may be referred directly to the Parliament for consideration of its general principles without the need for any additional report from a committee.

The committee Bill procedures have not been extensively used but the initiative was taken in January 2001 when the first formal proposal for a Bill – subsequently the Protection from Abuse (Scotland) Act 2001 – was considered by the Parliament[5]. The proposal was supported by the Executive and the debate was dubbed 'a testament to the flexibility and power of our new Parliament and its procedures'[6]. Other committee Bills which have been enacted include the Scottish Parliamentary Standards Commissioner Act 2002, the Commissioner for Children and Young People (Scotland) Act 2003, the Interests of Members of the Scottish Parliament Act 2006 and the Scottish Parliamentary Pensions Act 2009[7].

1 SOs, r 9.15.
2 Bills promoted by committees have not been a feature of legislative practice at Westminster but, on 3 June 2003, the House of Commons Public Administration Select Committee announced its intention to draft its own Civil Service Bill. For further discussion of the fate of that Bill see p 183.
3 *Scotland's Parliament* (Cm 3658) para 9.10.
4 Section 3.5, paras 18–20.
5 SP OR 24 January 2001, col 510.
6 Col 515.
7 These Bills were considered at Stage 2 by specially established committees. The Protection from Abuse (Scotland) Bill, promoted by the Justice 1 Committee, was considered by the Justice 2 Committee.

PRIVATE LEGISLATION AT WESTMINSTER AND HOLYROOD

8.25   The purpose of the legislation discussed so far is to make changes – by new law or by the amendment or repeal of existing law – to the general law of the land. A piece of legislation of this type is referred to, in both the Westminster and Scottish Parliaments, as a *public* Act. It is a public Act regardless of who initiated the Bill from which it emerged, whether a minister, an MP or MSP or, in the case of the Scottish Parliament, a committee. It is also a public Act, even though the generality of its application is qualified by its subject matter or by the territory to which it applies. Thus, a Fisheries Act or a Schools Act is a public Act, even though its subject matter is confined to fish and fishermen or to schools, pupils and teachers respectively. Such Acts have general (public) effect across the classes of person or organisation to which they apply. Similarly, a United Kingdom Act confined in its application to Wales or Scotland is a public Act despite the territorial or jurisdictional restriction. The Scottish Parliament could pass an Act restricted to the islands areas of Scotland but it would not thereby cease to be a public Act[1].

Both Parliaments do, however, recognise the need for another type of legislation and for a different procedure by which it should be handled. The distinction is drawn between the public legislation described above and *private* legislation. Private legislation is sought by persons or organisations whose aim is not to change the general law but instead to achieve a change in the law specifically in relation to them. They might want to be excused from the application to them of a particular restrictive rule. Thus, two individuals forbidden to marry under the general law because of the closeness of their relationship would need a change in the law, confined to them alone, to permit them to marry. More usually, a local authority might seek special powers, over and above those generally available, to control a nuisance or to impose a new parking regime within their area. Similarly, a public body, or indeed a commercial company, may seek powers to acquire land compulsorily to enable a particular development to take place.

All such legislation is different from public legislation because of the very specific results sought for the benefit of its promoters. Procedurally, this has two main consequences. First, the promoter has to be given access to parliamentary procedures which are usually restricted to the Parliament's own members. Secondly, the procedures for consideration of a private rather than a public Bill have to be designed to ensure not only that the promoter has the opportunity and responsibility for establishing the need for legislative change but also that any opponents of the proposal, who may have very substantial reasons to object because their property or other interests are affected, have a clear opportunity to have their day in court. In debate on a public Bill, the primary responsibility for testing its merits falls on parliamentarians, even if, in some cases (and especially in the Scottish Parliament), they may call upon external experts to give evidence. In the case of private legislation, members are required to adopt a more dispassionate, 'quasi-judicial' role and to decide on a Bill's merits in the light of arguments presented for and against. Of course, in some instances, private Bills may attract no objections and be unopposed, in which case the task of the parliamentarians is more straightforward.

1 The University of St Andrews (Postgraduate Medical Degrees) Act 2002, and the Council of the Law Society of Scotland Act 2003 and the Breastfeeding etc (Scotland) Act 2005 are all public Acts of the Scottish Parliament.

Private legislation in the Westminster Parliament

8.26 The Westminster Parliament has evolved two distinct approaches to private legislation. Neither can be dealt with comprehensively here and, since July 1999, the Westminster procedures have less relevance to Scotland because most private legislation is likely to be within the competence of the Scottish Parliament. Prior to 1999, however, Scottish business had a substantial impact on Westminster procedures and its influence continues.

The primary response of the Westminster Parliament to the special requirements of private legislation has been to adapt the standard committee stage on public Bills to enable an inquiry into the need for the powers or exemption sought in a private Bill. The promoter and objectors have the opportunity to call and to cross-examine witnesses. Private Bill procedure is inevitably an expensive matter for the parties and it was largely with a view to abating the expense for Scottish promoters that an alternative procedure was developed. The need to attend committee inquiries at Westminster was removed and the opportunity to have substitute inquiries conducted in Scotland was provided by the Private Legislation Procedure (Scotland) Act 1899, replaced later by an Act of the same name in 1936 (PLP(S)A 1936). While leaving open the option of standard private legislation procedure for Bills which 'raise questions of public policy of such novelty and importance[1]' that they ought to be dealt with in that way, PLP(S)A 1936 requires applicants for private powers to petition the Secretary of State (on 27 March or 27 November in any year) requesting the issue of a 'provisional order'. Once issued, the order is appended to a brief 'confirming' Bill which is introduced into Parliament and usually passed without substantive debate[2]. The real debate takes place at the stage prior to the making of the provisional order when an inquiry is held (usually in Scotland) by four commissioners, normally two MPs and two peers. Since the arrival of the Scottish Parliament, it is now unlikely that there will be much demand for private legislation relating to Scotland at Westminster[3]. There have been only two confirmation Acts since 1999[4]. One additional procedural complication is that Westminster procedures give recognition to 'hybrid Bills' – Bills which are predominantly public in character but which touch upon particular private interests by, for instance, providing for the acquisition of specific land. Such Bills attract special procedures in committee to enable evidence to be heard for and against those provisions[5].

1 PLP(S)A 1936, s 2.
2 But not always. For discussion see the *Report of the Joint Committee on Private Bill Procedure* (HL Paper 97, HC Paper 625 (1987–88)).
3 PLP(S)A 1936 was amended by SA 1998, Sch 8, para 5 to exclude its use to confer powers wholly within the legislative competence of the Scottish Parliament.
4 Comhairle Nan Eilean Siar (Eriskay Causeway) Order Confirmation Act 2000 and Railtrack (Waverley Station) Order Confirmation Act 2000.
5 Erskine May, *Parliamentary Practice* (eds WR McKay etc, 23rd edn, 2004) pp 483–484.

Private legislation in the Holyrood Parliament

8.27 The Scottish Parliament's procedures for consideration of private Bills have been the focus, over the past decade, of what might at first seem like a surprising amount of attention. That attention is a reflection, however, of the significant part which private Bills have played in delivering major public infrastructure projects in Scotland. Recent reforms – principally the enactment of the Transport and Works (Scotland) Act 2007 – should reduce the role which private legislation might be expected to play in Scotland and we may expect rather less of a focus on the procedures which are in place to deal with private bills. Early recognition of the need for procedures to handle private legislation was provided by SA 1998, s 36(3)(c) which enabled the making of special standing orders for private Bills. The initial versions of the Parliament's standing orders did contain such provision[1] but that was very much a holding measure, pending full consideration by the Parliament itself of how best to deal with private legislation in the longer term. The rules were a curious procedural mix, providing for special consideration by committees but, from PLP(S)A 1936, retaining a provision restricting the introduction of private Bills to 27 March and 27 November each year. While this might be appropriate to the provisional order procedure under PLP(S)A 1936, its purpose in the Scottish Parliament was not obvious. At all events, private legislation became an early topic for review by the Procedures Committee of the Parliament and, following investigation by a Private Bill Working Group, the Committee reported in November 2000 with recommendations including proposals for new standing orders[2]. The rules were subsequently adopted as Chapter 9A of the Parliament's standing orders. No private Bills had been introduced under the original rules. An important preliminary question for the Procedures Committee had been which approach to private legislation to adopt. Should it be similar to the standard in-house procedure used at Westminster for almost all private Bills, except those relating to Scotland? Or should it be a simplified version of the provisional order procedure in PLP(S)A 1936, with functions split between the Parliament and the Scottish Executive? In the Committee's view, a 'Parliament-led' system was preferable, as it was more accessible and participative. The Parliament was directly involved throughout. Because the wholly parliamentary approach needed only a change of standing orders rather than new legislation, it could also be adopted quickly. In the event, practical experience of dealing with private Bills led to re-consideration of that Parliament-led system as the most appropriate mechanism for authorising 'public works'. Following an inquiry in 2005, the Procedures Committee noted that the system had come under a great deal of strain (particularly in terms of parliamentary resources) because of the large number of transport infrastructure bills which had been introduced in the preceding three years. The Committee recommended that the government take forward legislation to enable such projects to be dealt with under a procedure which was driven by ministers (rather than Parliament) and which had greater similarities to the process for obtaining planning consent for major developments (see SP Paper 334, 4 May 2005). The Committee's recommendations were in due course taken forward in the shape of the Transport and Works (Scotland) Act 2007, the consequence of which is that very few major transport projects will now be taken forward by primary legislation of the Parliament. One exception is likely to be a Bill to authorise a new Forth Crossing, for which purpose (amongst others) the Standards, Procedures and Public Appointments Committee has recommended changes to the standing orders to allow for hybrid bills to be introduced in the Parliament[3].

The Private Bill rules provide for the introduction of a Bill on any sitting day of the Parliament. It must be lodged with the Clerk along with accompanying documents including a statement by the Presiding Officer as to whether the Bill is within the legislative competence of the Parliament, explanatory notes and a promoter's memorandum setting out the Bill's objectives, alternatives considered and consultation undertaken. Other documents are to include a funding statement and a promoter's statement concerning affected heritable property and an undertaking to pay the fee determined by the Parliamentary corporation[4]. Private Bills and their accompanying documents are printed and published[5]. Within 60 days of the introduction of a Bill, objections may be lodged by those who consider that their interests would be adversely affected, and a list of objectors is published[6].

On the introduction of a private Bill, the Parliament establishes a private Bill committee of not more than five members. Special rules exclude members resident in, or who represent, an area affected by the Bill and provide that members may be absent from meetings in exceptional circumstances only[7]. Private Bill procedure is divided into three stages. The preliminary stage involves consideration of the general principles of the Bill by the committee and preliminary consideration of the objections, following which the Parliament decides whether the Bill should proceed[8]. If the Bill proceeds, it is referred back to the private Bill committee for detailed examination at the consideration stage[9]. Where the Bill is a 'works Bill'[10] or a Bill which would confer powers of compulsory purchase the Bill Committee can direct the Parliamentary corporation to appoint – for the purposes of the consideration stage – an 'assessor' to consider and report to the Committee on outstanding objections (SOs r 9A.8.2A). The role of the assessor is akin to that of a reporter at a planning inquiry, taking evidence and producing a report for the Parliament[11]. Where an assessor is appointed, the promoter and objectors (who may be grouped for the purpose) are to be invited to attend to give evidence or to provide written evidence or both. Standing orders make no detailed provision for how private Bill committees should conduct the evidence-taking proceedings but the Procedures Committee assumed that promoters and objectors should be able to lead evidence and to cross-examine witnesses on the other side[12]. Legal representation would be permitted and, although the Committee did not accept that parties (especially objectors) would necessarily be disadvantaged by the lack of legal representation, the Procedures Committee proposed that the Scottish Executive should be invited to consider extending the legal aid scheme to these inquiries[13]. After the taking of evidence, the consideration stage on a private Bill follows a similar procedure – consideration of amendments and sections – as that adopted for public Bills. The same is true of the third and final stage at which the Parliament decides whether a private Bill is to be passed[14] and there is equivalent provision too for matters such as reconsideration by the Parliament following reference of a Bill to the Supreme Court[15].

A private Bill introduced in one session falls if it has not been passed before the end of that session. The Bill may, however, be introduced within 30 days of the beginning of the next session and, if the consideration stage has been completed, in the terms agreed at the end of that stage[16].

Private legislation passed by the Parliament include the National Galleries of Scotland Act 2003, the Robin Rigg Offshore Wind Farm (Navigation and Fishing) (Scotland) Act 2003, the Stirling-Alloa-Kincardine Railway and Linked Improvements Act 2004, the Edinburgh Tram (Line One) and (Line Two) Acts of 2006, the Waverley Railway (Scotland) Act 2006, the Glasgow Airport Rail Link Act 2007, and the Edinburgh Airport Rail Link Act 2007.

1 See both SI 1999/1095 and the December 1999 version of the Parliament's standing orders, r 9.17.
2 *Second Report of the Procedures Committee* SP Paper 204.
3 SP Paper 299, 16 June 2009.

4   SOs, rr 9A.1, 9A.2. At the time of writing, the standard fee is £5,000 with a reduced fee for
    Bills relating to 'charitable, religious, educational literary or scientific purposes whereby no
    private profit or advantage is derived' or is 'promoted by a person other than a local authority,
    and is one from which the Promoters appear unlikely to derive substantial personal or corpo-
    rate gain' (guidance on Private Bills, Annex J).
5   SOs, r 9A.4.
6   SOs, r 9A.6
7   SOs, r 9A.5.
8   SOs, r 9A.8. There is provision also for a Bill to be referred back for further consideration in
    committee.
9   SOs, r 9A.9.
10 See above.
11 An assessor was appointed to consider objections to the Glasgow Airport Rail Link Bill and to
    the Edinburgh Airport Rail Link Bill.
12 *CSG Inquiry* para 70.
13 *CSG Inquiry* para 76.
14 SOs, r 9A.10.
15 SOs, r 9A.11.
16 SOs, r 9A.7.5–11.

THE MAKING OF SUBORDINATE LEGISLATION BY MINISTERS

Introduction

8.28   The rationale for delegated law-making by ministers has already been explained in Chapter 6[1]. So too have the forms that such delegated legisla-tion may take and the tension that it produces between the demands for the effectiveness of government and, on the other hand, maintaining some meas-ure of democratic control. That tension is nowhere better reflected than in the procedures adopted for the actual making of delegated legislation. Most of the point of delegating powers to ministers is to exempt them from the degree of scrutiny and control that both Parliaments try to exercise in relation to primary legislation. There is a will to surrender much of that control but, on the other hand, both Parliaments are reluctant to release ministers from all supervision of the exercise of their powers[2]. This reluctance is demonstrated at two, quite different, points.

1 Delegated legislation may also, of course, be made by bodies other than ministers. The procedures required for the making of local authority byelaws are laid down in the Local Government
   (Scotland) Act 1973.
2 For parliamentary scrutiny of proposed EU legislation, see p 50.

Control of legislation conferring powers on ministers

8.29   The first is at the stage when the relevant Parliament is considering a Bill which contains provisions for the delegation of power to ministers. Such provisions come under the scrutiny of the Parliament, especially in commit-tee (Westminster) or at Stage 2 (Holyrood), and members will wish to estab-lish whether the delegation of power to ministers is justified at all and, if so, whether the powers are cast too broadly, leaving the Bill itself a mere 'skel-eton'; whether the powers include 'Henry VIII' clauses to amend primary legislation; whether there are sufficient requirements to consult affected persons prior to the making of the regulations; and whether the provisions for parliamentary scrutiny of the delegated legislation[1] are sufficient. To assist in this process of Bill scrutiny prior to conferring delegated powers, both Parliaments have specialised committees. At Westminster, there is the Deregulated Powers and Regulatory Reform Committee in the House of Lords[2] and, in the Scottish Parliament, this is one of the functions of the Subordinate Legislation Committee[3].

1 See below.
2 On the origins of the Committee, see C M G Himsworth 'The Delegated Powers Scrutiny Committee' [1995] PL 34. Such a committee was first recommended in the report of the (Scott/ Donoughmore) Committee on Ministers' Powers (Cmd 4060, 1932).
3 See C Himsworth 'Subordinate Legislation in the Scottish Parliament' (2002) 6 Edin LR 356 for the work of the Committee in its first three years. See also CT Reid (2002) 6 Edin LR 380 and (2003) 24 Stat LR 187.

Control of ministers' exercise of powers

8.30   The second point at which both Parliaments demonstrate a wish to impose a measure of supervision and control over the delegated law-making process is when the orders or regulations have been made, or have at least been published in draft form. Here, parliamentary scrutiny takes different forms. In the first place, ministers are subject to the general principles of accountability and are answerable to their respective Parliaments for the making of delegated legislation, or for the failure to make it. They are answerable for the subsequent impact of delegated legislation. Questions may be asked by MPs or MSPs; parliamentary debates may be initiated; and inquiries may be conducted by parliamentary committees which have the impact (or anticipated impact) of delegated legislation as their main focus. It should be borne in mind too that these standard parliamentary mechanisms for scrutiny and control are accompanied by the standard mechanisms for the judicial control of ministerial activities. The making of delegation legislation is subject to judicial review in much the same way as other executive acts[1]. Thus, even if no special steps were taken to scrutinise delegated legislation, the ordinary principles of parliamentary and legal accountability would apply.

However, special steps have also been taken. Some apply to delegated legislation at large. Others, while made available in standard form, need to be applied to particular rule-making powers by the primary legislation (sometimes called the 'parent Act') which confers them. In the first category are rules contained in the Statutory Instruments Act 1946 (SIA 1946) which regulate most delegated law-making by UK ministers. Similar rules have been extended to the Scottish Ministers. Also in this first category is the provision made by both Parliaments for the 'technical' scrutiny of delegated legislation made by ministers. In the second category are the rules laid down in many Acts of Parliament and now in Acts of the Scottish Parliament which require that the delegated legislation which they authorise must be brought to the attention of the relevant Parliament by being 'laid' before that Parliament (at Westminster, either the

Commons alone or both Houses) and, in most cases, is also made subject to an approval procedure.

1 See p 388.

Statutory Instruments Act 1946

8.31   To take these measures in order, the principal contribution of SIA 1946 was to adopt recommendations made 14 years earlier by the Committee on Ministers' Powers[1]. That Committee had complained about the confusing range of types of ministerial order then available and the varying degrees of formal publication required. The variety of practice impeded knowledge of the orders in force and endangered the rule of law. In response, SIA 1946 created the device of the 'statutory instrument' and then attached to all such instruments certain standard characteristics. It was not intended to affect the content of instruments promulgated nor their overall quality or quantity, but to impose proper procedural controls.

As noted earlier[2], most statutory powers to make delegated legislation take one of two forms. The first is, as a matter of legal form, conferred on the Queen in Council and exercisable by Order in Council. The second is conferred directly upon a minister, typically in the style of 'the Secretary of State', who is authorised to make the rules, regulations or order permitted by the parent Act. In either case, the Act may have imposed some prior procedural requirement including, for instance, the obligation to consult other persons or organisations. The contribution of SIA 1946 is to add further procedural requirements to a process which would otherwise be complete once the Order in Council or rules have been formally made. The Act applies to all statutory Orders in Council and also to all legislative powers delegated to ministers and stated to be exercisable by statutory instrument. Standard requirements are laid down for the numbering; printing and publishing (by the Stationery Office); and citation of all statutory instruments. Certain instruments may be exempted from the need for publication. Despite the standard requirement of publication, it was held, in an early case under SIA 1946, that, even without publication, an instrument is nevertheless valid once made and, if this is required by the parent Act, laid before Parliament[3]. However, SIA 1946 does itself provide a defence in criminal proceedings involving an alleged breach of a statutory instrument where it is proved (a) that a statutory instrument has not been issued by the Stationery Office unless, on the other hand, it is proved (b) that reasonable steps have been taken to bring the instrument to the notice of the public or of persons likely to be affected or of the person actually charged[4].

The rules in SIA 1946 apply to statutory instruments including, since July 1999, those instruments which extend to Scotland but which continue to be made by the Secretary of State for Scotland or other UK ministers in the exercise of powers which have not been devolved to the Scottish Ministers. As respects delegated legislation made by the Scottish Ministers, it is for the Scottish Parliament to make equivalent provision for the numbering and printing of instruments made and the Interpretation and Legislative Reform (Scotland) Bill to make such provision was introduced in the Parliament on 16 June 2009.

Transitional provision was made – and has remained in place for more than a decade – by an order under SA 1998[5]. The order created the new category of 'Scottish statutory instrument' being a statutory instrument, other than an 'excepted instrument', made by a member of the Scottish Executive[6] or by any other person with power to do so, within devolved competence, under an Act, whether of the UK or the Scottish Parliament[7], a definition which includes Orders in Council made within devolved competence. 'Excepted instruments' include those which continue to be made by a UK minister (but with the agreement of a member of the Scottish Executive) or by a UK and a Scottish Minister jointly[8]. The order requires that, immediately after it is made, a Scottish statutory instrument must be sent to the Queen's Printer for Scotland for numbering (SSI 1999/1 and so on) and for printing and sale. Local instruments may be exempted[9]. The limited defence to criminal proceedings provided by SIA 1946 is extended to Scottish statutory instruments[10] and there is provision for the preparation and publication of an annual edition of Scottish statutory instruments[11].

1   Cmd 4060.
2   See p 143.
3   *R v Sheer Metalcraft Ltd* [1954] 1 QB 586.
4   SIA 1946, s 3(2).
5   Scotland Act 1998 (Transitory and Transitional Provisions) (Statutory Instruments) Order 1999, SI 1999/1096.
6   Or by a Scottish public authority with mixed functions or no reserved functions.
7   Scotland Act 1998 (Transitory and Transitional Provisions) (Statutory Instruments) Order 1999, SI 1999/1096, arts 3, 4.
8   Scotland Act 1998 (Transitory and Transitional Provisions) (Statutory Instruments) Order 1999, SI 1999/1096, art 4(3).
9   Scotland Act 1998 (Transitory and Transitional Provisions) (Statutory Instruments) Order 1999, SI 1999/1096, arts 5, 6 and 7.
10 Scotland Act 1998 (Transitory and Transitional Provisions) (Statutory Instruments) Order 1999, SI 1999/1096, art 8(3).
11 Scotland Act 1998 (Transitory and Transitional Provisions) (Statutory Instruments) Order 1999, SI 1999/1096, art 9.

Technical scrutiny

8.32   Another important procedure in the Westminster Parliament which has been modified for adoption at Holyrood is that known as the 'technical' scrutiny of delegated legislation. Practically all statutory instruments and some other types of rules and orders are required to be laid before Parliament at the time of their making or sometimes in draft, prior to their formal making. This is not a requirement of SIA 1946 (or the Scottish transitional order) but it is routinely imposed by Acts which provide the delegated powers. The laying of an instrument brings it formally to the notice of the Parliament in which it is laid and this is a procedure frequently, but not necessarily, linked to an opportunity (which may, in practice, also be merely formal) given to that Parliament to approve or reject the instrument (see below). In the Westminster Parliament, the requirement is most commonly to lay an instrument before *both* Houses, although some instruments of a financial character are required to be laid only in the House of Commons. In the Scottish Parliament, there is not the complication of two chambers and the rules on laying are straightforward where they derive from Acts of the Scottish Parliament. Many such requirements have already been imposed and the standing orders of the Parliament make the necessary procedural provision[1]. However, many powers now vested in the Scottish Ministers derive from Acts of the Westminster Parliament and, for these, the original obligation to lay an instrument before one or both Houses at Westminster has been translated into an obligation to lay it before the Scottish Parliament[2].

Once laid, instruments fall within the scrutinising jurisdiction of committees in the two Parliaments. At Westminster there is a Joint Committee on Statutory Instruments which considers instruments laid before both Houses and a Commons Committee for instruments laid only before that House. They share the same terms of reference which require the Committees to draw instruments to the special attention of Parliament on any of a number of specified grounds or on any other ground which does not impinge on the merits of the instrument or on the policy behind it. The specified grounds are that the instrument imposes a charge on public revenues; that it is excluded from challenge in the courts; that it purports to have retrospective effect; that there has been unjustifiable procedural delay; that there are doubts about whether it is intra vires; that it requires elucidation; or that its drafting appears defective[3].

In the Scottish Parliament powers virtually identical to those of the Westminster Committees have been given to the Subordinate Legislation Committee[4], the committee already charged with the scrutiny of Bills in the Parliament which contain proposed powers to make delegated legislation[5].

1 SOs, ch 14.
2 SA 1998, s 118.
3 HC standing orders 1998, r 151.
4 With the additional ground that an instrument raises a devolution issue.
5 SOs, r 10.3. For the Committee's powers to scrutinise Bills, see p 246.

Merits scrutiny

8.33   It has been the usual practice of the Westminster Parliament, when conferring powers to make delegated legislation, to go further than to require merely that instruments should, when made, be laid before Parliament. An Act of Parliament may, as mentioned earlier, impose requirements on ministers to consult with bodies outside Parliament before making delegated legislation. With or without such a statutory requirement, ministers will, in any event, usually engage in extensive consultation with relevant interest groups. Much more frequently, however, statutes reserve the possibility of additional scrutiny by Parliament itself and it has already been pointed out that the question of whether scrutiny should be required is an important question for Parliament and, in the House of Lords, the Delegated Powers and Regulatory Reform Committee checks this aspect of a Bill as it proceeds. The same question now arises in the Scottish Parliament and in its Subordinate Legislation Committee.

The way in which the scrutiny of instruments is sought is by one of two main procedural devices. The first is for the Act which confers the delegated law-making power to provide that any orders or rules made are subject to annulment by resolution of either House of the Westminster Parliament (or of the Commons only) or, as the case may be, by resolution of the Scottish Parliament. While the power to annul has to be conferred by the empowering Act itself, further contributions have been made by SIA 1946. That Act provides that, where an enactment requires a statutory instrument to be laid before Parliament, the instrument must be laid before the date on which it is to come into force[1]. It also standardises the period during which resolution to annul may be passed at 40 days[2]. Conventional practice at Westminster then supplements the requirements of SIA 1946 to ensure that ministers will lay an instrument not less than 21 days before it is to come into force. This is intended to provide a real opportunity for a negative resolution to be considered before the instrument takes effect. In the Scottish Parliament, a translation section of SA 1998 converts the Westminster procedures[3] and then the transitional rules extend provisions equivalent to those in SIA 1946 to Scottish statutory instruments[4]. They go further, however, by giving legal status to the 21-day convention[5], a period which the Interpretation and Legislative Reform (Scotland) Bill would extend to 28 days.

Sometimes the legislature goes beyond the negative resolution procedure and provides instead that an instrument cannot be brought into effect at all unless the instrument (or a draft of the instrument) has been positively approved by resolution. Once again, at Westminster this is a requirement normally attached to both Houses and an affirmative resolution from each is needed before an instrument can come into force or, if approved in draft, before the final version of the instrument can be made. Such requirements in pre-SA 1998 legislation have the effect, in relation to orders to be made in devolved areas, of requiring the approval of the Scottish Parliament[6].

These standard procedures, now established in both Parliaments, provide, on their face, a clear hierarchy of scrutiny and control. Wishing to retain some measure of supervision of a process which they recognise must largely be driven by ministers, the Parliaments have reserved the right to be informed (by laying only); the right to annul (by negative resolution); and the right to withhold consent (by use of the affirmative resolution procedure). The idea of a formal hierarchy has been broadly recognised in practice by the allocation of a procedure appropriate to the significance of the power delegated. Thus, the negative resolution procedure is effectively treated as standard and has been the most widely deployed at Westminster. The requirement merely to lay is used more sparingly in situations where no further degree of control is sought. Perhaps paradoxically, this has been taken to include commencement orders even though the impact of the use or non-use of such orders may, of course, be considerable. The Delegated Powers and Regulatory Reform Committee of the House of Lords has expressed concern about one aspect of this – the quantity of unimplemented legislation on the statute book[7] – and has sought to monitor the situation. At the other end of the scale, there has been a recognition of the desirability of subjecting particularly important instruments to the affirmative resolution procedure. Many financial measures are included in this category for instance the annual finance orders distributing funds to local authorities[8]. Sometimes an order which establishes a new administrative scheme from a very skeletal statute may be subject to the affirmative resolution procedure in the first instance, but with succeeding orders subject to only the negative procedure[9]. The Scottish Parliament, in addition to inheriting Westminster's hierarchy of powers now exercised by the Scottish Ministers, has adopted broadly the same approach to the order-making powers it itself creates and the Interpretation and Legislative Reform (Scotland) Bill does not herald radical reform. In the construction of its budget procedures, the Parliament paid special attention to the control appropriate to the modification of the terms of Budget Acts by order[10] and care was taken to impose the affirmative resolution procedure in respect of orders to amend such Acts. A 'super affirmative'[11] level of control, under which an order is not only subjected to be affirmative resolution procedure but is also required to be put out for wider consultation prior to the resolution, was attached to powers to designate parks under the National Parks (Scotland) Act 2000.

Despite the apparent rationality underlying the imposition of these form of control, all is not what it seems. Effective scrutiny in all degrees is subject to restrictions not apparent on the face of the rules formally laid down. At Westminster there have been three main impediments to serious control. First, the domination of party politics extends from procedures on primary legislation into those on secondary legislation. Despite the formal opportunities for the rejection of a statutory instrument, whether by annulment or by withholding approval, it would be almost unthinkable for a government with a stable majority in the House of Commons to 'lose' an instrument in this way. Options in the House of Lords are, of course, different but, in practice, that House has acted with great restraint[12]. There is no equivalent to the 'Parliament Acts' procedure for the overriding of resistance by the Lords but consideration has been given to such procedures in the context of House of Lords Reform[13]. At Holyrood, a majority loyal to the Executive has prevented upsets, although substantial pressure brought undertakings for change when a draft Census Order was considered by the Parliament. As one MSP said, 'It might not yet be all power to the committees but it is some power'[14]. It is possible that, over time, the slightly more relaxed party discipline may produce different results.

The second barrier to serious scrutiny and control is more technical. With very limited exceptions, an instrument may be only either entirely approved or entirely rejected. This is a situation which could be changed and suggestions have indeed been made at Holyrood that the Parliament's capacity to amend instruments could be enhanced. In the meantime, however, the limitations of an all-or-nothing vote do restrict mature scrutiny of an instrument which even the Opposition would not wish to reject as wholly unwanted but would simply like to amend. The third obstacle at Westminster has been the lack of available parliamentary time. A back-bench MP might put down a motion to annul an instrument but time for a debate on the motion will not be allocated. This is a situation which has been alleviated somewhat by the practice of referring such motions to delegated legislation committees (but these committees cannot pass or even recommend a motion to annul[15]) and then, since 30 November 1999, the expansion of Commons business into Westminster Hall. At Holyrood the consideration of instruments falls in the main to the subject committees. Although occasionally threatened[16], there has not yet been a motion to annul an instrument on the floor of the chamber – the current administration avoided such a motion by opting to revoke the Justice of the Peace Courts (Sheriffdom of South Strathclyde, Dumfries and Galloway) Order 2009[17] when a motion to annul was passed by the Justice Committee on 5 May 2009[18]. The Committee was unhappy about the proposals for closure of certain Justice of the Peace (formerly District) Courts within that sheriffdom).

1 SIA 1946, s 4.
2 SIA 1946, ss 5–6.
3 SA 1998, s 118.
4 SI 1999/1096, arts 10–15.
5 SI 1999/1096 art 10(2).
6 SA 1998, s 118.
7 *First Report of Select Committee on Delegated Powers* (HL Paper 9 (1993–94)), paras 11–12.
8 Local Government Finance Act 1992, Sch 12, the powers under which are now exercised by the Scottish Ministers. See the Local Government Finance (Scotland) Order 2008, SSI 2008/33.
9 See, for example Bankruptcy and Diligence etc (Scotland) Act 2007, s 224(3), (4)(b)(ii).
10 See p 289.
11 The term was first used to described the scrutiny attached to the extremely wide powers delegated by the Deregulation and Contracting Out Act 1994. Similar provisions are contained in Part 2 of the Public Services Reform (Scotland) Bill which was introduced in the Scottish Parliament on 28 May 2009.
12 There have, however, been occasional exceptions, where the House of Lords has refused to comply – in relation to sanctions under the Southern Rhodesia Act 1965 in 1968; and the Greater London election rules in 2000.
13 HC Public Administration Committee (HC Paper 494 (2001–02)).
14 SP OR 16 Feb 2000, col 1100. See also, on an order under the Children (Scotland) Act 1995, the Education Culture and Sport Committee, 29 January 2002.
15 A Beith 'Prayers unanswered' (1981) 34 *Parl Affs* 165.
16 See, for example Education, Culture and Sport Committee, 22, 29 January 2002 and, in connection with the Public Transport Users' Committee for Scotland Order 2006 (SSI 2006/250) see SP OR 13 June 2006, col 3878.
17 SSI 2009/115.
18 See the Justice of the Peace Courts (Sheriffdom of South Strathclyde, Dumfries and Galloway) Revocation Order 2009, SSI 2009/180 and SP OR, Justice Committee, 5 May 2009, col 1741.

Subordinate legislation under SA 1998

8.34   Finally, and as a little appendix to the consideration of instruments by one or other Parliament, a note should be added on the exceptional case of the subordinate legislation introduced by SA 1998 itself which requires some special forms of scrutiny for certain devolution-related orders. Some instruments to be made by Order in Council, such as those amending SA 1998, Sch 4 or 5 (competence of the Scottish Parliament) require approval in draft not only by both Houses of the Westminster Parliament but also by the Scottish Parliament[1]. An Order in Council to prescribe the list of offices disqualifying the holder from membership of the Scottish Parliament needs the approval of that Parliament[2]. Although the general constitutional justification for these approvals may be clear, they create a situation in which orders promoted, in effect, by United Kingdom ministers require approval by the Parliament of which they are not themselves members[3].

1 SA 1998, s 30 and Sch 7.
2 SA 1998, s 15 and Sch 7.
3 For discussion, in relation to the Scottish Parliament (Disqualifications) Order 2003, SI 2003/409, see SP OR 9 January 2003.

Chapter 9

The Parliamentary Accountability of Government

INTRODUCTION

9.1   In the White Paper *Scotland's Parliament* it was stated that '(t)he Scottish Parliament will hold the Executive to account for its actions'[1] and it was one of the 'key principles' adopted by the Consultative Steering Group in *Shaping Scotland's Parliament* that 'the Scottish Executive should be accountable to the Scottish Parliament and the Parliament and Executive should be accountable to the people of Scotland'[2].

These statements reflect two important ideas. The first is the general principle of the accountability of governments. The primary purpose of governments is, of course, to govern. They must also ensure the adequate financing of their operations. They must, if necessary, obtain legal authority for their actions by promoting the passing of new legislation. It has, therefore, to be an important role of constitutions to assist in bringing about the conditions under which governments can discharge these functions efficiently on behalf of the people they are elected to serve. It is, however, of equal importance that the powers of government should not be unconstrained and that those in power should be accountable for their actions. They should be in a position in which they can be held responsible for what they do. In some measure, this may be seen as a means to ensure the greater effectiveness of governments. Governments which know that they are subject to scrutiny and that they may be called to account for their failings may be expected to try to maintain or improve their standards. The merit of accountability is also, however, to be seen in terms of the need for the deliberate control of executive power. Whether one has in mind the behaviour of Scottish or English monarchs prior to the seventeenth century or the tendencies to abuse of power by modern governments, it is assumed to go without saying that governments must be held to account. In democracies, this has to imply an ultimate accountability to 'the people' but it is also recognised that this may need to be operationalised by a variety of different means and that some of these may be rather indirect. The ballot box may be an important symbol of direct democratic accountability but in representative democracies it has required substantial supplementation. There is in the United Kingdom a reliance on the differentiation of both the principles and also of the methods of accountability. The task of maintaining the legal accountability of government and the rule of law has been substantially, but not exclusively, allocated to the courts[3]. Such legal accountability has broadened to embrace accountability to the standards imposed by the European Convention on Human Rights, with a reliance, but again not exclusively, on the courts. The creation and expansion of the powers of ombudsmen have, to an extent, separated off the accountability which is maintained by the insistence on standards of good administration in government[4]. Similarly, the imposition and the monitoring of standards of ethical conduct operate as a distinct mechanism of accountability. For much longer, there have been forms of financial control over government and, in particular, procedures for the audit of government accounts which also operate to strengthen the general process of accountability[5].

All these forms of accountability involve, in addition to the separate roles of courts, ombudsmen and auditors, a strong role for Parliament. However, the aspiration contained in the opening statements of this chapter – that the Scottish Government should be accountable to the Scottish Parliament – refers not so much to these specific accountabilities but more to that form of general political accountability which is represented by the principle that ministers are, at Westminster, responsible to Parliament for their actions. The UK Government's aim was to see this position replicated in Scotland. 'The relationship between the Scottish Executive and the Scottish Parliament will be similar to the relationship between the UK Government and the UK Parliament'[6]. Just how far that aim has been fulfilled is a matter for debate, but certain comparisons can be made between the rules applicable in the two systems. Pages 254–259 set out, in summary form, the present theory and practice of ministerial responsibility. This is necessarily based primarily on the Westminster Parliament but it is possible to draw on some discussion of the Scottish position too. In pp 259–270 the forms of procedure designed to maintain accountability in both Parliaments are discussed. Pages 270–275 deal with the role of ombudsmen and pp 275–277 deal specifically with the Scottish Parliament and its public petition procedure. The separate rules on financial accountability and on legal accountability are dealt with in Chapters 10 and 13 respectively.

Since access to relevant information is a vital component of maintaining accountability. the implementation of the Freedom of Information Act 2000 and the Freedom of Information (Scotland) Act 2002 have been of great importance. These Acts are discussed in Ch 12 below but their provisions supporting individual citizen access to information and, indirectly, MP and MSP access to information through parliamentary channels should be borne in mind[7].

1 Cm 3658, 1997, para 4.7.
2 Section 2, para 2.
3 See ch 13.
4 See below.
5 See ch 10.
6 *Scotland's Parliament* para 2.6.
7 For discussion of the impact of the 2000 Act on parliamentary questions see Fifth Report of the Public Administration Committee (2004-05) HC 449-1, para 6 and the case of *Office of Government Commerce v Information Commissioner* [2008] EWHC 774 (Admin).

MINISTERIAL RESPONSIBILITY – AN INTRODUCTION

9.2   First a word on terminology. In the discussion so far, the ideas of 'accountability' and 'responsibility' of ministers have been used more or less interchangeably and this practice will continue. Plainly, the two words can be used in contexts which make one preferable rather than the other. Equally, however, the meanings elide in general usage and a choice is often made simply on grounds of elegance. Ministers have duties and responsibilities and, whilst it would be clumsy to speak of a responsibility to Parliament for their responsibilities, it is perfectly acceptable to speak of accountability without change of meaning. The current *Civil Service Code* refers to ministers' 'accountability to Parliament'[1] and the current UK *Ministerial Code* states that 'Ministers have a duty to Parliament to account, and be held to account, for the policies, decisions and actions of their departments and "next steps" agencies'[2]. 'Accountability' here embraces both the idea of giving an account of policies, decisions and actions and of being held responsible for them. However, it has to be acknowledged that, for the purpose of restricting the scope of responsibility and especially the scope of blameworthiness, distinctions have sometimes been drawn between the broader obligations of accountability and the narrower or more focused obligations implied by responsibility. It is a distinction to which we should return while, in the meantime, continuing to use the terminology more or less interchangeably. It is, in any event, not merely questions of language which make a principle routinely stated to be fundamental to the working of the constitution so uncertain in its content. It would be surprising if a principle which is described as constitutional, but which is so intimately bound up in the workings of politics, were not of disputed content.

However, some things are clearer than others. Firstly, it is *ministers* who are described as responsible. This, in turn, has three main consequences. The first is that the principle of ministerial responsibility is designed to protect those over whom the minister presides – the departmental civil servants – from the obligation publicly to defend the actions of the department. There is nothing very exceptional in this. In most organisations, those who lead find it operationally necessary or desirable to represent the organisation publicly, whether to take praise or blame and without regard to the steps which may be taken *internally* to attribute responsibility where it more accurately lies. Constitutionally, however, this principle also operates to distinguish the publicly accountable politician from the unaccountable and often 'anonymous' civil servant[3]. Secondly, the principle distinguishes ministers from other, non-departmental, holders of public office. Ministers are responsible to Parliament but chief constables and chairs of quangos are not. Thirdly, ministers are responsible only in respect of those matters which are within their departmental remit. This may be broad – and the Prime Minister's remit may be interpreted *very* broadly – but it does impose limits. Similarly, it is a responsibility owed to *Parliament*. This has consequences not only for the nature of the obligations of accountability themselves but also for their priority over obligations to others. Ministers must, for instance, 'bear in mind the desire of Parliament that the most important announcements of government policy should be made, in the first instance, in Parliament'[4].

Beyond this, however, there is much indeterminacy, an indeterminacy which arises out of the twin circumstances which underpin the constitutional situation of governments on the Westminster model. On the one hand, they owe their very existence to the will of Parliament and can be removed by it[5]. On the other hand, governments are in a position to impose a considerable degree of discipline and control on a majority of Parliament's members. Governments are, therefore, at the same time, both acutely vulnerable to Parliaments but also protected from them. The position of individual ministers is further shaped by the solidarity (formally described as 'collective responsibility') which is extended to and demanded of them[6]. Except in circumstances where the alleged failing of a minister relates directly to a question of personal behaviour, whether by virtue of unacceptable personal relationships or of dishonesty, a Prime Minister will tend always to extend the cloak of protection, at least for a while. The political backdrop also produces a starker and more restricted range of outcomes. In particular, the idea of responsibility has been overlaid by the rather absurd notion that proof of error will always demand a resignation. Resignation may be too severe a penalty for mistakes apparently made blamelessly, at least from the point of view of the affected minister. Unrepentant denial of responsibility may be the only practical alternative and it is not surprising when, for instance, prisons prove to be insecure[7] ministers react very defensively.

In the modern working of the UK constitution, there are two principal questions which remain unresolved. The first is how the rhetoric of the asserted responsibility to Parliament of ministers for the entire working of their departments and executive agencies can be reconciled with the practical reality that ministers cannot possibly be directly involved in, or even know about, the vast range of actings and decision-making in their departments. Doctrine demands that it is *ministers* who must indeed be responsible, in the main because doctrine also demands that civil servants should be protected. But common sense, not just the common sense of ministers but also of parliamentarians and outsiders, tells us that the responsibility of ministers across the entire range of activities, especially if it carries with it the risk of blame and sanctions, perhaps to the extent of loss of office, is impractical and illusory. There is a circle here which cannot be squared. However, successive attempts at a reconciliation have been made and this is what prompted the reformulation of the doctrine following the Crichel Down affair of half a century ago when, following the resignation of the Minister of Agriculture because of the mistakes and inefficiency of his officials in the handling of the return to farmers of requisitioned land, the Home Secretary of the time (Sir David Maxwell Fyfe) sought to distinguish between situations with varying degrees of ministerial involvement – ranging from a civil servant's carrying out a ministerial order to a civil servant's taking action completely unknown to the minister – to determine the appropriate degree of responsibility. The Home Secretary's analysis also incorporated varying degrees of seriousness of the decisions made and of the fault of the civil servant so that no clear conclusions can be drawn beyond the bald statement that ministers are indeed constitutionally responsible to Parliament and that they must 'render an account' of their stewardship[8]. There have been attempted distinctions between matters of 'policy' for which ministers have a responsibility, and matters of 'administration' for which they have, at most, a reduced level of responsibility[9]. This is a distinction which has acquired a higher profile since the arrival of executive agencies and the special relationship between ministers and their chief executives[10]. Most prominently, reliance has been placed on a distinction, already mentioned, between 'responsibility' for some matters and, on the other hand, 'accountability', an obligation merely to inform and give an account, for the rest[11]. Another distinction has been drawn between 'constitutional accountability', as delivered through the convention of ministerial responsibility and 'managerial accountability'[12]. While none of these accounts[13] supplies a wholly persuasive reconciliation of the dilemma, it does also appear that an accommodation of a sort has been reached. The element of responsibility which involves an obligation to provide information, as we shall see when considering parliamentary mechanisms below, has been strengthened. On the other hand, political responsibility (in the sense of ministerial vulnerability to Parliament) has become marginalised as a serious element of governmental accountability as a whole. As long ago as 1956, Professor SE Finer reduced questions of responsibility to the political relationship between a minister, the Prime Minister and their party[14] and nothing much seems to have changed there. The weakness of crude political responsibility need not necessarily be a cause of distress if greater confidence can be placed in the other structures of accountability which have been built around it. If this is the case, ministerial responsibility as vulnerability to raw political pressure in Parliament can safely take on a more residual role.

The second, and related but also more subversive, question is whether the ministerial responsibility which does survive beyond the obligation to inform is really best seen as a responsibility to *Parliament* at all or whether instead it is better seen as a responsibility to the public, in relation to which Parliament exercises, along with other institutions, only a facilitative role. There are, of course, no formal constitutional rules to guide us here. We are in the domain of convention and such 'rules' as there are must derive from today's observable practice – not from statements in classic texts, nor even from the words of a statement of practice agreed between Parliament and government. Parliament will, almost inevitably, wish to assert the continuing vitality of the doctrine. It is in the government's political interest to assert its own constitutional accountability[15], whether or not supported by the facts. There is, however, nothing new in suggesting that ministers owe a responsibility which is, at least, shared between Parliament and public. Nor is it new to suggest that the BBC's 'Question Time' (or indeed 'Newsnight') has a higher political prominence than Parliament's own. But today it is perhaps truer to say that the hugely greater political power of the mass media combined with a more subservient and less autonomous role for Parliament have redrawn the constitutional lines of responsibility. Winning and maintaining media support on key issues and scoring highly in opinion polls[16], rather than support in Parliament, are seen as the truer tests of governmental performance. Praise or blame in Parliament may be an insecure guide to fortunes in the country. Ministerial accountability is ultimately more a state of mind and a political fact than a constitutional doctrine.

Whatever the real condition of ministerial responsibility to the UK Parliament, it was, in name at least, the equivalent doctrine which was received into Scottish practice. In language similar to the UK Code, the *Scottish Ministerial Code*[17] states that 'Ministers have a duty to the Parliament to account, and be held to account, for the policies, decisions and actions taken within their field of responsibility'[18]. Later, it is stated that 'Ministers should seek to uphold and promote' the key principles which guided the work of the Consultative Steering Group, including that 'the Scottish Executive should be accountable to the

Scottish Parliament and the Parliament and Executive should be accountable to the people of Scotland'[19]. One of the *Code*'s highest obligations is to 'give accurate and truthful information to the Parliament.' Ministers who knowingly mislead Parliament are expected to resign[20].The wording of the Scottish Code may, however, be intended to produce, or to reflect a somewhat different relationship between ministers and the Scottish Parliament from that at Westminster. The tendency to coalition or minority government can produce a different balance between executive and Parliament and different relationships of accountability. The fact that there is not, in the practice of the Scottish Executive, a direct alignment between the distribution of functions of ministers and departments or directorates[21] may dilute the idea of the responsibility of one for the other. The starting point, however, has been one of assumed equivalence. Although powers are vested in the Scottish Ministers and, for instance, parliamentary questions are addressed to the Scottish Executive as a whole[22], individual accountabilities among the members of the Executive are, as indicated in the *Code*, plain enough. Scottish practice is also acquiring its own portfolio of high-profile cases. The resignation of Dr Richard Simpson MSP as a deputy minister was forced on 26 November 2002 after it had been revealed that he had spoken of the striking firefighters in highly disparaging tones[23]. That was a matter of personal behaviour but, as a matter of departmental responsibility, there was no doubt, when severe problems occurred at the Scottish Qualifications Authority, about the ministerial accountability of Sam Galbraith MSP, the Minister for Education. He was exposed to the first vote of no confidence in the Parliament and, although that challenge was unsuccessful and the minister did not resign, he was subsequently removed from his position[24].

Since June 2008, the Scottish Ministerial Code has made provision for the First Minister as 'ultimate judge of the standards of behaviour expected of a Minister' to refer matters, as he deems appropriate, to a panel of independent advisers on the Code[25]. The advisers are the two former Presiding Officers and their first inquiry related to a complaint that the First Minister himself had misled Parliament. The panel's principal conclusion was that he had not[26].

1 *Civil Service Code* para 3. In this context 'Parliament' means both the UK and Scottish Parliaments.
2 *Ministerial Code: A Code of Conduct and Guidance on Procedures for Ministers* (July 2007) para 1.2(b). For 'next steps' or 'executive' agencies, see p 186.
3 Sometimes a civil servant sheds anonymity, as was the case in the high-profile appearance of Alastair Campbell before the House of Commons Foreign Affairs Committee on 25 June 2003. More routinely, in his capacity as Principal Accountable Officer, Sir John Elvidge appears before the Scottish Parliament's Public Audit Committee (see eg 14 Jan 2009).
4 *Ministerial Code* para 27. See House of Lords Communication Committee report, Government Communications, 26 January 2009, First Report of Session 2008–09, HL Paper 7).
5 This is made explicit in relation to the Scottish Parliament by the Scotland Act 1998 (SA 1998), ss 45(2), 47(2), 48(2) and 49(4)(c).
6 On collective responsibility, see p 163.
7 A cause of embarrassment to James Prior in 1983 and Michael Howard in 1995 and in 2009 to First Minister Alex Salmond and Cabinet Secretary for Justice Kenny McAskill.
8 HC Debs, 20 July 1954, cols 1285–1287.
9 For a recent discussion of this and other terminological distinctions, see D Woodhouse 'The Reconstruction of Constitutional Accountability' [2002] PL 73.
10 For executive agencies, see p 186.
11 For example, Treasury and Civil Service Committee *The Role of the Civil Service* (HC Paper 27 (1993–94)).

12 Woodhouse [2002] PL 73.
13 For some further useful analysis, see R Mulgan (2000) 78 Public Administration 555.
14 (1956) 34 Public Administration 377.
15 In the Scottish Executive *Partnership Agreement* of May 2003 it was declared: 'We will support robust parliamentary arrangements to hold the Executive to account.'
16 See D Woodhouse 'Ministerial responsibility in the 1990s: when do ministers resign?' (1993) 46 Parl Aff 277.
17 Reissued June 2003.
18 Para 1.1(b).
19 Para 3.1.
20 See also text at n 00 below. And note the ministerial apology for inaccurate information inadvertently provided at SPOR 4 Feb 2009, col 14643.
21 See p 187 above.
22 See p 261 below.
23 Perhaps for related reasons, he lost his seat in the May 2003 elections.
24 See also p 264 n 3 below.
25 See the Scottish Ministerial Code para 1.4; SPOR 18 June 2008 col 9826 et seq.
26 Report, March 2009.

PARLIAMENTARY MECHANISMS

9.3   It is valuable to carry forward this preliminary consideration of ministerial responsibility as we now turn to the mechanisms established in both Parliaments to hold ministers to account. We should bear in mind the flexibility and even ambiguity in the concept of responsibility and the question whether it is best seen as responsibility to the people, with the relevant Parliament acting simply as the agent of the people, albeit formally the most important agent, in holding the executive to account; or whether the Parliament is better seen as the primary accountee. The actual function of parliamentary mechanisms will, in any event, depend on political conditions of the time – the balance of parties in the Parliament, the political vulnerability of the government (especially if a minority government) and whether the government is drawn from a single party or is the product of a coalition or partnership. The effectiveness of parliamentary scrutiny may also depend on the structures of government adopted, including the use, or not, of executive agencies. It will depend too upon quite practical considerations such as the availability of time. The Scottish Parliament maintains an emphasis upon a strong committee system. But committees quickly devour the time of members and the strains of squeezing committee meetings into a day and a half of the parliamentary week have had to be accommodated. A related question is the divided loyalty of back-bench members. They are interested in the scrutiny of the executive but it is an interest which usually has to be combined with loyalty to their party (whether or not it is in government); ambition for personal advancement which is usually seen in terms of advancement in a party; and the need for most members to maintain a high profile in their own locality. Members are fighting the next election as well as a scrutinising the executive. If an MP or MSP appears to be pressing the government with questions in either the chamber or a committee, he or she will also have an eye on the party whip, as well as on what will appear on the parliamentary website and in the national or local newspapers.

Issues of accountability may arise in virtually all aspects of parliamentary business. Whatever the business, ministers are aware that they are subject to the scrutiny of their parliamentary colleagues and, although a line is often drawn between scrutiny of law-making and of executive action, ministers are as vulnerable to critical examination of their proposals in both. It is, however, possible to identify certain parliamentary procedures as devoted principally to executive scrutiny, and these may usefully be divided into three: parliamentary questions; debates on the initiative of opposition parties or of individual members; and the work of select or subject committees.

Parliamentary questions

9.4   Probably the most distinctive and potentially the most incisive mechanism for demonstrating the accountability of ministers to MPs and MSPs is the parliamentary question. Questions have historically been prominent at Westminster and, if the record of the first three sessions of the Scottish Parliament is anything to go by, MSPs at Holyrood have shown an enthusiasm for questions which has expanded the answering function of the Scottish Government far beyond that of the Scottish Office in the pre-devolution period.

Questions at Westminster

9.5   In the House of Commons[1], question time has established itself as central to ministerial accountability. A government statement has agreed that 'questions are a highly effective means of holding the Executive to account. A well-aimed question can benefit a Member simply by enabling them to obtain information. It can also benefit the Government, perhaps by requiring attention to a detail, which had been insufficiently considered, perhaps by allowing the Government to put its case across'[2]. On a rota basis, questions are put to departmental ministers for about an hour on sitting days except Fridays, and to the Prime Minister for half an hour on Wednesdays. The practice of the House, policed in the first instance by its Clerks, confines questions to matters within the departmental responsibility of ministers and acknowledges that ministers cannot be compelled to answer questions which trespass upon areas where the public interest demands secrecy[3] or where the cost of obtaining information would be excessive. The limits of responsibility exclude questions about institutions outwith central government, such as local authorities. Current practice on questions about the work of (executive) agencies has shifted from an earlier practice of leaving chief executives to respond by letter to ministerial answers. Special rules were adopted by resolution of the House in October 1999[4] to ensure that UK ministers may not, in general, be required to answer questions on matters devolved to the Scottish Parliament or to the National Assembly for Wales[5]. Ministers are expected to answer questions purely on devolved matters by making it clear that such questions should be addressed to the relevant devolved administration. It is, however, acknowledged that a clear dividing line cannot always be drawn where, for instance, a question relates to a reserved matter which is executively devolved to the Scottish Ministers[6]. It is, in practice, often the case that issues overlapping the division of competences arise in questions to the Secretary of State for Scotland, including, commonly, questions about meetings between the Secretary of State and the First Minister.

The effectiveness of questions depends only in part upon their formally permitted scope but much more on matters of procedure and style. Pressures on parliamentary time make it necessary to ration access by MPs who may put down no more than two questions for oral answer which are then subject to a draw ('shuffle') for priority status while the opportunity for important supplementary follow-up questions is regulated by the Speaker. MPs are often unhappy about 'evasive or unhelpful replies' letting ministers 'off the hook'[7]. As the *Ministerial Code* stipulates, 'it is of paramount importance that Ministers give accurate and truthful information to Parliament' and ministers should refuse information only in the public interest and in accordance with relevant statutes and the Freedom of Information Act 2000 [8] (although for the difficulties which can arise where questions are answered by reference to the Freedom of Information Act see *Office of Government Commerce v Information Commissioner*[9]). Changes to the rules on the submission of questions have enabled questions for oral answer to be submitted as little as two sitting days beforehand (four days in the case of questions to the Secretaries of State for Scotland, Wales and Northern Ireland, to enable information to be gathered from the devolved administrations) to ensure greater immediacy of impact[10]. Unanswered oral questions join other 'unstarred' questions for written answer. Such written answers, published in Hansard and often replete with the facts and figures of governmental performance, are a rich source of information and are a significant further indicator of accountability.

1   Similar arrangements operate in the House of Lords.
2   Cm 5628, 2002, para 2.
3   And see *Ministerial Code* para 1.2(d).
4   HC Debs 25 October 1999 col 774. A similar practice was adopted in relation to the 'Stormont' government in Northern Ireland.
5   See also the HC Procedure Committee *Fourth Report* (HC Paper 185 (1998–99)) – 'The Procedural Consequences of Devolution', Devolution Guidance Note 1: 'Common Working Arrangements'.
6   See also Devolution Guidance Note 13: 'Handling of Parliamentary Business in the House of Lords'.
7   HC Paper 622 (2001–02), para 48.
8   Para 1.2(d).
9   [2008] EWHC 774.
10 HC Debs, 29 October 2002 cols 813–814. See HC SOs 22(5).

Questions at Holyrood

9.6   In the Scottish Parliament the standing orders make provision for questions to the Scottish Executive[1]. Questions must be in writing (in English) and lodged with the Clerk of the Parliament. They must relate to a matter for which the First Minister, the Scottish Ministers or the Scottish Law Officers have general responsibility and must be brief, clearly worded and address a specific point. They must not, however, express a point of view; they must not contain offensive language; they must not breach any enactment or rule of law or be contrary to the public interest. Nor may they be in breach of the general '*sub judice*' rule of the Parliament – questions may not refer to any matter in relation to which legal proceedings are active[2] except to the extent permitted by the Presiding Officer[3]. To be admissible, a question must comply with these requirements but will be inadmissible if the information it seeks has been provided in response to a similar question in the previous six months. Disputes as to admissibility are to be determined by the Presiding Officer. A question must specify whether it is an oral question or a written question.

Written questions are published in the Parliament's Business Bulletin and must usually be answered within 14 days. A question concerning a matter for which he or she is alone responsible must be answered by the First Minister; similarly in respect of the Law Officers. All other questions may, in terms of the standing orders, be answered by any member of the Scottish Executive but, in practice, questions will be answered by the minister with direct responsibility. Answers (along with questions) are published in the Official Report. Oral questions are answered at the weekly periods of question time (usually held on Thursdays) – with 30 minutes for First Minister questions and with questions to the Scottish Executive divided between 'themed' questions (40 minutes) focused on specific topics rotating from week to week and 'general' questions (20 minutes) on other topics – subject to prescribed timetables for the lodging of questions and to selection procedures to bring questions down to manageable numbers. Questions may also be asked of the Scottish Parliamentary Corporate Body[4].

At First Minister's question time, a question must usually, of course, be answered by the First Minister but provision is made for another member of the Government to answer if the First Minister is unable to attend. Supplementary questions (required to be on the same subject matter and to be brief) from any MSP may follow, at the discretion of the Presiding Officer. Often this is used to enable senior opposition leaders to intervene. At the 'general' and 'themed' question times, relevant members of the Scottish Executive and junior ministers answer questions[5]. A supplementary question may follow from the MSP who put the question and, at the discretion of the Presiding Officer, from other members as well. Special provision is made for emergency questions[6]. An oral question 'of an urgent nature' may, if lodged by an MSP by 10 am on a day when the Parliament is meeting, be referred to the Presiding Officer who, if he or she thinks it sufficiently urgent, will allow the question to be put and answered at some appropriate point in the meeting[7].

In the course of the first session of the Parliament, the process of parliamentary questions had established itself at the heart of the Parliament's procedures. The volume of questions quickly reached a high level. During the second session (2003–2007), the total number of oral questions was 9084, written 32482, and, to the First Minister, 2812. The volume of business has, however, produced problems for both the Executive and the Parliament. There is a limit of ten days for a response to a written question but ministers may initially offer 'holding answers'. As an alternative to a formal question MSPs may contact officials directly in order to pursue points of information. But, of course, simply obtaining the information requested may not be the sole motivation of a parliamentary question: the opportunity to apply political pressure on ministers and publication in the official record may be important. Another issue in the Scottish Parliament, as at Westminster, has been that of the question 'inspired' or 'planted' by the Executive. It is required that all questions initiated by the Government are identified as such.

1 SOs, rr 13.3–13.8. The Parliament also publishes *Guidance on Parliamentary Questions* (4th ed 2007).
2 For the purposes of the Contempt of Court Act 1981, s 2.
3 SOs, r 7.5.
4 SOs r 13.9.
5 The Law Officers are usually required to answer questions within their responsibility.
6 SOs, r 13.8.
7 See, for example, SP OR 20 December 2001 col 5067, on the impact on island communities of a strike by ferry staff. To Feb 2009, only 6 emergency questions had been submitted.

Debates on the initiative of opposition parties (including motions of no confidence) and of individual members

9.7   At Westminster, opposition parties are anxious to use opportunities available to them to debate issues of their choosing and in a way designed to hold the government to account. Rarely used but potentially of high political profile is the motion of no confidence in the government[1]. More routinely, there are regular debates in both the main Commons chamber and, since November 1999, the parallel chamber in 'Westminster Hall', on matters proposed by the opposition parties. Away from these relatively high-profile debates and sometimes late at night, individual MPs have the opportunity to initiate short 'adjournment debates' in which they raise matters of more specific concern – frequently of relevance to their own constituency – and elicit a ministerial response.

At Holyrood, similar opportunities are available. Standing order provision is made for motions of no confidence – whether in relation to the Scottish Executive as a whole, or an individual member of the Executive, or a junior minister[2]. To be included in the business programme of the Parliament, such a motion must have the support of at least 25 members. Two such motions were debated in the first and second sessions of the Parliament. They were not successful[3]. It is also the specific responsibility of the Parliamentary Bureau to ensure that the business programme includes debates initiated by persons and bodies other than the Executive[4]. There must be at least 12 half-sitting days in each parliamentary year in which priority is given to the business of committees; there must be at least 16 half-sitting days devoted to business chosen by opposition political parties and groups; and, at the end of each meeting of the Parliament, there is a period of up to 45 minutes for any members' business.

On general debates in the chamber, it was the observation of the Procedures Committee[5] that, while these provided the opportunity for challenging the Executive, debates tended to be highly predictable because they were structured around motions and amendments which reinforced party differences. The Committee proposed that there might, in addition, be 'subject-based debates' in the Parliament in which there would be no specific motion and no vote. General debates in the chamber have, in the main, focused, as would be expected, on matters devolved to the Parliament and Executive, although important opportunities have also been taken to debate reserved matters such as the European Constitution[6] and, in January 2003, the possibility of an attack on Iraq[7]. As well as providing an opportunity for discussion of the topic under debate, these occasions have been used to air differences as to whether reserved matters are suitable for debate in the Parliament[8] and whether the formal scope of the Parliament's powers should be extended.

Debates on members' business have provided an opportunity for the discussion of motions which are non-controversial and on topics which usually raise either local constituency and regional issues or general campaigns or causes in which the sponsoring MSP is interested[9]. As the Procedures Committee has noted, the debates pass without a vote and attendance is usually small. The level of attendance does not, however, undermine the rationale for such business. The debates provide opportunities to raise important local issues with the Government, or to press very specific issues which might otherwise not be capable of being pursued. They often attract specific audiences to the public gallery and, since they are rarely of a party political nature, they tend to be free of partisanship. The Procedures Committee thought that, perhaps as a result, these debates frequently attain a quality and freshness which general debates lack[10]. The Committee proposed that the value of members' business might be enhanced by removing the selection of motions from the Parliamentary Bureau (perhaps by substituting a ballot) and, on some occasions at least, by holding the debates at a more popular time in the parliamentary day.

1 On 28 March 1979, the Callaghan government failed to repel a motion of no confidence and was forced into the dissolution of Parliament.
2 SOs, r 8.12.
3 The first (on 13 December 2000) was directed at Sam Galbraith for his handling of the SQA examinations affair and the second (on 15 February 2001) at Sarah Boyack for her handling of road transport policy. In the second session, Malcolm Chisholm faced a confidence motion on health service provision (30 Sept 2004). It was reported in May 2009 that, when Cabinet Secretary Kenny MacAskill came under threat of a no confidence vote following a prison escape, the First Minister in turn threatened that the whole Government would instead resign (Times, 23 May 2009). For the consequences for ministers of a resolution that the Executive no longer enjoys the confidence of the Parliament, see p 168.
4 SOs, r 5.6.
5 *CSG Inquiry* paras 486–497.
6 SP OR, 5 December 2002, col 16141.
7 SP OR, 16 January 2003, col 17013. See also 13 March 2008, col 7042.
8 SP OR, 16 January 2003, col 17013. Other debates have been on the drink drive limit, the Glasgow passport office, human trafficking and the Commonwealth.
9 *CSG Inquiry* paras 498–506.
10 *CSG Inquiry* para 499.

Select and subject committees

9.8   Whatever the strengths and weaknesses of the parliamentary mechanisms so far considered, it is in scrutiny by committee that first Westminster and now Holyrood have invested most trust and resources in recent times. The general structure of parliamentary committees has been noted in Chapter 4 and, in particular, the provision made in the House of Commons for the post-1979 system of departmental select committees and then, at Holyrood, the setting up of the 'subject' committees of the Parliament with remits intended to combine the functions of both the Commons select committees and its public bill (formerly standing) committees.

Select committees at Westminster

9.9   Despite early reservations about the potential of House of Commons select committees to fail because of their political domination by the governing party or because of their lack of resources, there is today no doubting their high level of productivity in the use of their powers 'to call for persons, papers and records' to conduct serious inquiries in their areas of focus. Through their reports, much information is put into the public domain. The only major targets of criticism have been, since devolution in 1999, the committees tracking the 'territorial' departments – the Northern Ireland Affairs, Scottish Affairs and Welsh Affairs Committees. Individual inquiries continue to be held[1] but questions hang over these committees, as they have done over their related departments. Although a standing committee rather than a select committee and, therefore, not a committee to hold inquiries, the Scottish Grand Committee has held occasional debates on Scottish matters since devolution but has not met since 2002/03[2].

It is difficult to assess the overall contribution of select committees in seeking to secure the accountability of the executive to Parliament. An exchange of views between the Liaison Committee of the House of Commons – a committee consisting of the chairman of all select committees – and the Government nicely illustrates the issues. The Committee entitled a report issued in 2000 'Shifting the Balance: Select Committees and the Executive'[3]. In it, it took as its starting point the proposition that, despite the best efforts of select committees, in practice governmental power has always outstripped parliamentary control. Prior to 1979 and the creation of the new committees, it had been an unequal struggle and governments had always had the upper hand. The new system had been a success. Independent scrutiny of government had been achieved. Ministers and civil servants had been questioned and forced to explain policies. On occasion, short-sighted policies and wrongdoing had been exposed. The system had been a source of unbiased information, national debate and constructive ideas. The political process had been made less remote and more accessible to the citizen. The system had shown the House of Commons at its best: working on the basis of fact, not supposition or prejudice; and with constructive co-operation rather than routine disagreement. On the other hand, success had not been unalloyed and questions had arisen about the overall effectiveness of the system. After two decades – and especially in the present climate of constitutional change – it was time for some further reform and modernisation.

The Committee prefaced its proposals with a statement of what it called the 'realities of select committee work'. It is an interesting list (some points have already been touched on) which is as relevant to the consideration of the work of committees at Holyrood as it is to those at Westminster:

(1)   Select committees have to operate within a constitutional framework in which, unlike the position in the United States, there is no separation of powers, and a stronger party system. Ministers are also members of

Parliament, and are sustained in office by Parliament. The relationship is thus more subtle, the Liaison Committee said, but there is no reason why select committees should not call ministers to account.

(2) Select committees are affected by party loyalty and organisation, which structure the way in which Parliament and its institutions work. In turn, careers have generally been shaped by party service and the floor of the House rather than by work on select committees.

(3) Because select committees are bodies created by and subordinate to the House itself, the exercise of their formal powers is eventually subject to the will of the House, in which the government of the day is likely to have a majority. A particular application of this is the powers committees have to ensure the attendance of those they wish to interview, especially civil servants. A general agreement on access to civil servants has been made under the 'Osmotherley rules'[4] but, in the case of a refusal supported by ministers, a committee would need the backing of an order of the House as a whole which, because of the government's majority, would be very unlikely to be forthcoming[5].

(4) There is no easy route to success. A determined and hard-working committee, in which members are prepared to devote substantial effort and put the interests of the citizen and taxpayer first, can be extraordinarily effective.

(5) Within their powers, and subject to any instruction from the House, committees are entirely independent. It is up to them to decide how to do their job, set their priorities, and select and run inquiries.

(6) The scarcest resource in the committee system is members' time. The credibility of the system depends upon members being fully involved in the work of committees, being prepared to put in the necessary preparation and study as well as taking part in the committee's programme. Additional staff resources may improve the quality of a committee's work, but should not be the means of increasing a committee's output at the cost of member involvement.

Against that background, the Committee made a number of reforming proposals. The Liaison Committee itself should be reconstituted as the Select Committee Panel with an important new task of proposing the membership of select committees, rather than the Committee of Selection which is more readily dominated by party whips. The functions of select committees should be extended and strengthened, especially in relation to the scrutiny of secondary legislation, draft Bills and treaties. Committees should hold 'confirmation hearings' for major public appointments. Steps should also be taken to improve attendance at select committees and also the status of the committee chairman who might be paid a salary or receive additional financial allowances. Select committee reports should be given a higher priority for debate by the House of Commons, and the quality of government replies to reports should be improved. There should be a relationship of constructive co-operation between committees and the government. There should be more use of joint working between committees. 'Joined-up government' must be scrutinised by joined-up committees. Committee staffing should be strengthened. Committee reports should be made more attractive and should be given wider publicity.

Although the government gave a formal welcome to the Liaison Committee's report and affirmed the success of the select committee system – it was indeed 'an entrenched part of our constitutional arrangements' – it also recorded a number of robust reservations[6]. The government rejected the Committee's call for new procedures for the appointment of select committee members. Creating a Select Committee Panel might waste the time of the House and might be less effective in achieving party balance in committee membership and chairmanship. The government was strongly opposed to giving select committees powers equivalent to those of US Congressional committees in confirmation hearings on official appointment. Officials should not become political footballs and, unlike the US position, UK ministers responsible for making appointments were directly accountable to the legislature. (A practice of holding 'confirmation hearings' for appointments to the Bank of England's Monetary Policy Committee was, however, introduced by the Treasury Select Committee[7]. More recently, the Government proposed in The Governance of Britain[8] the broader adoption of pre-appointment hearings[9]. In July 2009 the Health Committee reported on the Appointment of the Chair of the Food Standards Agency[10]. The government welcomed the development of 'constructive co-operation' between departments and select committees, while noting also the impact of the burden of increasing committee activity on ministers. In particular, the involvement of select committees in the pre-legislative scrutiny of draft Bills was to be encouraged but would not always be possible because of the priority to be given to legislation already embarked on its formal passage through Parliament. One innovation in select committee practice has been the twice-yearly appearances now made by the Prime Minister for questioning by the Liaison Committee of the Commons[11].

Has the balance shifted? Has the balance of power changed between select committees on behalf of Parliament as a whole and the executive departments they scrutinise? Certainly activity has increased and well-publicised investigations such as that of the Foreign Affairs Committee into *The Decision to go to War in Iraq*[12] in June 2003 do much to raise the profile and, therefore, perhaps the influence of committees as a whole. Similarly, there is no doubting the influence of the Treasury Select Committee in its work on a series of reports on the Banking Crisis in 2009[13]. But the overriding constraints imposed by the political underpinnings of parliamentary government will always loom large.

Important areas of activity in which Westminster committees have made a significant contribution and, joining the Public Accounts Committee[14] in which party politics are less prominent have been those of justice/constitutional affairs where each House has a committee and human rights where the Joint Committee has been especially active in its critique of the Government.

1   Poverty in Scotland, Experience of the Scottish Elections, and Employment and Skills for the Defence Industry during 2007-08. Recently the Scottish Affairs Committee had lively encounters with Sir Kenneth Calman as Chair of his Commission on Devolution. See 11 June 2008 and 11 Feb 2009.
2   In 2002–03, the Committee debated the Scottish Fishing Industry (10 December 2002) and the Scottish Economy. For the demise of its legislative role, see p 220.
3   HC Paper 300 (1999–2000).
4   Guidance now published by the Cabinet Office as 'Department evidence and response to select committees'.

5 For problems with securing the attendance of Lord Birt, the PM's Strategy Adviser, see Public Administration Select Committee (2005–06) HC 690.
6 The Government's Response to the First Report from the Liaison Committee on Shifting the Balance: Select Committees and the Executive (Cm 4737, 2000).
7 Third Report (HC Paper 571 (1997–98)). And see eg HC Paper 1009 (2007–08).
8 1997.
9 Paras 74-76, 80. See also the First Report of the Liaison Committee 2007–08, HC 384.
10 2008-09, HC 856.
11 See eg HC Paper 257 (2008–09).
12 HC Paper 813 (2002–03).
13 See 2008–09 HC 402, 416,519,656.
14 See p 292.

Subject committees at Holyrood

9.10   At Holyrood, many of the same questions are also relevant since many of the same constraints on committee activity apply. On the other hand, the Holyrood committees have been created in a parliamentary environment deliberately designed to give them a strong role from the start. The subject committees of the Parliament have a standing obligation to examine matters within their remit and to report to the Parliament. As well as their legislative duties, they are to 'consider the policy and administration of the Scottish Administration'[1]. For each committee, the scope of its powers is then further defined – generally in such a way as to map on to the responsibilities of the department in the Scottish Executive to which it relates. As to their investigative powers, a committee may *invite* any person to attend its proceedings for the purpose of giving evidence or to produce documents in that person's custody or control[2]. In addition the power of the Parliament to *require* persons to attend to give evidence and to produce documents, conferred by SA 1998, s 23, has been extended to committees[3]. That power is, however, confined to evidence and documents concerning subjects 'for which any member of the Scottish Executive has general responsibility'. Special provision is made in respect of persons 'outside Scotland'[4]. Such persons may be required to attend or to produce documents only in connection with the discharge by that person of functions of the Scottish Administration or of a Scottish public authority[5] or a cross-border public authority and again only where those functions are within the general responsibility of a member of the Scottish Executive[6]. The intention is to narrow accountability to the Scottish Parliament to those matters which do not also attract accountability at Westminster. To similar effect, UK ministers (or former ministers) and civil servants (or former civil servants) may be summoned only in respect of matters within the general responsibility of a member of the Scottish Executive and expressly *not* in the case of matters where responsibility is shared with the Scottish Ministers, ie the relevant member of the Scottish Executive should be the principal target of the committee. Requirements to attend may not be imposed on judges or tribunal members[7]. No witness may be obliged to answer questions or to produce documents in circumstances where in judicial proceedings a court would permit a refusal to do so[8] – for example, where there would be a risk of self-incrimination.

The Scottish Executive has issued guidance on the appearance and questioning of civil servants at Holyrood committees (equivalent to the 'Osmotherley rules'

268

at Westminster[9]). This emphasises that officials give evidence on behalf of their ministers and under their direction and approval. Officials are accountable to ministers and are subject to instruction. They are not directly accountable to the Parliament. They may be called upon to give a full account of Executive policies or of their own actions. But their purpose in doing so is to contribute to the process of ministerial accountability, not to offer personal views or judgments on matters of political controversy[10]. There is, in practice, a substantial contribution made by civil servants to the work of committees and, in the report on its CSG inquiry, the Procedures Committee was anxious, without disturbing the formal constitutional position, to encourage a closer relationship of partnership between the two[11].

In the course of the first session of the Parliament, UK ministers were called upon to give evidence on several occasions, the first being the European Committee's questioning of Peter Hain MP in November 2001[12]. Since then UK ministerial appearances have been sparse but have included Anne McGuire MP[13] and Vera Baird MP[14]. In guidance issued by the UK government[15], it has been stressed that, while circumstances in which a UK minister may be required to attend a committee of the Scottish Parliament will be rare and while a minister's overriding responsibility is to Westminster, any invitation to attend 'should be treated with as much care and courtesy' as an invitation to attend a Westminster select committee.

Subject committees have conducted a number of inquiries leading to the publication of important reports[16]. The Local Government Committee investigated possible reform of local government finance and this led, inter alia, to the Executive's agreement to modify the 'capital consents' regime[17]; the Health and Community Care Committee recommended that personal care for the elderly should be free[18]; the Justice 1 Committee's report on prison estates was influential in the eventual decision not to close Peterhead Prison[19] and the Health and Community Care Committee reported critically on the Executive's risk assessment procedures in relation to the planting of genetically modified crops[20]. Perhaps of highest profile were the investigations carried out by the Enterprise and Lifelong Learning Committee[21] and the Education, Culture and Sport Committee[22] into the calamitous conduct of the Higher examination procedures by the Scottish Qualifications Authority which led to the 'no confidence' debate in the chamber on 13 December 2000.

As already noted in Chapter 4, the work of the subject committees figured prominently in the '*CSG Inquiry*' conducted by the Procedures Committee. The committees had made a substantial impact although concerns had been expressed about some aspects of their work, including complaints of too much secrecy, instability caused by changes of membership and general time pressures. On the other hand, at least one committee, the Justice 2 Committee was able to comment in generally favourable terms on its scrutiny work in the first session. Members believed that the relationship between the Committee and ministers had matured. The rigour of its questioning had produced a more open-minded response from ministers[23].

Although there have been some notable committee reports in the second and third sessions[24] their prominence seems to have declined. It may be that, at least during the second session, the time and resources of committees were diverted towards their legislative rather than scrutiny activities.

1   SOs, r 6.2.2(a).
2   SOs, r 12.4.1.
3   SOs, r 12.44.14.1 and see SA 1998, s 23(8).
4   A phrase not further explained in SA 1998.
5   See p 209.
6   SA 1998, s 23(2).
7   SA 1998, s 23(7). A protection is also extended to procurators fiscal. Members of the judiciary are, of course, free to attend committee hearings if they wish, as the Lord President and others did at Justice Committee hearings on the Judiciary and Courts (Scotland) Bill in 2008.
8   SA 1998, s 23(9).
9   *Scottish Executive Evidence and Responses to Committees of the Scottish Parliament*, (February 2001). See also resolution of the Scottish Parliament: SP OR 1 November 2000 col 1245.
10 A 'Protocol between Committee Clerks and The Scottish Executive' provides detailed guidance on how Committees are to secure written or oral evidence from the Scottish Executive.
11 Paras 513–548.
12 SP EU OR 5 November 2001, col 1275. Another was the appearance of Eliot Morley MP before the Rural Development Committee on 18 Feb 2003 (col 4330).
13 Procedures Committee 1 March 2005.
14 Equal Opportunities Committee, 2 Dec 2008.
15 Devolution Guidance Note 12 'Attendance of UK Ministers and Officials at Committees of the Devolved Legislatures'.
16 A list of successes to that point was set out in the Presiding Officer's Constitution Unit lecture of 29 January 2003.
17 *Sixth Report* (2002) SP Paper 551.
18 *Sixteenth Report* (2002) SP Paper 219.
19 *Sixth Report* (2002) SP Paper 612.
20 *First Report* (2002) SP Paper 743.
21 *Sixth Report* (2002) SP Paper 225.
22 *Eleventh Report* (2002) SP Paper 234.
23 Justice 2 Committee, Session 1 Legacy Paper 2003.
24 See eg the Report on Child Poverty by the Local Government and Communities Committee, 2009, SP Paper 267.

Parliamentary and other ombudsmen[1]

9.11   Forty years on, it is puzzling to recall how difficult it was in the 1960s to make the case, against its more conservative opponents, for establishing a United Kingdom parliamentary ombudsman. In the period since the Parliamentary Commissioner Act 1967 (PCA 1967) was brought into effect, however, that case has become more familiar and, with experience of the actual operation of the office of the parliamentary ombudsman, it has been given greater strength. The principal reason for the creation of the ombudsman was the weakness of the other parliamentary mechanisms for accountability. These served some useful purposes but they tended to fail where individuals had specific complaints about mistreatment by civil servants. The complaints might be about serious injustices done or they might be about quite minor flaws in administrative behaviour, such as delay or rudeness, which nevertheless caused offence or inconvenience. Collectively such failings, great or small, have been grouped together as 'maladministration'. Often, however, they do not readily lend themselves to resolution by either the courts or Parliament. The courts deal only with alleged illegality, whether in judicial review proceedings or in ordinary actions, and often only rather inefficiently and at some considerable expense. Many complaints of maladministration do not actually involve illegality and, even if they do, the prospects for successful resolution by litigation are not good. Nor are such complaints always susceptible to resolution by parliamentary means. While an MP or MSP may ask a parliamentary question or write to a minister on behalf of a constituent, this is rarely appropriate where the circumstances are complex or contested or both and a systematic inquiry into all the circumstances is necessary. It is not satisfactory to have such an inquiry carried out by civil servants who will have considerable advantages over the complainant in terms of access to information held on files or by other civil servants and whose impartiality will obviously be doubted by the aggrieved complainant. The ministerial response to a complaint will often fail to satisfy the complainant for these reasons. Equally, other parliamentary mechanisms, while appropriate for other purposes, are not well designed to handle the individual complaint. Select committees of the House of Commons and committees at Holyrood may be successful in addressing complaints of general policy failure but they are less well equipped to conduct inquiries into complaints by individuals. Nor do they have the resources to do so[2].

At Westminster in the 1960s, these arguments led to the creation of the parliamentary ombudsman by PCA 1967 and, because the arguments have been judged to remain sound, have led to a general strengthening of the office – though not going as far as some would wish – in subsequent years. They are arguments which were adapted to produce the case for the creation of local government ombudsmen[3]; health service ombudsmen[4]; and most recently the Scottish Public Services Ombudsman. SA 1998, required the Scottish Parliament to make provision for the investigation of complaints made to MSPs in respect of action taken by or on behalf of a member of the Scottish Executive or any other office-holder in the Scottish Administration. On a permissive basis, the Parliament could extend the scope of any provision it made to other public bodies, and, indeed to the Parliamentary corporation. Initially, temporary provision was made for the creation of the office of Scottish Parliamentary Ombudsman[5], very much along the lines of the Westminster counterpart and, indeed, with the offices held by the same person. This was followed by the Scottish Public Services Ombudsman Act 2002 (SPSOA 2002), creating for Scotland an ombudsman whose jurisdiction includes not only the Scottish Executive and Administration but also Scottish local government and the health service. In this brief account of the work of the parliamentary ombudsmen, we start with the UK Parliamentary Commissioner for Administration and move on to the Scottish Ombudsman.

1 For a recent review, see M Seneviratne *Ombudsmen: Public Services and Administrative Justice* (2002).
2 For the handling of petitions by committees of the Scottish Parliament, see p 275 below.
3 In Scotland, by the Local Government (Scotland) Act 1975, Pt II.
4 By the National Health Service (Scotland) Act 1972 and later the Health Service Commissioners Act 1993.
5 Scotland Act 1998 (Transitory and Transitional Provisions) (Complaints of Maladministration) Order 1999, SI 1999/1351.

UK Parliamentary Commissioner for Administration

9.12 The ombudsman's constitutional contribution depends on four main characteristics of the office: (1) its independence; (2) the investigatory powers; (3) the quality of investigations carried out; and (4) the supporting contributions of a parliamentary committee. With these in place, the ombudsman has the potential to ensure the righting of individual wrongs; the potential too to achieve the wider reform of administrative systems where her[1] investigations may have exposed systemic deficiencies; and the important deterrent role of the scrutineer whose invisible presence may often be felt by administrators as they make decisions affecting the interests of individuals. Just as the knowledge that the powers of courts may be invoked to expose illegality may encourage decision-making within the law, so too the ombudsmen may have a similarly encouraging effect. The parallel has been marked by the publication within the civil service of a pamphlet called *The Judge over your Shoulder*[2] which addresses questions of judicial review[3], while *The Ombudsman in your Files*[4] provides an account of situations which might attract criticism as maladministration.

The independence of the ombudsman is secured in her appointment by the Crown and security of tenure resembling that of senior judges. She holds office during good behaviour but may be removed, like senior English judges only following an address from each House of Parliament[5]. Her salary is, again like judicial salaries, a charge on the Consolidated Fund[6]. The function of the ombudsman is to investigate complaints by individuals (or a body of persons, but not a public authority) who claim to have suffered 'injustice in consequence of maladministration' by any of the government departments or public bodies listed in PCA 1967, Sch 2[7]. With effect from the implementation of devolution in 1999, the list of departments was amended to remove the Scottish Executive and devolved public bodies[8]. They became instead subject to investigation by the Scottish Ombudsman. Just as courts are, in principle, confined to legal issues when involved in judicial review and are not in general, permitted to stray into broader policy matters[9], so too the ombudsman is statutorily confined to questions of maladministration. Certain types of administrative function are excluded from investigation[10], sometimes controversially. Many would accept that action affecting relations with foreign governments should be excluded and so too the commencement or conduct of civil or criminal proceedings. But the exclusion of action relating to commercial transactions or action in respect of civil service personnel matters define the ombudsman's jurisdiction in ways which make it unnecessarily narrow. Another restriction normally prevents the ombudsman from conducting an investigation where a legal remedy is available[11] and the ombudsman may not question the merits of a decision taken without maladministration[12].

Procedurally, a complaint must reach the ombudsman in writing and by way of an MP[13]. This requirement that access be via an elected member has both a practical and a more broadly constitutional aspect. It provides the opportunity for complaints to be scrutinised prior to their submission to the ombudsman, and for incompetent or frivolous complaints to be filtered out. It also ensures that MPs are integrated into the constitutionally significant process of the investigation of complaints against executive bodies on behalf of Parliament. On the other hand, ombudsmen themselves have joined those who criticise the restriction because of the tendency to deter individuals from pursuing their complaints. Considering the range of public bodies against which complaints may be made, numbers of complaints are small and they should not be discouraged by procedural barriers[14].

The investigations themselves are conducted by the ombudsman's staff in private, with powers in reserve to compel the production of evidence[15]. The outcome is a report which may, if appropriate, recommend a remedy but the ombudsman has no direct power to enforce a recommendation. The report is to Parliament and there may be a special report if an injustice has not been remedied[16]. The ombudsman is a *parliamentary* commissioner whose independent powers of investigation have greatly extended the reach of Parliament's function to scrutinise administrative activity. She remains dependent, however, for the implementation of her recommendations, upon the status and influence of her parliamentary support. For this purpose, the specific support of a parliamentary committee has been crucial for the UK ombudsman. This, at least, was the case until 1997 when the Parliamentary Commissioner Select Committee had a remit dedicated to the office. It is not so clear that the Public Administration Committee which now embraces the ombudsman's work in a wider remit is having the same beneficial effect.

1 The current ombudsman is Ms Ann Abrahams.
2 Treasury Solicitor (4th edn, 2006).
3 See p 374 below.
4 Cabinet Office (revised edn, 1997).
5 PCA 1967, s 1.
6 PCA 1967, s 2 (as amended). For the Consolidated Fund, see p 280.
7 PCA 1967, s 5(1).
8 Scotland Act 1998 (Consequential Modifications) (No 2) Order 1999, SI 1999/1820.
9 See p 378 below.
10 PCA 1967, s 5(3), Sch 3.
11 PCA 1967, s 5(2).
12 PCA 1967, s 12(3).
13 PCA 1967, s 5(1).
14 The Annual Report of the PCA for 2007-08 recorded receipt of 7,341 new cases received during that year. Only 290 statutory investigations were completed. See HC Paper 1040 (2007–08).
15 PCA 1967, s 8.
16 PCA 1967, s 10. See, for example, *Equality under the law? The treatment of widowers by the Inland Revenue and the Department for Work and Pensions* (HC Paper 122 (2002–03)); *The Prudential Regulations of Equitable Life* (HC Paper 809 (2002–03)); *Tax Credits: Getting it wrong?* (HC Paper 1010 (2006–07)); *Trusting in the Pensions Promise* (HC Paper 984 (2005–06)).

Scottish Public Services Ombudsman

9.13　As far as Scotland is concerned, the UK parliamentary ombudsman's role continues in relation to 'reserved' departments such as the Inland Revenue and the Department for Work and Pensions. In relation to the devolved areas, early consultations by the Scottish Executive indicated a preference for consolidating into a single ombudsman office the transitional Scottish

Parliamentary Ombudsman, the health service ombudsman and the local government ombudsman as well as the housing association ombudsman[1]. The principal objective was to merge the different offices into a 'one-stop shop', headed by a single ombudsman, with substantially integrated powers of investigation, and the SPSOA 2002[2], passed by the Scottish Parliament and brought into effect on 23 October 2002, made the new provision. Apart from the merger of the offices, the model of PCA 1967 is broadly maintained with the exception that:

(a)   The ombudsman is appointed by the Queen on the nomination of the Scottish Parliament[3] rather than simply on the nomination of the government (SPSOA 2002, s 1). Dismissal would require a resolution of the Parliament to that effect to be passed by a two-thirds majority of the total number of the MSPs (SPSOA 2002, sch 1, para 4).

(b)   The scope for investigations has been extended to include not only action taken by an authority but also any 'service failure' ie any failure in a service provided or failure to provide a service (SPSOA 2002, s 5(1), (2)).

(c)   Complaints to the ombudsman are not subject to any 'MSP filter' and may be made whenever a person claims to have sustained injustice or *hardship* in consequence of maladministration or service failure (SPSOA 2002, s 5(3)).

(d)   Investigations may also be carried out pursuant to a request by the public authority affected (SPSOA 2002, s 2(2)) but only when it has been alleged publicly that one or more members of the public have sustained injustice or hardship and the authority has taken all reasonable steps to deal with the matter (SPSOA 2002, s 5(5)).

(e)   All reports on investigations must be sent, in addition to the person aggrieved and authority affected, to the Scottish Ministers, whether or not it was a member of the Scottish Executive against whom the complaint was made, and must be laid before the Parliament (SPSOA 2002, s 15). In the case of a failure to remedy any injustice or hardship, a special report may follow (SPSOA 2002, s 16).

The impact of this integrated ombudsman model will be interesting to observe. Despite the involvement, perhaps only formal or symbolic, of the Parliament in the ombudsman's appointment, the broad span of her jurisdiction and the loss of the MSP filter tends to disengage the office from any specifically parliamentary lines of accountability. The ombudsman has become more free-floating, as may be appropriate for someone receiving complaints from a wide range of sources. On the other hand, the system of reporting to the Scottish Ministers and the Scottish Parliament may have oddly centralising consequences in relation to complaints against local authorities. It would cut sharply across existing lines of accountability if the Scottish Ministers or the Parliament took steps to encourage or compel local authority compliance with a critical report[4]. Since 2006, the ombudsman has appeared before the Local Government and Communities Committee (previously Local Government and Transport) to discuss the annual report. On one occasion, however, this was an opportunity for abrupt questioning about the case of *Argyll and Bute Council v SPSO*[5].

1 See *Modernising the Complaints System* (SE 2000/84, 2000) and *A Modern Complaints System* (SE/2001/139, 2001). See also B Thompson 'The Scottish Public Services Ombudsman: Revolution or Evolution?' in A Maharg and T Mullen (eds) *Public Law in Scotland* (2006).
2 Subject to approval by the Scottish Parliament, the scheduled list of bodies subject to investigation may be amended by Order in Council. See, for example, SSI 2002/468.
3 On 27 June 2002, the Parliament nominated Professor Alice Brown as the first holder of the office. From April 2009, the ombudsman has been Mr Jim Martin.
4 But see the suggestion made by the ombudsman that the Parliament might hold to account a defaulting local authority – Local Government and Transport Committee 5 Dec 2006 col 4389.
5 2008 SC 155 and see para 9.14 below.

Ombudsman decisions in the courts

9.14   Despite the rules which are intended to prevent ombudsmen from encroaching on issues which are appropriately decided by courts, there is no doubt that there are points at which illegality and maladministration overlap and that, in any event, ombudsmen and courts become partners in the broader goal of checking administrative misbehaviour. On the other hand, it is sometimes the case that the decisions of ombudsmen are themselves challenged in the courts. A succession of English cases has established that ombudsmen are indeed susceptible to judicial review[1] and the case of *Argyll and Bute Council v SPSO*[2] made it clear that, where the ombudsman misinterprets statutory provisions (here, the Community Care and Health (Scotland) Act 2002), a decision and recommendation flowing from that misinterpretation must be struck down[3]. The case of *R(Bradley) v Secretary of State for Work and Pensions*[4] explored the question of whether the rejection by a public authority of an ombudsman's finding of maladministration or subsequent recommendation is challengeable. The English Court of Appeal held that successful challenge would be confined to those extreme situations where *Wednesbury* unreasonableness[5] could be established.

1 See *R v Parliamentary Commissioner for Admininstration, ex p Dyer* [1984] 1 All ER 375; *R (Cavanagh) v Health Service Commissioner* [2004] EWHC 1847; *R (Parish) v Pensions Ombudsman* [2009] EWHC 32.
2 2008 SC 155.
3 And see para 9.13.
4 [2009] QB 114.
5 See p 378 below.

PUBLIC PETITIONS

9.15   The right of citizens to petition one or other of the Houses of the Westminster Parliament, principally the House of Commons, has an important history and a symbolic constitutional significance. Public petitions may range over diverse subject matter and 'may pray for an alteration of the general law or the reconsideration of a general administrative decision, and they may also pray for redress of local or personal grievances'[1]. Provision is made in the standing orders of both Houses for the presentation of a petition by a member of the relevant House, in the case of the Commons normally at the adjournment. Procedural restrictions and a very low level of use have, however, produced a low profile for petition procedures at Westminster.

When the Scottish Constitutional Convention came to make its proposals for establishing the Scottish Parliament, it insisted on the need for the Parliament to encourage the greatest possible involvement by the people of Scotland and for arrangements to be put in place to ensure that the Parliament remained responsive to their wishes and values. It made a specific recommendation that standing orders should be adopted to enable electors directly to petition the Parliament[2]. This was a theme taken up by the Consultative Steering Group who declared it to be an important principle that the Scottish people should be able to petition the Parliament. Public petitions should be encouraged and there should be clear and simple rules as to form and content. The Parliament should accept all petitions for which the remedy sought would be within its competence. A decision on the action to be taken should depend on the strength and depth of support for the petition and not simply on the number of signatories. A Committee for Petitions should be established to decide, in the first instance, how each petition should be processed[3].

These recommendations were carried forward into the standing orders of the Scottish Parliament and these provide for a Public Petitions Committee to be established[4] and for its procedures[5]. A petition may be brought by an individual person, a body corporate or an unincorporated association in a form determined by the Public Petitions Committee. The Committee has two functions in respect of any petition lodged. It must first decide whether the petition is admissible. It will be inadmissible if it requests the Parliament to do anything which, in the opinion of the Committee, the Parliament clearly has no power to do. Although a test of admissibility based on the competence of the Parliament seems appropriate, this version adopted in the standing orders is curiously phrased. The Parliament's own powers are, of course, primarily legislative and many petitions will not be directly aimed at a change in the law. This is not a merely technical matter. It reflects an ambiguity inherent in the purpose of petition procedures in a modern Parliament. It is unclear how a Parliament should respond to petitions, given the relative sophistication of other procedures for the handling of the complaints and concerns of citizens. Should a petition procedure merely operate as a channel towards those other procedures – designed mainly to secure a response from the Government rather than the legislature – or should it offer some quite separate response?

The standing orders of the Parliament offer a number of procedural options for the Petitions Committee as it exercises its second function, that of deciding what action should be taken on a petition judged to be admissible. Following consideration of the petition, the Committee may (a) refer the petition to the Scottish Ministers, any other committee of the Parliament or any other person or body for them to take such action as they consider appropriate; or (b) report to the Parliamentary Bureau or to the Parliament itself; or (c) take any other appropriate action. The Committee has issued its own web-based guidance on the submission of public petitions which, in addition to explaining the mechanics of how petitions are to be made, explains some of the limitations of the process. The Parliament does not have the power to interfere with or overturn the executive decisions of other public bodies in Scotland, such as the decisions of local authorities on planning applications or school closures. Nor can the committee recommend action in relation to cases which are or have been subject to court or tribunal proceedings. Petitions must be in the public interest and should not, for instance, ask the Parliament to do something which may be unlawful.

As with much of the early work of the Parliament, it is difficult to form a concluded view of the petition work handled so far[6]. Certainly petitioning has proved popular and receipt of the 1000th petition was recorded in October 2006. Petitions have been lodged by a wide variety of individuals and organisations including residents' associations, community councils, local authorities, political parties and pressure groups. Issues raised have been personal, local and national. Many have had a sympathetic reception and many petitioners appear personally before the Committee. At other points the Petitions Committee has expressed concern about the burdens imposed by petitions and the undue expectations raised. Committee members have been apprehensive about the risks of manipulation by professional or other powerful interest groups. There is an early frustration expressed about individuals who bombard the Parliament with strings of petitions: one petitioner had lodged over 30 petitions by June 2000.

In 2006 the Public Petitions Committee commissioned a report on the operation of the system to that point[7]. This confirmed the popularity of the procedure. Most (53%) of petitions had been from individuals, with five accounting for 11% of all petitions. 30% of all petitions had over 100 signatures. Petitioners were disproportionately older, male and middle class. 58% were graduates. In its consideration of petitions, the Committee had shifted from a concentration on questions of admissibility to a concentration on merits. Rather than referring petitions to other committees, it was investigating many more itself. No substantial proposals for reform were made, except some rather tentative suggestions for a form of 'appeal' to a reviewing panel.

In the meantime, it is the case that the process has revealed some substantial concerns and prompted substantial inquiries by the Committee[8].

It will be interesting to see how the petitions process does develop. Despite the generally positive reaction so far, the early experience raises questions about the value to the parliamentary system as a whole of a mechanism which may turn out to add little to the procedural resources already available to MSPs. Legitimate complaints will probably be directed to the same destination in the end. Some less worthy concerns, or those already fully aired in the political process, may receive undeserved attention. In the meantime, however, there can be little doubt that the best-known petition ever was that supported by 43,000 signatures to retain acute services at Stobhill Hospital in Glasgow[9]. It was on the strength of her own support for this cause that the independent MSP Dr Jean Turner secured election to the Parliament for the Strathkelvin and Bearsden constituency on 1 May 2003.

1 Erskine May, *Parliamentary Practice* (ed W McKay 23rd edn, 2004, ch 34).
2 *Scotland's Parliament, Scotland's Right* pp 24 and 26.
3 *CSG Inquiry*, s 3.6, paras 13–18.
4 SOs, r 6.10.
5 SOs, rr 15.4–15.6.
6 For an early review, see P Lynch and S Birrell 'Linking Parliament to the People' (2001) 37 Scottish Affairs 1.
7 CJ Carman, *Assessment of the Scottish Parliament's Public Petitions System 1999–2006*. SP Paper 654.
8 See, for instance, its investigation into the availability on the NHS of cancer treatment drugs – SP Paper 133 (2008).
9 Petition PE 354.

Chapter 10

Public Finance

INTRODUCTION

10.1   Financial issues retain a centrality and vitality in any modern constitutional account. Sometimes they become hidden behind a veil of technicality and complexity which serves to distort their significance, but financial matters are frequently of concern not only to those in government but also to ordinary citizens in their relations with governments. Individuals have an acute interest in the taxes and charges imposed on them as well as in the financial benefits which may come their way. Financial questions are also very important in the shaping of relations between the Executive and the legislature and relations between devolved and central institutions. A chapter on 'Financing Devolution' was prominent in the 2003 report of the House of Lords Select Committee on the *Constitution on Devolution: Inter-Institutional Relations in the United Kingdom*[1].

In this chapter, United Kingdom-level issues and Scotland-level issues are considered in parallel under five broad headings. In the first place, pp 280–282 on the UK level of government take a brief look at the annual cycle of financial decision-making by government and Parliament, as to both the raising and the spending of public money. There are the procedures leading to the passing of the annual Finance Act which contains proposals for new or amended taxes and then the decisions made by governments on their expenditure plans and the parliamentary procedures available for their scrutiny and approval. At Westminster, procedures for both types of decisions have been progressively refined over many years and they remain under review. They are procedures in which the House of Commons has its clearest pre-eminence over the House of Lords and in which it also claims to assert its strongest controls over the executive – there can be no imposition of taxation nor any expenditure without statutory authority. However, it is also an area in which the executive asserts a powerful right of initiative and does, in practice, maintain substantial overall control. The rules governing the equivalent processes in Scottish government require rather different treatment. Thus, at pp 282–285, the system by which the annual grant of funds is made by the Secretary of State is considered and then, at pp 285–288, the power of the Scottish Parliament to vary the rate of income tax payable by Scottish taxpayers. At pp 288–291, the system by which the Scottish Executive proposes and the Scottish Parliament approves expenditure on an annual basis is outlined. Finally, at pp 291–293, a mainly Scottish consideration is given to procedures for the audit of accounts and the parliamentary supervision of those procedures at both levels of government.

1 *Second Report* (HL Paper 28 (2002–03)), hereinafter *Inter-Institutional Relations*. That chapter is drawn on heavily in what follows. For the government's response to the report, see Cm 5780. For a most valuable and wide-ranging account of Scottish public finance, see D Heald and A McLeod 'Public Expenditure' in *SME Reissue* Constitutional Law.

FINANCIAL PROCEDURES: WHITEHALL AND WESTMINSTER[1]

10.2   Discussion of financial procedures is apt to become very complex and technical. It starts, however, from two elementary propositions. The first is that governments need financial resources to do the job of governing and that, subject to economic constraints which will vary from time to time, they must, by one means or another be given these resources. Governments have statutory duties to perform: they have political programmes to which they are committed and on which they must deliver. Secondly, however, it is constitutionally important that governments' access to and use of resources are subject to appropriate forms of scrutiny and control. These two phenomena interact but at their centre is *parliamentary control*, exercised almost exclusively by the House of Commons rather than the House of Lords[2] and deriving from Parliament's successful claims to control asserted in the seventeenth century. The Crown and the Crown's ministers must be financially accountable to Parliament and Parliament insists that it controls both the income (by taxation) and expenditure of governments. This quickly links with the second form of *control by the courts*. The courts will strike down as invalid any attempt by the executive either to raise or to spend money which does not have the authority of an Act of Parliament[3]. The third form of control is that performed by the independent operations of the Comptroller and Auditor General, the National Audit Office and the accounting officers in individual government departments. These are carried out under the authority and supervision of Parliament but under conditions which are substantially free from political control. At the points where the House of Commons authorises taxation or expenditure it inevitably behaves in a way which reflects the close political alliance between a government and its Commons majority. When officials appointed to be independent of both government and Parliament perform their tasks of financial scrutiny, they should, and it seems do, operate quite differently.

The focus for any study of the process of government financing and its control is what is known as the Consolidated Fund. The Consolidated Fund is held at the Bank of England and is managed by the Treasury, the government department headed by the Chancellor of the Exchequer which co-ordinates the financial affairs of all other departments and formally initiates all financial decision-making. Most income to the Fund derives from taxation and all taxation requires the authority of an Act of Parliament. All expenditure from the Fund requires authority by an Act of Parliament, almost all of it by authority of an annual Act of Parliament – the Appropriation Act – passed in the year to which the expenditure relates. It is by the need for parliamentary assent to these statutes authorising both taxation and expenditure that the most direct forms of parliamentary control are, at least in theory, assured. At the same time, it should be borne in mind that there are other opportunities for scrutiny available. When new legislation is passing through Parliament as a Bill, one of the issues for consideration will be the cost of the new proposals. This is formally recognised in the need for the passing of a money resolution on the motion of a minister, following the Bill's second reading, but questions about the financial resources which the Bill's proposals will require – whether they are thought to be too much or too little – will often be relevantly discussed at all stages. The other point at which financial matters are constantly raised is in select committee investigations into the activities of ministers and their departments. Questions of extravagance and waste may be the principal targets but underspending may equally be an issue.

1 This is necessarily a highly simplified summary of some very complex material. *Government Accounting* (2000, but with periodic amendments) contains accessible commentary despite its function as a Treasury guide for government departments. See also Erskine May, *Parliamentary Practice* (ed Sir William McKay, 23rd edn, 2004) chs 29–33.
2 An interesting recent adjustment to this position has been the scrutiny (from April 2003) of the Finance Bill by a sub-committee of the House of Lords Economic Affairs Committee. The Committee's approach was intended to be wholly technical and not 'to challenge Commons financial privilege' – see *Third Report* (HL Paper 121 (2002–03)). The Chancellor of the Exchequer has appeared before the Committee. See eg 3 February 2009.
3 *A-G v Wilts United Dairies* (1921) 37 TLR 884.

Taxation

10.3   Statutory authority is required for all forms of taxation. Much of that authority derives from statutes which remain in force over long periods, with the need only for authority for changes in the tax rates from time to time. Other taxes, including, above all, income tax, require the rate to be stipulated for each financial year (1 April to 31 March). Sometimes entirely new forms of taxation are proposed and the vehicle for establishing any new regime and for achieving the other categories of change is the annual Finance Act. Only a minister, on behalf of the Crown, may propose a new tax or level of tax[1].

The Finance Bill incorporates proposals first announced by the Chancellor of the Exchequer in the Budget speech which is currently delivered in the House of Commons in March or April each year. The Budget, preceded by a pre-Budget statement in November, is the occasion for the Chancellor to publish[2] not only proposals for new taxes and for changes in tax rates but also, as a background to the proposals, substantial information on the state of the UK economy. Because some tax changes must come into effect immediately, they are announced before the Finance Bill can be debated and enacted into law, and authority for the collection of tax at the new rates is given in the form of resolutions, approved by the House of Commons, whose own authority derives from a statute passed for this purpose, currently the Provisional Collection of Taxes Act 1968[3].

1 The same applies to expenditure proposals. See Erskine May p 853. Both taxation and expenditure involve 'charges, whether as a charge upon the people or a charge upon public funds, the initiative for which must come from the Crown'.
2 In the speech itself but also in a range of additional Budget documents.
3 The need for such statutory authority, rather than a simple reliance upon the resolutions themselves, was established in the landmark case of *Bowles v Bank of England* [1913] 1 Ch 57. Normally, preparatory work in advance of the launch of a new tax does not require specific statutory authority – but see the Planning–gain Supplement (Preparations) Act 2007.

Expenditure

10.4   Just as statutory authority must be given for the raising of taxes paid into the Consolidated Fund, so also must there be statutory authority for expenditure by departments out of the Fund. For the most part, this is the process historically known as 'supply' for the government's purposes and then the 'appropriation' (ie allocation) of the total amount to the several departments. Exceptions to the standard route to parliamentary approval are those payments which, mainly for 'separation of powers' reasons, but in some cases on more technical grounds, are protected from the need for direct annual approval. The most prominent payments to be 'charged on the Consolidated Fund'[1] are judicial salaries and pensions but others include the salaries of the Speaker of the House of Commons, the Comptroller and Auditor General, the Parliamentary Ombudsman and also the Civil List[2]. These cases apart, the processes of supply and appropriation operate formally on an annual cycle and involve the submission of proposals of estimated expenditure by departments and the Treasury in the light of current spending guidelines which are, under present practice, published pursuant to the 1998 comprehensive spending review[3]. The estimates are scrutinised by select committees and approved by resolution of the House of Commons, following 'estimates day' debates. The spending proposals are then carried forward into a Consolidated Fund (Appropriation) Bill which, on enactment, becomes an Appropriation Act[4].

1 In *Government Accounting*, described as 'Consolidated Fund standing services' (para 27.2.7).
2 Also charged on the Fund in this way are payments of interest on the national debt and payments to the European Union.
3 *Modern Public Services for Britain: Investing in Reform* (Cm 4011). Each spending review covers a period of three financial years. See, for example, *Meeting the Aspirations of the British People* (Cm 7227, 2007) in respect of 2008–09, 2009–10 and 2010–11.
4 That procedure is supplemented each year by the passing of a further Act – a (confusingly named) Consolidated Fund Act – whose main purpose is to make initial spending provision for the next following financial year, effective before that next year's Appropriation Act can be passed.

FUNDING OF SCOTTISH GOVERNMENT BY WESTMINSTER

10.5   In *Scotland's Parliament*, the White Paper which preceded the Scotland Bill in 1997, the United Kingdom government set out its proposals for the funding of devolved Scottish government[1]. With one significant change – the introduction of the Scottish Parliament's limited power of tax variation discussed at pp 285–288 below – it was to be business as usual. Funding would come from the UK government itself and would be allocated on an annual basis according to the same principles on which funds were allocated to the Scottish Office prior to devolution. Since 1978–79, immediately prior to the aborted introduction of devolution under the Scotland Act 1978, there had been in place a scheme for the distribution to Scotland (and also to Wales and to Northern Ireland) of annual grants – 'block' grants – to provide for domestic services within the remit of the Scottish Office[2]. The amounts to be allocated to Scotland (and the other territories) were made in accordance with a formula which initially took account of the relative assessed 'needs' of the territories (largely population-based but also encompassing factors such as poverty and sparcity of population) but which, in subsequent years, was adjusted in accordance with the percentage increase (or decrease) in resources allocated for parallel services in England. That adjustment was made by the application of a population-based formula (the 'Barnett' formula[3]) to enable expenditure in Scotland, Wales and Northern Ireland to grow proportionately.

Although the principles for funding allocations could be broadly carried forward to apply to devolved Scottish government, the mechanisms for making the allocation had to be changed. Instead of being simply an accounting device for the division of resources internally within the UK governmental machine, it had to be a mechanism for the transfer of funds from one government to the other. This was very simply done, as far as the Scotland Act 1998 (SA 1998) is concerned, in s 64(1) and (2). Section 64(1) establishes a separate Scottish Consolidated Fund[4]. Then SA 1998, s 64(2) provides: 'The Secretary of State shall from time to time make payments into the Fund out of money provided by Parliament of such amounts as he may determine.' Nothing is said in SA 1998 itself about the amount that should be paid annually nor what relation it should bear to amounts paid, for example, to Wales or Northern Ireland. No mention is made of the Barnett formula. All of that has been left to less formal documentation issued by HM Treasury[5], setting out the principles of public expenditure allocation across the United Kingdom, the working of the formula and other practical matters.

These procedures established for the funding of Scottish devolved government have not gone uncriticised[6]. There are perhaps three main complaints:

1 Cm 3658, Ch 7.
2 See *Scotland's Parliament*, Annex B, para 4.
3 Named after Lord (Joel) Barnett, former Chief Secretary to the Treasury.
4 Subsequent provisions deal with payments into and out of the Fund – SA 1998, ss 64, 65. See pp 288–291 below for expenditure from the Fund.
5 The arrangements launched in 1999 are comprehensively and authoritatively described in the Treasury document *Funding the Scottish Parliament, National Assembly for Wales and Northern Ireland Assembly: A Statement of Funding Policy* (5th edn, Oct 2007).
6 For critical appraisal, see D Heald and A McLeod 'Beyond Barnett? Financing Devolution' in J Adams and P Robinson (eds) *Devolution in Practice* (2002) and (2002) 41 Scottish Affairs 5. See also *Inter-Institutional Relations* ch 3.

(a) Reliance on the block grant

10.6   The near-total reliance of the Scottish Parliament and Executive upon grant aid from the UK government has been criticised. Unless and until the Scottish Parliament makes use of its own limited tax-varying power, Scottish government depends almost entirely for its income upon what the UK government, in its discretion, decides to provide – the other principal sources being income derived from non-domestic rates and council tax collected by local authorities[1], as well as a small amount in charges for services provided. Some might say that there should be no problem with that, provided that the funds provided are sufficient – on which, see below. Others, not necessarily of a nationalist persuasion, argue differently. There *is* something inherently wrong about a model of democratic government which has no control, or virtually no control, over the resources available to it. Accountability is undermined because politicians will tend to pass the blame for their failures in government to those who, they claim, are underfunding them. This was a complaint made about the Scotland Act 1978 (SA 1978) model. It is a complaint addressed, to an extent, by the tax-varying power which, at least, permits marginal adjustments. But some would go much further in asserting the need for a 'fiscal autonomy' which enables the Scottish Executive and Parliament to raise funds from a range of sources and at levels which they themselves can determine. Because of the challenge it might present to the economic and fiscal integrity of the United Kingdom[2], and thus to the principles underpinning the current devolution settlement, autonomy of this sort seems unlikely to be conceded and, for the time being at least, there will be a continued dependence upon grant aid. Even under the present grant regime, one source of flexibility which *is* available to the Scottish Executive and which might prove useful despite obvious political constraints is its own power to reduce levels of grant to Scottish local authorities, forcing them to raise higher levels of council tax. Indirectly, this would produce savings for the Executive which it could divert to expand other programmes. This was all considered by the Calman Commission which reported in June 2009[3]. The Commission's recommendations on 'strengthening accountability in finance' were at the core of their report. They proposed that the Scottish budget's near-total reliance on the block grant and the Barnett formula should be reduced. The existing tax-varying power should be replaced by a new Scottish rate of income tax, applicable to both the basic and higher rates of tax. The rates levied by the UK government should be reduced by 10 pence in the pound (with a consequential reduction in the block grant), leaving the Scottish Parliament to substitute a rate of its own choosing[4]. In addition, certain other taxes – stamp duty land tax, the aggregates levy, landfill tax and air passenger duty – should be devolved to the Scottish Parliament and the Parliament should be empowered to introduce further new taxes with the agreement of the UK Parliament. In response to calls from many quarters, the borrowing powers of the Scottish Ministers should be extended to enable an increase in capital investment. These proposals did not meet with universal approval[5] but their adoption by the 'Unionist' parties for discussion was immediate[6].

1 See p 200.
2 See *Inter-Institutional Relations* para 105.
3 See p 63 above.
4 Income tax on savings and distributions would not be devolved but half of the yield would be assigned to the Parliament's budget.
5 See eg D Scott and others 'Long-term planning is threatened by report' Scotsman 17 June 2009.
6 The funding of devolution has been under investigation by other bodies. In July 2009 the (Holtham) Independent Commission on Funding and Finance for Wales made its first report to the Welsh Assembly Government and, also in July 2009, the House of Lords ad hoc Barnett Formula Committee issued its report – 2008–09, HL 139.

(b) The system of grant allocation

10.7   The lack of transparency and impartiality in the determination of amounts of grant payable to Scotland and the other territories[1] has also been questioned. One change which might have been introduced at the time of devolution was some form of independent board or commission to oversee the process of grant distribution[2]. In a constitutional environment which has become similar to that in federal countries, there would be an advantage in having such an independent body to make recommendations for grant distribution according to relatively objective economic criteria rather than leaving distribution to the hidden judgment of politicians. Disputes between different parts of the United Kingdom might be lessened as a result.

1 The use of 'territories' may be unfamiliar but it is the terminology adopted in UK government official documents.
2 See Constitution Unit *Scotland's Parliament: Fundamentals for a New Scotland Act* (1996), ch 5; and *Inter-Institutional Relations* paras 102 and 107.

(c) The amount of funding

10.8   It is certainly true that, whether or not because of the lack of an independent grants commission, disputes have arisen[1]. On the one hand, it is argued by some in Scotland that the distribution formula which once favoured Scotland because it deliberately recognised its greater funding needs now discriminates against Scotland because the formula for *amending* levels of expenditure operates, as was intended (or was, at least, wholly predictable), to reduce differentials between territories and thus to leave Scotland without the advantage it once had. There is a 'Barnett squeeze' on Scottish expenditure which arguably should be remedied by a new needs assessment which would find in favour of a greater allocation to Scotland in future. There is, on the other hand, an argument mainly associated with London and the north-east of England to the effect that some at least of the English regions are already being *underfunded* in comparison with Scotland. Poignant comparisons have been drawn between the funding of schools in Northumbria and the Scottish Borders[2]. Such disputes are likely to increase if regional government in England is extended and pressure to revise Barnett will grow[3]. A quite separate matter of controversy under the scheme of distribution is that the Scottish funding entitlement includes not only the moneys payable to the Scottish Executive itself but also those payable to the Scotland Office for non-devolved purposes. The House of Lords Committee recommended that the distribution by formula should relate only to the Executive's own funding[4].

1 Nicely documented in the memorandum by I McLean published as evidence to the HL Committee on the Constitution (*Inter-Institutional Relations*).
2 *Inter-Institutional Relations* para 3.2.
3 A recommendation to review the system was made by the House of Commons Select Committee on the Office of the Deputy Prime Minister. See *Reducing Regional Disparities in Prosperity* (HC Paper 492 (2002–03), para 75).
4 *Inter-Institutional Relations* para 105.

THE SCOTTISH PARLIAMENT'S TAX-VARYING POWER[1]

10.9   This chapter is not, in general, one in which specific forms of taxation are discussed, even in outline. The principles of parliamentary control over taxation at Westminster are of constitutional significance but the actual taxes imposed are beyond the scope of a constitutional study. In the Scottish Parliament, however, the power to increase or decrease the basic rate of income tax for Scottish taxpayers contained in SA 1998, Pt IV is important.

As explained in the last section, Scottish government is largely financed by grant paid by the UK government. It is not within the legislative competence of the Parliament to enact new general powers to tax[2] and if it were not for the tax-varying power, the Parliament and Executive would therefore, be compelled to operate within the financial limits of the grant. It is true that there might be scope for adjusting the charges made for some services provided – proposals for road tolls/parking charges are an example. And, as already noted, there might also be scope for the Scottish Executive to reduce the grant it makes to local authorities and force the local authorities to make up the shortfall by increasing levels of council tax. The financial and political limitations on the use of such measures are in practice, however, likely to keep their effect very marginal.

This situation would create a difficulty because it is a principle of some con-stitutional importance that bodies established to be democratically accountable to their electorates – whether they are states in a federal system of government or local authorities – should also have a form of financial accountability. As the Scottish Constitutional Convention put it: 'In the Western democracies all principal levels of national and local government have powers over taxation'. While the Parliament's income will be principally based on totals of expendi-ture set at UK level, the power to vary the rate of tax is vital if the Parliament is to be properly accountable. Critics of the proposal to establish a Parliament in Scotland repeatedly state that such a power is essential for an effective Par-liament'[3]. A tax-raising or tax-varying power had not been included in SA 1978 but it was proposed in the 1997 White Paper that 'the Scottish Parliament should be able to raise limited income at its own hand by means of a defined but limited power to vary income tax in Scotland'[4].

A little paradoxical in these circumstances was the Scottish Labour Party's own commitment, prior to the Scottish Parliament elections in 1999, not to make use of the tax-varying power in the course of the first Parliament. This was an undertaking reconfirmed in 'Partnership for Scotland', the statement which formed the basis of the coalition agreement between the Scottish Labour Party and the Scottish Liberal Democrats in May 1999. The undertaking was further reconfirmed in the second coalition agreement, *A Partnership for a Better Scotland*, in May 2003. And this has remained the policy of the SNP Government since 2007. As a practical matter, therefore, the provisions in SA 1998, Pt IV are unlikely to be implemented in the immediate future but their significance remains as an opportunity for an alternative political direction and, perhaps, for their eventual use at a later stage in the life of the Parliament. Prior to the Budget Acts of 2008 and 2009 the Liberal Democrats *did* indicate a wish that the powers be used.

SA 1998, Pt IV makes provision for the three core elements of the scheme, to which are added some supplementary rules. The core elements are (a) the Parliament's power to decide, by resolution, to vary the basic rate of income tax for Scottish taxpayers; (b) the identification by definition of those Scottish taxpayers; and (c) the provision made to accommodate the future impact on the scheme of any wider changes to the general structure of income tax in the United Kingdom. Thus:

1 See S Eden 'Taxing times ahead for the Scots' 1998 SLT (News) 57.
2 SA 1998, Sch 5, Pt II, S A1.
3 *Scotland's Parliament: Scotland's Right* (1995) p 27.
4 *Scotland's Parliament* (Cm 3658) para 7.1.

The resolution of the Scottish Parliament

10.10   On the motion of a member of the Scottish Executive[1], the Parliament may pass a resolution providing for the basic rate of income tax to be increased or reduced for Scottish taxpayers by up to 3 per cent[2]. The resolution must relate to a particular year of assessment, but may subsequently be cancelled[3]. Importantly, the scope of the tax variation is such as to exclude tax on savings income[4].

1 SA 1998, s 74(5).
2 Using only whole or half numbers: SA 1998, s 73(1).
3 SA 1998, ss 73(1), 74(1). A resolution may be passed no more than 12 months in advance but provision is made to accommodate different timetables for the determination of tax rates in the UK Parliament: SA 1998, s 74(2), (3).
4 SA 1998, s 73(3).

The definition of 'Scottish taxpayers'

10.11   One of the trickiest questions in any scheme intended to apply to a particular group of UK taxpayers not previously identified in the tax legislation is the precise definition of the members of the group. Challenge to their increased liability by aggrieved taxpayers is clearly a possibility and the rules must, therefore, be clear and robust.

A person is defined as a 'Scottish taxpayer' if, in the first place, he or she is treated, for general income tax purposes, as resident in the United Kingdom for the year in question. Secondly, Scotland must be the part of the United Kingdom with which he or she has the 'closest connection' during that year[1]. To be a Scottish taxpayer, a person must satisfy one or more of three tests to establish a 'closest connection' with Scotland: (a) if, during the year of assessment, the person spends at least a part of the year in Scotland; and, for at least a part of that time, his or her principal UK home is located in Scotland and the home is made use of as a place[2] of residence; and the times in that year when Scotland is where the person's principal UK home is located comprise (in aggregate) at least as much of that year as the times (if any) when the location of that home is not in Scotland[3]. For the purposes of this test, an individual's principal UK home is located in Scotland if the person has a place of residence in Scotland and, in the case of a person with two or more places of residence in the UK, Scotland is the location of such one of those places as at that time is his or her main place of residence in the UK[4]; or (b) if the number of days which the person spends in Scotland in the relevant year is equal to or exceeds the number of days spent elsewhere in the UK[5]. For these purposes an individual spends a day in Scotland if, but only if, he or she is in Scotland at the end of that day but, on the other hand, an individual spends a day elsewhere in the UK if, but only if, he is in the UK (but not in Scotland) at the end of that day[6]; or (c) if the person, for the whole or part of the year of assessment is an MP for a Scottish constituency, or a Scottish MEP, or an MSP[7].

In summary, therefore, a Scottish taxpayer is to be identified by reference to the location of his or her principal home, or by days spent in Scotland, or, in a few cases, by virtue of membership of a Parliament.

1 SA 1998, s 75(1).
2 Which includes a place on board a vessel or other means of transport: SA 1998, s 75(6).
3 SA 1998, s 75(2)(a), (3).
4 SA 1998, s 75(5).
5 SA 1998, s 75(2)(b).
6 SA 1998, s 75(4).
7 SA 1998, s 75(2)(c).

Changes to income tax structures

10.12   When the tax-varying power was devised it was admitted that attaching it to the basic rate of income tax left it vulnerable to changes in the general UK tax structure[1]. If that structure changed, then the impact of the use of the tax-varying power might be substantially altered and the initial assumption that a full 3 per cent variation would produce about £450m could become badly wrong. The need to amend the rules of the tax-varying power could arise. Provision for this is made in the SA 1998 by imposing on the Treasury the obligation to respond to any proposals to modify the income tax regime which would have 'a significant effect on the practical extent' of the Parliament's tax-varying power. The Treasury must make a statement of whether an amendment of the power is required and, if so, its proposals for doing so[2]. Such statements have been made annually[3], all being to the effect that no amendment was required. If amendments are ever proposed they must be confined to income tax (not affecting savings or distributions) and must satisfy conditions intended to keep the 'practical extent' of the tax-varying power at a level similar to that in 1997–98 and that the effect on levels of the after-tax income of Scottish taxpayers generally would not be significantly different from the effect in previous years[4].

1 *Scotland's Parliament* paras 7.13–7.14.
2 SA 1998, s 76(1), (2).
3 See, for example, the statement made in the Budget Policy Decisions chapter of the April 2009 Financial Statement that a one-penny change in the Scottish variable rate in 2009–10 could be worth approximately plus or minus £350 m (in 2010–11, £360m) in a full year.
4 SA 1998, s 76(3)–(7).

THE AUTHORISATION OF EXPENDITURE BY THE SCOTTISH GOVERNMENT

10.13   As we turn to expenditure by the Scottish Government, the parallels between the procedures which operate at the United Kingdom level and the procedures which have now been established in Edinburgh are quite close. At their centre is the authority for payments to be made from the Scottish Consolidated Fund.

SA 1998, s 65 provides that sums may be paid out of the Fund under two main forms of authority. The first is where sums have been statutorily charged on the Fund and it is by this means that judicial salaries, as with their UK equivalents, are made payable without the need for further parliamentary approval year by year[1].

The other authority for payments conferred by SA 1998 is for sums paid out for the purposes of meeting the expenditure of the Scottish Administration (or other statutory purpose) in accordance with rules made by or under an Act of the Scottish Parliament[2]. Those rules have been laid down by the Public Finance and Accountability (Scotland) Act 2000 (PFA(S)A 2000)[3]. This provides that the use of resources for any purpose by the Scottish Administration and by other bodies reliant upon the Scottish Consolidated Fund must be authorised by a Budget Act passed by the Parliament[4]. Such authorisations relate to a particular financial year and the use of resources must not exceed the amount authorised for the year and purpose[5]. Thus the principal authority for expenditure is the annual Budget Act but PFA(S)A 2000 also authorises emergency funding arrangements at the beginning of a financial year if a Budget Act has not yet provided routine authorisation. Pro rata expenditure may be incurred on the basis of the previous year's figures[6]. There is also provision for the exceptional funding of 'contingencies' not otherwise authorised. Such funding is permitted only on the authority of the Scottish Ministers and then only where it is necessarily required in the public interest and reasons of urgency make the use of standard procedures not reasonably practicable. There are also strict financial limits. Any use of the power must be reported to the Parliament[7].

The adoption of the use of an annual Budget Act as the standard means of authorisation of expenditure followed discussion of alternatives[8]. The possibility of setting budgets to cover more than a year at a time had been considered but rejected because this might prejudice parliamentary scrutiny and would not dovetail well with UK requirements for financial control. Another possibility had been a procedure for approval of expenditure by secondary rather than primary legislation. It had, however, been accepted that the importance of this function demanded primary legislation and that an annual Budget Act should be required. On the other hand, the case for the use of secondary legislation for budget revisions later in the course of a financial year was accepted. It would be unnecessarily burdensome to insist on repeated recourse to primary legislation and, despite the model of successive Appropriation Bills at Westminster, the use of revising orders would be simpler[9].

The Parliament's standing orders provide the procedure for Budget Bills[10]. In line with practice at Westminster, a Budget Bill may be introduced only by a member of the Scottish Executive and it need not be accompanied by a financial memorandum, explanatory notes or a policy memorandum[11]. At Stage 1 the Bill must be referred immediately to the Parliament for consideration of its general principles without the need for a committee report and Stage 2 must then be taken in the Finance Committee. Certain of the other standard procedural provisions on Bills are then suspended but it is specifically provided that (a) Stage 3 may begin no earlier than 20 days after the introduction of the

Bill; but (b), if Stage 3 is not completed within 30 days from introduction, the Bill falls. Amendments to a Budget Bill may be moved only by a member of the Scottish Executive. Specific provision is also made for the possibility that a Budget Bill is itself dependent upon the Parliament's passing a tax-varying resolution as the source of additional revenue. If, in those circumstances, the tax-varying resolution is rejected, the Budget Bill falls[12]. If, for any reason, a Budget Bill falls or is rejected, a replacement Bill in the same or similar terms may be introduced at any time[13].

To take a recent example, the Budget (Scotland) Act 2009 (B(S)A 2009) – made provision for the authorisation of expenditure in 2009–10 in respect of both the Scottish Administration and other bodies. Specific amounts were attributed to eleven itemised 'purposes' for which resources could be used by the Scottish Administration[14] and to four direct-funded bodies – the Forestry Commissioners, the Food Standards Agency, the Scottish Parliamentary Corporate Body and Audit Scotland[15]. Then B(S)A 2009, s 7 provided for its own amendment to enable the amounts of authorised expenditure to be revised. Subject to prior approval of a draft of the order by the Parliament, the Scottish Ministers may amend the amounts specified in the Act[16].

The procedures just described relate to the formal stage at which the Parliament gives its approval by statute to the Government's proposals for forward spending. However, it is important to recognise that those procedures come at the end of a much longer annual process which starts with the Government's publication of its spending proposals produced on a three-year cycle in line with the UK spending reviews. The Scottish Budget Spending Review 2007 covered the three financial years from 2008-09 and, in non-review years, the Government simply publishes a draft budget in respect of the one year following and concludes with the publication of the Budget Bill by 20 January. That is a timetable agreed between the Parliament and the Scottish Ministers in 2005[18]. As well as the overall timetable, the agreement deals with the content of the two stages of the process prior to the introduction of the Budget Bill[19]. Following proposals originally made by FIAG[20] and the CSG[21], the intention has been to provide the Parliament's Finance Committee, subject committees and the Parliament in plenary session the opportunity to scrutinise the budget proposals. At Stage 1 the general expenditure proposals are available; at Stage 2, during October and November, detailed proposals (usually presented by 20 September) can be scrutinised, concluding with a chamber debate based on a report produced by the Finance Committee, after consultation with subject committees.

Quite apart from the annual budget process, it is also a function of the Finance Committee to scrutinise the financial memoranda which accompany Bills introduced into the Scottish Parliament. This is intended to ensure that the Parliament is in full possession of relevant financial information in advance of taking decisions on the general principles of Bills.

1   See SA 1998, s 119(3) – a provision which is itself 'entrenched' in relation to judicial salaries by SA 1998, Sch 4, paras 4(3), 5(a). See Scottish Consolidated Fund Receipts and Payments Account 2007–08, SG/2008/172 (Dec 2008) (note 4). See also p 309 below.
2   SA 1998, s 65(1)(c).
3   Temporary provision was made for the period up to 31 March 2000 by the Scotland Act 1998 (Transitory and Transitional Provisions) (Finance) Order 1999, SI 1999/441. The passing of

the Act followed a period of consultation on the (Scottish Office) Financial Issues Advisory Group (FIAG) Report *Principles of the Scottish Parliament's Financial Procedures* (November 1998). See *Consultation Paper on a Financial Framework for the Scottish Parliament* (July 1999).

4 PFA(S)A 2000, s 4.

5 PFA(S)A 2000, s 1(3) defines 'the use of resources' as 'their expenditure, consumption or reduction in value'. PFA(S)A 2000 has incorporated the UK terminology of resource accounting – see Government Resources and Accounts Act 2000, s 27.

6 PFA(S)A 2000, s 2. These arrangements may be adjusted by a Budget Act – see, for example, the Budget (Scotland) Act 2009, s 6.

7 PFA(S)A 2000, s 3. Additional authority for contingency funding may also be made in a Budget Act – see the Budget (Scotland) Act 2009, s 4.

8 For a summary, see the policy memorandum which accompanied the Public Finance and Accountability Bill.

9 See Subordinate Legislation Committee, 1 Feb 2000.

10 SOs, r 9.16.

11 For standard procedure on Bills, see p 226.

12 SOs, r 9.16.7.

13 SOs, r 9.16.8.

14 B(S)A 2009, s 1 and sch 1.

15 B(S)A 9 s 2 and sch 3. Provision was also made for the application of receipts for specified purposes: see B(S)A 2009, ss 1, 2 and schs 1, 2, 3; and for certain capital expenditure and borrowing, see B(S)A 2009, s 5 and sch 5.

16 For an order amending the Budget (Scotland) Act 2008, see SSI 2008/424.

18 *Agreement on the Budgeting Process*, SP Paper 155, Session 1 (2000).

19 See also SOs, r 5.8.

20 See n 3 above.

21 *CSG Report* s 3.4 and Annex 1.

GOVERNMENT ACCOUNTING AND AUDIT

10.14 The detailed rules of government accounting are well beyond the scope of this work. There are, however, some aspects of the rules on accounting and audit which are of the highest constitutional importance. These rules operate in support of the appropriation procedures already considered and they add an important further dimension to the parliamentary procedures for the scrutiny and control of government action dealt with in Chapter 9. They involve the work of significant independent scrutineers of government in the form of the Comptroller and Auditor General and the National Audit Office at the United Kingdom level and, in Scotland, the Auditor General for Scotland and Audit Scotland; the specialised functions of the Public Accounts Committee of the House of Commons and the Public Government Audit Committee of the Scottish Parliament; and the work of 'accounting' (United Kingdom Government) and 'accountable' (Scottish Government) officers who, while senior civil servants whose loyalties are usually channelled through ministers, owe a special loyalty to their respective auditors. In this account the focus is on the Scottish arrangements introduced by SA 1998 and PFA(S)A 2000[1].

Although the United Kingdom Parliament deliberately left to the Scottish Parliament the task of making detailed provision in this area, SA 1998 does contain certain of the core rules[2]. SA 1998, s 69 provides for the appointment of an Auditor General for Scotland by the Queen, on the nomination of the Parliament[3]. Like the Comptroller and Auditor General, the Auditor General for Scotland enjoys formal security of tenure equivalent to that of a senior judge in that no recommendation may be made to the Queen for removal from office unless the Parliament approves by a two-thirds majority[4]. The independent operation of the Auditor General is sought to be further assured by a provision that he or she must not be subject to the direction or control of any member of the Scottish Executive or of the Parliament[5].

The duties of the Auditor General are laid down in outline by SA 1998[6] and then in more detail by PFA(S)A 2000. There are two main functions. The first is the approval of any payment from the Scottish Consolidated Fund, on the request of the Scottish Ministers. Such payments are approved only if authorised[7]. In this way the Auditor General is acting as the independent scrutineer and enforcer of the rules on expenditure approval.

Secondly, the Auditor General is responsible for the audit of the accounts of the Scottish Ministers, the Lord Advocate and other persons and bodies to whom sums are paid out of the Scottish Consolidated Fund[8]. For this purpose, the staff of a body known as Audit Scotland assist the Auditor General. Audit Scotland consists of the Auditor General, the Chairman of the Accounts Commission for Scotland[9] and three other members appointed jointly by the first two[10]. The audit process has a dual aspect. On the one hand, it is an examination of whether accounts have been properly kept. A report on such audits must be submitted to the Scottish Ministers who, in turn, must publish the report and lay a copy before the Parliament[11]. On the other hand, the Auditor General may initiate examination into the economy, efficiency and effectiveness (value for money audit) of any of the bodies subject to scrutiny. In determining whether to carry out such an examination, the Auditor General must take into account any proposals made by the Parliament and he may report the results to the Parliament[12]. For the purposes of discharging these functions the Auditor General is entitled to all documents and information reasonably required[13]. In addition, the work of the Auditor General is assisted by the contribution required of the principal accountable officer for the Scottish Administration, the 'most senior member of the staff of the Scottish Administration' ie the Permanent Secretary[14]. Accountable officers are stated to be answerable to the Parliament for the exercise of their functions which, in addition to ensuring the general propriety and regularity of the finances of their part of the Administration, include special obligations if they consider that something inconsistent with the proper performance of their functions is being required of them by ministers. In such an event accountable officers must obtain written authority from ministers before taking the action, and send a copy to the Auditor General[15]. These arrangements and the personal responsibilities they impose place accountable officers in a special relationship with ministers which is quite different from their usual position as civil servants[16].

In the Parliament, it is the responsibility of the Public Audit Committee to consider and report on accounts and reports by the Auditor General which are laid before the Parliament[17]. At Westminster, the Public Accounts Committee of the House of Commons has achieved a reputation as the most powerful and independent of select committees. It is, by convention, always chaired by an opposition MP. At Holyrood, standing orders provide that the convener of the Public Audit Committee must not be an MSP who represents a political party represented in the Scottish Executive. No minister may be a member of the Committee[18].

1   For arrangements at the UK level, see Government Accounting chs 3 and 4.
2   Under SA 1998, transitional provision was made, pending the passing of the necessary further legislation by the Scottish Parliament, for the period to 31 March 2000 by the Scotland Act 1998 (Transitory and Transitional Provisional) (Finance) Order 1999, SI 1999/441.
3   SA 1998, s 69(1). Provision for the salary and pension of the Auditor General is to be made by the Parliament: PFA(S)A 2000, s 13.
4   For the procedure to dismiss a Court of Session judge, see p 304 below.
5   SA 1998, s 69(4).
6   SA 1998, s 70(1)(c), (2).
7   PFA(S)A 2000, s 5. For the categories of authorised payments, see pp 288–291 above.
8   SA 1998, s 70(1), (2), (9) and PFA(S)A 2000, ss 21–22. Accounts themselves are required by SA 1998, s 70(1) and PFA(S)A 2000, s 19.
9   The body responsible for the audit of the accounts of Scottish local authorities under the Local Government (Scotland) Act 1973. The composition and functions of the Accounts Commission were modified by PFA(S)A 2000 to transfer responsibility for the audit of bodies, including the Health Service, to the Auditor General.
10 PFA(S)A 2000, ss 10–11 and sch 2. Audit Scotland's own accounts are audited by the Scottish Commission for Public Audit, a body consisting of the convener of the Parliament's Public Audit Committee and four other MSPs: PFA(S)A 2000, ss 12, 19 and 25.
11 PFA(S)A 2000, ss 21, 22.
12 PFA(S)A 2000, s 23.
13 PFA(S)A 2000, s 24.
14 PFA(S)A 2000, s 14. The Clerk of the Parliament is principal accountable officer for the Parliamentary corporation: PFA(S)A 2000, s 16.
15 PFA(S)A 2000, s 15(8).
16 See *Scottish Ministerial Code* (June 2008) paras 6.2–6.5.
17 SOs, r 6.7.
18 SOs, r 6.7.2.

Chapter 11

Courts and the Independence of the Judiciary

INTRODUCTION

11.1

'An independent judiciary is a feature of every democracy which is worth the name.'[1]

'The role of the courts as resolver of disputes, interpreter of the law and defender of the Constitution requires that they be completely separate in authority and function from all other participants in the justice system.'[2]

'A judge shall exercise the judicial function independently on the basis of the judge's assessment of the facts and in accordance with a conscientious understanding of the law, free of any extraneous influences, inducements, pressures, threats or interference, direct or indirect, from any quarter or for any reason.'[3]

There is something striking and compelling about these statements. They contain a direct appeal to the doctrine of the rule of law and the importance of judges in sustaining it. Coming from Scottish, Commonwealth and United Nations sources, there is an assertion of universality. The first, as a statement about the United Kingdom, which does not in its system of parliamentary government make strong claims to sustain the principle of the separation of powers, it is a very bright reassertion of one aspect of that principle. The judiciary should be independent. What this means (and how far it is advanced) is the main focus of this chapter. In chapter 13, consideration is given to the principal constitutional functions of the Scottish judiciary, with a particular focus on the processes of public law and constitutional adjudication.

For reasons to be explained, the main focus here will be upon the higher judiciary. They have a special significance in the constitutional order but it is valuable also to recognise that (a) the judicial system of Scotland extends to include the lower courts upon which, in quantitative terms, the main burdens fall; (b) the judges in the courts of the system as a whole are discharging a wide variety of different functions; and (c) on the other hand, there are many other persons and bodies who would not be included in the 'judiciary' but who are undoubtedly carrying out functions of a judicial character. It is a reminder of the limitations of a crude application of the idea of the separation of powers[4].

1 Lord Cullen of Whitekirk 'The Judge and The Public' 1999 SLT (News) 261.
2 *Beauregard v Canada* [1986] 2 SCR 56 at 73 per Dickson CJ.
3 The Bangalore Principles of Judicial Conduct, 2002, as endorsed by the United Nations Human Rights Commission, 2003.
4 See p 27.

The judicial system and judicial functions

11.2   As to the judicial system proper, this is taken to include the full range of civil and criminal courts from the justice of the peace courts of very limited criminal jurisdiction and staffed in the main by lay justices[1]; the sheriff courts organised across the six sheriffdoms and with very extensive civil and criminal jurisdictions; through to the Court of Session whose civil jurisdiction is both original (mainly before a single judge in the Outer House) and appellate (in the Inner House constituted in Divisions – the First Division presided over by the Lord President, the Second by the Lord Justice-Clerk and Extra Divisions appointed by the Lord President and usually under the chairmanship of the most senior of the judges comprised in the Division[2]). Civil cases may be taken on appeal (since October 2009) to the UK Supreme Court whose membership of 12 Justices is expected always to include two Scottish judges who will sit in Scottish cases. The replacement of the long-standing system of civil appeals to the Appellate Committee of the House of Lords[3] has a significance which may be more apparent than real. Broadly the role of the Supreme Court replicates that of the House of Lords and in particular, there is provision that the creation of the Supreme Court is not to affect the 'distinctions between the separate legal systems of the parts of the United Kingdom'[4] and that a decision of the Court[5] is 'to be regarded as the decision of a court of that part of the United Kingdom'[6]. The senior criminal jurisdiction is vested in the High Court of Justiciary, sitting at first instance or, under the presidency of the Lord Justice General or more usually the Lord Justice-Clerk, on appeal. There is no further general right of appeal in criminal cases.

Since devolution in 1999, however, a special form of appeal has been created – in both criminal and civil cases – under which the determination of a 'devolution issue' may be appealed or referred from the High Court and the Court of Session to the UK Supreme Court[7].

Although all these courts must be included in a full description of the Scottish judicial system, it is not difficult to see that the courts and those who preside over them are carrying out a huge range of functions. There is the broad distinction to be drawn between criminal business, in which the Crown will almost always be the prosecuting party, and civil business usually involving private parties but including cases where public bodies are involved. This latter portion of civil business, in turn, includes contractual disputes or reparation cases arising, for instance, out of the alleged negligence of a public authority or its employees. Also included in civil cases are those arising in the Court of Session as petitions for judicial review in the exercise of the court's supervisory jurisdiction[8] or in the form of statutory appeals in the sheriff court or Court of Session against decisions made by public bodies[9]. While cases at all levels and of all types demand certain standards of fairness and impartiality it is clear that, from the point of view of their constitutional significance, the many activities carried on by those collectively known as the judiciary vary greatly. Low-level trials of minor traffic and other regulatory offences in JP courts, mainly involving the resolution of disputes over facts, bear little resemblance to the hearing of appeals on difficult points of law in the Inner House or the Supreme Court. Sentencing in criminal cases, although treated as a judicial function, bears little relation to most other forms of judicial activity and merges more into the administration of penal policy largely undertaken by other authorities. Sheriffs, although mostly involved in civil and criminal cases, are also required to undertake functions which clearly straddle the boundary between judicial and executive and are administrative in character. They make licensing decisions and hear administrative appeals in matters such as child welfare and mental health[10].

This mix of functions is also reflected on the administrative side of the divide between judicial and executive institutions. So-called 'administrative tribunals' vary greatly in function and mode of operation but they are as much involved in adjudication as courts themselves. Some include judges and other lawyers in their membership. Others have an entirely lay membership but they have an adjudicative role and their work involves many of the same problems of doing justice between individuals or between an individual and a public authority. This mix of functions extends right into central government itself. Civil servants as planning reporters decide most appeals from local authorities to the Scottish Ministers on planning matters, holding, if necessary, public local inquiries in the process[11]. Some of the most important planning appeals fall to be decided by the relevant member of the Scottish Government, currently the Minister for Communities, and the Scottish Ministers also retain the power to recall particularly important appeals which would otherwise be dealt with by a reporter[12]. Such decisions are undoubtedly judicial (or 'quasi-judicial') in character.

Even though it is easy to see, therefore, that those whom we correctly regard as part of the judiciary, broadly defined, are often discharging functions of no great constitutional significance and sometimes not of a judicial nature at all and, on the other hand, many judicial tasks are carried out by members of the executive, there *is* good reason for paying special attention to the situation of the senior judiciary, by which is principally meant the judges of the Court of Session and of the Supreme Court. They have a direct responsibility for the most important tasks of adjudication where the interpretation of the powers of the executive and the legislature are most at issue. This adjudicative role is the principal subject matter of Chapter 13. In addition, the senior judiciary have a supervisory responsibility, exercised through procedures of appeal and review, over the standards of adjudication by inferior courts and by ministers and other administrative bodies. This is done partly on the basis of standards generated by the courts themselves but increasingly also by the application of standards derived from the European Convention on Human Rights (ECHR)[13]. The Court of Session and, in England, the High Court also assume responsibility for seeking to keep open access to the courts. They will, for instance, interpret narrowly statutory language intended to restrict access[14]. They will treat, equally critically, delegated legislation which, without specific authority, restricts access to the courts[15].

1   Criminal Proceedings etc (Reform) Scotland Act 2007 as amended. For an account of the origins and history of justices of the peace in Scotland, see the opinion of Lord Hope of Craighead in *Clark v Kelly* 2003 SLT 308.
2   2008 Act s 46.
3   The last appointment to the House of Lords was that of Lord Kerr of Tonaghmore in June 2009.
4   Constitutional Reform Act 2005, s 41(1).

5 Other than a decision on a devolution matter. See p 416.
6 Ibid, s 41(2).
7 See ch 13. Again, with effect from October 2009. Previously, these appeals were taken to the Judicial Committee of the Privy Council (JCPC) to which appeals from certain professional bodies still go, along with appeals from a limited number of Commonwealth countries.
8 See ch 13.
9 See ch 13.
10 For a general introduction see I D Macphail *Sheriff Court Practice* (3rd edn by T Welsh 2006) vol 1, ch 27
11 Town and Country Planning (Scotland) Act 1997, Sch 4 and Town and Country Planning (Determination of Appeals by Appointed Persons) (Prescribed Classes) (Scotland) Regulations 1987, SI 1987/1531.
12 See, for example, *Lafarge Redland Aggregates Ltd v Scottish Ministers* 2000 SLT 1361.
13 Particularly in the context of ECHR, art 6 which has, as its central concern, the requirements of due process or procedural fairness.
14 *Watt v Lord Advocate* 1979 SC 120, applying *Anisminic Ltd v Foreign Compensation Commission* [1969] 2 AC 147. For a recent example, see *Homer Burgess Ltd v Chirex (Annan) Ltd* 2000 SLT 277.
15 *Singh v Home Secretary* 1993 SC (HL) 1.

The importance of judicial independence

11.3   If the higher judiciary are to continue to discharge the functions already allocated to them and to take on others, it is necessary that the right conditions for high-quality decision-making are created and maintained. In this context 'quality' refers only partly to ideas of accuracy or technical sophistication in the application of the law. There is an expectation that judges will have the knowledge and skills required but also that they will be enabled to deploy these skills, both individually and collectively, in conditions which protect decision-makers from inappropriate influences or pressures and which enable the judiciary to maintain their legitimacy within the constitutional and political system as a whole. These conditions are often referred to, in shorthand, as 'judicial independence'.

As the reference to 'legitimacy' suggests, the importance of judicial independence does not rest merely on the extent to which it actually protects judges from inappropriate influences or pressures or ensures quality decision-making. Arguably as important in this context is the impact which the principles of judicial independence – and the degree to which these are maintained – have on public confidence in the judicial system. That such confidence is considered to be a key value is evidenced by the now famous maxim, repeated in various different guises over the years, that 'justice must not only be done but must manifestly be seen to be done'. Indeed, in practice, complaints of a lack of judicial independence are invariably accompanied by a concession that there has been no actual prejudice or bias on the part of the judge involved but simply that the circumstances provide the opportunity for unfairness or the appearance of bias[1]. Interestingly, in one recent case it was made clear that confidence in the judiciary is not a 'one-way' process: 'A litigant is entitled to expect integrity of the judge, but he in turn must give the judge his trust. That is the only basis on which litigation can be conducted in an atmosphere of confidence rather than suspicion.'[2]

Views on exactly what *in fact* is required to ensure judicial independence change over time. They change in the light of changes in the duties assigned to judges and as a consequence of diminishing deference to the judiciary and more exacting scrutiny of the judicial system. Undoubtedly the issue of judicial independence has become more prominent in recent years as the judiciary are increasingly being asked to determine disputes which are perceived as having an overtly 'political' dimension. This is particularly true in the field of human rights where, following the implementation of the Human Rights Act 1998 (HRA 1998) and devolution legislation in Scotland, Wales and Northern Ireland, there have been a number of high-profile cases in which the position taken by the courts has been criticised in the media, occasionally even by government ministers[3]. The threats to maintaining independence also vary, although there is a recurring assumption that the most persistent threat comes from the executive branch of government[4]. This is not merely because of the seventeenth-century inheritance but because central government, in the exercise of its very substantial powers, will often wish to press those powers to their limits. It is a frequent litigant in the courts and usually in cases where the rights of weaker parties are at stake. The Crown is also the prosecutor in virtually all criminal cases.

Historically, the expression 'judicial independence' has been treated by the Scottish courts as a reference to all those safeguards – institutional and jurisprudential – put in place to ensure high-quality decision-making. However, there has in recent years been increasing recognition of a distinction between the concepts of judicial *independence* and judicial *impartiality*[5]. The emergence of this distinction can be seen in domestic case law under the influence of both evolving Commonwealth standards and the interpretation and application of the ECHR, art 6 which guarantees that, in the determination of his or her civil rights and obligations or of any criminal charge against him or her, an individual is entitled to a 'fair and public hearing within a reasonable time by an independent *and* impartial tribunal established by law'. In the context of the Canadian Charter of Rights and Freedoms, the distinction between independence and impartiality has been illuminated in this way:

> 'Although there is obviously a close relationship between independence and impartiality, they are nevertheless separate and distinct values or requirements. Impartiality refers to a state of mind or attitude of the tribunal in relation to the issues and the parties in a particular case. The word "impartial" ... connotes absence of bias, actual or perceived. The word "independent" ... reflects or embodies the traditional constitutional value of judicial independence. As such, it connotes not merely a state of mind or attitude in the actual exercise of judicial functions, but a status or relationship to others, particularly to the Executive Branch of government, that rest on objective conditions or guarantees.'[6]

Crudely put, the idea of judicial *independence* may be thought to refer to external, institutional or systemic safeguards to protect the judiciary as a whole from inappropriate influences while judicial *impartiality* concerns, much more directly, the circumstances of the individual decision-maker in any given case and personal, subjective factors which may influence the decision-maker in a way which is considered to be illegitimate. This concept of judicial impartiality accords most closely with that protected by the well-established common law rule against bias[7].

It is clear, though, that while it may be possible to separate the *concepts* of judicial independence and judicial impartiality, in *practice* one is very much dependent upon the other and indeed the Scottish judiciary have been equivocal about whether they consider the distinction to have value even as an analytical tool[8]. In a lecture in 2002 on the topic of 'judicial independence'[9], Lord Hope of Craighead, Justice of the Supreme Court and former Lord of Appeal in Ordinary and Lord President of the Court of Session, addressed three principal questions: (1) What purpose does judicial independence serve? (2) Is our judicial independence at risk of being compromised? (3) How can judicial impartiality be preserved? In answer to his first question, Lord Hope said that judicial independence serves the one very specific purpose of preserving the judge's impartiality. On the question of the risks of compromising judicial independence, he referred to the centrality of security of tenure as a way of ensuring impartiality[10] and acknowledged that security's vulnerability to erosion at the hands of the executive. As to how judicial impartiality might be preserved, Lord Hope's starting point was the Commonwealth's *Latimer House Guidelines*[11]. They are described as 'Guidelines on good practice governing relations between the Executive, Parliament and the Judiciary in the promotion of good governance, the rule of law and human rights' and they address, in turn, questions of judicial autonomy, funding and judicial training.

An important new statutory contribution to the regulation of Scottish courts and to securing their independence has been delivered in the form of the Judiciary and Courts (Scotland) Act 2008 ("2008 Act). When fully implemented[12], this will provide new rules on judicial independence itself, the administration of the courts under a new Scottish Court Service presided over by the Lord President of the Court of Session as Head of the Scottish Judiciary, judicial appointments, judicial conduct and removal from judicial office[13].

1   See pp 312–316 below.

2   *Robbie the Pict, Petitioner* 2003 SCCR 299 per the Lord Justice Clerk Gill at para 8.

3   For example, in February 2002 Collins J in the English High Court upheld a challenge to the application of the Nationality, Immigration and Asylum Act 2002, s 55 in terms of which a number of persons seeking asylum in the UK had been refused state support. The court concluded that the refusals were unlawful and constituted a breach of certain of the applicants' Convention rights. The Home Secretary, David Blunkett, in an interview with the BBC, was reported to have said that he was 'fed up with having to deal with a situation where Parliament debates issues and judges overturn them'. For the decision see *R(Q) v Home Secretary* [2003] EWHC 195, affirmed by the Court of Appeal at [2004] QB 36.

4   'Threats to judicial independence usually come from governments irked by a judiciary fulfilling its traditional role of standing between the executive and the citizen': Lord Steyn 'Democracy Through Law' [2002] EHRLR 723 at 726.

5   See eg *Gillies v Secretary of State for Work and Pensions* 2006 SC(HL) 71 para 38 (per Lady Hale of Richmond).

6   *Valente v The Queen* (1985) 24 DLR (4th) 161 per Le Dain J.

7   As to which see pp 312–316 below.

8   For example, in *Starrs v Ruxton* 2000 JC 208 Lord Prosser expressed the view that while independence and impartiality were concepts which were 'inextricably interlinked', nevertheless the requirement of independence was an additional substantive requirement and was wider than impartiality (at 232). By contrast, in *Clancy v Caird* 2000 SC 441 Lord Sutherland described the Canadian approach as unnecessarily analytical (at 445) and Lord Coulsfield was of the view that independence and impartiality are so closely related as to be difficult to distinguish (at 459–460).

9   'Judicial Independence' 2002 SLT (News) 195.

10   Citing Lord Fraser of Tullybelton 5 *Stair Memorial Encyclopaedia*, paras 663–665.

11 So called because they were the product of a colloquium which was held at Latimer House in June 1998 and attended by lawyers and judges from 20 Commonwealth countries. The Guidelines were subsequently annexed to the Commonwealth Principles and reissued (with an Edinburgh Plan of Action) in 2009.
12 By 1 June 2009, most provisions had been implemented with the exception of Pt 2 Ch 4 on judicial conduct. See SSIs 2009/83 and 2009/192.
13 For discussion of the background to the Act as well as of its provisions in detail, see the Current Law Statutes Annotations by J Harrison and C Himsworth.

JUDICIAL INDEPENDENCE

11.4   In the United Kingdom the conditions of judicial independence, as well as varying over time, are only in part the result of direct legal intervention. Much depends instead on constitutional practice with only the sporadic intrusion of legal rules many of which have, over time, lost the significance they once had. However, a bold new and explicit statement is now provided by s 1 of the 2008 Act. Without seeking to define what is meant by 'independence', the section[1] imposes on the First Minister, the Lord Advocate, the Scottish Ministers, MSPs and other persons responsible for matters relating to the judiciary or the administration of justice an obligation to 'uphold the continued independence of the judiciary'. In particular, the First Minister, the Lord Advocate and the Scottish Ministers must not seek to influence particular judicial decisions through any special access to the judiciary and must have regard to the need for the judiciary to have the support necessary to enable them to carry out their functions. Some may doubt whether these declaratory statements will have any practical effect. They do, however, have an undoubted symbolic impact.

As to the more specific rules relating to the manner in which judicial independence is safeguarded, the subject is divided into two parts: first, the appointment of judges; and second, the creation of conditions conducive to high-quality and independent decision-making by the judiciary as a whole. Thereafter, under the head of 'Judicial impartiality' there is a discussion of the legal principles, developed almost entirely by the courts themselves, which seek to ensure that in any specific case the parties involved can have confidence in the neutrality of the decision-maker involved.

1 Following a similar rule in s 3(1) of the Constitutional Reform Act 2005.

Judicial appointments

11.5   Judicial appointments are made formally by the Crown. Members of the Supreme Court (including the Scottish judges) are appointed on the recommendation of the Prime Minister[1]. Below that level, the rules have been changed in line with the broader arrangements for devolution under SA 1998. Except to ensure the 'continued existence' of the High Court of Justiciary and the Court of Session, SA 1998 does not, in general, make the judicial system of Scotland a reserved matter[2] but s 95 does make special provision for the appointment and removal of judges. Thus it is for the Prime Minister to make recommendations for appointment to the two most senior judicial positions in the Court of Session and the High Court of Justiciary: the Lord President and the Lord Justice-Clerk[3]. However, a recommendation may be made only of a person nominated by the First Minister and the First Minister is, in turn, required first to consult the Lord President and the Lord Justice-Clerk (unless either office is vacant)[4]. In the case of other judges of the Court of Session, sheriffs principal and sheriffs, it is for the First Minister (again after consultation with the Lord President) to make recommendations on appointments[5]. In respect of both nominations for the two most senior posts and recommendations for the others, the First Minister is required to comply with any requirements imposed by another enactment. Such requirements have been laid down by the 2008 Act.

Recommendations for appointment as Court of Session judges cannot be made unless the individual concerned has, in turn, been recommended by the Judicial Appointments Board for Scotland (the JAB) (s 11(1)). Originally established on a non-statutory basis in 2002 to replace an appointments process which was left very much in the hands of the Lord Advocate[6] the JAB has a membership of ten, divided into three categories. The three "judicial members", appointed by the Lord President are a Court of Session judge, a sheriff principal and a sheriff[7]. The two legal members "appointed by the Scottish Ministers are a practising advocate and solicitor and there are five "lay members" (one of whom is designated the Chairing Member) also appointed by the Scottish Ministers[8]. Using procedures including public advertisement and interview, the Board must have regard to the need to encourage diversity – one of the principal reasons for establishing the Board at all was to seek to draw the judiciary from a broader base – but tempered also by the need to assess legal knowledge, skills and competence and, as the Act expressly stipulates, to select "solely on merit" (ss 12–16). Both the Scottish Ministers and the Lord President may issue procedural guidance to the Board[9].

The Board's task of balancing the need for diversity with the obligation to select on merit is not a simple one[10]. A prior requirement for any appointment, however, is legal qualification. Article 19 of the Treaty of Union originally required that candidates be advocates of at least five years standing – a position modified to include sheriffs and solicitor advocates[11].

In addition to Court of Session judges, the Board's remit includes most temporary judges (except those who hold or have held certain judicial offices), sheriffs principal and sheriffs[12]. In respect of the two last offices, the formal prerequisite for appointment is legal qualification for at least ten years[13]. JP recommendations are not within the Board's remit.

Recommendations to the First Minister for nomination to the Prime Minister for appointment as Lord President or Lord Justice Clerk are made not by the Board but by a smaller ad hoc panel established for the purpose, chaired by the Board's Chairing Member, another lay member of the Board and two judges[14].

Even taking into account its earlier years on a non-statutory basis, it is too early to assess the significance in practice of the creation of the Judicial Appointments Board. Critics have expressed doubts about both its procedures and its recommendations[15] but the relative disengagement of the process from ministerial domination (especially that of the Lord Advocate) and the transparency of the criteria and procedure of the Board must be counted as considerable advantages. The old system of appointments on the basis of 'nods and winks' has passed[16].

1 Constitutional Reform Act 2005 s26. Initially the Court comprised the then serving Lords of Appeal in Ordinary (s 24). Prime ministerial recommendations follow processes involving the participation of a selection commission and the Lord Chancellor (ss 26–31).
2 SA 1998, Sch 5, Pt I, para 1. But see SA 1998, Sch 5, Pt II, S L1, which does reserve the determination of judicial remuneration, and p 309 below.
3 The Lord President, carrying the title of Lord Justice-General when sitting in the High Court of Justiciary.
4 SA 1998, s 95(1)–(3). The wording of SA 1998, s 95(3), which refers to 'persons' nominated by the First Minister, was quite deliberate draftsmanship: it enables the First Minister to identify two or three candidates for consideration by the Prime Minister (HL Debs, 6 October 1998, col 403).
5 SA 1998, s 95(4). In the case of nominations under SA 1998, s 95(2) and recommendations under SA 1998, s 95(4), the First Minister is also to comply with any requirement imposed by any enactment.
6 The scheme adopted in the 2008 Act followed consultation on a succession of reforming proposals from the Scottish Executive (both Labour/Liberal Democrat and SNP): Judicial Appointments: An Inclusive Approach (2000)'; Strengthening Judicial Independence in a Modern Scotland (2006); Proposals for a Judiciary (Scotland) Bill (2007); and the Judiciary and Courts (Scotland) Bill itself. For discussion, see the Annotations at p 301 n 13 above.
7 The Board also makes recommendations for shrieval office – see below.
8 2008 Act sch 2.
9 2008 Act ss 15–16.
10 See eg the evidence of Board members to the Parliament's Justice Committee – SPJCOR 5 May 2009.
11 Law Reform (Miscellaneous Provisions) (Scotland) Act 1990 as amended.
12 2008 Act s 10.
13 Sheriff Courts (Scotland) Act 1971 s 5(1).
14 2008 Act ss 19–20 and sch 3. A similar panel was convened prior to the appointment of Lord Hamilton as Lord President in 2005.
15 See the Annotations at p 301 n 13 above.
16 See the evidence of Roy Martin QC at SP JC OR 5 May 1009 col 1724.

Safeguarding independent adjudication

11.6   These recent developments apart, there has been little about the process of *appointing* judges that has been designed to guarantee their 'independence'. Much more attention, however, has been paid to rules, whether or not strictly rules of law, which are intended to protect judges from inappropriate pressures while carrying out their functions. Some operate as restrictions on the behaviour of others; some on their own behaviour. Some are aimed at the conduct of individual cases; some at a judge's position in general. In many instances, the purpose of the protective rules does not differ greatly from that of the rules designed to protect the independence of many other officials or employees. It is, for instance, usually considered appropriate that university teachers should be able to perform their functions of research, teaching and examining without the sort of influences which might affect the independence of their research or cause them to be unfair in their examining decisions. Security of tenure may be considered important but so too are codes of behaviour, whether externally or self imposed. A degree of accountability both to students and to a wider public is important and most would agree that a teacher who is too incapacitated, by illness or otherwise, should not continue in office. Although some of the rules concerning judges are more formalised, the comparison with such other positions is easily made. In the case of judges, as with others, there is a substantial reliance upon their behaviour and the behaviour of others being regulated without the need for legal intervention at all. In almost all cases, there is room for reasonable disagreement as to whether the lines which mark the limits of acceptable behaviour have been drawn at the right place.

Security of tenure

11.7   There are a cluster of rules and practices, which may be described as 'constitutional' in the broadest sense, which are designed to protect a judge's independence while in office. Traditionally most prominent among these has been the assurance of security of tenure. There is no more inappropriate influence than the threat of loss of office and it has been considered important, since the Claim of Right 1689, that the tenure of Court of Session judges has been *ad vitam aut culpam*: for life or until fault[1]. Since 1959 that position has been qualified by provisions for compulsory retiral at age 70, but extendable to 75[2].

REMOVAL OF COURT OF SESSION JUDGES   Important provisions concerning the dismissal of Court of Session judges are contained in SA 1998. As noted above, this Act amended appointment procedures to adapt to the introduction of devolved government. For dismissals, rather more was required because, in contrast with the position in other parts of the United Kingdom, formal procedures for dismissal had never been laid down[3]. It was presumed that dismissal would have been by the Crown on the advice of ministers and *culpa* would have had to be established. But there was not, for instance, the protective mechanism originally provided by the Act of Settlement 1700 and latterly by the Senior Courts Act 1981, that a judge in England and Wales or Northern Ireland cannot be dismissed without an address presented to the Crown by both Houses of Parliament[4].

SA 1998 now requires that a judge may be removed from office only by the Queen, on the recommendation of the First Minister, and such a recommendation may be made only if the Scottish Parliament, on a motion by the First Minister, resolves that such a recommendation should be made[5]. If the motion is in respect of the Lord President or the Lord Justice-Clerk, the First Minister must first have consulted the Prime Minister[6]. A motion to dismiss a judge may be made only if the First Minister has received a written report from an independent tribunal appointed under SA 1998 which concludes that 'the person in question is unfit for office by reason of inability, neglect of duty or misbehaviour' and gives reasons for that conclusion[7]. 'Neglect of duty' and 'misbehaviour' continue the old test of *culpa* but it will be noticed that dismissal for 'inability' – presumably on the grounds of severe illness or other incapacity – is added[8].

As to the constitution and operation of the tribunal itself, some rules are laid down by SA 1998[9] but others are provided by ch 5 of the 2008 Act. A tribunal must be established by the First Minister when he is requested by the Lord President to do so and may be formed in such other circumstances as the First Minister thinks fit. The tribunal must be chaired by a member of the JCPC. The second member must be another senior judge; the third is someone qualified as an advocate or solicitor for at least ten years; the fourth must be a person who is not, and never has been, legally qualified. Provision is made for the suspension from office of a judge who is subject to investigation by the tribunal.

This quite detailed statutory procedure to be followed before the removal of a Court of Session judge can be effected may be viewed as an appropriate safeguard of judicial independence and a necessary protection for the judiciary against arbitrary removal. It also sends an important message about the accountability of the judiciary to Parliament and to the public at large.

REMOVAL OF SHERIFFS   Machinery for terminating the appointment of a sheriff is provided by the Sheriff Courts (Scotland) Act 1971 (SC(S)A 1971), as amended by the 2008 Act. Section 12(A) provides that a sheriff (or sheriff principal) may be removed from office by the First Minister by order, subject to annulment by the Scottish Parliament. The Scottish Ministers may, however, act only in response to a report in writing following investigation by a tribunal similar to that required for a Court of Session judge, save that the second judicial member must be a sheriff principal or sheriff. A report justifying dismissal must be to the effect that the sheriff is unfit for office by reason of inability, neglect of duty or misbehaviour.

Two sheriffs were removed under an earlier procedure which involved investigation by the Lord President and the Lord Justice Clerk and an order by the Secretary of State. The first was Sheriff Peter Thomson in 1977 for associating himself with a Scottish Plebiscite campaign. In 1992 Sheriff Ewen Stewart was dismissed on grounds of inability based on a report focusing on his behaviour in court. He had, for instance, constantly interrupted proceedings and this indicated an underlying defect of character which had continued despite prior warnings. Sheriff Stewart's petition for judicial review of the Secretary of State's order[10] on the grounds that he was not subject to an 'inability' in the narrow sense of physical or mental infirmity and that his investigation had not been in accordance with the rules of natural justice was rejected in the Court of Session[11] and in the House of Lords[12].

TEMPORARY SHERIFFS AND SECURITY OF TENURE   The unfortunate circumstances which have led to the use of the powers to dismiss sheriffs are likely to remain rare occurrences and the new provisions made by SA 1998 for the dismissal of Court of Session judges are likely to be even more rarely invoked. In both cases they preserve security of tenure – which itself safeguards the judiciary against the threat of loss of office – in all but the most extreme conditions. The safeguard of security of tenure *ad vitam aut culpam* was not extended, however, to the temporary sheriffs who were introduced in 1971 and were, until 1999, widely used in the Scottish courts. Under SC(S)A 1971 the Secretary of State could appoint temporary sheriffs in circumstances where a sheriff was ill or otherwise unable to perform his duties; when there was a vacancy; or when, for any other reason, it appeared expedient to do so to avoid unnecessary delays[13]. Although not much used in its early years, this apparently restricted power came to be relied on to provide extensive support for the permanent sheriffs. By 1985 there were 88 permanent sheriffs and 61 temporary sheriffs and by 1999 the corresponding numbers were 110 and 129 respectively. The proportion of work, in terms of total sheriff court days, carried out by temporary sheriffs was nearly 25 per cent[14]. SC(S)A 1971 provided that the appointment of a temporary sheriff would subsist 'until recalled by the Secretary of State',[15] although in practice the Secretary of State developed a policy whereby temporary sheriffs were appointed for a fixed, but renewable, one-year term[16].

The use of temporary sheriffs came under challenge from two directions. The principal challenge arose in *Starrs v Ruxton*[17] in which the Appeal Court of the High Court of Justiciary was asked to consider whether the relative lack of security of tenure enjoyed by temporary sheriffs gave rise to difficulties under the ECHR, art 6. Specifically, the court was invited to rule on whether the Lord Advocate – in pursuing the prosecution of the two accused before a temporary sheriff – was acting in a manner which was incompatible with the rights of the accused to trial before an 'independent and impartial tribunal'[18]. While the court focused on the question of a temporary sheriff's security of tenure it was, nevertheless, presented with a good deal of information about the practical operation of the appointment of temporary sheriffs, a process in which the Lord Advocate's leading role was obvious despite the formal allocation of the statutory powers to the Secretary of State and, from 1 July 1999, the Scottish Ministers[19]. The most prominent feature of the system that had operated in recent years was that virtually all temporary sheriffs were appointed for a period of a calendar year. In holding that, for the purposes of the Convention, a temporary sheriff was not an independent and impartial tribunal, the court made clear that it was not objectionable that temporary sheriffs were, like their permanent counterparts and Court of Session judges, appointed by the Executive but that their tenure was too precarious to satisfy the requirements of ECHR, art 6(1). The provision in SC(S)A 1971 that a temporary sheriff's appointment subsisted only 'until recalled by the Secretary of State'[20] conferred a power of recall which appeared 'to be exercisable at pleasure'[21] and 'the use of the one year term suggests a reservation of control ... [which] reinforces the impression that the tenure of office by the individual temporary sheriff is at the discretion of the Lord Advocate'[22]. It should be repeated that the fact that temporary sheriffs were, like other members of the judiciary, appointed by the Executive and, in particular, effectively on the nomination of the head of the prosecution system, was not relied on by the court, although these issues had been raised in argument[23]. Lord Reed accepted that issues of perception in this area were important. There was a risk, in any situation where judges were appointed by the Executive, that they might be perceived as having attained their position as a result of the Executive's favour, and therefore as being obligated to the Executive. But perceptions, he said, 'are of course relevant only if they have some objective justification, rather than being the product of mere cynicism'[24].

The impact of the decision in *Starrs v Ruxton* was immediate. The use of temporary sheriffs was ended with the Deputy First Minister confirming to the Scottish Parliament just a few hours after the decision that he had 'asked the Justice Department to suspend the availability of temporary sheriffs for new civil or criminal business'[25]. Additional permanent sheriffs were rapidly recruited. The decision also raised doubts about appointments to district courts and practice was changed there too. In a second challenge concerning temporary sheriffs, an issue was raised not as to their impartiality but as to whether the widespread use of temporary sheriffs already noted in *Starrs* went so far beyond the scope anticipated and permitted by SC(S)A 1971 as to be an abuse of the powers of appointment and therefore *ultra vires*. If such a challenge had been upheld, the consequences for the validity of judgments over many years – much longer than the period since the 'incorporation' of the ECHR in May 1999 – might have been considerable. In *Gibbs v Ruxton*[26] , however, the Appeal Court held that the power to appoint temporary sheriffs was not one which was confined to situations of illness, vacancy of office or short-term emergencies but could be used to provide a long-term and large pool of temporary sheriffs for deployment as needs arose. Their Lordships reserved their opinion on whether, had they found the appointment of a temporary sheriff to have been *ultra vires*, the consequence would have been that the acts and decisions of those temporary sheriffs would be held to be invalid.

Related doubts extended to the appointment of temporary judges in the Court of Session and the High Court but in *Clancy v Caird*[27] it was held by an Extra Division, on report from a case conducted by T G Coutts QC, sitting as a temporary judge, that temporary judges appointed for three-year terms[28] were to be regarded as sufficiently independent and impartial for the purposes of ECHR art 6[29]. Then in *Kearney v HM Advocate*[30] the Judicial Committee of the Privy Council held that there could be no grounds for challenge to the conduct of a criminal trial by a temporary judge. The case provided the opportunity for Lord Hope of Craighead to conduct a substantial review of both the history and modern practice of the appointment of temporary judges, including his own involvement as Lord President (paras 10–54).

Judicial Incapacity

11.8   Quite distinct from questions of dismissal, the 2008 Act provides for the circumstances in which the office of Lord President is vacant or the Lord President is incapacitated or suspended[31]. His functions become exercisable by the Lord Justice Clerk. Similar provision is made for the Lord Justice Clerk to be replaced, in the same circumstances, by the senior Inner House judge.

Judicial Conduct

11.9   Until recently the Scottish legal system lacked any formal rules applicable in cases of judicial misconduct short of behaviour which might warrant dismissal. Normal procedures for the appeal or review of decisions in individual cases might provide a remedy in some circumstances. And doubtless informal interventions by senior judges or even the Lord Advocate were other possibilities. But it is a sensitive area. Important questions of the individual and institutional autonomy of judges are at stake. There is a tension between autonomy and accountability.

The passing of the 2008 Act, however, and, in particular, its formal designation of the Lord President as the Head of the Scottish Judiciary brought an opportunity to introduce a new approach (ss 28–34). The Lord President may make rules (to be published) for the investigation and determination of matters concerning the "conduct" (a term not defined in the Act) of judges (including sheriffs)[32]. Following any such investigation, the Lord President may give the judge formal advice, a formal warning or a reprimand[33]. Somewhat controversially, these processes are to be overseen by a Judicial Complaints Reviewer, appointed by the Scottish Ministers with the consent of the Lord President.

Another conduct-related provision added by the 2008 Act gives the Lord President (or, if unavailable, the Lord Justice Clerk or other senior judge) the power to suspend a judicial office holder (judge or sheriff) if he considers that it is "necessary for the purpose of maintaining public confidence in the judiciary" (s 34).

1   *Mackay and Esslemont v Lord Advocate* 1937 SC 860.
2   See the Judicial Pensions Act 1959, the Judicial Pensions Act 1981, and the Judicial Pensions and Retirement Act 1993, s 26(7) and Sch 5. For a discussion , see W Finnie 'Judicial Tenure and Judicial Pensions' 1993 SLT (News) 213.
3   See C M G Himsworth 'Securing the tenure of Scottish Judges: A somewhat academic exercise?' [1999] PL 14.
4   Act of Settlement 1700, s 3 and Senior Courts Act 1981, s 11(3).
5   SA 1998, s 95(6), (7).
6   SA 1998, s 95(10)(b).
7   SA 1998, s 95(10)(a).
8   For the English rule on permanent infirmity, see Senior Courts Act 1981, s 11.
9   SA 1998, s 95(8), (9).
10 Until 1999 and devolution, removal orders were made by the Secretary of State, subject to annulment by resolution of either House at Westminster.
11 *Stewart v Secretary of State for Scotland* 1996 SC 271.
12 *Stewart v Secretary of State for Scotland* 1998 SC (HL) 81.
13 SC(S)A 1971, s 11(2).
14 These figures were supplied to the court by the Solicitor General in *Starrs v Ruxton* 2000 JC 208 at 216–217.
15 SC(S)A 1971, s 11(4).
16 In *Starrs v Ruxton* 2000 JC 208, it was suggested that, as there was nothing in SC(S)A 1971, s 11 to empower the Lord Advocate to impose any term or condition on the appointment of a temporary sheriff, the adoption of such a policy may raise questions of vires (at 227–228 per Lord Justice General Rodger). That specific point was not argued before the court and their Lordships reserved their opinion on it.
17 *Starrs v Ruxton* 2000 JC 208.
18 The accused were in fact, and as one would expect in the sheriff court, prosecuted at the instance of the local procurator fiscal but in the course of the proceedings in the High Court it was accepted on behalf of the Lord Advocate that in both solemn and summary proceedings he is represented by the procurator fiscal. That the challenge was taken against the prosecutor at all – rather than against the temporary sheriff concerned – was a consequence of the rather disjointed way in which the ECHR was given effect in Scotland. HRA 1998 – in terms of which a court is a public authority and is bound itself to act in a manner which is compatible with Convention rights – came into force throughout the UK on 2 October 2000. However, as a member of the Scottish Executive, the Lord Advocate had been required (by virtue of SA 1998, s 57) to act compatibly with the Convention rights with effect from 20 May 1999 (SI 1998/3178). Characterising the challenge in *Starrs v Ruxton* 2000 JC 208 (which was taken in July 1999) as a challenge to the Lord Advocate as a means of addressing the position of temporary sheriffs was a tactic employed by a defence team keen to employ Convention rights arguments as soon as possible.

19 An interesting side-issue was explored briefly by Lord Reed when he questioned (*Starrs v Ruxton* 2000 JC 208 at 251) whether the transfer of authority to the Scottish Ministers had been effective. If the powers exercisable under SC(S)A 1971, s 11 were held to be incompatible with the Convention rights they could not be within 'devolved competence'; could not be transferred to the Scottish Ministers; and had, therefore, been retained by the Secretary of State. That only functions which are exercisable (and exercised) in a manner which would be within the legislative competence of the Scottish Parliament are actually transferred by SA 1998, ss 53, 54 has been described as 'washing': see R Reed and J Murdoch *A Guide to Human Rights Law in Scotland* (2nd ed, 2008) para 1.24.

20 SC(S)A 1971, s 11(4).

21 *Starrs v Ruxton* 2000 JC 208 at 226.

22 *Starrs v Ruxton* 2000 JC 208 at 228.

23 *Starrs v Ruxton* 2000 JC 208 at 241.

24 *Starrs v Ruxton* 2000 JC 208 at 241.

25 SP OR 11 November 1999, col 574.

26 *Gibbs v Ruxton* 2000 JC 258.

27 *Clancy v Caird* 2000 SC 441. See also, approving *Starrs v Ruxton* 2000 JC 208, Millar v Dickson 2002 SC (PC) 30.

28 Under the Law Reform (Miscellaneous Provisions) (Scotland) 1990, s 35(3).

29 As a preliminary issue the court had also held that the case raised a 'devolution issue' (see p 397 below) because the Scottish Executive's provision of judicial resources amounted to an 'act' for the purposes of SA 1998, s 57(2) (Lord Penrose at 473).

30 2006 SC(PC) 1.

31 2008 Act, Part 2, Ch 2. These provisions replace the Senior Judiciary (Vacancies and Incapacity) (Scotland) Act 2006 which was passed hurriedly in case of the need to respond to the Lord President's absence through illness.

32 In England the Judges' Council has published a Guide to Judicial Conduct which, drawing on the Bangalore Principles (p 295 n 3 above) lays down a series of principles and rules on which judicial behaviour should be based.

33 In April 2009 the Lord Justice General publicly criticised a temporary judge who had summarily jailed a rape witness.

Judicial salaries

11.10   Historically, at least, an important further condition of judicial quality and independence has been the assurance of substantial salaries for judges and their protection from the need for annual parliamentary debate and approval. The *Latimer House Guidelines* emphasise the importance of protection of judicial funding from political interference: 'funds, once voted for the judiciary by the legislature, should be protected from alienation or misuse. The allocation or withholding of funding should not be used as a means of exercising improper control over the judiciary.'[1]

The determination of judicial salaries is a reserved matter under SA 1998[2] and is made formally by the Secretary of State[3] but on the recommendation of the Senior Salaries Review Body[4].

It has been considered appropriate that the funding of judicial salaries should not be the subject of parliamentary (and, therefore, potentially party political) debate. At Westminster this meant ensuring that judges should be paid out of the Consolidated Fund without the need for specific appropriation[5]. The same mechanism has been extended to apply in the Scottish Parliament[6]. While the provision of substantial salaries should ensure that the judiciary are less vulnerable to corruption than they otherwise might be, it remains a criminal offence to attempt to bribe a judge and, of course, an offence to accept such a bribe[7].

1 *Guidelines* I, 2.
2 SA 1998, Sch 5, Pt II, S L1.
3 Administration of Justice Act 1973, s 9. For the sheriff court, see Sheriff Courts (Scotland) Act 1907, s 14.
4 See Review Body on Senior Salaries *31st Report* 2009, Cm 7556.
5 For the Consolidated Fund and Scottish Consolidated Fund see ch 10.
6 See SA 1998, s 119(3), Sch 4, para 5(a) and Sch 8, para 9(b).
7 See G H Gordon *The Criminal Law of Scotland* (3rd edn, 2001) (hereafter Gordon) vol II, para 49.04.

Liability of judges

11.11   The very considerable weight which is attached to providing judges with security of tenure and with financial security is a recognition of the importance of ensuring their independence from the executive. That independence should enable the judiciary to decide even politically controversial matters without fear of or favour from the government of the day. But judges, in order to remain 'independent', must also be protected from the threat of reprisals from those who are directly affected by their acts or decisions. It is a longstanding principle of Scots law that a judge enjoys absolute immunity from civil liability for anything done by him in the exercise of his judicial office[1], even if his actions would otherwise give rise to a claim for damages for, for example, defamation or wrongful imprisonment[2].

This common law principle has been supplemented in relation to damages for infringement of Convention rights under HRA 1998 with a distinction being made between damages for judicial acts done in good faith and those which are not[3].

1 See *Haggart's Trs v Lord President Hope* (1824) 2 Sh App 125.
2 There appears to be just one statutory exception to this general rule: the Criminal Procedure (Scotland) Act 1995, s 170(1) provides for damages to be payable to any person who has been wrongfully imprisoned by a justice of the peace (or stipendiary magistrate) in summary proceedings and it is proved that the justice or magistrate acted maliciously and without probable cause. The immunity of sheriffs was questioned by temporary judge T G Coutts QC in *Russell v Dickson* 1997 SC 269: 'It does ... seem to be inequitable by today's standards that a man can spend five days in prison unreasonably and improperly without compensation from some quarter being awarded to him' (at 278).
3 HRA 1998, ss 8, 9. In the case of judicial acts done in good faith damages are only available in cases involving a breach of ECHR, art 5(5) (unlawful arrest or detention).

Public criticism of judges

11.12   In addition to being protected from civil liability for the decisions which they make, judges are also protected to a limited extent by the criminal law from undue public criticism of themselves and their decisions. It is a common law crime to slander or 'murmur' a judge[1] (although the last successful prosecution for such an offence was more than a century ago[2]) and criticism of a judge or of a court may amount to contempt of court. This is undoubtedly a difficult area: it is not easy to assess precisely what might today amount to murmuring[3], particularly when the need to protect the judiciary from criticism must be balanced against the rights of individuals and of the media to comment upon the justice system. The prosecution of a genuine offence should not 'degenerate into an oppressive or vindictive abuse of the Court's powers'[4] and this is also an area in which the ECHR is of some relevance. The European Court of Human Rights 'has repeatedly emphasised the importance of freedom of expression for democracy'[5] and will scrutinise domestic laws which prevent or simply discourage criticism of the state and those who represent it. While the Court has, understandably, focused on the freedom to criticise politicians it has also been willing to assess the compatibility with ECHR, art 10 (freedom of expression) of penalties imposed on those who publicly question or disparage the judiciary[6]. A special instance of this arises in relation to the law of contempt whose purpose is the maintenance of the authority and impartiality of the judiciary and the prevention of wilful challenge or affront to the authority of the court[6].

By convention, members of the Westminster Parliament, and to a greater extent UK ministers, have sought to avoid public criticism of the judiciary and the decisions made in individual cases and this is reflected in parliamentary practice[8]. Notwithstanding that convention, criticisms have been made from time to time[9] and it would appear that, following devolution, members of the Scottish Executive and Scottish Parliament have been somewhat less restrained than their UK counterparts. While the First Minister rather mildly remarked that a decision of Sheriff Gimblett[10] concerning the legality of the UK's Trident programme had come as 'a surprise'[11], more robust Scottish parliamentary criticism of judges has addressed such matters as the interpretation by a High Court judge of the Scots law of rape[12] and the approach of the Inner House to questions of the validity of Skye Bridge tolls[13]. There was particularly virulent and public debate in September 2007 arising out of the abrupt ending by Lord Clarke of the murder trial in the infamous 'World's End' case. Public criticism of the Crown Office brought a defence from the Lord Advocate which, in turn, was interpreted as a criticism of Lord Clarke. A letter from the Lord President expressed concerns about the need for judicial independence to be protected – attracting, in turn, a response from the First Minister at question time in the Scottish Parliament[14].

1 See *SME Reissue* Constitutional Law para 603 and Gordon vol II, para 50.03.
2 *HM Advocate v Robertson* (1870) 42 SJ 336.
3 In *HM Advocate v Robertson* (1870) 42 SJ 336, the offence was committed by the sending of letters to the Lord Chancellor and the Home Secretary complaining of the official and personal conduct of a sheriff including allegations to the effect that the sheriff involved had misused his official powers and had engaged, amongst other things, in following Mr Robertson home and trying to pick a fight with him.
4 Gordon vol II, para 50.03.
5 J McBride 'Judges, Politicians and the Limits to Critical Comment' (1998) 23 EL Rev (HRS) 76.
6 See *Anwar* 2008 JC 409.
7 *De Haes v Belgium* (1998) 25 EHRR 1.
8 Erskine May *Parliamentary Practice* (ed Sir William McKay, 23rd edn, 2004))
9 See p 300 n 3.
10 See p 103, n 10.
11 SP OR 28 October 1999, col 147.
12 During a debate on the matter Dr Winnie Ewing MSP declared that she was 'happy to murmur Lord Abernethy in this particular matter' and that she had no doubt that 'Lord Abernethy has made a fool of himself' (SP OR 25 April 2002 col 73). Lord Abernethy's ruling was reviewed,

and the law on this matter restated, by an Appeal Court bench of seven: *Lord Advocate's Reference (No 1 of 2001)* 2002 SLT 466.
13 See the proceedings of the Public Petitions Committee of the Scottish Parliament (SP OR 5 February 2002, col 1559 ff).
14 SPOR 27 Sept 2007, col 2227.

JUDICIAL IMPARTIALITY

Introduction

11.13   The issues raised in *Starrs v Ruxton* and the other cases discussed above concerning the ways in which the circumstances of a judge's appointment and tenure of office may be treated as detracting from his or her independence form part of a wider concern about the maintenance of judicial impartiality. It has recently been reaffirmed at the highest level that: 'One of the cornerstones of our legal system is the impartiality of the tribunals by which justice is administered.'[1]. This principle manifests itself in the common law rules of natural justice, and in particular the 'rule against bias'[2], and has been added to by the requirements of ECHR, art 6. Where this principle is infringed by a judge then his or her decision may be challenged[3] and, ultimately, overturned.

1 *R v Bow Street Metropolitan Stipendiary Magistrate, ex parte Pinochet Ugarte (No 2)* [2000] 1 AC 119 at 140 per Lord Hope of Craighead.
2 There is a very substantial body of case law and scholarship about the content and application of the rules of natural justice which cannot be treated fully here. See further at 378–380 below.
3 By way of appeal or judicial review (as to which, see ch 13).

The rule against bias

11.14   The rule against bias requires, as a fundamental principle, that a person may not be a judge in his or her own cause. If such a clash of interest arises, a judge[1] is disqualified from sitting and the judge should disclose the conflicting interest and, unless all parties waive any objections, they might have, withdraw ('recuse' himself or herself) from the case[2]. If there is no such disclosure, the decision in the case cannot stand. The application of the principle that a person should not be a judge in his or her own cause is not at all confined to those situations where a judge is actually biased and wrongly brings improper considerations to bear when hearing or deciding the particular case before him or her. Such behaviour would plainly be unlawful. The significance of the principle is in its extension to include circumstances where there is an *appearance* of bias. The use of the language of 'appearance' or 'perception' is not unproblematic[3] but it has usually been the practice of the courts to identify two main forms of *apparent bias*. As explained by Lord Browne-Wilkinson in *ex parte Pinochet Ugarte (No 2)*[4], the principle may be applied literally – where the judge is in fact a party to the litigation or has a financial or proprietary interest in its outcome. In this case, the mere fact that the judge is involved in one of these ways is sufficient to cause *automatic* disqualification. The second application of the principle is where the circumstances – for example the judge's conduct or behaviour or, for instance, friendship with one of the parties – may give rise to a suspicion that the judge is not impartial. In these cases there is no automatic disqualification. Instead an assessment has to be made – either by the individual judge when the case comes before him or by an appeal court after the event – as to whether the circumstances are sufficiently serious to warrant the judge's disqualification. The formulation of the test to be applied by the courts in making that assessment has been the subject of recent cases which are discussed below.

1 Or, indeed, in arbitrations an arbiter (cf *Sellar v Highland Rly Co* 1919 SC (HL) 19).
2 *R v Bow Street Metropolitan Stipendiary Magistrate, ex parte Pinochet Ugarte (No 2)* [2000] 1 AC 119 at 140.
3 See also *Starrs v Ruxton* 2000 JC 208.
4 *R v Bow Street Metropolitan Stipendiary Magistrate, ex parte Pinochet Ugarte (No 2)* [2000] 1 AC 119 at 143.

Automatic disqualification

11.15   Historically, cases of 'automatic' disqualification have arisen where the judge has had a direct financial interest in the case: the classic, oft-cited, example being where the judge was found to be a shareholder in a company which was one of the parties to the case[1]. Where such an interest was present it was irrelevant how small the interest actually was[2]. Recently, however, in the *Pinochet* case the concept of 'automatic disqualification' was further developed. The case itself was famous as that in which the House of Lords set aside an earlier decision of the House itself on the grounds that one of the judges in the case, Lord Hoffmann, had a disqualifying interest by virtue of his undisclosed links with Amnesty International, an organisation which had intervened in the proceedings[3]. It was held that these links with Amnesty International brought Lord Hoffmann within the first head of disqualification. The Lords were clear that he could not be regarded as a party to the proceedings[4], nor could he be said to have had a financial or proprietary interest in the outcome – but then, in the peculiar circumstances of these criminal proceedings to determine the susceptibility to extradition of General Pinochet, nor did Amnesty International[5]. Through his involvement in the organisation, however, Lord Hoffmann shared its interest in the promotion of its cause[6]. That was sufficient to establish the circumstances of automatic disqualification[7].

1 *Dimes v Grand Junction Canal Proprietors* (1852) 3 HL Cas 759. The judge involved was the Lord Chancellor. See also *Sellar v Highland Rly Co* 1919 SC (HL) 19.
2 *Wildridge v Anderson* (1897) 25 R (J) 27.
3 Lord Hoffmann was not a member of Amnesty International itself but was an unpaid director and chairman of an associated charity. For a detailed comment on the case, see T H Jones '*Judicial bias and disqualification in the Pinochet case*' [1999] PL 391.
4 *R v Bow Street Metropolitan Stipendiary Magistrate, ex parte Pinochet Ugarte (No 2)* [2000] 1 AC 119 at 134.
5 *R v Bow Street Metropolitan Stipendiary Magistrate, ex parte Pinochet Ugarte (No 2)* [2000] 1 AC 119 at 134.
6 *R v Bow Street Metropolitan Stipendiary Magistrate, ex parte Pinochet Ugarte (No 2)* [2000] 1 AC 119 at 135.
7 The extension of the long-standing principle in *Dimes v Grand Junction Canal Proprietors* (1852) 3 HL Cas 759, to include the 'promotion of a cause' interest in *ex parte Pinochet (No 2)* has since been considered in *Locabail (UK) Ltd v Bayfield Properties Ltd* [2000] QB 451.

Disqualification on other grounds

11.16   Because *ex parte Pinochet* (No 2) was decided on the basis of automatic disqualification, the House of Lords was not required to examine closely
the other category of disqualification beyond noting that it was, for the English courts, based on the test laid down in *R v Gough*[1]: 'is there in the view of
the court a *real danger* that the judge was biased?'. There was, however, an
acknowledgment that a review of that decision might be needed in the light
of the reopening of a gap between the 'real danger' test in *Gough* and, on the
other hand, decisions in other jurisdictions where the question was 'whether
the events in question give rise to *a reasonable apprehension or suspicion* on
the part of a fair-minded and informed member of the public that the judge was
not impartial'[2]. Lord Hope, in particular, explained that, in Scotland, the courts
had applied the 'reasonable suspicion' test[3] but he also observed that, although
the tests were described differently, their application by appellate courts was
likely in practice to lead to results which were so similar as to be indistinguish-
able. They were founded on the same broad principle. The judge must be seen
to be impartial[4].

Whichever test is adopted, there will obviously be some uncertainty as to how
it is to be applied in the circumstances of particular cases and this was an issue
addressed in an important decision in the English Court of Appeal intended
to provide guidance for other courts and tribunals. In *Locabail (UK) Ltd v
Bayfield Properties Ltd*[5] the court started with the requirement of ECHR, art
6; moved on to the 'automatic disqualification' test of *Dimes* and *Pinochet*;
but then acknowledged the much greater importance in practice of the 'real
danger' test in *Gough*. Surveying the authorities, the court concluded:

> 'It would be dangerous and futile to attempt to define or list the factors
> which may or not give rise to a real danger of bias. Everything will depend
> on the facts, which may include the nature of the issue to be decided. We
> cannot, however, conceive of circumstances in which an objection could
> be soundly based on the religion, ethnic or national origin, gender, age,
> class, means or sexual orientation of the judge. Nor, at any rate ordinarily,
> could an objection be soundly based on the judge's social or educational
> or service or employment background or history, nor that of any member
> of the judge's family; or previous political associations; or membership of
> social or sporting or charitable bodies; or Masonic associations; or previ-
> ous judicial decisions; or extra-curricular utterances (whether in textbooks,
> lectures, speeches, articles, interviews, reports or responses to consultation
> papers); or previous receipt of instructions to act for or against any party,
> solicitor or advocate engaged in a case before him; or membership of the
> same Inn, circuit, local Law Society or chambers. By contrast, a real danger
> of bias might well be thought to arise if there were personal friendship or
> animosity between the judge and any member of the public involved in the
> case; or if the judge were closely acquainted with any member of the public
> involved in the case, particularly if the credibility of that individual could
> be significant in the decision of the case; or if, in a case where the cred-
> ibility of any individual were an issue to be decided by the judge, he had
> in a previous case rejected the evidence of that person in such outspoken

terms as to throw doubt on his ability to approach such person's evidence with an open mind on any later occasion; or if on any question at issue in the proceedings before him the judge had expressed views, particularly in the course of the hearing, in such extreme and unbalanced terms as to throw doubt on his ability to try the issue with an objective judicial mind; or if, for any other reason, there were real ground for doubting the ability of the judge to ignore extraneous considerations, prejudices and predilections and bring on an objective judgment to bear on the issues before him. The mere fact that a judge, earlier in the same case or in a previous case, had commented adversely on a party or witness, or found the evidence of a party or witness to be unreliable, would not without more found a sustainable objection. In most cases, we think, the answer, one way or the other, will be obvious. But if in any case there is real ground for doubt, that doubt should be resolved in favour of recusal. We repeat; every application must be decided on the facts and circumstances of the individual case. The greater the passage of time between the event relied on as showing a danger of bias and the case in which the objection is raised, the weaker (other things being equal) the objection will be.'[6]

This statement concerning the factual circumstances which may or may not lead to a judge's disqualification for apparent bias appears to be comprehensive. It does not, however, eliminate all difficulty. For one thing, it does not make any clear distinction – in terms of their relative significance – between the various factors listed as potentially relevant or irrelevant to disqualification. Are we to take it that the judge's own Masonic associations are to be weighed equally with his brother's previous employment background? Another difficulty is that the lists of the irrelevant factors suggested by the court are qualified in an important way: they apply only 'ordinarily' and this, of course, leaves open the possibility that such factors will be important in an 'extraordinary' case. Very little guidance is given to assist in identifying such a case.

What *Locabail* demonstrates, however, is the desire to see questions of bias move away from 'subjective' personal and private attributes of the judge's character, his or her opinions and his or her family and social connections to issues more directly relevant to how he or she has behaved while fulfilling his or her judicial role. Nevertheless, the bottom line is that every case will turn very much on its own facts. So, for example, in Scotland a sheriff was disqualified where he made, at a social occasion, disparaging remarks about striking miners and afterwards did not recuse himself from hearing cases involving such miners[7]. While *Locabail* suggests that a judge's 'extra-curricular utterances' will not normally give rise to apparent bias, it was held that Lord McCluskey's published remarks about the ECHR 'would create in the mind of an informed observer an apprehension of bias on the part of Lord McCluskey against the Convention and against the rights deriving from it'[8]. And in an interesting series of cases the Inner House held that, where it was suggested that a judge's membership of a private society gave rise to apparent bias, it was appropriate for such a judge to recuse himself from deciding whether it did give rise to such bias[9]. Ultimately, however, it was held that no such bias had been established[10].

315

The decision in *Locabail* focused on this lengthy narration of the factors which may or may not give rise to a 'real danger' of bias (subject, of course, to the proviso that 'everything will depend on the facts'). It did not revise the wording of the test itself. In *Porter v Magill*[11] the House of Lords (and, in particular, Lord Hope of Craighead) revisited that question. The difference between the English 'real danger' test and the 'reasonable apprehension' test applied in Scotland and beyond had been commented upon in *ex parte Pinochet Ugarte* and Lord Hope noted that the latter test placed more emphasis on the perceptions of the reasonable member of the public looking at all the facts of the case than on those of the reviewing court. Drawing on the decision of the Court of Appeal in *In re Medicaments and Related Classes of Goods (No 2)*[12], he recommended the 'modest adjustment' of the *Gough* test which had been suggested there. In Lord Hope's view, to resolve any conflict between England, Scotland and the Commonwealth, the test of apparent bias should be restated as being 'whether the fair-minded and informed observer, having considered the facts, would conclude that there was a real possibility that the tribunal was biased'.[13] Whether this does, in fact, resolve the tensions between the 'real danger' and 'reasonable apprehension' tests remains to be seen[14]. In *Davidson v Scottish Ministers (No 2)*[15] the House of Lords held that where Lord Hardie had decided an issue on the basis of his interpretation of s 21 of the Crown Proceedings Act 1947, having earlier, as Lord Advocate, having expressed a view on the matter, there was, applying *Porter v Magill*, a risk of apparent bias. In *Helow v Home Secretary*[16] it was held that the Lord Ordinary's membership of the International Association of Jewish Lawyers (whose publication *Justice* included fervently pro-Israeli articles) should not disqualify her from hearing an asylum appeal brought by a Palestinian activist. The "fair-minded observer" is someone who always reserves judgment until both sides of the argument are fully understood. She is not unduly sensitive or suspicious. She is not to be confused with the complainant but is someone with a measure of detachment[17].

1 *R v Gough* [1993] AC 646. For discussion of the emergence of the test, see *Locabail (UK) Ltd v Bayfield Properties Ltd* [2000] QB 451 at 475–476.
2 *R v Bow Street Magistrate, ex parte Pinochet Ugarte (No 2)* [2000] 1 AC 119 at 136, citing, as an example the Australian case *Webb v R* (1994) 181 CLR 41.
3 See *Bradford v McLeod* 1986 SLT 244; *Doherty v McGlennan* 1997 SLT 444.
4 *R v Bow Street Magistrate, ex parte Pinochet Ugarte (No 2)* [2000] 1 AC 119 at 142.
5 *Locabail (UK) Ltd v Bayfield Properties Ltd* [2000] QB 451. References deleted.
6 *Locabail (UK) Ltd v Bayfield Properties Ltd* [2000] QB 451 at 480.
7 *Bradford v McLeod* 1986 SLT 244.
8 *Hoekstra v HM Advocate (No 2)* 2000 SLT 602.
9 *Robbie the Pict v HM Advocate* 2003 SCCR 99.
10 *Robbie the Pict, Petitioner* 2003 SCCR 299.
11 *Porter v Magill* [2002] 2 AC 357.
12 *In re Medicaments and Related Classes of Goods (No 2)* [2001] 1 WLR 700.
13 *Porter v Magill* [2002] 2 AC 357 at 494.
14 Some subsequent Scottish cases have referred both to the test in *Porter v Magill* [2002] 2 AC 357 and also to the test set out by Lord Hope in *Millar v Dickson* 2002 SC (PC) 30: 'grounds which would be sufficient to create in the mind of a reasonable man a doubt about the judge's impartiality' (at 54). See *Mellors, Petitioner* 2003 SLT 479 and *Robbie the Pict, Petitioner* 2003 SCCR 299.
15 [2005] 1 SC (HL) 7.
16 2009 SC(HL) 1.
17 Ibid. Lord Hope of Craighead, para 2. See also *Johnson v Johnson* (2000) 201 CLR 488; *Gillies v Secretary of State for Work and Pensions* 2006 SC(HL) 2.

A brief assessment

11.17 The law relating to automatic disqualification for apparent bias, and the formulation of the test for disqualification where the judge does not have a pecuniary interest and is not 'promoting a cause' in the sense which arose in *ex parte Pinochet Ugarte* have been the subject of much scrutiny in recent years. Despite this, and despite the subtle reworkings of the tests to be applied, questions remain.

Is the dichotomy between the tests for automatic disqualification and the remaining grounds sustainable? There have been suggestions of a '*de minimis*' exception to automatic disqualification[1]; there is a blurring of the interest of the judge with that of a spouse, partner or family member[2]; and there must be an underlying doubt now about which interests in which entities should disqualify automatically. The circumstances of the *Pinochet* case – the extremely unusual position of Lord Hoffmann and his involvement in the promotion of the cause of Amnesty International and the court's desire to ensure that, in a case of such political sensitivity, it should be beyond reproach – may have extended the 'automatic' test too far. It might have been more difficult to have established a 'real danger' of bias on the part of Lord Hoffmann[3].

In another recent development, the European Court of Human Rights has thrown further light on the question of judicial impartiality, this time in the situation where a judge's position may be compromised by prior involvement in some aspect of the case while performing some other role in government. In *McGonnell v UK*[4] the Bailiff of Guernsey had presided over the Royal Court in an appeal on a planning matter and the Strasbourg Court held that the Bailiff's prior involvement in the making of the rules which had to be applied in the case was capable of casting doubt on his impartiality. He had presided, as Deputy Bailiff (a government office), over the States of Deliberation (a legislative body) when the measure was adopted. The court noted that there was no suggestion that the Bailiff was subjectively prejudiced or biased but held that he lacked the required 'appearance' of independence or 'objective' impartiality[5]. The applicant had legitimate grounds for fearing that the Bailiff may have been influenced by his prior participation in the adoption of the measure: that doubt in itself, however slight its justification, was sufficient to vitiate the impartiality of the Royal Court[6]. In its defence of Mr McGonnell's application, the UK pointed to previous case law of the Strasbourg court which indicated that the ECHR did not require 'compliance with any particular doctrine of separation of powers'[7]. The Court was careful to agree with this submission, emphasising that states were not obliged to 'comply with any theoretical constitutional concepts as such'. But for Mr McGonnell the question was not a theoretical one: the Bailiff had, in fact, been directly involved in his case in a manner which cast doubt on the objective impartiality of the court[8].

If the recent cases have indeed provided reasons to question the division between the supposedly distinct categories of apparent bias, they have also quite explicitly reopened the debate between those who favour the 'real danger' test and those who prefer that of the 'reasonable suspicion'. It may be that, in some cases at least, the tests will produce similar results but there *is* a conceptual difference nicely captured by the fear that the reliance on 'real danger' impinges on the requirement that justice should appear to be done[9]. There is a link here with *Starrs* and also with *McGonnell*. As Lord Reed said in *Starrs*, the importance of a court being perceived to be independent is that it must command public confidence[10]. But is it the perception of the judge of a 'real danger' or is it the judge's perception of a public suspicion reasonably held? If an analogy may be drawn here with decision-making in the face of scientific uncertainty, there is a division between those who would rely on the scientific analysis of the judge and those who would insist on the application of a precautionary principle.

1   *Locabail (UK) Ltd v Bayfield Properties Ltd* [2000] QB 451 at 473.
2   *Locabail (UK) Ltd v Bayfield Properties Ltd* [2000] QB 451 at 473.
3   *R v Bow Street Metropolitan Stipendiary Magistrate, ex parte Pinochet Ugarte (No 2)* [2000] 1 AC 119 at 135.
4   *McGonnell v UK* (2000) 30 EHRR 289.
5   Adopting the test applied in *Findlay v UK* (1997) 24 EHRR 221.
6   *McGonnell v UK* (2002) 30 EHRR 289 at 308.
7   *McConnell v UK* (2000) 30 EHRR 289 at 307, and see, in particular, the concurring opinion of Sir John Laws sitting as an ad hoc judge.
8   See also *Procola v Luxembourg* (1996) 22 EHRR 193.
9   *R v Bow Street Metropolitan Stipendiary Magistrate, ex parte Pinochet Ugarte (No 2)* [2000] 1 AC 119 at 142.
10 *Starrs v Ruxton* 2000 JC 208 at 252.

JUDGES AND POLITICS

11.18   The previous sections of this chapter have considered the legal rules which have been put in place to ensure that individual judges are protected, collectively and individually, from inappropriate influences which might otherwise affect the way in which they exercise their judicial functions. We have also seen the important consequences of judicial impartiality for the individuals whose rights and obligations are determined by those judges. However, the significance of judicial independence goes beyond the need to guarantee dispassionate adjudication of disputes brought before the courts: there are wider constitutional considerations which must be satisfied. We have referred elsewhere[1] to the importance of the separation of powers and – perhaps more relevant in the United Kingdom – to the need, in ensuring the accountability of any one branch of government, to maintain the autonomy of those other individuals or institutions who must exercise that control. Particularly in the context of constitutional adjudication, therefore, it is important that the judiciary enjoy sufficient independence from the legislature whose laws they must interpret and apply and from the executive whose actions they must review and sometimes overturn.

These wider considerations are recognised partly in rules imposed by law but also, in the British constitutional tradition, by conventions observed by members of the judiciary themselves. Again, in the traditional British way, current arrangements are perhaps more the product of piecemeal evolution than of principled and deliberate design. Thus, members of the judiciary are disqualified by law from membership of the House of Commons and the Scottish Parliament[2] but while there is no bar to their membership of political parties as such, by convention, members of the judiciary do avoid associating themselves publicly with a particular political party[3] and overt support for a political campaign may constitute grounds for removal under the statutory procedures described earlier[4]. The English judiciary are exhorted to 'exercise their freedom to talk to the media, with 'the greatest circumspection'[5] and they are similarly expected to take care with contributions to public debate in general[6]. Nevertheless, it is increasingly common for members of the judiciary to contribute to debates on law reform, the legal system and matters of constitutional importance. Indeed, many of their contributions are referred to in this book.

Interestingly, it seems that while the independence of the judiciary is promoted by a deliberate distance from party political activity, judges are also protected against the imposition of penalties for expressing criticism of the legislature or the executive. In *Wille v Liechtenstein*[7] the European Court of Human Rights held that the refusal by Prince Hans-Adams II of Liechtenstein to reappoint the applicant to judicial office following their disagreement over the interpretation of the constitution and the jurisdiction of the Liechtenstein Constitutional Court amounted to a violation of the applicant's ECHR, art 10 right to freedom of expression.

As to the judiciary's formal separation from Parliament and the executive, until recently, the issue was dominated in the United Kingdom by, (a) the former constitutional position of the Lord Chancellor and (b) the status of the former Law Lords and (c) the appointment of senior judges to conduct inquiries into matters of political controversy or great public interest. The reform of the position of the Lord Chancellor (the combination of the office with that of Secretary of State for Justice; the separate creation of the Lord Speaker of the House of Lords and the designation of the Lord Chief Justice as head of the English judiciary under the Constitutional Reform Act 2005) and the creation of the UK Supreme Court have removed the first two concerns from the constitutional agenda. Item (c) retains its vitality.

1   At p 38.
2   House of Commons Disqualification Act 1975, Sch 1, para 1 and SA 1998, s 15; and see p 73. In terms of the Scottish judiciary this covers judges of the Court of Session, the chairman of the Scottish Land Court, sheriffs principal, sheriffs and stipendiary magistrates.
3   Guidance for judges published by the English Judges' Council makes clear that: 'A Judge must forego any kind of political activity and on appointment sever all ties with political parties' (*Guide to Judicial Conduct*, 2004 (updated to 2008)).
4   See pp 304–305.
5   Guide to Judicial Conduct para 8.1.1. The English rules were formerly promulgated as the 'Kilmuir rules'.
6   Ibid para 8.2.
7   *Wille v Liechtenstein* (2000) 30 EHRR 558; and see 'Freedom of Expression: Disqualification from Public Office' (2000) EHRLR 196.

Judicial inquiries

11.19   The Law Lords, as we have seen, are for the moment both members of the legislature and members of the judicial branch of government. In that former capacity they may be involved, by virtue of their membership of a House of Lords select committee for example, in scrutiny and perhaps criticism of the work of government. Somewhat analogous to this scrutinising role – but with important differences – is the involvement of senior judges in what may broadly be described as 'judicial inquiries'. These may take a number of different forms and go by a variety of different names. Royal Commissions are frequently chaired by judges[1], public inquiries may be permitted by statutes dealing with particular subject areas[2], and judges may be appointed to chair inquiries under the Inquiries Act 2005[3]. In recent years inquiries involving Scottish judges have included Lord Cullen's inquiries into the shootings at Dunblane Primary School in March 1996[4] and the Paddington rail crash[5], Lord Clyde's inquiry into the removal from children from Orkney following claims of child abuse[6] and inquiries by Lords Coulsfield[7] and Bonomy[8] respectively into aspects of civil and criminal procedure. Recently Lord Gill has been undertaking an inquiry into civil justice and Lord Penrose an inquiry into NHS infections from blood products. The (McKie) Fingerprint Inquiry is chaired by The Rt Hon Sir Anthony Campbell, a retired Northern Ireland appeal court judge.

The desirability of judicial involvement in such inquiries and the implications of that involvement for judicial independence are not easy to assess. On the one hand it is clear that there is a public appetite for 'judicial' scrutiny of the executive. There is a perception that in relation to issues of intense political controversy – particularly where doubts have been cast as to the probity of government action – the 'truth' is more likely to come out at the hands of a judge than at those of elected politicians. So, for example, in July 2003 when the House of Commons Select Committee on Foreign Affairs published its report on the use of military intelligence by the government in the lead-up to the Iraq war[9] the leader of the Liberal Democrats, Charles Kennedy, criticised the report as incomplete and demanded that an 'independent judicial inquiry' be appointed[10]. Indeed, the establishment of a judicial inquiry can become, itself, a campaigning objective: the establishment of the Saville Inquiry into 'the events of Sunday, 30th January 1972 which led to loss of life in connection with the procession in Londonderry on that day'[11] followed one such campaign.

There is no doubt that such inquiries can provide much-needed scrutiny[12] and may be a useful addition to the various mechanisms for accountability of the executive which are explored elsewhere in this book[13]. However, this method of scrutiny does not fall squarely within our traditional understanding of the judicial role – while evidence is heard and conclusions are reached, such an inquiry is not a 'court case' and does not produce any legally binding decision or order – and is more akin to the kind of political inquiry which is ordinarily carried out by parliamentary committees. Although the involvement of a judge may appear to add 'legitimacy' to an investigation[14], this legitimacy may be more apparent than real and sceptical observers may see the appointment of a judge as an attempt to 'pass the buck'. From the perspective of independence of the judiciary we should remain alert to the potential difficulties of involving judges in a process which may lead them to criticise government or to propose legislative or administrative changes. Their status as judges inevitably gives such proposals weight but it may also bring them dangerously close to overstepping the bounds of their constitutional role. This was particularly evident in the case of the Hutton inquiry[15].

1 For example, the Royal Commission on Local Government in Scotland 1966–69 was chaired by Lord Wheatley.
2 For example, the Public Inquiry into the Piper Alpha Disaster, chaired by Lord Cullen, was established in terms of the Offshore Installations (Public Inquiries) Regulations 1974, SI 1974/338. See Cm 1310.
3 Formerly the Tribunals of Inquiry (Evidence) Act 1921.
4 Cm 3386.
5 The *Ladbroke Grove Rail Inquiry*. Lord Cullen was appointed by the Health and Safety Executive, with the consent of the Deputy Prime Minister (the minister responsible for transport), under the Health and Safety at Work etc Act 1974, s 14.
6 *Report of the Inquiry into the Removal of Children from Orkney in February 1991* (HMSO).
7 *Report by Working Party on Court of Session Procedure* (2000).
8 Lord Bonomy *Improving Practice – The 2002 Review of the Practices and Procedure of the High Court of Justiciary.*
9 *The Decision to go to War in Iraq* (HC Paper 813 (2002–03)).
10 Reported by the BBC on 8 July 2003. A public inquiry into the death of David Kelly was later established under Lord Hutton. This reported ((2003–04) HC 247) in Feb 2004 amidst great controversy.
11 Better known as the 'Bloody Sunday Inquiry'. The terms of reference for the inquiry were announced by Prime Minister Blair on 29 January 1998 (HC Debs, cols 501–503). Although chaired by a Lord of Appeal in Ordinary, the two other Members of the inquiry are senior members of the Canadian (Hon W Hoyt) and Australian (Hon J L Toohey) judiciary. The inquiry continues.
12 See M Flinders 'Mechanisms of judicial accountability in British Central Government' (2001) 54 *Parl Aff* 51.
13 See ex p chs 9 and 10.
14 See G Drewry 'Judicial inquiries and public reassurance' [1996] PL 368.
15 See note 10 above.

AN APPRAISAL

11.20 It should be apparent from even a brief consideration of the issues discussed in this chapter that the concepts of judicial independence and impartiality raise difficult questions. The variety of legal rules and institutional mechanisms which have been put in place to preserve the independence of the judiciary do not always present a coherent picture. Senior judges themselves disagree not only on what is required to preserve judicial independence but on how to express the requirements: a point illustrated by the recent cases, discussed at pp 312–316 of this chapter, concerning the common law test for apparent bias. In a quite different environment, judges have encountered difficulties in defining exactly what judicial independence demands in terms of sentencing practice. In proceedings on the Criminal Justice and Licensing (Scotland) Bill the Lord Justice General and the Lord Justice Clerk raised "constitutional" objections to the creation of a Sentencing Commission for Scotland with a power to issue sentencing guidelines for use by the judiciary[1]. Whilst the issue of statutory guidelines by the Parliament would be acceptable, the issue of guidelines by a quango (or at least one without a judicial majority) was not.

Perhaps one reason for the difficulties which surround this topic is that, at least on the face of it, judicial independence is an umbrella under which a number of competing, and even contradictory, concerns attempt to shelter. There is the recognition that the judiciary requires to be protected from undue influence, principally from government but also from the parties before them. However it is also acknowledged that those affected by judicial decision-making need some protection from the judiciary. They are entitled to expect that determinations about their legal rights and obligations – affecting their liberty, personal status, family and property – are not affected by what might be described as 'non-legal' and irrelevant considerations such as a judge's personal views about race, religion or politics. At a more fundamental constitutional level, it is understood that the independence of the judiciary is essential to preserve the rule of law by controlling, where necessary, the exercise of legislative and executive power and by upholding the rights of individuals and minority groups. Yet this desire to ensure government 'according to law' is tempered by a further concern that the judiciary themselves ought not to overstep the bounds of their role by interfering unnecessarily with the work of government.

Again, while it is accepted that reform of the judicial system may be necessary to deal with threats to judicial independence and to preserve public confidence – by, to take a current example, completely removing senior judges from the legislature – it is equally important to the preservation of public confidence that judges are seen to be robust and that the work of the courts is not disrupted by frequent, sometimes trivial, accusations of bias. Over-zealous pursuit of an absolutely impartial tribunal is not only futile but is damaging if it is allowed to go too far and concern for impartiality must be considered in light of the problems caused by delays and the perceived advantages to be gained by individuals who may stall legal proceedings by raising objections to an adjudicator's independence.

1 See SP JC OR 12 May 2009.

Chapter 12

Citizen and State

INTRODUCTION

12.1   Any constitution has to define not only the different institutions of the state[1] and their interrelationships but also the relationships between the state and the members of its population. The state exercises powers over its people, some of which may be very burdensome, but it also confers benefits. Individuals have rights to those benefits and must, to an extent, enjoy protection from state powers. Equally, however, they have responsibilities to both the state and to each other. It is, therefore, necessary for constitutions to define the extent of the powers exercisable by the state against the individual and then the extent to individuals may be protected from the use of those powers. In very large measure those protections are conferred, in the modern law, in the form of the rights deriving from the European Convention on Human Rights (ECHR), and these are discussed below, along with an analysis of a selection of the principal powers exercisable by the police and authorities which impinge most acutely on individual liberty. Before doing so, however, we should consider the concept of citizenship and, in summary form, some elements of the closely-related law of immigration.

1 Although the state is the entity to which citizenship normally relates, the European Union also attributes rights to its citizens (EC Treaty Art 19).

CITIZENSHIP

12.2   We have referred so far to the relationship of 'individuals' to the state but we quickly find that individual persons have to be differentiated one from another to produce a variety of different relationships which vary according to the status of each individual and the area of state activity with which we are concerned. Different degrees of connection with the state define different rights and responsibilities. We shall find that it is, in principle, mere presence within the United Kingdom which determines access to the general rights under the ECHR[1]. For the purposes of specific areas of law, however, rights are defined by the legislation concerned. Levels of university fees, for example, vary according to whether students are 'settled' in the United Kingdom and have been 'ordinarily resident' here for at least three years[2]. General rules as to equality and non-discrimination[3] apply without special regard to citizenship and Art 14 of the ECHR which prohibits discrimination has been held to have similar effect[4]. It was indeed on this ground that in *A v Home Secretary*[5] the House of Lords held that, despite the closely entwined immigration aspects of the case, distinctions between UK national and foreign terrorist suspects could not be sustained. But in the United Kingdom, as in other countries, the core concept of citizenship serves to define a degree of connection or belonging to the country which then serves as a common framework for determining the rights and responsibilities of those classed as citizens. To an extent, the need for a definition of citizenship is driven by the demands of international law. States are, however, free to determine their own rules[6].

In the United Kingdom the process of defining citizenship has followed a complex historical pattern which has produced some difficult modern rules which are badly in need of reform[7]. The historical complexity derives from the slow emergence of the legal concept of citizenship, as opposed to that of being a 'British subject', and the fluctuating pressures (both opportunities and constraints) of disengagement from the British Empire. These led, in particular, to rules which, since the British Nationality Act 1948, have been required to decouple rights to citizenship of the United Kingdom from the rights to settle ('right of abode') in the country[8]. The British Nationality Act 1981 which, in its time, attempted to simplify the law but has since been frequently amended[9] now provides for six different categories of citizens[10]: British citizen, British overseas territories citizen, British overseas citizen, British national (overseas), British protected person and British subject. All but the first two are, however, 'residual' in the sense that they are transitional categories to which no new members can be admitted and are, therefore, in decline. The principal way in which British citizenship may be acquired under the 1981 Act is by birth in the United Kingdom where the mother is a British citizen[11] or adoption where the adopter is a citizen. Alternatively, citizenship may be acquired by registration (by right or by decision of the Secretary of State)[12] or by naturalisation[13]. Citizenship may be renounced by notice/declaration to the Home Secretary, a step required by any citizen who wishes to apply for citizenship of a country whose laws deny the option of dual citizenship – not a position adopted in the United Kingdom. It is, however, possible for the Home Secretary to deprive a person of British citizenship where (a) that person is also a national of another state and (b) the Home Secretary is satisfied that deprivation would be conducive to the public good[14].

A separate source of ambiguity in relationship to citizenship is the tendency to use the term to define *political* as opposed to legal rights and responsibilities. The Conservative Government's *Citizen's Charter* of 1991 and, more recently, the Labour Government's focus since 2006 on "Britishness" are illustrations of the promotion of political rather than strictly legal purposes. Reforms proposed by the Goldsmith review[15] sought a simplification of the law but also, as a part of the political strengthening of citizenship, proposed a group of measures designed to 'enhance the bond of citizenship', such as citizenship education and citizenship ceremonies.

In the meantime, however, the existing legal rights and responsibilities of citizenship may be summarised[16]:

Right of abode and free movement

- Right of abode and freedom of movement in the UK;
- Freedom of movement within the Common Travel Area and the European Economic Area;
- Expectation of issue of a British passport

Right of protection – and duty of allegiance

- Entitled to request that the State exercises diplomatic protection where they have suffered a wrong at the hands of another State;
- Entitled to request consular assistance when abroad;
- Entitled to domestic protection;
- Duty of allegiance to the Crown;
- Duty to obey the law when in the UK – liable for certain offences in the UK even if committed abroad

Civic rights

- Right to vote where registered as resident in Westminster and European Parliamentary elections, in local and devolved elections;
- Right to vote in Parliamentary and European Parliamentary elections where valid overseas declaration made (contingent upon UK residence and registration in preceding 15 years);
- Right to stand in elections, subject to residence requirements in local elections;
- Duty to provide information for purpose of electoral registers on request;
- Right to campaign in referendum if resident in UK or appearing on one of the electoral registers

Although the reforms of the substantive categories of citizenship proposed by Goldsmith have not yet been undertaken, one initiative which has been embarked upon is that of the simplification of the routes open to would-be citizens (from non-EEA countries)[17]. In some measure the current Borders, Citizenship and Immigration Bill implements these proposals, with provision for temporary residence, a period of probationary citizenship, and then permanent residence citizenship.

1 See p 330.
2 Education (Fees and Awards) (Scotland) Regulations SSI 2007/152.
3 See now the current Equality Bill which will consolidate and extend the law in this area.
4 See *int al Belgian Linguistics Case (No 2)* (1968) 1 EHRR 252.
5 [2005] 2 AC 68.
6 *Nottebohm* Case (*Liechtenstein v Guatemala*) ICJ Reports 1955, 4.
7 For brief account of the history and the current rules, together with proposals for reform, see Lord Goldsmith, *Citizenship: Our Common Bond* 2008 (Goldsmith).
8 The Commonwealth Immigrants Act 1962 and the Immigration Act 1971.
9 British Nationality (Hong Kong) Act 1997, British Overseas Territories Act 2002; Nationality, Immigration and Asylum Act 2002.
10 Goldsmith paras 17, 18, 27 and Annex C.
11 Or 'settled' in the UK ie 'ordinarily resident' without immigration restrictions.
12 1981 Act s 1(3), (4).
13 Ibid s 6.
14 British Nationality Act 1981 s 40(2) as amended by the Immigration, Asylum and Nationality Act 2006, s 56. Citizenship acquired by registration may also be revoked on grounds of fraud or concealment of a material fact.
15 See note 7.
16 Goldsmith Report 5–6.
17 *The Path to Citizenship: Next Steps in Reforming the Immigration System* (Home Office, 2008); *Government response to the consultation* (2008).

IMMIGRATION CONTROL[1]

12.3   It has already been noted that the development of the law of citizenship has been closely entwined with the development of the right to enter and live in the United Kingdom – the right of abode. There has been the need for controls – still contained in the Immigration Act 1971, as amended – to be imposed on all those who, in terms of the British Nationality Act 1981, lack British citizenship and, therefore, the right of abode.

As also already noted, however, there are two categories of non-citizen which receive special treatment – a special treatment which extends to their position under immigration law. These are citizens of the Republic of Ireland[2] and citizens of other EU states[3] and of Iceland, Liechtenstein, Norway and Switzerland[4]. Though liable to deportation, these categories are not subject to the normal immigration controls.

Immigration control is in the hands of a Home Office agency known (since 2008) as the UK Border Agency. The Agency implements and enforces an elaborate and complicated code of regulations contained in the Immigration Act 1971 (as comprehensively amended[5]) and the Immigration Rules made (and, again, frequently amended) under s 3(2) of the Act for application by immigration officers at ports and airports of entry. The Act and Rules create different categories of would-be entrants to the country, by reference to their need (or not) for a visa and the purpose of their visit – as short-term visitor, student, au pair, employee or (on a 'points-based' system) as highly skilled migrants, entrepreneur migrants, investor migrants and some others[6]. Under this system, minimum points totals must normally be achieved, by reference to levels of education, other qualifications, age, previous earnings and wealth.

Separately the Act and Rules (Parts II, IIA and IIB) make provision for applications made by those who seek admission as refugees claiming protection under the Geneva Convention 1951 ie on the grounds of a well-founded fear of being persecuted for reasons of race, religion, nationality, membership of a particular social group or political opinion but is unable or unwilling to see protection in his or her own country. Decisions made by immigration officers may be taken on appeal to the Asylum and Immigration Tribunal[7] and thereafter, on statutory review, to the Inner House of the Court of Session – with some matters, eg a refusal of leave to appeal by the Tribunal, subject to common law judicial review[8]. If the decision was made on the grounds of national security, the appeal lies to the Special Immigration Appeals Commission[9], with further review by the Court of Session.

1 For a comprehensive introduction, see RM White *Immigration* SME Reissue 2003.
2 1971 Act s 2 as amended.
3 Immigration Act 1988 s.7.
4 Switzerland, although not a member of the European Economic Area (cf Iceland, Liechtenstein and Norway which are), is defined as an 'EEA State' by the Immigration (EEA) Regulations 2006, SI 2006/1003.
5 And to be further amended by the Borders, Citizenship and Immigration Bill 2009.
6 Special, recently controversial, provision is made for former members of the Brigade of Gurkhas.
7 Asylum and Immigration (Treatment of Claimants etc) Act 2004 and SI 2005/230 (as much

amended) . Appeals to the Tribunal are decided by one or more Tribunal members 'immigration judges', with the possibility of a reconsideration by a differently constituted panel.
8 In *Tehrani v Home Secretary* 2007 SC (HL) 1 the House of Lords held that, in the judicial review of decisions of the Asylum and Immigration Tribunal, both the Court of Session and the English Administrative Court had jurisdiction.
9 Special Immigration Appeals Commission Act 1997.

DEPORTATION, REMOVAL AND EXTRADITION

12.4   Just as British citizenship carries with it the right to enter and reside in the United Kingdom, British citizens are not subject to powers to remove or deport them. Non citizens, however, have no such immunity. They are subject to two principal powers. First, the regime of immigration control itself necessarily incorporates a power to remove those in breach of the rules as a means of their enforcement. Secondly, they are subject to a power of the Home Secretary to deport when this would be conducive to the public good or where a trial court has recommended deportation after conviction of an offence punishable with imprisonment[1]. In the latter case, such recommendations may, like other sentencing decisions, be appealed to the High Court of Justiciary[2]. Once an order to remove or deport has been made, the decision may be appealed to the Asylum and Immigration Tribunal (as above).

Quite different considerations arise where a person physically present (and whatever their citizenship or residence status) in the United Kingdom may be subjected to extradition proceedings designed to ensure his or her removal to another country for the purpose either of standing trial for a criminal offence or for punishment in respect of conviction of an offence.

The modern law is contained in the Extradition Act 2003 and this contains two distinct statutory schemes. Part 1 of the Act relates to 'category 1' countries, defined as those which are EU member states[3]. Part 2 relates to 'category 2' countries, which are all those other countries designated for extradition purposes. The principal difference between the two is that proceedings under Part 1 are almost entirely judicial but that proceedings under Part 2 also involve the intervention of the Home Secretary.

Part 1 proceedings begin with the submission by the appropriate judicial authority of the other country of an arrest warrant to, for Scotland, the Crown Office[4] which then ensures its execution and the commencement, by the Lord Advocate[5], of proceedings before the sheriff of Lothian and Borders[6]. The Act requires the sheriff to decide whether the offence specified in the warrant is an extradition offence[7]; whether any specified "bars to extradition" (e.g. double jeopardy or the passage of time or conviction in absence) apply[8]; and whether the person's extradition would be compatible with Convention rights[9]. If satisfied on all counts, the sheriff must order the person's extradition. There is a right of appeal to the High Court of Justiciary[10] As examples of such appeals, see *Goatley v HMA*[11] and *La Torre v HMA*[12] in which questions about devolution issues in relation to the Lord Advocate's role and the absence in Scotland of appeals to the House of Lords in criminal cases on grounds of were raised. See also *Campbell v HMA*[13] in which the views of Lord Bingham in *Dabas v High Court of Justice in Madrid*[14] on the interpretation of Part 1 of the 2003

327

Act in the light of the European Council Framework Decision of 13 June 2002 were adopted (para 2).

Meanwhile, extradition to category 2 countries is handled rather differently under Part 2 of the Act. The principal modification is that, as with the earlier treaty-based regimes, the Home Secretary has a significant role. In the first place, it is he who initiates the procedure by certifying the incoming request as valid[15] and forwards it (once again, in Scotland, to a sheriff in Lothian and Borders) for consideration. More importantly, the judicial stage ends not with an order to extradite but, subject to an appeal to the High Court Justiciary, with the return of the case to the Home Secretary for further consideration[16] including the issue of whether the death penalty might be imposed in the receiving state[17]. In the absence of specified factors requiring him not to do so, the Home Secretary must order the person to be extradited.

1   Immigration Act 1971 s 3.
2   See eg *Alili v HMA* 2008 SCCR 566.
3   All EU states have ratified the European Council Framework Decision of 13 June 2002, which Part 1 of the 2003 Act transposes into UK law.
4   S 2.
5   S 191.
6   S 67(1)(b) interpreted as *any* sheriff of the sheriffdom.
7   S 10.
8   Ss 11–20.
9   S 21.
10 Ss 26, 216(9).
11 [2006] 2008 JC 1.
12 [2006] HCJAC 56.
13 [2008] HCJAC 11.
14 [2007] 2 AC 31 at para. 4.
15 S 70.
16 S 92.
17 S 94.

LIMITATIONS ON STATE POWER AND PROTECTION OF THE INDIVIDUAL

12.5   It has been noted above that the overarching concept of citizenship does much to define the relationship between individuals (both citizens and non-citizens) and the state. In particular, citizenship in large measure determines a person's right to reside permanently in the United Kingdom and whether he or she could be required to leave. But, even if the current law of citizenship were to be reformed, it could never provide a detailed account of all the rules which determine the relationship between state power and individual freedoms. For the most part, in the law of Scotland, we look to the particularities of the extent of state power and individual freedom, as defined in specific rules contained mainly in statute, but also in the common law. A selection of some of the higher-profile instances of such power-freedom contexts is provided in pages 344–352 of this chapter. However, those specific instances have to be understood within the context, on the one hand, of the European Convention on Human Rights (ECHR) and the Human Rights Act 1998 (pp 329–344) and, on the other, of the statutory 'information' rights of individuals (pp 352–361). The law across the entire scope of this chapter is in flux – especially, in recent years, because of the enactment of substantial terrorist (or anti-terrorist) legislation by the Westminster Parliament. The principal components are the Terrorism Act 2000, the Anti-Terrorism, Crime and Security Act 2001, the Prevention of Terrorism Act 2005, the Terrorism Act 2006. The detailed content of this legislation cannot be considered here. However, the impact of terrorism legislation is taken into account at relevant points of this chapter.

HUMAN RIGHTS

12.6   When describing in Chapter 1 our 'model' constitution, we suggested it would be natural to include within that constitution a list of rights and freedoms which were to be regarded as 'fundamental', to be enjoyed by citizens and others to whom the state has responsibility, and which were enforceable in the courts, against the state itself. However, one consequence of the absence of a written constitution in the UK has been the concomitant absence of a 'Bill of Rights' in the sense understood in other democracies around the world. The traditional doctrine of the supremacy of Parliament (see p 106) to which the courts have given effect precludes the striking down of Westminster legislation on any grounds, including on grounds of interference with individual rights. Similarly, so far as executive (rather than legislative) action is concerned, historical explanations are grounded in an assertion that the state is generally free to act in whatever manner it sees fit, unless it is expressly prohibited from particular conduct by the legislature[1]. As we have seen, (pp 108–109) the higher courts have in recent years suggested that parliamentary supremacy may not be absolutely unqualified – particularly where individual rights and freedoms are at risk. This new approach may be viewed by some as little more than a change of tone or shift of emphasis but, as we will see, it has been accompanied by the use by the courts of still relatively new mechanisms for the protection of human rights.

In this chapter we discuss the institutional framework which has been created following the incorporation of the European Convention on Human Rights by the Human Rights Act 1998 (HRA 1998) and describe the substantive rights which have been conferred by HRA 1998. Our treatment of this area is necessarily brief: there is significant literature available elsewhere[2] which we do not attempt to replicate. In Chapter 13 we describe in more detail the manner in which human rights issues come to be adjudicated upon in the British courts and the approach which the courts have adopted to their determination. We have, elsewhere, described the manner in which the 'Convention rights' also place limits on the legislative competence of the Scottish Parliament[3] and the devolved competence of Scottish Ministers[4] and, again in Chapter 13, we consider the way in which this further 'incorporation' of the ECHR – and the interplay between SA 1998 and HRA 1998 – has been dealt with by the courts.

1 See, for example, *Malone v Commissioner of Police of the Metropolis (No 2)* [1979] Ch 344 discussed below in the context of wire taps.
2 See in particular, R Reed and J Murdoch, *A Guide to Human Rights in Scotland* (2nd ed, 2008); A Lester, D Pannick and J Herberg (eds), *Human Rights Law and Practice* (3rd ed, 2009); R Clayton and H Tomlinson, *The Law of Human Rights* (2nd ed, 2009); A Boyle et al (eds), *Human Rights and Scots Law* (2002).
3 P 139.
4 [1935] KB 249.

The European Convention on Human Rights

12.7   The prominence that we and others give to HRA 1998 is quite understandable in light of its particular role within the United Kingdom legal order.
But the drafters of HRA 1998 did not, of course, begin with a blank canvas.
The Act is, and was quite deliberately intended to be, a vehicle by which certain
rights contained in an international agreement to which the United Kingdom
is a party – the European Convention on Human Rights (ECHR)[1] – become
enforceable at a domestic level in the British courts.

As has been described elsewhere[2] the ECHR was one product of the European
movements which had arisen 'simultaneously and spontaneously' in western
European democracies 'in response to the threat to fundamental human rights
and to political freedom which had all but overwhelmed the European conti-
nent in the [Second World] War and which reappeared after the War in new
forms of totalitarianism'[3]. The United Kingdom signed the ECHR in 1950 and
ratified it in 1951 and in doing so committed itself, as a matter of international
law, to compliance with the ECHR in its treatment of individuals – citizens
and others – over which it had jurisdiction. As an international treaty, however,
the ECHR did not confer rights or obligations as a matter of the domestic law
of the United Kingdom[4] and the principal mechanism available to individuals
who believed their rights had been infringed by the UK, and wished to vindi-
cate those rights, was an application to the European Court of Human Rights
in Strasbourg (ECtHR)[5]. While a relatively large number of such applications
were made to the ECtHR by British citizens, and in many of those the United
Kingdom was found to have breached the Convention, success for an applicant
could represent a pyrrhic victory: while binding in international law, a favourable decision from the ECtHR did not automatically result in a remedy being
afforded the applicant at a domestic level. In some cases, of course, such decisions did lead to changes in domestic law with the express purpose of giving
effect to the ECtHR's interpretation of the ECHR[6].

The ECHR was the product of work carried out by the Council of Europe,
and the Council has continued to play an important role in promoting observance of the ECHR. While the ECtHR is concerned with the adjudication of
individual disputes, the Council has a much wider role in raising awareness
of human rights issues, engaging in public education projects, encouraging
cultural exchange and participating in activities designed to assist in the development of emerging democracies through, for example, election monitoring.

The rights protected by the ECHR reflect the concerns of those who drafted
it: civil and political rights and freedoms drafted predominantly in 'negative'
language, requiring governments and state apparatus to refrain from interfering with those rights and freedoms. Those rights are described in more detail
below.

The ECHR is not, of course, the only international human rights instrument to
which the United Kingdom is a party and other such instruments adopt a more
expansive approach to the rights they seek to protect. The Universal Declaration of Human Rights[7], for example, provides that everyone has the 'right to

work, to free choice of employment, to just and favourable conditions of work and to protection against unemployment' (article 23) as well as a right to 'rest and leisure, including reasonable limitation of working hours and periodic holidays with pay' (article 24). Perhaps unsurprisingly, the Universal Declaration is not binding, per se, even in international law and has not been 'incorporated' in the domestic law of the United Kingdom. By contrast, although it does not say so explicitly on the face of the Act, the Children (Scotland) Act 1995 was intended, amongst other things, to give effect in Scots law to a number of the principles set out in the 1989 United Nations Convention on the Rights of the Child[8]. Space does not permit a more detailed discussion of these and other treaties to which the United Kingdom is party but special mention should be made of one further human rights instrument: the proposed Charter of Fundamental Rights of the European Union. The Charter was drafted by a Convention established by European Council in 1999 and the text of the draft Charter was approved by the Council, the European Parliament and the European Commission in 2000. The Charter sets out a range of civil, political, economic and social rights and freedoms which it is intended will be enjoyed by all those resident within the EU (whether as citizens of the EU or otherwise): including, for example, a right to 'protection of personal data' (article 8), a freedom to 'conduct a business in accordance with Community law and national laws and practices' (article 16), and an obligation on the EU to 'respect cultural, religious and linguistic diversity' (article 22). The text borrows extensively and deliberately from the ECHR[9] but is intended to reflect not only the ECHR but, amongst other things, the 'constitutional traditions and international obligations common to the Member States' (preamble). The Charter forms part of the Lisbon Treaty (see pp 53–54) and will have direct legal effect within EU member states – except the United Kingdom which has secured an 'opt out' – as and when the Lisbon Treaty is ratified.

1 Formally the Convention for the Protection of Human Rights and Fundamental Freedoms of 4 November 1950.
2 See Lester, Pannick & Herberg, op cit, pp 4–8 and C Ovey and R C A White, Jacobs & White *The European Convention on Human Rights* (4th ed, 2006) pp 1–6.
3 Ovey and White, op cit, p3.
4 For discussion of the limited use made of the ECHR by English and Scottish courts prior to the passing of HRA 1998 see p 390.
5 The right of individual petition to the ECtHR was accepted by the United Kingdom in 1966 and for a discussion of the timing of that acceptance see Lester, Pannick & Herberg, op cit, pp 8–9. The ECtHR has been the subject of reform by virtue of both the 11th and 14th Protocols to the ECHR the aim of each being to enable the Court to deal more efficiently with its large and ever growing caseload. See, for example, L Caflisch, *The Reform of the European Court of Human Rights: Protocol No 14 and Beyond* (2006) 6 HRL Rev 403.
6 For example, in *Campbell and Cosans v United Kingdom* (1982) 4 EHRR 165 the applicants, both parents of children in Scottish schools, complained that the possibility of their children being subject to corporal punishment represented a breach of Article 3 ECHR (inhuman and degrading treatment) and of Article 2 of the First Protocol to the Convention (rights of parents to have their children educated in conformance with their own religious and philosophical convictions). The ECtHR rejected the Article 3 complaint but upheld that under Article 2, Protocol 1 and this judgment led to the abolition of such corporal punishment in state schools: see s 48A of the Education (Scotland) Act 1980.
7 Adopted by the United Nations General Assembly in 1948.
8 The Convention was ratified by the United Kingdom on 16 December 1991. For discussion of the Convention and the 1995 Act, see K M Norrie, *Children (Scotland) Act 1995* (revised edition, 1998) and A Cleland and E Sutherland, *Children's Rights in Scotland* (2nd ed, 2001).

9 Indeed, the preparation of the Charter was driven at least partly in response to the opinion of
the European Court of Justice that it would not have been possible for the EU to accede directly
to the ECHR without amendment of the EC Treaty: see Opinion 2/94, [1996] ECR I-1759. The
development of a human rights jurisprudence by the ECJ, and the history of the Convention and
drafting of the Charter, are also topics treated extensively elsewhere: see P Alston, *The EU and
Human Rights* (1999); G de Burca, 'The Drafting of the European Union Charter of Fundamental Rights' 2001 26 EL Rev 126; S Peers and A Ward (eds), *The EU Charter of Fundamental
Rights: Politics, Law and Policy* (2004); N Nic Shuibhne, 'Margins of appreciation: national
values, fundamental rights and EC free movement law' 2009 34 EL Rev 230.

The move to incorporation of the ECHR

12.8   HRA 1998 was a flagship policy for the first Blair government. The
enactment of a Bill of Rights by the 'incorporation' of the ECHR had been
forecast by the Labour Party prior to the 1997 general election[1] and then in the
White Paper Rights Brought Home[2]. The government saw incorporation as an
integral part of its 'comprehensive programme of constitutional reform' which
was aimed at increasing individual rights, decentralising power, opening up
government and reforming Parliament. The White Paper described the continuing effect on the British people of non-incorporation as 'a very practical one.
The rights, originally developed with major help from the United Kingdom,
are no longer actually seen as British rights. And enforcing them takes too
long and costs too much'[3]. The elimination of the delay and of the expense
involved in enforcing rights protected by the ECHR in Strasbourg was seen as
one of the many benefits of incorporation. Other advantages included the fact
that 'the rights will be brought much more fully into the jurisprudence of the
courts throughout the United Kingdom and their interpretation will thus be far
more subtly and powerfully woven into our law' and that 'British judges will
be enabled to make a distinctively British contribution to the development of
the jurisprudence of human rights in Europe'[4]. Perhaps most important, in the
view of the government, was what it perceived to be evidence of the failure of
the then existing arrangements: the number of cases in which the United Kingdom had been found to have violated rights protected by the Convention. While
such violations could not be attributed to one single cause, an important factor
was the lack of any 'framework within which the compatibility with Convention rights of an executive act or decision can be tested in the British courts'[5].

As was made clear in Rights Brought Home[6], the Human Rights Bill which
became HRA 1998 was the successor to a line of (private members') Bills
which from 1987 onwards had unsuccessfully sought to incorporate the Convention. All had failed in Parliament because of the lack of governmental support. The two main political parties had previously resisted incorporation and
it was a resistance which extended beyond politicians. Many commentators
opposed the trend towards what they saw as the transformation of matters of
social and political debate into issues about rights; and their transfer from political fora, above all Parliament, into the courts for resolution[7]. The general arguments for and against incorporation provided a platform for a more specific
debate about which bodies or authorities should be bound, in domestic law, by
the terms of the Convention. In the view of the protagonists, much would be
gained by making ministers, local authorities and other public bodies subject to

the Convention. But what about the Westminster Parliament itself? Should Parliament enact a Bill of Rights which would restrict future Parliaments, requiring them always to enact laws which complied with the Convention? Some would say that this was essential if the risks of 'elective dictatorship'[8] were to be overcome: Parliament itself represented the biggest threat to human rights and should be restrained. But could Parliament restrain future Parliaments by passing a new Human Rights Act or did the doctrine of legislate supremacy[9] prevent this? Could the difficulty be overcome by the use of a device similar to that used in ECA 1972, s 2(4)[10]? Would the courts treat a provision which required them to apply the terms of HRA 1998 (and of ECHR) in preference to the terms of a later Act with the same respect as they now accorded ECA 1972?

1   In particular by a 1996 consultation document entitled '*Bringing Rights Home*'.
2   Cm 3782.
3   Cm 3782, para 1.14.
4   Cm 3782, para 1.14.
5   Cm 3782, para 1.16.
6   Cm 3782.
7   See KD Ewing 'The Human Rights Act and Parliamentary democracy' (1999) 62 MLR 79; N Lyell 'Whither Strasbourg? Why Britain should think long and hard before incorporating the European Convention on Human Rights' (1997) 2 EHRLR 132; KD Ewing and C A Gearty 'Rocky Foundations for Labour's new rights' (1997) 2 EHRLR 146.
8   See Lord Hailsham *The Dilemma of Democracy* (1978) ch XX.
9   See p 106.
10 See p 115. Such a device was included in a draft Bill promoted by Lord Lester: see 'The Mouse That Roared: The Human Rights Bill 1995' [1995] PL 198.

The Human Rights Act 1998

12.9   In the event, HRA 1998 steered a new path of some ingenuity through this difficult area. It sought to compel future legislative compliance with the terms of the Convention, while (as is discussed in the following chapter) also acknowledging the continuing force of the Westminster Parliament's legislative supremacy.

The 'Convention rights'

12.10   HRA 1998 sets out (most but not all of) the rights guaranteed by the articles and protocols of the ECHR; names them 'the Convention rights'; and provides that they are to have effect for the purposes of the Act[1].

The Convention rights which by virtue of HRA 1998 are to have effect are (in summary):

THE RIGHT TO LIFE (ECHR, art 2): Everyone's right to life is to be protected by law. However, causing a person's death will not be regarded as a breach of article 2 where that is the result of defending another person from unlawful violence, making a lawful arrest or preventing the escape of a detained person, or taking lawful action to quell a riot or insurrection. This article has been interpreted as not only requiring the state to refrain from taking life unlawfully but as requiring positive measures to be put in place to enable, for example, the review by the courts or other bodies of the use of lethal force by the state and to take effective operational measures to protect the lives of those in the care of the state[2].

THE PROHIBITION OF TORTURE (art 3): No one is to be subjected to torture or to inhuman or degrading treatment or punishment[3].

THE PROHIBITION OF SLAVERY AND FORCED LABOUR (art 4): No one is to be held in slavery or servitude or required to perform forced labour[4].

THE RIGHT TO LIBERTY AND SECURITY (art 5): Everyone has the right to liberty and security of the person and deprivation of liberty is permitted only in specific circumstances (for example after conviction by a competent court, for the purpose of bringing a suspect before a court or, in the case of a minor, for the purpose of educational supervision) and so long as the detention is in accordance with procedures set down by law[5].

THE RIGHT TO A FAIR TRIAL (art 6): In the determination of his civil rights and obligations or of any criminal charge against him, everyone is entitled to a fair and public hearing within a reasonable time by an independent and impartial tribunal established by law. Art 6 goes on to make provision in relation to accessibility of legal proceedings, the presumption of innocence in criminal cases and, again in relation to charges of criminal offences, the giving of adequate time and facilities for the preparation of a defence, availability of legal advice, cross-examination of witnesses and access to an interpreter where necessary. It is one of the most cited and litigated articles of the ECHR and is frequently pled in tandem with claims of breach of common law standards of fair process (see p 378)[6].

THE PROSCRIPTION OF PUNISHMENT WITHOUT LAW (art 7): No one is to be held to be guilty of a criminal offence in relation to conduct which was not an offence when the conduct was committed. This article is concerned with the particular unfairness which arises from retrospective application of the criminal law[7].

THE RIGHT TO RESPECT FOR PRIVATE AND FAMILY LIFE (art 8): Everyone has the right to respect for his private and family life, his home and his correspondence albeit that this right may be interfered with by the state so long as the interference is lawful and necessary 'in the interests of national security, public safety or the economic well-being of the country, for the prevention of disorder or crime, for the protection of health or morals, or for the protection of the rights and freedoms of others'. There is extensive domestic and Strasbourg case law on the proper interpretation of the various different elements of art 8 – what is private life, family life, what amounts to a person's[8] home[9] and their correspondence[10] – and as is discussed below (p 359) art 8 has been a significant driver in the development of the common law of confidence so as to give greater protection to individual privacy.

THE RIGHT TO FREEDOM OF THOUGHT, CONSCIENCE AND RELIGION (art 9): Everyone has the right to freedom of thought, conscience and religion including the freedom to change a religion or belief and to manifest[11] that religion or belief in 'worship, teaching, practice and observance'. Again this freedom may be subject to limitations provided those are prescribed by law and are necessary in the interests of public safety, protection of public order, health or morals or for the protection of the rights and freedoms of others[12].

FREEDOM OF EXPRESSION (art 10): Everyone has the right to freedom of expression, including the right to hold opinions, receive and impart information and ideas without interference by public authority and regardless of frontiers. This article does not prevent the licensing of broadcasting, television or cinemas and the exercise of the freedoms conferred by article 10 'since it carries with it duties and responsibilities, may be subject to such formalities, conditions, restrictions or penalties as are prescribed by law and are necessary in a democratic society, in the interests of national security, territorial integrity or public safety, for the prevention of disorder or crime, for the protection of health or morals, for the protection of the reputation or rights of others, for preventing the disclosure of information received in confidence, or for maintaining the authority and impartiality of the judiciary'[13].

FREEDOM OF ASSEMBLY AND ASSOCIATION (art 11): Everyone has the right to freedom of peaceful assembly and association with others including the right to form and join trade unions. The freedom should not be restricted except as prescribed by law and where necessary in the interests of national security, public safety, protection of health or morals or protection of the rights and freedoms of others. Article 11 does not prevent restrictions being imposed on the exercise of these rights by members of the armed forces, the police or the 'administration of the State'.

THE RIGHT TO MARRY AND FOUND A FAMILY (art 12): Men and women of marriageable age have the right to marry and to found a family, according to the national laws governing the exercise of this right[14].

THE PROHIBITION OF DISCRIMINATION (art 14): The enjoyment of the Convention rights is to be secured 'without discrimination on any ground such as sex, race, colour, language, religion, political or other opinion, national or social origin, association with a national minority, property, birth or other status. This prohibition of discrimination is not 'free standing' – it applies only where another Convention right is engaged – and does not, therefore, provide general protection against discrimination on grounds of sex, race or sexuality in employment in the manner provided for by EU legislation[15].

PEACEFUL ENJOYMENT OF POSSESSIONS (art 1 of protocol 1): Every natural or legal person is entitled to the peaceful enjoyment or his possessions. No one shall be deprived of their possessions except in the public interest and subject to the conditions provided for by law and by the general principles of international law. Article 1 of protocol 1 does not, however, prevent laws being put in place to control the use of property in accordance with the general interest or to secure the payment of taxes, contributions or penalties[16].

THE RIGHT TO EDUCATION (art 2 of protocol 1). No one is to be denied the right to education and in making provision relating to education and teaching the state must respect the right of parents to ensure that such education and teaching conforms with their own religious and philosophical convictions[17].

THE RIGHT TO FREE ELECTIONS (art 3 of protocol 1). States are to hold free elections at reasonable intervals by secret ballot and under conditions which will ensure the free expression of the people in the choice of the legislature[18].

ABOLITION OF THE DEATH PENALTY (arts 1 and 2 of protocol 6). The death penalty is abolished, albeit that states may continue to make provision for the death penalty in respect of acts 'committed in time of war or of imminent threat of war'.

1   HRA 1998, s 1(1)–(3), Sch 1. The Convention rights have effect subject to any designated derogation or reservation from ECHR which has been entered into properly by the UK – see HRA 1998, ss 1(2), 14, 15 and Sch 3. Such a derogation, from ECHR, art 5(1) (liberty and security of the person), was intimated to the Secretariat General of the Council of Europe by the UK on 18 December 2001 in relation to the extended power to detain contained in the Anti-terrorism, Crime and Security Act 2001. The derogation was implemented at a domestic level by the Human Rights Act 1998 (Designated Derogation) Order 2001. Derogations must, however, be justified by reference to art 15 ECHR which provides that such a derogation may be made 'in time of war or other public emergency threatening the life of the nation' and must be limited to 'the extent strictly required by the exigencies of the situation'. The United Kingdom's derogation was held by the House of Lords (*A v Secretary of State for the Home Department* [2005] 2 AC 68) and by the ECtHR (*A & Others v United Kingdom* (2009) 26 BHRC 1) not to have been justified inasmuch as it represented a disproportionate and discriminatory (in treating nationals and non-nationals differently) response to the admitted public emergency faced by the United Kingdom. The 2001 Order was quashed by the House of Lords and the UK withdrew its derogation on 16 March 2005.
2   See *R (Sacker) v HM Coroner for West Yorkshire* [2004] 2 All ER 487; *R (Gentle) v Prime Minister* [2008] 1 AC 1356. There have been failed attempts in the UK and before the ECtHR to argue that art 2 confers a positive right (which must be protected by the state) to choose to end one's life, for example by assisted suicide or euthanasia (see *R (Pretty) v DPP (Secretary of State for the Home Department intervening)* [2001] 1 AC 800; and *Pretty v United Kingdom* (2002) 35 EHRR 1) although if the state chooses to make provision for such a right that will not necessarily amount to a breach of the article.
3   This is one of the most 'absolute' rights guaranteed by the ECHR and is not limited by any exceptions in the way in which, for example, arts 8, 10 and 12 are limited. It is intended to prevent the state from engaging in, or permitting, the use of force or ill-treatment, particularly in relation to detained persons. Cases involving the United Kingdom have concerned, for example, interrogation techniques used by the security forces in Northern Ireland (*Ireland v United Kingdom* (1978) 2 EHRR 25) and the use of corporal punishment on the Isle of Man (*Tyrer v United Kingdom* (1978) 2 EHRR 1). The success of Scottish prisoners in arguing that the practice of 'slopping out' amounted to degrading treatment and a breach of art 3 has been one of the most significant Scottish examples of the use of the Convention since the incorporation of the ECHR by the HRA (and by SA 1998, see p 139): *Napier v Scottish Ministers* 2005 1 SC 229 and see A Lawson and A Mukherjee, 'Slopping out in Scotland: the limits of degradation and respect' 2004 6 EHRLR 645.
4   In 2005, the Joint Committee on Human Rights expressed concerns that certain provisions of the Children and Adoption Bill – which became the Children and Adoption Act 2006 – relating to the imposition of unpaid work as a penalty for breach of a contact order were likely to breach art 4. See Joint Committee on Human Rights, Fifth Report of Session 2005–2006, Legislative Scrutiny: Second Progress Report, HL 90/HC 767.
5   The compatibility of this article with aspects of the United Kingdom's anti-terrorism laws has been particularly controversial and has brought the courts into direct conflict with the

UK government and parliament. As noted above (n 1), the derogation from art 5 which was felt by the United Kingdom government to be required by provisions of the Anti-terrorism, Crime and Security Act 2001 was found not to be justified by reference to art 15 ECHR. The offending provisions themselves – allowing for indefinite detention without trial of certain non-nationals – were held, as had been anticipated by the government, to breach the art 5 rights of those detained (*A v Secretary of State for the Home Department* [2005] 2 AC 68). Parliament responded to this ruling by introducing a system of 'control orders' – effectively house arrest – under the Prevention of Terrorism Act 2005. The procedure by which these control orders have been made was the subject of successful challenge in 2009 on the grounds that they breached the art 6 rights of the individuals concerned: *Secretary of State for the Home Department v F* [2009] UKHL 28, 10 June 2009.

6   See in particular Lester, Pannick & Herberg op cit p 277–348 for much more detailed treatment than could be given here.

7   For an example of the court declining to find a breach of art 7 see *R (McFetrich) v Secretary of State for the Home Department* [2003] 4 All ER 1093 concerning differences in sentencing policy affecting a prisoner transferred from Scotland to England.

8   The ECtHR has made it clear that art 8 rights can in some circumstances be enjoyed by legal persons such as companies as well as by individuals: see *Societe Colas Est v France* (2004) 29 EHRR 373 and *Wieser v Bicos Beteiligungen GmbH v Austria* (2008) 46 EHRR 54.

9   Which may include business premises: see *Niemietz v Germany* (1992) 16 EHRR 97.

10   Interference with the correspondence and other communications of prisoners has been the subject of particular litigation in the Scottish courts: see *Beggs v Scottish Ministers* 2006 SC 649 and *Potter v Scottish Ministers* 2007 SLT 1019.

11   There has been a great deal of debate about the extent to which external, physical symbols of religious belief are 'manifestations' of religious belief. Even where they are, it may be lawful to place restrictions on the wearing or exhibiting of those symbols: see *R (SB) v Governors of Denbigh High School* [2007] 1 AC 100 (a jilbab (headscarf) worn by a Muslim schoolgirl was such a manifestation but it was not a breach of her art 9 rights to require her to adhere to the school's dress code which excluded the jilbab); *R (Playfoot) v Governing Body of Millais School* [2007] EWHC 1698 (Admin) (a 'purity ring' was not a manifestation of Christian belief and art 9 not engaged by a school dress code which forbade the wearing of it); and *R (Watkins-Singh) v Governing Body of Aberdare Girls' High School* [2008] EWHC 1865 (Admin) (a religious bangle worn by a Sikh schoolgirl was a manifestation of her religious beliefs).

12   The protections afforded by art 9 are enjoyed principally by individuals although in some cases churches or other 'collective' entities may act on behalf of individual members of the church in claiming a breach of art 9 rights. See the discussion in Reed and Murdoch, op cit pp 665 to 691.

13   Art 10 is concerned with, amongst other things, rights to engage in the expression of views which may be unpalatable or offensive to 'majority' or 'mainstream' views. This includes the expression of racist opinions or opinions which might provoke religious division (*Jersild v Denmark* (1995) 19 EHRR 1); expressions of support for unlawful activity including terrorism (*Norwood v United Kingdom* (2005) 40 EHRR SE11); political speech (*R v BBC, ex parte ProLife Alliance* [2004] 1 AC 185); and advertising (*Stambuk v Germany* (2003) 36 EHRR 1059). See the discussion below (p 359) concerning those provisions of HRA 1998 which seek to balance art 8 rights with the freedom of the press protected by art 10.

14   States are entitled to exclude same sex couples from the right to marry (*Rees v United Kingdom* (1986) 9 EHRR 56) but not transsexual persons (*Goodwin v United Kingdom* (2002) 35 EHRR 447).

15   And for discussion of the concept of 'other status' see *Kjelsden, Busk Madsen and Pedersen v Denmark* (1976) 1 EHRR 711; and *R (S) v Chief Constable of Yorkshire Police* [2004] 1 WLR 2196.

16   Art 1 of protocol 1 is concerned with rights of property and with the interference with or deprivation of property by the state. Obvious examples concern confiscation or compulsory acquisition of property – which may be permissible provided proper procedures are followed (and art 1, protocol 1 claims are frequently combined with claims about breaches of art 6) and appropriate compensation is paid.

17   See *Campbell and Cosans v United Kingdom* (1982) 4 EHRR 293.

18   See *Hirst v United Kingdom* (No 2) (2006) 42 EHRR 41 and p 74 n 20.

Public Authorities and Convention Rights

12.11   HRA 1998, s 6(1) provides that it is unlawful for a public authority to act in a way which is incompatible with a Convention right[1]. The definition of 'public authority' for the purposes of HRA 1998, s 6 is not straightforward and has been the subject of considerable debate and, recently, reform. Firstly, it provides that 'public authority' includes any 'court or tribunal'[2]. By requiring courts themselves to comply with Convention rights – and not just to enforce compliance by others – it is argued that HRA 1998 has what is described as 'horizontal effect'[3]. Thus, in developing and applying the common law, even in disputes involving only private parties, the courts must do so in a manner which is compatible with the Convention rights of the parties before them[4]. Secondly, HRA 1998 provides that a public authority also includes 'any person certain of whose functions are functions of a public nature'[5] but qualifies this definition with the proviso that even where a person has some public functions 'in relation to a particular act, a person is not a public authority ... if the nature of the act is private'[6]. This part of the definition of 'public authority' has been a cause of difficulty for the English courts in particular[7]. Decisions about what constitutes a 'public function' and, as a consequence, which bodies should be bound to act compatibly with the Convention rights inevitably involve judgments by the courts in areas which are close to the boundary between law and politics. In response to concerns in some quarters about the interpretation of 'public authority' by the courts and the impact which that might have on the protection of individual rights, the Joint Committee on Human Rights has on a number of occasions called for amendment of the definition so as to ensure an expansive rather than restrictive application of HRA 1998[8]. Very specific provision has now been made by the Health and Social Care Act 2008 which does not amend the definition of public authority in HRA 1998 but which does provide that a person 'who provides accommodation, together with nursing or personal care, in a care home for an individual under arrangements made with [the person] under the relevant statutory provisions is to be taken for the purposes of subsection (3)(b) of section 6 of the Human Rights Act 1998 to be exercising a function of a public nature in doing so'[9].

The question of whether a public authority has acted unlawfully in terms of HRA 1998, s 6(1) may be raised in proceedings in 'the appropriate court or tribunal'[10], for instance in an application for judicial review[11]. Breach of Convention rights has, therefore, become a very important new ground for judicial review.

1   This general rule is subject to a number of exceptions and qualifications. For instance, in line with HRA 1998, ss 3, 4 (see below) there is an exception in the case of acts unavoidably required by 'primary legislation'.
2   HRA 1998, s 6(3)(a).
3   For discussion, see D Oliver 'The Human Rights Act and Public Law/Private Law Divides' (2000) 4 EHRLR 343; R Buxton 'The Human Rights Act and Private Law' (2000) 116 LQR 48; N Bamforth 'The true "horizontal effect" of the Human Rights Act 1998' (2001) 117 LQR 34; A L Young 'Remedial and substantive horizontality: the common law and *Douglas v Hello! Ltd*' [2002] PL 232; K Hughes 'Horizontal privacy' (2009) 125 LQR 244.
4   Similarly, the obligation imposed on the courts by HRA 1998, s 3 to interpret primary and subordinate legislation in a manner compatible with Convention rights is relevant in even 'private' disputes.

5   HRA 1998, s 6(3)(b). Excluded from this part of the definition of 'public authority' are 'either House of Parliament or a person exercising functions in connection with proceedings in Parliament'.

6   HRA 1998, s 6(5).

7   See, in particular, *Poplar Housing and Regeneration Community Association v Donoghue* [2002] QB 48; *R (Heather) v Leonard Cheshire Foundation* [2002] 2 All ER 936; *Marcic v Thames Water Utilities* [2002] QB 929; *Aston Cantlow and Wilmcote with Billesley Parochial Church Council v Wallbank* [2004] 1 AC 546 and *L v Birmingham City Council* [2008] 1 AC 95.

8   Joint Committee on Human Rights, Seventh Report of Session 2003-04, 'The Meaning of Public Authority under the Human Rights Act', HL Paper 39/HC 382; Joint Committee on Human Rights, Ninth Report of Session 2006-07, 'The Meaning of Public Authority under the Human Rights Act', HL Paper 77/HC 410.

9   Health and Social Care Act 2008, s145.

10 HRA 1998, s 7(2). For Scotland, see the Human Rights Act 1998 (Jurisdiction) (Scotland) Rules 2000, SSI 2000/301, r 3 of which provides that for the purpose of this section the appropriate court is 'any civil court of tribunal which has jurisdiction to grant the remedy sought'; and Act of Adjournal (Criminal Procedure Rules Amendment No 2) (Human Rights Act 1998) 2000, SSI 2000/315.

11 In all cases, proceedings are subject to the applicant's being a 'victim' for the purposes of the ECHR and subject also to restrictions as to remedies: see HRA 1998, ss 7(1), (3) and 8.

Territorial extent of the Human Rights Act

12.12   Particularly, though not exclusively, as a consequence of the United Kingdom's recent involvement in conflicts in Afghanistan and Iraq, questions have arisen about the extent to which the United Kingdom – through its armed forces – is bound to act compatibly with HRA 1998 where it is operating overseas. It has been held that the application of HRA 1998 depends on the extent to which the United Kingdom exercises 'effective control' of a territory and that, even where effective control of a particular territory is absent, HRA 1998 does apply to activity within British embassies, military bases and the like[1].

1   See *R (Quark Fishing Ltd) v Secretary of State for Foreign and Commonwealth Affairs* [2006] 1 AC 529; *R (Al-Skeini) v Secretary of State for Defence* [2008] 1 AC 153; *R (Hassan) v Secretary of State for Defence* [2009] EWHC 309 (Admin).

Commissions, Commissioners and Others

12.13   HRA 1998 is concerned predominantly with the imposition of an obligation on public authorities to act compatibly with Convention rights. The natural arena within which debates about the scope and meaning of those rights will take place is the courts and the approach of the courts to determining disputes about the rights conferred by HRA 1998 is discussed in chapter 13. It can be, and is, argued by many, however, that the protection of human rights is about much more than the legal enforceability of those rights and the determination of individual disputes in an adversarial contest. Rather, respect for individual rights requires changes in culture within public authorities, public education and awareness-raising about the importance of rights and the application of political pressure to the legislature and the executive to ensure an ongoing focus on the protection of rights.

The perceived need for an official 'flagbearer' for human rights at a domestic level, with a role perhaps comparable to that of the Council of Europe at the

European level, has led in recent years to the creation of commissions and commissioners with broad remits in relation to the promotion and protection of human rights[1]. The Scottish Commission for Human Rights Act 2006 (SCHRA 2006) created the Scottish Commission for Human Rights which now 'trades as' the Scottish Human Rights Commission[2]. The Commission is a statutory corporation comprising a chair (currently Professor Alan Miller) and up to four other members. It has a 'general duty…through the exercise of its functions under this Act, to promote human rights and, in particular, to encourage best practice in relation to human rights', which rights include but are not limited to the Convention rights[3]. To enable it to fulfil this general duty, the Commission has a range of powers including the power to review and recommend changes to 'any area of the law of Scotland' and 'any policies or practices of any Scottish public authorities'[4]. It may also publish information, provide advice, conduct research and provide education and training[5] and it may consult, act jointly with, co-operate with or assist any other person[6]. SCHRA 2006 makes quite careful provision about the manner in which the Commission can become involved in legal proceedings. It is expressly prohibited from providing assistance (which includes advice, guidance and grants) to or in respect of any person in connection with any claim or legal proceedings to which that person is or may become a party[7]. However, the Commission may with the leave, or at the invitation, of the court[8], intervene in legal proceedings for the purpose of making a submission to the court on an issue arising in the proceedings. The provision of SCHRA 2006 which confers this power removes any doubt about the '*vires*' of an attempt by the Commission to intervene in relevant proceedings but does not give the Commission a right of intervention: it will continue to be a matter for the court to decide whether or not to allow such an intervention. The power conferred on the Commission relates to civil proceedings only and excludes children's hearings proceedings[9]. The extent of the Commission[er]'s power to intervene in proceedings was the subject of considerable debate at Stage 1 of the Bill's passage[10].

Because not all aspects of human rights protection in Scotland are devolved under SA 1998 (see p 129), the Great Britain Commission for Equality and Human Rights (CEHR) also has a role to play in Scotland. The CEHR was created by the Equality Act 2006 (EA 2006)[11] and took over the responsibilities formerly discharged by the Equal Opportunities Commission, the Commission for Racial Equality and the Disability Rights Commission. It was given new powers and duties in relation to human rights, with specific provision being made for Scotland to take account of the 'reserved/devolved' boundary. So, EA 2006 provides that the 'Commission shall not take human rights action in relation to a matter if the Scottish Parliament has legislative competence to enable a person to take action of that kind in relation to a matter'[12]. 'Human rights action' is defined by reference to a list of other provisions of EA 2006 but includes the promotion of the understanding of the importance of human rights, encouraging good practice in relation to human rights and encouraging public authorities to comply with section 6 of HRA 1998. In addition, despite its general duty to take account of 'any relevant human rights' in discharging certain of its functions, the CEHR shall not, in the course of discharging those functions 'consider the question whether a person's human rights have been contravened if the Scottish Parliament has legislative competence to enable a person to consider that question'[13]. The potentially unhelpful consequences of these provisions are intended to be ameliorated by provisions which permit the CEHR to take action with the consent of a person 'established by Act of the Scottish Parliament' and whose 'principal duties relate to human rights and are similar to any of the Commission's duties under section 9'[14] and to act jointly or cooperate for a purpose relating to human rights and connected with Scotland[15]. The CEHR has somewhat wider powers in relation to legal proceedings than does the Scottish Commission for Human Rights, being entitled to 'institute or intervene in legal proceedings, whether for judicial review or otherwise, if it appears to the Commission that the proceedings are relevant to a matter in connection with which the Commission has a function'[16]. To avoid any doubt about the CEHR's title and interest to raise proceedings, it is provided explicitly that it is to be 'taken to have title and interest in relation to the subject matter of any legal proceedings in Scotland which it has capacity to institute, or in which it has capacity to intervene, by virtue of subsection (1)'[17].

Amongst a range of other provisions of EA 2006 relating to Scotland, those concerning the constitution of the CEHR are particularly noteworthy. The Commission is to be comprised of between 10 and 15 Commissioners including at least one who has been appointed with the consent of the Scottish Ministers and who 'knows about conditions in Scotland'[18]. The current 'Scottish' Commissioner is Ms Morag Alexander. In addition, the CEHR is required to establish a 'Scotland Committee' the role of which is to advise the CEHR about the exercise of its functions so far as they affect Scotland and with whom the CEHR is obliged to consult before it exercises a function in a manner likely to affect persons in Scotland[19]. Finally, mention should also be made of the Scotland's Commissioner for Children and Young Persons (SCCYP[20]). The SCCYP's general function is to promote and safeguard the rights of children and young people[21] and he has a wide range of powers in the exercise of which she must have regard, amongst other things, to any relevant provisions of the United Nations Convention on the Rights of the Child[22]. The current commissioner is Tam Baillie who took office in May 2009, replacing the first commissioner Professor Kathleen Marshall.

In addition to the role to be played by the commissions described above, there are a number of other bodies, formal and informal, which play a role in generating public debate and discussion about human rights protection and in providing mechanisms of political accountability. At a parliamentary level, the Scottish Parliament has a cross-party group on human rights which meets on a regular basis but which, in terms of status and output, cannot match the Westminster Parliament's Joint Committee on Human Rights. That Committee has proved influential in provoking debate and holding the Westminster Parliament and UK government to account in relation to the impact of both legislation and executive action human rights.

1   In addition to the Scottish and Great Britain Commissions discussed below, the Northern Ireland Human Rights Commission was established in 1999 by the Northern Ireland Act 1998 following the Good Friday Agreement. For discussion of the power of the NIHRC to intervene in legal proceedings see *R (Northern Ireland Human Rights Commission) v Greater Belfast*

Coroner [2002] HRLR 35 and for criticism of the Commission in using its powers to intervene in legal proceedings in the public interest see *Re E (A Child)* [2009] 1 AC 536 per Lord Hoffmann at p 542.

2 See www.scottishhumanrights.com. The Bill which became SCHRA began life as the Scottish Commissioner for Human Rights Bill.

3 SCHRA 2006, s 2.

4 SCHRA, s 4.

5 SCHRA, s 3.

6 SCHRA, s 5.

7 SCHRA, s 6.

8 Which in this context means only the Sheriff Court, Court of Session and Land Court: SCHRA, s 14(9). Section 14(8) provides that this specific power is 'without prejudice to the Commission's capacity to intervene in any proceedings before any court or tribunal under an enactment or in accordance with the practice of the court or tribunal'.

9 SCHRA, s 14.

10 See Stage 1 Report, SP Paper 508, 23 February 2006.

11 EA 2006 was principally concerned with reform of the institutional arrangements for protection of rights and preventing discrimination. So far as reform of the substantive rights in respect of which the CEHR is to have responsibility, this is being undertaken via the Equality Bill currently before the Westminster Parliament.

12 EA 2006, s 7(1).

13 EA 2006, s 7(3).

14 EA 2006, s 7(4).

15 EA 2006, s 7(5).

16 EA 2006, s 30(1).

17 EA 2006, s 30(2).

18 EA 2006, s 2 and Sch 1, para 2(3). Similar provision is made for the appointment of a Commissioner with the consent of the Welsh Ministers and who knows about conditions in Wales.

19 See EA 2006, s 2 and Sch 1, paras 16 to 23. Again, similar provision is made for a Wales Committee.

20 Created by the Commissioner for Children and Young People (Scotland) Act 2003.

21 Ibid, s 4(1).

22 Ibid, s 5(2).

Further reform: A Bill of Rights for the United Kingdom?

12.14   At the outset of this chapter we referred to the importance of relationships between the state and individual: to the benefits which individuals can derive from the exercise of state power and to the importance of providing protections for the individual against the abuse of power by the state. In the years since the incorporation of the ECHR by the HRA 1998 there has developed another debate about the relationship between the state and the individual which sits alongside those which concern rights and protections against state power: that is a debate about responsibilities owed by individuals to one another and to the state itself and the extent to which the enjoyment of fundamental rights is conditional upon the discharge by individuals of those responsibilities. The cruder versions of this debate play out fairly regularly in the pages of the tabloid press, usually in response to a decision of the courts which is perceived to have put the interests (and Convention rights) of an undeserving individual – perhaps a delinquent youth, a hardened criminal or a terrorist suspect – before those of the wider community. Beyond the sensationalist headlines, however, a more sophisticated version of the debate is also taking place and has been given life by the current UK government through its Governance of Britain project and, in particular, its tentative proposals for a Bill of Rights for the United Kingdom. One of the other principal protagonists in the debate has been the Joint Committee on Human Rights whose work has been described above.

In its 2007 Green Paper 'The Governance of Britain'[1], the government announced that it wanted to 'forge a new relationship between government and citizen'. A range of issues were discussed in the Green Paper but a chapter was dedicated to the 'citizen and the state' and canvassed a number of options which, if implemented, might convey to individuals 'a better sense of their British identity in a globalised world'[2]. Options included offering to everyone within the UK 'an easily understood set of rights and responsibilities when they receive citizenship', the launch of a Youth Citizenship Commission and greater investment in education and integration of new citizens to the United Kingdom. In addition, the government asked Lord Goldsmith QC to carry out a review of citizenship, 'looking both at legal aspects and other issues including civic participation and social responsibility'[3]. The outcome of that review was the 2008 report 'Citizenship: Our Common Bond' ('the Goldsmith report', also discussed above at pp 324–325), the predominant focus of which was identifying the distinctions between citizens and other non-citizen residents (such as, for example, those seeking asylum) and seeking to analyse whether those distinctions were rational and defensible. A persistent theme was the importance of identifying responsibilities as well as rights of citizens and Lord Goldsmith recommended that the government consider the formulation of a statement of rights and responsibilities 'which is not intended to be justiciable but will draw on existing rights and duties and rely on those other laws and enactments for their force'[4].

This consideration was to take place as part of the government's wider project of examining the case for a 'British Bill of Rights' which had been adverted to in the Green Paper and by Prime Minister Brown in 2007 when the Green Paper was published[5]. In fact, the initiative so far as discussion about a Bill of Rights was concerned was taken from the government fairly forcefully by the Joint Committee on Human Rights which launched its own inquiry into the need, if any, for such a Bill of Rights. It took evidence from a range of sources – including on one occasion sitting in a Committee Room of the Holyrood Parliament[6] – and in August 2008 produced a comprehensive report in which it concluded that the United Kingdom should adopt a Bill of Rights[7] which would go further than HRA 1998 in conferring a number of new rights including certain social and economic rights but which would not result in a constitutional revolution by giving powers to the courts to strike down primary legislation. So far as responsibilities were concerned, the Joint Committee was clear: 'rights cannot be contingent on performing duties or responsibilities. We recommend that a Bill of Rights and Freedoms should not include directly enforceable duties. However, we acknowledge that responsibilities are implicit in human rights instruments. On that basis, and to that end we suggest that the language of responsibilities could have a role to play in a Bill of Rights and Freedoms, perhaps in the Preamble to the Bill'[8]. Although not described as such, the further Green Paper published by the government in March 2009 – 'Rights and

Responsibilities: developing our constitutional framework'[9] – was in large part a response to the Joint Committee's work and may be viewed as something of a 'retrenchment'. Conceding that the enjoyment of fundamental rights could not be contingent upon the fulfilment of responsibilities, the government nevertheless continued to place significant emphasis on the importance of responsibilities[10] and on the idea of a Bill of Rights *and* Responsibilities. Given that the government also concluded, however, that this Bill of Rights and Responsibilities was not to be legally enforceable and, further, that it was not intended that legislation in this area be brought forward before the next general election, it appears that further reform is some way off.

1   Cm 7170, 2007.
2   Ibid, para 185.
3   Ibid, para 193.
4   The Goldsmith report, para 31.
5   HC Deb 3 July 2007 col. 819.
6   On 10 March 2008.
7   29th Report of Session 2007–08, A Bill of Rights for the UK?, HL Paper 165, HC 150.
8   Ibid, p 6.
9   Cm 7577, 2009.
10 The government sought to identify responsibilities which it could be said were already well-established within the UK. It suggested that in the criminal justice sphere there 'are a number of duties that may be said also to imply an obligation to uphold the law' (Cm 7577, para 2.28) for example in relation to money laundering legislation where there are obligations to disclose information in certain circumstances; and identified other areas, for example in relation to education and child welfare, where new duties might be identified.

POLICE POWERS OF DETENTION AND ARREST

12.15   Reflected in Art 5 of the ECHR are the threats to individuals of the powers of public authorities to deprive them of their personal liberty. Inevitably, the extent of these powers, their limits, and the protections afforded to individuals are a matter of concern, especially since, in the modern law, these powers range widely. A selection may, however, be made under the headings of police powers to detain and arrest, with associated powers to search the person and property and to question suspects. These are treated in the pages which follow. At pages 349–352 below, we move on to the powers of the police and other authorities to maintain public order (including restraints on behaviour in public and the conduct of processions).

But first a word on the police service itself. Many of the powers to be discussed in this section and that which follows are exercisable by public bodies – in the main, ministers at the Scotland or UK level (or civil servants on their behalf) or local authorities – which are established, organised, and accountable in familiar ways[1]. The police service, however, is a special case. It has a tripartite structure[2]. Policing in Scotland is organised at a local level in that local authorities, acting through joint boards to produce eight police authorities[3], provide decentralised provision of premises, equipment and pay for the forces in their areas[4]. They have the important task of appointing the chief constable[5] – the second element. From that point, however, police management diverges from that of other services. Instead of council control over policy and practice in the force, with the local democratic accountability which that implies, it is the chief constable to whom these responsibilities are directly given[6]. One obligation retained by the police authority is that of meeting the cost of any damages awarded against the chief constable where a member of the force has been held liable in a civil action[7].

The third element in the constitutional structure of the police is the Scottish Ministers who have significant powers of central control over police authorities and chief constables. In particular, police funding is very largely a matter for ministerial control[8], as well the size of forces and the general regulation of police organisation[9]. In addition, the provision of some support services for police forces has become the responsibility of the recently established Scottish Police Services Authority which, on a centralised basis, provides information, forensic and training services (including the Scottish Police College and the Scottish Crime and Drug Enforcement Agency)[10]. Complaints against the police are now handled by the independent Police Complaints Commissioner for Scotland[11]. Despite the important contributions, however, of the Scottish Ministers and the centralised agencies, the decentralisation of much operational control to the police authorities and the chief constables ensures that the tradition of avoiding a single national police force has been maintained[12].

Although the governance of police forces as a whole is in the hands of the Scottish Ministers, the police authorities and the chief constables, most police powers are vested in individual officers and, in so far as constables exercise powers which may affect individual liberty, they do so against the background of two important principles. The first is the rule of law[13] itself which seeks to ensure that no invasion of individual rights at the hand of a public official is permitted unless authorised by law which may have its source either in statute or in common law. We shall find that, in the modern law, statute dominates but the police also have common law powers. We should also note, however, that, when obtained, the consent of the individual affected normally removes the need for specific legal authority. For instance, the police need legal authority for a search of premises or of a person. A search conducted with consent, however, is lawful in itself.

The second informing principle derives from art 5 of the ECHR which, subject to specified exceptions, provides that 'everyone has the right to liberty and security of person'. Any laws which confer powers on the police must themselves be compatible with the Convention's requirements.

As we turn to specific police powers, these are dominated by the powers of detention and arrest. In the absence of legal authority, a purported arrest or detention leaves a person free to resist, short of force involving 'cruel excess'[14], any physical constraint and absolves that person from any vulnerability to prosecution for obstruction of the police in the execution of their duty[15].

The principal statutory powers to detain are contained in ss 13–14 of the Criminal Procedure (Scotland) Act 1995[16]. The Act prescribes the circumstances in which the powers may be exercised, the extent of the core and ancillary powers, and the restrictions attached to their exercise. Section 13 provides that where a constable has reasonable grounds for suspecting that a person has committed or is committing an offence at any place he or she may require *that person* (at that place or at any place where the constable is entitled to be) to give his (or her) name and address and may ask for an explanation of the suspicious circumstances; and require *any other person* whom the constable believes to have relevant information to give their name and address (subs (1)). A suspect may be required (with reasonable force) to remain with the constable while the name and address are verified (if that can be done quickly) and the explanation noted (subss (2)–(4)). A person in either category is guilty of a criminal offence if, without reasonable excuse, they fail to comply and may be arrested without warrant (subss (6), (7)). There is also, however, a requirement that the constable informs a suspect of his or her suspicion and of the general nature of the offence and of why the suspect is being asked to remain. A witness must be informed of the suspicion and why the constable requires a name and address. Both must be informed that a failure to comply may be an offence (subs (5)).

Whilst the powers under s 13 are quite limited, those under s 14 are much more intrusive. Where a constable has reasonable grounds for suspecting[17] that a person has committed or is committing a serious offence (an offence punishable by imprisonment), the constable may, for the purpose of facilitating investigations, detain the suspect and take him (or her) as quickly as is reasonably practicable to a police station or other premises or place (subs (1)). It seems clear that a detention may be effected in either a public place or on private property. If on private property, however, entry on the property in the absence of a warrant must be done with consent[18]. Once detained, a person may be questioned and may be searched – using powers applicable also to an arrest (see below) (subs (7)). Reasonable force may be used (subs (8)).

Five protections for the person detained are prescribed:

(1)   At the time of detention the suspect must be informed of the suspicion, the general nature of the offence and the reason for detention (subs (6)).

(2)   Although the suspect may be questioned, he or she is under no obligation to answer a question beyond provision of name and address – and the suspect must be so informed (subs (9)).

(3)   The suspect is entitled to have intimation of the detention sent to a solicitor (or other person reasonably named) without unnecessary delay, and to be informed of this requirement (s 15(1), (2)).[19]

(4)   The police are obliged formally to record details of the detention (times, places, suspected offence, details of intimation under s 15) (s 14(6)).

(5)   And, most importantly, a detention is limited to a maximum period of six hours – although a detention must be terminated earlier if the person is arrested[20]; detained under another enactment (there can be no re-detention under s 14); or there are no longer any grounds for detention (subss (2)–(5).

Whilst the powers exercisable under ss 13 and 14 of the Criminal Procedure (Scotland) Act 1995 are the most commonly exercised statutory powers of detention, they do not stand alone. There are many others, the most prominent of which are those under s 24 of the Misuse of Drugs Act 1971, s 59 of the Civic Government (Scotland) Act 1982 (in respect of *int al* drunkenness), s 6 of the Road Traffic Act 1988 (drink driving), and s 41 of the Terrorism Act 2000[21].

In addition to all of these, however, police officers have common law powers of arrest. Statutory powers of detention were introduced to plug gaps in the common law powers but not to replace them entirely. Common law powers of arrest divide into the power to arrest under the authority of a warrant issued by a competent court[22] and the power to arrest without a warrant. Few problems arise in the execution of a warrant to arrest, normally accompanied by a warrant to search persons and premises. On the other hand, arrest without warrant at common law is more problematic. As with the statutorily conferred powers, however, the key components are the power of arrest itself, ancillary powers (especially the power to search), procedural requirements, and protections afforded to individuals[23].

As to the power itself, on the authority of the mid-nineteenth century case of *Peggie v Clark*[24] which has received consistent support to the present day, the exceptional circumstances which justify an arrest without seeking a warrant are that there are reasonable grounds to suspect that the person has committed an offence but *also* that a prompt arrest is justified by the seriousness of the crime (eg murder) and/or the risk that the offender may abscond[25].

Whatever the source of authority to make an arrest or detention, the arrest or detention is not effective without both an appropriate statement of intention to arrest or detain on the part of the police officer and, as necessary, the use of an appropriate degree of physical restraint. As to the words to be used, no precision is required but they must make clear that the person's freedom is being curtailed[26]. On the physical aspect, there too the rules are applied flexibly. It is plain, however, that a degree of physical restraint is required[27]. There is not an effective detention under s 14 of the 1995 Act if the words of detention are shouted to an escaping potential detainee but not accompanied by any actual physical restraint[28].

Once a lawful detention or arrest *has* been effected certain consequences follow. In particular, the police may undertake a personal search of the suspect[29] and 'relevant physical data' may be taken – a term which includes fingerprints, skin records and other samples[30]. Premises may also be searched – normally under authority of a warrant, in which case lawful search will be confined to the subject matter of the warrant save where plainly incriminating evidence of another crime is 'stumbled across'[31].

Also very important to the circumstances of arrest and detention is the power to question the suspect. Apart from the specific obligation already mentioned to inform a suspect of the right to contact a solicitor and a general rule that police questioning must cease at the point of a formal charge, there is no prescribed code for police behaviour during a period of vulnerability (especially to misplaced admissions of guilt) of suspects under arrest or detention. In a long series of cases, the Scottish courts have insisted, perhaps unhelpfully, simply on a general test of 'fairness' to the accused[32]. It has been assumed that the admissibility of evidence resulting from questioning in the absence of a solicitor is subject to the same general test of fairness[33]. A recent decision of the European Court of Human Rights may, however, require that issue to be revisited[34].

Such formulations of a test for lawfulness of police actions arise in the context of subsequent criminal trials in which the admissibility of evidence against the accused may be challenged. Only if the questioning was 'fair', will the evidence, which may be crucial to the prosecution case, be admissible. This reminds us that questions of the lawfulness of police action, not just in relation to questioning but also to other powers of arrest, detention and search, usually arise in this context. It is at least formally possible that a civil action might be raised (including a petition for judicial review) or a complaint lodged with the Police Complaints Commissioner in relation to an alleged breach of the rules but, in practice, most such issues are resolved as questions of admissibility in subsequent trials[35]. Such cases frequently turn, sequentially, on the lawfulness of the arrest or detention; the lawfulness of any subsequent search; and, if *prima facie* unlawful, whether that can be excused in all the circumstances, despite the countervailing arguments based on the rule of law and individual liberty, on grounds of the technicality of the breach or the good faith (rather than, for instance, an unfair trick) on the part of the police[36].

1 See chs 6 and 7.
2 Governance arrangements for Scottish police are currently under review. See the report of the (Tomkins) Independent Review of Policing in Scotland (January 2009).
3 Police (Scotland) Act 1967 s 1.
4 *Ibid.*
5 *Ibid* s 2.
6 Duties are also allocated to individual constables by s 17.
7 Police (Scotland) Act 1967 s 39.
8 *Ibid* s 32.
9 *Ibid* s 26.
10 Police, Public Order and Criminal Justice (Scotland) Act 2006 Pt 1, Ch 1.
11 *Ibid.* Pt 1, Ch 2.
12 There have, however, been concerns that the 'National Police Board' to be established in the wake of the Tomkins review (note 2 above) may be a sign of an increasing development of a national force.
13 See Ch 2.
14 *Wither v Reid* 1980 JC 7. See also *Gililes v Ralph* 2008 SLT 978.
15 Police (Scotland) Act 1967 s 41.
16 Originally enacted as ss.1, 2 of the Criminal Justice (Scotland) Act 1980.
17 *Wilson v Robertson* 1986 SCCR 700; *Houston v Macdonald* 2000 SLT 333.
18 *Gillies v Ralph* 2008 SLT 978.
19 *Paton v Ritchie* 2000 JC 271.
20 In *Jones v HMA* 2008 JC 78 it was held that the arrest need not be for the same offence as the detention.
21 And Sched 8. See also s 44 for powers to 'stop and search'.
22 Criminal Procedure (Scotland) Act 1995 ss 34 and 135.
23 There is a presumption that common law powers are to be interpreted restrictively. See *Gillies v Ralph* 2008 SLT 978.
24 1868 7M. 89.
25 Ibid. See, in particular, Lord President Inglis and Lord Deas.
26 *Forbes v HMA* 1990 SCCR 69.
27 *Muir v Magistrates of Hamilton* 1910 1 SLT 164.
28 *Gillies v Ralph* 2008 SLT 978.
29 *Adair v McGarry* 1933 JC 72.
30 1995 Act s 18(2)–(7B).
31 *HMA v Hepper* 1958 SLT 160.
32 See eg *Chalmers v HMA* 1954 SLT 177; *Miln v Cullen* 1967 SLT 35; *Codona v HMA* 1996 SLT 1100; *Peebles v HMA* 2007 SLT 197.
33 *Paton v Ritchie* 2000 SCCR 151.
34 *Salduz v Turkey* (App no 3691/02) 26 April 2007.

35 See, in addition to the cases cited in n 32, *HMA v Hepper* 1958 SLT 160; *Jones v HMA* 2008 JC 78.
36 *Lawrie v Muir* 1950 SLT 37. And see *Henderson v HMA* 2005 1 JC 301.

THE MAINTENANCE OF PUBLIC ORDER

12.16   As with the police powers regime in general, the development of the powers of the police and other public authorities to maintain public order (mainly on the streets but also in places to which the public may have access) has been a story of successive stages of statutory intervention, whilst never wholly ousting the residual availability of common law powers. Once again, the starting point is that, in the absence of powers deriving from one or other source, members of the public, whether acting individually or collectively, are broadly free to behave as they please in public places and, subject to the private rights of landowners and others, in private places as well. Restraint of that freedom requires specific legal authority. And this is an historic approach to liberty which has been reinforced by the ECHR, arts 10 (freedom of expression) and 11 (freedom of assembly and association).

In the modern law, the range of restraining powers available may usefully be divided into those which impose controls *in anticipation* of the possibility of disorder and those, on the other hand, which enable a response to *an immediate threat of or actual* disorder.

It is in the realm of anticipatory controls that the contribution of statute has been particularly important. The common law offers little, although the early case of *Deakin v Milne*[1] is perhaps authority for a police intervention to restrain a peaceful march in circumstances where those targeted are well intentioned but where, nevertheless, there has been a tendency for disorder to result – at the hand of others. The legitimacy of such precautionary measures taken against people who have not (or have not yet) disturbed the peace was also considered in cases such as *O'Kelly v Harvey*[2], *Duncan v Jones*[3] and *Thomas v Sawkins*[4] but the law has been recently reviewed and restated in *Austin v Metropolitan Police Commissioner*[5] where the English Court of Appeal held, following police action to contain demonstrators in Oxford Circus in London, that containment was lawful in the circumstances because necessary to prevent an imminent breach of the peace by others. It was subsequently held by the House of Lords[6] that the containment did not amount to a breach of Art 5 of the ECHR. It was a question to be measured by the degree of intensity of the restriction but, in those particular circumstances, the containment did not amount to a deprivation of liberty[7].

The decisions in *Austin* join that in *R (Laporte) v Chief Constable of Gloucestershire*[8] where the preventative action taken had been the stopping by the police of a bus load of would-be protestors 5 kms short of their destination of a US air base. It was held that, since there was not, at the time, any reasonable apprehension that an actual breach of the peace was imminent, the bus was not lawfully stopped. Only if the means adopted were the only practicable way of preventing an imminent breach of the peace would restraint of an innocent party be justifiable[9].

The Civic Government (Scotland) Act 1982[10] imposes controls on the holding of processions in public[11]. With some exceptions, such processions require local authority permission in advance (subject to appeal to the sheriff) and offences are committed by those who act in breach of this requirement or in breach of conditions laid down in a permission granted. A person proposing to hold a procession in public must give at least 28 days written notice to the local authority and to the chief constable, specifying date, time, route[12], likely number of participants, arrangements for control and the person's name and address (s 63(3)). This requirement does not normally apply to 'processions commonly or customarily held'[13] and local authorities may themselves modify the requirements (subss (4), (11)).

In response to the notice the local authority must deliver (at least two days before the proposed procession) an order either prohibiting the procession or imposing conditions as to date, time, duration, route and prohibiting its entry into a public place – defined as a public road or any place to which the public has access (as of right or with permission) on payment or otherwise[14]. There is an appeal to the sheriff against the local authority's order (s 64). Those who hold or take part in an unauthorised procession or act in breach of a condition commit a criminal offence (s 65).

In addition to these anticipatory measures, statutory powers are also available to the police to take measures 'on the day'. In relation to a public procession already being held or where people are already assembling with a view to taking part, the most senior police officer present at the scene is given certain powers of control[15]. If, having regard to the time, place or circumstances in which the procession is being held (or intended) and to its proposed route, that officer 'reasonably believes' that either it may result in serious public disorder, serious damage to property or serious disruption to the life of the community or the purpose of the organisers is to intimidate others, that officer may 'give directions' imposing conditions on the organisers and those taking part or prohibiting entry into any specified public place (subs (1)). Knowingly to fail to comply is a criminal offence, unless because of circumstances beyond the control of the organiser or participant (subss (4), (5)). Incitement to commit such an offence is also an offence (subs (6)). Persons suspected of these offences may be arrested.

Under the same circumstances of anticipated serious disorder etc. the senior police officer may give directions (as to place, maximum duration or maximum number of persons) in the case of organisers of and participants in a public assembly – defined as an 'assembly of 20 or more persons in a public place (defined as above) which is wholly or partly open to the air.'[16]

A later addition to the Public Order Act 1986 was another power to plug the gap left by the earlier focus on 'public' places, because of increasing resort by demonstrators to private land[17]. This power has an anticipatory aspect to it in that it enables the chief constable to apply to the local authority to order the prohibition of 'trespassory assemblies' in its area. Such an application may be made if the chief constable reasonably believes that an assembly (of 20 or more persons) is proposed to be held without permission on private land (in the open air) to which the public has no right (or a limited right) of access[18] and may result either in serious disruption to the life of the community or significant damage to a site of historical, architectural or scientific importance (s 14A). An order made by the local authority must be in writing (or recorded in writing as soon as practicable) and may apply to a period of no more than four days or to an area greater than a circle with a radius of five miles from a specified centre (subss (6), (8)). It may, however, be revoked or varied (subs (7)). Breach of an order is a criminal offence (s 14B (1), (2)) and a constable in uniform may arrest suspected offenders (s 14B(4)). A constable in uniform may also direct a person reasonably believed to be on his or her way to a prohibited assembly not to proceed with the direction of the assembly, with the same consequences as to committing an offence for non-compliance and power of arrest (s 14C). In the circumstances of a demonstration at Stonehenge it was held in *DPP v Jones*[19] that the public's right of access to a public road nearby was not a 'limited right of access' to which the section could apply. The public's rights included that of use of the roadway for peaceful assembly.

Section 1 of the Public Order Act 1936 makes it an offence for any person (in a public place or at a public meeting) to wear uniform signifying association with any political organisation or with the promotion of any political object. The term 'uniform' is not defined but *O'Moran v DPP*[20] made clear that a full uniform was not required but that items such as dark berets, dark glasses and dark clothing (though perhaps not merely a lapel badge), taken together and in the circumstances, suffice. The 1936 Act also created a number of offences relating to the organising and equipping of paramilitary forces (s 2). Those offences remain on the statute book but have largely been overtaken by the Terrorism Act 2000, Part II of which enables the proscription of terrorist organisations (listed in Sch 2 to the Act to include various Ireland-related organisations and many others including Al-Qa'ida). A number of related offences are created including those of membership of and support for such organisations (ss 11–12) and wearing items of clothing (s 13) in public in such circumstances as to arouse reasonable suspicion of membership or support. In *Rankin v Murray*[21] it was held that neck chains, pendants or rings with a prominent 'UVF' symbol would suffice.

Accompanying the core provisions directed towards public processions and meetings are a variety of other statutory provisions:

(1)   Related to the 'trespassory assemblies' above, there is additional provision for the regulation of 'raves' (100 or more persons)[22].

(2)   It is an offence to act in a disorderly manner at election meetings[23] or at public meetings in general[24].

(3)   It is an offence to stir up racial hatred (in public or in private)[25].

(4)   It is an offence to publish a statement encouraging terrorism[26].

In addition, an important weapon in the common law armoury of the police is the offence of breach of the peace. In its modern application, the basis of the offence is doing anything which is 'genuinely alarming and disturbing in its context, to any reasonable person'[27].

---

1   (1882) 10R. (J.) 22. But see the English case of *Beatty v Gillbanks* (1881–82) LR 9 QBD 308 to contrary effect.

2   (1883) 14 LR 1R 105.

3   [1936] 1 KB 218.
4   [1935] 2 KB 249.
5   [2008] QB 660; [2008] 1 All ER 564.
6   [2009] 1 AC 564.
7   Lord Hope of Craighead at para 18.
8   [2006] UKHL 55; [2007] 2 All ER 529.
9   See eg Lord Rodger of Earlsferry at para 90.
10 As amended, esp by the Police, Public Order and Criminal Justice (Scotland) Act 2006.
11 A public procession means a procession in a public place – defined by the Public Order Act 1986 s16 as a public road or any place to which at the material time the public has access on payment or otherwise, as of right or by virtue of express or implied permission.
12 The recent case of *Kay v Metropolitan Commissioner* [2009] 2 All ER 935 has raised doubts (in relation to the Public Order Act 1986 s 11) about whether processions (in that case, a mass cycle rally) which lack organisers and a route are 'processions' which can be regulated at all.
13 Subs (7).
14 See note 10 above.
15 Public Order Act 1986, ss 12(1), (2), (11).
16 Public Order Act 1986, ss 14, 16.
17 Criminal Justice and Public Order Act 1994, s 70, inserting ss 14A–14C into the 1986 Act.
18 Such a right of access does not include access rights (the right to roam) under the Land Reform (Scotland) Act 2003.
19 [1999] 2 AC 240.
20 [1975] QB 864.
21 2004 SLT 1164.
22 Criminal Justice and Public Order Act 1994 ss 63-66.
23 Representation of the People Act 1983 s 97.
24 Public Meeting Act 1908 s.1.
25 Public Order Act 1986 s 18.
26 Terrorism Act 2006 s 1.
27 *Smith v Donnelly* 2002 JC 65; *Miller v Thomson* 2009 SLT 59.

INFORMATION RIGHTS

12.17   A rapidly developing area of law in recent years has been the regulation – by legislation and by the courts – of access to, and use of, information. That regulation can pull in different directions depending on the nature of the information involved: an increased emphasis on openness and access to *official* information is matched by recognition of the importance of protecting *private* information. In the former case, greater access to information is founded upon the belief that information is essential to accountability and, equally, that accountability is essential to the wider project of an informed population. In the latter case, development has been accompanied, and to some extent caused, by heightened public anxiety about the security of personal information and fears about the increasingly sophisticated surveillance and information gathering techniques used by law enforcement agencies[1].

1   For comprehensive treatment see P Coppel, *Information Rights* (2nd edn, 2007) and J Macdonald, R Crail and C Jones (eds) *The Law of Freedom of Information* (2nd edn, 2009).

Official Secrets

12.18   In matters of public access to official information, the United Kingdom had a notoriously bad record. It has been said that the twentieth century saw the growth of a secrecy culture which was unfavourably compared with more liberal regimes elsewhere, including the United States. Such comparisons are not easily or accurately made but they produced a critique of the British position which, by the end of the century, saw the beginnings of substantial change.

Two principal legal characteristics were associated with the growth of secrecy. The first was the severity with which the secrets of government were protected by the Official Secrets Act 1911 and, latterly in a modified form, by the Official Secrets Act 1989 (OSA 1989). The latter protects from disclosure without lawful authority any information about security and intelligence (OSA 1989, s 1), defence (OSA 1989, s 2), international relations (OSA 1989, s 3) and criminal investigations (OSA 1989, s 4). To make a 'damaging disclosure by a member of the security and intelligence services' is a criminal offence. Secondly, there was lacking in the United Kingdom any general right of access to official information. Some types of documents and information held by local authorities were required to be put into the public domain[1] and certain types of personal information could be demanded by individuals[2]. But, until the passing, by the Westminster Parliament, of the Freedom of Information Act 2000 (FOIA) and, by Holyrood, of the Freedom of Information (Scotland) Act 2002 (FOISA), there was no generally assured right of access to information.

1 Local Government (Scotland) Act 1973, Pt IIIA.
2 For example, Access to Personal Files Act 1987.

Freedom of Information

12.19   FOIA and FOISA came into effect fully on 1 January 2005 and make very similar – though not identical – provision to ensure a substantial degree of statutorily guaranteed access to information held by public authorities exercising, on the one hand, reserved functions and, on the other, devolved functions in Scotland. In summary, FOISA creates a broad right to information by providing that any person who requests information from a Scottish public authority which holds it is entitled to be given it by the authority (FOISA, s 1(1)). Scottish public authorities are defined to include the Scottish Ministers, the Scottish Parliament (and the Parliamentary Corporate Body[1]), non-ministerial office holders in the Scottish Administration (including, for example, the Chief Inspector of Prisons and procurators fiscal), local authorities, National Health Service bodies, educational institutions such as colleges and universities, chief constables and a long list of Scottish quangos (FOISA, s 3 and sch 1).

With that general entitlement in place, the most important remaining sections of FOISA are those which (a) grant exemptions from the general entitlement and (b) provide for the enforcement of the duty to supply information. The exemptions in Part 2 extend to information reasonably accessible by other means (FOISA, s 25); information whose disclosure is prohibited by law (FOISA, s 26[2]); information being held for publication within 12 weeks and certain information deriving from programmes of research (FOISA, s 27); information whose disclosure would, or would be likely to, 'prejudice substantially relations between' governments (including devolved governments) in the United Kingdom (FOISA, s 28); information held by the Scottish Administration and relating to the formulation or development of government policy, ministerial communications, advice by any of the Law Officers or the operation of any ministerial private office (FOISA, s 29). 'Ministerial communications' means any communications between ministers (members of the Scottish Executive and junior Scottish Ministers) and includes, in particular, communications relating to proceedings of the Scottish Cabinet or of its committees. Other exemptions extend to information which would be likely to prejudice substantially the maintenance of the convention of the collective responsibility of the Scottish Ministers[3], inhibit the free and frank provision of advice or otherwise prejudice substantially the effective conduct of public affairs (FOISA, s 30[4]); information required for the purpose of safeguarding national security (FOISA, s 31); information which would prejudice substantially international relations (FOISA, s 32) or certain commercial interests (FOISA, s 33). And further exemptions apply to information relating to certain public investigations (FOISA, s 34), law enforcement (FOISA, s 35), certain confidential communications (FOISA, s 36), court records (FOISA, s 37), personal data (FOISA, s 38), certain audit functions (FOISA, s 40) and communications with the Queen (FOISA, s 41). Special arrangements have been made for the provision of environmental information[5].

Whenever one of the exemptions applies, the duty to give information to a person requesting it applies only to the extent that the exemption is not 'absolute' (ie those exemptions contained in FOISA, s 25 (information otherwise accessible), s 26 (disclosure prohibited), s 36(2) (entailing breach of confidence), s 37 (court records), and s 38 (personal data)) and 'in all the circumstances of the case, the public interest is disclosing the information is not outweighed by that in maintaining the exemption' (FOISA, s 2). There is also provision for the refusal of information if its provision would entail excessive cost (FOISA, s 12)[6] or if a request is vexatious or repeated (FOISA, s 14).

Essential to the process of enforcing the provisions of FOISA is the Scottish Information Commissioner, an officer appointed by the Queen on the nomination of the Scottish Parliament[7] and with the same security of tenure as the Public Services Ombudsman (FOISA, s 42)[8]. The Commissioner has certain general functions including the promotion of good practice under FOISA but his most important function has been the making of decisions on applications from anyone dissatisfied with the response from an authority to a request for information (FOISA, s 47). The Commissioner may issue enforcement notices requiring an authority to take action (FOISA, s 51) and the Commissioner's decisions are appealable on a point of law to the Court of Session (FOISA, s 56)[9].

It may fairly be said that over the past four years freedom of information law has had a significant impact on public attitudes to access to official information and, through its use by the media, has contributed to (some would say generated) a number of high profile political 'scandals'. In particular, access to information about amounts of money claimed by MSPs at Holyrood and by MPs at Westminster led to the resignation of individual politicians[10] and, at least indirectly, to the resignation of the Speaker of the House of Commons in May 2009[11]. It is anticipated that the reach of freedom of information will be extended in the near future to certain areas of the private sector through the use of powers conferred on Ministers of the Crown and the Scottish Ministers by FOIA and FOISA respectively to 'designate' individuals and corporations as public authorities for the purposes of freedom of information[12].

1   See, for example, Decisions 008/2005 and 09/2005 (Scottish Parliament) and 033/2005 (Scottish Parliamentary Corporate Body) of the Scottish Information Commissioner, available at www.itspublicknowledge.info/home/ScottishInformationCommissioner.asp
2   See *Dumfries and Galloway Council v Scottish Information Commissioner* 2008 SC 327.
3   For collective responsibility, see p 163.
4   See *Scottish Ministers v Scottish Information Commissioner* 2007 SC 330; 2007 SLT 274.
5   FOISA, ss 39 and 62 and the Environmental Information (Scotland) Regulations 2004, SSI 2004/520.
6   As to which see the Freedom of Information (Fees for Required Disclosure) (Scotland) Regulations 2004, SSI 2004/467. Fees can be charged for the provision of information in certain circumstances: see FI(S)A 2002, s 13 and the Freedom of Information (Fees for Disclosure under Section 13) (Scotland) Regulations 2004, SSI 2004/376.
7   Mr Kevin Dunion was nominated by the Parliament on 12 December 2002 and renominated for a second term on 24 January 2008.
8   See p 274 above.
9   And ultimately to the House of Lords: see *The Common Services Agency v Scottish Information Commissioner* 2008 SC (HL) 184.
10 David McLetchie, MSP resigned as leader of the Scottish Conservative Party in October 2005 in the face of criticism of expenses claims which related to taxi journeys between the Holyrood Parliament and the Edinburgh law firm at which he worked (see Decision 033/2005 of the Scottish Information Commissioner at www.itspublicknowledge.info).
11 The Westminster Parliament resisted in the courts the UK Information Commissioner's direction that expenses claims made by MPs should be made public. Ultimately defeated (see *Corporate Officer of the House of Commons v Information Commissioner* [2008] EWHC 1084 (Admin)), MPs first contemplated changes to FOIA to exempt their expenses information from disclosure before accepting that publication was inevitable. Scheduled for July 2009, disclosure by Parliament was pre-empted by the leaking to, and publication by, the Telegraph Newspapers over a number of weeks in May and June, of highly damaging revelations about the types of claims made by MPs of all parties. Speaker Martin's failure to maintain the confidence of the House in connection with potential reform of the expenses and allowances system resulted in his resignation (see HC Debs, 19 May 2009, col 1323).
12 See FOIA, s 5 and FOISA, s 5. See also Scottish Government Discussion Paper – Coverage of the Freedom of Information (Scotland) Act 2002, November 2008.

Data Protection

12.20   While freedom of information legislation confers rights on individuals to obtain official information, the focus of data protection law is on the rights of individuals to obtain – and to regulate the use of – their own personal information.

The Data Protection Act 1998 (DPA 1998), an Act of the Westminster Parliament, is the vehicle by which the UK gives effect to the requirements of the EC Data Protection Directive[1]. As the Directive acknowledges, the European internal market requires that 'personal data should be able to flow freely from one Member State to another, but also that the fundamental rights of individuals should be safeguarded'. Those fundamental rights include rights protected by the European Convention on Human Rights and the Directive can be seen, in part, as further developing principles first recognised by the Council of Europe's 1981 Convention for the Protection of Individuals with regard to Automatic Processing of Personal Data[2].

The Convention's title reveals one of the key preoccupations which informed the drafting of the Convention and, in due course, the Directive: the exponential growth of electronic storage and automated processing of personal information over the last 3 decades. As a consequence of this preoccupation, DPA 1998 focuses on personal information which is (or is intended to be), 'processed by means of equipment operating automatically in response to instructions given for that purpose' or is 'recorded as part of a relevant filing system'[3]. DPA1998 is a lengthy and complex Act but its key elements involve (1) providing a definition of the concept of 'personal data'; (2) conferring rights on individuals to obtain access to their own personal data; and (3) imposing duties on those 'data controllers' who process personal data.

Personal data is defined as data which 'relate to a living individual who can be identified (a) from those data or (b) from those data and other information which is in the possession of, or is likely to come into the possession of, the data controller' (DPA1998, s 1(1)). The definition 'includes any expression of opinion about the individual and any indication of the intentions of the data controller or any other person in respect of the individual' (DPA1998 s 1(1)). A subset of personal data is 'sensitive personal data' to which more stringent requirements apply. Sensitive personal data is personal data consisting of information as to an individual's racial or ethnic origin, political opinions, religious beliefs or other beliefs of a similar nature, trade union membership, physical or mental health or condition, sexual life, and history of criminal conduct or prosecution.

Litigation about data protection has been relatively rare but the House of Lords recently considered the definition of personal data in *Common Services Agency v Scottish Information Commissioner*[4]. The key issue addressed by the court was when an individual can be 'identified' from information held by a data controller. Their Lordships holding that where sufficient steps can be taken by the data controller to anonymise data in its own hands – for example, in the case of statistical information, by making it difficult to 'unravel' statistics internally so as to identify the individuals represented by those statistics – then the data may cease to be 'personal data' at all[5].

DPA1998 is chiefly concerned with the protection of 'data subjects': the individuals who are the subject of personal data (DPA1998, s 1(1)). Data subjects have a variety of rights relating information about them which are set out in the Act's 'subject information provisions' (DPA1998, s 27(2)). A data subject is entitled to be informed by any data controller, in response to a properly constituted request, whether any of his personal data are being processed by or on behalf of that data controller, and if so to be given a description of the personal data concerned, the purposes of the processing and the recipients or classes of recipients to whom the data are or may be disclosed. The data subject is also entitled to have communicated to him in 'intelligible form' the personal data held by the data controller and any information available to the data controller as to the source of those data (DPA1998, s 7). Importantly, individuals are entitled not only to know what information is held about them but also how that information may be used: a data subject is entitled, where his personal data is processed by automatic means for 'the purpose of evaluating matters relating to him such as, for example, his performance at work, his creditworthiness, his reliability or his conduct, has constituted or is likely to constitute the sole basis for any decision significantly affecting him', to be informed of the 'logic involved in that decision-taking' (DPA1998, s 7).

The rights of individuals to access their own personal data are not absolute. There are a variety of exemptions contained in DPA1998 itself – for example, personal data which has been processed for the purposes of assessing suitability for judicial office or appointment as a QC are exempt from the subject information provisions (DPA1998, Sch 7, para 3) – and others have been added by statutory instrument[6].

In addition to these rights to obtain information, DPA1998 also seeks to protect individuals by placing obligations on data controllers in relation to their use of data. A data controller is defined for most purposes as 'a person who (either alone or jointly or in common with other persons) determines the purposes for which and the manner in which any personal data are, or are to be, processed' (DPA1998, s 1). Data controllers include government and public authorities but the definition extends far beyond the public sector. The definition of "processing" is extremely wide and includes obtaining, recording or holding the information or data and carrying operations on the information or data, including organising or altering of the information or data, consulting or using the data, and disclosing and destroying the data (DPA, s 1). Importantly, a data controller must comply with the "data protection principles" in relation to all personal data with respect to which he is the data controller (DPA1998, s 4(4)). The requirements of the data protection principles include the fair and lawful processing of personal data, that personal data which is held is 'accurate and, where necessary, kept up to date' and that appropriate steps are taken to prevent the unauthorised use or accidental loss or destruction of personal data.

While DPA 1998 does confer some rights which can be enforced by individuals through the courts[7], the Act is chiefly policed by the UK Information Commissioner. The Commissioner is appointed by the Queen[8] for a term of up to five years (which may be renewed but is subject to an overall maximum of fifteen years' service) and has wide ranging powers of investigation and enforcement. These include new powers to issue fines ('monetary penalty notices') for serious breaches of the data protection principles – a response to concerns raised by a number of high profile incidents of the loss or inadvertent disclosure of large amounts of personal data by government departments, financial institutions and others[9] which are expected to come into force in late 2009. Appeals against decisions of the Information Commissioner may be taken to the Information Tribunal (also established by DPA 1998, s 6) and thereafter to the courts.

1 Directive 95/46/EC of the European Parliament and of the Council of 24 October 1995 on the protection of individuals with regard to the processing of personal data and on the free movement of such data. Data Protection is reserved to Westminster (see 128) by SA1998, s 30 and Schedule 5, Part II, Section B1.
2 The 1981 Convention refers to the potential adverse effects which unfettered processing might have on rights of privacy, non-discrimination and fair trial and on other 'legitimate interests' such as employment and consumer credit.
3 DPA 1998, s 1(1).

4 2008 SC (HL) 184. This was an appeal against a decision of the Scottish Information Commissioner directing the release of information about the occurrence of leukaemia in children living in Dumfries and Galloway. The decision was resisted by the CSA on the grounds that the information was exempt under s 38 of FI(S)A, being personal data the release of which would breach the data protection principles. FI(S)A incorporates the definition of personal data in DPA1998 for the purposes of the s 38 exemption and the case is therefore of relevance to the interpretation of DPA1998 notwithstanding its roots in a freedom of information request.

5 See also *Durant v Financial Services Authority* [2003] EWCA Civ 1746, [2004] FSR 28 in which the Court of Appeal considered the meaning of the words 'relate to a living individual' which appear in the definition of personal data. As this case and *CSA v Scottish Information Commissioner* demonstrate, arguments about this definition can be highly technical, if not to say esoteric.

6 See, for example, the Data Protection (Subject Access Modification) (Health) Order 2000, SI 2000/413; the Data Protection (Subject Access Modification) (Social Work) Order 2000, SI 2000/415; the Data Protection (Subject Access Modification) (Education) Order 2000, SI 2000/414; the Data Protection (Miscellaneous Subject Access Exemptions) Order 2000, SI 2000/419.

7 See, for example, DPA 1998 s 13 which entitles an individual to compensation in some circumstances if they have suffered damage and/or distress as a consequence of a contravention of the Act by a data controller.

8 DPA 1998, s 6. The current Commissioner, Christopher Graham, replaced Richard Thomas in June 2009. The UK Commissioner has additional responsibilities for enforcement of UK – rather than Scottish – freedom of information law.

9 See the Criminal Justice and Immigration Act 2008, s144.

Privacy Rights

12.21   Historically, the British courts have not recognised any general right of privacy or any presumption against the intrusion by the state – or by others such as the press – into the private affairs of individuals. This is in contrast to the constitutional protection of privacy which exists in states such as France, Canada or the USA. As we have seen, specific protections are now offered by the DPA 1998 in relation to the processing of personal data, and we describe below (p 360) the role of Regulation of Investigatory Powers legislation in relation to surveillance and intelligence gathering. In addition, there have been two separate (but related) developments over the last decade or so which have significantly extended the legal protection of privacy within the UK.

The first was the incorporation of the ECHR by HRA 1998 (see p 333). As noted above, art 8 provides that 'Everyone has the right to respect for his private and family life, his home and his correspondence'. A qualified right, interference with it is permitted where that is 'in accordance with the law and is necessary in a democratic society in the interests of national security, public safety or the economic well-being of the country, for the prevention of disorder or crime, for the protection of health or morals, or for the protection of the rights and freedoms of others'. The component parts of the protection – relating to private life, family life, home and correspondence – may be infringed individually or cumulatively. Article 8 has been held by British courts to be breached by the taking, and retaining by the police, of photographs of an individual who was engaged in wholly lawful activity[1] but not necessarily by different approaches to parental rights and responsibilities taken by the law in relation to married and unmarried fathers[2] or by a practice of attaching to all external telephone calls from prisoners a pre-recorded message making it clear to the recipient that the call was coming from within a prison[3].

As may be expected, the particular 'rights or freedoms of others' which most frequently collide with those protected by article 8 – and which are relied upon by the media in particular to justify the publication of personal information – are those referred to in article 10 ECHR: rights to freedom of expression, including the freedom to 'hold opinions and to receive and impart information and ideas without interference by public authority and regardless of frontiers'. For many of the same reasons as justify freedom of information laws – the importance of scrutinising and holding to account those who exercise the powers of the state – special significance is attached to the rights of journalists to bring to public attention information which public officials and politicians might prefer to keep secret. The potential risks to democracy of limitations on those rights are recognised by section 12 of HRA 1998. Section 12 applies 'if a court is considering whether to grant any relief which, if granted, might affect the exercise of the Convention right to freedom of expression' – the most obvious example of which would be a court considering an application for an interdict to prevent publication or broadcast. In such circumstances the court is required to take steps to ensure that the person against whom the order is sought is given the opportunity to put their case[4]. The court is also under a duty to have 'particular regard to the importance of the Convention right to freedom of expression and, where the proceedings relate to material which the respondent claims, or which appears to the court, to be journalistic, literary or artistic material', the extent to which the information concerned is already (or about to be) in the public domain and whether it is in the public interest for it to be published[5].

The fact that the ECHR has been incorporated in domestic law does not, of course, preclude applications to the European Court of Human Rights by individuals who believe the UK has failed to give proper respect to their article 8 rights. Over the past decade the UK has been found guilty of such failure in relation to, for example, the release to the public of CCTV pictures of a man who attempted suicide in a public place[6] and the long-term retention by the police of DNA samples taken from individuals who had not been convicted of any crime[7].

The second recent development in the protection of individual privacy has been the extension, particularly by the English courts, of the common law of confidence: that the law which recognises and enforces duties to keep information confidential either because such a duty has been set out expressly (for example in a contract) or because the it is to be implied from the nature of the information and the circumstances in which is has been communicated by one person to another. Traditionally concerned with the rights of commercial parties to maintain the confidentiality of business information, the last ten years have seen breach of confidence being used by individuals, particularly 'celebrities', to restrain the publication of personal information about, and photographs of, them. This development of the law of breach of confidence, following the incorporation of the ECHR, is not coincidental and may be viewed as an example – sometimes more or less explicit – of the 'horizontal' application of the Convention described above (p 338). Many recent cases involve not only breach of confidence and of Convention rights through publication of personal information but breach of article 8 in acquisition of that information by the media[8].

1 *Wood v Commissioner of Police of the Metropolis* [2009] EWCA Civ 414.
2 *D v Children's Reporter* 2008 GWD 1-10.
3 *Potter v Scottish Prison Service* 2007 SLT 1019. It was conceded that art 8 rights were engaged but not that they had been infringed.
4 HRA 1998, s12(2).
5 See, for example, *Attorney General's Reference No 3 of 1999: Application by the British Broadcasting Corporation to set aside or vary a Reporting Restriction Order* [2009] UKHL 34
6 *Peck v United Kingdom* (2003) 36 EHRR 41.
7 *S v United Kingdom*; *Marper v United Kingdom* (2009) 48 EHRR 50.
8 See *Douglas v Hello! Ltd (No 1)* [2001] QB 967; *Campbell v Mirror Group Newspapers Ltd* [2004] 2 AC 457; and *Mosley v Newsgroup Newspapers Ltd* [2008] EMLR 20. For discussion, see N A Moreham, 'Privacy in the common law', (2005) 121 LQR 628.

Regulation of Investigatory Powers

12.22   Finally, one further area in which there has been statutory intervention is in the field of surveillance and intelligence gathering by law enforcement agencies. As has been noted, interference with the rights to private life, family and home protected by article 8 is permissible provided certain conditions are met. Amongst those conditions are that the interference is 'in accordance with the law'. One difficulty which the UK faced in complying with this condition was the absence of any general legal regime governing the circumstances in which public authorities might engage in activity such as telephone tapping, interception with correspondence or electronic communications and the gathering of information using 'informants'. This absence, together with an approach to individual rights which held that so long as the state was not expressly prohibited by law from engaging in a particular activity it was free to do so[1] left individuals with little real protection against covert surveillance activity by the state.

The incorporation of the ECHR rendered the need for reform more pressing and resulted in the passing of the Regulation of Investigatory Powers Act 2000 (RIPA) and the Regulation of Investigatory Powers (Scotland) Act 2000 (RIPSA)[2]. As the policy memorandum to the Scottish bill explained, in order for an interference to be 'acceptable in ECHR terms…(a) a framework of controls must have a basis in law; (b) the law must define the scope and manner of the exercise of a public authority's functions with sufficient clarity to protect the individual from arbitrary interference and to ensure that it is the subject of effective control; (c) the law must be sufficiently accessible and precise; [and] (d) the exceptions which allow interference should be construed narrowly and interference with those rights should be necessary and proportionate to any offence". RIPA and RIPSA are designed to meet these criteria.

RIPSA applies to Scottish police forces, the Scottish Administration, Scottish health service bodies, Scottish local authorities, SEPA and the Scottish Crime and Drug Enforcement Agency and provides a scheme for the authorisation and control of directed surveillance activity (for example, using CCTV cameras to monitor the activity of specific individuals in a street or public park) intrusive surveillance (for example the use of a listening device placed in a car or in someone's home) and the use of 'covert human intelligence sources' (i.e. informants or 'undercover' investigators). RIPA regulates these activities in the remainder of the UK and also contains further provisions which apply in the whole of the UK, including Scotland (for example in relation to interception of communications).

Compliance with the requirements of RIPA and RIPSA is chiefly the responsibility of the Surveillance Commissioners appointed under each Act, although the Secretary of State and the Scottish Ministers, respectively, also issue codes of practice explaining how they expect public authorities to discharge their duties under the Acts. Complaints about the use of surveillance powers may be made by aggrieved individuals to the Investigatory Powers Tribunal, established under section 65 of RIPA. Perhaps more importantly, if an individual is able to demonstrate that surveillance activity has been carried out which is not in accordance with the requirements of RIPA or RIPSA this may enable him to prevent the use, in criminal proceedings against him, of any evidence obtained through that activity[3].

1 See *Malone v Commissioner of Police of the Metropolis (No 2)* [1979] Ch 344.
2 There had been limited earlier reform: see the Police Act 1997 and the Intelligence Services Act 1994.
3 See, for general discussion by the House of Lords of the range of issues raised by covert surveillance, *Re C's Application for Judicial Review* [2009] 2 WLR 782 and, for a Scottish example of exclusion of evidence obtained not in accordance with the requirements of RIPSA, see *HMA v Higgins* 2006 SLT 946. See also, B Goold, *Liberty and others v United Kingdom*: a new chance for another missed opportunity, [2009] PL 5.

Chapter 13

Public Law Adjudication

INTRODUCTION

13.1   A typical but not inevitable characteristic of a country which has a written constitution is a constitutional court. The constitution itself generates questions and disputes which must be resolved at the very highest level by a court of the highest prestige and authority. There may be an entrenched Bill of Rights whose guarantees must be upheld and, more generally, the status of the constitution as the supreme law within the state may require the ordinary laws enacted by the legislature to be measured against its precepts[1]. Equally, in countries with a federal system of government in which the constitutional rights of the states or provinces must be sustained, it is usually assumed that the task must fall to a constitutional court. There must be an umpire to decide between the claims of the state and federal governments and that will usually be a court[2]. What distinguishes courts performing functions such as these is not their name. They may or may not be designated 'constitutional courts'. The jurisdiction of the German Federal Constitutional Court is broadly paralleled by that of the Supreme Courts of the United States and Canada and of the High Court in Australia. The parallels are not exact. The German court has a more specialised role. It is competent to resolve disputes about the validity of legislation not only on the basis of 'concrete' facts after the legislation has been enacted but also 'abstract' disputes before legislation reaches the statute book[3]. In this respect it is to be contrasted with the French Constitutional Council (Conseil Constitutionnel) which (until constitutional reforms of 2008 are implemented) has powers to consider challenges to legislation *only* at the pre-enactment stage. Both of these courts are, however, to be contrasted with the highest courts of the United States, Canada and Australia[4] which, while much occupied with constitutional matters, operate also as final courts of general jurisdiction. Similarly, in these jurisdictions constitutional issues are not the exclusive preserve of the single highest court but, at least some of the time, arrive there only after they have been first raised, and provisionally answered, in courts below[5]. The task of constitutional adjudication is, in those systems, dispersed across the courts as a whole.

In the United Kingdom there has been no constitutional court on either of these models: its absence no doubt a consequence of Britain's constitutional tradition and, in particular, the lack of a written constitution. The sovereignty of Parliament and the problem which this presents for any claim to entrenchment of rules against interference by Parliament, whether in the form of a federal structure or of a Bill of Rights, have tended to restrict the 'constitutional' role for courts to the preservation of the will of Parliament and little more[6]. The claims to supremacy made on behalf of the Treaty of Union 1707 have, whatever their other strengths, never been sufficient to make the case for a new court[7]. The supremacy of EC law[8] has created, since 1 January 1973, a special role for UK courts (alongside courts in other member states) and has given rise to the argument that the ECJ should itself be regarded as a 'constitutional court' for the Community[9] but never that a new court to handle EC issues should be created for the United Kingdom.

Paradoxically, the London-based Judicial Committee of the Privy Council (JCPC) did, for many years, perform the functions of a surrogate constitutional court for countries of the Empire and Commonwealth and, to an increasingly limited extent, continues to do so[10]. Although the JCPC has also discharged certain functions as a court for the United Kingdom[11] and was indeed available to perform a constitutional role during the period of the Stormont Government in Northern Ireland[12], it has not achieved the status of a final court of appeal for either constitutional or general business and seems destined never to do so given the transfer to the new UK Supreme Court of the tasks previously assigned to it under the Scotland Act 1998 (SA 1998)[13], the Government of Wales Act 2006 (GWA 2006)[14] and the Northern Ireland Act 1998 (NIA 1998)[15] and we consider these below.

At the end of this chapter (at pp 413–417) we return to the subject of constitutional courts to consider why, for other reasons, a case has been increasingly strongly made for the creation of a constitutional court for the United Kingdom and whether the new Supreme Court – as a final court of appeal of general jurisdiction – has answered calls for a separate constitutional court.

In the meantime, it is acknowledged that, even in the absence of a single specialised court, there are functions which UK courts certainly are required to perform which are appropriately regarded as constitutional in character and which, in turn, attract many of the concerns about the need to create and sustain judicial independence which were considered in chapter 11. Among such functions to be treated as constitutional in character are the relatively new arrivals of adjudication under the Human Rights Act 1998 (HRA 1998) and under the devolution legislation for Scotland, Wales and Northern Ireland. But they also include decision-making deriving from the European Communities Act 1972 (ECA 1972) and, of much longer standing, civil liberties and administrative law adjudication. The linking feature is the challenge in the courts of the decisions, whether administrative or legislative, of public bodies of all sorts – often, but not inevitably, in litigation initiated by individuals to protect rights they believe have been or may be infringed.

As in other forms of litigation, the task of the courts in such cases is to establish the facts, if these are disputed, and to apply the law. Facts are not often the main focus of dispute in the superior courts. On the other hand, the application of the law, a process which may at first sound merely technical or mechanistic, is frequently very difficult. Three principal factors contribute to different degrees to make constitutional or public law adjudication problematic.

There is, first, the nature of the disputes which arise. They involve the challenge to decisions made by public bodies and public officials, often at the highest level and often involving bodies claiming a special legitimacy of their own deriving from their elected status. Sometimes they involve disputes between different public bodies[16] and, almost always, the outcome of the litigation will be politically (as well as legally) damaging to at least one of the parties. In some jurisdictions, and for some purposes, the acute political sensitivities involved have led courts to decline to adjudicate upon such essentially political questions. The courts have been unwilling to enter the 'political thicket' and have declared those issues non-justiciable[17]. This is not, however, an option for most courts most of the time. There is no avoiding the decision to be made, despite its political context: 'the courts should not be too eager to relinquish their judicial review function simply because they are called upon to exercise it in relation to weighty matters of state'[18].

This combines with the second characteristic – the flexibility of many of the rules to be applied. The political context would cause little difficulty for courts if the rules they applied were clear and unproblematic. This, however, is rarely the case. Whether they derive from common law or statutory sources, the rules which define the legal limits of the acts of public authorities are often open-textured and in need of interpretation as they are applied to particular facts. Courts are seen, therefore, to have a choice as to which interpretation to adopt. Judges may disagree publicly with other judges as to the decision to be reached and, against a background of political controversy, this inevitably makes the process more problematic and potentially fraught.

The third characteristic is the finality of much constitutional adjudication. A prominent feature of decision-making by a constitutional court or supreme court is that the court's decision is the last word on the matter at issue. Unless the procedures for formal constitutional amendment are invoked – and, given the difficulties of doing so, this is rare[19] – a court's decision on a matter of constitutional interpretation will be final and, where this is in effect a decision about the law-making competence of the country's legislature, may raise particularly acute questions about the power of unelected courts to 'trump' decisions of elected parliaments. The role of the courts appears to be 'countermajoritarian', and as such may be viewed as undemocratic and illegitimate[20]. There are different responses to this. On the one hand, there is the robust defence of the courts with the argument that it is wholly proper for them to uphold the protective mechanisms of the constitution – often designed to shelter weak minorities – against the oppression of a, sometimes temporary, majority in a legislature or indeed in wider society[21]. Another defence of the finality of the courts' role is that it is designed not to undermine a narrow version of majoritarian democracy but positively to sustain a broader rights-based democracy, in particular by monitoring and keeping open the processes of democracy themselves[22]. Whatever view is taken, however, there is no doubt that, when courts are placed in such a position of final decision-making, their constitutional status becomes much more contested. Until recently, this has not been an issue which has arisen in the UK constitutional order. The absence of the 'higher law' of a written constitution and the power of the Westminster Parliament, in theory at least, to undo almost any imaginable decision of any court have left 'final' power with Parliament. To a significant degree, however, the impact of the supremacy of EC law has undermined this position and, although the unlimited legislative powers of the Westminster Parliament have been explicitly retained in the terms of SA 1998[23], courts do now have the power to make decisions about the limits of the powers of the Scottish Parliament – a role which is, at least, analogous to that of a constitutional court[24]. Likewise, the powers given to superior courts by HRA 1998 to declare that provisions in Acts of the Westminster Parliament are incompatible with the Convention rights[25] are, while formally lacking the finality of much constitutional adjudication in other countries, similar in effect.

It is with these considerations in mind that we turn to the various categories of constitutional or public law adjudication in which courts may be involved. At pp 367–369, the courts' common law jurisdiction is discussed; then, at pp 369–388, the control of administrative action by administrative tribunals and by the courts, including the process of judicial review followed, at pp 388–390, by the use of judicial review in relation to delegated legislation. Pages 390–395 address the issues raised by HRA 1998 and pp 395–413 the resolution of devolution issues under SA 1998. The chapter concludes, at pp 413–417, with a return to the question of a constitutional court.

1 The remit and powers of a constitutional court in this context depend on the particular legal system in question. The Australian High Court, for example, is empowered to declare invalid Acts of a state legislature or of the Commonwealth Parliament if they conflict with the constitution, whereas the Swiss Federal Tribunal may declare invalid legislation emanating from the provincial ('cantonal') legislatures but has no such power in respect of laws passed by the Federal Assembly. See K C Wheare *Federal Government* (4th edn, 1963), especially ch IV.

2 But, for a contrary view, see, for example, P C Weiler *In the Last Resort: A Critical Study of the Supreme Court of Canada* (1974) ch 6.

3 See L Mammen 'A Short Note on the German Federal Constitutional Court and its Power to Review Legislation' 2001 EHRLR 433.

4 For the United States see L H Tribe *American Constitutional Law* (3rd edn, 2000); for Canada see P W Hogg *Constitutional Law of Canada* (5th edn, 2007); and for Australia see P Hanks *Constitutional Law in Australia* (2nd edn, 1996) (hereafter Hanks).

5 For example, the Australian High Court has original jurisdiction in respect of those matters specified in the Commonwealth constitution, ss 75 and 76 (for example all matters arising under any treaty and all matters in which a writ of mandamus or prohibition or an injunction is sought against an officer of the Commonwealth) but also hears appeals on constitutional matters from state supreme courts and from the Australian Federal Court. See Hanks pp 12–13 and, for an example of the latter type of appeal, see *Eastman v The Queen* [2000] HCA 29.

6 See p 106–110.

7 Although, interestingly, the Treaty provisions on the location of Scottish business gave rise to comments, made in the context of the UK government's announcement in June 2003 of its intention to create a new Supreme Court, concerning the need for a separate court building. See p 113, n 19.

8 See pp 115–117.

9 For discussion, see pp 47–48.

10 The JCPC continues to hear appeals on constitutional matters from a number of independent states including Jamaica, Barbados and St Lucia and from certain UK overseas territories and Crown dependencies. The JCPC also hears appeals 'by proxy' on behalf of the Sultan of Brunei from the Court of Appeal of Brunei: see *Bolkiah v Brunei Darussalam* [2007] UKPC 63. Appeals from New Zealand have ceased as a consequence of the New Zealand Supreme Court Act 2003. For a statistical breakdown, see the JCPC website at http://www.privy-council.org.uk.

11 For example, as the final court of appeal in relation to disqualification for election to the House of Commons, see *Re MacManaway* [1951] AC 161 (concerning the House of Commons (Clergy Disqualification) Act (1801)) and the House of Commons Disqualification Act 1975, s 7.

12 See p 402 below.

13 SA 1998, ss 32–34, 98, 103 and Sch 6 and see p 416 below.

14 GWA 2006, s 149 and Sch 9 (previously the Government of Wales Act 1998, s 109 and Sch 8), although the JCPC was not been called upon to determine any 'devolution issues' under either Act before the transfer of its devolution jurisdiction to the Supreme Court.

15 NIA 1998, ss 11, 79, 82 and Sch 10. Again, the JCPC had not been asked to determine any 'devolution issues' under this Act before the jurisdiction was transferred to the Supreme Court.
16 See, for example, *Scottish Ministers v Scottish Information Commissioner* 2007 SC 330 discussed at p 275 and *Argyll and Bute Council v Scottish Public Services Ombudsman* 2008 SLT 168 discussed at p 355 n 4.
17 For a discussion of the definition and scope of 'political questions' under the United States Constitution, see *Baker v Carr* 369 US 186 (1962). However, constitutional courts have often displayed an unwillingness to relinquish jurisdiction over a dispute simply because it raises issues of political controversy. The Supreme Court of Canada has, for example, been prepared to rule on the constitutionality of the Canadian government's decision to permit testing of US cruise missiles within its territory (*Operation Dismantle v The Queen* [1985] 1 SCR 441). By contrast, in *Gibson v Lord Advocate* 1975 SLT 134, Lord Keith was of the view that the question whether UK legislation, in this case ECA 1972, s 2, which altered Scots private law, was not 'for the evident utility' of the Scottish people (as required by the Act of Union 1707, Art XVIII) was not a justiciable issue for the court.
18 *Operation Dismantle v The Queen* [1985] 1 SCR 441 per Wilson J at 471.
19 For example, the Commonwealth Constitution of Australia may be altered only by a law passed by the Australian Parliament and approved by both a majority of electors throughout Australia and by a majority of the electors in a majority of the states (Commonwealth Constitution, s 128). Only eight alterations to the Commonwealth Constitution were approved between 1906 and 1977: see Hanks p 29.
20 The most sustained debate on this has been in the United States. For some of the most prominent contributions, see H Wechsler 'Towards Neutral Principles of Constitutional Law' (1959) 73 Harv LR 1; AM Bickel *The Least Dangerous Branch* (1962); and JH Ely *Democracy and Distrust* (1980) (hereafter Ely).
21 One famous example of such protection being the decision of the US Supreme Court in *Brown v Board of Education* 347 US 483 (1954) in which it rejected the racial segregation of public schools on the ground that such segregation breached the constitutional right of those black children affected to 'equal protection of the laws'.
22 See, especially, Ely and Lord Steyn 'Democracy through Law' (2002) 6 EHRLR 723.
23 SA 1998, s 28(7).
24 See, for example, the comments of Lord President Rodger in *Whaley v Watson* 2000 SC 340 at 348, 349 and of Lord Brodie in *Whaley v Lord Advocate* 2004 SC 78 at page 98,99. Both cases are discussed below at pp 404–406.
25 HRA 1998, s 4 and see pp 391–393 below. Such a declaration of incompatibility does not affect the validity, continuing operation or enforcement of the legislation in question, nor is it binding on the parties to the proceedings in which it is made (HRA 1998, s 4(6)).

COURTS AND THE COMMON LAW

13.2   It is now more than 120 years since Dicey wrote his *Introduction to the Study of the Law of the Constitution* and, for many purposes, his work has to be regarded as largely overtaken by the political and constitutional events of the last century. Certainly the developments affecting the constitutional role of the courts, to be discussed in the later sections of this chapter, would have surprised (and probably dismayed) him. The growth of administrative law would perhaps have seemed the greatest shock.

There is, however, one aspect of the role of the courts, as Dicey described it, which remains residually in place. It was part of his version of the doctrine of the rule of law that the general principles of the British constitution are the result of judicial decisions determining the rights of private persons in particular cases brought before the courts[1]. They are inductions or general propositions based on particular decisions pronounced by the courts[2]. Even statutes 'being passed to meet special grievances, bear a close resemblance to judicial decisions, and are in effect judgments pronounced by the High Court of Parliament'[3]. This was all to be sharply contrasted with the situation in most other states where it was the written constitution itself that laid down general principles. Dicey regarded this as a 'merely formal difference' which did not, necessarily, have any impact on those whose rights were protected in this way. It was not that liberty was less well secured in Belgium, for instance: it was simply that it was differently secured[4]. Historically it was almost entirely to decided cases that, in the United Kingdom, one looked for the law and it was there that the landmark principles of civil liberties and the limits to public power were to be found.

By the beginning of this century, practically all of this had changed. For the protection of the rights and liberties of individuals, we now look primarily to statutes – for instance, anti-discrimination legislation[5] – and, above all, to the rights protected by the ECHR and secured under HRA 1998. There are, however, four ways in which an important common law jurisdiction survives. The *first* is in relation to all those areas in which, despite the general encroachment of statute, public bodies invoke common law powers in the exercise of their authority and it falls to the courts to determine the limits of those powers. Good examples of this arise where ministers use powers deriving from the royal prerogative, such as the prerogative of mercy[6] or, until statute intervenes[7], the power to regulate the civil service[8]. Such powers are usually subject to regulation under judicial review procedures[9]. *Secondly*, subject to specific statutory exceptions, and, in the case of the Crown, the Crown Proceedings Act 1947, public authorities are generally subject to common law rules on the extent of their civil liability in contract or delict when they are alleged to have acted in breach of contract or, for instance, negligently. The interpretation of the statutory powers of authorities in such cases will always be relevant but the courts have been forced to evolve common law principles of liability against the statutory background. It is a process which continues to prove uncomfortable for the courts as they try to develop general rules as to how far statutory powers and duties will, on the one hand, create the conditions of civil liability or, on the other hand, provide immunity from it[10]. Questions of how far public bodies should be liable in damages when injuries (or physical damage) are caused by a failure to clear snow from roads[11]; or to extinguish properly a fire in a neighbouring property[12]; to provide supervision of schoolchildren in a playground[13]; or to protect local authority tenants from the violent conduct of neighbours[14] have exercised judicial minds. The traditional approach of the English courts to questions of negligence by public authorities – in terms of which some latitude was afforded to those public bodies and restrictions were placed on the circumstances in which, in the exercise of public functions, a duty of care was owed to individuals – was successfully challenged in the European Court of Human Rights as an infringement of the rights of such individuals to a 'fair trial' under ECHR, art 6[15]. Although the Strasbourg Court has now effectively conceded that its decision in *Osman v United Kingdom* was based on a misunderstanding of English law, the case has had lasting effects, encouraging arguments for a more generous (from the point of view of the claimant) approach to claims against public authorities[16]. *Thirdly*, it can reasonably be argued that, except for some procedural and remedial aspects regulated under statute, the whole of the law of judicial review developed by the Court of Session in the exercise of its inherent supervisory jurisdiction is a creation of the common law. Judicial review is dealt with separately at pp 374–390. *Fourthly*, the wider claim is sometimes made that it is an aspect of the inherent powers of the courts and, therefore, of the common law when they claim to be the guardians of the unwritten constitution. They, and not Parliament, are, it has been argued, the ones to determine the ultimate powers of Parliament; they are the ones to determine the legitimate limits of institutional reform of the central constitutional relationship; they are the final guardians of the fundamental rights of citizens. These are claims which have been addressed at other points in this book.

1   AV Dicey *Law of the Constitution* (10th edn, 1959) (hereafter Dicey) p 195. For discussion of the rule of law see p 30.
2   Dicey p 197.
3   Dicey p 197.
4   Dicey p 198.
5   For example (and for the moment) the Sex Discrimination Act 1975, the Race Relations Act 1976 and the Disability Discrimination Act 1995 (all as amended). For discussion of the current Equality Bill see p 342 n 11.
6   *R v Secretary of State for the Home Department, ex parte Bentley* [1994] QB 349 (cf the comments of Lord Roskill in *Council of Civil Service Unions v Minister for the Civil Service* [1985] AC 374 at 418); *McDonald v Secretary of State for Scotland* 1996 SLT 16. For discussion of potential for the reform of prerogative powers see p 155 n 9.
7   The UK government has accepted (for some time) the need to regulate the civil service by statute: see p 184.
8   Council of *Civil Service Unions v Minister for the Civil Service* [1985] AC 374.
9   See pp 374–388 below.
10 See A Mason 'Negligence and the Liability of Public Authorities' (1998) 2 Edin LR 3; D Fairgrieve 'Pushing Back the Boundaries of Public Authority Liability' [2002] PL 288; C Booth and D Squires, The Negligence Liability of Public Authorities (2006); and D Brodie 'Public authority liability: the Scottish approach' (2007) 11 Edin LR 254.
11 *Syme v Scottish Borders Council* 2003 SLT 601; *Goodes v East Sussex CC* [2000] 3 All ER 603.
12 *Burnett v Grampian Fire and Rescue Service* 2007 SLT 61.
13 *Hunter v Perth and Kinross Council* 2001 SCLR 856.
14 *Mitchell v Glasgow City Council* 2009 SLT 247.
15 *Osman v United Kingdom* (2000) 29 EHRR 245.
16 *TP v UK* (2002) 34 EHRR 2; *Z v UK* (2002) 34 EHRR 3; and see A Lidbetter and J George 'Negligent Public Authorities and Convention Rights – The Legacy of *Osman*' (2001) 6 EHRLR 599.

JUDICIAL CONTROL OF ADMINISTRATIVE ACTION

13.3   One of Dicey's best-known stances, deriving from his conception of the proper role of the ordinary courts in the application of the ordinary law, was his antipathy to what he called 'administrative law'. By this he meant the '*droit administratif*' applied by the Conseil d'Etat to officials of the French state. His objection was that the application of special law by special courts or tribunals to officials was an automatic breach of (his version of) the rule of law. Any special treatment meant unacceptable concessions and a compromise of one of the constitution's highest principles.

A full account of the development of administrative law in the United Kingdom during the twentieth century, despite these inauspicious beginnings, cannot be given here[1]. However, the ideological clouding of Dicey's assessment of the changing condition of the British state – and its effects on the law and the role of the courts – lifted eventually, to reveal a strong system of administrative law. The last century saw the emergence of state institutions with expanded powers. The state became more interventionist, initially broadly in the direction of establishing the 'welfare state' but also in *consequence* of the state's role as promoter or regulator of many forms of economic activity. Such intervention brought inevitable disputes between public authorities and those affected by their decisions and the task of managing and resolving these disputes has fallen both to the ordinary courts and to specially created tribunals of limited jurisdiction. Challenges to the administrative decisions of public bodies are generally dealt with in one of two different ways:

1 See, for example, PP Craig *Administrative Law* (6th edn, 2008) ch 2; Lord Clyde and DJ Edwards *Judicial Review* (2000) ch 2; Woolf et al *De Smith's Judicial Review of Administrative Action* (6th edn, 2007), ch 1.

(a) Statutory appeals

13.4   First, the twentieth century saw a substantial growth in procedures, provided by statute, for challenging decisions made by government officials. In situations where many thousands of decisions are being made annually by such officials, considerations both of fairness to each individual affected and also of efficiency and consistency of provision demand that those initial decisions should not be absolutely final. Mistakes of fact may have been made by the original decision-maker or the relevant statutory rules may have been misinterpreted or misapplied. Parliament responded to these risks by establishing a wide variety of mechanisms for appeal and review.

Administrative Tribunals

13.5   In the first edition of this book we commented on the absence of any serious effort within the United Kingdom to establish a coherent, comprehensive system of administrative courts of general jurisdiction. We referred, in passing, to the clustering of provision to deal, for instance, with related welfare benefits[1] but also to the hundreds of self-standing systems of appeal which represented the more general picture. The most common model of tribunal might involve a three-stage process, beginning with an appeal against the initial decision to a tribunal (typically of three persons including a legally qualified chair, or a single person); followed by a further right of appeal to another tribunal (often chaired by a judge); and then a right of appeal on grounds of law alone to the Court of Session (or, in England, the High Court). We noted then that this model was by no means universal and that the diversity – or, more unkindly, lack of coherence – in tribunal provision had given cause for concern.

At that time, in 2003, the then Lord Chancellor's Department had just announced its intention – in response to the Leggatt Review – to bring together most non-devolved central government tribunals within a single tribunal service. Since then significant steps have been taken to reform the institutional framework within which administrative tribunals operate and further reform is anticipated within the next several years[2].

THE LEGGATT REVIEW   Sir Andrew Leggatt was appointed in 2000 to conduct a review of the existing tribunal structure for which the UK government was responsible. His terms of reference were wide ranging: he was to "review the delivery of justice through tribunals other than ordinary courts of law, constituted under an Act of Parliament by a Minister of the Crown or for purposes of a Minister's functions" and to review whether in resolving disputes, tribunals ensured "…fair, timely, proportionate and effective arrangements for handling those disputes, within an effective framework for decision-making which encourages the systematic development of the area of law concerned, and which forms a coherent structure, together with the superior courts, for the delivery of administrative justice;…[that] administrative and practical arrangements for supporting those decision-making procedures meet the requirements of the European Convention on Human Rights for independence and impartiality;" and whether proper arrangements for funding and performance management were in place and whether tribunals "overall constitute a coherent structure for the delivery of administrative justice"[3]. Sir Andrew's report was published in August 2001[4] and contained a large number of recommendations for reform. Some of those related to concerns over judicial independence – a recommendation that there should be separation between the minister or other authority whose policies and decisions are tested by a tribunal, and the minister who appoints and supports the tribunal itself[5] – while many more focused on the importance of modernising and unifying the tribunal system. In addition, Tribunals for Users made specific recommendations in relation to individual tribunals including the Criminal Injuries Compensation Appeals Panel, Employment Tribunals, the Pensions Appeal Tribunal and the Social Security and Child Support Commissioners.

THE TRIBUNALS SERVICE   In part response to the Leggatt Review, the UK government created a new executive agency, the Tribunals Service, in 2006[6] to provide a centralised and unified system of administrative support for most non-devolved UK tribunals. The Framework Document which governs the Tribunals Service describes its primary tasks as being to provide a responsive and efficient tribunals administration, to contribute to the improvement of the quality of decision-making across government, to reform the tribunals justice system for the benefit of its customers and the wider public, and to promote and protect the independence of the judiciary[7]. The Tribunals Service is headed by a Chief Executive who is to be distinguished from the Senior President – the most senior member of the tribunals judiciary (see below).

THE TRIBUNALS, COURTS AND ENFORCEMENT ACT 2007   Establishing the Tribunals Service was a precursor to more significant structural reform of the tribunal system itself by the Tribunals, Courts and Enforcement Act 2007 (TCEA 2007). TCEA 2007 creates a new framework into which, on a gradual basis, many existing UK tribunals will be expected to move. That framework involves a two-tier structure: a First-tier Tribunal and an Upper Tribunal, with the Upper Tribunal being described as a 'superior court of record', i.e. that its decisions are binding on tribunals and chambers below[8]. The

First-tier and Upper Tribunals are then[9] sub-divided into 'Chambers' which are intended to deal with matters of a broadly similar nature. Currently, the First-tier Tribunal is divided into four such Chambers: the Social Entitlement Chamber, the Health, Education and Social Care Chamber, the War Pensions and Armed Forces Compensation Chamber and the Tax Chamber[10]. The Upper Tribunal is divided into three Chambers: an Administrative Appeals Chamber, a Finance and Tax Chamber and a Lands Chamber. The jurisdiction of each First-tier and Upper Tribunal Chamber is set out in some detail in the order establishing the Chambers[11]. So, for example, the First-tier Social Entitlement Chamber has assigned to it functions relating to asylum, criminal injuries compensation, social security benefits and a number of other areas including industrial accidents.

Of particular interest is the jurisdiction of the Administrative Appeals Chamber of the Upper Tribunal. That Chamber has jurisdiction to hear appeals against decisions of all of the First-tier Chambers except the Tax Chamber (which appeals, as might be anticipated, are heard by the Finance and Tax Chamber of the Upper Tribunal). The Administrative Appeals Chamber also has jurisdiction to hear appeals against the decisions of other tribunals which are not comprised within a First-tier Chamber (for example, decisions of the Pensions Appeal Tribunal in Scotland[12] and, perhaps most unexpectedly, enjoys first instance jurisdiction over certain matters which would previously have been dealt with by way of petition for judicial review in the Court of Session[13]. That jurisdiction is discussed in more detail below (pp 383–384).

In addition to establishing the First-tier and Upper Tribunals, TCEA 2007 also makes provision relating to the tribunals judiciary. It firstly extends the 'guarantee' of judicial independence conferred by s3 of the Constitutional Reform Act 2005 (see p 301) to members of a range of tribunals[14]. It also creates a new office of Senior President of Tribunals and confers on the Senior President a number of powers and functions including, for example, a power to make representations to Parliament about matters "that appear to him to be matters of importance relating (a) to tribunal members, or (b) otherwise to the administration of justice by tribunals"[15]. The first Senior President, Lord Justice Carnwath (who is also a Lord Justice of Appeal) has been extremely active in promoting the work of the new tribunals and has produced three separate reviews assessing the way in which TCEA 2007 has been implemented over the past two years[16].

Finally, TCEA 2007 abolished the Council on Tribunals (and its Scottish Committee) and replaced it with the Administrative Justice and Tribunals Council (AJTC) the role of which is to keep the whole system of administrative justice under review, to consider ways in which to make that system more accessible, fair and efficient and to make recommendations for change or for further research[17]. The AJTC must establish a Scottish Committee (and indeed a Welsh Committee).

SCOTTISH TRIBUNALS[18]   The Leggatt review acknowledged the potential difficulties created by devolution in achieving a consistent approach to tribunal organisation where certain tribunals deal with matters which are wholly reserved, others are concerned with matters which are wholly devolved (for example the Crofters Tribunal) and others which are formally cross-border public authorities (see p 210)[19]. The Scottish Committee of the AJTC is concerned with all administrative tribunals with a Scottish role and it produces its own annual report for laying before the Scottish Parliament. In addition, in 2006 the then Scottish Public Services Ombudsman, Professor Alice Brown, established an Administrative Justice Steering Group to report on, amongst other things, the likely impact of TCEA 2007 on Scotland. Its report was published in June 2009 and included proposals for 'rationalising' tribunal provision in Scotland and for further exploration of the potential for a unified Scottish tribunals service[20].

It is impossible to conclude that the system of tribunals which now operates within Scotland and the remainder of the United Kingdom is entirely coherent or comprehensive but it is evident that the field of administrative justice is one in which there has been considerable activity in the last five years and in which significant further activity may be expected.

1   The Appeals Service Tribunals under the Social Security Act 1998.
2   For discussion of the history of tribunals as a mechanism for resolving administrative disputes and recent reforms see: M Adler 'Tribunal Reform: proportionate dispute resolution and the pursuit of administrative justice' (2006) 69 MLR 958.
3   The terms of reference were announced on 18 May 2000 by the then Lord Chancellor Lord Irvine of Lairg in a speech to the Council on Tribunals Conference.
4   Tribunals for Users – One System, One Service (2001), hereafter 'Tribunals for Users'.
5   Tribunals for Users, para 2.23.
6   The Tribunals Service falls under the umbrella of the Ministry of Justice.
7   Available at http://www.tribunals.gov.uk/Tribunals/Publications/publications.htm
8   TCEA 2007, s3.
9   By order made by the Lord Chancellor but with the concurrence of the Senior President of Tribunals: TCEA 2007, s7 and see the First-tier Tribunal and Upper Tribunal (Chambers) Order 2008, SI 2008/2684 (as amended).
10 A General Regulatory Chamber is expected to be established in September 2009.
11 Ibid.
12 Ibid, para 7(a)(iii).
13 See TCEA 2007, ss 20, 21 and SI 2008/2684 para 7(b)(ii).
14 TCEA 2007, s1.
15 TCEA, s 2 and sch 1, para 13.
16 See the Tribunals Service website: www.tribunals.gov.uk
17 TCEA, s 44 and sch 7.
18 For the position pre-TCEA 2007 see S Craig, 'Tribunals in Scotland' in A McHarg and T Mullen (eds), *Public Law in Scotland* (2006).
19 Tribunals for Users, ch 11.
20 Administrative Justice in Scotland – The Way Forward (2009).

Appeals to the Courts

13.6   Although the powers of most 'administrative' tribunals relate to decision-making by central (including devolved) government, decisions by local authorities and other bodies also attract statutory appellate procedures, sometimes involving a first stage appeal to the Scottish Ministers. The best example of such an appeal is that available to applicants for planning permission who are aggrieved by decisions made in the first instance by local authorities[1]. In other cases, rights of appeal are direct to the courts. Appeals from decisions of the Scottish Information Commissioner, for example, are to the Court of Session (see p 354). A special feature of Scottish practice at this level has been the role of the sheriff as, in effect, a statutory appellate tribunal[2]. The powers of the sheriff vary from one form of appeal to another. Sometimes those powers are cast in quite narrowly defined terms leaving the sheriff with only questions of law to decide[3] but sometimes the statutory formulae which are used give the sheriff a much wider range of decision-making over matters of fact, law and even of policy. This dimension of the sheriff's jurisdiction raises interesting questions about the appropriateness of the use of judges to determine the issues allocated to them. Are sheriffs, whose expertise derives from their training in the law, the people who can best decide whether a child should be admitted to a particular school or a house should be demolished because of its poor condition? This is an area in which the principle of the separation of powers seems to be largely ignored[4].

Whatever form they take, statutory appeals have some characteristics in common. The circumstances in which an appeal may be lodged are defined (for example, when an adverse decision has been issued by an official). So too are the categories of person permitted to make the appeal (for example, the person in respect of whom the decision has been made); the period within which an appeal must be made; the tribunal or court to whom the appeal must go; the permitted grounds of appeal; the powers of the relevant tribunal including the procedures it must follow and its powers to grant remedies, whether interim or final; and the availability of any further appeal against the decision. The rules on these matters vary from one statutory scheme to another and sometimes they are themselves cast in statutory language which is imprecise and in need of interpretation by a tribunal or court.

There is, however, a sharp contrast between, on the one hand, all the statutorily defined procedures for appeal to a tribunal or court and, on the other, the second type of challenge referred to above – the procedure known as judicial review in the Court of Session.

1 Town and Country Planning (Scotland) Act 1997, ss 47–48 (as amended by the Planning etc (Scotland) Act 2006). See also appeals against decisions of the Scottish Environment Protection Agency (SEPA) under the Pollution Prevention and Control (Scotland) Regulations 2000 (as amended), SSI 2000/323, reg 22.
2 See p 297.
3 Licensing (Scotland) Act 2005, s 131.
4 For discussion, see G Little 'Local Administration in Scotland: the Role of the Sheriff' in W Finnie et al (eds) *Edinburgh Essays in Public Law* (1991). The structure of the civil courts system as a whole, including rights of appeal, is currently under review by the Lord Justice Clerk, Lord Gill. Lord Gill's report and recommendations were due to be published in summer 2009.

(b) Judicial review[1]

13.7   Judicial review provides, like statutory appeals, a procedure by which the decision of a governmental authority or official may be challenged. However, unlike statutory appeals which are available, by definition, only where the UK or Scottish Parliament by statute has made specific provision for them[2], judicial review is a procedure which has simply been asserted as a power of the Court of Session by the court itself. It is claimed to be inherent; to be of very long standing; and the rules concerning its availability have been the subject of development by the court. The origins and history of this supervisory jurisdiction were outlined by Lord President Hope in the leading case of *West v Secretary of State for Scotland*[3] which is discussed in more detail below.

What makes the development of judicial review interesting is the way in which the courts have sought to define their role in the supervision and control of public bodies. It is often suggested that this role has expanded and certainly the numbers of decided cases did grow substantially during the twentieth century and especially in the second half of the century. At the same time, the courts have sought to place this expansion within a principled framework which, while permitting and justifying growth, also explains the limits to that growth. Sometimes, however, these principles have been indistinct because they are not expressly and coherently articulated by the judges. Indeed, it is not so very long ago that judicial review was described as a 'wilderness of single instances'[4]. Latterly, however, greater efforts have been made to articulate the conceptual basis of judicial review.

A good starting point is the early twentieth-century case of *Moss' Empires Ltd v Glasgow Assessor*[5] in which Lord Kinnear stated that '[w]herever any inferior tribunal or any administrative body has exceeded the powers conferred on it by statute to the prejudice of the subject, the jurisdiction of the court to set aside such excess of power as incompetent and illegal is not open to dispute'[6]. The reviewing power of the court is, in principle, triggered whenever it is claimed that an 'administrative body' has exceeded its powers.

The essential preconditions for the exercise of this supervisory power of review by the courts are four:

1 For fuller discussion of judicial review in Scotland, see Lord Clyde and DJ Edwards *Judicial Review* (2000); *SME Reissue* Administrative Law; A O'Neill *Judicial Review in Scotland* (1999); and S Blair *Scots Administrative Law: Cases and Materials* (1999). Leading English works include HWR Wade and CF Forsyth *Administrative Law* (10th edn, 2009); PP Craig *Administrative Law* (6th edn, 2008); and Woolf et al, De Smith's *Judicial Review of Administrative Action* (6th edn, 2007).
2 Occasionally by statutory instrument, for example the Licensing of Venison Dealers (Application Procedures etc) (Scotland) Order 1984, SI 1984/922.
3 *West v Secretary of State for Scotland* 1992 SC 385.
4 See HWR Wade and CF Forsyth *Administrative Law* (10th edn, 2009) at p 15, quoting Tennyson *Aylmer's Field*, line 441.
5 *Moss' Empires Ltd v Glasgow Assessor* 1917 SC (HL) 1.
6 *Moss' Empires Ltd v Glasgow Assessor* 1917 SC (HL) 1 at 6.

Scope

13.8   There must have been conferred on the administrative or other body under review a power to act or a power to decide – described by Lord President Hope in the leading case of *West v Secretary of State for Scotland* as a 'jurisdiction'[1]. Typically, this jurisdiction will have been conferred – in primary or secondary legislation – by the Westminster or Scottish Parliament but it may also have derived from a prerogative source, and perhaps from elsewhere. It is possible that the 'jurisdiction' may have been conferred by an arrangement which does not involve a Parliament or any public authority at all. For example, Lord

Hope referred to the decision in *St Johnstone FC v SFA*[2] in which the Court of Session considered that it was competent to review decisions of the Council of the Scottish Football Association to fine or expel member clubs in accordance with the SFA's articles of association. Lord Hope, in citing this case, also sought to emphasise that in Scots law the availability of judicial review did not depend on the existence of some 'public law' element in the decision-making process, as is the case in England[3]. That being said, purely contractual disputes – such as that between Mr West and his employers, the Scottish Prison Service – were not amenable to judicial review. What was absent from the relationship between those parties was the necessary 'tripartite relationship'[4] in which (1) power is conferred (2) on a party 'to whom the taking of the decision is entrusted' and (3) whose decision affects the rights and obligations of another person[5].

1 *West v Secretary of State for Scotland* 1992 SC 385.
2 *St Johnstone FC v SFA* 1965 SLT 171.
3 There is a large body of case law and scholarship on the need for a 'public law' element in English judicial review proceedings. For general discussion, see the references cited at p 375 n 1 and, in particular, *O'Reilly v Mackman* [1983] 2 AC 237; *Cocks v Thanet District Council* [1983] 2 AC 286; *Roy v Kensington and Chelsea Family Practitioner Committee* [1992] 1 AC 624; and *Boddington v British Transport Police* [1999] 2 AC 143.
4 For the difficulties of this terminology, see W Finnie 'Triangles as Touchstones of Review' 1993 SLT (News) 51 and CMG Himsworth 'Further West? More Geometry of Judicial Review' 1995 SLT (News) 127 and for further judicial consideration of the "West test" see *Blair v Lochaber DC* 1995 SLT 407; *Wm Fotheringham & Son v British Limousin Cattle Society Ltd* 2004 SLT 485 and *Magnohard Ltd v United Kingdom Atomic Energy Authority* 2004 SC 247.
5 Referring to *St Johnstone FC v SFA* 1965 SLT 171, Lord Hope described the case as 'a clear example of the tripartite relationship to which we referred earlier, by which a decision making body – in this case the council – has been entrusted by an enabling body with a limited jurisdiction for decision taking in regard to others to which it must adhere' (*West v Secretary of State for Scotland* 1992 SC 385 at 400). There have been several petitions for judicial review taken against sports clubs in recent years, leading some to question whether the availability of the supervisory jurisdiction in such cases is in the interests of the parties or the administration of justice. See *Irvine v Royal Burgess Golfing Society of Edinburgh* 2004 SCLR 386; *Crocket v Tantallon Golf Club* 2005 SLT 663 and *Smith v Nairn Golf Club* 2007 SLT 909 and, for discussion, S Thomson, 'Golf Clubbing Judicial Review to Death' 2008 SLT (News) 221.

Grounds

13.9 Secondly, there must be an alleged excess or abuse in the exercise of this power or jurisdiction. In *West v Secretary of State for Scotland*, Lord Hope reaffirmed that there was 'no substantial difference' between English law and Scots law as to the grounds which the process of decision-making may be open to review[1]. A helpful restatement of the grounds of review was developed in *CSSU v Minister for the Civil Service* (the '*GCHQ*' case)[2] at the hand of Lord Diplock. There he noted that 'the English law relating to judicial control of administrative action has been developed upon a case to case basis' but that this development had reached the stage where 'one could conveniently classify under three heads the grounds upon which administrative action is subject to judicial review. The first ground I would call "illegality", the second "irrationality" and the third "procedural impropriety"'[3].

It must be borne in mind that this summary of the grounds of judicial review was indeed a *restatement*: Lord Diplock identified three seemingly straightforward labels under which a number of different – but well established – principles could be grouped. These are principles which have been, by and large, developed on an incremental basis by the courts themselves on a case-by-case basis. Indeed, Lord Diplock adverted to the possibility of further such development not only of these three categories, but potentially, of altogether new heads:

> "That is not to say that further development on a case by case basis may not in course of time add further grounds. I have in mind particularly the possible adoption in the future of the principle of "proportionality which is recognised in the administrative law of several of our fellow members of the European Economic Community[4].

A full account of those principles cannot be given here[5] but an outline may give a flavour of the complexity which Lord Diplock's labels disguise.

ILLEGALITY Illegality is arguably the broadest of the three categories identified by Lord Diplock as giving rise to a claim for judicial review. Indeed, at one level – and illustrating immediately the difficulties of terminology which are inescapable in this area – all three categories represent illegality (or 'unlawfulness') of one sort or another. Lord Diplock described the ground as follows:

> "I mean that the decision-maker must understand correctly the law that regulates his decision-making power and must give effect to it. Whether he has or not is par excellence a justiciable question to be decided, in the event of dispute, by those persons, the judges, by whom the judicial power of the state is excercisable"[6]

The concept of 'illegality' encompasses ultra vires, by which is meant that a decision-maker must act within the four corners of the statutory powers under which he or she acts, but it also extends beyond that straightforward principle. So, for example, where statute clearly empowers a public body to provide 'ferry services' across the river Tay that public body may not use those powers to carry on profit-making tourist trips[7]. More than that, though, even where legislation appears to confer very wide decision-making powers – 'discretion' – on a public body or government minister, the courts have asserted their right to regulate the manner in which those powers may be exercised. They must be used for proper and not improper purposes[8]; the public body must take account of relevant and not irrelevant considerations[9]; and it must not act with malice or bad faith[10]. Where one person or body is charged with making a decision or taking action they must not delegate their responsibilities to another body or person[11] (although there are a number of exceptions to this general rule[12]) and they must not abdicate their responsibilities altogether by refusing or failing to make any decision at all[13].

One area of complexity which falls within the broad ambit of 'illegality' but which is often discussed as a free standing ground of judicial review is that of 'error of law'. This concerns circumstances in which it is claimed that in the exercise of administrative discretion by a public authority, or in the determination of disputes by an adjudicator such as a tribunal or arbiter, the decision-maker has failed to apply properly the law which governs the decision-making process. This is one area in which the grounds of review north and south of the border are not quite in step[14]. In England, it has been held that all errors of law are capable of being challenged by way of judicial review whereas the Scottish approach has been to distinguish between errors of law which are 'intra vires' – that is permissible for the original decision-maker to make without being challenged – and those which are 'ultra vires' – impermissible and giving rise to the possibility of the decision being struck down[15].

IRRATIONALITY   Judicial review is frequently characterised by the courts as an exercise in assessing the legality rather than the merits of the decisions of public bodies, ensuring that they act within their lawful powers. However, of the three grounds identified by Lord Diplock 'irrationality' comes closest to a test of the substantive merits of a decision. Lord Diplock viewed irrationality as simply another term for what had come to be known as '*Wednesbury* unreasonableness'[16] albeit described in slightly different language. In *Wednesbury*, Lord Greene MR explained that "if a decision on a competent matter is so unreasonable that no reasonable authority could ever have come to it then the courts will interefere"[17] whereas Lord Diplock's characterisation was that:

> "By 'irrationality' I mean what can by now be succinctly referred to as '*Wednesbury* unreasonableness... It applies to a decision which is so outrageous in its defiance of logic or of accepted moral standards that no sensible person who had applied his mind to the question to be decided could have arrived at it. Whether a decision falls within this category is a question that judges by their training and experience should be well equipped to answer, or else there is something badly wrong with out judicial system"

However described, traditionally, the courts have treated this as a very difficult test for a petitioner to meet, requiring to be satisfied that the decision-maker's judgment is quite obviously flawed before substituting their own[18].

PROCEDURAL IMPROPRIETY   Finally, the courts have been concerned to ensure not only that a decision-maker acts within the parameters of their lawful powers but also that the manner in which those powers are exercised meets certain minimum standards. The third ground of judicial review identified by Lord Diplock – that of a 'procedural impropriety' – has been characterised as imposing a 'duty to act fairly'[19] on those exercising discretionary powers:

> "I have described the third head as "procedural impropriety" rather than failure to observe basic rules of natural justice or failure to act with procedural fairness towards the person who will be affected by the decision. This is because susceptibility to judicial review under this head covers also failure by an administrative tribunal to observe procedural rules that are expressly laid down in the legislative instrument by which its jurisdiction is conferred, even where such failure does not involve any denial of natural justice."[20]

It requires them both to observe any relevant statutory procedural requirements but also to comply with the precepts of 'natural justice', that is the common law rules of fair process, which have been developed by the courts themselves.

So far as procedural requirements contained in legislation are concerned, one question which arises is whether a failure to follow such a procedural requirement should have the consequence that the action taken by the public authority – which might but for the procedural failure be quite lawful – should be treated as being wholly invalid or whether it may survive. Sometimes the legislation under scrutiny will make express provision about what is to happen if procedural hurdles are not cleared but, where it does not, historically one way in which the courts have answered the question is by categorising statutory procedural requirements as being of one of two kinds: mandatory or directory. In the case of mandatory requirements a failure will result in the nullity of the public body's act whereas in the case of directory requirements a failure will not automatically lead to that result. Doubt has been case on the usefulness of this distinction[21] and though it continues to feature[22] other approaches have also found favour. In particular, the seriousness of the breach and the impact of the breach on the person(s) affected by the public body's action will influence the attitude of the courts[23].

In addition to such statutory requirements there are also, of course, the principles of natural justice which may be summarised as follows.

Firstly, the rule against bias – *nemo iudex in sua causa* – concerns the impartiality of the decision-maker himself. This concept is discussed in much fuller detail in Chapter 11 and involves, for example, a requirement that a decision-maker should not have any personal pecuniary interest in the outcome of the decision-making process[25], should not make a decision directly involving someone, such as a family member, with whom he has a close personal relationship[25], or having a direct impact on a company of which he is a director[26]. The rule against bias goes beyond a prohibition against the decision-maker actually acting in a partial manner towards one or other of the parties. Reliance is often placed on the dictum that 'justice must not only be done but must manifestly be seen to be done'[27] and decisions may be struck down where the circumstances are such that a 'fair-minded and informed observer, having considered the facts, would conclude that there was a real possibility that the tribunal was biased'[28].

Secondly, the right to a hearing – *audi alteram partem* – focuses on the rights of a party involved in a dispute or affected by an administrative decision to put their case fully and effectively to the court, tribunal or public body entrusted with decision-making powers. Although many cases have concerned the very specific issue of whether a party is entitled to an oral hearing before a decision is made, the right to a hearing encompasses wider concerns with fair procedure. Consideration has been given, for example, to the circumstances in which a person may be entitled to legal representation[29], to lead witnesses[30] and to test the evidence of an opponent whether by cross-examination or otherwise[31]. Questions have also concerned the right of a party to have appropriate notice of any case against him and to have access to evidence which may be used by his opponent or by the decision-maker in forming a view on the merits of his case[32].

Closely linked to these two main principles of natural justice are rules which concern when and to what extent a party is entitled to be furnished with the reasons for any decision which is made[33]. In addition, ECHR, art 6 concerns procedural fairness and a breach of that article (or indeed any other of those incorporated by HRA 1998) may now provide grounds for judicial review[34].

1 A position taken earlier by Lord Fraser in *Brown v Hamilton District Council* 1983 SC (HL) 1 at 42.
2 *CCSU v Minister for the Civil Service* [1985] AC 374.
3 *CCSU v Minister for the Civil Service* [1985] AC 374 at 410.
4 Ibid, and for discussion of proportionality see p 386.
5 See the works cited at p 375 n 1.
6 Ibid.
7 *Dundee Harbour Trustees v Nicol* 1915 SC (HL) 7. Nor, where a statute requires a local authority to provide a 'pure supply of wholesome water' will that permit the proactive fluoridation of the water supply as a purported public health measure: *McColl v Strathclyde Regional Council* 1983 SC 225.
8 *Highland Regional Council v British Railways Board* 1996 SLT 274; *Congreve v Home Office* [1976] QB 629; *Bromley London Borough Council v Greater London Council* [1983] 1 AC 768.
9 *Gerry Cottle's Circus Ltd v City of Edinburgh District Council* 1990 SLT 235; *Roberts v Hopwood* [1925] AC 579.
10 *Pollok School Co Ltd v Glasgow Town Clerk* 1946 SC 373; *R v Secretary of State for the Environment, ex parte Ostler* [1977] QB 122.
11 *Young v Fife Regional Council* 1986 SLT 331; *Dalziel School Board v Scotch Education Department* 1915 SC 234.
12 *Carltona v Commissioners of Works* [1943] 2 All ER 560; *R v Home Secretary, ex parte Oladehinde* [1991] 1 AC 254; Local Government (Scotland) Act 1973, s 56; and *cf R v Race Relations Board, ex p Selvarajan* [1976] 1 All ER 12; *Sommerville v Scottish Ministers (No 2)* 2008 SC (HL) 45.
13 *Kilmarnock Magistrates v Secretary of State for Scotland* 1961 SC 350; *British Oxygen Co Ltd v Minister of Technology* [1971] AC 610.
14 See SME Reissue, Administrative Law, paras 47 to 51.
15 See *Watt v Lord Advocate* 1979 SC 120.
16 *Associated Provincial Picture Houses Ltd v Wednesbury Corpn* [1948] 1 KB 223.
17 In *Associated Provincial Picture Houses Ltd v Wednesbury Corpn* [1948] 1 KB 223, Lord Greene MR referred to a decision 'so unreasonable that no reasonable authority could ever have come to it' ([1948] 1 KB 223 at 230). See the discussion at p 385 below.
18 *Secretary of State for Education and Science v Tameside Metropolitan Borough Council* [1977] AC 1014; *K v Scottish Legal Aid Board* 1989 SC 21; *Woods v Secretary of State for Scotland* 1991 SLT 197; *McTear v Scottish Legal Aid Board* 1995 SCLR 611; *Rooney v Strathclyde Police Joint Board* 2009 SC 73.
19 *Re HK (an infant)* [1967] 2 QB 617; *Errington v Wilson* 1995 SC 550.
20 Ibid.
21 *London and Clydeside Estates Ltd v Aberdeen District Council* 1980 SC (HL) 1 and *Wang v Commissioner for Inland Revenue* [1995] 1 All ER 367.
22 See, for example, *R v Birmingham City Council, ex parte Ireland* [1999] 2 All ER 609 and *Robinson v Secretary of State for Northern Ireland* [2002] NI 390.
23 See, for example, *Mitchell v North Lanarkshire Council* 2007 SLT 765 in which a petition for judicial review of a demand notice for Council Tax – on the grounds that the notice failed to refer to the recipient's right of appeal or to a colour pamphlet which ought to have been sent with the notice – was dismissed. Lord McEwan held that "it would be astonishing if Parliament having laid out a careful scheme for taxation then legislated in subordinate rules for the frustration of the scheme if the collection documents were not a model of clarity" (para 16).
24 *Dimes v Grand Junction Canal Proprietors* (1852) 3 HL Cas 759; *Sellar v Higland Railway Co* 1919 SC (HL) 19.
25 *Moncrieff v Lord Moncrieff* (1904) 6 F 1021.
26 *R v Bow Street Metropolitan Stipendiary Magistrate, ex parte Pinochet Ugarte (No 2)* [2000] 1 AC 119.
27 See *Barrs v British Wool Marketing Board* 1957 SC 72.
28 *Porter v Magill* [2002] 2 AC 357 per Lord Hope of Craighead at 494.

29 *Abbas v Home Secretary* 1993 SLT 502; *R v Home Secretary, ex parte Tarrant* [1985] QB 251.

30 *R v Hull Board of Prison Visitors, ex parte St Germain (No 2)* [1979] 3 All ER 545.

31 *R v Hull Board of Prison Visitors, ex parte St Germain (No 2)* [1979] 3 All ER 545; *Errington v Wilson* 1995 SC 550.

32 *Inland Revenue Comrs v Barr* 1956 SC 162; *Moore v Clyde Pilotage Authority* 1943 SC 457; *R v Criminal Injuries Compensation Board, ex parte Ince* [1973] 3 All ER 808; *R v Home Secretary, ex parte Fayed* [1997] 1 All ER 228.

33 *R v Civil Service Appeal Board, ex parte Cunningham* [1991] 4 All ER 310; *R v Higher Education Funding Council, ex parte Institute of Dental Surgery* [1994] 1 WLR 242.

34 *Anderson v Scottish Ministers* 2002 SC (PC) 63.

Title and Interest[1]

13.10   Thirdly, there must be someone (whether a natural or artificial person or group of persons) who has the necessary *locus standi* or title and interest to sue. The courts in both Scotland and England have been keen to insist that they are not simply available to all and sundry in judicial review proceedings. Judicial review may not be sought by someone with a merely academic interest in, or who is otherwise unaffected by, the act or decision of the public authority. In England, a person is statutorily required to have 'sufficient interest' in the case.[2] In Scotland, there has been no statutory definition of *locus standi* but the Court of Session has insisted on the need for both *title* – deriving from 'some legal relation' which gives the petitioner some right which the person against whom he or she raises the action infringes or denies[3] – and an *interest* which, will usually derive from the petitioner's pecuniary rights or status[4]. The practical consequences of the need to establish both title and interest may not be very great – of those motivated to raise the issue in the courts, there will usually be *someone* who satisfies the tests – but a question of concern has been the standing of representative voluntary organisations such as pressure groups. While in England, the courts appear to have taken a generous view[5], the Scottish *Age Concern* case[6] continues to impose a more restrictive regime. In that case Age Concern Scotland was held not to have the 'interest' necessary to challenge the legality of administrative guidance concerning the payment of cold weather allowances to elderly people. In reaching this view Lord Clyde took account of a number of factors including the fact that it had not been argued that 'the association or any of its members have claimed the benefit in question or are intending to do so ... [they] are not suing as a body of potential claimants but as a body working to protect and advance the interests of the aged'[7]. A variation on this approach to the standing of representative bodies was put forward by Lord Clarke in *Rape Crisis Centre v Secretary of State for the Home Department*[8] in which the petitioners – a limited company engaged in the provision of advice and support to rape victims and one of its employees – were held not to have the necessary 'title' to challenge the Home Secretary's decision to grant entry clearance to the United Kingdom to the boxer Mike Tyson. That decision was made under Immigration Rules which 'did not confer general duties owed to members of the public as a whole, creating between the [Home Secretary] and a member of the public ... [any] legal "relationship"'[9].

The limits placed on the involvement of pressure groups, voluntary associations and campaigning organisations in matters of sometimes very great controversy or public interest, by this approach to title and interest have been ameliorated somewhat by new rules concerning 'public interest intervention' in judicial review proceedings. Since 2000[10] it has been possible for a party who believes that proceedings for judicial review (which have been initiated by someone with title and interest) raise a matter of 'public interest' to apply for leave to intervene in those proceedings. Before leave is granted the court must be satisfied that a matter of public interest is at stake, that the applicant has relevant arguments to make and that the intervention will not 'unduly delay or otherwise prejudice the rights of the parties, including their potential liability for expenses'. Where intervention is allowed the intervener's submissions are normally to be made in writing, although an oral hearing may be held. There are no reported cases in which an application for public interest intervention in Scottish judicial review proceedings has been made, much less succeeded. However, in 2008 the NGO Liberty was given leave to intervene in the public interest in proceedings for contempt involving a Scottish solicitor who had criticised a trial judge following his client's conviction for terrorist offences. Notwithstanding that the rules of court applicable to such proceedings contain no express provision for intervention, Liberty were permitted to make written and oral submissions in relation to the implications of the proceedings for the solicitor's rights to freedom of expression under art 10 ECHR[11].

In a separate and recent development the rules of the Court of Session have been found to allow a number of interested parties to enter the process in the ongoing judicial review of the Damages (Asbestos-related Conditions) (Scotland) Act 2009 (see p 407 below) as additional 'respondents' to that judicial review. Eight individuals relied on a rule of court (RCS 58.8(2)). entitling any person on whom the petition for review was not originally served – but who contends that they are 'directly affected' by any issue raised in the review – to apply for leave to enter the process. Lord Uist, in granting the motion for leave to enter the process, expressed the view that the terms of the rule obviated any need for the individuals concerned to demonstrate title and interest to defend the petition[12]. It remains to be seen whether the Lord Ordinary hearing the merits of the petition will take a different view on the need to demonstrate title and interest.

1   See T Mullen, 'Standing to Seek Judicial Review' in A McHarg and T Mullen (eds), *Public Law in Scotland* (2006).
2   Senior Courts Act 1981, s 31(3).
3   *Dundee Harbour Trustees v D Nicol* 1915 SC (HL) 7 at 12, 13 (per Lord Dunedin).
4   *Swanson v Manson* 1907 SC 426 at 429 (per Lord Ardwall).
5   See, for example, *R v HM Inspectorate of Pollution, ex parte Greenpeace Ltd (No 2)* [1994] 4 All ER 329 (challenge to grant of permission for discharge of radioactive waste) and *R v Secretary of State for Foreign and Commonwealth Affairs, ex parte World Development Movement Ltd* [1995] 1 All ER 611 (successful challenge by pressure group to government's decision to grant aid for construction of Malaysian hydro-electric dam).
6   *Scottish Old People's Welfare Council, Petitioners* 1987 SLT 179.
7   *Scottish Old People's Welfare Council, Petitioners* 1987 SLT 179 at 187.
8   *Rape Crisis Centre v Secretary of State for the Home Department* 2000 SC 527.
9   *Rape Crisis Centre v Secretary of State for the Home Department* 2000 SC 527 at 535.
10 Act of Sederunt (Rules of the Court of Session Amendment No 5) (Public Interest Intervention in Judicial Review) 2000, SSI 2000/317 (as amended); and see R Charteris 'Intervention – in the Public Interest' 2000 SLT (News) 87. For the significance of third-party interventions in human rights litigation, see A Loux 'Writing Wrongs: Third-party Intervention Post-incorporation' in A Boyle et al (eds) *Human Rights and Scots Law* (2002).

11 See *Anwar*, 2008 JC 409 and JP Marshall, 'Liberty to intervene beyond judicial review' 2008 SLT (News) 187.
12 Unreported decision of Lord Uist of 8 May 2009.

Access to the courts

13.11   The final core prerequisite for judicial review is that access to the courts has not been prohibited or curtailed by statute. Judicial review is a power asserted by the courts but its scope and availability are open to manipulation by Parliaments. This may take two principal forms, sometimes in combination. The first is where there has been provision for a statutory remedy – typically an appeal to a court or tribunal – which may be used, as described above, by specified persons to challenge the administrative act or decision. The courts have, in general, taken the view that where such a statutory appeal has been provided, Parliament has impliedly excluded the residual option of judicial review[1]. The second form of statutory intervention has been where Parliament has gone further and has explicitly excluded review. In most cases, this has been in circumstances where statute has deliberately provided an appeal but restricted access to the appeal to a specified period of, for example, six weeks and then excluded any form of legal challenge thereafter[2]. In a few cases, the Westminster Parliament has simply excluded review, without access to any form of statutory appeal. Considerations of secrecy and state security have been used to justify some such use of provisions to 'oust' the jurisdiction of the courts in this way[3].

Another oft-cited example was the statutory attempt to close off all challenges to decisions ('determinations') made by a body known as the Foreign Compensation Commission. The Foreign Compensation Act 1950 provided that '[t]he determination by the commission of any application made to them under this Act shall not be called in question in any court of law'[4]. However in the leading case of *Anisminic Ltd v Foreign Compensation Commission*[5] the House of Lords showed great ingenuity, if not defiance, in holding that even such clear statutory rules did not exclude review of a determination which was demonstrably invalid through the legal error of the Commission. Despite a general attitude of deference to the will of Parliament – an attitude which the courts may in general be expected to extend to the Scottish Parliament – the courts are apt to respond more robustly when their own powers are at stake[6]. The courts' wish, and indeed obligation, to secure their powers of review against statutory intervention is strengthened by the terms of ECHR, art 6, especially since its incorporation by HRA 1998 and – with heightened impact on the Scottish Parliament – by SA 1998[7].

A rather different issue concerning access to the courts for the purposes of judicial review is raised by TCEA 2007[8] which for the first time empowers a court other than the Court of Session to consider first instance applications for judicial review. The Court of Session must in some cases and may in others transfer petitions for judicial review to the new Upper Tribunal (and specifically to the Administrative Appeals Chamber) to be heard there. An application *must* be transferred if all that is sought is an exercise of the supervisory jurisdiction of the Court of Session, if the application does not concern certain immigration and nationality matters[9] and if the application is of a type specified by an Act of Sederunt made with the consent of the Lord Chancellor. The only type of application so specified to date is an application which challenges a procedural decision or a procedural ruling of the First-tier Tribunal[10]. An application *may* be transferred if, again, all that is sought is an exercise of the supervisory jurisdiction, the application relates to matters which are not devolved and it does not relate to the citizenship and nationality matters described above[11]. The powers of the Upper Tribunal in relation to such cases are the same as the powers of review of the Court of Session in an application to the supervisory jurisdiction[12] and the Upper Tribunal is bound to apply the same principles of judicial review as would be applied by the Court of Session[13]. Whether in fact the approach of the Upper Tribunal to Scottish judicial review applications differs in a material way from that of the Court of Session remains to be seen.

Access to the courts may also, practically rather than legally speaking, be cut off by inadequate resources or by the fear that failure will lead to an adverse award of expenses running to tens or potentially hundreds of thousands of pounds. Where legal aid may not be available, the English courts have been prepared in limited circumstances to make a 'protective costs order': in essence an order which provides an 'insurance policy' to a litigant by making it clear that they will not be required to meet the other party's expenses if their case ultimately fails. Such an order will be made only where, amongst other requirements, the issues raised by the case are of 'general public importance'[14]. The Scottish courts have expressed a preparedness in principle to make such an order[15] but no such order has in fact been made to date.

Finally, and on the other side of the 'access' coin, persons aggrieved by the decision of a public authority are normally expected to exhaust all statutory remedies which they may have before pursuing a petition for judicial review[16].

1   See, for example, *O'Neill v Scottish Joint Negotiating Committee for Teaching Staff* 1987 SC 90.
2   For such time limits in a planning context, see *Hamilton v Secretary of State for Scotland* 1972 SC 72 and *Pollock v Secretary of State for Scotland* 1993 SLT 1173.
3   See, for example, the Prevention of Terrorism Act 2005, s 11 concerning appeals against certain decisions relating to the 'control orders' (as to which see p 336 n 5).
4   Foreign Compensation Act 1950, s 4(4).
5   *Anisminic Ltd v Foreign Compensation Commission* [1969] 2 AC 147.
6   See p 388.
7   See p 371.
8   See p 372 above.
9   The application must not call into question any decision made under the Immigration Acts or the British Nationality Act 1981 or under any instrument having effect under those Acts, or a decision made under any other provision of law which determines British citizenship, British overseas territories citizenship, the status of a British National (Overseas) or British Overseas citizenship: TCEA 2007, s 20(5). But see Borders, Citizenship and Immigration Bill 2008–09.
10 See Act of Sederunt (Transfer of Judicial Review Applications from the Court of Session) 2008, SSI 2008/357.
11 See TCEA 2007, s 20.
12 TCEA 2007, s 21(2).
13 TCEA 2007, s 21(3).
14 See *R (Corner House Research) v Secretary of State for Trade and Industry* [2005] 1 WLR 2600.
15 *McArthur v Lord Advocate* 2006 SLT 170.
16 See *British Railways Board v Glasgow Corporation* 1976 SC 24.

Judicial review and the constitution

13.12   The constitutional significance of judicial review hardly needs to be stated. It enables and indeed compels courts to determine whether the acts and decisions of public authorities are legally valid and thus whether they are, or can become, enforceable. The courts are there both for the protection of individuals (frequently also companies, other businesses and sometimes public bodies themselves) from unlawful activity by public authorities and also, where appropriate, to uphold the lawful acts of those authorities as they implement powers conferred by statute[1]. In so doing, the courts are, in either event, implementing the will of Parliament[2] and upholding the rule of law: a function simply described but sensitive in its operation.

It is sensitive because the striking down of decisions made by executive bodies – especially those such as local councils and ministers who are democratically elected and directly accountable to the electorate – is a serious matter. It reconfirms the need for a robust and independent judiciary but, in order to maintain their legitimacy, it also requires the judiciary to remain within their allocated domain. They must be seen to confine themselves to deciding the issues before them on legal and not political grounds. They must be seen not merely to substitute their views on how executive decisions should be made for the views of those whom a Parliament has designated for the task. This is a position frequently restated by the courts themselves[3] as a shield from criticisms that might otherwise be launched against them. However, two particular features of judicial review can still make the courts' task controversial. Both relate to the grounds of review.

The first is the problem of statutory interpretation and the evaluation, often in the light of loosely constructed criteria such as 'fairness' and 'reasonableness', of the lawfulness of administrative action. It might be thought, for instance, that Lord Diplock's 'procedural impropriety' would be relatively easy to detect. A decision-maker has either followed the statutory procedures laid down or he or she has not. But it is not as simple as that[4]. The courts have, in addition, adopted and applied their own standards of procedural propriety. They have applied tests of 'natural justice' (incorporating the need for impartiality of the decision-maker and the need to hear both sides before deciding), 'fairness' and, latterly, the obligation of decision-makers to respect the 'legitimate expectation' of a hearing prior to decision[5]. Much flexibility attaches to the interpretation of all those terms and indeed to the concept of 'unreasonableness'. On the one hand, unreasonableness may be viewed as synonymous with Lord Diplock's 'irrationality', itself a term giving a broad interpretative freedom to the courts. As we have seen, in the earlier classic English case of *Associated Provincial Picture Houses Ltd v Wednesbury Corporation*[6] Lord Greene referred to the sort of decision caught by this test as one 'so unreasonable that no reasonable authority could ever have come to it'[7]. But, while that case provided Lord Greene with the opportunity to warn against the intrusion by courts into the decision-making of bodies on whom Parliament has conferred the power to decide, it also enabled him to broaden the scope of reviewable unreasonableness to include cases where public bodies were claimed to have taken into account 'irrelevant considerations', failed to take into account 'relevant considerations' or used their powers for an 'improper purpose'. Once again, tests cast in such terms provide much freedom for courts.

In addition to such interpretative difficulties and the apparent threats to the legitimacy of the process of judicial review that they produce, there is a wider debate about expanding the grounds of judicial review. In his speech in the GCHQ case, Lord Diplock not only set out the existing grounds of review but also speculated that they might, in due course, be joined by others. In particular, he mentioned a test of 'proportionality'[8]. There are a number of different understandings of what such a test demands of decision-makers. One widely deployed is that the decision-maker should not 'use a sledgehammer to crack a nut'[9]. More prosaically, in the context of EC law, the test has been formulated as allowing a decision-maker to take measures which interfere with fundamental rights only so far as 'necessary and appropriate'[10]. Now, no one would deny, of course, that proportionality so defined is a desirable quality in decision-making. The question, as with tests of reasonableness and fairness, is whether the arbiter of these standards should be administrative bodies – who should be politically accountable for the proportionality of their decisions – or whether their judgment should be second-guessed by courts. For some, the extension of the reviewing courts' jurisdiction to embrace proportionality would be unproblematic. Either it would involve the same processes as deciding questions of 'irrationality' or be only a small extension of them; the obligation of United Kingdom courts to apply EC law[11] already requires the courts to use the proportionality tests and it would be logical to extend that use into non-EC issues; and, similarly, the need for courts to apply the terms of the ECHR involves the 'balancing' of individual rights against the public interest – a process which, again, closely resembles recourse to proportionality[12].

Against this, it is reasoned that the tests of rationality and proportionality involve quite different techniques. Judges are equipped to recognise a decision which is 'outrageous in its defiance of logic or of accepted moral standards'[13] when they see it. However, they have neither the skills nor the resources to undertake the balancing exercise demanded by the proportionality test[14]. The fact that EC law requires a particular response does not demand its extension. And the same applies to the ECHR: the obligation to balance rights does not carry with it the competence to balance wider policy issues.

Whatever the rights and wrongs of these arguments, it is probably true to say that the UK courts have not yet taken up the invitation trailed by Lord Diplock in GCHQ. The House of Lords took a firm negative stance on proportionality in *R v Home Secretary, ex parte Brind*[15] and, although there have been, for instance, dicta in *Daly*[16] and *Alconbury*[17] which suggest a greater sympathy towards arguments based explicitly or implicitly on a proportionality test, the formal position appears not to have shifted[18].

The debate about the proper limits of the grounds of judicial review is one which has been further complicated by a separate but related discussion about the more fundamental constitutional basis of judicial review. There has been a (perhaps rather contrived) tussle between those who see the function of judicial review as to uphold Parliament's will and those, on the other hand, who see the courts' authority to undertake judicial review as grounded not simply in obedience to Parliament but in the common law[19]. It may be that there is less at stake in this debate than meets the eye and, in any event, a truce seems to have been called around a compromise position. If, however, there really is an important disagreement here, it is one which would produce different views of the desirability and indeed the competence of the courts to extend their review jurisdiction into new areas. At the heart of all debates about the proper jurisdiction of courts of law – whether in relation to the expansion of judicial review into proportionality or the adoption of more pervasive human rights adjudication – is the question of whether greater trust and reliance should be placed in political or judicial accountability.

1   Advocates of each of these sometimes competing interests – protection of individual liberty versus facilitating the work of government – have been described, respectively as 'red light' and 'green light' theorists: C Harlow and R Rawlings *Law and Administration* (2nd edn, 1997).
2   But see p 391 below.
3   See *Associated Provincial Picture Houses Ltd v Wednesbury Corpn* [1948] 1 KB 223 and, in the planning context, Lord Hoffmann in *Tesco Stores Ltd v Secretary of State for the Environment* [1995] 2 All ER 636: 'If there is one principle of planning law more firmly settled than any other, it is that matters of planning judgment are within the exclusive province of the local planning authority or the Secretary of State' (at 657).
4   See eg p 379 above.
5   This 'legitimate expectation' can arise in a variety of ways, for example where a public authority gives an undertaking that a hearing will be held before a given decision is taken (see *A-G of Hong Kong v Ng Yuen Shiu* [1983] 2 AC 629) or where the individual involved has enjoyed the benefit of some right or licence and it is proposed that this be withdrawn or revoked by a public body (see *McInnes v Onslow-Fane* [1978] 3 All ER 211).
6   *Associated Provincial Picture Houses Ltd v Wednesbury Corpn* [1948] 1 KB 223.
7   *Associated Provincial Picture Houses Ltd v Wednesbury Corpn* [1948] 1 KB 223 at 230.
8   *CCSU v Minister for the Civil Service* [1985] AC 374 at 410.
9   See *R v Secretary of State for the Home Department, ex parte Brind* [1991] 1 AC 696 per Lord Ackner at 759.
10 See *R v Chief Constable of Sussex, ex p International Trader's Ferry Ltd* [1999] 2 AC 418 and *Commission v France* [1997] ECR I-6959.
11 See pp 48–50.
12 See p 395 below.
13 *CCSU v Minister for the Civil Service* [1985] AC 374 per Lord Diplock at 410.
14 In *R v Secretary of State for the Home Department, ex parte Brind* [1991] 1 AC 696, Lord Lowry expressed the view that the fact that proportionality was not an established principle of English law was 'no cause for regret' because, amongst other things '[t]he judges are not, generally speaking, equipped by training or experience, or furnished with the requisite knowledge and advice, to decide the answer to an administrative problem where the scales are evenly balanced, but they have a much better chance of reaching the right answer where the question is put in a *Wednesbury* form' ([1991] AC 696 at 767).
15 *R v Home Secretary, ex parte Brind* [1991] 1 AC 696.
16 *R (Daly) v Home Secretary* [2001] 2 AC 532. 'The infringement of prisoners' rights to maintain the confidentiality of their privileged legal correspondence is greater than is shown to be necessary to serve the legitimate public objectives already identified' (per Lord Bingham of Cornhill at 543).
17 *R (Holding & Barnes plc) v Secretary of State for the Environment, Transport and the Regions* [2001] 2 All ER 929: 'I consider that even without reference to the 1998 Act the time has come to recognise that this principle is part of English administrative law, not only when judges are dealing with community acts but also when they are dealing with acts subject to domestic law' (per Lord Slynn of Hadley at 976). The House of Lords disposed of a number of separate applications in this case, one of which had been raised by Alconbury Developments Ltd.
18 See *Somerville v Scottish Ministers* 2008 SC (HL) 45 in which their Lordships declined to address the question directly.
19 See C Forsyth (ed) *Judicial Review and the Constitution* (2000) and, for other contributions, PP Craig 'Constitutional Foundations, the Rule of Law and Supremacy' [2003] PL 92; C Forsyth

and M Elliot 'The Legitimacy of Judicial Review' [2000] PL 286; TRS Allan 'Doctrine and Theory in Administrative Law: An Elusive Quest for the Limits of Jurisdiction' [2003] PL 429; A Lever, 'Is Judicial Review Undemocratic?' [2007] PL 280.

JUDICIAL REVIEW OF DELEGATED LEGISLATION

13.13 As already seen, an important characteristic of judicial review is the breadth of its application across the full extent of decision-making by ministers, local authorities and other public bodies and officials. One aspect of its coverage is that it extends to include not only the 'administrative' decision-making of public bodies but also their law-making. When ministers, including the Scottish Ministers, make delegated legislation in the form of statutory instruments[1] or local authorities make byelaws, the validity of such delegated legislation may be questioned in judicial review proceedings[2]. If it fails the tests laid down by the Court of Session discussed at pp 376–381, the court may intervene. It is unsurprising, however, that the review of delegated legislation does raise some special questions which have required a response from the courts.

The relative generality of the scope of legislative rules rather than of specific decisions may prompt different problems of *locus standi*[3] – who is or might be relevantly affected by them? In addition, many rule-making powers are extremely widely drafted and this has caused the courts to take a view of the purposes for which the use of the powers was intended[4]. Courts have adopted a restrictive interpretation of powers to insist that the rights of individuals should not be adversely affected, unless clear language in the empowering statute justifies this. Thus, the courts will tend to take a narrow view of rules purporting to rely on a merely implied power to impose a tax or charge[5]; or to restrict professional freedom with retrospective effect[6]; or to restrict access to the courts[7]. In the absence of express statutory language, the courts will presume that it was not the legislature's intention to enact such intrusions into individual liberty. Another difference in the interpretation of powers of delegated law-making is that questions of fairness and natural justice[8] may take a different form. Nevertheless important issues about, for instance, the scope and thoroughness of consultation prior to rules being made have proved important[9].

Three other special characteristics of the review of delegated legislation deserve particular mention. One is the robust defence by the courts of their power to review a statutory instrument despite the fact that the instrument under review may previously have been approved under the affirmative resolution procedure[10] by the relevant Parliament[11] or, by default, under the negative procedure. The courts have sometimes suggested that they should be even more sparing in making a finding of irrationality in respect of an instrument approved not only by a minister but also by Parliament itself. A measure of additional deference is called for because of the constitutional relationship involved[12]. But it is clear that the deference accorded to Acts of the UK Parliament by virtue of the doctrine of the sovereignty of Parliament is not, in principle, extendable to other rules approved by Parliament[13]. A second special feature of the review of delegated legislation is that, if a challenge to the validity of an instrument is upheld, a question may arise as to whether the court is obliged to strike down the whole of the instrument, leaving it of no legal effect whatever, or whether the court may instead strike down the instrument only to the extent of its defective part or parts, leaving the rest of the instrument intact. Here the courts have taken the view that a finding of partial validity and partial invalidity is a legitimate outcome. Where it can be assumed that the rule-making authority would still have wished to issue the remaining rules if it had known in advance that others would be nullified, then a remedy incorporating a finding of partial invalidity is appropriate. If that interpretation of the will of the law-maker in that hypothetical situation *cannot* be made, then the whole document should be struck down[14].

The third special feature of the review of delegated legislation is that, in addition to its being challengeable in the ordinary way by application for judicial review, the validity of delegated legislation may also be challenged by way of defence to a criminal prosecution brought under the delegated legislation itself[15]. No one should be vulnerable to prosecution under rules which are themselves invalid, and a defence based on such invalidity may be raised in whatever court the prosecution is brought.

The reason for spelling out the court's approach to delegated legislation is that an obvious comparison may be drawn between, on the one hand, the judicial review of delegated legislation made by ministers under primary legislation (of both the Westminster and Scottish Parliaments) and, on the other, the review of primary legislation made by the Scottish Parliament under SA 1998. Both are reviewable on the grounds that the law-maker has gone beyond the limits of the powers laid down. As we shall see, however, there are also good reasons to suppose that the patterns of review will diverge[16].

1   Including Scottish statutory instruments. See pp 245–252.
2   See, generally, *SME Reissue* Administrative Law para 93 ff; HWR Wade and CF Forsyth *Administrative Law* (10th edn, 2009) ch 23; and PP Craig *Administrative Law* (6th edn, 2008).
3   See *Scottish Old People's Welfare Council, Petitioners* 1987 SLT 179; *Air 2000 Ltd v Secretary of State for Transport (No 1)* 1989 SLT 698.
4   See, for example, *R (Spath Holme Ltd) v Secretary of State for the Environment and Transport* [2000] 1 All ER 884.
5   *A-G v Wilts United Dairies* (1921) 37 TLR 884; *Scottish Milk Marketing Board v Ferrier* 1936 SC (HL) 39.
6   *Malloch v Aberdeen Corpn* 1973 SC 227.
7   *Kerr v Hood* 1907 SC 895; *Leech v Secretary of State for Scotland* 1993 SLT 365.
8   See, for example, *Bates v Lord Hailsham of St Marylebone* [1972] 3 All ER 1019.
9   *Agricultural, Horticultural and Forestry Industry Training Board v Aylesbury Mushrooms* [1972] 1 All ER 280; *R v Secretary of State for Social Services, ex parte AMA* [1986] 1 All ER 164; *Neizer v Johnston* 1993 SCCR 772; *MacGillivray v Johnston (No 2)* 1994 SLT 1012; *R (O'Callaghan) v Charity Commission for England and Wales* [2007] EWHC 2491 (Admin)
10 See p 250.
11 See *F Hoffmann-la Roche & Co AG v Secretary of State for Trade and Industry* [1975] AC 295. This case arose, of course, in relation to an instrument subject to procedures in the Westminster Parliament but there is no doubt that the same principle would apply (to even stronger effect) to an instrument approved by Holyrood. See also, more recently, *R (Javed) v Home Secretary* [2002] QB 129.
12 *East Kilbride District Council v Secretary of State for Scotland* 1995 SLT 1238, following *R v Secretary of State for the Environment, ex parte Hammersmith and Fulham London Borough Council* [1991] 1 AC 521; *cf R v Secretary of State for the Environment, ex parte Nottinghamshire County Council* [1986] AC 240.

13 And, in principle, even less deference is to be shown to prerogative legislation which is not the product of a 'democratic' parliamentary process but is in substance an exercise of executive power: see *R (Bancoult) v Secretary of State for Foreign and Commonwealth Affairs* [2009] 1 AC 453. In fact, in this case, a significant degree of latitude was afforded the government in deciding not to allow resettlement of former inhabitants of the Chagos Islands and the courts have also declined to review the exercise of some prerogative powers such as that to commit troops to armed conflict: *R (Gentle) v The Prime Minister* [2008] 2 WLR 879.

14 *DPP v Hutchinson* [1990] 2 AC 783; *Dunkley v Evans* [1981] 1 WLR 1522.

15 *MacGillivray v Johnston (No 2)* 1994 SLT 1012; *Robbie the Pict v Hingston (No 1)* 1998 SLT 1196; *Boddington v British Transport Police* [1999] 2 AC 143.

16 See p 405 and n 28.

HUMAN RIGHTS ADJUDICATION

13.14   It is undoubtedly the case that HRA 1998, fully implemented from 2 October 2000[1], has had a substantial effect upon the courts of the United Kingdom[2]. Related provisions in SA 1998[3] took effect over a year earlier as part of the rules defining the competence of the Scottish Parliament and the Scottish Executive[4] and their impact was significant[5]. In chapter 12 we discussed the process by which HRA 1998 was enacted and described the 'Convention rights' incorporated by the HRA 1998. We also explained the political and administrative structures which have been put in place which are intended to foster and maintain a 'rights culture' in Scotland and throughout the United Kingdom. Those aspects of human rights protection should not be underplayed but it nevertheless remains true that in any discussion of constitutional law and the legal protection of individual rights it is the work of the courts which demands most attention.

We have already described how Convention rights have become a new ground on which to seek judicial review and suggested the difficulties which face the courts in resolving human rights questions (p 385). In this section we discuss the approach of the courts to human rights questions before and after the passing of HRA 1998.

1 SI 1998/2882; SI 2000/1851.

2 See R Reed and J Murdoch *A Guide to Human Rights Law in Scotland* (2nd ed, 2008) Lord Irvine of Lairg 'The Impact of the Human Rights Act: Parliament, the Courts and the Executive' [2003] PL 308; S Shah and T Poole, 'The impact of the Human Rights Act on the House of Lords' [2009] PL 347.

3 SA 1998, ss 29(2)(d), 54, 57, 101 and 129(2). See also the GWA 2006, ss 81, 94 and Sch 9, and NIA 1998, ss 6, 7, 24, 71, 79 and Sch 10.

4 pp 139 and 177 above.

5 See, for example, the discussion of *Starrs v Ruxton* 2000 JC 208 at pp 306–307.

The pre-incorporation approach to fundamental rights

13.15   Although the pre-incorporation period has passed into history, it retains interest, for better or for worse, as one of great judicial creativity in the face of legislative and executive inactivity. The courts, especially in England, were energetic in their efforts to subject ministers and others to scrutiny on grounds of compliance with human rights[1]. There were two channels for this. The first was to insist that, despite the lack of formal incorporation of the

ECHR, its terms could be used as an interpretative aid, especially in circumstances of statutory ambiguity. Parliament could be presumed to have wished to comply with the United Kingdom's international obligations[2]. The English courts were willing to adopt such an approach quite early on. In Scotland, though, the position which prevailed for many years was that taken by Lord Ross in *Kaur v Lord Advocate*[3], to the effect that the courts would not have regard to the Convention even in cases of statutory ambiguity. Scots law was brought into line with the English approach only very shortly before incorporation of the Convention[4].

Secondly, it was argued that 'fundamental rights', even though secured (only) in the common law rather than in the ECHR, could be deployed to similar interpretative effect[5]. This led, in particular, to an insistence on a high degree of scrutiny in judicial review when the fundamental rights of individuals were at stake. Public decision-making should be subject to anxious scrutiny[6] in such circumstances. In a 'balancing' process familiar in the process of interpretation of the ECHR at Strasbourg (and latterly in UK courts themselves), the courts insisted that the need for a particular decision or rule be weighed against the countervailing rights of the individual.

1 See M Hunt *Using Human Rights Law in English Courts* (1997).
2 See *R v Secretary of State for the Home Department, ex parte Brind* [1991] 1 AC 696 per Lord Bridge of Harwich at 747, 748.
3 *Kaur v Lord Advocate* 1980 SC 319.
4 *T, Petitioner* 1997 SLT 724.
5 See *Derbyshire County Council v Times Newspapers Ltd* [1993] AC 534.
6 *Singh v Secretary of State for the Home Department (No 1)* 1998 SLT 1370.

The Human Rights Act 1998 and Legislation

13.16 We have discussed elsewhere (p 107) the potential difficulties, in the context of the United Kingdom's constitutional history, of attempts to 'entrench' human rights against infringement by a sovereign Westminster Parliament. HRA 98 acknowledges those difficulties directly in the way in which it provides for adjudication of human rights disputes by the courts: principally by denying the courts any power to strike down as invalid an Act of the Westminster Parliament and, instead, permitting at most a declaratory judgement that such an Act breaches Convention rights.

Section 3(1) of HRA 1998 provides that '[s]o far as it is possible to do so, primary legislation and subordinate legislation must be read and given effect in a way which is compatible with the Convention rights'. As well as assisting in the interpretation of Convention rights for the purposes of HRA 1998, s 6, this provision links with the other principal new power of the courts – the making of a declaration of incompatibility in relation to primary legislation.

The scheme of HRA 1998 is to make unlawful and, therefore, invalid any act of a public authority which is incompatible with a Convention right and this includes the making of what HRA 1998 defines as 'subordinate legislation'. Thus delegated legislation made by ministers and, importantly, Acts of the Scottish Parliament[1] are to be held invalid to the extent of their incompatibility.

Section 3(1) may assist in saving some such legislation where it is possible to read it as compatible with the relevant Convention right. How this provision applies in any individual case in practice is not always easy to predict[2]. It provides a starting presumption of compatibility but with unclear limits[3].

The same presumption is applied by HRA 1998, s 3(1) to the interpretation of 'primary legislation', ie Acts of the Westminster Parliament[4]. They too must be read as compatible if possible. If, however, that is not possible, the consequences are difficult. The court must continue to treat HRA 1998 as wholly valid and binding on the parties to the case[5]. This applies whether the Act was passed before or after the enactment of HRA 1998 and it is by this means that that Act is seen to uphold the principle of the supremacy or sovereignty of Parliament. What HRA 1998 does allow, however, is that senior courts (including the Supreme Court, the High Court of Justiciary sitting otherwise than as a trial court (ie on appeal), and the Court of Session) may make a 'declaration of incompatibility' where incompatibility with a Convention right is held to occur, HRA 1998, s 3(1) notwithstanding[6]. Declarations have been made relating to mental health[7], the legal status of transsexuals[8], the Home Secretary's involvement in fixing life sentences in England and Wales[9] and the regulation of travel abroad by individuals convicted of sexual offences[10]. Contrary to the contention of the Advocate General for Scotland, the Court of Session has confirmed that it is competent to bring a petition for judicial review for the sole purpose of obtaining a declaration of incompatibility[11].

All UK government Bills introduced since 24 November 1998 have had to be accompanied (prior to second reading) by a ministerial statement of compatibility with the Convention rights (or a statement that the government intends to proceed despite any incompatibility)[12]. Statements admitting incompatibility are unusual but have been made and the possibility reconfirms the freedom of Parliament to enact legislation of its choosing[13].

If a declaration of incompatibility is made, it is open to the Westminster Parliament to rectify the position by making the necessary legislative modification. In the case of provisions which do not affect reserved matters and are otherwise within its competence, the Scottish Parliament has the same powers. HRA 1998 does, however, also provide a 'fast-track' mechanism for a relevant UK minister or, as the case may be, the Scottish Ministers to make such a necessary modification by means of a 'remedial order' where there are 'compelling reasons' to do so. Such orders must be approved in draft by either both Houses of the Westminster Parliament or (again, as the case may be) by the Scottish Parliament[14].

The fact that a declaration of incompatibility is the only remedy available to an individual whose rights have been breached by an Act of the Westminster Parliament has itself been challenged as being incompatible with the ECHR. Although the Strasbourg Court has cast doubt on the adequacy of such a declaration and has held that an individual need not pursue a declaration of incompatibility at a UK level before making an application to Strasbourg, it has also said that it may be open to persuasion that declarations of incompatibility are an effective remedy if there is evidence that they lead, invariably, to changes in the law to remedy the incompatibility[15].

1   HRA 1998, s 21(1).
2   See *Advocate General for Scotland v MacDonald* 2002 SC 1; *Douglas v Hello! Ltd (No 1)* [2001] QB 967; *Gunn v Newman* 2001 SC 525; and D Bonner et al 'Judicial Approaches to the Human Rights Act' (2003) 52 ICLQ 549.
3   For the similar provision contained in SA 1998, s 101, see p 401.
4   HRA 1998, s 21(1). The definition of 'primary legislation' also includes Measures of the General Synod of the Church of England and any Order in Council made in exercise of Her Majesty's Royal Prerogative.
5   HRA 1998, ss 3(2), 4(6).
6   HRA 1998, s 4.
7   *R (H) v Mental Health Review Tribunal North & East London Region* [2002] QB 1, in consequence of which a remedial order was made to amend the Mental Health Act 1983, ss 72 and 73.
8   *Bellinger v Bellinger* [2003] 2 AC 467.
9   *R (Anderson) v Home Secretary* [2003] 1 AC 837.
10   *R(F) v Secretary of State for Justice* [2009] Cr App R (S) 47.
11   Unreported decision of Lord Woolman of 25 June 2009 in *M, as guardian of the Child JM v. Advocate General for Scotland* 2009.
12   HRA 1998, s 19 and SI 1998/2882.
13   When the Communications Bill – now the Communications Act 2003 – was introduced in November 2002 it was accompanied by a statement under HRA 1998, s 19(2) to the effect that the government was unable to state that the Bill's provisions were compatible with the Convention rights but that it, nevertheless, wished to proceed with the Bill: see HC Debs, 3 Dec 2002, col 785 ff. A similar statement was made on the introduction in 2004 of the Civil Partnership Bill which became the Civil Partnership Act 2004.
14   HRA 1998, s 10 and Sch 2. Special provision is made for urgent orders to be made, in the first instance, without the need for such approval (HRA 1998, Sch 4, paras 2(b) and 4). Three remedial orders (the Mental Health Act 1983 (Remedial) Order 2001, SI 2001/3712; the Naval Discipline Act 1957 (Remedial) Order 2004, SI 2004/66 (now repealed and replaced with new provisions) and the Marriage Act 1949 (Remedial) Order 2007, SI 2007/438 have been made so far at Westminster; but none at Holyrood. See also the 2001 Report of the Joint Committee on Human Rights on the making of remedial orders (HC Paper 473 (2001–02)).
15   *Burden v United Kingdom* (2007) 44 EHRR 51.

The Human Rights Act and the significance of Strasbourg jurisprudence

13.17   We described in Chapter 12 the approach which the courts have taken to the definition of 'public authority' in HRA 1998 in considering challenges to government (and in some cases private) action based on Convention rights arguments. We also discussed there the development of the common law by the courts – as public authorities themselves – in a manner which reflects the Convention rights of those whose rights are being determined. In determining when and to what extent there has been a breach of Convention rights, HRA 1998 provides some guidance to the courts in how to approach that task.

Section 2 of HRA 1998 provides that a court or tribunal, when determining a question which has arisen in connection with a Convention right, must take into account any judgment, decision, declaration or advisory opinion of the European Court of Human Rights[1]. This is logical in the light of the general aims of ECHR and HRA 1998: a degree of uniformity of interpretation of the Convention rights across all the 47[2] member states of the Council of Europe is desirable and it would do nothing to limit the number of UK applications to Strasbourg[3] if UK courts were known to be interpreting the Convention very differently from the Court of Human Rights. But 'taking account' of Strasbourg jurisprudence is not itself easy. The Court's decisions range widely across many types of proceedings and, of course, across many national jurisdictions. They have now been decided over many years and not always consistently. Strasbourg jurisprudence has also developed interpretative principles of its own which may or may not be of much assistance to UK courts. The Court has, for instance, developed the concept of the 'margin of appreciation' designed to give a sort of 'benefit of the doubt' to national authorities. They are afforded some latitude in deciding the manner in which, and the extent to which, individual rights are protected in light of their own assessment of local conditions and of the needs of their 'democratic society'[4]. But in national courts does the 'margin of appreciation' have relevance to their decisions about the acts of their own national authorities?

This issue is one of some controversy[5]. It is argued by some commentators that there is no need – and no justification – for national courts to accord the same respect to decisions of domestic governments as is appropriate where the adjudicator is an international court. However, since HRA 1998 came into force, the British courts have developed a concept, justified at least notionally by reference to the principle of the separation of powers, described initially as one of 'due deference' to a decision of the legislature or of the executive in areas where they have a 'discretionary area of judgment'. This concept was explained by Lord Hope of Craighead in *R v DPP, ex parte Kebilene*[6] in which he commented that in 'some circumstances it will be appropriate for the courts to recognise that there is an area of judgment within which the judiciary will defer, on democratic grounds, to the considered opinion of the elected body or person whose Act or decision is said to be incompatible with the Convention'[7]. There has been, since *Kebilene*, a move away from the language of 'deference', Lord Hoffmann expressing the view in *R (ProLife Alliance) v BBC*[8] that the word itself was inapposite:

> "I do not think that its overtones of servility, or perhaps gracious concession, are appropriate to describe what is happening. In a society based upon the rule of law and the separation of powers, it is necessary to decide which branch of government has in any particular instance the decision-making power and what the legal limits of that power are. That is a question of law and must therefore be decided by the courts."[9]

and that what is at the heart of the issue is which branch of government is best suited to the particular task at hand:

> "The principles upon which decision-making powers are allocated are principles of law. The courts are the independent branch of government and the legislature and executive are, directly and indirectly respectively, the elected branches of government. Independence makes the courts more suited to deciding some kinds of questions and being elected makes the legislature or executive more suited to deciding others. The allocation of these decision-making responsibilities is based upon recognised principles. The principle that the independence of the courts is necessary for a proper decision of disputed legal rights or claims of violation of human rights is a legal principle. It is reflected in article 6 of the Convention. On the other hand, the

principle that majority approval is necessary for a proper decision on policy or allocation of resources is also a legal principle. Likewise, when a court decides that a decision is within the proper competence of the legislature or executive, it is not showing deference. It is deciding the law."[10]

The limits of the 'discretionary area of judgment' in any given case will, of course, fall to be determined by the courts themselves but in deciding just where the line should be drawn – particularly, in recent years, in relation to issues of national security – the courts have been criticised by some as being too deferential and by others as insufficiently so[11].

Another feature of the Strasbourg Court's decisions has been the adoption of a principle of 'proportionality' in the balancing of rights of individuals against the policy needs of state authorities[12]. This, as already mentioned, has made a limited appearance in UK jurisprudence, in part because of human rights arguments raised prior to HRA 1998[13] and in part because of the adoption of the principle in EC law[14].

1 Indeed it must also take into account certain opinions and decisions of the (now abolished) European Commission on Human Rights and the Committee of Ministers.
2 As at July 2009.
3 The right to apply to Strasbourg, once proceedings under HRA 1998 (or, in relation to Convention rights, proceedings under SA 1998, GWA 1998 or NIA 1998) are completed, is not formally excluded by HRA 1998 and remains available under the Convention. One recent example of this was the successful application by a number of individuals who complained that the continued retention by the police of DNA samples taken from them, even after they had been acquitted of criminal charges, amounted to a breach of their art 8 right to respect for their private life. Their application to Strasbourg followed failed judicial reviews in the domestic courts including the House of Lords: see *R (S) v Chief Constable of South Yorkshire* [2004] 4 All ER.193 and *S v United Kingdom* (2009) 48 EHRR 50.
4 *Handyside v UK* (1976) 1 EHRR 737; *James v UK* (1986) 8 EHRR 123.
5 See, for example, S Atrill 'Keeping the executive in the picture' [2003] PL 41; Lord Irvine 'The Impact of the Human Rights Act: Parliament, the Courts and the Executive' [2003] PL 308; I Leigh 'Taking rights proportionately: judicial review, the Human Rights Act and Strasbourg' [2002] PL 265; D Pannick 'Principles of interpretation of Convention rights under the Human Rights Act and the discretionary area of judgment' [1998] PL 545.
6 *R v DPP, ex parte Kebilene* [2000] 2 AC 326.
7 *R v DPP, ex parte Kebilene* [2000] 2 AC 326 at 381. A similar respect for the 'discretionary area of judgment' of the legislature appears to be emerging in relation to the disposal of devolution issues under SA 1998. This is discussed at p 406 below.
8 [2004] 1 AC 185.
9 [2004] 1 AC 185 at 240.
10 Ibid.
11 See for example KD Ewing, 'The futility of the Human Rights Act [2004] PL 829; KD Ewing and JC Tham 'The continuing futility of the Human Rights Act' [2008] PL 668; and, in reply, A Kavanagh, 'Judging the judges under the Human Rights Act: deference, disillusionment and the "war on terror"' [2009] PL 287.
12 See *Handyside v UK* (1976) 1 EHRR 737; *Jersild v Denmark* (1995) 19 EHRR 1.
13 See pp 390–391.
14 See p 386.

THE SCOTLAND ACT 1998 AND DEVOLUTION ISSUES

13.18 That the Scottish Parliament is a Parliament of defined legislative competence is by now familiar. It may make laws only within the limits specified in SA 1998, ss 29–30 and Schs 4 and 5[1]. We have also noted that a number of devices are built into the law-making process which are designed to ensure that the Parliament does, in practice, operate within the limits laid down. For example, the minister in charge of an Executive Bill is required to state that the Bill's provisions are within the Parliament's competence[2]. Similarly, the Presiding Officer must state whether, in his or her view, the Bill's provisions are competent[3] Then, finally, SA 1998 provides for an interval of up to four weeks between the passing of a Bill and its submission for royal assent to give the opportunity to one or more of the Law Officers to refer the Bill to the Supreme Court if they suspect that its provisions are outside the Parliament's legislative competence[4]. If the Supreme Court considers that a provision in the Bill would not be within the Parliament's legislative competence, the Bill cannot proceed further without amendment[5].

It would have been possible for those who drafted the Scotland Bill to draw a line at that stage. They might have considered that these controls on the validity of legislation would have been sufficient and that SA 1998 could then provide that 'no provision in an Act of the Scottish Parliament may be challenged in any court' or words to that effect. Such a formula might, however, have been the cause of difficulty. It could not have protected a provision found later to be incompatible with EC law[6]or with a Convention right[7]and it would have raised difficult questions about the validity of a provision seen clearly to be trespassing upon reserved matters, especially where an individual claimed that an injustice was being done[8].

In the event, no such finality clause was included in SA 1998 and, by contrast, specific provision is made for dealing with legal challenges which may be made to the validity of an ASP after it has been enacted. These might be thought are most likely to arise in litigation in which the validity of a decision made by a member of the Scottish Executive depends in turn upon the validity of a provision of an ASP under which it purports to be made. By this route the validity of the provision conferring the power on the minister becomes an issue in the case. The most likely type of action in which this might arise is an application for judicial review but there is no reason why it should not arise, for example, in an action for damages for personal injury caused to an individual. The issue might arise in an action brought by an individual to recover money or property or as a defence to such an action brought by a public body. It might also arise as a defence to a criminal prosecution when a person seeks to establish that the provision under which he or she is charged was itself beyond the Parliament's competence.

It is also possible that a devolution issue may arise in proceedings which involve a dispute between the Scottish and UK administrations. This is facilitated by SA 1998, s 99 which makes provision for a 'division' of the Crown in certain circumstances. Thus, '[r]ights and liabilities may arise between the Crown in right of Her Majesty's Government in the United Kingdom and the Crown in right of the Scottish Administration by virtue of a contract, by operation of law or by virtue of an enactment as they may arise between subjects'[9] The section also provides for the transfer of property and liabilities between the Crown in these two capacities.

It is also possible to raise proceedings with the sole purpose of challenging the validity of an ASP. However, interestingly, it seems that in such circumstances the appropriate party against whom such proceedings should be raised is not the Parliament (or more precisely the Scottish Parliamentary Corporate Body (SPCB)) itself. In *Adams v Scottish Ministers*[10] – which is discussed in more detail below – Lord Nimmo Smith held that the SPCB was not the 'appropriate contradictor' of a petition for judicial review of an Act of the Parliament. In his view it was clear from SA 1998 (and the structure of s 28 in particular) that, following royal assent, an ASP 'has a specific character such that its enactment is not merely an Act of the Parliament. The Act has passed out of its hands.'[11] In such a case the Lord Advocate was the appropriate respondent[12].

In addition to litigation in which the legislative competence of the Parliament is challenged, SA 1998 also creates the possibility of challenging decisions of and subordinate legislation made by the Scottish Ministers where it is their own devolved competence which is at issue, rather than the validity of an ASP. A member of the Scottish Executive may be challenged on the use of powers claimed to be transferred to the Scottish Ministers under SA 1998, ss 53 and 54[13].

1   See pp 119–140.
2   SA 1998, s 31(1); and see p 228.
3   SA 1998, s 31(2); and see p 228.
4   SA 1998, ss 32–34 and pp 233–234.
5   SA 1998, s 32.
6   See pp 48–50.
7   Because of the designation by HRA 1998 of ASPs as 'secondary legislation'.
8   For consideration of this issue, including discussion of a finality clause included in the Scotland Bill of 1987 (introduced as a private member's Bill by Donald Dewar), see Scotland's Parliament (Constitution Unit, 1996) para 127.
9   SA 1998, s 99(1).
10 *Adams v Scottish Ministers* 2003 SLT 366.
11 *Adams v Scottish Ministers* 2003 SLT 366 at 377.
12 Lord Nimmo Smith's decision on this point has some practical importance. The Advocate General had suggested that the proceedings ought to have been against the SPCB and, had she been correct, as a consequence of SA 1998, s 40(3), the remedy of reduction of the Act would not have been available. The most which the petitioners could have obtained would have been a declarator to the effect that the ASP provision was 'not law'. For discussion of additional 'respondents' being permitted to enter proceedings to defend the validity of an ASP see p 382.
13 See pp 176–177.

Definition of 'devolution issues'

13.19   It has, therefore, to be envisaged that in a large number of situations, deriving in one way or another from the devolution of powers under SA 1998, there will be the potential for legal challenge to legislation or decisions made. However, SA 1998 does not seek to regulate the manner in which individual litigants may initiate their proceedings and, as already mentioned, this may often be by way of application for judicial review. But it does identify certain types of 'devolution issue' and then makes special provision for how these are to be handled by the courts. This includes a power of the law officers to raise such issues, on their own initiative, for resolution by the courts including, if necessary, by the Supreme Court.

The detailed provisions on devolution issues are provided by SA 1998, Sch 6, Pt I which starts by defining what is meant by a 'devolution issue' and then identifies six categories. The first relates to the powers of the Parliament itself:

(a)   a question whether an ASP or any provisions of an ASP is within the legislative competence of the Parliament.

The other five, in different ways, raise issues of Executive competence, starting with:

(b)   a question whether any function (being a function which any person has purported, or is proposing, to exercise) is a function of the Scottish Ministers, the First Minister or the Lord Advocate;

(c)   a question whether the purported or proposed exercise of a function by a member of the Scottish Executive is, or would be, within devolved competence.

And then two relating to compatibility with Convention rights and Community law:

(d)   a question whether a purported or proposed exercise of a function by a member of the Scottish Executive is, or would be, incompatible with any of the Convention rights or with Community law;

(e)   a question whether a *failure to act* by a member of the Scottish Executive is incompatible with any of the Convention rights or with Community law.

Then, finally:

(f)   any other question about whether a function is exercisable within devolved competence or in or as regards Scotland and *any other question* arising by virtue of this Act about reserved matters.

The list of defined devolution issues is qualified by the statement that a devolution issue shall not be taken to arise 'merely because of any contention of a party to the proceedings which appears to the court or tribunal ... to be frivolous or vexatious'[1]. Frivolity or vexatiousness apart, it will, in the first instance, be for the court in which a devolution issue is claimed to arise to decide whether it satisfies one of the definitions laid down[2] before going on to determine the issue itself. One question which may have to be resolved is the scope of paragraph (b). The question of whether or not a function is a function of the Scottish Ministers might raise issues of statutory interpretation, for example of the ASP which is claimed to confer the function, which have nothing at all to do with the devolution settlement established by SA 1998 and do not have the 'constitutional' flavour one would expect of such issues. Would it nevertheless be a 'devolution issue' attracting the special procedural provision made by SA 1998, Sch 6? The answer may be a formal 'yes' but producing a situation in which a court would, in the exercise of its discretion, decline to make any special order in relation to an appeal or reference[3].

1 SA 1998, Sch 6, para 2.
2 In *Starrs v Ruxton* 2000 JC 208 it was conceded by the Crown that for a procurator fiscal to prosecute before a court that was claimed to be not impartial as required by ECHR, art 6 was an act of the Lord Advocate and, therefore, raised a devolution issue. That a prosecution by the Lord

Advocate could give rise to a 'devolution issue' concerning the independence and impartiality of the court before which that prosecution was taken was affirmed in the JCPC by Lord Hope of Craighead in *Brown v Stott* 2001 SC (PC) 43. See also *Clancy v Caird* 2000 SC 441, especially Lord Penrose at 472.

3 See, for example, *Somerville v Scottish Ministers* (2008) SC (HL) 45 in which it was held by the House of Lords that Rule 80 of the Prisons and Young Offenders Institutions (Scotland) Rules 1994, SI 1994/1931, conferred functions on a prison governor which were distinct from those functions exercised by the Scottish Ministers.

Determination of devolution issues

13.20   Such questions of definition apart, SA 1998, Sch 6 makes four forms of special provision: (1) it ensures that, by way of the Advocate General or the Lord Advocate, as appropriate, proceedings may be brought on behalf of either the UK government or the Scottish Executive to resolve a devolution issue, for example as to the legislative competence of the Scottish Parliament or the devolved competence of the Executive[1]; (2) it requires notice to be given to both the Advocate General and the Lord Advocate of any devolution issue raised in order to enable either or both to participate in the proceedings if they wish to do so[2]; and then (3) the Schedule enables the reference of devolution issues to be made by inferior courts to either the Court of Session or the High Court of Justiciary and then for either a further reference or appeal from either of those courts to the Supreme Court[3]. In addition, (4) the Lord Advocate or Advocate General may *require* any court or tribunal to refer a devolution issue direct to the Supreme Court and they may themselves refer a devolution issue which is not the subject of proceedings[4].

SA 1998, Sch 6 also deals with certain ancillary, but practically important, matters concerning questions of procedure and expenses in cases involving devolution issues. SA 1998, Sch 6, para 37 permits the making of procedural rules which prescribe the stage in legal proceedings at which a devolution issue is to be raised or referred, which deal with the sisting of any proceedings under Sch 6 and which prescribe the manner and timing of intimation or notice of a devolution issues[5]. Additionally, in recognition of the extra cost to private parties which is likely to be incurred as a consequence of the regular involvement of Law Officers in devolution issues cases, SA 1998, Sch 6, para 36 makes special provision for the award of expenses to take account of that extra cost.

The Supreme Court is now the final arbiter of devolution issues. Section 40 of the Constitutional Reform Act 2005 (see below) provides that any decision of the Supreme Court on a devolution matter is not binding on the Supreme Court itself but is otherwise binding in all legal proceedings.

1 Para 4.
2 Paras 5–6.
3 Paras 7–12.
4 Paras 33–35. See *Clark v Kelly* 2003 SLT 308 and CM O'Neill 'Kirkcaldy to London via the Lord Advocate: Requiring a Reference to the Privy Council' 2001 SLT (News) 285.
5 See Act of Adjournal (Criminal Procedure Rules Amendment) (Miscellaneous) 2000, SSI 2000/65; Act of Adjournal (Devolution Issues Rules) 1999, SI 1999/1346; Act of Sederunt (Devolution Issues Rules) 1999, SI 1999/1345; Act of Sederunt (Proceedings for Determination of Devolution Issues Rules) 1999, SI 1999/1347; Act of Sederunt (Rules of the Court of Session Amendment) (Miscellaneous) 2000, SSI 2000/66; Employment Tribunals (Constitution and

Rules of Procedure) (Scotland) (Amendment) Regulations 2001, SI 2001/1460; Employment Tribunals (Constitution and Rules of Procedure) (Scotland) Regulations 2001, SI 2001/1170; Act of Sederunt (Rules of the Court of Session Amendment No 7) (Devolution Issues), SSI 2007/360; Act of Adjournal (Criminal Procedure Rules Amendment No 4) (Devolution Issues) 2007, SSI 2007/361; and Act of Sederunt (Proceedings for Determination of Devolution Issues Rules) Amendment, SSI 2007/362.

Questions of interpretation

13.21   On one view, however, the questions for the courts raised by devolution issues will not raise new difficulties. Questions about compatibility with EC law may not always be easy but they are not unfamiliar[1]. Disputes about compatibility with Convention rights are being dealt with by courts throughout the United Kingdom as they interpret HRA 1998[2]. As to the other issues which may arise, these will be largely resolved by the application of the normal principles of statutory interpretation with which the courts are familiar. Most judicial review of administrative action and of delegated legislation turns on statutory interpretation. It is, by no means, always easy but it is familiar. In some cases, the interpretation exercise involved – the comparison between what is prohibited by SA 1998 and what has been enacted in the ASP under review – may even be quite straightforward. With some precision, SA 1998, Sch 4 prohibits the modification of HRA 1998[3] and SA 1998, Sch 5 prohibits legislation on the subject matter of the Coastguard Act 1925[4]. Resolution of the question whether the Parliament has enacted law in either of these forbidden areas may, at least in some instances, not be difficult[5].

On the other hand, it is argued, the resolution of devolution issues may turn out to be fraught with difficulties. This is for two main reasons. Firstly, the language of SA 1998, especially in its definition of 'reserved matters' in Sch 5, is far from precise. On the contrary, the language is often very open-textured, imprecise and capable of a variety of meanings. This was, in large measure, deliberate: a very precise articulation of reserved matters was avoided for the very reason that it might cause difficulties for the Scottish Parliament and attract disputes in the courts. But general language has its own problems. Secondly, the division of the subject matter of legislation between devolved and reserved will always bring problems for the provisions of ASPs which quite evidently bridge the boundary. Are they to be treated as relating to reserved matters, and therefore unlawful, or not? In all constitutional systems which rely on the division of legislative powers on a functional basis, whether these are federal or devolved systems, there are bound to be difficulties in deciding whether legislation of mixed character should fall on one side of the line or the other. It has, of course, always to be remembered that disputes, if they arise, are quite likely to have consequences beyond the specific case to be decided. In particular, even if neither tier of government is directly involved in the litigation, the case may be politically very sensitive. It is one thing for a local authority or even a minister to be told that they have exceeded their powers. It may be quite another for a Parliament – the Scottish Parliament – to be told by a court that it has misbehaved. Political sensitivities will be even higher if the legislation under review had been passed by the Parliament in order directly to test the limits of its powers and of the devolution settlement.

SA 1998 does itself offer some assistance in the interpretation of legislation which appears to straddle the boundary of legislative competence[6]. Section 29(3) and (4) and Sch 4 have already been discussed in Chapter 5[7], especially the function of the 'purpose' test. Some further guidance is provided by SA 1998, s 101 which applies to the interpretation of provisions of Acts of the Scottish Parliament (or Bills for such Acts[8]) and provisions of subordinate legislation made or confirmed by a member of the Scottish Executive. Where such a provision 'could be read in such a way as to be outside competence' the 'provision is to be read as narrowly as is required for it to be within competence, if such a reading is possible, and is to have effect accordingly'[9]. This section echoes the wording of HRA 1998, s 3(1) and, in so far as it is concerned with compatibility with Convention rights as an aspect of competence, it may be assumed to have a similar effect[10]. It is less obvious what impact it may have on other aspects of legislative competence[11] but it seems fairly clear that, at the boundary between reserved and devolved matters, the intention is that the terms of a provision of an ASP are to be read as narrowly as is required to prevent its relating to reserved matters, if such a reading is possible. A provision which could be read as straying into the reserved area should not be so read, if that is possible. An example given by the Lord Advocate during debate on the Scotland Bill[12] was that of an ASP that might be passed to give a general power to the Scottish Ministers to hold referendums on matters of their choice. Without the inclusion of s 101 in SA 1998 the hypothetical Referendums Act might be held to be invalid simply because one of the many purposes for which it could be used would be the holding of a referendum on a reserved matter such as independence for Scotland or abolition of the monarchy. If, however, the Act were read 'narrowly' and confined in scope to its use for legitimate purposes, its validity could be saved[13].

It cannot, of course, be guaranteed that the examples discussed and resolved in a particular way by ministers in Parliament would be approached by the courts in the same way. It would be open to them to place their own interpretation on the terms of the ASP (or subordinate legislation or decision of the Scottish Ministers) under challenge in the light of their interpretation of SA 1998 itself. In many respects, this is a process which may be compared with the more routine and more familiar forms of statutory interpretation. Two characteristics do mark out the adjudication of the validity of ASPs (although not necessarily of the validity of executive acts by members of the Scottish Executive) as different. One general difficulty, which we have already mentioned, is the non-specific nature of much of the language of SA 1998, Sch 5, upon which cases may turn. This is different from many 'ordinary' statutes which are, on the whole, designed to achieve a high degree of precision. SA 1998, Sch 5, while precise at some points, is quite deliberately cast in looser terms elsewhere. The idea is to create a more flexible framework within which the Parliament can do its work without the constant threat of being caught out exceeding its powers in minor, technical ways. However, the inevitable result of giving greater flexibility to the Scottish Parliament is also to give greater flexibility to the courts in the way they are to handle this 'constitutional' adjudication in comparison with their more routine decision-making.

Secondly, questions then arise as to how the courts should use this flexibility available to them. In particular, should the review of the validity of the Acts of a Parliament attract a response different in kind from that meted out to public bodies of a lesser order? Should the courts start out with a stronger presumption of validity in the case of the Act of a Parliament than in the case of decisions of a local authority? Should the courts permit a Parliament a greater 'margin of appreciation'? Should they be more sympathetic, more forgiving to a Parliament? Should they take a broader, more generous view of the powers of a Parliament?

Arguments in favour of such an approach derive from the greater democratic legitimacy of a Parliament than, say, a minister acting under statutory powers and comparisons here have been drawn with the attitude adopted by courts to legislatures under written constitutions. In the United States and Canada, for instance, the courts have taken the view that the review of legislation under a constitution *is* different from the review of administrative action under a statute and does demand a different response. Significantly, the courts were seen to adopt an analogous approach in the review of Acts of the Stormont Parliament in Northern Ireland[14]. In *Gallagher v Lynn*[15] Lord Atkin treated the questions raised by the Government of Ireland Act 1920 as entirely comparable with those involving the distribution of powers between Parliaments in a federal system and assumed, in particular, that relevant Canadian authority could be aptly invoked[16].

1   See pp 115–119.
2   See pp 390–395.
3   SA 1998, Sch 4, para 1(f).
4   SA 1998, Sch 5, Pt II, S E3(a).
5   However, it is conceivable that the Scottish Parliament may enact legislation which, at least on its face, does not purport to stray into reserved matters or to modify an enactment protected by SA 1998, Sch 4. Whether such legislation would have the effect of impliedly repealing – either deliberately or accidentally – provisions which were outside the Parliament's competence may pose more difficult questions for the courts.
6   For a detailed discussion of these provisions of SA 1998 and their potential limitations see the written evidence of Iain Jamieson to the Calman Commission (of 31 August 2008) available at www.commissiononscottishdevolution.org.uk
7   See especially pp 130-136.
8   Which may also fall to be adjudicated upon by the Supreme Court (SA 1998, s 33).
9   SA 1998, s101(1), (2).
10 See p 391.
11 For example, in relation to compatibility with European Community law.
12 HL Debs, 28 Oct 1998, cols 1952–1956.
13 Although the referendum example does illustrate the Lord Advocate's point, it may be thought to be inappropriate. It assumes that an independence (or monarchy) referendum Act would be incompetent, which might not be the case – although an independence Act or a monarchy (abolition) Act plainly would be. This particular issue will come sharply into focus if the current Scottish government fulfils its commitment to introduce a bill to authorise a referendum on independence before the next Scottish general election.
14 See the works cited at p 62 n 23.
15 *Gallagher v Lynn* [1937] AC 863.
16 *Gallagher v Lynn* [1937] AC 863 at 870. For discussion, however, of the dangers in drawing such parallels too closely, see H Calvert *Constitutional Law in Northern Ireland* (1968) ch 11 and B Hadfield *The Constitution of Northern Ireland* (1989) ch III.

Challenges to Acts of the Scottish Parliament

13.22   Thus, it was inevitably a matter of interest from the start to see how the courts reviewing legislation made by the Scottish Parliament would approach their task under SA 1998. Comparisons with constitutional adjudication in other parts of the world had already been drawn[1] No doubt the Stormont experience would be called in aid.

But the starting point will always be the terms of SA 1998 itself, rather than guidance culled by analogy from elsewhere. The review of the Acts of a Parliament created by an Act of the UK Parliament is *not* the same as the review of the legislation of a Parliament created by a written constitution; and, especially where not only the interests of the UK government but also the interests of private individuals in Scotland are at stake it might be thought that the courts would be disinclined to use the discretion available to them to make strong presumptions in favour of the legality of ASPs. That being said, experience to date does not suggest any particular appetite on the part of the courts to interfere with the 'Will of Parliament' Three challenges to the validity of an ASP have been disposed of by the courts so far and a fourth is ongoing at the time of writing. Of the three, none has been successful but they have thrown some light on judicial attitudes. On the other hand, all three cases were confined almost entirely to human rights based arguments, which will not be elaborated in full in this account but which were, in their substance, very similar to the arguments which have been widely deployed in the significant number of challenges to the validity of executive action[2] under HRA 1998 and SA 1998 itself. New ground will be broken as and when an ASP is challenged on grounds of encroachment upon the 'reserved matters' of SA 1998, Sch 5.

In *Anderson v Scottish Ministers*[3] a challenge was made to the validity of the very first ASP, the Mental Health (Public Safety and Appeals) (Scotland) Act 1999 (MH(PSA)(S)A 1999). It was argued that a new power conferred on the Scottish Ministers by the Act to refuse to discharge a patient from hospital[4] if satisfied that detention is necessary to protect the public from serious harm was contrary to ECHR, art 5 which guarantees liberty and security of the person. The Inner House[5] found little difficulty in upholding the validity of MH(PSA) (S)A 1999 on the basis of cases decided by the Strasbourg Court[6] but some of the dicta in the case are interesting. Lady Cosgrove remarked, for example, that it represented 'a significant milestone in the development of Scots law: for the first time in its history the Court of Session [was] asked to strike down the Act of a legislature, the power to do so having been conferred on it by s 29(1) of the Scotland Act'[7] Lord President Rodger noted that the balance which has to be struck, first by the Scottish Parliament and then by the court, on all major human rights issues under the ECHR, is between the general interest of the community on the one hand and individual rights on the other. In so doing, it was right, as previous authorities showed[8] that 'the court should give due deference to the assessment which the democratically elected legislature has made of the policy issues involved'[9] In the field of human rights jurisprudence this inclination to give 'due deference' to the views of the legislature reflects the Strasbourg Court's doctrine of 'margin of appreciation' or its equivalent, expressed in the domestic context as the 'discretionary area of judgment'[10]. What may be of wider interest in relation to adjudication on the competence of the Scottish Parliament (and which remains untested) is whether it will be accorded a 'discretionary area of judgment' in cases where it is not a human rights infringement which is alleged but, for instance, a deviation into reserved matters.

In a case which did not itself relate to legislative competence, the former Lord President may have given a sign of a more restrictive view. *Whaley v Watson*[11] concerned a pre-emptive challenge attempted to the member's Bill to outlaw certain blood sports which Lord Watson proposed to introduce in the Scottish Parliament early in its first session. The petition for interdict, on grounds of breach of the advocacy rules[12] for MSPs contained in SA 1998, was rejected by Lord Johnston and by the First Division. In doing so, however, different views were expressed about the relationship between the courts and the Scottish Parliament and in the Division Lord Rodger expressed some criticism of the earlier views in the Outer House.

Lord Johnston, conceding that challenges to the legislative competence of the Parliament might later occur[13], took the view that, as far as its internal rules were concerned, the Parliament should be entitled to make its own determination and that pressure groups should not be able to challenge such a determination in the courts[14]. Lord Rodger took a sterner line. Lord Johnston had given 'insufficient weight to the fundamental character of the Parliament as a body which – however important its role – has been created by statute and derives its powers from statute. As such, it is a body which, like any other statutory body, must work within the scope of those powers. If it does not do so, then in an appropriate case the court may be asked to intervene and will be required to do so, in a manner permitted by the legislation. In principle, therefore, the Parliament like any other body set up by law is subject to the law and to the courts which exist to uphold that law'[15]. These references to the Parliament's equivalence to any other statutory body send out a signal of a restrictive judicial approach to the interpretation not only of the Parliament's powers to regulate its internal procedures but also its legislative competence. The suggestion is that any judicial obligation to defer to democratically elected Parliaments when determining the limits of an individual's human rights does not apply in relation to other categories of parliamentary decision-making.

A different, more deferential, approach to political considerations is evident from the decision in *Adams v Scottish Ministers* discussed below and also from the Northern Ireland case of *Robinson v Secretary of State for Northern Ireland*[16]. This concerned the challenge by a member of the Northern Ireland Assembly to the election of a First Minister and Deputy First Minister of the Assembly in contravention, it was claimed, of the provisions of NIA 1998. The House of Lords was keen to emphasise that 'the 1998 Act does not set out all the constitutional provisions applicable to Northern Ireland'[17] and that it retained 'scope for the exercise of political judgment[18]'. NIA 1998 was not intended to 'constrain local politicians and the Secretary of State within ... a tight straightjacket'[19] and the court declined to interfere with the political compromise which had been reached.

There was a return to Lord Rodger's dicta in *Whaley* in the second case so far decided on the legislative competence of the Parliament. This was *Adams v Scottish Ministers*[20] which was a sequel to *Whaley* because it was a challenge to the validity of the legislation which Lord Watson's Bill eventually became: the Protection of Wild Mammals (Scotland) Act 2002 (PWM(S)A 2002). This challenge was launched shortly before PWM(S)A 2002 was due to come into effect on 1 August 2002[21].

Mr Adams, the first petitioner, was a self-employed manager of foxhounds for the Buccleuch Hunt. He was joined in his challenge to PWM(S)A 2002 by three other individual petitioners and a variety of associations including a hunt supporters' club and a campaigning organisation, the Countryside Alliance[22]. The petitioners claimed that PWM(S)A 2002 was outside the competence of the Scottish Parliament because it breached their Convention rights under ECHR, arts 8 (respect for private life) and 14 (freedom from discrimination) and ECHR, Protocol 1, art 1 (protection of property and possessions). They also argued that in passing PWM(S)A 2002 the Parliament had been guilty of procedural impropriety and of *Wednesbury* unreasonableness[23]. Lord Nimmo Smith summarised the petitioners' complaints under this head as being that

> 'the Act is not a bona fide or reasonable exercise of limited legislative powers; it is unnecessary for the good government of Scotland; it involves oppressive or gratuitous interference with rights; it will have damaging and disproportionate economic and social effects; it is based on incompletely informed views as to the moral desirability or appropriateness of criminalising certain types of conduct; proceedings on the Bill were vitiated by procedural impropriety, especially owing to reformulation of its scope at stage 2; and the Scottish Parliament failed to take account of limitations on its legislative powers. They aver that the legislative powers of Parliament are limited because it can only enact legislation that is reasonable and necessary for the legitimate aims of good government in Scotland.'[24]

The petitioners sought reduction of PWM(S)A 2002 and, more immediately, an interim order disapplying the operation of the Act's commencement order pending final determination of the petition[25].

In rejecting the petition, Lord Nimmo Smith concentrated on the interpretation of the relevant Convention rights but also dealt with the other aspects of the challenge. In particular he held that it was incompetent to attempt to judicially review an ASP on traditional common law grounds. In coming to this view, his Lordship considered the nature of Acts of the Scottish Parliament. Notwithstanding the comments made by the Lord President in *Whaley* and notwithstanding the classification of Acts of the Scottish Parliament, by HRA 1998, as secondary legislation, his opinion was that such an Act is 'of a character which has far more in common with a public general statute than with subordinate legislation'[26]. What was significant for his Lordship was that 'the Scotland Act is clearly intended to provide a comprehensive scheme, not only for the Parliament itself, but also for the relationship between the courts and the Parliament' and that 'ss 28, 29, 100, 101 and 102 and Sch 6 are definitive of the extent of the court's jurisdiction and of the procedure to be followed when a devolution issue is raised. It necessarily follows that traditional common law grounds of judicial review are excluded, and that there is no room for the implication of common law concepts in considering the legislative competence of the Parliament'[27]. This is clearly contrary to the dicta of Lord Johnston in *Whaley v Watson* to the effect that 'fundamental irrationality' might invalidate an ASP.

The petitioners appealed to the Inner House but did not pursue their irrationality' argument there[28]. So far as the Convention rights challenge to PWM(S) A 2002 was concerned, the Inner House endorsed the conclusions reached by

Lord Nimmo Smith that there was no breach of the petitioners' Convention rights[29]. Their Lordships addressed directly the scope of the Scottish Parliament's 'discretionary area of judgment'[30] and were of the view that the key factors relevant to that issue were '(1) whether the Parliament had before it any proper factual basis for the conclusion that mounted foxhunting with dogs was cruel per se; and whether, if it had, it was entitled to make the judgment that the infliction of such cruelty by such means for the purpose of sport and recreation should be proscribed by law; and (2) whether the likely impacts of the legislation would be such that it should not be enacted.'[31]. On the question of the factual basis for the legislation, their Lordships were keen to distinguish the legislative from the judicial process:

> 'The factual basis upon which a legislature decides to enact a specific provision is not governed by the rules of admissibility and sufficiency of evidence that would apply in a court of law. A legislator is entitled to bring to bear on his decision his personal knowledge gained from his experience of life and from the representations that he may receive on current political topics from informants, pressure groups, committee witnesses, and so on. It is entirely for the judgment and experience of the individual legislator to decide which competing factual account he prefers. He is entitled to accept any account that in his judgment is reliable, no matter that it may be contradicted from other sources.'[32]

The court was satisfied that the competing views for and against the legislation had been fully canvassed before the Parliament, including views about the social and economic impacts of PWM(S)A 2002 and views about the extent to which it could be said fox-hunting was cruel. On the question of the Parliament's 'moral judgment' in this area, the Court considered that the Act 'represents a considered decision by the Parliament on a long-standing and highly charged public controversy. In our view, any judgment on that controversy is pre-eminently one for MSPs[33]....MSPs are elected on their policies on matters such as this.'[34].

A further challenge to PWM(S)A 2002 has also been disposed of. In *Whaley v Lord Advocate*[35], two party litigants sought judicial review of it on the grounds not only of breach of Convention rights (including, in this case, ECHR, arts 9 (freedom of conscience), 10 (freedom of expression), and 11 (freedom of assembly and association)) but also on the grounds that certain of its provisions did not comply with the United Kingdom's international obligations. In particular, it was argued that PWM(S)A 2002 breached the Rio Declaration on Environment and Development (1992), the Rio Convention on Bio Diversity (1992), the Final Act of the Helsinki Conference on Security and Co-operation in Europe (1975), the UN International Covenant on Economic, Social and Cultural Rights (1966), the UN International Covenant on Civil and Political Rights (1966) and the UN Declaration of Human Rights (1948).

In dismissing the petition at first instance, Lord Brodie referred to Lord President Rodger's opinion in *Adams v Scottish Ministers*, reiterating his comments to the effect that the Scottish Parliament is not a sovereign body. With reference to the submissions of the second petitioner (Mr Friend), Lord Brodie's view was that he was 'correct to say that the Scottish Parliament is governed by what is, in effect, a mini-constitution' by which was meant that, 'in the Scotland Act, the Convention and Community law, there are written sources of law which have primacy over what the Scottish Parliament may purport to enact'[36]. However, while the Convention and Community law were specifically referred to by SA 1998, s 29 as placing restrictions on the Parliament's legislative competence, similar limitations were not imposed in relation to the other international obligations to which the petitioners had referred. With respect to those measures the traditional approach of the courts, set out by Lord Dunedin in *Mortensen v Peters*[37] remained valid: they had no jurisdiction to set aside Acts of Parliament on the grounds of incompatibility with international law[38]. The second petitioner appealed against Lord Brodie's decision. So far as the Convention rights arguments were concerned, the court accepted that those issues had, by the time of this appeal, been considered and disposed of appropriately by the Inner House in *Adams* and they endorsed Lord Brodie's reasoning in relation to the appellant's arguments based on international law[39]. The House of Lords – to which the further appeal had gone rather than to the Judicial Committee of the Privy Council – also dismissed Mr Friend's complaints about the validity of PWM(S)A 2002 and rejected his contention that by refusing his petition for judicial review without hearing evidence the Lord Ordinary had breached his right under art 6 ECHR to a fair trial[40].

The most recent challenge to an ASP is the ongoing judicial review of the Damages (Asbestos-related Conditions) (Scotland) Act 2009 (DACSA 2009). DACSA 2009 was passed by the Scottish Parliament in response to the decision of the House of Lords in the case of *Rothwell v Chemical & Insulating Co Ltd & Others*[41] in which their Lordships held that a particular physical condition, asymptomatic pleural plaques (a type of scarring of the lungs), was not 'damage' for which the law of tort or delict would allow recovery of compensation[42]. The Act provides that asymptomatic pleural plaques (and two other asymptomatic conditions which also result from exposure to asbestos) are 'a personal injury which is not negligible'[43] and that accordingly 'they constitute actionable harm for the purposes of an action of damages for personal injuries'[44]. These provisions are retrospective and are to be treated as 'for all purposes as having always had effect'[45]. The petitioners, five insurance companies who will bear the cost of meeting compensation claims under employers' liability insurance policies, claim that DACSA 2009 infringes their Convention rights under art 6 and art 1 of protocol 1 ECHR. They also argue that the Parliament is guilty of irrationality and arbitrariness in legislating to compensate individuals for a condition which Parliament appears to have accepted is not itself harmful to health.

The petitioners first sought interim interdict to prevent the Scottish Ministers making a commencement order to bring DACSA 2009 into force pending the outcome of the judicial review. That application was refused by the Lord Ordinary, Lord Glennie, on 27 April 2009[46] who was prepared to accept that the petitioners had made out a prima facie case but that it was not a sufficiently strong prima facie case[47] as to warrant interference 'with the acts of a democratically elected body'[48].

When it became clear in early June of 2009 that the first hearing of the judicial review would not be completed before DACSA 2009 came into force, a further application was made, this time for interim suspension of the commencement order. This was also refused by the Lord Ordinary, Lord Emslie, who was hearing the substantive argument in the case, essentially on the grounds that the petitioners would not be prejudiced by the coming into force of the Act given the apparent willingness of the Scottish courts to sist individual actions for damages pending the outcome of the judicial review.

The Lord Advocate entered the process to defend the petition in the public interest, the Advocate General has not lodged answers to the petition on behalf of the UK government and, as noted above, a number of individuals who would benefit from the provisions of DACSA 2009 were given leave to participate as respondents to the judicial review and to defend the Act's validity.

1 See p 402.
2 And occasionally actions seeking declarations of incompatibility of UK Acts.
3 *Anderson v Scottish Ministers* 2002 SC 1. See B K Winetrobe 'Scottish devolved legislation in the courts' [2002] PL 31 and I Jamieson, 'Challenging the validity of an Act of the Scottish Parliament: some aspects of *A v The Scottish Ministers*' 2002 SLT (News) 71.
4 The State Hospital at Carstairs.
5 *Anderson v Scottish Ministers* 2001 SC 1. The decision of the Inner House was upheld in the JCPC which restricted itself to consideration of ECHR, art 5 and did not make more general comments on the principles to be applied in considering a challenge to an ASP.
6 *Guzzardi v Italy* (1981) 3 EHRR 333; *Winterwerp v The Netherlands* (1979) 2 EHRR 387.
7 *Anderson v Scottish Ministers* 2001 SC 1 at 36.
8 Lord Rodger cited, in particular *Soering v UK* (1999) 11 EHRR 439; *R v DPP, ex parte Kebilene* [2000] 2 AC 326; *Murray v UK* (1995) 19 EHRR 193; and *A-G of Hong Kong v Kwong-Kut* [1993] AC 951.
9 *Anderson v Scottish Ministers* 2001 SC 1 at 21.
10 See *R v DPP, ex parte Kebilene* [2000] 2 AC 326 per Lord Hope at 380 and the discussion at p 394 above.
11 *Whaley v Watson* 2000 SC 125, 340.
12 See pp 95–96.
13 Including the possibility of a challenge on the grounds of some 'fundamental irrationality' in the Parliament's approach to the legislation it passes (*Whaley v Watson* 2000 SC 125 at 134).
14 *Whaley v Watson* 2000 SC 125 at 134.
15 *Whaley v Watson* 2000 SC 125 at 348.
16 *Robinson v Secretary of State for Northern Ireland* [2002] NI 390. The claimant in these proceedings, Peter Robinson, is now First Minister of Northern Ireland.
17 *Robinson v Secretary of State for Northern Ireland* [2002] NI 390, per Lord Bingham of Cornhill at para 11.
18 *Robinson v Secretary of State for Northern Ireland* [2002] NI 390, per Lord Bingham of Cornhill at para 12.
19 *Robinson v Secretary of State for Northern Ireland* [2002] NI 390, per Lord Bingham of Cornhill at para 14.
20 *Adams v Scottish Ministers* 2003 SLT 366.
21 Protection of Wild Mammals (Scotland) Act 2002 (Commencement) Order 2002, SSI 2002/181.
22 For Lord Nimmo Smith's comments concerning the standing of these bodies, see 2003 SLT 366 at 386–389.
23 See p 95.
24 *Adams v Scottish Ministers* 2003 SLT 366 at 384.
25 Lord Nimmo Smith did not, as matters turned out, require to determine the application for interim orders. For discussion of the approach of Lord Glennie, and then of Lord Emslie, to that issue in the context of the ongoing challenge to the Damages (Asbestos-related Conditions) (Scotland) Act 2009, see below.
26 *Adams v Scottish Ministers* 2003 SLT 366 at 385.
27 *Adams v Scottish Ministers* 2003 SLT 366 at 385, 386.
28 The question of the Parliament's susceptibility to challenge on traditional common law grounds

has however been raised again in the most recent challenge to an ASP (see below) in which the petitioners argue that Lord Nimmo Smith's analysis is wrong.

29 *Adams v Scottish Ministers* 2004 SC 665.
30 Noting, by reference to Lord Hoffmann's comments in *R v BBC, ex parte ProLife Alliance* 2004 1 AC 185 (see p 394 above) that the "vocabulary of 'deference' is no longer seen as appropriate. It is a question of the court's deciding if the Parliament has complied with the Convention".
31 2004 SC 665 at 674.
32 2004 SC 665 at 675.
33 Citing *R v DPP ex p Kebilene* [2002] 2 AC 326, per Lord Hope of Craighead at pp 380–381 and *Brown v Stott* 2001 SC (PC) 43 per Lord Bingham of Cornhill at pp 58–59.
34 2004 SC 665 at 676.
35 *Whaley v Lord Advocate* 2004 SC 78.
36 *Whaley v Lord Advocate* 2004 SC 78 at p 107.
37 *Mortensen v Peters* (1906) 8 F (J) 93; and see p 107.
38 *Whaley v Lord Advocate* (20 June 2003, unreported) OH, Lord Brodie at paras 43, 44.
39 *Friend v Lord Advocate* 2006 SC 121.
40 *Friend v Lord Advocate* 2008 SC (HL) 107.
41 [2008] 1 AC 281.
42 See, for a critical view of the draft Bill which became DACSA 2009, M Hogg, 'Asbestos related conditions and the idea of damage in the law of delict' 2008 SLT (News) 301.
43 DACSA 2009, s 1(1).
44 DACSA 2009, s 1(2).
45 DACSA 2009, s 4(2) DACSA 2009 received Royal Assent on 17 April 2009 and a petition for judicial review was lodged almost immediately afterwards.
46 *AXA General Insurance, Petitioners* [2009] CSOH 57.
47 The test being, in Lord Glennie's view, as set out by Lord Goff of Chieveley in *R v. Secretary of State for Transport, ex parte Factortame* (No 2) [1991] AC 603: 'In the end, the matter is one for the discretion of the court, taking into account all the circumstances of the case. Even so, the court should not restrain a public authority by interim injunction from enforcing an apparently authentic law unless it is satisfied, having regard to all the circumstances, that the challenge to the validity of the law is, *prima facie*, so firmly based as to justify so exceptional a course being taken'. Lord Glennie also referred to *Infant and Dietetic Foods Association Ltd, Petitioners* 2008 SLT 137.
48 [2009] CSOH 57, para 19.

Challenges to acts or decisions of the Scottish Executive

13.23   While there have been only four challenges to Acts of the Scottish Parliament (two of which related to the same Act), a much greater number of devolution issues have been raised concerning the activities of the Scottish Executive. Disappointingly, perhaps, from the perspective of the constitutional lawyer, these have focused narrowly on Convention rights matters[1] – and, in particular, on questions relating to the fair trial requirements of ECHR, art 6 in criminal proceedings[2] – and not on wider questions of devolved competence.

Nevertheless, a few of these cases have raised interesting questions about the definition of 'devolution issues' under SA 1998, Sch 6. For example, in *HM Advocate v Campbell*[3] Lord Cameron of Lochbroom, in the High Court of Justiciary, was asked to rule on whether serving an accused person with a list of productions and witnesses referring to an identification parade – the circumstances of which identification parade were alleged to have infringed the accused's ECHR, art 6 rights – was a 'purported or proposed exercise of a function by a member of the Scottish Executive' so as to constitute a devolution issue under SA 1998, Sch 6, para 1(d). Lord Cameron took the view that until the Lord Advocate took steps to introduce evidence in the accused's trial there was no 'act' of the Lord Advocate giving rise to a devolution issue[4].

Similarly, in *BBC, Petitioners*[5], the BBC complained that the refusal by the High Court of Justiciary to allow it to broadcast the trial of the men accused of the Lockerbie bombing constituted a devolution issue under SA 1998, Sch 6, para 1(d). It argued that this refusal breached its rights under ECHR, art 10 (freedom of expression) and that the broadcasting restrictions which had been imposed were the result of action taken by the Lord Advocate because he had opposed the BBC's application for broadcasting rights. The Appeal Court of the High Court of Justiciary held that no devolution issue was raised because there had been no act or decision by the Lord Advocate. Although he had supported the application by the US government to have the trial broadcast on a limited basis for relatives of the victims, it was the court which made the decision.

1 See *County Properties Ltd v Scottish Ministers* 2002 SC 79; *Lafarge Redland Aggregates Ltd v Scottish Ministers* 2001 SC 298; *Clancy v Caird* 2000 SC 441.
2 See, for example, *Clark v Kelly* 2003 SLT 308; *HM Advocate v R* 2003 SLT 4; *HM Advocate v Beggs (No 4)* 2002 SLT 163.
3 *HM Advocate v Campbell* 1999 SCCR 980.
4 See also *Hoekstra v HM Advocate (No 5)* 2001 SC (PC) 37.
5 *BBC, Petitioners (No 2)* 2000 SLT 860.

Dual protection of human rights in Scotland

13.24 Special mention should be made of one particular issue which has exercised the courts and which has, ultimately, led to recent legislative reform: the overlapping protections for human rights contained in SA 1998 and HRA 1998. As noted elsewhere (p 338), HRA 1998 obliges public authorities – including the Scottish Parliament and the Scottish Executive – to act in a manner which is compatible with Convention rights. Separately, by virtue of section 57 of SA 1998, a member of the Scottish Executive 'has no power' to act in a way which is incompatible with Convention rights and further, in terms of section 54, the exercise of a function by the Scottish Ministers is outside of 'devolved competence' to the extent that such exercise of the function breaches Convention rights[1].

Questions arose in the courts about the way in which the SA 1998 and HRA 1998 were intended to interact in cases where it was claimed that the Scottish Ministers were guilty of a human rights violation. Was the 'victim' of the breach required to pursue their claim under HRA 1998 or under SA 1998 or both? What time limits applied to the bringing of such a claim? And what remedies were available to the courts should it find that there had been a breach of Convention rights?

These questions were considered and determined by the House of Lords in the case of *Somerville v Scottish Ministers (No 2)*[2] which concerned claims by prisoners that their 'segregation' in terms of the Prisons and Young Offenders Institutions (Scotland) Rules 1994[3] breached their rights under art 8 ECHR. The House of Lords was not asked to determine the merits of the art 8 complaint: rather the appeal was taken part way through the first instance judicial review proceedings in relation to a number of specific issues[4].

One very significant question was whether a claim for damages for breach of Convention rights by the Scottish Ministers was subject to the time limit in s 7(5) HRA 1998 which requires a person who claims that a public authority has acted in breach of s 6(1) of HRA 1998 (which itself requires the public authority to act compatibly with Convention rights) to bring proceedings with one year of the alleged breach[5]. This issue was of no small importance beyond the complaints of the four petitioners in this case: if the time limit did not apply then that exposed the Scottish Ministers to a much larger number of historic Convention rights claims (for example, in relation to 'slopping out' cases[6]). At first instance and on appeal to the Inner House the petitioners argued that they had no option but to raise their claim under SA 1998 and that the HRA 1998 time limit did not apply. The Scottish Ministers contended that the claim had to be brought under HRA 1998 and could not be brought under SA 1998 (and hence the one year time limit did apply). Their Lordships rejected the contention that only one of the two Acts was relevant:

> 'There can be no doubt that the Scottish Ministers are a public authority in terms of s 6(3) HRA and that, accordingly, under s 6(1) it is unlawful for them to act in a way that is incompatible with a Convention right. If the Ministers' decisions on the segregation of the appellants were indeed incompatible with the appellants' Convention rights, under s 6(1) the Ministers acted unlawfully in taking them. Equally, as already explained, under the Scotland Act, if the decisions were incompatible with the appellants' Convention rights, the Ministers acted ultra vires in purporting to take those decisions. Both Acts would apply in the circumstances.'[7]

That being the case, and subject to the one year time limit under HRA 1998, a victim of a breach of Convention rights was entitled to raise a claim under either Act or indeed under both. On the question of the one year time limit itself, on a plain reading of SA 1998, no time bar equivalent to that contained in s 7(5) HRA applied to claims brought against the Scottish Ministers under SA 1998.

Tied into the arguments on this point was a contention on the part of the Scottish Ministers that there was no power to make an award of damages under SA 1998 where those damages were intended to provide 'just satisfaction' for a Convention rights violation. If that was correct, claims for the specific remedy of damages in the context of a Convention rights breach would have to be made under HRA 1998 (and would by that route be subject to the one year limitation period). This was based in part in the Ministers' construction of s 100(3) of SA 1998 which provides that: 'This Act does not enable a court or tribunal to award any damages in respect of an act which is incompatible with any of the Convention rights which it could not award if s 8(3) and (4) of the HRA 1998 applied'. It was argued that this wording indicated the UK Parliament's intention that damages should not be capable of being awarded under SA 1998. Lord Rodger dismissed this argument in the following way:

> 'If you tell a French girl visiting you on an exchange that she cannot go out to a club if her parents would not allow her to go to a similar club in France,

you tell her two things: first, that she cannot go to the club if her parents would not permit her to do so in similar circumstances in France; but, secondly, that she can go to the club if they would permit it. Similarly, s 100(3) tells the court both what the Act does not enable it to do and what it does enable it to do. The court cannot award damages if it could not award them under s 8(3) and (4); but also the court can award damages if it could award them in respect of the act in question under s 8(3) and (4).'[8]

This part of the Lords' decision in *Somerville* led, ultimately, to the passing of the Convention Rights Proceedings (Amendment) (Scotland) Act 2009 (CRPASA 2009. See pp 136–137). The Act amends s 100 of SA 1998 to require (subject to limited transitional provisions) any proceedings (whether for damages or otherwise) in which it is claimed that the Scottish Ministers are guilty of a breach of Convention rights to be raised within a period of one year after the breach complained of. The court may waive that time limit where it is 'equitable having regard to all the circumstances'[9] and it does not apply at all where the breach complained of is the making of legislation[10].

1   SA 1998, s 54 provides that the exercise of a function is outside devolved competence to the extent that it would be outside the legislative competence of the Scottish Parliament to confer the function (or to confer it so as to be exercisable in that way) which includes, of course, conferring functions so as to be exercised in breach of Convention rights.
2   2008 SC (HL) 45. For discussion, see CMG Himsworth, 'Conflicting interpretations of a relationship: damages for human rights breaches' 2008 12 Edin LR 321 and I Jamieson, 'Remedies under the Scotland Act: implications of Somerville 2007 SLT (News) 289. Mr Jamieson's earlier article ('The Somerville Case' 2007 SLT (News) 111), in which he criticised the approach taken by the Inner House, was the subject of comment in the House of Lords. Lord Rodger noted that it had clearly influenced the arguments made on behalf of the petitioners and said that 'For my part, I would acknowledge the assistance that I have derived from it' (para 92).
3   SI 1994/1931.
4   These issues also included whether the exercise of functions by a prison governor under the applicable prison rules could be characterised as the exercise of those functions by the Scottish Ministers (see p 377 above) and the appropriate procedure to be adopted when a claim for public interest immunity was made in connection with documents which might be relevant to a litigation.
5   Section 7(5) provides that proceedings 'must be brought before the end of – (a) the period of one year beginning with the date on which the act complained of took place, or (b) such longer period as the court or tribunal considers equitable having regard to all the circumstances…'.
6   See p 336 n 3.
7   2008 SC (HL) 45 per Lord Rodger at para 107.
8   2008 SC (HL) 45 at para 124.
9   SA 1998, s 100(3B)(a) inserted by CRPASA 2009, s 1.
10 Although it does apply to a claim that a breach has resulted from a failure to legislate: SA 1998, s 100(3D).

Consequences of a successful challenge

13.25   As explained above, there has yet to be a successful challenge to an ASP. However, in recognition of the potentially serious consequences of a decision by the courts to invalidate all or part of an Act, or to strike down decisions or subordinate legislation of the Scottish Executive, SA 1998 makes special provision for judicial and executive action deemed necessary as a result of such a decision.

Firstly, SA 1998, s 102 applies where a court decides that all or part of an ASP is outside legislative competence or that a member of the Scottish Executive does not have power to make, confirm or approve any provision of subordinate legislation which he or she has purported to make, confirm or approve. In those circumstances the court in question may make an order '(a) removing or limiting any retrospective effect of the decision, or (b) suspending the effect of the decision for any period and on any conditions to allow the defect to be corrected'[1]. Such an order could be used to protect, for example, third parties who have relied on legislation subsequently held to be invalid. The section requires a court, when considering whether or not to make an order, to 'have regard to the extent to which persons who are not parties to the proceedings would otherwise be adversely affected'[2] and to give notice to the Lord Advocate and, where a devolution issue is involved, to the appropriate Law Officers[3].

Secondly, SA 1998, s 107 confers power on the UK government to make subordinate legislation containing such provisions as it deems 'necessary or expedient in consequence of (a) an Act of the Scottish Parliament or any provision of an Act of the Scottish Parliament which is not, or may not be, within the legislative competence of the Parliament, or (b) any purported exercise by a member of the Scottish Executive' which is or may not be an exercise or 'proper' exercise of their functions. This wide ranging power is similar to the power to make remedial orders conferred by HRA 1998[4]. It is to be noted that subordinate legislation made under this section may amend an ASP and may be made whether or not a court has been asked to rule on whether the Act is or is not within the legislative competence of the Parliament[5].

1 SA 1998, s 102(1).
2 SA 1998, s 102(3).
3 SA 1998, s 102(4)–(7).
4 See p 392.
5 See, for example, Scotland Act 1998 (Regulation of Care (Scotland) Act 2001) Order 2001, SI 2001/2478.

CONSTITUTIONAL ADJUDICATION AND THE SUPREME COURT

13.26　At the time when the Scotland Bill was being debated in the UK Parliament, the case was made for the creation of a new constitutional court for the United Kingdom[1]. The new business of devolution issues to be generated not only by SA 1998 but also by GWA 1998[2] and NIA 1998 needed a more radical response than that proposed by the use of the JCPC.

In essence this was an argument that, in acquiring the new devolved institutions, the British constitution had reached a new stage of maturity. The enhanced status accorded to the ECHR by HRA 1998 strengthened the case. At earlier stages of its development, the constitution was incapable – Northern Ireland in the Stormont years apart – of producing genuinely constitutional issues for resolution by courts. The supremacy of Parliament and the unitary nature of the state suppressed such issues. All that courts were empowered to do was to interpret and to apply the will of Parliament[3]. In legal, if not in political, ways, constitutional conflict was flattened. There was a need for a London-based court

413

(the JCPC) to act as a final court of appeal and to resolve constitutional disputes in the Empire and Commonwealth but there was no such need for a court with a domestic jurisdiction. The United Kingdom's accession to the European Community in 1973 did not change this situation greatly because that brought with it a 'constitutional' court of its own – the European Court of Justice – although without doubt that accession has brought a new 'constitutional' dimension to the work of the ordinary courts. They must now determine the extent to which British law – including Acts of the UK Parliament – complies with the requirements of EC law and, in appropriate cases, may be faced with the task of disapplying an Act of the UK Parliament which contravenes those requirements[4]. The same courts are also frequently involved in interpreting and applying EC law in circumstances which are not explicitly constitutional in character.

But, it was argued, the arrival of devolution and of HRA produced a new situation and the case for a new court with a domestic jurisdiction. For its advocates, this jurisdiction would be quite separate from that of courts dealing with matters of 'ordinary' law. It would extend to 'difficult and controversial decisions about where state power ends and where personal liberty begins; decisions about striking a fair balance between competing human rights; decisions about the respective powers and duties of the Parliament of Westminster and central Government and of the devolved legislatures and administrations'[5]. The very nature of these decisions gave rise to the need for a specially constituted court: they were 'properly justiciable but they will sometimes be politically and ethically controversial. That is why it is especially important to ensure that the independence, authority and legitimacy of the final court are securely protected'[6].

This case was bolstered by both principled and more pragmatic objections to the continued reliance on existing institutions. It was, at the very least, a constitutional oddity that, in the twenty-first century, one final court should be formally part of the legislature (the House of Lords) and the other a part of the executive (the Privy Council). Nor was this merely a historical curiosity. The incorporation of the ECHR with its insistence upon the guarantee of the right to a hearing by 'an independent and impartial tribunal' brought a heightened awareness of the need for institutional distance between the judiciary and the other organs of government. There was growing unease, even among the Law Lords themselves[7], about the participation of the United Kingdom's most senior judges in the country's legislature. However restrained their political contribution may have been in that forum, their dual roles were undesirable. That concern was further heightened by their increasing involvement in cases of a political nature and there was an even more focused concern about the multiple roles of the Lord Chancellor. Once treated as little more than a matter of constitutional amusement, the capacity of that office seriously to infringe the rules of judicial impartiality could no longer be overlooked. The participation of the UK government's most senior member in the Upper House in cases, a large proportion of which have a governmental or human rights interest, had ceased to be justifiable[8]. The combined effect of these central questions of constitutional principle, the arrival of the new business under the Acts of 1998, together with more pragmatic reasons of case management in an overloaded system produced a strong imperative for new arrangements[9].

Proposals for a new constitutional court were rejected by the new Labour government during the passage of SA 1998, GWA 1998 and NIA 1998. The Lord Chancellor, in debate on the Scotland Bill, described the government's programme of constitutional reform as 'incremental'[10] and recalled that the government 'came down ... as a matter of policy against a constitutional court in ... the White Paper, *Rights Brought Home*'[11]. However, referring to not only the new devolution legislation but to the Human Rights Bill, the Freedom of Information Bill and provisions for locally elected mayors, Lord Irvine suggested that perhaps 'after all that legislation beds down, longer-term thought should be given to the appropriateness of a specialist constitutional court'. No reference to this issue appeared in the Labour Party's manifesto for the 2001 general election.

Nonetheless, on 12 June 2003 the UK government announced a number of measures billed as 'part of the continuing drive to modernise the constitution and public services'. These included abolition of the Lord Chancellor's Department, to be replaced with a Department for Constitutional Affairs which would also take on the responsibilities of the Scotland and Wales Offices[12]; abolition of the post of Lord Chancellor, to be replaced with a Secretary of State for Constitutional Affairs who would no longer act as Speaker of the House of Lords and who would neither sit as a judge nor have any involvement in judicial appointments[13]; establishment of a new Judicial Appointments Commission for England and Wales[14]; and the creation of a new Supreme Court to replace the Law Lords.

Undoubtedly this last proposal was driven principally by the perceived need to ensure the independence and impartiality of the UK's highest court by removing the senior judiciary from the legislature. Arguably, this difficulty could have been cured relatively simply by removing the rights of the Law Lords to sit and vote in the House of Lords. Little more would have been needed. However, following publication in July 2003 of the government's consultation paper *Constitutional Reform: A Supreme Court for the United Kingdom*, it became clear that a number of other questions were to be asked about the arrangements for high-level adjudication – both constitutional and otherwise – in the UK and more far reaching reform has in fact been the result.

In setting out the case for reform, the consultation paper referred to the existing functions of both the Appellate Committee of the House of Lords and the JCPC, which functions raised 'questions about whether there is any longer sufficient transparency of independence from the executive and the legislature to give people the assurance to which they are entitled about the independence of the Judiciary'[15]. It noted that one consequence of the growth of judicial review in recent years has been that judges have been brought more into the 'political eye'[16] and that there was increased sensitivity to the 'anomaly of the position whereby the highest court of appeal is situated within one of the chambers of Parliament'[17]. The continuing role of the Lord Chancellor as head of the judiciary added to the perception that judicial independence might be compromised by the existing arrangements[18].

The government's proposals for reform were taken forward by the Bill which became the Constitutional Reform Act 2005 (CRA 2005) and the provisions of that Act concerning the independence of the judiciary, appointments to the new Supreme Court and modifications to the role and functions of the Lord Chancellor are discussed in other parts of this book. The remaining provisions of CRA 2005 appear less an attempt to create for the UK a more obviously 'constitutional' court than a reflection of a desire to streamline and modernise existing processes. So, in summary:

(1)   With effect from 1 October 2009, the jurisdiction of the House of Lords within the United Kingdom's legal systems has been abolished and the functions of the Appellate Committee vested in the Supreme Court. The Supreme Court may hear appeals from any order or judgment of the Court of Appeal in England and Wales in civil proceedings and in relation to Scottish appeals, an appeal 'lies to the Court from any order or judgment of a court in Scotland if an appeal lay from that court to the House of Lords at or immediately before the commencement of this section'[19].

(2)   As a necessary consequence of the abolition of the House of Lords' judicial role, a large number of 'miscellaneous', and in some cases obscure, statutory jurisdictions formerly exercised by the Lords have been transferred to the Supreme Court including, for example, appeals which may involve the appointment of assessors under the Nautical Assessors (Scotland) Act 1894, appeals against decisions of disciplinary committees established under the Agricultural Marketing Act 1958 and appeals under the Extradition Act 1989[20].

(3)   Also transferred to the Supreme Court is the jurisdiction formerly exercised by the JCPC in relation to devolution matters[21]. The JCPC's role as a final court of appeal for Commonwealth jurisdictions has remained unchanged[22].

(4)   CRA 2005 contains some explicit recognition of the distinct constituent legal systems of the United Kingdom and the importance of making provision for those legal systems. So, 'a decision of the Supreme Court on appeal from a court of any part of the United Kingdom, other than a decision on a devolution matter, is to be regarded as the decision of a court of that part of the United Kingdom'[23]. In the appointment of Justices to the Supreme Court, the Judicial Appointments Commission must consult the Lord Chancellor, the First Minister for Wales, the Secretary of State for Northern Ireland and the Scottish First Minister[24]. The UK government's consultation paper acknowledged that the previous arrangements for devolution issues to be dealt with by the JCPC provided 'more opportunities to have Scottish and Northern Ireland judges sitting on devolution issues'[25] and in consequence it intended to make 'arrangements which enable additional Scottish and Northern Ireland judges to sit in cases raising devolution issues where that is appropriate'[26]. That has been done by allowing for the appointment, as 'acting' judges, a person who holds office as a 'senior territorial judge' which term includes Inner House judges in Scotland and judges of the English and Northern Irish Courts of Appeal[27]. The Supreme Court will not be quorate unless comprised of a majority of permanent judges[28] but nevertheless at least in theory the Supreme Court could constitute itself along more 'territorial' lines where that was thought appropriate in individual cases. There

is no formal quota for Scottish and Northern Ireland judges but it is anticipated that the previous convention by which two Scottish judges were appointed to the House of Lords and sit on Scottish appeals will continue in the Supreme Court.

In its 2003 consultation paper the government stated unequivocally that '[t]here is no proposal to create a Supreme Court on the US model with the power to overturn legislation. Nor is there any proposal to create a specific constitutional court, or one whose primary role would be to give preliminary rulings on difficult points of law'[29]. A court with the power to strike down Westminster legislation would not fit with the British tradition in which Parliament is supreme[30] and there is no need for an exclusively constitutional court because, in the UK, there 'is no separate body of constitutional law which takes precedence over all other law'[31]. CRA 2005 may, it seems, be as far as the United Kingdom is prepared, for now, to move in the direction of a constitutional court.

1   See HL Debs 28 Oct 1998, cols 1963–1986.
2   Now GWA 2006.
3   See pp 106–110.
4   *R v Secretary of State for Transport, ex parte Factortame Ltd* [1991] 1 AC 603; *R v Secretary of State for Employment, ex parte Equal Opportunities Commission* [1995] 1 AC 1. For discussion, see pp 115–119.
5   HL Debs, 28 October 1998, col 1969 (Lord Lester of Herne Hill).
6   HL Debs, 28 October 1998, col 1969 (Lord Lester of Herne Hill).
7   See Lord Bingham of Cornhill 'The Evolving Constitution' (2002) 6 EHRLR 1 and Lord Steyn 'The Case for a Supreme Court' (2002) 118 LQR 382.
8   See also para 11.17.
9   See, for example, A Le Sueur and R Cornes 'The Future of the United Kingdom's Highest Courts' (Constitution Unit, 2001) and 'What Do the Top Courts Do?' (2000) 53 Current Legal Problems 53.
10 HL Debs 28 October 1998, col 1982.
11 HL Debs 28 October 1998, col 1982.
12 See p 185.
13 See p 319.
14 See p 302.
15 Para 2.
16 Para 2.
17 Para 2.
18 Para 3.
19 CRA 2005, s 40.
20 See CRA 2005, s 40 and Sch 9, Part I.
21 Devolution matters include both post-enactment devolution issues and any references under SA 1998, s 33. CRA 2005, s 40 and Sch 9, Part II.
22 See p 298 n 7 and 364.
23 CRA 2005, s 41(2).
24 CRA 2005, s 27.
25 Para 19.
26 Para 21.
27 CRA 2005, s 38.
28 CRA 2005, s 42.
29 Para 8.
30 Para 23.
31 Para 23.

Index

[all references are to paragraph number]